Praise for *Capitalism and Commerce in Imaginative Literature*

"This may be the definitive anthology on literature and business. It offers a truly remarkable range of perspectives and insights."—**Joseph L. Badaracco, Harvard Business School**

"We have too long spoken of the opposition between business and literature, but in this remarkable collection that distorted perception is not only corrected, but overridden. With impressive diversity of both topics and authors, this collection of essays highlights the synergies between commerce and culture. I have little doubt that this volume will also inspire future artistic endeavors with business as the central subject."—**Douglas Den Uyl, Vice President of Educational Programs, Liberty Fund**

"Marcel Proust famously said, 'The writer's work is . . . an optical instrument . . . to enable [the reader] to discern what, without this book, he would perhaps never have experienced in himself. And the recognition by the reader in his own self of what the book says in the proof of its veracity.' I can't think of more powerful application of this insight than in the new volume edited by Ed Younkins, *Capitalism and Commerce in Imaginative Literature*. In 28 extraordinarily diverse essays, the authors explore alternative worlds that might have been and could never be, as a means of exploring worlds readers couldn't possibly have experienced. The essays work as literature on their own, but their real importance is as thought experiments: What does it mean to be human, and what does it mean to engage in commerce. A *tour de force* for economist and literature scholar alike."—**Michael C. Munger, Duke University**

Capitalist Thought: Studies in Philosophy, Politics, and Economics

Series Editor: Edward W. Younkins, Wheeling Jesuit University

Mission Statement

This book series is devoted to studying the foundations of capitalism from a number of academic disciplines including, but not limited to, philosophy, political science, economics, law, literature, and history. Recognizing the expansion of the boundaries of economics, this series particularly welcomes proposals for monographs and edited collections that focus on topics from transdisciplinary, interdisciplinary, and multidisciplinary perspectives. Lexington Books will consider a wide range of conceptual, empirical, and methodological submissions. Works in this series will tend to synthesize and integrate knowledge and to build bridges within and between disciplines. They will be of vital concern to academicians, business people, and others in the debate about the proper role of capitalism, business, and business people in economic society.

Books in Series

Economic Morality: Ancient to Modern Readings by Henry C. Clark and Eric Allison
The Ontology and Function of Money: The Philosophical Fundamentals of Monetary Institutions by Leonidas Zelmanovitz
Andrew Carnegie: An Economic Biography by Samuel Bostaph
Water Capitalism: Privatize Oceans, Rivers, Lakes, and Aquifers Too by Walter E. Block and Peter Lothian Nelson
Capitalism and Commerce in Imaginative Literature: Perspectives on Business from Novels and Plays edited by Edward W. Younkins

Capitalism and Commerce in Imaginative Literature

Perspectives on Business from Novels and Plays

Edited by
Edward W. Younkins

LEXINGTON BOOKS
Lanham • Boulder • New York • London

Published by Lexington Books
An imprint of The Rowman & Littlefield Publishing Group, Inc.
4501 Forbes Boulevard, Suite 200, Lanham, Maryland 20706
www.rowman.com

Unit A, Whitacre Mews, 26-34 Stannary Street, London SE11 4AB

British Library Cataloguing in Publication Information Available

Library of Congress Control Number: 2015952394
ISBN: 978-1-4985-1929-8 (cloth : alk. paper)
eISBN: 978-1-4985-1930-4

∞™ The paper used in this publication meets the minimum requirements of American National Standard for Information Sciences—Permanence of Paper for Printed Library Materials, ANSI/NISO Z39.48-1992.

Printed in the United States of America

This book is dedicated to my parents, Russell and Anna Younkins,
whose example has encouraged me to read and to appreciate
both fiction and the world of business.

Contents

Preface

In my 2014 book, *Exploring Capitalist Fiction: Business through Literature and Film*, I summarized and analyzed twenty-five works of fiction in the form of novels, plays, and films. These works portray and discuss business activity and fictional business persons. Each of the twenty-five chapters provided an even-handed and sequential summary of a particular novel, play, or film along with some comments about the work's philosophical, managerial, and economic implications. The works were chosen because of their importance to the subject of business itself. They were not examined for their literary greatness but rather for their pedagogical value for business students and individuals in the business world. The twenty-five works were selected from the eighty plus novels, plays, and films that I have used in my MBA course, Business through Literature, over the years at Wheeling Jesuit University.

The underpinning premise of *Exploring Capitalist Fiction* was that fiction can be a powerful force to educate in ways that lectures, textbooks, articles, case studies, and other teaching methods cannot. Literature is not only enjoyable but also can be enlightening, inspiring, and a source of character formation. Literature is memorable and can make people more contemplative. *Exploring Capitalist Fiction* highlighted the lessons that individuals can learn from each work examined and can apply to his or her own life. Readers were invited to learn more about themselves.

Exploring Capitalist Fiction provided something like expansive teaching and learning notes including summaries for each novel, play, or film. Its intended audience included college students, business teachers, general readers, and people employed in the business world. It was not meant for scholars, did not examine existing scholarship, and was not a work of literary criticism.

Exploring Capitalist Fiction was a good start but there are many more riches to be found in the literary treatment of business. People who read the book told me that they would like to see additional studies of business fiction that would be more detailed, more in-depth, and written from a variety of perspectives. As a result, I called upon a number of individuals from a range of disciplines and perspectives to contribute to this anthology called *Capitalism and Commerce in Imaginative Literature: Perspectives on Business from Novels and Plays*. All of the contributors to this set of essays are committed to treating literary texts with integrity and believe that business should have a larger claim upon peoples' literary consciousness. In addition, they all value the important role of literature in dealing with the complexities of a capitalist culture. I asked the contributors to this volume to find and to write about works that intrigue and excite them.

This anthology provides a means to appreciate the richness and variety of fictional portrayals of businesses and businesspersons. The works selected for examination reflect the variety of philosophical, political, economic, cultural, social, and ethical perspectives that have been found over time in American society. The novels and plays analyzed include high literature, mid-range literature, popular literature, ancient epics, grand narratives, hero tales, masterpieces, ideological texts, science fiction, and more.

Thanks are due to the many contributors to this book. I am extremely grateful to them for their fine work. I am also greatly indebted to Paula Ullom, WJU Department of Business Administrative Assistant, who typed my portions of this anthology. Work on this volume was assisted by the BB&T Charitable Foundation. The BB&T Foundation provided a gift in 2006, which resulted in the founding of Wheeling Jesuit University's Institute for the Study of Capitalism and Morality. As is the case with all of my other books, I am indebted most of all to Carla Cash, Administrative Assistant in Wheeling Jesuit University's Institute for the Study of Capitalism and Morality, for the most capable and conscientious work in bringing this book to print.

Edward W. Younkins
Wheeling Jesuit University

Introduction

My 2014 book, *Exploring Capitalist Fiction,* left a lot unexplained. Readers told me that they wanted additional studies of business fiction. The result is this collection of essays called *Capitalism and Commerce in Imaginative Literature: Perspectives on Business form Novels and Plays.* The essays in this anthology are broader in scope, more detailed, and more in-depth than what I presented in my chapters in the earlier book. The authors include a variety of individuals from diverse perspectives and disciplines. There was, and still are, a great many works of literature out there waiting to be read and studied by business and economically minded individuals from many different viewpoints and fields of study. *Capitalism and Commerce in Imaginative Literature* provides a space to explore a wide range of fictional works and opinions.

What now follows is a brief preview and description of each of the in-depth, detailed, and discrete articles contained in this book. The chapters do not have to be read in progressive order to be of use and/or of interest to the reader. Reading the brief summaries in this Introduction may point a given reader to particular essays in the book. In turn, after reading certain chapters, the reader may decide to read the work or works of specific authors.

In the opening essay, I discuss the nature and uses of business fiction and provide a historical survey of many of the novels and plays within this genre. Some of these are popular works, some have artistic merit, and some have not only been well-received by the general population but have also earned praise from the literary community. Many devalue business, others are more favorable in the treatment of business values and business people, and a few have portrayed a career in business as honorable and heroic. This retrospective article takes a look at the changing image of business and the businessman during various time periods. This survey also demonstrates how business and organizations have changed and how successful ones have adapted in order to survive and prosper. Through literature, a person can learn about work-life from another person's point of view in a very different time, place, and context.

Epic, as the inner history of the emergence of the human race and its civilization, is interested in the history of the media by which human beings learned to trade and the ideas behind them. Those media include gift exchange and barter, the rise of local currencies, the consolidation of currencies into gold and silver, the birth of written or inscribed instruments including paper money, and post-print forms of currency. Frederick Turner's close study of the *Gilgamesh Epic*, the Biblical epics, the Japanese epic *Heike*, the Mayan *Popol Vuh*, the Nordic epics including the *Volsung Saga*, Shakespeare's Henry plays, and Melville's prose epic *Moby Dick* reveals that epic deals with changes in the nature of economic exchange and the coinages that carry it, and suggests healing advances to solve the economic crises of their times.

In "The Cost of War and the Profits of Peace in Aristophanes' *Acharnians*," Troy Camplin investigates Aristophanes' economic arguments, as presented in dramatic form in his *Acharnians*, against war. While many of Aristophanes' plays are explicitly antiwar, it is in the *Acharnians* that Aristophanes investigates the damaging effects of war on the economy in general and trade in particular. Using recent scholarship on the Athenian economy, Aristophanes' arguments are put into historical and economic context. Given that the pre-Peloponnesian War Greek economy was perhaps the strongest-growing economy in the world at the time—an economic situation the world would not see again for almost two millennia—we can begin to understand why it is Aristophanes thought his economic argument against the war would be a strong one. His argument may not have been persuasive to enough people at the time, but there is still much we can learn from Aristophanes' play about the damaging economic effects of war.

Allen Mendenhall examines the plural nature and meaning of the word bond in Shakespeare's *Merchant of Venice*, dispelling popular Marxist readings of the play as anti-market. This play is shown to be multifaceted and open to an array of interpretations favorable to commerce. Mendenhall challenges common perceptions of Shylock and suggests that the Venice of the play anticipates certain Hayekian notions about societies that accommodate competing interests and cultures.

Felix Livingston's "Human Action: Pursuing Happiness Inside and Outside the Happy Valley" uses a Samuel Johnson fable written in 1759 as context for exploring multiple facets of Ludwig von Mises' observations about unease that can produce human action. For Johnson, the human condition is such that hardly anyone is immune from experiencing unease. Whether a person is wealthy or poor, powerful or powerless, social or antisocial, intelligent or dumb, wise or imprudent, a sense of unease makes virtually everyone "think the lot of his neighbor better than his own." While Adam Smith's "parable of the poor man's son" touches on the onerous aspects of acquiring wealth endured by the poor because they have overvalued the rich man's status and amenities, happiness in Johnson's fable seems to be experienced by honorable traders who can freely pursue their own ends. The essay concludes by suggesting that entrepreneurs who are honorable in the sense of Alexis de Tocqueville and virtuous in the sense of Aristotle are most likely to overcome moral and physical challenges threatening themselves and their firms. They can achieve both wealth *and* happiness at the same time while fostering general human flourishing in a great extended order of peaceful social cooperation.

Many in the Capitalism movement have held economics on high as the science to convince people of the virtue of Capitalism and its necessary connection to dignified human flourishing. In his essay, Derek Yonai explains that neoclassical economics, with its hero of Max U, fails to inspire people to understand or defend Capitalism. The notion of having more people understand economics and thereby improving the ability to educate people about the power of the market is misleading. If by that we mean teach people more about neoclassical economics, this endeavor will continue to fail. As the Romantics understood, science without the humanizing passion of a poet leaves it cold and sterile. People will not understand or appreciate the awe that the new science brings to understanding the natural world. Economists need to stir people's passions if they want to convince others about the dignity, virtue, and morality of Capitalism. Much like the authors of the Romantic Era, we must return to nature and find what moves us in our souls to animate our economic presentation to others.

In "Elizabeth Gaskell's *North and South*: Industrial Energy versus 'The Idiocies of Rural Life,'" Paul Cantor analyzes one of the few works of nineteenth-century British literature that defends capitalism. The "North" and "South" of Gaskell's title refer to the urban, industrial north of England versus the rural, agricultural south. Gaskell initially seems to prefer the south to the north. Her heroine regrets moving from the peaceful, idyllic south to the polluted, crowded north. But Gaskell's heroine gradually learns to appreciate the energy, prosperity, and progressivism made possible by the burgeoning cotton industry in the north. She also comes to reconsider her idealized image of the south, once she realizes that its poverty produces ignorance, prejudice, superstition, and torpor. *North and South* thus reverses the celebration of the rural world characteristic of English Romanticism, and offers a positive image of capitalist and industrial development in such cites as Manchester. In particular, Gaskell appreciates what capitalism did for the economic emancipation of women. Far from viewing factory jobs as oppressive for women, Gaskell presents them as liberating women from the drudgery, indignity, and dependency of life as domestic servants.

According to Amy Willis, Horatio Alger remains one of the best-selling authors in American history, yet his books are barely recognized today. These stories are exemplars of both personal success and the morality of capitalism. They remain a critical part of our cultural capital, perhaps because they are illustrative of the "bourgeois virtues," also so important to the American character. That the clerisy, as Deirdre McCloskey puts it, have rejected Alger may be representative of their disavowal of capitalism as well.

In "Crony Capitalism in *The Gilded Age* by Twain and Warner and Its Relevance for Today," Michelle Albert Vachris uses the Public Choice framework to analyze themes in the novel that gave "The Gilded Age" era its name. Her paper provides some excerpts and assignments that could be incorporated into an undergraduate upper level field course in Public Choice, Public Sector Economics, or US Economic History. Examples from the novel are also compared to real-world events in the United States illustrating parallels between crony capitalism in today's economy and during the roots of the Progressive Era.

In her essay, Cynthia Hunter discusses how Henrik Ibsen's 1882 play, *An Enemy of the People,* addresses complex, relevant, and timeless sociopolitical issues. In the play, Dr. Stockmann discovers that the resort town's spa baths are polluted. The virtuous doctor is worried about the health threat to the spa's visitors. While he is concerned with morality and science, his brother, the Mayor, is concerned with the reputation of the baths and the expense of rectifying the problem. Initially, the doctor believes in the power of democracy and the ability of the citizens to see the truth of his report and their willingness to support him. However, when a democratic vote at a town meeting keeps him from reading his report, he voices a diatribe against the "common majority." The play illustrates how leaders can manipulate the people, but also how leaders tend to cater to what will be acceptable to the majority. There is also the issue of whether an employee (e.g., the doctor) should submit to authority (e.g., the Mayor) or should become a whistleblower. At the end of the play, Dr. Stockmann is dismissed, but he decides to remain in town to educate people to participate responsibly in the political process.

The aim of Zennure Köseman's "William Dean Howells' Work Ethic in *The Rise of Silas Lapham*" is to highlight how the meaning of acquiring success transformed in the 1880s in American literature by taking into consideration the work ethic of William Dean Howells in his famous fictional work, *The Rise of Silas Lapham.* The utmost significant theme of this literary work is about the change in the meaning of success from moral improvement into material prosperity. A historical and cultural analysis of this novel in Köseman's article depicts that for William Dean Howells, success is the accumulation of prosperity by means of reliance on the others.

Such a finding implies a Calumet loss of self-reliance in Howells' literary and historical period.

According to Michael Spindler, in his two major novels, *The Rise of Silas Lapham* (1885) and *A Hazard of New Fortunes* (1890), William Dean Howells explored and dramatized the tensions that come into play between leading an ethical life and succeeding in business. The business plot of *Lapham* centers on the difficulty of maintaining an equilibrium between self-interest and moral scruple in the face of the corrupting pressures of the Gilded Age, as Lapham, who is the embodiment of Jeffersonian individualism and the Protestant ethic, finds his moral code tested and ultimately vindicated. *Hazard* provides a much broader, more comprehensive representation of the conflict between ethics and capitalism, for it not only portrays the entrepreneur figure in Jacob Dryfoos but also includes a range of alternative social perspectives whether it be Conrad Dryfoos's Christian Socialism, Colonel Woodburn's patriarchalism, Lindau's socialism, or March's liberalism. Howells' increased radicalism is particularly evident in the strike scene where police violence against the strikers is closely associated with the entrepreneur's violence against his son. Both books are realistic explorations of the ways in which rapid economic change puts traditional ideologies to the test.

The depression of the 1890s was one of the most important economic events in American history. It rivaled in severity and in political drama the depression of the 1930s. American literature has had much to say about the latter, but what has it said about the former? Stephen Cox answers that question with respect to a variety of important authors, all of whom experienced the Panic of 1893. These authors represent a spectrum of political and economic attitudes. But, Cox finds, even those who were ideologically opposed to the capitalist system appear to have seen nothing of crucial importance about the depression of the 1890s. Cox observes that the federal government did little to end that depression, and the economy recovered fairly soon; but the depression of the 1930s was characterized by an extraordinarily slow recovery and a permanent institutionalization of governmental "solutions" to economic problems. The Crash of '93 was forgettable; the Crash of 1929, and the New Deal response to it, were not. The dominant culture of government intervention, introduced in the 1930s, continues to maintain "the story of a great depression—the depression of the 1930s—that required the creation of a giant welfare state. The story gives life to the state; the state gives life to the story."

In "Heroism Redefined: Integrating Mind and Emotion in *Calumet K*," Virginia Murr looks at Charles Bannon, the protagonist of Ayn Rand's favorite novel, *Calumet K*. Bannon is a businessman who saves the day with purposeful action, a keen sense of justice, and an unyielding sense of integrity. As heroic as his actions are, Bannon struggles with friendships and romantic love.

This struggle is a result of Bannon's view that emotions are inherently irrational and, therefore, detrimental to a successful life. Disconnected from his emotions, Bannon has been left to unconsciously navigate the emotional terrain of his life. Thus, Bannon's greatest achievement does not occur when he heroically saves the day, but when he begins to see the value of emotion as a tool of his rational mind—when he begins to integrate his mind and emotions.

Sarah Skwire explains that, in addition to their noteworthy charm and historical usefulness, Edna Ferber's stories about the traveling saleswoman Emma McChesney offer us the chance to consider an early and extended depiction of the characteristics of the successful businessperson, and to do so in light of more contemporary depictions such as Deirdre McCloskey's bourgeois virtues, Israel Kirzner's entrepreneurial instincts, and Michael Novak's idea of business as a calling. Emma McChesney is no cut out corporate caricature. She is a fully realized human being. She has a son she adores. She has friends and colleagues. She has a happy second marriage. She has dreams and desires. And she has a calling that is at least as important as all of those things. And her bourgeois virtues and entrepreneurial instincts combine with the strength of her calling to make her a model portrait of a business women from the previous, or any, century.

Gary Wolfram's essay discusses F. Scott Fitzgerald's depiction of New York in the 1920s. While ostensibly a story of failed romance, *The Great Gatsby* offers a commentary on the both the lifestyle of the wealthy of New York society and how one gets wealthy in a capitalist system. Rather than focusing on how entrepreneurs of the time were improving the lifestyle of the average American with the introduction of movies, penicillin, and vacuum cleaners, Fitzgerald portrays the wealthy as decadent party-seekers who were born to wealth, were blessed with luck, or engaged in bootlegging. Unfortunately this view of capitalism remains too prevalent today.

Few of the analyses of John Steinbeck's most autobiographical of novels, *East of Eden,* pay attention to its positive depiction of business and businessmen. With a nod to Churchill's conclusion that conservatism comes with age, Mimi Gladstein examines how, with time and experience, Steinbeck's depictions of the "evils" of big business in *The Grapes of Wrath* morphed into the portrayals of positive real and fictional characters whose business acumen is a key ingredient of the plot of this interweaving of his family's story with the archetypal pattern of Adam and Eve and Cain and Abel. Whereas abuse of workers and manipulation of markets are highlighted in *The Grapes of Wrath,* entrepreneurship and individual choice shine in *East of Eden.* The message to his sons was that they could elect their paths and his final protagonist chooses business to replace his father's losses in a failed venture.

Walter Block has a love-hate relationship with Objectivists and Ayn Rand, their leader and creator of the philosophy of Objectivism. On the one hand, he was converted to libertarianism by her, personally, and owes her a great debt of gratitude. On the other hand, she was a bitter opponent of libertarianism, and although she adhered to most of its tenets, this is not true of all of them, and Block is critical of her deviations from its principles. In his essay, Block focuses on her views on accepting government subsidies, and comments on political scientist Charles Murray's reaction to Ayn Rand.

Andrew Bernstein explains that the focus of Ayn Rand's fiction is the importance of values in human life. An individual's personal values—whether these are education, career, love, or the like—provide meaning, purpose, and joy in his or her life. A society's political system either supports or impedes an individual's quest for values: In a free society upholding individual rights, a person is at liberty to pursue his dreams; in a totalitarian state where individual rights are crushed, he or she does as the state dictates. Ayn Rand's four novels span the spectrum of political freedom and its lack, ranging from a relatively free society in *The Fountainhead* to a brutally repressive one in *Anthem.* Therefore, Ayn Rand's heroes, in their quest for values, are confronted by varying degrees of governmental impediments: Some face minimal statist interference, while others flee for their lives.

According to William Kline, *The Fountainhead* is a powerful vision of both business and ethics in which business is an art embodying the substantive style of the professional. Too often style is overlooked as meaningless puffery. Yet, there is an aesthetics to style: One can do something beautifully or the "same" thing in an ugly manner. When there is substance to style, there is both meaning and beauty. Substantive style, then, comprises the integrated character traits that embody skill, virtue, aesthetics, and mindset. The content and object of this style is determined both through personal ethics and the nature of the profession one chooses. *The Fountainhead* makes the argument that intermediary institutions like professional standards are crucial for flourishing lives within capitalism by providing just such content. In turn, capitalism's defense in *The Fountainhead* is that it allows for multiple such styles. Business ethics, far from being an oxymoron or ad hoc list of rules, helps us to flourish within a market economy by mapping out the different substantive styles required by different professions; enabling us to consciously choose how we work and live.

In my second essay, I discuss how *Atlas Shrugged* is very much a novel about business and businessmen. The purpose of this article is to describe Ayn Rand's treatment of business and businessmen in this novel. The paper begins with an explanation of how *Atlas Shrugged* demonstrates that wealth and profit are creations of the human mind. The next section compares, at a general level, the worldviews of the novel's business heroes and villains. This is followed by an in-depth analysis of the novel's main business protagonists—Dagny Taggart and Hank Rearden. The next part provides capsule summaries of other *Atlas Shrugged* business characters. The last section provides an account of how *Atlas Shrugged* is used in college-level business courses.

Business can be a powerful agent of human progress. Gennady Stolyarov II explores business concepts in three works of science fiction: Henry Hazlitt's *Time Will Run Back* (1951), Robert A. Heinlein's *Methuselah's Children* (1958), and Zoltan Istvan's *The Transhumanist Wager* (2013), each of whose protagonists are able to achieve world-transforming goals through the use of business enterprises. In *Time Will Run Back,* Peter Uldanov unintentionally finds himself in the role of the dictator of a one-world socialist dystopia and is able to transform it by incrementally unleashing economic freedom. In *Methuselah's Children,* the entrepreneur Ira Howard establishes a foundation for the furtherance of uncommonly long lifespans and the protection of especially long-lived humans. During the twenty-second century, the Howard Foundation enables its beneficiaries—the Howard Families—to escape persecution on Earth once their existence is discovered by the broader society. Led by Lazarus Long, the Howard Families seek a home among the stars, while their example motivates humans on Earth to seek out methods to extend lifespans for everyone. Zoltan Istvan's protagonist, Jethro Knights, also seeks to overcome death and live indefinitely. To this end, he creates a floating nation and massive research enterprise—Transhumania—aboard a seastead. Jethro harnesses many free-market principles to facilitate technological and economic growth, but he uses them only instrumentally in his quest to become an omnipotender—an all-powerful dictator who seeks to control the world's resources for the purpose of achieving a technological utopia.

Carl Horner discusses how, in John Updike's *Rabbit Is Rich*, Rabbit trades his love of adventure for fortune-making potential. Glistening with money, new cars, a house in Penn Park, and the plush greens and tees of country club golf, feeling power and attention and respect for the first time since high school basketball, "in these middle years it is so clear to him that he will never run"—never run from his Toyota dealership and never run again from his wife, "the keystone of his wealth." Harold C. Angstrom is his own "Fortune's hostage" trapped at the helm of his inherited kingdom, trapped upright and grinning in his coffin, his showroom—with no place left to run.

Theodore Pauls uses scenes from Roger Rueff's play *Hospitality Suite* to demonstrate applications of consumer behavior principles from three perspectives; the consumers', the marketers', and from the marketer as a consumer. These principles are extracted from both the setting and the script, offering insightful examples not readily observed through casually reading or watching the play. With the plays' simplicity of a single setting and only three primary characters, the underlying principles of consumer behavior are easily understood once drawn to the attention of the reader. The examination of the play from this perspective makes it an excellent tool for demonstrating and applying various consumer behavior principles, both simple and complex.

In his essay "Writing, Money, Markets, Slavery, and Unintended Consequences at the Beginning of History," Jeff Riggenbach examines Samuel R. Delany's *Return to Nevèrÿon*, a four-volume postmodernist novel set in a land its author sees as "on the brink of civilization," a land based on "what can, most safely, still be imagined about the transition from a barter economy to a money economy." Riggenbach regards Delany as displaying a keen understanding of what the economist Friedrich A. Hayek famously called "spontaneous order" as well as an insightful, if intuitive, grasp of what the same economist famously called "the fatal conceit"—the error of believing that human planners can so successfully design and centrally control the operations of a market that they will be able to achieve greater efficiency and prosperity than can be realized by leaving economic behavior up to the individuals engaged in it, that is, to the working of spontaneous order.

According to Matthew McCaffrey and Carmen Elena Dorobăt, George R.R. Martin's fantasy epic *A Song of Ice and Fire* brilliantly illustrates a number of basic principles of political economy. In particular, the richness of his world allows for a fascinating account of economic and political relations in human society, and the saga uses its fantasy setting to dramatize and explore important questions about power, conflict, and the state. This essay discusses three economic themes in *A Song of Ice and Fire*. First, Martin's novels illustrate some fundamental ideas about political institutions, showing that organized economic exploitation is the foundation of the state. Second, they dramatize the relationship between war-making and public finance, describing the immense (networks of) political power created through control of the treasury, as well as the political logic that drives Lord Baelish and the Lannisters from taxation to borrowing to inflation in order to sustain and conceal the crown's war debt. Third, the paper examines how the rhetoric of Westeros's ruling class prevents the emergence of institutions friendly to peace and social cooperation, especially in the form of market exchange.

Previous discussions of economics in the Harry Potter series have primarily focused on consumption and class, particularly noting ways in which consumption patterns signal "good" or "bad" characters, and the ways in which class is defined economically. There have been multiple, competing attempts to identify or label the economic structure in the books, with corresponding implications for the representation of business. Absent from most of these discussions is what it means to be a producer in the system Rowling depicts. Heather King's essay focuses on how characters in the novels become producers in the economic system, and the moral implications of this agency. Through the characters of Fred and George, mischief makers in chief and successful entrepreneurs, Rowling presents a vision of business and commerce that strengthens communal bonds and that is associated with the chaotic, creative, and comedic forces that ultimately defeat the sinister, centrally controlling, Voldemort.

Susan Brown's article "Race, Rules, and Real Estate in August Wilson's *Radio Golf*" analyzes the dilemmas faced by two middle-class African American men as they go about trying to revitalize an old black community now considered blighted and seized with crime. Using the resources available to them—electoral politics, eminent domain, and their own capital investments—they run into problems when the past catches up with them in the form of Old Joe Barlow and his legal claim to one of the houses that has been condemned to make way for new development—new housing, a Whole Foods grocery, a Barnes & Noble, and a Starbucks. While one man dreams of bringing back the past, the other dreams of advancing to a new future. In setting up this problem, Wilson evokes the injustices of the African American past and their influences on the present, which results in contradictions and ambiguities that cannot be easily resolved, and which mirror many of the problems African Americans face today when they try to reconcile their regard for the past and their desires in the present only to be thwarted by political and economic systems that are themselves riddled with contradictions.

RECOMMENDED READINGS

Badaracco, Joseph L. 2006. *Questions of Character: Illuminating the Heart of Leadership through Literature.* Boston: Harvard Business Review Press.

Berman, Russell A. 2007. *Fiction Sets You Free: Literature, Liberty, and Western Culture.* Iowa City: University of Iowa Press.

Bohanon, Cecil and Michelle Albert Vachris. 2012. "Economics and Literature: The Gains from Trade." In Hoyt, Gail and Kimmarie McGoldrick (Eds.). *The International Handbook on Teaching and Learning Economics.* Aldershot: United Kingdom: Edward Elgar Press: 223–33.

Borus, Daniel H. 1989. *Writing Realism: Howells, James, and Norris in the Mass Market.* Chapel Hill: University of North Carolina Press.

Brandis, R. 1961. "The American Writer Views the American Businessman." *Quarterly Review of Economics and Business* 1, no. 3, 29–38.

Brawer, Robert A. 1998. *The Fictions of Business.* New York: John Wiley and Sons.

———. 2001. "10 Great American Business Novels." *American Heritage Magazine* 52, no. 4 (June).

Burden, Charles. 1977. *Business in Literature.* New York: David McKay.

Cantor, Paul and Stephen Cox. 2010. *Literature and the Economics of Liberty.* Auburn, Alabama: Ludwig von Mises Institute.

Cashill, Jack. 1985. "Capitalism's Hidden Heroes: The Literary Establishment Contrives to Ignore the business Giants in the American Novel." *CNN Money* (February).

Cashill, John R. 1982. *The Capitalist as Hero in the American Novel.* Dissertation. West Lafayette, Indiana: Purdue University.

Cassady, Edward E. 1939. *The Business Man in the American Novel.* Dissertation. Berkeley: University of California.

Chamberlain, John. 1948. "The Businessman in Fiction." *Fortune* XXXVIII (November): 134–36, 139, 142, 14, 146, 148.

Coles, Robert.1987. "Storytellers' Ethics." *Harvard Business Review* (March–April).

———. 1987. "Gatsby at the B School." *New York Times* (October 25): 2.

———. 1989. *The Call of Stories: Teaching and the Moral Imagination.* Boston: Houghton Mifflin.

Courtemanche, Eleanor. 2011. *The "Invisible Hand" and British Fiction 1818–1860: Adam Smith, Political Economy, and the Genre of Realism.* New York: Palgrave.

Czarniawska-Joerques, Barbara and Pierre Guillet de Monthoux. 1994. *Good Novels, Better Management: Reading Organizational Realities.* Chur: Harwood Academic Publishers.

Darby, William. 1987. *Necessary American Fiction: Popular Literature of the 1950s.* Bowling Green, Ohio: Bowling Green State University Press.

Davies, Geoff, and Roger Hancock. 1993. "Drama as a Learning Medium." *Management Development Review* 6.

DeMott, B. 1989. "Reading Fiction to the Bottom Line." *Harvard Business Review* 67 (May-June): 128–34.

Egger, R. 1959. "The Administrative Novel." *American Political Science Review* 53, no. 2: 448–55.

Erskine, John. 1931. "American Business in the American Novel." *The Bookman.* LXXIII (July): 449–57.

Fienberg, Lorne. 1988. *A Cuckoo in the Nest of Culture: Changing Perspecitves on the Businessman in the American Novel, 1865–1914.* New York: Garland.

Fineman, Joel A. and Lori A. Merish. 2012. *All Business: Confronting the Ethical Dilemmas of Financial Evolution in Gilded Age Fiction.* Thesis: Washington, DC: Georgetown University.

Friedsam, H.J. 1954. "Bureaucrats as Heroes." *Social Forces* 32, no. 3 (March): 269–74.

Gailey, J.D., and Virsima Schaefer Carroll. 1993. "Toward a Collaborative Model for Interdisciplinary Teaching: Business and Literature." *Journal of Education for Business* (September-October).

Garaventa, Eugene. 1998. "Drama: A Tool for Teaching Business Ethics." *Business Ethics Quarterly* 8, no. 3: 535–45.

Georgi, Charlotte. 1959. *The Businessman in the Novel.* Chapel Hill: University of North Carolina Press.

Guroian, Vigen. 2002. "Why Should Businessmen Read Great Literature?" *Religion and Liberty* 12, no. 4.

Halsey, Van R. 1959. "Fiction and the Businessman: Society through All It's Literature." *American Quarterly* XI (Fall): 391–402.

———. 1956. *The Portrait of the Businessman in Twentieth Century American Fiction*. Thesis. Philadelphia: University of Pennsylvania.

Hansen, Drew. 2011. "Why Every MBA Should Read More Literature." *Forbes* (October).

Hapke, Laura. 2001. *Labor's Text: The Worker in American Fiction*. New Brunswick, New Jersey: Rutgers University Press.

Henderson, George L. 1999. *California and the Fictions of Capital*. New York: Oxford University Press.

Hoeller, Hildegard. 2012. *From Gift to Commodity: Capitalism and Sacrifice in Nineteenth-Century American Fiction*. Durham: University of New Hampshire Press.

Hoivik, Heidi von Weltzien. 2009. "Developing Students' Competence for Ethical Reflection While Attending Business School." *Journal of Business Ethics* 88: 5–9.

Horner, Carl. 1992. *The Boy inside the American Businessman*. Lanham, Maryland: University Press of America.

James, Harold. 1991. "The Literary Financier." *The American Scholar* 60, no. 2 (Spring): 251–57.

Jennings, Kate. 2001. "Best Business Books: Business Novels." *Strategy to Business* no. 25 (October).

Jobe, Linda Barnes Gardner. 1970. *The Businessmen in the American Novel*. Thesis. Lubbock: Texas Tech University.

Jones, Howard Mumford. 1953. "Literature and the Businessman." *Harvard Business Review* XXXI (January-February): 133–34, 136, 138, 140, 142.

Kaufmann, David. 1995. *The Business of Common Life: Novels and Classical Economics between Revolution and Reform*. Baltimore, Maryland: John Hopkins University Press.

Kavesh, Robert. 1955. *Businessmen in Fiction: The Capitalist and Executive in American Novels*. Hanover, New Hampshire: Amos Tuck School of Business Administration.

Kennedy, Ellen J. and Leigh Lawton. 1992. "Business Ethics in Fiction." *Journal of Business Ethics* 11: 187–95.

Lawson, Lewis A. 1961. "The Rogue in the Gray Flannel Suit." *College English* 22, no. 4 (January): 249–52.

Long, Elizabeth. 1985. *The American Dream and the Popular Novel*. Boston: Routledge and Kegan Paul.

Lown, Charles R. 1957. *Business and the Businessman in American Drama Prior to the Civil War*. Dissertation. Stanford, California: Stanford University.

Lynch, Deidre. 1998. *The Economy of Character: Novels, Market Culture, and the Business of Inner Meaning*. Chicago: University of Chicago Press.

Lynn, Kenneth S. 1956. "Authors in Search of the Businessman." *Harvard Business Review* XXXIV (September-October): 116–24.

Mahalik, Christa. 2010. *Merchants, Barons, Sellers, and Suits: the Changing Images of the Businessman through Literature*. New Castle upon Tyre: Cambridge Scholars.

McAdams, Tony, and Roswitha Koppensteiner. 1992. "The Manager Seeking Virtue: Lessons from Literature." *Journal of Business Ethics* 11.

McGuire, Joseph W. 1960. "Bankers, Books, and Businessmen." *Harvard Business Review* 38, no. 4 (July-August): 67–74.

McTague, Michael J. 1979. *The Businessman in Literature: Dante to Melville*. New York: Philosophical Library.

McVeagh, J. 1981. *Tradeful Merchants: The Portrayal of the Capitalist in Literature*. London: Routledge and Kegan Paul.

Meakin, D. 1976. *Man and Work: Literature and Culture in Industrial Society*. New York: Holmes and Meier.

Miller, Stephen. 1987. "The Three Voices of American Literature." pp. 223–57 in *Capitalism and Equality in America*. Edited by Peter L. Berger. Lanham, Maryland: Hamilton Press.

Morson, Gary Saul. 1996. *Narrative and Freedom: The Shadows of Time*. New Haven, Connecticut: Yale University Press.

Moses, Michael Valdez. 1995. *The Novel and the Globalization of Culture*. Oxford: Oxford University Press.

O'Rourke, W. (ed). 1977. *On the Job: Fiction about Work by Contemporary Writers*. New York: Vintage Books.

Pollard, Arthur. 2009. *The Representation of Business in English Literature*. Indianapolis: Liberty Fund.

Rajski, Brian. 2011. "Corporate Fictions: Cameron Hawley and the Institutions of Postwar Capitalism." *Textual Practice* 25, no. 6: 1015–31.

Russell, Norman. 1986. *The Novelist and Mammon: Literary Response to the World of Commerce in the Nineteenth Century*. New York: Oxford University Press.

Sarachek, Bernard.1995. "Images of Corporate Executives in Recent Fiction." *Journal of Business Ethics* 14: 195–205.

Shell, Marc. 1993. *The Economy of Literature*. Baltimore, Maryland: Johns Hopkins University Press.

Smith, Henry Nash. 1964. "The Search for a Capitalist Hero: Businessmen in American Fiction." In *The Business Establishment*. Edited by Earl F. Cheit. New York: Wiley.

Smith, Howard R. 1959. "The American Businessman in the American Novel." *Southern Economic Journal* XXV (January): 265–302.

Spindler, Michael. 1983. *American Literature and Social Change*. Bloomington: Indiana University Press.

Stedmond, J.M. 1962. "The Business Executive in Fiction." *Dalhousie Review* XLII (Spring): 18–27.

Taylor, D.J. 2007. "In Search of Novels about Working Life." *The Independent* (May).

Taylor, Walter Fuller. 1964. *The Economic Novel in America*. New York: Octagon.

Turner, Frederick. 1999. *Shakespeare's Twenty-First Century Economics: The Morality of Love and Money*. Oxford: Oxford University Press.

Uzzell, Thomas H. 1958. "The Novel that Says Something." *The English Journal* 47, no. 5 (May): 255–58.

Van Nostrand, Albert D. 1959. "Fiction's Flagging Man of Commerce." *English Journal* XLVIII (January): 1–11.

———. 1959. "After Marquand, the Deluge." *The English Journal* XLVIII (February): 55–65.

Ward, R.J. 1982. "Business in the American Novel: The Fictional Treatment of the Market Society." *Bulletin of Bibliography* 39: 195–200.

Ward, Thomas. 1990. *The Businessman in American Popular Literature of the 1950s.* Thesis. Muncie, Indiana: Ball State University.

Watts, Emily Stipes. 1982. *The Businessmen in American Literature.* Athens: The University of Georgia Press.

Watts, Michael, and Robert F. Smith. 1989. "Economics in Literature and Drama." *Journal of Economic Education* 20, no. 3 (Summer): 291–307.

Watts, Michael. 1999. "Using Literature and Drama in Undergraduate Economic Courses." In *Teaching Economics to Undergraduates: Alternatives to Chalk and Talk.* Edited by W.F. Becker and M. Watts. Cheltenham, United Kingdom: Edward Elgar.

———. 2002. "How Economists Use Literature and Drama." *Journal of Economic Education* 33, no. 4 (Fall): 377–86.

Westbrook, Wayne W. 1980. *Wall Street in the American Novel.* New York: New York University Press.

Williams, Oliver F. 1997. *The Moral Imagination: How Literature and Films can Stimulate Ethical Reflection in the Business World.* Notre Dame, Indiana: University of Notre Dame Press.

Younkins, Edward W. 2014. *Exploring Capitalist Fiction: Business through Literature and Film.* Lanham, Maryland: Lexington Books.

Zayani, Mohamed.1999. *Reading the Symptoms: Frank Norris, Theodore Dreiser, and the Dynamics of Capitalism.* New York: Peter Lang.

Zimmerman, David A. 2006. *Panic! Markets, Crises, and Crowds in American Fiction.* Chapel Hill: University of North Carolina Press.

———. 2011 "Novels of American Business, Industry, and Consumerism." pp. 409–25 in *Cambridge History of the American Novel.* Edited by Leonard Cassuto, Clare Eley, and Benjamin Reiss. Cambridge, United Kingdom: Cambridge University Press.

Chapter 1

Capitalism and Commerce in Novels and Plays

Edward W. Younkins

The underpinning premise of this article is that fiction can be a powerful force to educate students and employees in ways that lectures, textbooks, articles, case studies, and other traditional teaching approaches cannot. Works of fiction can address a range of issues and topics, provide detailed real-life descriptions of the organizational contexts in which workers find themselves, and tell interesting, engaging, and memorable stories that are richer and more likely to stay with the reader longer than lectures and other teaching approaches. Imaginative literature can enrich business teaching materials and provide an excellent supplement to the theories, concepts, and issues that students experience in their business courses. Reading novels and plays is an excellent way to develop critical thinking, to learn about character, and to instill moral values.

This article will begin by discussing the nature and uses of business fiction. It will then provide a historical survey of works within this genre. Over the years, writers have produced hundreds of novels and plays that focus on capitalism and commerce. This article examines a broad scope of writers and their works, their varying concerns about the world of business, and the changing depictions of business and business persons in fiction. Literary treatments of commerce and people in the business world have been varied with a number of them being complex and nuanced. Many of these highlight the tremendous power of stories that deal with ethical dilemmas in business.

THE NATURE AND USES OF BUSINESS FICTION

Imaginative literature has contributed to the progress of civilization and to the dynamism of society. Fiction empowers individuals' imaginations to transcend the empirical constraints that circumscribe them. Fiction sets people free both as writers and as readers by cultivating their potentials to self-reflect, to devise alternatives to the present, and to freely choose among those options. Literature is a means to study the individual human capacity for imagination and expression. Narrative makes sense out of reality and provides a backdrop from which to view the place of morality in one's life. By reading literature, people are studying the human condition.

The autonomy of imaginative literature mirrors the freedom and independence of the individual human person. Fiction can help people to realize their individuality and their ability to envision, to express, to choose, and to pursue their possibilities for living a flourishing and happy life. The point of reading fiction is to make people reflect about what they believe in and what they want to get out of life. Literature dramatizes how a person in a particular culture and context, given his individual talents and motivations, defines himself, makes choices, and acts. Because literature is, in part, an expression of the culture within which it is produced, it can also supply a tool for examining the social history of that culture. Because literature possesses historical substance, reading fiction from various time periods and places allows one to gain a big-picture explanation of the evolution of civilization.

Reading literature contributes to a richer life. Fiction permits individuals to encounter people who they would never get to meet, travel to places they would never get to go, and to experience situations they would never get to experience. Fiction takes readers beyond their own individual experiences of life. Literature from very different times and places can be a source of pleasure and appreciation here and now. Such works can help a person to shape his general attitude toward life.

Literary texts can be sources of inspiration and character formation and can develop one's capacity to empathize with others. They can provide insights into the subtleties of human nature. They can teach significant truths about the human condition revealing how people think and act. Imaginative fiction presents a variety of fully developed literary characters with a wide range of beliefs, desires, and behaviors. Literature transmits profundity of thought, fullness of emotion, and insight into various characters' value systems. It can be inspiring to see different characters grow and change throughout a fictional work—at times the reader almost feels as though he is growing and changing with them. An individual can take on roles vicariously through reading. Fiction gives the reader the opportunity to know and to follow various characters and to see why they take certain courses or actions. Fiction allows people to observe a wide range of motives, traits, and behaviors. Different perspectives are attained because fiction helps readers see scenarios from various points of view. Stories can enable readers to identify with characters who are quite different from themselves. This can help in understanding the many types of people they encounter in life. Characters in a story can have an impact on the character of the reader. A person's own moral conduct and responses can be affected by the moral imagination of writers. Every fictional work has the potential to prompt a person to make changes in his own life.

Business is the great story of the last several hundred years. Work is an essential and intrinsic part of human existence—a person's identity is frequently defined by the work he performs. Imaginative literature can impart an understanding of the business world and how it works. All of the elements of outstanding fiction are present in every business day including heroism, cowardice, comedy, tragedy, absurdity, romance, genius, stupidity, morality, immorality, catastrophe, emotion, competence, incompetence, independence, teamwork, politics, conflicts, dilemmas, opportunities, threats, decision-making, make or break moments, and so on. Reading fiction dealing with business issues can sensitize and enlighten us to the nature and complexities of the business world.

Literature offers portraits of characters as employers, employees, managers, leaders, consultants, and other professionals and as regular human beings with a variety of drives, desires, and ambitions. Fiction offers superb descriptions of the situations, circumstances, and organizational settings in which workers find themselves. Reading literary texts enables people to observe the issues within large and appropriate contexts—context must be established. The reader is able to encounter descriptions of a variety of successful and unsuccessful, moral and immoral, men and women in different work situations. Stories can serve to stimulate the moral imagination, to increase one's understanding of moral dilemmas, and to enhance moral competence. Fiction can heighten a person's ability to relate to complex ethical matters facing the individual and the organization. Literature can strengthen a manager or other employee's ability to resolve specific moral issues. Imaginative literature can be an especially valuable resource for managers attempting to comprehend and to resolve human problems in business. Fiction can help a manager to understand his own needs and the needs of the people whom he manages for things such as individuality, identity, challenges, power and control, responsibility, self-respect and self-esteem, acceptance and recognition, personal integrity, and self-fulfillment.

The use of fiction, including novels and plays can enrich teaching materials in both educational and business settings. Fiction can be a powerful force to teach, educate, and move students and employees in ways that lectures, case studies, textbooks, articles, and anecdotes cannot. Although cases can be complex, they cannot compare with the multifaceted nature of storytelling. In fiction, we know much more about the characters than in case studies. In addition, readers or viewers can empathize with the characters. Fiction more closely mimics reality and illuminates the full context of a situation.

It follows that fiction generates insights that are conceivably different from those emanating from the study of cases. Not only do novels and plays offer an expanded view of businessmen and business relationships, they can also sometimes serve as a way to experience real events that occurred in the past. Studying such works helps people understand what happened in the past so that they can learn to avoid making similar mistakes in the future or, more positively, learn what to do from successful actions taken in prior situations.

Studying fictions of business can provide insight to often inexperienced business students with respect to real-life situations. They can address a multitude of issues and topics and can frequently better transmit a lesson or message than traditional teaching approaches can. Novels and plays have the ability to tell interesting stories and the potential to stick with the reader longer than lectures, case studies, textbook chapters, etc. Literary passages are much more engaging and memorable for most students and other audiences. Fiction can be a great supplement to the theories that students encounter in their business curriculum. Studying business fiction helps business students to relate their various business classes, such as management, marketing, organizational behavior, finance, operations management, and to real-life situations like takeovers, market crashes, layoffs, etc.

Everyday business people deal concurrently with multiple issues. Novels and plays are thus realistic because they tend to present several issues together in the context of a story. Fiction can tell a more complete story by dealing with multiple subjects and by demonstrating how issues interact and interrelate. Also, the situations and characters found in fictional works are more realistic than the abstractions found in textbooks and case studies.

Fiction can be used to teach, explicate, and illustrate a wide range of business issues and concepts. Many fictional works address human problems in business such as managing interpersonal conflict and office politics; using different styles of management; the potential loss of one's individuality as a person tends to become an "organization man"; the stultifying effect of routine in business; the difficulty in balancing work life and home life; hiring and keeping virtuous employees; maintaining one's personal integrity while satisfying the company's demands for loyalty, conformity and adaptation to the firm's culture; communication problems a business may experience; fundamental moral dilemmas; and depersonalization and mechanization of human relationships. Fictional works tend to describe human behavior and motivations more eloquently, powerfully, and engagingly than texts, articles, or cases typically do. Literary authors are likely to develop and present ideas through individual characters. They depict human insights and interests from the perspective of individuals within an organizational setting. Reading imaginative literature is an excellent way to develop critical thinking and to learn about values and character.

Many novels and plays, are concerned with the actual operation of the business system. Some deal directly with business problems such as government regulation, cost control, new product development, labor relations, environmental pollution, health and safety, plant openings and closings, tactics used and selection of takeover targets, structuring financial transactions, succession planning, strategic planning, the creation of mission statements, the company's role in the community, and social responsibility. Assessing fictional situations makes a person more thoughtful, better prepared for situations, and better able to predict the consequences of alternative actions. Fiction can address both matters of morality and practical issues. There are many fine selections in literature which prompt readers to wrestle with business situations.

Older novels and plays can supply information on the history of a subject or topic. They can act as historical references for actual past instances and can help students to understand the reasons for successes and failures of the past. Older literature can provide a good history lesson and can help people to understand the development of our various businesses and industries. These stories can be inspiring and motivational and can demonstrate how various organizations and managers were able to overcome obstacles, adapt, and survive. Fictional works are cultural artifacts from different time periods that can be valuable when discussing the history of business. Many fictional works present history in a form that is more interesting than when one just reads history books.

A case can be made that reading the works of playwrights who have taken business persons and a business-oriented culture as their literary subject may be even better than novels for teaching business concepts and for instilling moral values. Plays can more distinctly address the interaction of characters thus enabling the reader to become more involved in their situations. Drama can be a more efficient teaching tool than novels because plays can attend to the same number of business issues in a briefer format. A play's dynamic scenarios more nearly map reality and illuminate a situation's full context. Passages in a play can be used in role playing and readers' theater. This form of active learning can depict a more complete portrait of the business world.

Throughout history, business and the businessman have not fared especially well in business fiction. There have been many unflattering depictions of business, businessmen, and capitalism. Many have often attacked business and industry for destroying an old communal order based on equality and have lamented the businessman's preoccupation with material success and the dominance of large dehumanizing organizations in people's lives. A great many novelists and playwrights, have been repelled by business and have criticized the businessman's lack of culture and interest in education. Notably, writers of artistic merit are likely to be hostile and negative toward business ideology.

Fortunately, some fictional works do characterize business and the businessmen in a more favorable, more realistic, even heroic image by emphasizing the possibilities of life in a free society, the inherent ethical nature of capitalism and the businessman, the strength and self-sufficiency of the hard-working businessman, and the entrepreneur as wealth creator and promoter of human economic progress. Positive images of business, businessmen, and capitalism do exist but more are needed in order to illustrate the value of free enterprise, innovation, and personal initiative.

Business fiction is a heterogeneous collection of writings. Depictions of business and the businessman have changed over time. Literary attitudes in a given time period and part of the world, and for a specific author, are frequently partial, particular to a given social class, and reflective of the author's political convictions. For example, European attitudes toward business have been more negative than the attitudes of Americans who have great faith in progress and who believe in the necessity of material progress. In addition, writers are likely to set their fiction within the professional environment with which they are familiar.

THE BEGINNINGS OF BUSINESS FICTION

The tradesman has been portrayed in English literature ever since Geoffrey Chaucer's time in the fourteenth century. Chaucer himself was controller of customs and royal business projects for many years. In his *The Canterbury Tales,* he paints a positive portrait of a merchant as a worthy and respectable man. During this time a new merchant class with business values was slowly but steadily becoming a factor in a world traditionally controlled by the Church and land owners. In the sixteenth century, we find Shakespeare frequently showing respect and honor for the tradesmen. Shakespeare was a fine businessman in his own right possessing knowledge of commerce, contracts, and finance. His play *The Merchant of Venice* (1596) is essentially about business ethics with its main theme being a disagreement about a contract between the Jewish money lender, Shylock, and the Christian merchant, Antonio, which has to be decided by a judge. Shakespeare's play focuses on the gradual acceptance of interest on loans in the European business world. In addition, the father of the English novel, Daniel Dafoe, started out as a businessman and displayed admiration for the merchant in his works. Beginning with Dafoe, novels have delivered treatments of business and the businessman that are varied, complex, and nuanced resulting in a new literary genre. The businessman was a familiar character in the sixteenth century and the manufacturer became a common figure later.

We will now take a retrospective look at the changing image of business and the businessman in fictional works during various time periods. In doing so, a number of notable works will be mentioned and briefly discussed. This survey will also demonstrate how business and organizations have changed and how the successful ones have been adaptive in order to survive. Through literature, a person can learn about work-life from another person's point of view in a very different time and place.

THE PRE-CIVIL WAR ERA

In the eighteenth century, business was still seen as respectable and virtuous. By the first half of the nineteenth century, business and the businessman were beginning to become objects of reprobation. Criticisms were levied at individual businessmen as there were very few American corporations in existence during the first half of that century. Fictions of this era tended to portray salesmen and individual proprietors as uncultured and selfish men who lack scruples. The few corporations that did exist tended to be state-granted monopolies for accomplishing public works. During this period many state officials were bribed by such corporations in order to be granted the required licenses. For example, railroad companies and government officials engaged in unprecedented political and financial corruption.

Two of the best pre-Civil War American works of business fiction are Herman Melville's *Bartleby the Scrivener: A Story of Wall Street* (1853) and *The Confidence Man* (1857). Bartleby is a mysterious clerk and copyist on New York's Wall Street who politely refuses to do work. His employer is a kind and compassionate man. The story is of the relationship between a manager and an uncooperative, inert employee. *Bartleby* can perhaps be viewed as an early ancestor of the recent film, *Office Space*, a satire of helpless employees doing mindless jobs in a bland company. In *The Confidence Man* a master con man or Yankee peddler assumes a variety of forms as he transforms into different characters on a steamboat going from St. Louis to New Orleans. The confidence man is a master of duplicity and deception. The lesson in this novel is that a person is known by what he or she appears to be. The great English author, Charles Dickens, had visited America in 1842 during which he sensed the emerging image of the American businessman as a con man. In his *The Life and Adventures of Martin Chuzzlewit* (1844), he tells of a young Englishman who changes into a confidence man when he travels to America. Of course, the young man is no match for the American con man and he returns defeated and chastised to England. Dickens also authored *A Christmas Carol* (1843), in which he provided an image of a miserly and greedy businessman in the character, Ebenezer Scrooge. In addition, his 1848 novel *Dombey and Son* centered around a family-owned shipping business.

Elizabeth Gaskell's *North and South* (1855) is a classic of Victorian literature and the Industrial Revolution. This novel deals with the disagreement and possible harmonization of the worldviews prevalent in idyllic, gentrified, and agricultural Southern England and in the brutal industrial North. In *North and South* a woman moves with her family from the peaceful South to settle in a busy working city. She initially experiences culture shock as she goes from living in the naturalness and beauty of the South to the unnaturalness of the industrial North. She meets a hard-working, self-made industrialist who has become a leading manufacturer of cotton fiber. He is a willful taskmaster who does not interact with his workers on a personal level. Both the woman and the industrialist need to change and they do. The story is about how people from different cultural backgrounds and social spheres go from dislike of each other to understanding and respecting each other's views. Each one is transformed into a more tolerant, rounded, and thoughtful person. There is a merging of dissimilar types. She grows to accept and to appreciate the work ethic, progress, and productivity, and he learns to relate to his employees on a human level. The novel is defined by the resolution of numerous interrelated conflicts: North vs South, industrialists vs working class, wealthy class vs leisure class, life as work vs life as aesthetic appreciation, industry vs agriculture, and so on.

THE POST-CIVIL WAR ERA

In American fiction, the revulsion and animus toward business and the businessman were well developed by the time of the Civil War. Business power had accumulated during the Civil War and expanded throughout the following decades. Following the Civil War, there appeared a variety of novels dealing with success, financial and political corruption and scandals, and economic reforms. The materialistic philosophy and economic system of the Gilded Age promoted a widespread sense of distrust. Many novels after the Civil War disparaged capitalism by emphasizing the contradiction between business sentiments and higher cultural and moral ones.

Horatio Alger is famous for his rags-to-riches glorified stories of small merchants such as *Ragged Dick* (1868), *Strive and Succeed* (1871), and *Paul the Peddler* (1871). Alger's literary optimism was a function of the prevailing beliefs of his times in individualism and laissez-faire economics. Alger emphasized that hard work is the key to success. In his popular improvement tales, his hero characters earn their living through their efforts, self-discipline, self-reliance, and good luck. Diligence and thrift play a part, but usually, in the end, occurrences such as inheritance or finding a proper patron help to move the hero to the station of the rich. It is interesting to note that Richard Kimball's earlier novel, *Undercurrents of Wall Street* (1862), ends like Alger's novels with an intervention—a large inheritance that rescues the protagonist from destitution. This also occurs in Charles Bellamy's later 1879 novel, *The Breton Mills.* Alongside the Horatio Alger type of businessman who makes good through his own efforts plus chance was the Scrooge-like miser warped by his ruthless struggle for material rewards. The image of the businessmen put forth by the followers of Dickens is one of greed, miserliness, unethical business dealings, and exploitation of, and insensitivity to, the needs of employees. Then after the Civil War in the 1870s there was rampant political and moral corruption inflamed by the national mania for speculation. This corruption was dealt with in several novels.

Mark Twain and John Dudley Warner's *The Gilded Age* (1873) portrays speculation as a national pastime. The novel satirizes every type of speculation imaginable. It is a tale of corrupt Washington politicians conniving with private land and stock speculators who lobby them. The mania for stock and land speculation following the Civil War was intensified by the railroad explosion and financial scandals in Washington during the Grant administration and on Wall Street between 1868 and 1872. The novel recommends moral reform rather than economic reform. Anthony Trollope's *The Way We Live Now* (1873) was also set at the time of the financial madness of the early 1870s and the financial crash of 1873. Trollope's satire of speculation and deception is an indictment of a corrupt society. Trollope's financier protagonist makes a pretense of wealth and respectability and almost succeeds in a manipulative scam of enormous proportions.

Two 1875 novels break ground and provide the model for the modern financial Wall Street novel. These are John W. DeForest's *Honest John Vane* and Josiah G. Holland's *Sevenoaks: A Story of Today.*

There were sweeping transformations in the economy after the Civil War. Industry grew rapidly, cities mushroomed, large groups were dislocated, there was an influx of immigrant foreign workers, labor/industrial conflict grew, economic protests became common, and the leaders of industry became "robber barons" within a short number of years. America was changing from a nation of individual entrepreneurs and small farmers to one of factory workers in routinized jobs. Many of the factory workers were immigrants who felt more at home in America than in Europe because they were free of the class structure of Europe.

Henrik Ibsen's 1882 play, *An Enemy of the People*, begins with Dr. Thomas Stockmann's discovery that the water at the town resort's spa baths are contaminated. He is concerned about the serious health threat to the visitors to the spa. The doctor expects to be praised for his discovery but then the people find out how much the needed improvements will cost. His brother, the Mayor, refuses to believe the truth of science and turns the "common majority" against the doctor by expressing doubt about the test report's findings. The mayor manipulates the proceedings of the town meeting so that the doctor cannot read his findings. At first, Stockmann believes in the power of democracy and the capabilities of the people who he believes will see the truth of his report and will support him. Then, when democratic principles are used at the meeting to keep him from reading his report, he delivers a tirade against the democratic majority. Dr. Stockmann is great example of virtue ethics. He is honest, courageous, impartial, objective, just, truthful, rational, and independent. He has integrity and refuses to abandon his principles. This play resonates with relevant current issues and concerns such as hydraulic fracking, pipelines, climate charge, contamination of drinking water, and man-made organic chemicals.

Although an engineer in H.H. Boyesen's *A Daughter of the Philistines* (1883) is critical of the financial machinations of Wall Street speculators, he also comments favorably on the material, moral, and intellectual progress in the United States and expresses his belief in American notions of freedom, quality workmanship, and social welfare. Another 1883 social novel, *The Bread-Winners*, by John Hay deals with a former captain in the army who organizes a group of Civil War veterans to keep law and order and to protect property rights when a strike occurs. This antilabor novel is more against labor organizers than it is against the workers themselves.

THE ERA OF SOCIAL DARWINISM, REALISM, AND NATURALISM

The appearance of freewheeling private enterprisers led to regulations such as the Interstate Commerce Act of 1887 and the Sherman Antitrust Act of 1890. By 1890 there were a large number of critics who advocated the replacement of capitalism with socialism. Novelists helped pave the way for the passage of the early antitrust laws. The period between the end of the Civil War and the end of World War I produced hundreds of novels dealing with business, financial speculation, trusts, labor relations, economic crises, and so on. During the 1880s there was a great deal of labor/industrial conflict. There were economic crises including a depression during the 1890s. In addition, by 1900, there was the establishment of the great industrial trusts and the proliferation of mergers. As a result, the railroads and the large manufacturing firms were accused of engaging in ruinous competition.

Success novels, reflecting the belief in Social Darwinism, existed alongside reform and utopian novels that began to appear in the 1880s. The success novels treated corporate empire builders as visionaries, heroes, creators, as well as manipulators. In the success novels acquiring riches proved one's mastery over the environment and his fitness to survive. Utopian novels were numerous in the last decade of the nineteenth century. By then social protest novels were gaining popularity. The discontent and unrest of the 1890s stemmed from the prevailing notion that industries were getting to be too institutionalized and that wealth was becoming too concentrated. The reform novels were intended to explain structural problems beyond the control of any one individual. By 1900, novelists were capitalizing on the widespread distrust of business, especially big business. Their works were keeping pace with the huge transformations in the business world. Since the late 1800s, authors have been quick to criticize monopoly power, employment practices, and income distribution.

William Dean Howells is more realistic and kinder to the businessman than many of his contemporary writers. His novel, *The Rise of Silas Lapham* (1885), is the classic realistic novel of American business and has received a great deal of literary acclaim. Howells did not reduce his hero to caricature and he illustrated the complexities of moral action in the real world. Silas Lapham is depicted as uncultured but he is not shown to be necessarily immoral. He is portrayed as a sympathetic and motivated individual who intended to make something of himself from his early years on. Howells shows that man is a free agent and that the choices in one's life determine his character. Lapham is a newly rich industrialist who rose from the backwoods of Vermont to run a successful mineral paint business. His wife blames him for what she perceives as mistreatment of a former business partner. He tries to make amends. This, along with some other events, causes Lapham to spin headlong toward financial ruin. At the end of the story, he finds peace and continues to manufacture a small line of paints. By the end of the story, Lapham has come back from financial collapse and is happy running a small version of his former business. Howells is not as kind to the businessman in his *A Hazard of New Fortunes* (1890). In this novel Jacob Dryfoos represents the dishonest individual in the marketplace. Dryfoos becomes a corrupt speculator on Wall Street. Dryfoos, Howell's version of the contemporary robber baron, fails to repent by the end of the story. Howells paints a distressing portrait of the newly rich Dryfoos. Like Lapham, Dryfoos begins as a farmer possessing traditional virtues. Then natural gas is found under his land. He sells his farm to Standard Oil for a large sum of money, discovers stock speculation, is stricken with "boom fever," becomes rich through luck rather than through talent, and experiences spiritual and moral decay. What he gains in money, he loses in happiness. In the novel, Howells illustrates the disintegrating effects of suddenly acquired wealth.

In *Looking Backward* (1888), Edward Bellamy describes a new egalitarian American social, political, and economic order in which a technocratic elite manages nationalized industries. This best-selling utopian novel played a large role in shaping public opinion regarding equality. In the novel America has evolved into a cooperative society in which the government owns all of the capital. The people are motivated by pride and each citizen receives the same amount of credit to spend. America has evolved into a command economy made up of one great trust. Another socialist writer, Jack London, penned an interesting, dystopian, futuristic, socialist, and muckraking novel, *The Iron Heel* (1908), twenty years after Bellamy's work. In London's novel, written from the workers' point of view, there are great divisions between the classes and a powerful oligarchy and dictatorship of monopoly capitalists or plutocrats uses terror to run the country and to deny worker's rights. *The Iron Heel*, focuses on political and social changes. In this tale of despair, socialism eventually creates a Utopian society. Another important novel written by London is his *Burning Daylight* (1910). It centers on the moral corruption and physical depravity that stems from the country's obsession with business.

In Mark Twain's *A Connecticut Yankee in King Arthur's Court* (1888), the hero, Hank Morgan, a type of tinkerer or efficiency expert, gets hit over the head at work and awakens to find himself in sixth-century medieval England which is suffering from economic problems. The inventor attempts to improve England's economic, communications, and transportation systems. The resourceful and skilled Morgan wants to free people from ignorance and superstition. He advances the notions of free enterprise and private property. Morgan introduces a new currency in an attempt to promote economic recovery. He also introduces a stock exchange and utilizes knights as traveling salesmen. His actions led to a war that breaks up King Arthur's realm. At one point, the mechanic tries to explain to a group of workers the difference between real wages and nominal wages. He discusses that most people tend to resist changes and he is able to improve life in medieval England in only small ways. The decade of the 1890s then gave us two fine business-related novels: Henry B. Fuller's *The Cliff-Dwellers* (1893) and Robert Herrick's *The Gospel of Freedom* (1898). Fuller's novel supplies a sense of the complexity of the business world that includes capitalists, bankers, lawyers, brokers, marketers, industrialists, insurance agents, and so on. Herrick attempts to define real success by exploring the relationship between commitment to oneself and commitment to others.

The Great God Success (1901) by progressive journalist, David Graham Phillips, deals with the newspaper industry and explores a variety of social problems. This naturalistic novel casts the businessman in a Darwinian manner and attacks yellow journalism with its sensationalized features, eye-catching headlines, and lack of well-researched stories.

Naturalistic writers such as Frank Norris and Theodore Dreiser portrayed the businessman in Darwinian scale, cornering a commodities market, establishing a trust, or through some other grand endeavor. The philosophy of naturalism does not find any distinctive significance in man. Nature is thus indifferent toward men but nevertheless natural laws do provide social benefits. The goal of literary naturalism is to represent in abundant and objective detail that man is a small, finite, and limited being determined by heredity and by social, economic, and psychological factors. In his novels, Norris depicts the naturalism, romance, and adventure of business.

In Frank Norris's novels, economic processes are huge, impersonal forces—the business system is ultimately controlled by natural forces. His novels demonstrate the impersonality, power, and pervasiveness of market forces. In his *The Octopus* (1901) independent wheat—farmers become pawns at the mercy of the great railroads, politicians, and natural forces beyond their control. In Norris's vision of orderly determinism evil is short-lived. *The Octopus* provides a historical look into a specific struggle between railroad executives and independent wheat farmers in an expanding California. Norris's 1903 novel, *The Pit*, looks at an attempt to corner the wheat market in Chicago. The title refers to the trading room of the Chicago Board of Trade. For his story, the author drew upon a historical speculative grain corner of 1897–98. In this novel, Norris senses and foresees the possibilities of speculation and Wall Street. In *The Pit* economic laws collide with natural laws. The natural law wins as the speculators and financiers, who attempt to interfere with the natural order of the wheat cycle, are soundly defeated. This novel is about both the romance, excitement, and fascination of business warfare and speculation and the rapacity and greed that can stem from commercial struggles. It teaches that business can be adventurous, but that it can also have corrosive effects.

Several notable business novels appeared during the first decade of the 1900s. *Calumet K* (1901) by Samuel Merwin and Henry Webster is a Midwestern novel centered around the building of a two million bushel grain elevator. The principal character is Charlie Bannon, a heroic mid-level manager, who has been charged by his company to construct the elevator. The competent hero faces a series of obstacles and complications that threaten the completion of the project. Bannon loves his work and is a great example of the achieving moral individual. He is motivated to achieve what is best for his company and for himself. It is no wonder why *Calumet K* was philosopher-novelist Ayn Rand's favorite novel. In contrast, in Robert Herrick's *The Memoirs of an American Citizen* (1905) tainted money is required for the "success" of the protagonists similar to the case in Norris's *The Pit*. Herrick's main character is proud to be a creator, revels in his possessions, and is ultimately condemned on moral grounds.

Another novel by Merwin and Webster celebrating unregulated competition in American business is the *The Short Line War* (1899). This novel describes the struggle between two railroads for control of a profitable feeder line.

Upton Sinclair's *The Jungle* (1906) is well known for bringing about the United States' meat inspection system. This proletarian novel gained meteoric notoriety because of its graphic depiction of terrible slaughterhouse conditions, thus prompting reform of the meat packing industry and the passage of the Food and Drug Act. *The Jungle* is a powerful study of the working conditions in the Chicago stockyards. It describes the exploitation of workers and explains how economically disadvantaged and low-skilled workers have a very small chance to better themselves and to move up the economic ladder. The novel details the corruption, waste, and exploitation of Chicago's "Packingtown." Ernest Bramah's *Secret of the League* (1907) tells the story of the overthrow by businessmen of a left-wing socialist government in England. The weapon of the businessmen in the economic war against socialist government is a mass boycott of coal, a heavily state-subsidized industry.

George Bernard Shaw's play, *Major Barbara* (1906), explores a conflict of values between a father and his daughter. Andrew Undershaft is an armaments manufacturer and his daughter, Barbara, is a major in the Salvation Army. Both have strong convictions. She rejects her father because of his materialism and of the business that he is in. He derides her and the Salvation Army's self-congratulatory saintliness. Barbara becomes disillusioned when she discovers that the Salvation Army has accepted money from her father. That organization exists in order to save the souls of the poor who need to eat and he supplies money to that organization. The lesson is that donations can always be used for good purposes no matter what their source happens to be. They decide to visit each other's workplace. She discovers that her father is a benevolent and visionary leader who runs a model factory, provides for his employees' needs in order to elicit their productivity, and as a result, is able to amass a large fortune. At the Salvation Army he sees people intent on saving souls. He also sees that some of the poor pander to the altruistic instincts and saintliness of the workers who provide them with food and shelter.

Theodore Dreiser's trilogy of desire is about the ruthless and manipulative business titan, Frank Cowperwood, who believes that he is superior to the moral and legal codes restraining other individuals. Cowperwood has reasoned that the law of civilization is the same as the law of the jungle. The strong feed on the weak and the only choice is to kill or be killed. Like Frank Norris, Dreiser portrays the captains of industry and finance as heroic but manipulative creators and organizers. It is evident that Dreiser admired and sympathized with his nonconformist superman-hero in *The Financier* (1912). *The Titan* (1914), and *The Stoic* (1947). In these novels, Cowperwood shows contempt for conventional notions of morality. Dreiser's best known book in this trilogy, *The Financier* takes a look back at the financial disasters of the 1870s. The Darwinian Cowperwood seeks satisfaction in wealth, women, and power. He bribes, cheats, and lies to gain these. He becomes a streetcar magnate in Philadelphia. The man without a conscience rises, falls, and rises again. His motto is "I satisfy myself." He is unrepentant after being found guilty of legally questionable acts. Undeterred, he restores his fortune after being released from prison by taking a bear position in the midst of the great panic of 1873. Throughout his life he uses opportunities presented to him by the limitations and weaknesses of others.

In *The Titan,* Cowperwood goes to Chicago from Philadelphia with the goal of being a power in the city. He first gains control of the gas companies, and then he struggles to gain control of the city's street railway franchises. In his efforts he buys politicians and engages in bribery. Cowperwood outmaneuvers and bankrupts several opponents with the help of his political allies. His financial rivals elicit the outrage of the common people and the press against Cowperwood who is deemed to be a treat to the city. When there is a public demand for public ownership of all street railings, Cowperwood's enemies retract their opposition to his attempt to monopolize. However, in the end he fails to obtain the fifty year franchise for his railway that he had deserved.

In *The Stoic*, the sixty-year-old Cowperwood goes to London where he intends to build, develop, and take over an underground railway system throughout the city. He dies and the young woman who he loves uses his money to search for wisdom in India. She is moved by the poverty that she sees there, returns to the United States, and promises to erect a free hospital for the poor who live in Manhattan's East Side, as was Cowperwood's desire. Her action helps to make amends for Cowperwood's acquisitive desire and to portray him as a benefactor of public welfare.

Dreiser does not attack the immorality of the world he describes in his novels. Dreiser understands Cowperwood's faults but he does not pass judgment on him. Like Norris, Dreiser views businessmen as amoral individuals in the era of trusts, monopolies, political corruption, and financial manipulation. Dreiser writes about the unconquerable self-made man who reached his successful position without the benefit of formal education.

In addition to his trilogy of desire, Dreiser published *An American Tragedy* (1925). The breadth and depth of this complex novel attempts to contain the entire American experience. Clyde Griffiths, a poor boy from a working class background, attempts to break free from his family and to enter the upper echelons of American society. He struggles, has a little success, but mostly endures a life of suffering. Too many forces, including lack of education and economic conditions, work against him. The novel illustrates that hereditary, environmental, social, and economic forces determine a person's destiny. For most Americans, their dream can never come true because of class distinctions, social restrictions, inherited wealth, and other factors. In *An American Tragedy,* Dreiser also highlights the shallowness and moral poverty of the rich.

Upton Sinclair's *The Moneychangers* (1908) is a fictional account of the Great Panic of 1907. The novel provides a behind-the-scene description of that panic. This tale of banker omnipotence illustrates the political influence existed by the rich and how the media is controlled in order to affect public opinion. The most powerful man on Wall Street deliberately brings on a financial disaster in order to destroy a rival trust company and to cause a crash in the stock market, a run on America's banks, and a nationwide depression. He brings the country down in one quick stroke in order to teach the masses to fear and to respect the nation's monied interests. *The Moneychangers* also shows how depositors and stockholders both share the blame for and consent to, their own predicament. The destructive effects of speculation and over-leveraging that underpinned the 1907 financial panic led to the implementation of the Federal Reserve System. Sinclair's *The Metropolis* (1908) addresses the huge disparity between the upper and lower classes of society and the cruelty and injustice that exist in more prosperous societies.

Will Payne was a financial journalist and novelist who wrote about both the positive and negative aspects of capitalism and business in his fictional works. With respect to ethics, he illustrated that businessmen are as good or as bad as those in other professions. They do not always behave morally but people are better off because of capitalism. In his provocative novels he invites his readers to consider the dynamic and long-term effects of capitalism. He wrote nine novels including *Jerry the Dreamer* (1896), *The Money Captain* (1898), *Mr. Salt* (1903), and *The Automatic Capitalists* (1909).

Edna Ferber penned three books in her adventures of Emma McChesney series: *Roast Beef Medium* (1913), *Personality Plus* (1914), and *Emma McChesney and Co.* (1915). Emma is a bright, stylish, divorced, Midwest sales representative for a skirt company. In her mid-thirties, she has a teenage son and a talent for business and for dealing with people. She is a honest, hardworking, highly motivated, highly respected, and knowledgeable career woman around 1910 or so. These three volumes realistically chronicle the life of an entrepreneurial woman in the early twentieth-century business world.

Abraham Cahan's *The Rise of David Levinsky* (1917) is a great example of immigrant fiction as well as of business fiction. In the form of a thirty year memoir, it tells the story of the process of adaptation to American life by a Russian Jewish immigrant. Despite his early years of poverty, the protagonist becomes extremely successful financially in the American ready-to-wear clothing industry. He becomes rich in things of the world at the expense of his inner spirit. At the end he realizes that he is no different than he was as a child and that money and power alone cannot make one happy. Unlike many other novelists who explored American business, Cahan paid a great deal of attention to the details of the functioning of business itself.

FROM THE DECADE OF EXCESS TO WELFARE AND WARTIME

In the 1920s literary satire rather than outright condemnation of business and the businessman was the preferred vehicle for literary critics of capitalism. Before Sinclair Lewis's *Babbitt* (1922) the businessman had consistently been portrayed as a rugged individualist. *Babbitt* fiercely satirizes the way in which bourgeois culture and standardized mass consumption have affected society. In this novel, Lewis provides a harsher perspective on the businessman than did earlier writers such as Howells. Babbitt gives up his individuality to conform to the values of his community and lives for what others consider to be respectable. Babbitt is a complacent, prosperous, middle-class citizen who is depicted as a helpless victim of social pressure. The author devotes a large section of the novel to describe Babbitt's typical working day. Babbitt dislikes hard work. By the end of the story he realizes and admits that his life is not fulfilling.

Garet Garrett's novel *The Driver* (1922) tells the story of a Wall Street speculator, financier, and entrepreneur, Henry Galt, who acquires control of a failing railroad. When the railroad declares bankruptcy Galt assumes a leadership position in the company and, through his great vision and work ethic, turns it into a spectacular success. The story occurs in the wake of the great panic of 1893. As he succeeds the government conspires with his competitors to regulate and control him. *The Driver* tells how the government cannot get the economy out of recession but, instead, how people like Galt can through investments and productive work.

Upton Sinclair's *Oil* (1927) provides a picture of Southern California's early oil industry. It is set during the early Southern California oil boom and encompasses the Harding Administration's Teapot Dome Scandal, World War I, and the Red Scare. This novel of social injustice includes senators, oil barons, oil workers, small investors, and much more. It is a story of greed, corruption, and class warfare. The tale is of a willful, entrepreneurial, and energetic oil magnate who builds an empire through ruthlessness and bribery of public officials. The oil baron has an idealistic pro-worker son who has become aware of working class Americans' exploitation and struggles.

Certain novels of the 1920s and 1930s look at class differences and class warfare. One of America's best known and most loved novels is F. Scott Fitzgerald's *The Great Gatsby* (1925). It is a story of social stratification and of "old money" versus "new money." The novel centers on an ambitious, self-made man with huge hopes and dreams in an era of excess. Unfortunately, Gatsby could never escape his lowly background. He fails when he encounters the vicious "old rich" world of emptiness, moral decay, and extravagant parties. The best works of the 1920s such as *The Great Gatsby*, Booth Tarkington's *The Plutocrat* (1927), and Sinclair Lewis's *Babbitt* and *Dodsworth* (1929) were more separated from the everyday actualities of business than novels before them or since them. Lewis's Sam Dodsworth is a noble businessman who has the dream of creating an attractive and practical product. Much later Fitzgerald supplied a portrait of a strong-minded, compassionate head of a major Hollywood movie studio in his unfinished *The Last Tycoon* (1941). The dictatorial tycoon understands his responsibilities to all of his constituencies. He knows what he wants to accomplish and is adept at playing to the strengths, weaknesses, and personalities of others including actors, screenwriters, directors, and others. This movie producer exhibits a command and control management style.

Alice Tisdale Hobart's *Oil for the Lamps of China* (1933) tells the story of a salesman, inventor, and field inspector who is sent to China during the turmoil of China's Nationalist Revolution of the 1920s in order to capture that nation's untapped market. He is devoted to his job and he wants to bring progress to China in the form of oil and oil lamps.

In Sinclair Lewis's *Work of Art* (1934) three generations of a family live and work in inns, boarding houses, and hotels. The main character is inspired by the ideal of perfection that he had learned from a traveling salesman. He is a virtuous businessman who believes that running a great hotel can be a work of art. He dreams of running a perfect hotel. Never satisfied, he imagines what a perfect hotel can be like but he never attains that dream as he experiences the joys and frustrations of operating a business in the real world.

A great deal of the literature of the 1920s and 1930s is of the left. The crash and the Great Depression brought about a new wave of literary social criticism and calls for the federal government to lead the economy. John Dos Passos's *USA* trilogy consisting of *The 42nd Parallel* (1930), *1919* (1932), and *The Big Money* (1936) present the story of America from 1910 until 1930. In these works Dos Passos presents a mixture of stories, news items, biographical sketches of important figures, and narrations. He tells the stories of a variety of people. His complex trilogy condemns both capitalism and socialism. In *The Big Money* Dos Passos speaks for the decade of the Depression. In it he continues to interweave fiction, biography, and documentary-style newsreels to witness the pursuit of the American Dream from various vantage points. The author describes two different nations within the United States during the 1920s. This social and political novel contrasts the world of speakeasies, prohibition, and stock speculation with the world of the rebelling working class, the labor movement, labor-management warfare, and immigrants. Much later Dos Passos wrote *Midcentury: A Contemporary Chronicle* (1961) in which he focuses on the damaging nature of labor involvement with racketeering and the Mafia. The author illustrates how union leaders become like monopolistic capitalists when they invest union funds for private gain. He also condemns big corporations and big government. Dos Passos rebuffs the NLRB for its inability to control violence and racketeering in unions.

In *The Grapes of Wrath* (1939), John Steinbeck proposes fundamental questions regarding social justice, land ownership and stewardship, and the proper role of government. This is the story of tenant farmers in Oklahoma driven away by drought, depression, and large companies that wanted to take their land back. They are told that there are "orders from the bank" to force them off the land. Fruit growers in California print flyers asserting the existence of abundant well-paying jobs. This is untrue and when they arrive in California there are so many migrant workers seeking employment that wages are set at extremely low levels. Then, of course, there are the company stores that charge disproportionately high prices compared to the wages received. The necessity of large-scale government intervention during bad economic times appears to be a major lesson in *The Grapes of Wrath.*

The famed poet, William Carlos Williams began a trilogy of business novels about an immigrant family with *White Mule* (1937). The other two novels in the series are *In the Money* (1940) and *The Build-Up* (1946).

THE POST-WORLD WAR II ERA

During and immediately following World War II the reputation of business improved. The fine novels celebrating commerce are *The Fountainhead* (1943) by Ayn Rand and *Mildred Pierce* (1941) by James M. Cain. Then there is Budd Schulberg's *What Makes Sammy Run*?, a story of the rise and fall of a Jewish boy born in New York's Lower East side who escapes the ghetto and climbs the ladder of success through deception and betrayal. The post-World War II period also witnessed a reconsideration of the large corporations as the source of stultifying conformity. A company's demands for loyalty and devotion called for managers to dedicate their lives and efforts first and foremost to the corporation placing one's individuality and family in the background. The fictional image of the middle-level "organization man" was that of an individual having to choose between his personal values and the company's demands. Corporate life was becoming a major challenge for the individual. After World War II the emphasis of literary authors switched from one which includes the entire system of business to one confined to specific segments of that system. Some business sectors such as advertising seem to hardly even receive a fair depiction in fiction. For example, Frederic Wakeman's *The Hucksters* (1946) is a popular satiric exposé of the radio advertising business. Samuel Hopkins Adams's business novel *Plunder* was released in 1948. *Plunder* chronicles the career of an industrialist involved in dirty politics. Is this anti-business novel the reader is shown characters manufacturing defective airplanes, ships, armor plate, and shells. In addition, some corrupt Washington insiders attempt to fix the Army-Navy football game.

Arthur Miller's play *Death of a Salesman* (1949) is the tragic story of a man who wants to believe that he is a success and who is unable to admit failure. Willy Loman is a self-deluded man whose aspirations were much higher than his achievements. The unsuccessful salesman thinks that popularity, personality, and charisma are equal to success. He is not impressive or well-liked and creates fantasies to cover up his failures. *Death of a Salesman* provides a portrait of the coming apart of a man who has chosen the wrong career path and who is now at the end of that path. Willy is a man who worships success and popularity, but who achieves neither of them. He was a failure as a salesman and he was not loved by his friends and his family. He is a man living in a delusional world as a shield against reality. He wanted to "succeed" by being well-liked and personally attractive as opposed to becoming successful through skill and hard work. Willy did not know himself and he had all of the wrong dreams. He did not like being a salesman and he was not good at it. However, he liked working with his hands doing carpentry work and he was good at it. Unfortunately, carpentry was not his chosen career path.

Another Miller play, *All My Sons* (1947) tells the story of a manufacturer, Joe Keller, who averted financial failure by sending cracked cylinder heads to the Army Air Force during the war. These defective parts caused the deaths of twenty-one pilots. He sets up his business partner to take the blame and to go to jail. Keller becomes a rich man, but in the end his actions come back to haunt him. One of his sons had gone missing during the war. Keller faces an awful truth when he discovers that his son had learned about his father's deed and had intentionally flown to his death in revulsion to his father's lack of moral integrity.

In *Point of No Return* (1947) by John P. Marquand, Charles Gray, son of upper-middle-class New England Yankee parents, rises into aristocracy at an elite bank in New York City. Although he has escaped his former small town lifestyle, it still affects him. The successful banker attempts to free himself from a life that seems to be stereotyped and preordained. During a period of time when he is under consideration for a huge promotion, he revisits the town where he was brought up. He struggles to become a vice-president but resents the conformity required. Our sympathetic protagonist gets the promotion but the promotion does not fulfill his life. Gray then understands the superficiality and artificiality of the inter-office rivalry with another manager for the vice-presidency. He also comes to the realization that he would not have done anything differently. When success is thrust upon him he understands that he is part of a system and that he cannot do anything about that. *Point of No Return* thus reflects the doctrine of social determinism. Deterministic philosophy underpins this novel as well as others depicting the "organization man."

In 1951, noted economist Henry Hazlitt released his futuristic novel *Time Will Run Back*. The novel is set in the year 2100 some 150 years after the victory of socialism over capitalism. A new reluctant leader, who grew up on an island isolated from the workings of the global socialist political state, senses that there is something wrong with the socialist policies. He and his friend engage in Socratic-style discussions and rethink the economic basis of the system. They gradually rediscover the free market and attempt to implement new policies. The clever plot includes an assassination attempt, the founding of a new nation, and a love story. Reading *Time Will Run Back* is a great way to learn about free market economics.

THE MIDDLE-CLASS WORLD OF THE 1950s AND 1960s

Former businessman turned novelist, Cameron Hawley, truly understands and accurately portrays the world of business. His 1952 novel, *Executive Suite*, attained great success. The story begins with a crisis when the president of a furniture company suddenly and unexpectedly dies before he could develop a succession plan. The company is left in disarray with five vice-presidents competing for the top position. The story details the resulting office politics, machinations, and power struggles. In the end, the vice-president of product research and development is pitted against the vice-president of finance for the position of president. The foreman runs the factory and the latter keeps a close look at the costs. The hands-on factory man makes an impassioned speech explaining that the firm's success depends upon producing quality product. Profit results from doing good work. He wants to give consumers better furniture and the workers more fulfilling jobs. As a result, the controlling shareholders choose him for the position and, in turn, he selects the finance man to be his executive vice-president.

Hawley's 1955 novel *Cash McCall* is the story of a justified and benign corporate raider who benefits himself and society by acquiring poorly managed companies and bringing them back to economic health. He is misperceived by many to be a dishonorable tycoon who merely takes over firms, lays off workers, and sells the assets for huge profits. He is actually a man of moral integrity who acquires failing companies, improves them to turn them around, and then sells them to make an earned profit. McCall makes changes to a firm and frequently finds ways to attain synergy with other companies. *Cash McCall* celebrates the power of capitalism and portrays business as an honorable activity. Cameron Hawley went on to write two more novels about the drama of business, *The Lincoln Lords* (1960) and *The Hurricane Years* (1968).

Sloan Wilson's *The Man in the Gray Flannel Suit* (1955) provides a snapshot of life in the United States during the post-World War II era. The novel tells the story of Tom Rath, a returning World War II veteran and educated white collar worker. He longs for a safe, uneventful corporate existence after the chaos of the war. His goal is to balance his fragmented professional and personal lives. Rath values his personal, familial, and social needs more than he values gaining a promotion and moving up the corporate ladder. The sympathetic hero recognizes the costs of success. He understands that a man only has so much time and energy and therefore must choose between work or leisure and job or family. Rath rediscovers his integrity when he faces the choice between being like his mentor, Hopkins, who totally devotes his life and energies to the corporation while destroying his relationships with his wife and daughter or settling for a lesser, more comfortable position with commensurate earnings and status. Work comes first for the dedicated Hopkins but not for Rath, the corporate suburban nine to five man.

A large number of business novels thematically and/or stylistically similar to *Point of No Return* and *The Man in the Gray Flannel Suit* appeared between the late 1940s and the early 1960s. Many dealt with the submergence of the individual businessman in the culture of the corporation. These works provide a variety of images of middle-level executives as well as CEOs. Some noteworthy novels in this category are: *The Big Wheel* (1949) by John Brooks; *The Power and the Prize* (1954) by Howard Swiggett; *Company Man* (1956) by John G. Burnett; *Sincerely, Willis Wade* (1957) by John P. Marquand; *The Durable Fire* (1957) by Howard Swiggett; *Venus in Sparta* (1958) by Louis Auchincloss, *The Big Company Look* (1958) by J. Harry Howells, *The View from the Fortieth Floor* (1960) by Theodore White, and *Revolutionary Road* (1961) by Richard Yates.

Not all business fiction of this period concerns the individual working for a large corporation. For example, in Bernard Malamud's *The Assistant* (1957), the small businessman is portrayed as a sympathetic antihero. A Jewish businessman has owned his small neighborhood grocery store for more than twenty years. He is a hard-working, trusting, honest, and compassionate man who readily grants credit to the neighborhood's poor. Nevertheless, he is being put out of business by his rival, a store run by a large supermarket chain corporation. In addition, Saul Bellow's *Seize the Day* (1957) tells the story of an out of work salesman who is a failure in a prosperous world. He is a man who lacks entrepreneurial talent but who hungers for money and freedom.

Yielding to the temptations of easy money he tries his hand in the volatile commodity futures market. *Seize the Day* depicts the alienation, isolation, and despair of a low man in a society in which people worship only money.

Portraying a totally different world is Ayn Rand's monumental *Atlas Shrugged* (1957). This novel depicts businessmen as heroic protagonists whose pursuit of profit is profoundly moral. It tells the story of the last stages of conflict between producers and looters who live by very different moral codes. The heroes are rationally purposeful and the villains are not. The productive men of the mind reject destructive government edicts and the looters' doctrine of altruism, and go on strike by withdrawing from society. By doing so, they illustrate the role of the mind in human existence. The mind is shown to be the fundamental source of wealth and profits. This novel of ideas also has the ability to induce intense emotions.

Sometimes a Great Notion (1964) by Ken Kesey is the tale of a small, independent, family-owned logging business in Oregon. Henry Stamper is the patriarch of the family and his son, Hank, symbolizes individualism and self-sufficiency. The heroic, hardworking family members are anti-union and against anyone who attempts to tell them what to do. They fight for what they believe in and their family motto is "Never give an inch." Their business is not a union shop so they continue to work when the unions strike the other logging operators in the area. The Stampers have a contract with a big lumber company to provide logs. They pursue a great quest to supply the logs and succeed through their indomitable will despite union violence and sabotage.

God Bless You Mr. Rosewater or *Pearls before Swine* (1965) by Kurt Vonnegut, Jr. tells the story of egalitarian Eliot Rosewater, the president of a philanthropic foundation set up by his old-wealth family. Motivated by his equal love of everyone he decides to distribute the funds among all of the deserving and non-deserving poor of his county. He tries to love everyone equally merely because they are human. Eliot does not understand that the true nature of love involves discrimination and exception making. Eliot seems to feel guilty for the wealth that he has inherited. His father is a conservative senator who is an elitist and who represents the ethic of capitalism. The senator views the indiscriminate distribution of money and love as devaluing of human beings. The sentimental Eliot wants individual people to be kind and to share. Philanthropy is shown to be an individual and personal choice and action. In general, the novel is against both business and government.

Louis Auchincloss's *The Embezzler* (1966) tells the story of a struggle to succeed in a world dominated by corporate greed and corporate giants. It is a tale of crooked financial practices and the fall of the head of a brokerage firm. The novel reflects real Wall Street scandals and still has relevance today. The satiric *Office Politics* by Wilfrid Sheed also appeared in 1966. The novel revolves around the power struggles, disloyalty, and backstabbing that occurs in a publishing house. The chief editor and his two senior editors constantly fight over the magazine's focus and content. When the chief editor suffers a heart attack the others compete for the top position. When the charismatic chief editor returns he restores order because of his effective leadership including the mastery of office politics.

UNSETTLING TIMES: THE 1970s AND 1980s

Society, business organizations, and ideas about success and fulfillment were being restructured and transformed during the several decades following World War II. Ideas were changing regarding the American Dream, the good life, social progress, what constituted a good society, the role of government, social responsibility, and so on. During the 1950s, the fragmented world of employees was constrained by corporate culture and hierarchy. By the 1970s, the growing complexity of American society was leading to the loss of all traditional ideals, authorities, morals, and sanctions. These changes are reflected in the fiction of that era.

Joseph Heller's black comedy *Something Happened* (1974) is the story of the American Dream gone wrong. It takes place in a corporate office where work is routinized and where process has replaced product. Slocum, the "hero," is alienated, unhappy, and beset by constant vague anxieties. The goal of the troubled Slocum is to have no rivals or enemies. He understands the corporate culture and produces (i.e., spins) data to ensure that nobody is unhappy and that the status quo is maintained. He is a proponent of bureaucracy and corporate gospel and understands that getting ahead depends upon one's attitude, style, and appearance. The organization values and rewards style rather than substance. He puts up a façade of niceness in an environment of entropy, irrationality, and immorality. The troubled Slocum loses touch with himself and with reality.

JR (1975) is William Gaddis's easy money novel about a boy who learns about the stock market in a sixth grade class. He becomes a child capitalist and amasses a fortune in paper holdings. He uses a phone booth in his school to create a diversified paper empire beginning with a mail-order shipment of surplus Navy forks. He incorporates, has stockholders, and puts together a team of grown-up marketers, financiers, and administrators. The boy has a thoroughly materialistic value system and mindset. Ultimately, he loses his fortune.

Ben Flesh, the hero of Stanley Elkin's comic 1976 novel, *The Franchiser*, endeavors to help people acquire whatever they need or want. He serves his customers democratically and equally while at the same time pursuing his individual business interests through franchises and within the world of huge corporations. Ben wants to homogenize the country by having the same stores appear all across the country. He wants to obliterate regional destinations. He uses money obtained at low costs to buy a variety of franchises that shape the American landscape in 1970's America, complete with gas shortages and rolling blackouts. Ben's vitality is evident as we observe him relishing existence in a world of possibilities. There are a number of other interesting business novels of the late 1970s including: *Not a Penny More, Not a Penny Less* (1976) by Jeffrey Archer; *The Moneychangers* (1975) by Arthur Hailey; *Rich* (1979) by Graham Masterton; and *Takeover* (1979) by Herb Schmertz and Larry Woods.

Rabbit Is Rich (1981) by John Updike in the third novel is a series of four that reveal the life of Harry "Rabbit" Angstrom. The others are *Rabbit Run* (1960), *Rabbit Redux* (1971), and *Rabbit at Rest* (1990). Our endearing but self-absorbed and directionless hero is a former high school basketball star who sold cars and attained "success" through luck by marrying into a family business. The middle-aged Harry now enjoys prosperity as the chief sales representative during the late 1970s at a Toyota agency in a medium-size city in Pennsylvania. The dealership is owned by his wife and his mother-in-law. The novel offers a look back at America in 1979 and into the early 1980s. This snapshot of that period of time includes inflation, gas shortages, the Carter administration, consumerism, the OPEC oil crisis, the Iran hostage situation, and much more. The novel is rich with respect to the issues and problems of the time. Rabbit is now reasonably comfortable, affluent, and his family is firmly in the middle class. American brand car sales are declining because of their low gas mileages. Harry's Toyotas sell because of their high mileage per gallon and their low maintenance costs. He belongs to the Rotary Club and he and his wife enjoy the country club life. Rabbit's son Nelson desires to work as a salesman at the Toyota agency but this would mean dismissing the company's top salesman. Rabbit knows that Nelson lacks competence and maturity and that he possesses a sense of entitlement. Rabbit feels like an economic prisoner when his wife and mother-in-law overrule him and hire Nelson to work at the dealership. The novel does a good job of illustrating problems of an intergenerational family business. There are problems of succession and of accommodating the next generation. Harry is never really happy. He says that people never are because they either want something that they don't have or are fearful of losing what they do have. He thinks that there is always someone out there who wants to get him. Both Rabbit and America are running out of gas. Both have reached middle-age. The novel's theme is entropy as evidenced by the economically vulnerable and spiritually deficient Harry "Rabbit" Angstrom. The novel discusses economic and business issues throughout. For example, it is argued that it is government and those in debt who benefit from inflation. With respect to business, we hear talk about profit margins and pricing of various cars, financing percentages, carrying costs of cars in the lot, what percentage a car salesman makes on new and used cars, and so on.

In David Mamet's 1984 play *Glengarry Glen Ross*, the reader is able to witness the interactions between real estate salesmen, potential customers, and managers in a small, Chicago office in the early 1980s. This study of human interactions shows four small-time real estate hustlers competing for their very jobs while attempting to revolt and unite against a ruthless, inexperienced, vapid, and heartless company-man boss who answers to his superiors downtown. Anger drives the characters in this bleak world in which selling real estate is a hard way to make a living. The premium leads are reserved for closers only. The salesmen try to sell vacation and retirement land to less than financially ideal clients. One desperate and despairing salesman in his fifties, was once a great salesman, but is now struggling to make sales. Two others are shown discussing an opportunity to steal their own company's best leads and then to offer to sell them to a competitor. These representatives of a dying breed will do just about anything to get a sale. They manipulate, scheme, make up stories, improvise, and cheat in order to connive people into buying land. The salesmen are sly and convincing when talking to clients. Ultimately, the office is broken into and the premium leads are stolen by one (or more) of the salesmen who did not have access to them. This play is an insightful study of human interrelationships among desperate and despairing cutthroat salesmen who despise their cruel, hostile, and heartless boss.

Nice Work (1988) by David Lodge is set in the Thatcherite mid-1980s in a fictitious city in the English Midlands. It tells the story of the collision of two different worlds, lifestyles, and personalities. An Industry Year Shadow Scheme, a government program intended to foster mutual understanding between university and collegiate communities, has a faculty member shadow a local industrialist for a period of eight weeks. Both of the chosen participants are disinterested in taking part in the project. They have preconceived ideas about each other. The female faculty member is an expert on the nineteenth-century factory novel. She is an ardent feminist devoted to the study of women in the Victorian industrial novel who has never been inside an actual factory. The other person is the practical, hard-working managing director at a casting and engineering firm. They are skeptical and lack appreciation for the other's mode of life. Adversarial at first, the two become understanding of the other's point of view. During their voyage of discovery, they try to make sense of each other's worlds. Their constant and lively debates force both characters to reexamine their assumptions with respect to business, politics, literature, and so much more.

Jerry Sterner's 1989 play *Other People's Money*, a great primer on the nature, operations, and nomenclature of takeovers, presents two sides of the hostile takeover and subsequent liquidation story line. Corporate raider, Larry "The Liquidator" Garfinkle, wants to take over an outmoded, debt-free wire and cable company that has a lot of cash. His method is to target companies with undervalued assets. Larry plans to sell off the assets of the takeover target firm. The company is worth more if it is liquidated. Larry wants to maximize shareholder wealth by taking the money and investing it in some viable more technologically advanced industry. New England Wire and Cable's aging chairman, Andrew "Jorgy" Jorgenson, is a traditionalist and supporter of community values who doesn't want to see hundreds of people out of work. Jorgy is an idealistic, passionate, and paternal businessman who runs the company based on sentiment and who has pride and faith in his stockholders. The climactic scene is a proxy fight in a shareholders' meeting. It is a battle for control of the board of directors between Larry, who would make the shareholders money, and Jorgy, who would continue business in the dying copper wire industry. They both deliver impassioned speeches, which are masterpieces, explaining the principles underlying their respective positions. The play portrays Larry as a moral, likeable, even heroic person. He wants to make money for the stockholders including retired people who are not rich, while freeing resources to produce things that people want more than copper wire. The play illustrates that an efficient and productive economy has the ability to change and that takeovers are necessary for the efficient operation of a market economy. Unfortunately, some people will be out of work but people are flexible and adaptable to changing conditions.

There are a number of other good 1980s novels that fall under the business novel rubric including: *The Power Players* (1980) by Arlo Sederberg; *The Broker* (1981) by Harold Q. Masur; *Money: A Suicide Note* (1984) by Martin Amis; *Confessions of a Taoist on Wall Street* (1984) by David Payne; *Cash* (1981) by Paul-Loup Sulitzer; *Small Business* (1986) by Tom Parker; *Bonfire of the Vanities* (1987) by Tom Wolfe; *The Palace* (1988) by Paul Erdman; *The Real World* (1984) by Christopher Knowlton; and *Strong Medicine* (1984) by Arthur Hailey, among others.

THE CONTEMPORARY PERIOD

William H. Morris's 1992 novel, *Motor City* (also known as *Biography of a Buick*) is a tale of media manipulation, dealer pressure, and espionage at General Motors in 1954. This novel offers an optimistic and romantic portrayal of the cultural and social landscape of flourishing and energetic America of the 1950s.

Roger Rueff's play *Hospitality Suite* (1992) deals with the American way of conducting business. It is the story of three salesmen for a company that sells a generic product, industrial lubricants. They are attending a trade convention and have rented a hospitality suite in their efforts to land a big deal with a potential client who represents the largest account that their company would ever have signed. They wait to meet their "Big Kahuna" who has the potential to validate both the company's and the salesmen's existence. The youngest and most inexperienced of the three unknowingly has a long discussion with the "Godot" of this story. Unfortunately, the greenhorn salesman talks about religion rather than business. The devoted born-again Christian values selling his religion more than he values selling his company's product. He does not seem to be aware of his obligation to his company. Later, after being given specific business directions from the two seasoned salesmen, the young man goes to a private gathering where he again speaks with the critical potential client and again he preaches God's word rather than the company's word. Much of the play involves the three salesmen and what they have to say about business, salesmanship, religion, the human condition, human purpose, success, honesty, and the meaning of life.

Bombardiers (1995) by Po Bronson tells the story of a dysfunctional San Francisco bond trading office named Atlantic Pacific. This accurate satire of a high-pressure brokerage house was penned by a former insider of the industry. In the brutally competitive environment a new, young bond salesman ignores the house rules. The novel features a variety of fearful and greedy brokers who engage in outrageous deals. The story provides a good primer on the concepts and language of finance.

The hero of Philip Roth's *American Pastoral* (1997) is the owner of a ladies' glove factory in mid-century Newark, New Jersey, who sees his life fall apart due to political and social unrest. Radical movements threaten his family and his factory. He is a good and kind employer who treats his craftsman employees well, but he is not perceived that way by outsiders. The owner appreciates human work and initiative and he respects each and every employee who possesses expertise in each manufacturing process. The hero believes that a properly made glove reflects a superior world. It follows that people can flourish through their common efforts to strive for perfection. This is done when each employee contributes to the manufacturing process and to the goals of the company.

Tom Wolfe's *A Man in Full* (1998) is primarily about two characters. One, Charles Croker, is a middle-aged conglomerate king who has a real estate empire. The other man, Conrad Hensley, works in one of Croker's frozen food warehouses and is about to be laid off from his job due to downsizing that the bank has recommended. Croker's real estate business is on the brink of collapse. Both men experience tests of character. Hensley, a man in full, discovers Stoicism and realizes that happiness lies in not permitting oneself to be controlled by external events.

Gain (1998) by Richard Powers is a historical novel about the origins and development of a soap company and how its later years brought the threat of cancer to nearby residents. In *Gain* two stories of different scale are juxtaposed and woven together. The novel describes the rise of Clare, a small soap company, into a multinational corporation over a period of a hundred years or so. From one perspective, it tells the story of enthusiasm, courage, and financial triumph. Not only does it illustrate the benefits of industry, it also shows its dark side. The author offers a good blend of American history, economics, management, marketing, technology, and environmentalism in this work. He also provides a parallel story of a woman real estate agent stricken with ovarian cancer which may have been caused by using Clare products or by living nearby a Clare factory.

Radio Golf (2005), a play by August Wilson, deals with the business plans and political ambitions of Harmond Wilks, an energetic young urban redeveloper who aspires to be the first black mayor of Pittsburgh, Pennsylvania. His golf loving partner is helping him to redevelop Pittsburgh's Hill district. They plan to demolish the blighted part of the Hill district and to redevelop it into apartments, a parking garage, and businesses such as Whole Foods, Barnes and Noble, and Starbucks. A problem comes when a man claims that one of the homes scheduled to be razed belongs to him. He says that he had not received notice from the city that it was auctioning his house because of nonpayment of taxes. Wilks discovers that the man is correct and that Wilks and his partner have no legal claim to it even though they had "purchased" it at the auction. He devises a plan to build around the house. However, both Wilks's partner and Wilks's wife are against that idea. His morals and ideals are challenged when he is torn between attempting to further his political career, making money for his real estate firm, saving his marriage, and acting in as honorable and moral manner.

Max Barry's *Company* (2006), like the comic strip *Dilbert*, is a parody of the corporate mindset. A new hire at the Seattle-based Zephyr Holdings witnesses the wholesale irrationality of company policy. He also realizes that none of the employees have an idea of what the company actually does. As a result, he undertakes a crusade to understand the firm's mission, policies, and so forth. *Then We Came to the End* (2007) by Joshua Ferris is about life in 2001 in a Chicago advertising firm where many layoffs are occurring. All of the copywriters and designers are in constant fear of being fired. Written in the first person plural "we," the novel tells the story of office politics, deadlines, pranks, stress, rumors, arguments, threats, laughter, tears, and much more. Work in this downward-spiraling office is depicted as both boring and vibrant and both as something to be avoided and as essential to people's lives.

We have now arrived at our brief analysis of the treatment of business and businessmen in fiction. A large number of works of business fiction have appeared and continue to be published. Some of these are popular works, some have artistic merit, and some have been both well-received by the general population and have also secured a high place in literary canon. Many have treated business and the businessman with derision and hostility while others have held them up for admiration. Many are literary devaluations of business as a way of life, others have generally been more favorable in their treatment of business values and businesspeople, and a few have depicted a career in business as honorable and heroic. The fictional image of business has been varied and has included: (1) overemphasis of the faults and weaknesses of business and the businessman thereby providing a distorted picture; (2) depictions of how business has changed and developed over time; (3) challenges at work; (4) the conflict between personal values and the company's demands; (5) the need for self-analysis and self-management as a first concern in managing a firm; (6) celebration of the opportunity and energy of business life; and (7) positive romantic portraits of businessmen as active creators in free markets.

Business fiction can be an alternative source of insight to the academic observations of social scientists. Fiction permits the unique individuality and richness of variation of its characters. The writer or filmmaker as artist is able to reshape reality in accordance with his own values. Positive business novels such as *Atlas Shrugged*, *Cash McCall*, *Executive Suite*, and *Sometimes a Great Nation* can serve as a guidepost for a new direction in business fiction.

This author would like to see someone write a novel (or perhaps a series of novels) that creates a fictional world, gathering place, or afterlife of characters that brings together characters from numerous authors of business novels and plays and characters from various business films. Just think how interesting it would be to see the interactions between characters such as Silas Lapham, Frank Cowperwood, David Levinsky, George Babbitt, Jay Gatsby, Tom Rath, Willy Loman, Cash McCall, Hank Stamper, Ben Flesh, and Larry Garfinkle. Are there any aspiring novelists out there who would want to take on this project?

NOTE

This article is an edited and expanded version of material found in the Conclusion of my *Exploring Capitalist Fiction* (Lexington Books, 2014).

REFERENCES

Adams, Samuel Hopkins. 1948. *Plunder*. New York: Random House.

Alger, Horatio, Jr. [1871] 2010. *Paul the Peddler or Fortunes of a Young Street Merchant*. Whitefish; Mt: Kessinger.

———. [1868] 2005. *Ragged Dick; or Street Life in New York*. Fairfield, Iowa: 1st World.
———. [1871] 1911. *Strive and Succeed or the Progress of Walter Conrad*. New York: New York Book Company.
Amis, Martin. 1984. *Money: A Suicide Note*. New York: Penguin.
Archer, Jeffrey. [1976] 2010. *Not a Penny More, Not a Penny Less*. London: Pan MacMillan.
Auchincloss, Louis. 1966. *The Embezzler*. Boston: Houghton Mifflin.
———. 1958. *Venus in Sports*. Boston: Houghton Mifflin.
Barry, Max. 2006. *Company*. New York: Vintage Books.
Bellamy, Charles. [1879] 2011. *The Breton Mills*. Charleston, South Carolina: Nabu Press.
Bellamy, Edward. [1888] 2009. *Looking Backward 2000–1887*. Oxford: Oxford University Press.
Bellow, Saul. [1957] 1996. *Seize the Day*. New York: Penguin.
Boyesen, Hjalmar Hjorth [1883] 2009. *A Daughter of the Philistines*. Charleston, South Carolina: Bibliolife.
Bramah, Ernest. [1907] 2013. *The Secret of the League: The Story of a Social War*. Worcestershire, United Kingdom: Read Books, Ltd.
Bronson, Po. 1995. *Bombardiers*. New York: Random House.
Brooks, John. 1949. *The Big Wheel*. New York: Harper and Brothers.
Burnett, John G. 1956. *Company Man*. New York: Harper and Brothers.
Cahan, Abraham. [1917] 1993. *The Rise of David Levinsky*. New York: Penguin.
Cain, James M. [1941] 1989. *Mildred Pierre*. New York: Vintage Books.
DeForest, John W. [1875] 2010. *Honest John Vane*. Whitefish, MT: Kessinger.
Dickens, Charles, [1843] 2010, *A Christmas Carol*. London: HarperCollins.
———. [1848] 2002. *Dombey and Son*. London: Penguin.
———. [1844] 1997. *Martin Chuzzlewit*. London: Wordsworth.
Dos Passos, John. [1932] 2000. *1919*. Boston: Mariner Books.
———. 1961. *Midcentury A Contemporary Chronicle*. Cambridge, Massachusetts: Riverside Press.
———. [1930] 2000. *The 42nd Parallel*. Boston: Mariner Books.
———. [1936] 2000. *The Big Money*. Boston: Mariner Books.
Dreiser, Theodore. [1925] 2010. *An American Tragedy*. New York: Signet.
———. [1912] 2008. *The Financier*. New York: Penguin.
———. [1947] 1981. *The Stoic*. New York: Signet.
———. [1914] 1925. *The Titan*. Garden City, New York: Garden City Publishing.
Elkin, Stanley. [1976] 2001. *The Franchiser*. Chicago: Dalkey, Archive Press.
Erdman, Paul. 1988. *The Palace*. New York: Doubleday.
Ferber, Edna. [1915] 2010. *Emma McChesney and Company*. Whitefish, Montana: Kessinger.
———. [1914] 2002. *Personality Plus: Some Experiences of Emma McChesney and Her Son, Jock*. Urbana-Champaign, Illinois: University of Chicago Press.
———. [1913] 2001. *Roast Beef Medium: The Business Adventures of Emma McChesney*. Urbana-Champaign, Illinois: University of Chicago Press.
Ferris, Joshua. 2007. *Then We Came to the End*. New York: Little, Brown, and Company.

Fitzgerald, F. Scott. [1925] 2004. *The Great Gatsby*. New York: Scribner.
———. [1941] 2010. *The Last Tycoon*. London: Penguin.
Fuller, Henry B. [1893] 2010. *The Cliff Dwellers*. Buffalo, New York: Broadview Press.
Gaddis, William. 1975. *JR*. New York: Alfred A Knopf.
Garrett, Garet. [1922] 2014. *The Driver*. Charleston, South Carolina: Nabu Press.
Hailey, Arthur. 1984. *Strong Medicine*. Garden City, New York: Doubleday and Company.
———. 1975. *The MoneyChangers*. New York: Doubleday and Company.
Hawley, Cameron. 1955. *Cash McCall*. Boston: Houghton Miffin.
———. 1952. *Executive Suite*. Cambridge, Massachusetts: The Riverside Press.
———. 1968. *The Hurricane Year*. Boston: Little, Brown, and Company.
———. 1960. *The Lincoln Lords*. Boston: Little, Brown, and Company.
Hay, John. [1883] 1901. *The Bread-Winners: A Social Study*. New York: Harper and Brothers.
Hazlitt, Henry. [1951] 2007. *Time Will Run Back*. Auburn. Alabama: Ludwig von Mises Institute.
Heller, Joseph. [1966] 1974. *Something Happened*. New York: Simon and Schuster.
Herrick, Robert. [1898] 2013. *The Gospel of Success*. Charleston, South Carolina: Nabu Press.
———. [1905] 1963. *The Memories of an American Citizen*. Boston: Harvard University Press.
Hobart, Alice Tisdale. [1933] 1946. *Oil for the Lamps of China*. New York: Bantam.
Holland, Josiah G. [1875] 1884. Sevenoaks: *A Story of To-day*. New York: Charles Scribner's Sons.
Howells, J. Harry. 1958. *The Big Company Look*. New York: Doubleday and Company.
Howells, William Dean. [1890] 2001. *A Hazard of New Fortunes*. New York: Penguin.
———. [1885] 1983. *The Rise of Silas Lapham*. New York: Penguin.
Ibsen, Henrik. [1882] 1999. *An Enemy of the People*. Mineola, New York: Dover.
Kesey, Ken. [1964] 1988. *Sometimes a Great Notion*. New York: Penguin.
Kimball, Richard. [1862] 2010. *Undercurrents of Wall Street*. Charleston, South Carolina: Nabu Press.
Knowlton, Christopher. 1984. *The Real World*. New York: Atheneum.
Lewis, Sinclair. [1922] 2007. *Babbitt*. Charleston, South Carolina: Bibliolife.
———. [1929] 1995. *Dodsworth*. New York: Signet.
———. 1934. *Work of Art*. New York: Doubleday, Doran, and Co.
Lodge, David [1988] 1989. *Nice Work*. New York: Viking Penguin.
London, Jack. [1910] 1913. *Burning Daylight*. Berkeley, California: Regent Press.
———. [1908] 2006. *The Iron Heel*. New York: Penguin.
Malamud, Bernard. [1957] 2003. *The Assistant*. New York: Farrar, Straus and Giroux.
Marquand, John P. [1947] 1949. *Point of No Return*. Boston: Little, Brown and Company.
———. [1954] 1955. *Sincerely, Willis Wade*. Boston: Little, Brown, and Company.
Mamet, David [1984] 1994. *Glengarry Glen Ross*. New York: Grove Press.

Masur, Harold Q. 1981. *The Broker*. New York: St. Martin's Press.
Masterton, Rich. 1979. *Rich*. New York: Simon and Schuster.
Melville, Herman. [1853] 2004. *Bartleby the Serivener: A Story of Wall Street*. Hoboken, New Jersey: Melville Printing House.
———. [1857] 1990. *The Confidence Man: His Masquerade*. London: Penguin.
Merwin, Samuel and Henry Kitchell Webster. [1901] 1999. *Calumet "K."* New Milford, Connecticut: Second Renaissance Books.
———. [1899] 2009. *The Short Line War*. Charleston, South Carolina: Bibliolife.
Miller, Arthur. [1947] 2000. *All My Sons*. New York: Penguin.
———. [1949] 1977. *Death of a Salesman*. New York: Penguin.
Morris, William H. 1992. *Motor City*. New York: Alfred A Knopf.
Norris, Frank. [1901] 1994. *The Octopus*. New York: Penguin.
———. [1903] 1994. *The Pit: A Story of Chicago*. New York: Penguin.
Parker, Tom. 1986. *Small Business*. New York: W.W. Norton and Company.
Payne, David. 1984. *Confessions of a Taoist on Wall Street*. Boston: Houghton Mifflin.
Payne, Will. [1896] 2009. *Jerry the Dreamer*. Charleston, South Carolina: Bibliolife.
———. [1903] 2010. *Mr. Salt*. Whitefish Montana: Kessinger.
———. 1909. *The Automatic Capitalists*. Boston: R.G. Badger.
———. [1898] 2012. *The Money Captain*. Charleston, South Carolina: Nabu Press.
Phillips, David Graham. [1901] 2010. *The Great God Success*. Portland, Oregon: Gregorius Publishing.
Powers, Richard. 1998. *Gain*. New York: Farrar, Straus, and Giroux.
Rand, Ayn. 1957. *Atlas Shrugged*. New York: New American Library.
———. [1943] 1994. *The Fountianhead*. New York: Plume.
Roth, Philip. 1997. *American Pastoral*. New York: Vintage Books.
Rueff, Roger. 1992. *Hospitality Suite*. Transcend Press.
Schmertz, Herb and Larry Woods. 1979. *Takeover*. New York: Simon and Schuster.
Schulberg, Budd. [1941] 1993, *What Makes Sammy Run?* New York: Vintage.
Sederberg, Arlo. 1980. *The Power Players*. New York: William Morrow and Company.
Shakespeare, William. [1596] 2010. *The Merchant of Venice*. New York: Simon and Schuster.
Shaw, George Bernard. [1906] 2001. *Major Barbara*. New York: Penguin.
Sheed, Wilfrid. 1966 *Office Politics*. New York: Farrar, Straus and Giroux.
Sinclair, Upton. [1908] 1947. *Metropolis*. London: T. Werner Laurie.
———. [1927] 2007. *Oil*. New York: Penguin.
———. [1906] 2006. *The Jungle*. New York: Penguin.
———. [1908] 2014. *The Money Changers*. London: Heritage Publishing.
Steinback, John. [1939] 1999. *The Grapes of Wrath*. New York: Penguin.
Sterner, Jerry. 1989. *Other People's Money: The Ultimate Seduction*. Scranton, Pennsylvania: Applause Theatre.
Sulitzer, Paul-Loup. [1981] 1986. *Cash*. Secaucus, New Jersey: Lyle Stuart.
Swiggett, Howard. 1957. *The* Durable Fire. Boston: Houghton Mifflin.
———. 1954. *The Power and the Prize*. New York: Ballantine.
Tarkington, Booth. 1927. *The Plutocrat*. New York: Doubleday, Page, and Co.
Trollope, Anthony. [1873] 1995. *The Way We Live Now*. London: Wordsworth.

Twain, Mark. [1888] 2001. *A Connecticut Yankee in King Arthur's Court*. Mineolas, N.Y.: Dover.
Twain, Mark and John Dudley Wainer. [1873] 2001. The *Gilded Age: A Tale of Today*. New York: Penguin.
Updike, John. 1990. *Rabbit at Rest*. New York: Alfred A. Knopf.
———. 1960. *Rabbit Run*. New York: Alfred A. Knopf.
———. 1971. *Rabbit Rud*ux New York: Alfred A. Knopf.
———. 1981. *Rabbit Is Rich*. New York: Alfred A. Knopf.
Vonnegut, Kurt, Jr. [1965] 2006. *God Bless You, Mr. Rosewater*. New York: Dial Press.
Wakeman, Frederic. 1946. *The Hucksters*. New York: Rinehart and Company.
White, Theodore. [1960] 1966. *The View from the Fortieth Floor*. New York: Mayflower-Dell.
Williams, William Carlos. [1940] 1967. *In the Money*. New York: New Directions.
———. [1946] 1968. *The Build-Up*. New York: New Directions.
———. [1937] 1967. *White Mule*. New York: New Directions.
Wilson, August. 2005. *Radio Golf*. New York: Theatre Communications Group.
Wilson, Sloan. [1955] 2002. *The Man in the Gray Flannel Suit*. Cambridgc, Massachusetts: Da Capo Press.
Wolfe, Tom. [1998] 2005. *A Man in Full*. New York: Dial Press.
———. 1987. *Bonfire of the Vanities*. New York: Farrner, Straus and Giroux.
Yates, Richard. [1961] 2000. *Revolutionary Road*. New York: Vintage.

Chapter 2

Epic and the Medium of Exchange

Frederick Turner

The Austrian economists have shown us that the market, with its language of pricing, is a mode of discovery, of knowledge, and of the communication of knowledge. The Romans were wise when they made Mercury (the root of words like "mercantile," "commerce," "merchant," and "market" itself) not only the god of messages but also the god of merchants. And as god of messages and thus of the rhetoric that makes messages effective, Mercury also became the god of poets.[1]

The core genre of poetry is epic. Epics are among the oldest known poems in the world, and the hymn, the other primordial poetic form, could not make sense without the appropriate body of epic narrative to give it reference and weight. I have argued in *Epic: Form, Content, and History* (Turner, 2012, 13) that the unanimity of the world's great epics and their correspondence in content with the evolutionary history of our species mark the form as the way we humans have defined, experienced, and answered the question of our origins: how did we become human?

Any history of the emergence of the human species would necessarily include as central the elaboration of gift exchange and barter, the rise of local currencies, the consolidation of currencies into gold and silver, the birth of written or inscribed instruments including paper money, and the explosion of electronic and virtual forms of currency. Epic is the inner history of the emergence of the human race, and as such it is deeply interested in the origins and conflicts of these types of exchange.

This remark is not to be taken as the fairly standard "Theory" assertion that literature simply reflects the economic infrastructure of its time. We need not insult the intelligence of the epic composers by supposing that they were mere unconscious pawns of the then current discourse of knowledge, money, and power. Because the trade of such poets is to blaze trails and make words do new things, they are far less liable to be pawns than the most perspicacious of critics and theorists, who are necessarily bound to the vocabularies of their academies and professions; far more likely to be questioning the very currency of their own discourse.

The interest of the epic poets in the evolution of economic value is both historical and critical. There is a tantalizing relation of similarity and difference between the meaning of a word and the value of a coin; between naming a thing and stamping a coin with an inscription; between meaning and means. Epic poets can, as did Ezra Pound,[2] go seriously off the rails in their understanding of economics and currency; but their interest in it—no pun intended—is not misplaced. Just as the epic impulse is often renewed when a change in the medium of communication forces a reconsideration of our whole language for understanding the world, so epic often responds brilliantly to a change in the medium of economic exchange and the consequent reevaluation of our whole sense of value itself.

A few examples of epic's play with the changing means of exchange may indicate the scope of thc subject. One of the most striking examples is the Gilgamesh poet's deep interest in the inscription itself, which, whether upon stone or baked clay, is inseparable from the technology of city wall building itself. Mesopotamians literally built their cities out of the medium of their currency. Of course the origin of the cuneiform writing in which the poem comes down to us was in early Mesopotamian business contracts:

> Therefore, several major inventions follow each other in time: the cylinder seal is followed by the bulla, and finally the tablet and script appear together, as if one could not come without the other. In parallel with the third invention, writing on the surface of bullae began. . . . These innovations can be credited to the Uruk society considered in its entirety. . . . (Glassner, Bahraini, and Van de Mieroop, 1993, 115–16)

The cylinder seal is actually the first use of printing, in the sense of a duplicable sign: a carved stone cylinder was rolled over a clay surface to leave a unique image representing the ownership or authority of the seal owner. The use of the bulla (the same word is used for the Papal Bull as from the shepherd of the Christian flock) is exceptionally interesting. A contract between a landowner and a shepherd was sealed by placing a number of different shaped calculi or small stones—with different colors representing different types of sheep—into the hollow of a small round clay vessel and then sealed shut and baked. When the shepherd brings the sheep in from pasture, the two parties break the seal, revealing the exact numbers of the sheep in the contract, enabling the contractors to compare the present flock with the original (with losses or gains according to the quality of its management), and concluding the contract. This system was extended to all sorts of merchant and trader contracts. After a time the contract was written on the surface of the bulla with the newly invented cuneiform autograph writing. Later, the tablet itself embodied the meaning of the bulla.[3]

So the tablets of the *Gilgamesh* text would necessarily have been associated in the mind of a reader with the storage and legal exchange of economic value, as if our stories were inscribed on coins or written on banknotes or composed in the form of property deeds. The epic is indeed a contract, even a bank or a treasury. The code of Hammurabi is thus both a formalization of this contract system and a logical analysis of the values implicit in the epic story.

The Biblical epics themselves take on huge new significance in the light of this association. Noah's ark contains the token animals as a bulla contains the token sheep. Abraham, Isaac, Jacob, Joseph, and Moses are shepherds: Abraham is carrying out a shepherd's contract when he sets out to sacrifice his son on Mount Moriah, and the ram that God gives him instead is the calculus within the bulla, the sign instead of the reality. When Jacob contracts with Laban to receive Rachel, Laban's daughter, in exchange for his stock management services, and Laban cheats him by switching daughters, it is a story of how someone might substitute the wrong ewe for the one specified by the calculus inside the bulla. On Mount Sinai Moses receives two tablets of stone inscribed personally by God using his finger as the stylus, containing the Law. The tablets are broken when the chosen people choose to make a golden calf, and the Law is reinscribed when the covenant is renewed. The ark of the covenant, then, is a portable contract seal between human shepherds and the divine landowner; and the ark, like a bulla, contains the scrolls of the epic of Exodus as Noah's ark contains the seeds of new life on Earth.

Another example of the promise for future scholarship along these lines is the currency crisis during the Heian period in Japan, which helped to precipitate the Gempei Wars that the *Heike* describes (McCullough, 1991). The reason why the samurai and the temples had so much power to reduce government to chaos was the *shoen* (manor) system of feudal land tenure, which virtually did away with money as such. In the absence of a government-issued currency, payment for goods and services came to be made in kind—in units of rice, for example, or lengths of silk—so that all economic exchanges became personalized as gifts. The result was the constant danger of misunderstanding and personal affront,[4] the fetishizing of objects of exchange, the substitution of social rank for earned financial wealth, and the ancestral rice field as the foundation of all value (Morris, 1964). The *Heike* can be seen as a perceptive analysis of the tragic consequences. The *Heike* begins with two bad gifts that epitomize the economic collapse of the Heian period: the gift to the Emperor by Tadamori, Kiyomori's father, of the Buddhist

Tokujojuin Temple, and the Emperor's return gift to Tadamori of a province and of courtier privileges in the Palace, against precedent (McCullough, 1991, 23–27). The epic ends with the extermination of both the Heike clan and the Emperor's direct lineage.

Composed in 1371, and recounting the events of the 1180's, the *Heike* reflects by implication the economic history that followed the triumph of the Minamoto and the reunification of Japan. Under the new regime Japan adopted the Chinese coinage, and an age of prosperity, trade, and technological advance followed. About the time the *Heike* appeared, Japanese coiners began to make imitations of the Chinese Song and Ming coins (which, however, were undervalued compared to the originals).[5] The *Heike* reads in this light as a rich and complex response not only to the tragedy of the civil war but to an epochal change in the means of economic value and exchange. Kakuichi, the author, revalues the often brutal, pragmatic, and unscrupulous actions of the poem's protagonists by setting them again and again in the context of the classical Chinese past (as Plutarch elevates his Roman magnates and warlords by pairing them with the classical Greek leaders in the *Lives*).[6] He recognizes sadly and ashamedly that Japan had failed, and had to recover its values by borrowing those of its ancient rival and mentor, China. At the same time he yearns for a finer, more absolute, more perfect form of honor and commitment than could be found in his own more mercantile and economically leveled world of money exchange. And by implication the poem itself becomes a new gold standard, a new repository of value—and remains so in the Japanese imagination, as the epic films of Kurosawa attest.

A similar analysis of the *Popol Vuh* might focus on the curious role of cacao in the poem's intricate symbolism of resurrection.

> At the beginning of Part Three of the *Popol Vuh*, the authors introduce Hun Hunahpu, and his brother Vucub Hunahpu, asking us to drink to the Father of the Hero Twins. Tedlock interprets this as raising a calabash gourd of chocolate, the traditional drink of K'iche' "Masters of Ceremony" *nimchokoj* (possibly from K'iche' *chokola'j*, connoting the gathering of food and drink, specifically cacao, for a banquet). This symbolic drinking from the skull of Hun Hunahpu precedes the story of the origin of the calabash, and the story of Hun Hunahpu, which then unfolds. (Tedlock, 1996: 249, 322). (Bergmann, 1969)

The point here is that the cacao bean was an important form of currency throughout the Maya lands. So when the epic characterizes itself as a toast to the memory of the first hero, One Hunahpu, the vessel—the calabash—is his skull, and the drink is the unit of Mayan currency roasted and ground up to make a nourishing and stimulating drink. The drink itself is related to the liquid that the skull spits into Blood Moon's hand, which virginally impregnates her with the hero twins who will become the sun and moon of the first day. The roasting, grinding up, and dissolving of the cacao—making it no longer a unit of currency, realizing its value—are imaged in the burning, grinding, and drowning of the hero twins; they resurrect as catfish, and the iconology of Mayan myth associates the catfish shape with the shape of both the maize kernel and the innards of the cocoa bean. Here we have indeed a sacrament that unites the resurrected god-hero, the creation of humankind, the food staples of the society, and the common unit of currency; and the epic poem is the words that call the sacrament into being, the *hoc est enim corpus meum.*

When standardized Roman gold currency appears in northern Europe, the epic poets respond, as we have already seen, with a searching symbolic analysis of its moral and social effects. Beowulf and the heroes of the *Nibelungenlied* and the *Volsungssaga* all contend with the dragon and his hoarded gold. Wagner is, I believe, right in interpreting the story of the Nibelungs as a warning against the concentration of value (and human obligation and human love) in unchanging metal. One of the great kennings for the action of the epic poet is to "unlock his word-hoard."[7] The danger of the dragon's hoard is that its value is not circulated; the response of the poet is to unlock the word-hoard, to give away something (words) that can be duplicated and owned by everybody in common. As the early medieval economy developed, powered by national gold currencies, great prosperity, cities, and alienation arose together, the epic poem, which is commonly owned, helps redress the moral loss.

In the Volsung saga, Regin is the smith who forges Sigurd's sword, but he is also the storyteller, the poet's alter ego. As Sigurd's mentor, he teaches him many languages and the runes of writing. Regin's brother Fafnir is the dragon who has deprived the storyteller of his inheritance. With Regin's advice Sigurd slays Fafnir and releases the treasure. But Sigurd is tempted by the gold, slays Regin and keeps the treasure for himself. This killing of the adviser/poet/smith turns the treasure into a curse. Further, we find out what is the meaning of the death of the dragon, lest we should be in any doubt about it: Fafnir's blood confers the classic poet's gift of being able to understand the language of the animals. Sigurd tastes it, and "when the blood from the serpent's heart touched his tongue, he could understand the speech of birds" (Brock, 66). The tragic equation is complex: the gold-hoard is a word-hoard as in *Beowulf*; if we try to keep it for ourselves, even if we have, as Regin has, a right to half of it, it will be our destruction; and Sigurd the dragon-slayer is a poet-slayer and will be destroyed in turn, because of the mutual jealousy of Gudrun and Brynhild over the gold ring of Odin, Andvaranaut (which is the divine supplement to the otter's ransom that completes the gold-hoard). The odd implication is that the poet who is telling this story is a ghost, who is haunting his murderer, but who redeems the curse of the gold by unlocking his word-hoard and circulating the currency of the poem.

Whenever Odysseus encounters in his journeys a decisive moment in which his identity as the rightful king of Ithaca is defined and established, the image of the olive-tree, its domestication, and its fruit (both food and cosmetic) becomes of central importance. Now the great wealth of the Greeks, which gave them the leisure to compose poetry, create great architecture, and pioneer the arts of science and philosophy, was largely based on the trade in olive oil (and on wine, too, which plays a similarly important part in such episodes). When Odysseus saves himself and his men from the bestial/divine Polyphemus, he does so with the aid of a stake of wild olive, which he has "domesticated" by sharpening in the fire. He rotates it in Polyphemus's one eye as a shipwright drills a hole in the deck planking to step the mast. The image includes both product and its conveyance. Again, when Odysseus arrives naked, chilled and half-drowned on the shore of Phaiakia, whence he will begin his recovery of his kingdom, he takes shelter under twin olives, one wild and one domesticated. He must himself be domesticated: when he appears naked before Nausicaa and her girls, he is described as being like a mountain lion. But he covers his nakedness with an olive branch and so proclaims his civilized shame and modesty. And having washed off the brine, he oils his body like a civilized athlete.

And of course the right answer to Penelope's trick suggestion that he move their bed is that the bedpost is a rooted olive tree that cannot be moved: as a refined hybrid strain of domesticated olive is grafted to the hardy stock of a wild olive, so their civilized marriage is grafted to the wild stock of their sexual and reproductive relationship. So the history of Odysseus is also a symbolic history of the archaic Greek economy. Now we may see why in Odysseus's various fictions about his identity, he is often a merchant, a trader.

Most epics deal in some way with staples, whether economic or fiscal: rice, wheat, maize, sheep, olives (as in the Odyssey), cattle (as in *The Cattle Raid of Cooley*), bananas (in the case of the *Mwindo* epic of the Congo Nyanga people), or baked clay, cacao beans, gold, seal stamps, or printed paper. Epic is, among other things, a meditation upon the backing of our currencies.

That meditation also concerns how grosser and more physical relationships of valuation may become the templates for, and explanation of, higher and more refined forms of meaning and value. The Greek concept of the *tokos*, the offspring of a sexual union, the interest on a loan, the likeness that is the basis of a metaphor, and the student's production of ideas that resemble those of his teacher, perhaps originated in the metaphorical connections we have noticed in the *Odyssey*. Marc Shell explores these ideas in his seminal book *Money, Language, and Thought: Literary and Philosophic Economies from the Medieval to the Modern Era.*

> Socrates, for example, is said to deposit in his interlocutors partial falsehoods or likenesses of the whole Idea that the god has deposited with him. These seminal parts are homogeneous with the Idea in the same way that monetary interest is homogeneous with its principal or that a child is homogeneous with its progenitors. Socrates' maieutic art ensures that from these likenesses are generated, by a series of intellectual births and rebirths from the minds of his interlocutors, intellectual offspring ever more like the Idea. (In the same way the hypotheses figured on the divided line approach the Idea ever more closely.) Thus Socrates husbands the Idea as if he were a midwife, and he draws intellectual hypotheses out of and to the Idea as if he were a banker drawing out compound interest from a financial deposit or hypothec.
>
> Greek dialecticians thus articulate the relationship of genuses with species in terms of monetary differentiation and elucidate intellectual hypothesizing in terms of monetary hypothecation. (Shell, 131)

But just how secure is the tower of values that can be built upon some staple or fundamental currency? Sometimes, as in the Indian *Mahabharata*, there is an explicit questioning of any such foundation. The central and precipitating episode in the whole poem is the game of dice between Yudisthira, the Pandava heir to the throne of Dhritarashtra, and Duryodhana, the bitter and tragic dispossessed son of the old blind king.[8] Yudisthira gambles everything away, including his kingdom, his wife, his brothers, and himself, losing to Duryodhana's enchanted dice (Vyasa, 1973, 90–103). Is the wager's result legitimate? What is the meaning of property, possession, itself? The *Bhagavadgita* section of the poem explores in depth the meaning of this question. Perhaps the whole of the phenomenal world is a game, the paper currency or play-money of Brahman, a consensual illusion.

In Shakespeare's *Henriad* (*Richard II*, 1 *Henry IV*, 2 *Henry* IV, *Henry V*, recognized as Shakespeare's entry in the epic stakes), there is a profound and extended meditation on the means of economic exchange, especially in connection with the issue of sovereignty and its legitimation. By Shakespeare's time there was a robust metallic currency and the beginnings of currency standardization, theories of fiscal soundness, inflation and deflation, and the emergence of the issues of coining and counterfeiting.[9] Sir Thomas Gresham had already formulated his Law that bad money drives out good. Shakespeare's dramatic epic tetralogy must find a way to "redeem from broking pawn the tarnished crown" of England (*Richard II*, II. i. 293.). My book *Shakespeare's Twenty-First Century Economics* argues that one of the core metaphors of the whole tetralogy concerns the validity of coinage.

What if there is a serious question about the legitimacy of the stamp or inscription with which a coin of the realm is impressed? Who has the right to mint a coin? What if the king, whose image is on the coin, is not a legitimate king? What makes a king legitimate anyway? A sufficiently large number of counterfeit coins will debase a currency; a counterfeit king can debase a whole commonwealth.

In the Battle of Shrewsbury, which forms the climax of *Henry IV, Part One,* Henry IV uses a tactic that secures victory over the rebel armies arrayed against him, but which smacks of dishonor and symbolizes all too graphically the political problems of his regime. He has a number of his followers put on his own heraldry and coat armor, effectively disguising themselves as the King himself. A coin of baser metal is stamped, so to speak, with the true seal of the monarch. Several of these fakes are killed by Douglas, his Scottish opponent. The King survives to see his enemies slain or captured; but the rebellions continue, because the doubt as to Henry's legitimacy remains. Nobody can tell for sure which is the real king, and there are many claimants to the throne. Henry is a counterfeit king.

This is not to say he is not a good king in many ways. He has the mettle, discipline, and intelligence of a true king—his blood, in Shakespeare's metaphor, is vigorous and potent. He has the right metal to be king, but the inscription has been improperly acquired, and thus his coinage, so to speak, is suspect. Here it is a case of having the right metal but the wrong inscription. Shakespeare plays with this idea throughout all four plays, punning on the colloquial terms for the coins of the realm—"crown" (five shillings), "royal" (ten shillings), "cross" (the inscription on the "tails" side of various coins), and "sovereign" (one pound). How can the English monarchy, Shakespeare asks, recover its legitimacy? And how can its economy regain its vigor and stabilize its currency, and so renew the basic fertility of its soil, its productiveness, and its health in the international markets (symbolized by participation in Europe's great project of the Crusades)? The plays are full of references to the financial instabilities of civil war economies. One can "buy land now as cheap as stinking mackerel"; worse, one can "buy maidenheads as they buy hobnails, by the hundreds" (II. iv. 362, 365). Hotspur, before the battle, puns on "crown" (the top of the head) and "crown" (the coin):

We must have bloody noses and cracked crowns
And pass them current too.

(1 *Henry IV,* II.iii.93–4)

The implication is that to engage in rebellion is to use as legal tender (pass current) a coin that is cracked and thus defaced and devalued—but whose metal may be good nevertheless.

All of these anxieties are summed up in Henry's first speech to his lords in *Henry IV, Part One.*

So shaken as we are, so wan with care,
Find we a time for frighted peace to pant

And breathe short-winded accents of new broils
To be commenced in stronds afar remote.
No more the thirsty entrance of this soil
Shall daub her lips with her own children's blood,
No more shall trenching war channel her fields,
Nor bruise her flow'rets with the armed hoofs
Of hostile paces. . . .

Forthwith a power of English shall we levy,
Whose arms were molded in their mother's womb
To chase these pagans in those holy fields
Over whose acres walked those blessed feet
Which fourteen hundred years ago were nailed
For our advantage to the bitter cross.

(1 *Henry IV,* I.i.1.)

The metaphor Henry uses for the soldiers' service to God in the Crusades is a mixed one. The soldiers are "engaged," a word like "mortgaged," implying the pledge of personal property or person itself as security for a sum of money. The passage also refers to the "impressing"—or we would say "press-ganging" of soldiers by forced conscription into an army, and the acceptance by the recruit of payment—the "cross" or the "king's shilling"—for his military service. And of course all this is based on the by now familiar process of pressing or stamping a coin, the British warrior shaped in the mold of the British womb and the cross of the British military uniform. In the ideal state of the kingdom, the "blood" to which Henry alludes so graphically at the beginning of his speech, the true wax or metal of England, must be properly molded and stamped with the cross of royal legitimacy if it is to carry value.

But can the sovereign be merely the most recent winner in the political struggle? Surely not. Prince Hal must legitimately succeed to a crown that was not itself legitimately attained by succession. Though Hal is of kingly metal, the inscription or stamp of his sovereignty has been defaced. How does one make a counterfeit coin (made of genuine metal) into a true "crown" or "royal" or "sovereign" of the realm?

The answer, when we express it in terms of coinage, is obvious: remelt the coin, and restamp it with a legitimate head of state. The answer is less obvious when we try to put it in terms of public policy and the necessary rituals of succession. Hal knows that the solution is not to join his father in the unscrupulous *Realpolitik* and treachery by which he maintains an uneasy seat on the throne. Hal seeks out an alternative father, one who is apparently free of all the hypocrisies of social power, and who embodies the ease and creativity of nature itself. He finds this alternative father in the fat highwayman Falstaff. Falstaff's solution to Hal's problem is that if nature has given a man kingly metal, the stamp doesn't matter: "Never call a true piece of gold a counterfeit," says Falstaff to Hal; "Thou art essentially made, without seeming so" (1 *Henry IV*, II.iv.491–93). If Hal is a true piece of gold, he cannot be a counterfeit king. He is truly made out of sovereign essence and has no need to appear so.

Falstaff is a misuser of the King's press, that is, someone who recruits soldiers in an illegal fashion for private profit, using the writ and seal authority of the monarchy. The word "press" itself alerts us to the deep relationship between the acts of minting and of conscription: both are ways to imprint, or impress, or stamp, the free material of nature for state use. The connection is underlined when Falstaff pretends to be dead on the battlefield in order to save his life. His defense against the charge of being a counterfeiter is that he is after all alive, and that life itself has a genuineness that trumps any kind of civilized, inscribed value, any such "trim reckoning" as honesty or honor (1 *Henry IV,* V.i.135). He argues that in denying the Apolline prerogative to stamp the raw material of life, he is himself genuine metal. The paradox is summed up in Falstaff's very name: he is a "false staff." To counterfeit a counterfeit is to be genuine. If, Falstaff points out, death is the counterfeit of life—a dead body is a mere simulacrum of a living one—to counterfeit death "is to be no counterfeit, but the true and perfect image of life indeed" (1 *Henry IV,* V.iv.115–19). The "staff" of life is the (etymologically related) "staple," the foundational commodity that supports an economy. Is Falstaff a false staple? Or a fallen staple that must be raised again in a new way?

The theoretical solution to Hal's problem is to remelt the counterfeit coin of his inheritance and restamp it with a legitimate head of state. But this is in practice a long process—Hal must, for example, wait for his father to die. He cannot continue the defiling series of murders for the sake of power. Though he has already explicitly rejected his father's way, Hal's psychological coinage must take some shape in the meantime. In the deepest symbolism of the play, the placeholder head that is inscribed on Hal's coin is the Boar's Head, the sign of the tavern where he and Falstaff hang out. Falstaff is the ritual King of the May, the Lord of Misrule, the embodiment of our animal nature. He is the boar, the sacrificial beast that must first be prepared for his role—the sins of the community heaped on his back—and then immolated for the health of the land.

The first step, then, in Hal's solution to the paradox of his inherited illegitimacy is to replace the King's head with the boar's head as his personal sign, replace the fake king with the authentic beast. Falstaff is authentic in that he embodies the fundamental substance of the English national character—that substance that we find in Sir Bercilak (the jolly castellan in *Sir Gawain and the Green Knight*), in the Host and the Miller in the *Canterbury Tales*, in Dr. Johnson and Samuel Pickwick and even in Benny Hill. John Bull is the cartoon version of this mythic figure. Falstaff is invested by Shakespeare with all the imagery of traditional animal sacrifice festivals—the roasted Manningtree ox with the pudding in his belly, the Bartholomew boar-pig, the fat kine of Pharaoh's dream, the sow that has overwhelmed all her litter but one. These are images of great meat-feasts, of satisfied hunger, of carnival (literally, flesh-rites), of the fertility of the land that gives us such good things and provides us with a surplus to tide us over the winter. Falstaff is a huge relief from the starved dry politicking of the historical chronicle.

But of course so far Hal does not yet have a solution. We cannot have a man-beast for a king. The coin of the realm must have another stamp than the slavering and greedy snout of the boar (the heraldic sign of the brutal Richard III, be it noted, well known to Shakespeare's audience of course). As soon as Falstaff is given the friendship of the Prince, he immediately abuses it, using it to commit highway robbery with impunity and to sell draft exemptions to the soldiers he has impressed into the king's service (another example, in the light of our discussion of Henry IV's proposed draft for the crusades, of Shakespeare's astonishing poetic economy). The problem with people who live like animals is that the big ones eat up the little ones; as Falstaff himself puts it, referring to one of the victims of his con games, "If the young dace be a bait for the old pike, I see no reason in the law of nature but I may snap at him" (2 *Henry IV,* III.ii.330–33).

But at least part of Hal's problem is solved. By consorting with Falstaff he has, as it were, reduced himself to a sort of Everyman; he has erased the stamp of his father and is now in the condition of Adam, with the potential to become anything he chooses: "I am now of all humors that have showed themselves humors since the old days of goodman Adam to the pupil age of this present twelve o'clock at midnight" (1 *Henry IV,* II. iv.92–95).

The Boar's Head tavern is a place where Hal is liberated from his ordinary identity and can play any role he likes. It is, among other things, the space of theater art itself. In the course of the ensuing scene Hal engages in a series of amateur theatricals, taking the parts of a bartender, a rich young drunk, the rebel Harry Hotspur, his own father the king, and himself as a dissolute young prince being scolded by his father. He is actually preparing himself to be the representative of all his people, since he has become, in play, each of them in turn.

Most important of all, he has thoroughly detached himself from his identity as an interested political party in the power struggle. He is thus in a position to "renormalize," as mathematicians say, the paradoxical situation in which he has been placed as the potential inheritor of stolen property. (To renormalize is to cancel out one mathematical absurdity with another, leaving an equation of finite real quantities that can be solved.) The manner in which this task is to be performed is explained symbolically in the episode of the Gad's

Hill robbery. The Prince has agreed to help Falstaff and his companions rob some rich travelers on the Canterbury road. But by prearrangement Hal does not rendezvous with Falstaff; instead he waits until Falstaff has completed his holdup, and in disguise with his friend Poins he in turn robs the robbers, and turns the whole affair into a joke. Later he repays the money ("with advantage"—interest) to its proper possessors. It is just in this fashion that he will restore the legitimacy of the English throne: he must in some sense steal it from the thief (his father), commit a second crime to erase the first.

This act of counter-usurpation is in turn symbolized by the scene in which Hal encounters his father for the last time on Henry's deathbed. In error, Hal believes that his father is already dead, and pitying his father for the terrible burden of the crown that has destroyed him, Hal takes that same crown up from the pillow where it lies and tries it on himself, as if to wrestle with the antagonist that has defeated his father. But Henry is not yet dead; he awakens to find his son wearing the crown, and bitterly upbraids him for his unseemly haste. Hal apologizes and they are reconciled at the end, but the act of counter-usurpation has been symbolically performed. And the symbolism is not empty, for throughout both *Henry IV* plays Hal has been psychologically and politically distanced from his father—so much so that at one point Henry wishes aloud that his son had been exchanged in the cradle with the chief rebel, Harry Hotspur. Significantly, when Hal comes to the throne, he discards the nickname "Hal," and adopts the name of the rebel, "Harry," as his familiar appellation. Hal has robbed the robber; or, to put it in terms of coinage, he has reminted the coin of sovereignty. And, like Abraham, he has changed his name or inscription.

But Hal does not keep the money stolen from the travelers on Gad's Hill. The very name—"God's Hill"—connotes that the events that happen there, between London and Canterbury, the civil and the spiritual capitals of Britain, are of a ritual importance matching that of the martyrdom of the Archbishop Thomas a` Becket. Another Henry, the Second, had been the cause of Thomas' death in much the same fashion as Henry IV had been the death of Richard II. Hal has expiated the crime, but he must still, so to speak, make restitution, return the money. To whom does he owe the crown? The answer is, to the people of England. Hal now proceeds to pay it back, and the paying is the work of his reign. His royalty consists, so to speak, in the continuous paying of "royalties" to the people of the land, who are the authors of the authority over which he has copyright. The play in which Hal receives his true title, Henry V, is Shakespeare's vision of what a genuine king should be, that is, the leader whose constant work is the emancipation of his subjects. When Hal, now Henry V, wanders his camp on the eve of the battle of Agincourt, speaking incognito with the common soldiers and presenting himself as Harry Le Roy and the servant of England, there is a distinct premonition of the ideal role of the American president, the first citizen, the ruler as recycler of sovereignty back to the people. It is a reversal of Henry IV's stratagem of disguising his followers as himself. Instead of betrayal and execution, which are the fate of rebels against the counterfeit King Henry IV, the loyal soldier who challenges the disguised Harry gets a glove full of gold coins. The restoring of the stolen property is a process, one that is never-ending, and one that constitutes the true function of sovereign rule (Turner, 1999, 103–11).

Shakespeare's incomparably acute analysis of the relationship between core political and core economic meanings can act as a lens for viewing many other epics. When in Herman Melville's epic novel *Moby Dick* Ahab, for instance, nails the doubloon to the mast of the *Pequod* as his reward to the first sailor to sight the white whale, Melville is basically revisiting the same set of problems but in the light of the American experience. The doubloon, with its mystical inscription, is a glowing symbol of sovereignty:

> On its round border it bore the letters, REPUBLICA DEL ECUADOR: QUITO. So this bright coin came from a country planted in the middle of the world, and beneath the great equator, and named after it; and it had been cast midway up the Andes, in the unwaning clime that knows no autumn. Zoned by those letters you saw the likeness of three Andes' summits; from one a flame; a tower on another; on the third a crowing cock; while arching over all was a segment of the partitioned zodiac, the signs all marked with their usual cabalistics, and the keystone sun entering the equinoctial point at Libra. (Melville, 1952, 428)

But what is sovereignty? After all, by offering the doubloon Ahab is usurping the "joint-stock" business legality of the voyage, substituting his own autocratic purpose for the democratic purpose of the *Pequod.* And when the offer is made it exposes nakedly the profoundly questionable nature of sovereignty itself. As each other member of the crew comes before the coin and interprets it, the meanings multiply into meaninglessness. If Melville has an answer, it is more, in the American spirit, like a question. If the autocratic and charismatic spirit of the old heroism can no longer serve the democratic regime, can sound business interest, combined with the brotherly charity he celebrates everywhere in his epic (and especially in chapter 94, "A Squeeze of the Hand") make an adequate substitute? Ishmael is saved by his blood-brother's (and fellow-businessman's) coffin; can this "whale of a book" provide a new basis for sovereignty?

It is no coincidence that the date of first publication of *Moby Dick*, 1851, falls exactly between two epochal events in the history of American currency, both in his lifetime. The first was the dissolution in 1836 by Andrew Jackson of the Second Bank of the United States. This act resulted in the issuance by about 1,600 local state-chartered private banks of private paper money currencies in over 30,000 varieties of design, which were very easily counterfeited. The resulting financial chaos, bank failures, and circulation problems, and the deflationary depression of 1837–41 would have marked Melville's early manhood. Combined with the impending near-bankruptcy of the Federal Government, the banking collapse already constituted a crisis of financial sovereignty at the time *Moby Dick* was being written; the outbreak of the Civil War in 1861 and the printing of the Confederate dollar ratified the breakdown. Like the sailors on the *Pequod* who each have their own version of the meaning of the coin, the various colored banknotes constituted a cacophonous excess of significations. Ahab's autocratic gold is all that holds them together. The other great economic event in Melville's later life, but anticipated symbolically in *Moby Dick*, was the issuance in 1862 by the Federal Treasury of the first national gold-backed paper currency, the Greenback, which began to stabilize the system but which ushered in what Melville feared might become an imperial presidency.

Melville cannot have failed to recognize the implications of these economic changes for a writer of printed books. The technology and legitimacy of both minting and counterfeiting were now no different from the technology and legitimacy of epic-writing. Was his own currency good or bad? Was brotherhood on the large scale more properly federalism or confederacy? What made paper and ink valuable? Can a paper nation be valid? Can we all get back on the same page, and use the same dollar? Though in later life, as *The Confidence-Man: His Masquerade* attests, Melville's answers were more pessimistic, and the excess of significances more cacophonous, in *Moby Dick* the epic answer, the possibility of true refounding, is still open. Perhaps one reason for his later darker vision was the lack of response that his nation showed to his great epic novel, and the failure of his verse epic *Clarel*. *Clarel* treats of a pilgrimage to the Holy Land that raises more pluralistic problems than it solves. It is very clear, though, what kind of questions Melville is asking. His pilgrimage plays the same role in *Clarel*, though at much greater length, that Henry IV's proposed crusade does in Shakespeare's play: the aborted search for a foundation or founding.

Epic, as many have noted, is an art of memory: literally in the first ages, when scops and guslers and blind *biwa hoshi* had to memorize their vast performances; more figuratively and more comprehensively, when written epic was the stored memory of a whole culture. So there is another deep relation between epic and money that this analysis indicates; for money, as we see from its origins in the bulla, is originally a way of keeping track of obligations when the numbers of participants in a market are too great to keep track of, the time between the sealing and consummation of a contract too long, the quantities and varieties of goods too complex to entrust to brain circuitry. Our bank account relative to the prices and to our needs is a precise memorial of the consensus of our society (including ourselves) about what our obligations are, what is our moral status as social beings, lest we forget our promises.

Epic is the container, or rule-set, the bulla in which the moral calculi of our ethical lives lie undisturbed by fraud and natural bias—the ark in which the breeding-stock of our stories can safely ride out the flood. One might speculate, then, that the neglect and disfavor epic has suffered in the last hundred years or so in avant-garde circles is a grand cultural effort to throw off our responsibilities and lighten the ethical burden of our humanity. Like Falstaff, we "owe God a death" but would "be loath to pay Him before his day," as he says in his famous speech on the folly of honor (1 *Henry IV*, V.i.126–41). We deny death, but if we do not honor our promises, we have broken the moral link between our past, present and future selves, and so death—moral death, perhaps more weighty than physical death—is everywhere in our lives, not just at the end. And where, without epic, is the bulla or ark wherein our accounting lies safe?

Today we face a new set of challenges in the light of our economic technology: our currency is now basically cybernetic. Paper and coin are now just markers of our real wealth, which is a configuration of virtual ones and zeros preserved in optical and electronic circuitry and vouched for by a consensual illusion. We have recently (in 1987, 2001, and 2007) experienced three massive collapses in the sovereignty of our money—the savings and loan crash, the dot com[10] crisis and the mortgage meltdown. Meanwhile intellectual property and copyright have become battlegrounds, and we are becoming aware of how grievously we are in debt to the planetary ecosystem, having ignored our promises. Any epic composed today would necessarily take as one of its explicit or implicit goals to reground our economic exchange system, found a new one, or find a way to make it work without the need for any ground at all. And such an epic would inevitably exist at some stage of its composition and publication in the same ghostly medium as our money.

Indeed, we may even be in a position to reverse the familiar Austrian mantra that market pricing is a distributed information system, operating by an Invisible Hand. The major forms of literature—especially epic, which always explores the boundaries of the known world—are themselves distributed information systems. As inciters and coaches of desire and expectation through narrative suspense and stories of achieved or unachieved goals, they shape the wishes of their users. Without those wishes there would be no demand, and without demand no incentive for supply. The Invisible Hand may not be so invisible after all. Perhaps—as advertisers well know—it is the story that sells the product. And the stories are there for us all to read.

NOTES

1. This essay summarizes and develops themes explored in two earlier monographs by the author: *Shakespeare's Twenty-First Century Economics: The Morality*

of Love and Money (Oxford University Press, 1999) and *Epic: Form, Content, and History* (Transaction Publishers, 2012). As these books may be unfamiliar to the reader of this one, and as the point of this essay relies heavily on conclusions drawn in the earlier research, substantial passages from those two books are allowed to stand unaltered in the context of a body of new material and within an argument that is new.

2. See Canto XLV on "usura"; and Redman, Tim. *Ezra Pound and Italian Fascism*, Cambridge University Press, 2009.

3. Seals not unlike these are still used by dock authorities and businesses to ensure against theft or tampering, and equivalent quantum cryptographic seals are in the works for valuable electronic information.

4. In another tragic island epic, *Njal's Saga*, the law fails and violence erupts when Njal adds a cloak to the agreed monetary weregild for Hoskuld's death, a gift that Flosi, the recipient, takes as an insult to his manhood.

5. Currency Museum of the Bank of Japan.

6. Immediately following the initial invocation of the Gion Shoja temple bell, the comparison is made:

> In a distant land, there are the examples set by Zhao Gao of Qin, Wang Mang of Han, Zhu Yi of Liang, and Lushan of Tang, all of them men who prospered after refusing to be governed by their former lords and sovereigns, but who met swift destruction because they disregarded admonitions, failed to recognize approaching turmoil, and ignored the nation's distress. (McCullough, 23)

7. "Him se yldesta andswarode, werodes wisa, wordhord onleac."—*Beowulf*, l. 258.

8. Another version of the Jacob and Esau story?

9. One of the charges against Shakespeare's friend and rival Christopher Marlowe in his trial for treason and heresy was that Marlowe had claimed that he had as much right to coin money as did the Queen. See Turner, Frederick. "The School of Night" *Corona* 4 (1986).

10. The "m" in ".com" is of course our old friend Mercury.

REFERENCES

Anonymous. 1996. Dennis Tedlock, translator. *The Popol Vuh*, Touchstone.

Anonymous. 2007.Translator unknown. *The Cattle Raid of Cooley*, Forgotten Books.

Anonymous. 1990. Jesse Byock, translator. *The Saga of the Volsungs*, University of California Press.

Bergmann, John. 1969. "The Distribution of Cacao Cultivation in Pre-Columbian America." *Annals of the Association of American Geographers* 59: 85–96.

Cook, Robert. 2001(1997). Translator and editor. *Njal's Saga*, Penguin Classics.

Glassner, Jean-Jacques, Bahraini, Zainab; Van de Mieroop, Marc. 2003. *The Invention of Cuneiform: Writing in Sumer*. Johns Hopkins University Press.

Grofe, Michael J. 12/30/2014. *The Recipe for Rebirth: Cacao as Fish in the Mythology and Symbolism of the Ancient Maya*, www.famsi.org/research/grofe/GrofeRecipe ForRebirth.pdf (consulted 12/30/2014).

Homer, C.1000 BCE? Robert Fitzgerald, translator (1963). *The Odyssey*, Doubleday Anchor.
McCullough, Helen Craig, 1991 (1988). Translator and editor. *The Tale of the Heike*, Stanford University Press.
Melville, Herman 1952 (1851). *Moby Dick*. Modern Library.
Morris, I. 1964. *The World of the Shining Prince; Court Life in Ancient Japan*, Oxford University Press.
Pound, Ezra, 1993 (1948). *Cantos of Ezra Pound*, New Directions.
Redman, Tim. 2009. *Ezra Pound and Italian Fascism*, Cambridge University Press.
Rureke, Shekarisi, Daniel Biebuyck, Kahombo C. Mateene 1989. *The Mwindo Epic from the Banyanga (Zaire)*. U. of California Press.
Shakespeare, William, G. Blakemore Evans. 1974. Editor. The Riverside Shakespeare, Riverside.
Shell, Marc. 1993. *Money, Language, and Thought: Literary and Philosophic Economies from the Medieval to the Modern Era*. Johns Hopkins University Press.
Turner, Frederick. 1999. *Shakespeare's Twenty-First Century Economics: The Morality of Love and Money*. Oxford University Press.
Turner, Frederick. 2012. *Epic: Form, Content, and History*. Transaction Publishers.
Vyasa, poet, and Buck, William, translator, 1973. *Mahabharata*, University of California Press.

Chapter 3

The Cost of War and the Profits of Peace in Aristophanes' *Acharnians*

Troy Earl Camplin

The comic playwright Aristophanes is most famous for his antiwar plays, which make up a majority of his extant plays. In fact, the earliest play we have by Aristophanes (though the third play he wrote) is an antiwar play: *Acharnians*. It was written when Aristophanes was, at twenty, too young to participate in the competition. Nevertheless, it managed to win first prize.

The war Aristophanes opposed was the Peloponnesian War, which Athens was fighting against Sparta and their allies. The primary argument Aristophanes makes against the war in his *Acharnians* is an economic one. Indeed, issues of trade and economics are the driving force in the play. War, as Aristophanes demonstrates, is primarily beneficial to the already-wealthy, but harms the poor, primarily due to disruptions in trade and the destruction of property. Ironically, as Aristophanes also points out, it is the poor who most support the war effort.

In many ways, the play is an absurd fantasy—or, perhaps, a staged thought experiment. The main character, Dikaeopolis, grows frustrated with his fellow citizens' support of the war, and manages to secure a peace with the Spartans that applies only to him and his household. He then goes to his country home and sets up a market, where he proceeds to trade with people from different cities with whom Athens is presently at war. Dikaeopolis' neighbor happens to be the wealthy general Lamachus, with whom Dikaeopolis refuses to trade, and against whom we are to compare Dikaeopolis. Indeed, the play ends with Lamachus returning from battle worn, hungry, and wounded while Dikaeopolis is enjoying his peaceful life with food, drink, and sex.

In *The Morality of Laughter*, F. H. Buckley points out that when a writer (joke teller, etc.) tries to get us to laugh, they are trying to get us to join them in laughing at something morally inferior to ourselves. Or, in the case of self-deprecating humor, at who we are versus who we think we ought to be.

Aristophanes is inviting the Athenians to laugh at themselves and all of their shortcomings when it comes to their own decision making within the Athenian democracy. Not only does Aristophanes make fun of the decisions being made regarding war and peace, he makes fun of the very way the Athenians conduct business at the *ekklesia* (the democratic assembly). Watching the play, the Athenians are made to:

> . . . experience the weakness of their premier democratic institution at first hand. They see citizens arriving late, including most disgracefully their elected officials. They see special interest groups blatantly helping themselves to public funds. They see attempts to hoodwink the *demos*, that is themselves, as broader questions of war and peace are glossed over, as those who will not toe the party line are ejected from the meeting, and as the interests of the countryside are ignored in favour of the city. (Whitehorne, 36)

Naturally all of these are moral failings which ought to be ridiculed, and which ought to induce laughter. Given that the people guilty of such behavior would have been in the audience, and given that the rest of the city would thus be laughing at them by laughing at the play, one can imagine the degree of discomfort this likely created for some people. At the same time, considering that the war continued with widespread popular support, it seems the shame the play no doubt induced was hardly long-lasting.

Nevertheless, Aristophanes makes several points in his play about the relationship between economics and war. It is these relationships which I will primarily be investigating. However, we need to start first with the context in which Aristophanes was writing. Thus, I will briefly discuss in section two the cultural context of the play's performance at the Great Dionysia. In section three, I will then discuss the nature of the Athenian economy. These two sections will create the context for discussing the *Acharnians* itself and what Aristophanes is saying about war and peace in section four. Section five concludes.

THE GREAT DIONYSIA

To really understand the play, we need to understand the cultural context of the play. Aristophanes' plays were performed in the Great Dionysia of Athens, a four-day long festival celebrating Dionysus. Central to this celebration was performances at the theater. So important were these performances that those chosen to participate as actors or members of the chorus were exempt from military duties. However, it is also notable that so rigorous were the practices and the skills needed to perform the plays that chorus members in particular were considered to be superior to regular soldiers when it came to maneuvers. Given the fact that so many of Aristophanes' plays were antiwar, it is somewhat ironic that the training his chorus members received would have made them better soldiers.

The city sat around the theater according to their demes. Among the demes was Acharnia, so the Acharnians themselves would have been viewing Aristophanes' depiction of them as the comic chorus. Each day of the festival had different types of performances. On the first day of the festival, "Before the plays were performed for this great gathering of citizens, four rituals were celebrated, which turned the theatre into a vivid political spectacle" (Goldhill, 224). The festival opened with the sacrifice of piglets, their blood sprinkled around the choral area, and wine was poured out to the gods. This sacrifice was performed by "the ten generals, that is, the ten most important military and political leaders of the state" (224). This was followed by the announcement of the names of Athens' civic benefactors, including those who financially supported the plays everyone was going to see. Athens was not supported by taxes, but rather by the voluntary donations of the wealthiest in Athens. This was a time to recognize those contributions. Third came the parade of tribute, during which time the tribute other cities paid to Athens for Athens' protection was paraded before the audience. It is also notable that there would have been dignitaries from those cities attending the Great Dionysia. And finally, the fourth ceremonial ritual involved the parading of the war orphans. "In Athens, if a boy's father died fighting for the state, the boy was brought up at state expense, educated at state expense, and at the end of this maintained childhood was presented with armour and weapons by the state, to take up his place in the state's fighting forces" (226).

As we can see, the opening rituals all involved the celebration of war and the role of the military in Athens. This was then followed by the performances of a type of poetry called dithyrhambs, in celebration of Dionysus. The next several days would have seen the performances of three tragic trilogies with their satyr plays. The final day would have been the performances of the comedies. All of these were also competitions, with the Athenian citizens voting on their favorite dithyrhambs, tragic four-part plays, and comedies. It is perhaps equally notable that while the festival began with a celebration of the Athenian war state, it ended—at least, when Aristophanes was writing—with comedies making fun of that very state and/or, at least, of the most important citizens within that state.

It is notable that Aristophanes' plays were often winners. And the *Acharnians* in fact won first place. It is also notable that Aristophanes was sued by at least one of the people he attacked (something he makes fun of in *Acharnians*). Given that Aristophanes was so popular, we should not be surprised to learn that he won the lawsuit. However, we might be surprised to learn that that same man who lost his lawsuit against Aristophanes went on to win reelection. Of course, this was the same democracy that consistently voted awards for Aristophanes' antiwar plays, then turned around and voted to continue the very same war Aristophanes was criticizing. Ironically, they often voted for the wars by listening to the same demagogues Aristophanes criticized in his award-winning plays. It is often a fine line between paradox and contradiction, and sometimes the paradoxes that drove the complexity inherent in democratic governance crossed over into outright contradictions such as these. Unfortunately for Athens, the main difference is that paradox drives the creation of complexity while contradiction causes collapse. These contradictions eventually led to the collapse of Athens.

THE ATHENIAN ECONOMY

Analyses of the Athenian economy suggest that it was a strong economy based on a combination of farming and trade. There were no taxes on the citizens, though the Athenians taxed "imports and exports at 2%" (Bergh and Lyttkens, 295). Other than that, with the exception of grain, trade was unregulated. Bergh and Lyttkens also suggest that in Athens "imports represent 50% of yearly income" (297), meaning trade was central to the Athenian economy. This central importance of trade also suggests why Aristophanes would pick it as a central theme of *Acharnians*.

The Greeks, and the Athenians among them, tended to practice the kind of virtue ethics we find in Aristotle's *Nicomachian Ethics*. That is, everything was supposed to be balanced—moderation in everything. Thus, one should be neither too rich nor too poor, as either were, as far as the Greeks were concerned, sources of evil. "The poor did evil out of necessities, and the rich did evil out of arrogance [hybris]" (Ameniya, 61). Social pressure against being too wealthy resulted in the wealthy becoming donors to the city's various projects—whether war or cultural projects like the Great Dionysia. In addition, according to Ameniya, "it was generally considered dishonorable to gain profit from trade, but honorable if the profit came from farming" (63). At the same time, Whitehorne argues that the Athenians saw themselves as being "shrewd and quick witted at driving a bargain in the marketplace" (38). The fact that so many people continue to see gaining profit from trade as dishonorable while at the same time priding themselves in being able to drive a hard bargain in the marketplace suggests not much has changed in the last 2,500 years.

Of course, Athens was likely not unique among the Greek city-states in the strength of its economy. The Greek city-states, being unified by language and culture, were in a position to both cooperate and to compete with each other. They cooperated on protection against foreign invasion, and they cooperated through trade. They competed as well on the production of goods and on attracting poets, philosophers, and teachers (sophists). Aristotle, for example, was not a native Athenian, but was rather a resident foreigner. This competition led to widespread economic growth and cultural innovation. As Bergh and Lyttkens observe, "While Athens often stands out, competition among poleis encouraged institutional innovation and imitation" (281). The cooperation through trade, however, obviously broke down and is, according to Aristophanes, one of the main causes of the Peloponnesian war. Aristophanes seems to be encouraging the Athenians to return to this state of paradoxical tension by creating a microcosmic model in Dikaeopolis' action of declaring his own peace, thus engaging in a kind of innovation which Aristophanes hopes his fellow Athenians will imitate—scaled up, this means, of course, Athens itself declaring peace with the Spartans and their allies.

Of course, with trade regulations of any kind—including even such a small tax on imports and exports as Athens had—the conditions are created for corruption. In *Acharnians*, there is a group of people Aristophanes labels the "Informers." These Informers are people who report regulation violations. Of course, if there are Informers, there have to be regulations to inform about. These were the import taxes, of which it seems that there was increasing suspicion that the Megarians were avoiding:

Some of our own people here—I'm not
saying the city; please remember that –
I do not say the city but a gang
of spurious obnoxious hooligans
who kept denouncing the Megarians
for importing jackets without paying the tax.
If they saw a cucumber or a rabbit,
a piglet, clove of garlic, lump of salt,
"Megarians!" they'd shout and confiscate the lot,
then sell it off at a knockdown price—(Aristophanes, 28)

So it seems that there were people in Athens who were taking advantage of the fact that Athens taxed imports at 2 percent to rob tax-evaders of their goods and then sell those very goods at the kinds of prices one can only ask for if you've gotten the goods for free. When the Megarians complained, Athens' officials refused to do anything about it. In fact, the situation led to "the so-called Margarian Decree of 432 BC, which had barred Megara from any trade with Athens and her empire" (Whitehorne, 2005: 38). So the Megarians went to the Spartans for help. The Athenians' refusal to do anything about the problem even after Sparta intervened led to the war.

In other words, Aristophanes has his protagonist tell the Athenians "how in many ways the Spartans are the wronged party" in the war (Aristophanes, 20). In the play he is telling this to the *Acharnian* chorus. The Acharnians were the poorest citizens in Athens. They had once been farmers, and were now reduced to producing charcoal because of the war. In fact, it is the Acharnians who have suffered most from the war because, as Whitehorne observes, "In any war it is always the poor who have the most to lose and who are the first to lose it" (42). And yet, it is also the poor who are most supportive of those same wars—perhaps for the very reason that they have lost so much and they blame those with whom the country is at war.

DIKAEOPOLIS—THE JUST CITY

The main character of Aristophanes' *Acharnians* is Dikaeopolis, whose name means "just city," from *dike*, meaning "just," and *polis*, meaning "city." The implication here is that the actions of Dikaeopolis are the actions of a just city—that Dikaeopolis is a microcosm of the city. This being the case, we should look to Dikaeopolis' actions to see how Aristophanes believes a just city acts.

The play begins with Dikaeopolis attending the Assembly meeting at the Pnyx. The Pnyx is where decisions on war and peace were decided. He is there waiting for everyone to show up. He's the only one there on time, so we get to hear him deliver a monologue on how much he longs for peace, loathes being in town, and is homesick for his village. Finally, everyone manages to show up. Shortly thereafter, ambassadors to the King of Persia arrive. They were sent to Persia to try to get financial support for Athens. The war the Greeks had had with Persia is, of course, the reason for the Athenian hegemony in Greece, so it is ironic that, when that hegemony falls apart with the resulting Peloponnesian war, Athens seeks aid from Persia. The ambassadors report that they have in fact procured the money, but they are soon proven to be liars. It is at this point that Dikaeopolis tells Amphitheus in front of the assembly

Do this for me, will you?
Take these eight drachmas and go and hatch
A private truce with Sparta:
Just for me, my siblings, and my wife. (11)

By the time the assembly dissolves, Amphitheus returns "with a load of truces" from the Spartans—but he comes being chased by "some Acharnian veterans" who want to keep the war going in revenge for their farms being destroyed (14). While Dikaeopolis chooses the "pledge to last thirty years over land and sea" (15), Amphitheus runs away from the approaching Acharnians. Dikaeopolis leaves, saying, "As for me, I'm rid of war and destitution; / I'm off to live it up at the Country Dionysia" (15).

The Country Dionysia is the country version of the Great Dionysia, or City Dionysia, being held in the city of Athens. Not everyone could attend the Great Dionysia, so there were smaller, more local versions of the celebration as well. At home, at the Country Dionysia, Dikaeopolis sacrifices to Dionysus, asking that the "truce of Thirty Years of Peace / be a success . . . " (17). During this sacrifice, the Acharnian Chorus arrives and threaten Dikaeopolis, accusing him of being a traitor. Needless to say, he riles them up more when he observes, as I noted above, that he could show them "how in many ways the Spartans are the wronged party" (20). He then goes onto identify the trade war with Megara as the cause of the war, which causes the Acharnian Chorus to split (30).

> In *Acharnians*, Dikaeopolis' argument (496–556) that Athens shares responsibility for the war—an eminently rational assertion—persuades half of the Chorus to take his side, but it hardens the other half against him, opposition which crystallizes in the appearance of Lamachus. The Chorus is only fully united behind Dikaeopolis when he insists (597–625), with more rhetorical élan than merit, that the war only benefits rich Athenians. Thus, charges of private, secret profiteering effectively sever the remainder of the chorus, all of whom understand themselves as poor, from Lamachus, an advocate of the war and a member of Dikaeopolis' evil rich. (McGlew, 1997: 37)

Since Lamachus is working to keep the war going, and is profiting from keeping the war going, Dikaeopolis declares that "And I for my part announce free trade between me and all Spartans, Megarians, and Boeotians—but not Lamachus" (33). Since Lamachus is gaining from the war, Dikaeopolis does not believe he should gain from trade with those with whom he is at war.

Dikaeopolis sets up a trading booth where "all the people of Peloponnese, / of Megara and Boeotia are free to trade / and to sell to me" (39). And immediately, a Megarian arrives and tries to sell his two girls, who he has dressed up as pigs. Dikaeopolis, knowing they are girls, buys them for "a rope of garlic" and "a peck of salt" (43)—two things which Megara had once imported to Athens. The implication here is that either Dikaeopolis is a brilliant trader and the Megarian is a foolish one, or that Megara itself has been so devastated that they need the very things they once produced in such excess they could export them. And worse, the amount of garlic and salt is "a ridiculously small amount" (Whitehorne, 38). As a result of this transaction, the chorus is quite impressed:

How lucky he is, this man, did you
See how beautifully his plan

Is working out?
In the market see him sit
Amid the fruits of his design. (44)

Indeed, his trading post continues to work out, as a Boeotian arrives after the choral interlude to sell locusts and

Oregano, chamomile, lamp wicks, doormats,
Daws, ducks, cormorants, coots,
Plovers, snipe, quail . . . (46)
Geese, hares, foxes, moles,
Hedgehogs, cats, badgers, weasels, Lake Copais eels (47)

Dikaeopolis is most excited about the eels because "we've waited six years for her" (47). The eels are a delicacy, and the war—which included Boeotia—had stopped the import of eels from that region. Dikaeopolis' excitement could have signaled to the Boeotian that he could have sold his eels at a premium, except that Dikaeopolis—perhaps realizing this—decides to take the eels as "a substitute for the market tariff" (47). That is, he imposes the same tax on trade that had led to the war. And he does it in order to take advantage of the trader—and so the trader won't take advantage of his excitement over the eels.

After Dikaeopolis extracts the "market tariff," we can see in the exchange with the Boeotian several elements of free trade. The Boeotian is not interested in trading for money—Athenian money would probably not be well accepted in cities at war with Athens. He is, rather, interested in bartering for "something Athens 'as and us Boeotians 'aven't" (47). This of course demonstrates the concept of mutual benefits of trade. The Boeotians have things—eels, especially—which the Athenians want, and the Athenians have things the Boeotians want. Both cities have suffered not just the usually-identified costs of war, but the loss inherent in trade between states. Indeed, when Dikaeopolis offers sardines or pottery, the Boeotian replies,

Mm! Sardines or pottery? It ain't a match:

We 'ave 'em both back 'ome.
Got to be som'at we don't 'ave any of
And you 'ave much too much of . . . See? (48)

The Boeotian understands the reasons countries engage in trade: to get things one doesn't have, or doesn't have enough of. Hearing the principles underlying trade, Dikaeopolis strikes upon a brilliant idea: he offers the Boeotian *Informers*, of which Athens has far too many, and which the Boeotian lacks. The Boeotian thinks he could make a fortune on them since they are "chock-full of . . . money tricks" (48). Fortunately, an Informer named Nicarchus shows up to denounce the Boeotian, and Dikaeopolis has Nicarchus packed up like china for the Boeotian to take away (48–49). Dikaeopolis has managed to find something of little value to Athens and trade it for something of much more value. After all, one does not engage in a trade unless, as the Boeotian understands, value increases for both parties. In fact, given that Dikaeopolis sees Informers as being detrimental to society—harming the economy and having been a cause of the war—from Dikaeopolis' point of view, he has a double increase in value. He traded something that destroys value for something of value.

Does this mean that Dikaeopolis has cheated the Boeotian? Only if one thinks the value Dikaeopolis puts on the Informer is relevant or should be relevant to the value the Boeotian puts on the Informer. According to the subjective theory of value, the price of what Dikaeopolis is selling has as a floor of how much Dikaeopolis values it and a ceiling of how much the Boeotian values it. Whatever price that emerges between the floor and ceiling is by definition a fair price for both parties. It doesn't matter if the floor is zero; if the Boeotian is willing to pay something, then that is a fair price for him. And it is no less fair for the Boeotian if he finds out later that Dikaeopolis would have given the Informer away than it is for Dikaeopolis to learn later that the Boeotian would have paid more. The bottom line is that no transaction would have taken place if both parties didn't view themselves as better off from it. Thus, Dikaeopolis is acting justly in regards to his interactions with the Boeotian.

So one way in which Dikaeopolis is a "just city" is because he is willing to engage in trade. A just city is one in which value is increased through mutual trade. Both parties leave better off, meaning wealth has increased. Aristophanes is demonstrating that wealth increase through trade is just. This is to be contrasted with the way people like Lamacus make money, through the continuation of the war. If we keep in mind the argument that the Athenians viewed farming as a noble way to become wealthy, but trade/exchange as a less noble way. Aristophanes is arguing that, even if the Athenians look down on making money through exchange, they should look down on war profiteering even more. This is why Dikaeopolis refuses to trade with Lamachus, who has made his money with the war.

The history of farmers supporting the war is also no doubt one of the reasons Dikaeopolis refuses to share his truce with Dercetes, who wants 5 years of the truce so the Boeotians will stop raiding his farm. It has already been noted that the people in the country were both the hardest hit by the war and the biggest supporters of the war. Dercetes sees Dikaeopolis profiting from the peace, and it is now that Dercetes wants some peace for himself. One could view this as selfishness on the part of Dikaeopolis; however, why should he endanger the life of his family when Dercetes could, after all, hash out a peace treaty for himself, as Dikaeopolis had done? Further, we can see that Dikaeopolis is willing to provide others with peace. When the Best Man arrives asking Dikaeopolis for "a dollop of peace" for the bridegroom so he won't "get called up for a campaign," Dikaeopolis takes pity on the bride and gives "her a spoonful" of the truce so they can at least make it through the wedding night without the groom getting drafted into the war (55). The "just city" does not draft people—at the very least, not on their wedding day. That this is brought up in the play suggests it was something that happened more than a few times.

We can gather from this that Aristophanes' view of what makes a "just city" is a combination of peace and free trade—with each contributing to the other, and both bringing about wealth for the city. As Paul Ludwig observes, with Dikaeopolis, "Aristophanes shows a nonimperial reaping economic benefits that Athens desires but cannot acquire because of the war being fought to save her imperial status" (2007: 482). One simply cannot have it both ways. More, the just city is one that is generous toward those who find themselves in a bad situation through no fault of their own—such as the bridegroom—but which allows people to reap what they have sown. Dercetes and, certainly, Lamachus fall into the latter category. When Lamachus returns from battle with a twisted ankle and a cracked head from the fall (60), it is clear that this is what he deserves. Dikaeopolis shows him no pity; quite the contrary, Dikaeopolis enters drunk with two dancing girls (61). War brings you poverty (unless you're a war profiteer) and destruction, as demonstrated by Dercetes' and the Acharnians' situation, and wounds and pain, while peace brings you prosperity, feasts, drink, and sex. That is, with peace, all the good things in life return—and will return to Athens.

CONCLUSION

While there are certainly aspects of Athenian society which we today would find abhorrent, such as the selling of human beings, we shouldn't make the mistake of missing the real message of Aristophanes' play. We sometimes have to remember that we should not make such judgments about ancient societies as we do about contemporary ones. Several of the transactions Dikaeopolis engages in involves the buying and selling of human beings. It is easy to condemn the Athenians for engaging in such actions, but the Athenians and every other society on earth at the time would have wondered what all the fuss was about. Slavery was a normal part of society, and no one really thought to question it. The fact that we have moved well beyond questioning it to unambiguous condemning it is an indication of just how far humans have come in their moral evolution.

Thus, when dealing with the transactions that take place in *Acharnians*, we have to take our own contemporary moral positions out of it and just consider the kinds of transactions which are taking place, and how the war has affected those transactions. Consider just how far the Megarians, who in effect started the war by going to the Spartans to complain about the Megarian Decree (which of course, is the real cause of the war, if we don't count the import tax that was being exploited by a few unethical Informants that led to it), have fallen because of the war. The Megarian has to sell his own daughters as sex slaves in order to buy salt and garlic—which had once been Megara's main exports. One presumes Megara is most in favor of a war being fought on their behalf. Yet look at what they have been reduced to. Even a society such as Athens in which slavery was the norm would surely see a man selling his own daughters as sex slaves to be a pitiful condition to have been reduced to. Indeed, Paul Ludwig goes so far as to argue that

> Aristophanes has carefully exhibited conditions in which the ostensibly just response of disgust and indignant refusal to buy would accomplish nothing for the sufferers. The situation is so bad in Megara that the girls want to be sold (733–35, 778–80). By buying them, Dikaiopolis sees to it that they and their father do not starve while simply purchasing his own interest: willing slave girls at low cost. (2007: 482)

In other words, what most if not all would consider a situation of exploitation is in fact a situation in which everyone—even the sold girls, in this case—are better off. The idea that being sold into slavery could make one better off is certainly anathema to our modern sensibilities, but we must, again, keep in mind ancient attitudes regarding slavery. To the Athenian audience, this would most definitely have seemed a better situation for the girls than leaving them to starve.

Attempting to create pity for the Megarians and reminding the Athenians of the luxuries they are missing because they cannot trade with the Boeotians can be contrasted with the attempt to create distain for Lamachus, with whom the Athenians would have presumably felt empathy. Lamachus was, after all, an actual general and hero to the Athenians. It is a bold move to suggest that he is an unethical war profiteer. Yet these are the kinds of reversals Aristophanes is making in his comic play. Comedies are of course full of reversals, but it is a bold comic who invites people to engage in a bit of self-deprecating humor and to laugh at their heroes. Yet this is precisely what Aristophanes was asking his audience to do. More, he was asking them to reconsider their valuation of war profiteering over profiting through trade.

In this play, Aristophanes also manages to address something that we might typically think of as a modern concern: income inequality. But as we have seen above, the Athenians were in fact quite concerned with this, considering both great wealth and great poverty to be sources of vice. Aristophanes shows us that Lamachus' great wealth comes from his profiting from the war, while the Acharnians' great poverty comes from the devastation caused by the war. It is the war state which exacerbates inequality. Meanwhile, mutual gains through trade make everyone better off, meaning greater equality. Whatever inequality that might arise from mutual trade is not a result of one group growing poorer as another grows richer, such as we see in the war economy, but rather from network effects that emerge when one person is engaging in more mutually beneficial transactions than are other people. The Megarian, the Boeotian, and Dikaeopolis are all wealthier for having traded with each other, even if Dikaeopolis is better off than either the Megarian or the Boeotian because he traded with both, while each only traded with him. This is how the wealthy get wealthier in a free market economy such as Dikaeopolis tried to create—by making others wealthier as well.

As we know from history, Athens did not heed Aristophanes' plea for them to return to their old values, to return to peace and increased prosperity for all. They continued with the war for many years—and through many more award-winning antiwar plays by Aristophanes—with the result that Athens eventually collapsed and lost to Sparta and their allies. A weakened Greece was then open to defeat by Macedon and rule by King Philip II. The independent city-state system was destroyed and Greece became unified under first Philip II, then Alexander the Great. One has to wonder if this would have happened had the Athenians listened to Aristophanes and traded war for peace and profiteering for free trade.

REFERENCES

Amemiya, Takeshi. 2004. "The Economic Ideas of Classical Athens." *The Kyoto Economic Review* 73(2): 57–74.

Aristophanes. 2005. *The Complete Plays*. Paul Roche, tr. New York: New American Library.

Bergh, Andreas and Carl Hampus Lyttkens. 2014. "Measuring Institutional Quality in Ancient Athens." *Journal of Institutional Economics*, 10: 279–310 doi: http://dx.doi.org/10.1017/S174413741300043X

Buckley, F. H. 2005. *The Morality of Laughter*. Lansing, Michigan: The University of Michigan Press.

Goldhill, Simon. 2004. *Love, Sex and Tragedy: How the Ancient World Shapes Our Lives*. Chicago, Illinois: University of Chicago Press.

Ludwig, Paul W. 2007. "A Portrait of the Artist in Politics: Justice and Self-Interest in Aristophanes' *Acharnians*." *American Political Science Review*, 101 (3).

McGlew, James. 1997. "After Irony: Aristophanes' *Wealth* and Its Modern Interpreters" *The American Journal of Philology* 118 (1): 35–53.

Whitehorne, John. 2005. "O City of Krnaos! Athenian Identity in Aristophanes' Acharnians." *Greece & Rome*, 52: 34–44 doi: 10.1093/gromej/cxi001.

Chapter 4

A Time for Bonding

Commerce, Love, and Law in The Merchant of Venice

Allen Mendenhall

A bond is an agreement, the unification of individuals or groups under mutual terms. Parents may bond affectionately with their children just as friends may bond affectionately with one another. Marital bonds join spouses in a sacred contract that confers conjugal rights and duties. A bond is also a security for a debt. Banks may issue and underwrite bonds with fixed interest rates or correlative maturity dates in exchange for the promise of repayment. Bonds may be defeasible, high-yield, low-yield, covered, subordinated, or perpetual. They may be backed by liens or mortgages. There are government bonds, municipal bonds, fiduciary bonds, war bonds. A bond may be an instrument or the name for a type of covenant between persons. Love is not just a bond but something within a bond, if we believe the Countess in Shakespeare's *All's Well That Ends Well.*[1]

In light of this rich multiplicity of meaning, the referent for the isolated term *bond* is not immediately clear but, instead, contextual. Serviceable explanations for *bond* depend upon the situation in which it is employed and the circumstances with which it is surrounded. The diverse meanings for *bond* have in common a reciprocal obligation or indebtedness that is voluntarily undertaken: a bond, whatever else it does, secures a promise or duty. Sometimes that promise or duty is implicit, as with romantic bonds between monogamous lovers. The term *bond* is thus pregnant with possibility, yielding manifold associations. "The word itself," submits Frederick Turner, "contains a fascinating amalgam of positive and negative connotations" (Turner, 1999, 1). This essay considers the role of bonds and bonding in William Shakespeare's *The Merchant of Venice* ("*Merchant*") to undermine the notion that "Shakespeare was anti-market" in the play (Ward, 1998, 212).[2] *Merchant* is instead as multifaceted and polysemous as the term *bond* and open to an array of interpretations favorable to commerce and business.

I set out, then, to dispel the popular and predictable assumption that Shakespeare's portrayal of Shylock and economics in *Merchant* disparages money, markets, and material prosperity. This assumption runs that because Shakespeare rendered Shylock as the central villain, Shylock's business practices (e.g., usury) and by association business more generally are also villainous in the play. Although it may seem careless or craven to do so, I will neither critique individuals who advance this erroneous assumption nor scrutinize their work, first because there are too many such individuals for the allotted space of this essay and second because I prefer to treat Shakespeare's text on its own terms, attentive to the diversity and range of possibilities that it offers. The presiding focus will be on Shakespeare, not his interpreters, except where I seek to establish historical context, acknowledge an unoriginal point, or supplement my own analysis with the reasoning of a more seasoned scholar of the Bard. Accordingly, I pretermit any investigation or evaluation of the *merits* of secondary sources or commentaries on *Merchant*, even those expositing a Marxist, materialist, new-historicist, or other "*ist*" perspective at odds with my thesis. This essay is not a forum for passing such judgment or an argumentative fray in which swords are drawn and the goal is to trump and trample. I am not out to conquer each critic's estate, looting what is useful and discarding what is not and in this way establishing my kingdom. Those hoping for a conquest of the field and a laying waste of rivals must look elsewhere.

Nor do I purport to have reached the best or only reading of the play. Shakespeare was too clever to be cabined. Building on the work of others without making them my subject, I propose not only that the "interactions between Antonio, Shylock, and Portia—that is, between merchant, usurer, and landlord—play out the new set of economic interactions that accompanied the birth of capitalism," but also, and more importantly, that these interactions, with their various forms of bonding, validated rather than indicted the nascent market system (Long, 2012). This is not a novel proposition. There was a time when it might have gone without saying. However unoriginal, it is also timely and significant. By concentrating on bonds, I hope to shed light on a particular aspect of an already tested thesis that needs further development. In this regard I am following Turner's lead. His book *Shakespeare's Twenty-First Century Economics* sought "to sort out very carefully what is indeed good about bonds, to examine the dangers and pitfalls in their use that the anti-money tradition warns about, and to find a way of thinking about the economic element of our lives that is not hypocritical" (Turner, 1999, 5). Turner casts his eye on *Merchant*, and this essay is intended to complement and complicate his analysis without relying on it or rehashing it.

The representation of bonds in the play reveals that Shakespeare anticipated some premises of a Hayekian legal order in which multiple competing attitudes and cultures may coexist and coordinate within one operative system. The stability of the Hayekian system inheres not in the fixity but in the fluidity of the law within certain prescribed and secure parameters. Hayek's evolutionary approaches and paradigms—his views on constitutionalism, for instance—would not have been recognizable to Shakespeare and his contemporaries, except perhaps in embryonic form, but looking back at Shakespeare through the lens of Hayek enables us to examine how Shakespeare portrayed the emergent conditions of capitalism, including those involving bonding, in a manner that substantiates a few of Hayek's most recognized legal hypotheses.

Shylock insists on strict literalism as the paramount legal hermeneutic. "I crave the law," he boasts, "[t]he penalty and forfeit of my bond." Antonio prizes leniency, never charging interest on his loans and berating Shylock for doing just that. The resolution Portia contrives at the end of the play is somewhere between strict and lenient; it's an awkward yet absolute compromise cunningly configured to sustain a relative peace between enemies. Her judgment, a mode of discretionary justice, frees up the characters from the harsh ramifications of their bond while ensuring the finality of the ruling against Shylock and in favor of Antonio. "[T]he essence of the law is its fixity. Only a Portia," says Allan Bloom, "indifferent to the law but aware of its power, can manipulate it" (Bloom, 1981, 27). Portia becomes, Bloom adds, "a representative of the law and interjects herself as such between the warring Jew and Christian," revealing that equitable arbitration is sometimes necessary to achieve constructive solutions when the litigating parties are at uncompromising odds and the law (or the putative law) is at its most severe (Bloom, 1981, 27).

Shakespeare uses the term *bond* or its variant thirty-two times in *Merchant*. The first occurrence is in Act I, Scene III, in which Shylock agrees to loan three thousand ducats to Bassanio, without interest, for a term of three months. *Bond* appears eight times in Act I, Scene III, and *bondman* once. Shylock mentions "bond" as part of his haggling: "Well, then, your bond; and let me see; but hear you; / Methought you said you neither lend nor borrow / Upon advantage." This remark comes shortly after Shylock expresses his hatred for Antonio, who lends money without interest (i.e., "lends out money gratis") to his clients, a practice that not only frustrates Shylock, a competitor, but also brings down the "rate of usance" in all of Venice.

Antonio, who agrees to serve as a surety in the deal, prods Shylock into the contract by emphasizing the potential benefits of loaning to an enemy rather than a friend: "If thou wilt lend this money, lend it not / As to thy friends; for when did friendship take / A breed for barren metal of his friend? / But lend it rather to thine enemy, / Who, if he break, thou mayst with better face /

Exact the penalty." The money thus secured, Bassanio intends to court Portia, a beautiful heiress whose father's will conditions her marriage on a lottery: the suitor who chooses the correct casket among three (made of gold, silver, and lead, respectively) will win her hand. The bond between Antonio and Shylock thereby enables a romantic relationship and a business partnership even as it authorizes punitive possibilities. "Money and love are inextricably linked in *The Merchant of Venice*," and not necessarily in a manner that privileges the latter over the former (Yoshino, 1997, 189).

Here we witness the beginnings of Shakespeare's playfulness regarding the plural nature and meaning of bonds. "What is going on in the drama of *The Merchant of Venice*," it has been said, "is the transformation of the language of courtly love into commerce" (Critchley and McCarthy, 2004, 9). It is not only courtly love, however, but virtuous love or *philia*, even if characters like Shylock and Antonio remain at loggerheads both legally and culturally. Moreover, it is not a "transformation" of language but a teasing out of the multiplicity and complementarity of love and commerce that effectuates the transaction between Antonio and Shylock and empowers the plot to go forward. Shylock and Antonio enter their bond in the spirit of "friendship" and "love," despite Antonio's negotiation tactic of highlighting tensions between him and Shylock. Although Shylock's "kindness" appears duplicitous, all parties to the contract voluntarily submit to terms that are mutually desired and beneficial. The contractual provisions are harsh ("let the forfeit / Be nominated for an equal pound / Of your fair flesh, to be cut off and taken / In what part of your body pleaseth me") but reached under no coercion, duress, mistake, or deception. Antonio, like Shylock, is aware of the grave consequences of breaching the agreement, and both men are able to set aside their religious differences and openly to assent to concurrent legal obligations. Shylock and Antonio's pact suggests that men who otherwise would not cooperate or associate with each other will nevertheless do so when motivated by financial interests, material gain, or passionate romance. Most importantly, Shylock never intends to exact the grotesque and gruesome remedy provided by the suretyship agreement until several Christian characters conspire against him and make off with his daughter, Jessica, as well as his ducats, in order to marry Jessica to Lorenzo.

Shakespeare develops the economic elements of love in the play's opening act in which Antonio articulates his "want-wit sadness" to Salarino and Solanio and discusses his troubles with merchandise and investment. The reader is immediately located in the context of commerce and business. Bassanio arrives on the scene, and Antonio announces his affection for Bassanio in terms of value. "Your worth," he says, "is very dear in my regard." There's a double-meaning to "worth": Antonio prizes not only Bassanio's excellent character and companionship but also his property and possessions. We know that Bassanio's financial wealth and purchasing power, which are presently strained in light of recent misadventures involving trade ships, are very dear to Antonio because they facilitate Antonio's pursuit of Portia, who is universally venerated such that "the wide world" is not "ignorant of her worth." Like Antonio, Portia has value both in character and in wealth. One of Bassanio's first remarks about her is that "in Belmont is a lady richly left." He later conflates "her beauty with her wealth" (Yoshino, 1997, 190–91). Lest there be any doubt that Shakespeare is linking love and money in these examples, he has Bassanio state, "To you, Antonio, / I owe the most, in money and in love, / And from your love I have a warranty / To unburden all my plots and purposes / How to get clear of all the debts I owe." The implication of these lines is that to love a friend for his "worth" is also to owe him a "debt" because of the feelings and devotions that friendship confers and engenders. Love is at once a product and a medium of exchange; when traded between persons, it represents the fruits of an unspoken contract, a manifestation of the loyalty and sentiment shared between people. It is, in every sense of the word, a bond; accordingly, in Act II, Scene IV, Salarino mentions "love's bond new-made" to be memorialized by "seal" as if by contract—language that recalls Antonio's promise in Act I, Scene III, to "seal" his bond with Shylock, a bond that even Shylock deems "merry."

Seizing again upon the relationship between love and bonding in Act II, Scene VIII, Salarino, recounting Antonio's conversation with Bassanio, explains that Shylock's bond with Antonio, because of its severity, has only deepened the friendship between Antonio and Bassanio. Antonio's speech to Bassanio, as reported by Salarino, references Bassanio's "love" twice in the same sentence in which Shylock's bond receives comment. Although cast in these lines in a negative sense, the bond appears to strengthen the friendship and fraternity between the borrower (Bassanio) and his surety (Antonio). Encouraging Bassanio not to dwell on "the Jew's bond which he hath of me," Antonio issues an imperative ("Be merry") that recalls Shylock's own language about a "merry bond" in Act I, Scene III. It is not in spite of Shylock's bond but because of it that Bassanio is able to "employ [his] chieftest thoughts / To courtship and such fair ostents of love / As shall conveniently become [him] there." The bond between Shylock and Antonio, whatever the characters might say about it, serves as a necessary precondition for the eventual marriage of Portia and Bassanio and even of Jessica and Lorenzo. Moreover, it generates the possibility of friendly unification among two adherents to different religious doctrines and teachings: "For the first time in the history of the bond plot Shakespeare raises the expectation of a potential friendship developing ironically from this vital loan request, if only the Christian will humble himself as much as the Jew already has" (Alscher, 1993, 9).

Act III, Scene I features Shylock's most famous monologue:

> [. . .] I am a Jew. Hath
> not a Jew eyes? Hath not a Jew hands, organs,
> dimensions, senses, affectations, passions; fed with
> the same food, hurt with the same weapons, subject
> to the same diseases, healed by the same means,
> warmed and cooled by the same winter and summer as
> a Christian is?

This monologue, which continues for several more lines, underscores the fundamental and organized presuppositions that differentiate the cultural and religious convictions of Shylock from the Christian milieu and practices in which he is immersed and with which he must contend. Bloom submits that "Shylock and Antonio are Jew and Christian," and by that he means character types,[3] and these character types "are at war as a result of their difference in faith. It is not that they misunderstand each other because of a long history of prejudice and that enlightenment could correct their hostility; rather, their real views of the world, their understanding of what is most important in life, are so opposed that they could never agree," except, that is, to tie themselves together in contract for their mutual benefit (Bloom, 1981, 17). Acknowledging what appears to be Shakespeare's implicit if ambiguous personal preferences, Bloom concludes that "Shakespeare to some extent gives justification to the Christian reproach that the Jews had lost the one most important thing and carried on only the empty forms of their law" (Bloom, 1981, 21). Yet the laws of the governmental institutions in commercial Venice must accommodate both Jew and Christian, not just notionally but practically. The law not only recognizes the status of these men as autonomous persons and their dignity as human beings but also tolerates equally the conceptual categories they represent (i.e., the caricatured principles of Judaism and the caricatured principles of Christianity) to ensure a constructive heterogeneity and a peaceful, prosperous society.

When Shylock learns of Antonio's pending bankruptcy due to the loss of his vessels at sea,[4] Shylock repeats three times, "Let him look to his bond." Should Antonio or Bassanio breach his agreement with Shylock, as in fact they will, Shylock will be within his contractual rights to demand immediate satisfaction of the debts owed to him and guaranteed by the suretyship.[5] On this basis Shylock eventually will seek the contractual remedy of specific performance, the pound of Antonio's flesh constituting the "unique damages" requisite to such an award (Fortier, 2007, 209–10, 214). For Shylock the bond is nearly sacred, as it represents on some level his standing as a Jew and a religious outsider in the Venetian community. He even swears by "our holy Sabbath" to maintain the integrity and effect of the bond. Salerio concedes the legal soundness of Shylock's position, bellowing with a hint of irony that "none can drive him [Shylock] from the envious plea / Of forfeiture, of justice and his bond." Salerio is not merely blowing smoke: Portia proposes to "deface the bond" in Act III, Scene II, by paying Shylock "six thousand ducats," then "double six thousand" ducats, "and then treble that," but Shylock is unremitting and will entertain no remedy besides that which his contract with Antonio and Bassanio memorializes. "I'll have my bond," he says, "speak not against my bond; / I have sworn an oath that I will have my bond."

As if his position were not clear enough, and to emphasize his unwavering commitment to the plain terms of the agreement, he repeats, "I'll have my bond; I will not hear thee [Antonio] speak: / I'll have my bond; and therefore speak no more. / I'll not be made a soft and dull-eyed fool, / To shake the head, relent, and sigh, and yield / To Christian intercessors. Follow not; / I'll have no speaking: I will have my bond." He repeats this sentiment in Act IV, Scene I, stating, "What judgment shall I dread, doing / Were in six parts and every part a ducat, / I would not draw them; I would have my bond." Shylock suggests, moreover, that the ramifications of any failure to satisfy the bond would affect the credibility and stability of the entire legal system of Venice: "To have the due and forfeit of my bond: / If you deny it, let the danger light / Upon your charter and your city's freedom." This is no small charge against a cosmopolitan city renowned for its "commercial spirit" that "causes men to moderate their fanaticism" (Bloom, 1981, 16). The laws of Venice in fact "were not respected for themselves [but] were obeyed because they were the foundation of the city's prosperity" (Bloom, 1981, 16). Such laws attained their credibility and authority by harmonizing conflicting mores and traditions and by tolerating irreconcilable differences in belief. "Shylock's claim against Antonio rests entirely on that law [or that legal system]," Bloom expounds in this regard, "and he is perfectly aware of its commercial roots" that made Venice "a model city for the new political thought" (Bloom, 1981, 16). The following lines, spoken by Shylock, substantiate Bloom's point: "The Duke cannot deny the course of law. / For the commodity that strangers have / With us in Venice, if it be denied, / Will much impeach the justice of his state; / Since that the trade and profit of the city / Consisteth of all nations."

Thus far the language of the play has not borne out the hypothesis that Shakespeare portrayed Shylock's financial motives or economic statements in the negative; if anything, only Shylock's embrace of rigid legalism suffers ignominy under Shakespeare's pen. Shakespeare reveals the humane potential of contractual freedom and the interpersonal character of business ventures by having Antonio agree to guarantee Shylock's loan to Bassanio, in effect repairing Antonio's relationship with Shylock and deepening his friendship with Bassanio while setting in motion the courtship of Bassanio and Portia. Portia rejects the wooing advances of the landed nobility and aristocracy, who, rendered as comically flawed, travel to Belmont from various countries; she favors instead the more common man whose financial dependence is inextricably tied to the speculative ventures of businessmen. Shylock undertakes great risk in loaning money to Bassanio, despite his checkered history with Antonio, who has publically criticized him. Shylock's surprising willingness to loan money to an enemy causes Antonio to remark, "The Hebrew will turn Christian: he grows kind." The potential for friendship among enemies is shattered only when a few Christian characters furtively conspire to unite Jessica to Lorenzo in a clandestine marriage. The profit motive brings together adversaries, whereas religious differences and hostilities—the impetus behind Jessica's elopement—set those adversaries apart again. Given the despicable cruelty and harshness of the Christian characters toward Shylock—they treat him as an "inexecrable dog," spit on him, and kick him—it simply will not do to assume Shylock as representative of all that is bad about economics while Antonio and others signal an unqualified Christian good in contradistinction to the profit motive and the charging of interest. If Shylock were only concerned about money and wealth, why would he turn down such lavish offers to pay off Antonio's debt? Shylock is no Iago; he is as much victim as villain, devastated as he is by the knowledge that Jessica has exchanged the ring that he "had [of his] wife when [he] was a bachelor." A lenient master who is enraged by his daughter's elopement, he is after revenge more than riches. His character is far superior to that of his foolish, lazy, vulgar, and idiotic servants such as Launcelot. If Shylock is representative of a single thing, it cannot be nascent capitalism or greed or financial self-interest. Any reading of the play that assigns to him these categories is in fact a misreading.

Shylock is cast as the stock Pharisee only *after* he is wronged. "The pound of flesh, and it only," one commentator has revealed, "is the wages of Shylock's carefully nursed revenge" (Yoshino, 1997, 196–97). Shylock's blinkered legalism is out-of-keeping with his earlier profit motive and openness or agreeability with an enemy. "I crave the law," he announces in his suddenly vengeful state, "[t]he penalty and forfeit of my bond." "Till thou canst rail the seal from off my bond," he says later, "Thou but offend'st thy lungs to speak so loud: / Repair thy wit, good youth, or it will fall / To cureless ruin. I stand here for law." So he stands, even when the mechanical technicalities of the law turn against him in ways he has either overlooked or misapprehended. Without treating the law as arbitrary or fungible, Portia brings about "a credible reconciliation" between Shylock and Antonio, one that "depends on each adversary cooperating with her directions to extend a visible mercy or compassionate understanding toward the other" (Alscher, 1993, 1). Bloom likewise notes Portia's mediating role: "She becomes," he observes, "a representative of the law and interjects herself as such between the warring Jew and Christian" (Bloom, 1981, 27). If the bond at issue once functioned to enable romantic and fraternal affection, it now operates to secure a relative peace between incompatible positions and worldviews. "The law of Venice can force them [Antonio and Shylock] to a temporary truce," Bloom suggests, "but in any crucial instance the conflict will re-emerge, and each will try to destroy the spirit of the law; for each has a different way of life which, if it were universalized within the city, would destroy that of the other. They have no common ground" (Bloom, 1981, 17). The bond that ties together adversaries, while enabling romantic love among and between some characters, nevertheless highlights the impregnable barriers between the Jewish and Christian types that Shakespeare constructs for narrative ease and metaphorical import. Antonio nevertheless learns "from his experience that the taking of interest is infinitely preferable to the pledging of securities such as a pound of flesh" (Turner, 1999, 70). The law as conceived and applied by Portia forces him to reconsider his premises from the perspective of an adversary—and of the prudent businessman.

Act IV, Scene I involves the climactic court scene in which Shylock and Antonio confront one another, in person, before Portia, who will determine Antonio's fate. At this point Portia has already revealed to Nerissa, her lady-in-waiting, her plan to "wear my dagger with the braver grace / And speak between the change of man and boy / With a reed voice, and turn two mincing steps / Into a manly stride, and speak of frays / Like a fine bragging youth." She and Nerissa will cross-dress, in other words, and once "accoutred like young men" will act as though Portia is a doctor of laws, or a law clerk, administering justice and adjudicating disputes in the Duke's Venetian courtroom. Bassanio attempts to settle the case on Antonio's behalf by tendering Shylock double and then triple the amount of the original loan, but Shylock unmercifully insists on exacting a pound of Antonio's flesh. Portia appears to support Shylock, saying, "[T]here is no power in Venice / Can alter a decree established: 'Twill be recorded for a precedent, / And many an error by the same example / Will rush into the state: it cannot be." Although she says that Shylock's "suit" is "[o]f a strange nature," she submits that "in such rule that the Venetian law / Cannot impugn you as you do proceed." Praising Portia as a "Daniel come to judgment," Shylock demands that a judgment be entered against Antonio immediately: "When [the bond] is paid according to the tenour. / It doth appear you are a worthy judge; / You know the law, your exposition / Hath been most sound: I charge you by the law, / Whereof you are a well-deserving pillar, / Proceed to judgment: by my soul I swear / There is no power in the tongue of man / To alter me: I stay here on my bond." Antonio himself conveys a preference for swift judgment: "Make no more offers, use no farther means, / But with all brief and plain conveniency / Let me have judgment and the Jew his will." Portia readies the others for the judgment by telling Antonio to "prepare your bosom for [Shylock's] knife." That the bond calls for the pound of flesh to be exacted "nearest [Antonio's] heart" draws attention to the metaphorical implications of the judgment and the plural meaning of the bond: it is not just the contractual relationship but the potential for friendship that is about to be carved apart. Just before the judgment is to be perfected, Bassanio and Antonio profess their love for one another.[6] Portia then explains to Shylock—turning his literalism against him—that the judgment calls for the removal of a pound of flesh but "no jot of blood." If any blood should be drawn, then Shylock must forfeit his lands and goods to Venice. There being no way to cut a pound of flesh without drawing blood, Shylock finds himself in a precarious situation. Portia tells him that

The law hath yet another hold on you.
It is enacted in the laws of Venice,
If it be proved against an alien
That by direct or indirect attempts
He seek the life of any citizen,
The party 'gainst the which he doth contrive
Shall seize one half his goods; the other half
Comes to the privy coffer of the state;
And the offender's life lies in the mercy
Of the duke only, 'gainst all other voice.
In which predicament, I say, though stand'st;
For it appears, by manifest proceeding,
That indirectly and directly too
Thou hast contrived against the very life
Of the defendant; and thou hast incurr'd
The danger formerly by me rehearsed.

With these words, Shylock is defeated. The Duke pronounces that, as a consequence of the legal proceeding, Shylock shall render half his wealth to Antonio and half to Venice, but Antonio pleads that he will forego his share if Shylock converts to Christianity. The Duke concedes; Shylock acquiesces. The litigation comes to a close.

As she does with the election of caskets, whereby she interprets her father's decree to both preserve the integrity of the rules while generating an equitable result, here Portia maintains the law of Venice while sparing it from accusations of severity or absurdity. In both cases, moreover, she affords the parties a choice: Shylock, for instance, may elect from possible outcomes or remedies. Portia's ruling could mean "the allegorical triumph of Christian mercy over Judaic justice. Christ said that he had come to fulfill the law not destroy it, and Shakespeare's characters have learned how to follow Christ's merciful example" (Willson, 1995, 713). Then again, that reading might be too tidy.

There is merit to the claim that the play is anti-Semitic. One commentator states that "[n]o one can ignore the anti-Semitic nature of the play's Christian characters" (Willson, 1995, 707). Harold Bloom calls Shylock "the most problematical" of "Shakespeare's displaced spirits" (Harold Bloom, 2010, 1) whose "representational force is handled so strangely by Shakespeare and ultimately so inadequately" (Harold Bloom, 2010, 2). Harold Bloom believes there to be "no legitimate way in which *The Merchant of Venice* ought to be regarded as other than an anti-Semitic text" (Harold Bloom, 2006, 151). Such accusations of anti-Semitism have been rebutted. Turner, for instance, makes a strong case for reading the depiction of Shylock as highly sympathetic, especially in the context of Shakespeare's own time and place (Turner, 1999, 85–88). Turner is far from alone on this score. Peter Alscher has noted alternatives "to those performances and those academic readings of the comedy that see the Jew as necessarily defeated, Antonio exonerated, and Portia consistently on Antonio's side" (Alscher, 1993, 2).[7] Alscher points out that Portia affords Shylock a "visibly dignified exit" (Alscher, 1993, 1) that highlights the manner in which he, "contrary to our expectation," shows "his adversary credible Jewish mercy," in effect swapping places with Antonio as the more just and merciful man (Alscher, 1993, 11). It cannot escape remark that Antonio is far from an ideal Christian: He has hated Shylock long before the suretyship was ever established and has kicked and spat on Shylock for no justifiable reasons; therefore, conflating Shylock's depiction with condemnation of capitalism is an error. Portia is the only vindicated character by the play's end, and the penalty she enacts at the behest of the Duke—that Shylock be forced into Christianity—can be read as a mere cover or ploy because it is impossible to enforce, Shylock's inner thoughts and beliefs being unknowable to anyone but himself. Although it would seem unusual and highly suspect to do so, even Christians could adopt the more orthodox practices of the Jewish faith without betraying their own private doctrines; it is conceivable, then, that Portia has artfully allowed Shylock to carry on as usual, his quotidian lifestyle being mostly unchanged. By enforcing her decree, she has answered Shylock's complaint that "[t]here is no force in the decrees of Venice," the law of Venice being in this instance the mere recognition of the literal terms of a voluntarily ratified contract. If these provisions are harsh, it is only because the parties to the contract have made them so.

For the purposes of this essay, perhaps the most telling gloss on Shakespeare's portrayal of Shylock comes from Allan Bloom:

> Shakespeare does not understand Judaism, for he saw it from the outside; he looked at it, as no man rightfully can, from a purely political point of view. But he was personally less interested in the question of Judaism than in man's conviction that it was of the nature of man to have varying opinions about the

> highest things and that such opinions become invested in doctrine and law and bound up with established interests. When confronted with one another, these opinions must quarrel. Such is life, and that must be accepted with manly resolution. (Bloom, 1981, 31)

On this view the Christian and the Jew are divided by a constructive agonism that, paradoxically, can be channeled toward societal harmony in the form of legal order. Hayek's jurisprudence is premised on the notion that quarrel and conflict are natural and inevitable. Rather than aspiring to perfection or institutionalized syllogisms, the optimal legal system, according to Hayek, accommodates a vast body of rules that sometimes conflict. Hayek teaches that "perfectionism of one kind or another [. . .] has often destroyed whatever degree of decency societies have achieved" (Hayek, 2011, 54). Rejecting teleology, he writes against centrally directed power by which select experts "assume that in their authority lies superior wisdom and thus the right to impose their beliefs on others" (Hayek, 2011, 54). Portia enjoys immense power in her station as a jurist, but the operation of her judgment depends upon a legal framework that precedes and controls her actions. Her power is limited to the case at hand. She is not a central command directing an entire polity but rather one minor authority in a presumably vast network of jurists bound by principles of law. She does not invent the law; she is confined by it. Her resolution fits within an existent legal framework and does not alter that framework or recommend a new framework. It is bothersome that Shylock is forced to convert to Christianity, but that outcome is in many ways preferable to the alternative outcomes; it provides Shylock a respectable exit and a way to continue to practice his religion in secret. Considered in light of the cosmopolitan ethos and commercial laws of Venice, this judgment reveals that a free system cannot be realized perfectly (Hayek, 2011, 59). Far from perfect or ideal, Portia's judgment, in its historical and cultural context, nevertheless signals the underpinning values of a system that does "minimize coercion, or its harmful effects, even if it cannot eliminate it completely" (Hayek, 2011, 59). It would be inappropriate to evaluate Portia's judgment by contemporary standards and through the paradigms of twenty-first-century democracy. Portia's judgment reflects a graceless leniency unique to Venice, which is characterized by "entirely different conditions, often in conflict with one another" (Hayek, 2011, 60). Rather than causing a disabling stasis, the agonism within the system facilitates offsetting, neutralizing conflicts. The agonism in Venice is a condition for its opposite: tolerance. In terms of love, such agonism mirrors the biological and genetic conflicts and differences between male and female that are fundamental to reproductive gain and sexual unity or complementarity.

Shakespeare's rendering of Shylock and bonds is not susceptible to reasonable characterization as antimarket or anti-money or anti-interest or other such labels. If anything, the contractual relationship between Antonio, Bassanio, and Shylock—in addition to these characters' respective drives for love and profit—bring together longtime adversaries who, absent economic incentives, would never cooperate. Antonio's criticisms of Shylock are ironic in light of the fact that he comes to embrace Shylock's views on interest by the end of the play. The business ventures at the background of the narrative motivate a just and merciful system that not only accommodates diverse attitudes and cultures but also facilitates peace and stability among rivaling factions. Even when a contract appears to be pressed into the service of punishment rather than restorative justice, the law as interpreted by Portia allows for the flexibility and latitude that preserve the integrity of the system while saving a man's life. Whether a system is reasonable that would entertain and hence validate a contract with terms in which a man's life is at stake (or for that matter would dignify a will with such strange marital conditions for Portia) is another matter. The same could be said of a system in which one judge is entitled to such wide discretion in matters so grave. But verisimilitude is not as telling as narrative resolution: it is not so important that this contract would have been *void ab initio* in the real Venice or that the powers of a single judge would never have been so unbridled because the entertaining falsity of the situation is what gives the play its appeal. Situating the action in Venice only bolsters Shakespeare's positive characterizations of commerce and contract. It is not superficial or sanguine to extrapolate from the treatment of bonding in the play a more general conjecture about the role of markets in a port setting—Venice—known for its commerce, trade, business, and tolerance. Nowhere besides Venice would the plot of *Merchant* have been able to run its course. The law of Venice is far from perfect, but it is, paradoxically, the imperfection of the law that facilitates the equitable resolutions that, in turn, lend credence to the similarly paradoxical notion that the system is both rigid and flexible enough to yield constructive results in legally ambiguous situations. "While the court may be biased against individual aliens," submits Kenji Yoshino, "it has bound itself, at a higher level of generality, to the principle that aliens will be treated fairly" (Yoshino, 1997, 210). In this system, procedural particulars give way to more general principles of jurisprudence. What was true before the trial scene is true afterward: "Stable laws enabled Venetian businessmen to carry on their trade" (Willson, 1995, 709). Any case taken in isolation may display imperfections, but in the aggregate the system is sufficiently adaptable—within clearly delineated restrictions of law—to facilitate free mobility and exchange. The market and the legal system work in concert, each reinforcing the other.

Turner rightly remarks that "almost all the critics would like to read *The Merchant of Venice* as a subversive argument against private ownership, as a rejection of the animal roots of human economics symbolized by eating, as a condemnation of usury, as a rather ill-managed warning against marrying for money, as a protest against the restrictions of inheritance and tribal identity, as an attack on the commercialization of work, and as a straightforward endorsement of the distinction between personal and property rights, with a strong preference for personal rights" (Turner, 1999, 68).

Turner humbly concedes that these critics are "partly correct in some of their contentions," but he concludes that "a close examination of the play shows that Shakespeare's view is much deeper, wiser, and more subtle, and can serve—as their model of its meaning cannot—as a guide for a future economics in which the strengths of market capitalism have been fully incorporated" (Turner, 1999, 68). This essay supports Turner's position. The overarching purpose of this essay has been to challenge the commonly accepted and too easily assumed notion that *Merchant* displays "a generally harsh critique of the workings of early modern capitalist practices" (Lim, 2010, 366). Shakespeare instead employs bonds and bonding and all of the metaphorical import of those words to validate a commercial system whose steady locomotion is guaranteed by laws protecting just and general principles. The laws of Venice reflect an underlying commercial ethos by which people are encouraged to avoid violence in order to facilitate widespread cooperation and material prosperity.

The fact of the matter is that *Merchant* does not fit into neat little boxes of economic thought. "Different conceptions of the economic and social realities of late sixteenth-century England," after all, can "lead to different interpretations" of "Shylock's and Antonio's roles" (Rosenshield, 2002, 29). For that reason, all readings of the play that attribute to Shakespeare antimarket or anti-commerce sentiments should be eyed with suspicion. By incorporating Hayek I have sought to do more than reveal the pro-market and pro-commerce elements of the play: I have highlighted the way in which the commercial culture in Venice influenced the legal system on which free economic exchange depended. Having focused primarily on bonds, I have not addressed the role of rings and caskets as marital commodities in the plot, even if doing so might have supported my linkage of commerce and commercialism with love and affection. My silence on this topic should not demean its importance. A study of it would yield valuable returns. This essay is not and cannot be exhaustive in its treatment of commerce and markets in *Merchant*, but it can, and I hope does, open up new directions for further study.

NOTES

1. The Countess exclaims that her "love hath in't a bond." In this essay all references to Shakespeare's plays, including *The Merchant of Venice*, come from *The Yale Shakespeare*, edited by Wilbur L. Cross and Tucker Brooke.

2. Ward is not expressing his own view but summarizing that of Christopher Hill in *Liberty Against the Law: Some Seventeenth Century Controversies.*

3. "Antonio and Shylock are [. . .] not merely individuals who differ; Shakespeare, rightly or wrongly, has presented them as types, representatives of Judaism and Christianity. Each acts according to the principles of his faith. They do not differ because they are men who have idiosyncrasies, but because their principles are opposed; those principles are not their own, but are derived from their respective religions" (Bloom, 1981, 17–18).

4. Antonio writes in a letter to Bassanio, "my ships have all / miscarried, my creditors grow cruel, my estate is / very low, my bond to the Jew is forfeit."

5. I pretermit any discussion of the historical accuracy of Shakespeare's rendering of Venetian contract law as accepting as valid a contract to forfeit a pound of human flesh.

6. Whether their relationship is homoerotic is an issue that exceeds the scope of this essay.

7. Alscher discusses the history of performances of Shylock's role, including a longstanding trend to depict a "dignified, indeed prophetic Hebrew who towered physically, and with stature of character, above his Christian tormentors" (Alscher, 1993, 3). This Shylock "was the social and racial victim, not the bloodthirsty aggressor" (Alscher, 1993, 3).

REFERENCES

Alscher, Peter. 1933. "I would be friends with you . . .: Staging Directions for a Balanced Resolution to *The Merchant of Venice Trial Scene*." *Cardozo Studies in Law & Literature*, vol. 5, 1–33.

Bloom, Allan with Harry Jaffa. 1964. *Shakespeare's Politics*. Chicago and London: University of Chicago Press, 1981.

Bloom, Harold. 2010. "Introduction," in *William Shakespeare's Merchant of Venice*, Bloom's Modern Critical Interpretations. Edited by Harold Bloom. New York: Bloom's Literary Criticism.

———. 2006. "An Essay By Harold Bloom," in William Shakespeare's *The Merchant of Venice*, Annotated Shakespeare. Edited by Burton Raffel. Yale University Press, 2006.

Critchley, Simon and Tom McCarthy. 2004. "Universal Shylockery: Money and Morality in *The Merchant of Venice*." *diacritics*, vol. 34, no. 1, 3–17.

Cross, Wilbur L. and Tucker Brooke, editors. 1993. *The Yale Shakespeare*. New York: Barnes & Noble Books.

Fortier, Mark. 2007. "Shakespeare and Specific Performance." *Law and Humanities,* vol. 1, Issue 2, 209–20.

Hayek, F. A. 2011. *The Constitution of Liberty: The Definitive Edition*. 1960. Chicago, Illinois: University of Chicago Press.

Hill, Christopher. 1996. *Liberty Against the Law: Some Seventeenth Century Controversies*. London: Penguin.

Lim, Walter S. H. 2010. "Surety and Spiritual Commercialism in *The Merchant of Venice*." *SEL: Studies in English Literature 1500–1900*. vol. 50, no. 2, 354–81.

Long, Melanie. 2012. "Merchantry, Usury, Villainy: Capitalism and the Threat to Community Integrity in *The Merchant of Venice*." *Anthropoetics*, vol. 17, no. 2.

Rosenshield, Gary. 2002. "Deconstructing the Christian Merchant: Antonio and *The Merchant of Venice*." *Shofar: An Interdisciplinary Journal of Jewish Studies*. vol. 20, no. 2, 28–51.

Turner, Frederick. 1999. *Shakespeare's Twenty-First Century Economics: The Morality of Love and Money*. New York and Oxford: Oxford University Press.

Ward, Ian. 1998. "Law, Liberty and Literature." *Anglo-American Law Review*, vol. 27, 188–220.

Willson, Michael Jay. 1995. "View of Justice in Shakespeare's *The Merchant of Venice* and *Measure for Measure*." *Notre Dame Law Review*. vol. 70, Issue 3, 695–726.

Yoshino, Kenji. 1997. "The Lawyer of Belmont." *Yale Journal of Law & the Humanities*, vol. 9, 183–216.

Chapter 5

Human Action

Pursuing Happiness Inside and Outside the Happy Valley

Felix R. Livingston

> "Every man ought to read *Rasselas* and every wise man will read it over half a dozen times in his life. Indeed, a man would do well to read it once a year at least, for never was wisdom better put, or more enduringly." (Belloc, 173–74)

Ludwig von Mises observed that human action animated by reason and understood through the use of reason has one and only one end— "the attainment of pleasure, the avoidance of pain" (Mises 1936, 96). When people feel a sense of unease for whatever reason, they imagine how this unease can be purposefully removed, and they act by replacing what they consider to be an inferior situation with another condition that they expect will produce greater happiness (97). Samuel Johnson's only extended work of prose fiction, *The History of Rasselas: Prince of Abissinia,* cogently illustrates Mises' thinking for many different kinds of individuals living under varied circumstances. Published in 1759, Johnson's story revolves around Rasselas, the fourth son of a powerful emperor of Abissinia (a kingdom in northeast Africa that is now Ethiopia), a wise confidant named Imlac who serves as Rasselas' spiritual and physical guide, his sister Princess Nekayah and her favorite servant and close friend Pekuah. Throughout Johnson's tale there are abundant insights about human aspirations and frustrations in the pursuit of happiness. He explores the unease experienced by many individuals, from those living an idyllic life in a land of lotus-eaters to others who must continually work to provide for a basic subsistence; from highly educated scholars to people whose minds "sit stupid in the gloom of perpetual vacancy"; from an old man who is close to "that hour which nature cannot long delay" to youthful individuals preoccupied with frivolous enjoyments; from social authorities occupying high political station to others leading obscure and simple lives; and from traders actively engaged in market exchange to self-reliant hermits and others living a quiet pastoral life. While the fable's main characters are frustrated in the search for a *choice of life* that will make them happy, their failed quest provides context for how a confluence of "law in the sense of abstract rules" and Aristotelian virtues in the *practice* of entrepreneurship can produce general happiness even when adherence to these rules heightens risk and diminishes material gain.

HAPPINESS AND UNEASE IN THE LAND OF LOTUS-EATERS

Johnson's story begins in a place of unparalleled beauty and abundance. The "happy valley" is lush with vast green meadows, all forms of exotic shrubs, plants and flowers, and a lake fed by fresh water streams lined with fruit bearing trees. There are no predators in the valley so that all grass and berry eating animals frolic and roam freely. The valley contains the "blessings of nature" while excluding its "evils," and its inhabitants are supplied with all of life's necessities. There is also an opulent palace in the valley that holds the riches of generations of Abyssinian emperors and provides its current occupants with complete security (Johnson, 7–9).

Rasselas, his siblings, their servants and other attendants are confined in the "happy valley" by their father. Surrounded by mountains with sole access provided by a hidden iron gate, no one can enter or leave this place without the emperor's permission. Once a year the guarded gate opens to the sound of music, and the emperor enters with a variety of talented musicians and dancers. "The appearance of security and delight" provided to residents of the happy valley creates significant competition among outsiders to produce new schemes of pleasure in hopes of being chosen to permanently live in this seemingly idyllic place. During his eight day long visit the emperor immediately grants all requests made by his children and other occupants of the valley to enhance their enjoyment and reduce the chance that they may become bored during the forthcoming year. The emperor's children experience all possible forms of pleasure and repose in the happy valley, and to further convince them of their good fortune he employs sages who tell them about how calamitous social life is beyond the mountains where no one can be trusted.

Most of the emperor's children are content, but Rasselas experiences an increasing sense of unease. In his mid-twenties, he begins avoiding social gatherings and he takes solitary walks in silent meditation. Instead of attending sumptuous banquets he prefers sitting under shade trees and quietly observing animal life. Everyone is puzzled by this behavior, and one of his old teachers follows him and hears him talking to himself. Rasselas mutters that while animals can quench their thirst by drinking, and can satiate their hunger by eating, he is not content with being full, and that things that please him one day are not enjoyed the following day. "I can," says Rasselas, "discover within me no power of perception which is not glutted with its proper pleasure, yet I do not feel myself delighted. Man has surely some latent sense for which this place affords no gratification, or he has some desires distinct from sense which must be satisfied before he can be happy" (10–11).

During the following day the sage attempts to counsel Rasselas by pointing out that there is no danger in the happy valley. When he asks Rasselas how it's possible to be unhappy when all wants are abundantly supplied in perfect security, Rasselas replies: "That I want nothing or that I know not what I want, is the cause of my complaint; if I had any known want, I should have a certain wish; that wish would excite endeavor . . . But, possessing all that I can want, I find one day and one hour exactly like another, except that the latter is still more tedious than the former" (12–13).

The philosopher Robert Nozick illuminates the emptiness of a life dedicated exclusively to experiencing pleasure (Nozick, 42–45). Nozick wonders what might happen if an "experience machine" were invented making it possible for an individual to experience a false reality by simply floating in a tank of liquid and plugging into the machine with electrodes connected to his or her brain. Each person would be able to choose any of life's many experiences from a catalog, and could periodically unplug and leave the tank for a short time to decide whether or not to continue a current experience or to plug into a new one. Pleasures provided by the experience machine would be completely realistic so that once people are plugged in they would have no idea that they are floating in a tank.

Nozick suspects that most people, if given this opportunity, would not want to plug into the experience machine or into any other hypothetical machine such as a transformation machine that could transform us into the kind of person we want to be, or a result machine that could create a world of our choosing and place us in it as we might want. People who would reject using these machines want to "do certain things, and not just have the experience of doing them." They want to create themselves the kind of person they want to be (43).

Rasselas imagines cultivating his virtues as a means of achieving happiness. He pretends to engage in an assortment of wild adventures that always end with praiseworthy actions such as detecting fraud, fighting oppression, or otherwise relieving distress, all of which are imagined to produce happiness in others. On one occasion he becomes so involved in a make-believe encounter that he breathlessly chases the pretend plunderer until he reaches the foot of the mountain. It is at this point that Rasselas recognizes the uselessness of these childlike fantasies (Johnson, 14–15). As Aristotle observed, we only acquire the moral virtues by actually exercising them. Just as "men become builders by building and lyre players by playing the lyre; so too we become just by doing just acts, temperate by doing temperate acts, brave by doing brave acts" (Aristotle, Bk. 2, Ch. 1). The happy valley is Rasselas' experience machine. He is unhappy because he is not free to discover a reality that is deeper than the artificial world created by his father.

When an old teacher counsels Rasselas and explains that he would be happy if only he could see how miserable people are outside the happy valley, Rasselas immediately experiences desire, a sensation that has been missing in his life. Enlivened by the prospect of observing life on the outside, Rasselas focuses entirely "upon the means of escaping from the valley of happiness." Knowing that it will be impossible to get past the guards and then to open the heavy iron gate, Rasselas concludes that the only way out will be to somehow surmount the mountain "that hinders at once the enjoyment of pleasure, and the exercise of virtue" (Johnson, 15–16).

DISCOVERING A POET'S LEARNING AND A MEANS OF ESCAPE

Rasselas spends the next few months exploring the mountains to find a way out. His hopes are dashed when he discovers that the summits are too steep to scale and that a cavern through which the lake's water discharges is full of broken rocks and passages too narrow to traverse. After encountering an engineer residing in the valley who has constructed a number of ingenious mechanical devices, his hopes are raised when he discovers that the inventor has been working on a flying device. The inventor will only work on his "sailing chariot" if Rasselas pledges not to reveal this project because he fears that his innovation might fall into the wrong hands and enable savages to swoop down from the sky to plunder their victims. Following a year of work the contraption is launched from a small cliff overlooking the lake, and the inventor and his machine plunge into the water. "His wings, which were of no use in the air, sustained him in the water, and the prince drew him to land, half dead with terror and vexation" (20).

Following this debacle, heavy seasonal rains cause Rasselas to stay in the palace and he becomes intrigued by a poet who will later become his confidant and guide in the search for a *choice of life* that Rasselas hopes will make him happy. Imlac's poems touch on various conditions of humanity and demonstrate considerable knowledge of life outside the valley. Rasselas asks Imlac thousands of questions common to most people but unknown to the prince because of his confinement, and in hopes of learning still more he commands Imlac to narrate his history and explain how he came to live in the happy valley.

Imlac begins his story by lamenting that his life as a scholar has been to "talk in public, to think in solitude, to read and to hear, to inquire, and answer inquiries," to wander "about the world without pomp or terror," and to remain unknown and unvalued by all but his fellow scholars (22). Rasselas learns that Imlac's father was a successful merchant who wanted Imlac to follow in his footsteps and to eventually become the "the richest man in Abissinia." His father gave him 10,000 gold pieces and told Imlac that if he could double the amount in four years he would be made his father's partner. Despite an education that prepared him for this task, Imlac secretly despised his father's focus on accumulating wealth, and he had no intention of achieving his father's wishes. He traveled extensively for the next twenty years and rather than invest his father's money Imlac drank "at the fountains of knowledge, to quench the thirst of curiosity" (23–24).

Early in his travels, Imlac "found that Poetry was considered as the highest learning, and regarded with a veneration somewhat approaching to that which man would pay to the Angelick Nature." Desiring to become a revered poet, he studied the works of famous writers but he soon concluded "that no man was ever great by imitation." Imlac then turned his "attention to nature and to life" (27). After reciting knowledge required for a poet to exhibit the "portraits of nature" and the passions of man, Imlac tells Rasselas about his encounters in Palestine with Europeans. He observes that compared to natives of Abissinia, they seem to be "almost another order of beings" who can obtain anything they want: "a thousand arts, of which we never heard, are continually laboring for their convenience and pleasure; and whatever their own climate has denied them is supplied by their commerce" (29). Imlac attributes the advanced state of European nations to superior knowledge, and he describes ignorance as "a vacuity in which the soul sits motionless and torpid for want of attraction; and, without knowing why, we always rejoice when we learn, and grieve when we forget" (31–32).

After passing through regions of Asia; "in the more civilized kingdoms as a trader, and among the Barbarians of the mountains as a pilgrim," Imlac at last desired to return home where he hoped to be welcomed by his father and friends, and to delight his "old companions with the recital" of his adventures and wisdom. Upon his return Imlac's hopes were shattered when he discovered that his father had been dead for fourteen years and had bequeathed his wealth to other sons "who were removed to some other provinces." Most of Imlac's companions from early years had also disappeared, while others could barely remember him or viewed him as "corrupted by foreign manners." In addition, Imlac attempted to open a school but was forbidden by nobles of the kingdom to teach, and his proposal to a lady who was fond of his conversation was rejected because his father had been a merchant. Wearied by these disappointments, Imlac resolved to hide himself from the world, "and depend no longer on the opinion or caprice of others." When the opportunity presented itself, he bid "farewell to hope and fear" and resigned himself "with joy to perpetual confinement" in the happy valley (32–33).

When Rasselas asks if he has found happiness in the valley, Imlac responds that "I know not one of all your attendants who does not lament the hour when he entered this retreat." Imlac believes he is less unhappy than most because of his considerable experiences and memories, which he "can vary and combine at pleasure." Imlac points out that the only people living in the valley who seem to be completely at ease are those "whose minds have no impression but of the present moment, are either corroded by malignant passions, or sit stupid in the gloom of perpetual vacancy." He also observes that "There may be community of material possessions, but there can never be community of love or of esteem." Some individuals will always be more pleasing than others, and "he that knows himself despised will always be envious; and still more envious and malevolent, if he is condemned to live in the presence of those who despise him" (34).

Rasselas confesses to Imlac that he has long wanted to escape from the valley in order to deliberately make his *choice of life*. Imlac agrees to help but warns that "The world, which you figure to yourself smooth and quiet as the lake in the valley, you will find a sea foaming with tempests, and boiling with whirlpools: you will be sometimes overwhelmed by the waves of violence, and sometimes dashed against the rocks of treachery" (35).

When the rainy season ends, Rasselas and Imlac discover that parts of the mountain have been washed away. They find a "small cavern, concealed by a thicket," and over a period of several days they dig their way through the mountain to daylight. As they plan their final escape they learn that Rasselas' favorite sister, princess Nekayah, has been secretly watching them. She is "equally weary of confinement," and wants to join Rasselas and Imlac in their escape. After making their plans and gathering "jewels sufficient to make them rich whenever they came into a place of commerce," Rasselas, Imlac, Nekayah and her favorite maid Pekuah make their way through the mountain's hidden cavern during the next night of a full moon and they strike out on an adventure to discover how life is lived and whether or not happiness is possible outside the happy valley (35–39).

HAPPINESS AND UNEASE OUTSIDE THE HAPPY VALLEY

Rasselas and Nekayah are nervous and uncertain about how to conduct themselves outside the happy valley, and Imlac helps with this transition by taking them to Cairo where they spend two years learning the local customs and language. Imlac believes that Cairo is a city that will give Rasselas an opportunity to learn about "the various ranks and conditions of mankind" from which he can make a *choice of life* that most suits him. Rasselas is perplexed that everyone he sees seems to be happy while his own mind remains restless and uneasy. Imlac comforts him with the observation that "Every man may, by examining his own mind, guess what passes in the minds of others: when you feel that your own gaiety is counterfeit, it may justly lead you to suspect that of your companions not to be sincere." Moreover, Imlac points out that unease for some is unremitting because "Every man is placed in his present condition by causes which acted without his foresight, and with which he did not always willingly cooperate." Thus, hardly anyone "does not think the lot of his neighbor better than his own" (40–43).

Believing that his wealth can help him avoid the human foibles described by Imlac, Rasselas begins his quest to survey the world and make a *choice of life* that will produce happiness. His first experiment is to visit and observe "young men of spirit and gaiety" whose primary interests are "to gratify their desires" and who spend all their time "in a succession of enjoyments." Rasselas becomes "weary and disgusted" after a few days when he finds their "laughter without motive" and their pleasures "gross and sensual." Before continuing his search for a *choice of life*, Rasselas advises the young men that "Perpetual levity must end in ignorance; and intemperance, though it may fire the spirits for an hour, will make life short or miserable." They respond by staring at him in silence and then driving him away with a "general chorus of continued laughter" (43–44).

Rasselas next encounters a professor who discourses "with great energy on the government of the passions. His look was venerable, his action graceful, his pronunciation clear, and his diction elegant." The Stoic philosopher compares "reason to the sun, of which the light is constant, uniform, and lasting; and fancy to a meteor, of bright but transitory luster, irregular in its motion, and delusive in its direction." Rasselas tells Imlac that this is a man whose life is worthy of emulation, and that happiness is sure to come to those who look with "indifference on those modes or accidents to which the vulgar give the names of good and evil," and who "arm themselves against the shafts of malice or misfortune, by invulnerable patience." Imlac warns Rasselas that teachers of morality "discourse like angels, but they live like men." The wisdom of this observation is soon made visible when the philosopher withdraws himself from social life because of the untimely death of his daughter. Rasselas discovers that "wisdom has no strength to arm the heart against calamity," and he continues his search elsewhere for a *choice of life* "convinced of the emptiness of rhetorical sound, and the efficacy of polished periods and studied sentences" (44–46).

Rasselas decides to visit a venerable hermit who lives on the Nile several hundred miles from Cairo to determine if "felicity, not found in public life can be found in solitude" and whether an older and virtuous man can teach him "any peculiar art of shunning evils, or enduring them." During the journey, taken with Imlac and princess Nekayah, Rasselas passes through an area where shepherds are tending their flocks with lambs playing in the fields. Imlac suggests that because this is a life often celebrated by poets and other writers "for its innocence and quiet" they should visit the shepherds in their tents to see if the search for a *choice of life* can be ended in "pastoral simplicity." They are surprised to find people "so rude and ignorant, so little able to compare the good with the evil of the occupation, and so indistinct in their narratives and descriptions, that very little could be learned from them." The shepherds' hearts seem to be permanently "cankered with discontent" because they feel "condemned to labor for the luxury of the rich" (46–47).

On the third day of their journey they reach the hermit who lives comfortably in a multi-roomed cavern in the side of a mountain, and he offers them food and a place to stay for the night. When he is asked for advice about a *choice of life*, the hermit replies that every form of life is good if lived well by removing ourselves "from all apparent evil." The hermit relates that he began living alone fifteen years earlier because of his disappointment as a soldier at being passed over for a promotion that was given to a younger less able officer. At first he "rejoiced like a tempest-beaten sailor at his entrance into the harbor" but once the novelty wore off he became "unsettled and distracted," and that while his solitude enabled him to "escape the example of bad men" he also gave up "the counsel and conversation of the good." Now ashamed that he could not remove himself from vice, without also "retiring from the exercise of virtue" he informs Rasselas that he is ready to return to civilization, and he joins Rasselas, Imlac and Nekayah on their return trip to Cairo (49–51).

Rasselas next joins "an assembly of learned men, who met at stated times to unbend their minds, and compare their opinions." One topic of conversation is the hermit's return to Cairo. A participant suggests that the hermit will likely resume his isolated existence, and then later "if shame did not restrain, or death intercept him," will return once again to Cairo. He further observes that "The hope of happiness is so strongly impressed," that even experiences producing misery may be painted by the imagination as desirable when viewed at a sufficient distance. Another conversation begun by a philosopher instructs the assembly that "The way to be happy is to live according to nature, in obedience to that universal and unalterable law with which every heart is originally impressed; which is not written on it by precept, but engraved by destiny, not instilled by education, but infused at our nativity." Following the philosopher's loquacious monologue about the virtues of living according to nature and his obscure answer to a question asking what is meant by living according to nature, Rasselas concludes that nothing more can be gained from these sages who frequently become more confusing the longer they talk (51–53).

Rasselas and his sister hatch a plan to divide their experiments: Rasselas will explore "the splendor of courts," while Nekayah will focus on learning about the "shades of humbler life." Rasselas expected to find that happiness is felt by kings who are "approached with reverence, and heard with obedience," and who have the power to extend their "edicts to a whole kingdom." He imagined that there surely can be no pleasure exceeding that produced by "thousands all made happy by wise administration." Rasselas surprisingly found the lives of individuals occupying high stations to be "a continual succession of plots and detections, stratagems and escapes, faction and treachery." All those he studied in power were either carried away in chains or murdered. For her part, Nekayah found people whose thoughts were narrow, whose wishes were low, and whose "merriment often artificial. Their pleasures, poor as they were, could not be preserved pure, but were embittered by petty competitions and worthless emulation." Many seemed to love triflers like themselves, and their affections were "seldom fixed on sense or virtue, and therefore seldom ended but in vexation." Their grief and their joy were transient and their minds were "unconnected with the past or future, so that one desire easily gave way to another." Rasselas and Nekayah conclude that happiness is not to be found either in lowly private homes or in the high courts of political authorities (54–56). They further agree that "visible happiness" is not always found "in proportion to visible virtue. All natural and almost all political evils, are incident alike to the bad and good." The benefits of virtue are "quietness of conscience, (and the) steady prospect of a happier state . . . (both of which) may enable us to endure calamity with patience" (60–61).

At this point, a discouraged Rasselas is close to ending his search for a life that might make him happy. Imlac suggests that a fruitful diversion from their unrequited quest will be to visit the pyramids. "To judge rightly of the present we must oppose it to the past; for all judgment is comparative, and of the future nothing can be known" (67). During their travel to the pyramids Imlac, Rasselas, Nekayah and Pekuah experience an unforeseen calamity. Pekuah is kidnapped and held for ransom; Imlac, Rasselas and a distraught Nekayah return to Cairo without her; a ransom is finally paid that reunites a joyful Nekayah and Pekuah; and Nekayah and Rasselas resume their search for a *choice of life* in Cairo (69–73).

Rasselas has learned much since leaving the happy valley and he informs Imlac that he has decided "to devote himself to science, and pass the rest of his days in literary solitude." Imlac warns Rasselas that before making this *choice of life* he needs to be aware of its hazards and he arranges for Rasselas to visit a world renowned astronomer "who has spent forty years in unwearied attention to the motions and appearances of the celestial bodies, and has drawn out his soul in endless calculations." Notwithstanding his vast comprehension, capacious memory, integrity, and benevolence, the astronomer is clearly experiencing a sense of unease. Imlac discovers that the cause of this is the astronomer's belief that he can control the weather, and he worries about how this can be done justly, since mistakes in the distribution of rain and sunshine can wreak havoc around the globe. Imlac explains to Rasselas that the astronomer's delusion is not uncommon when imagination predominates over reason. "To indulge the power of fiction, and send imagination out upon the wing, is often the sport of those who delight too much in silent speculation." Further, Imlac warns that "Of the uncertainties of our present state, the most dreadful and alarming is the uncertain continuance of reason." The intellectual who fixates on a favorite conception, and who "feasts" on its "luscious falsehood" even when "offended with the bitterness of truth," eventually begins to regard fiction as reality. When "false opinions fasten upon the mind, life passes in dreams of rapture or of anguish" (88–94).

During an evening when Rasselas and his sister are walking along the bank of the Nile they spot an old man that Rasselas remembers from the assembly of sages. They are curious to ask this person "whose years have calmed his passions, but not clouded his reason" if it is youth alone that struggles with vexation, "and whether any better hope remains for the latter part of life." Rasselas and his sister are soon disappointed by the man who complains about the pains he has suffered from the "vicissitudes of life"; the irrelevance of praise that he can no longer share with his friends and relatives who are dead; the uselessness of riches and tedium of employment near the end of his life; the regret of "time squandered upon trifles, and more lost in idleness and vacancy"; and of the many opportunities of accomplishing good left unstarted and the many more that were never finished. As he departs, the old man says that he is eager for the "hour which nature cannot long delay" so that he can "possess in a better state" the happiness he wasn't able to find and the virtue he never attained. Unsurprisingly, the old man leaves Rasselas and Nekayah "not much elated with the hope of long life" (95–97).

Johnson concludes his story in Cairo with Rasselas and his sister comparing "the different forms of life which they had observed, and with various schemes of happiness which each of them had formed." The princess was most impressed with people they encountered who possessed knowledge, and she imagines becoming a scientist and then founding a college of learned women to communicate wisdom, "and raise up for the next age models of prudence, and patterns of piety." Rasselas imagines administering justice in a little kingdom, although he isn't sure how this can be done, and he can't decide on "the limits of his dominion" or "the number of his subjects." Rasselas and Nekayah, both realizing that their dreams can never be achieved, decide to return to Abissinia (108).

ACHIEVING WEALTH *AND* HAPPINESS

In the entirety of Johnson's story, it is the possession of wealth rather than its accumulation that invariably produces a sense of unease. Rasselas was unhappy living in a place of unparalleled beauty, abundance, and security, and a well-funded Imlac traveled and drank "at the fountains of knowledge" only to retire in despair "to perpetual confinement" inside the valley's guarded iron gates. Although Imlac's father was "honest, frugal and diligent" in his acquisition of wealth, once he became rich he was forced to spend considerable time concealing it from province governors intent on plundering his holdings (22). A final example is provided by a rich man encountered by Rasselas and his companions outside of Cairo on their way to see the hermit. He lives in "a stately palace built upon a hill surrounded with woods," and when Rasselas comments about how cheerful people seem to be who are living on the estate, the man replies that "appearances are delusive. My prosperity puts my life in danger; the Bassa of Egypt is my enemy, incensed only by my wealth and popularity." The man informs Rasselas that the protection he is receiving from "princes of the country" is tenuous, and that "as the favor of the great is uncertain, I know not how soon my defenders may be persuaded to share the plunder with the Bassa." Rasselas learns that much of the man's accumulated treasure has already been moved to another country and he is fully prepared to evacuate his mansion and gardens for his enemies to despoil (47–48).

Unlike Johnson's tale describing the unease of being wealthy, Adam Smith's parable of the poor man's son primarily focuses on the sacrifices necessary for acquiring wealth. In *The Theory of Moral Sentiments*, published the same year as Johnson's *History of Rasselas*, Smith suggests that a lifelong obsessive pursuit of wealth can produce material well-being but can also leave a person exhausted and miserable. The poor man's son "whom heaven in its anger has visited with ambition," finds inadequate everything about his condition and he admires everything about being rich.

> "He finds the cottage of his father too small for his accommodation, and fancies he should be lodged more at his ease in a palace. He is displeased with being obliged to walk a-foot, or to endure the fatigue of riding on horseback. He sees his superiors carried about in machines, and imagines that in one of these he could travel with less inconveniency . . . He is enchanted with the distant idea of this felicity." (Smith, 181)

To accumulate wealth the poor man's son labors relentlessly to acquire the needed education that he uses during long hours and countless years that leaves barely enough time for sleep. "Through the whole of his life he pursues the idea of a certain artificial and elegant repose which he may never arrive at," and "in the last dregs of (his) life, his body (is) wasted with toil and diseases, (and) his mind (is) galled and ruffled by the memory of a thousand injuries and disappointments which he imagines he has met with from the injustice of his enemies, or from the perfidy and ingratitude of his friends." He realizes too late that he has sacrificed real tranquility for ends that are "mere trinkets of frivolous utility" (181). For Smith, the unease of individuals who feel compelled to pursue riches is caused by a deception of overrating the benefits of wealth compared to being poor (149). While this is socially beneficial in that it "rouses and keeps in continual motion the industry of mankind" (183), real happiness is produced by a clear conscience, good health, and freedom from debt, which the poor can easily enjoy. Smith even suggests that "the beggar, who suns himself by the side of the highway, possesses that security which kings are fighting for" (185).

In the *History of Rasselas*, there is no indication that either Imlac's father or the rich man outside of Cairo experienced difficulty in acquiring their riches, and the state of mind of Imlac's father at life's end is unknown. What is made clear, however, is that it was not a deception that made Imlac's father want to continue to accumulate wealth even when he was already quite rich. Imlac tells Rasselas that "some desire is necessary to keep life in motion, and he, whose real wants are supplied, must admit of fancy" (Johnson, 23). Thus, Johnson doesn't rule out the possibility that one can pursue wealth and be happy at the same time. Rasselas, in fact, observes such a circumstance when he first encounters entrepreneurs in Cairo. He sees merchants "from all the corners of the earth," and everyone seems to be "equally happy." Imlac tells Rasselas that "men of every character and every occupation" are found in Cairo because "Commerce is here honorable." Everywhere Rasselas goes in Cairo he finds "gayety and kindness." It is a city that seems to overflow "with universal plenty," and nothing is "withheld either from want or merit." Gold and silver coins are freely exchanged by traders (41), and it was gold coins that paid for Rasselas' experiments and Imlac's adventures (23), bought access to the Stoic philosopher (45), and secured Pekuah's freedom from her kidnappers (88). There is also much giving in Cairo, "and every heart melts with benevolence" (40–41).

Although Imlac tells Rasselas that the perception of general happiness in Cairo may not be entirely accurate, the city's radiant environment along with Aristotle's conception of virtue can provide a window into how Cairo's entrepreneurs may actually be experiencing a happiness in their *choice of life* that was so elusive for Rasselas and Imlac. If traders are free and secure enough to use their own means to pursuit their private ends, and if wealth is acquired through acts of entrepreneurship of the type that make commerce in Cairo honorable, then the possibility of achieving both wealth *and* happiness is heightened.

For Aristotle, all human action is aimed at achieving some good that is perceived differently by different people at the same time, and differently by the same people at different times depending on circumstances. When a person is sick he may imagine that health is the ultimate good, while if he is poor and in good health he may believe that wealth is the primary good. Wealth and pleasure, which are commonly viewed as final goods worthy of pursuit, are actually different ways, sometimes unsuccessful, of achieving the ultimate end in human life, which is happiness (Aristotle, Bk. 1, Ch. 7).

Aristotle viewed the moral virtues as a mean between excess and deficiency. Courage lies between rashness and cowardice, temperance rests between self-indulgence and insensibility, liberality is the mean between prodigality and meanness, and justice is bounded by doing injustice on the one side and suffering injustice on the other (Bk. II, Ch. 6–8). Because circumstances determine when a particular action is excessive, deficient or correct, practical wisdom is required to act correctly at the correct time and the correct place. Thus, judgment is an intellectual virtue necessary for exercising the virtues of character (Bk. VI, Ch. 12). Living a good life entails understanding and achieving excellence in the practice of virtues associated with a desired end.

Enjoyment can be realized when excellence is achieved in any number of activities such as playing chess, composing a play, or creating an architectural rendering of a complex building. In an extended social order, that was already present in ancient Athens but not understood by Aristotle (Hayek, 45–46), it can also be the work of a producer, trader, or creator of a new business. Excellence in any area is determined by evolved standards generally accepted by people actively engaged in that activity. How excellence is achieved and the kind of enjoyment that is experienced depend on a person's judgments about actions that are appropriate as well as what kind of person he or she wants to be. For example, excellence in playing chess requires a study of multiple openings, an understanding of the nuances of complex middle game strategies, and a memorization and mechanical precision of play in the end game. Similarly, excellence in launching, operating and liquidating a business involves discernment of the most strongly felt needs of customers, understanding management techniques that can be applied to efficiently operate and grow a business, quick adaptation to unforeseen changes in product and resource markets, and knowing when and how to liquidate a business to harvest the fruits of ownership.

If winning is all that matters in chess or other contests, some players may choose to cheat if they can get away with it. Similarly, if profit is all that matters for entrepreneurs, then some will not hesitate to do anything they can inside and outside the law to achieve their ends. In *Democracy in America*, Alexis de Tocqueville provides clues concerning how entrepreneurs can be dishonorable even when using legal means to achieve their ends. He observed that for a social group to improve its standing in society it is in the group's best interest to praise and encourage those practices of members who strengthen the group and to condemn behavior that weakens or undermines the group. Using honor and dishonor to allocate praise and blame respectively, is one way to accomplish this (Tocqueville, 626). Because "The prerequisite for the existence of property, freedom, and order, from the time of the Greeks to the present" has been the same: "law in the sense of abstract rules" (Hayek, 30), entrepreneurs are honorable, in the sense of Tocqueville, when they preserve or strengthen general rules of property and justice, and they are dishonorable when their actions serve to weaken the extended social order's requisite institutions. A vibrant and honorable commercial society, such as the Cairo seen by Rasselas, is characterized by entrepreneurs who take into consideration how their actions affect private property rights and the Rule of Law. They avoid taking an action that is personally advantageous but detrimental to the extended social order. Such "motives of rational action, provided people think them significant" are just as important "as those normally called economic" (Mises 1936, 99–100).

Entrepreneurs who forgo short-run tainted advantages are making only provisional sacrifices "in exchange for a much greater ultimate benefit" (Mises 1927, 33). Others, known today as crony capitalists, willingly violate general rules and in doing so create disadvantages for their non-preferred competitors. It's fortunate that most entrepreneurs still adhere to general rules of property and justice even though they must sometimes endure greater risk and less material success than the cronies. The violators betray entrepreneurs who hold themselves to a higher standard, and they deceive their customers, taxpayers and political authorities with partial truths justifying their special treatment.

Aristotle believed that achieving honor, while considered the highest final good by individuals of superior refinement, does not consistently produce happiness because criteria for this distinction can be twisted to arbitrarily withhold or take away honor from a deserving person. It is because of this that Aristotle regarded virtue as a superior means of achieving happiness (Aristotle, Bk. 1, Ch. 5). Aristotelian honor in the *practice* of entrepreneurship has its own rewards and can pave the way to happiness.

Consider the following definition of a practice:

> Any coherent and complex form of socially established cooperative human activity through which goods internal to that form of activity are realized in the course of trying to achieve those standards of excellence which are appropriate to, and partially definitive of, that form of activity, with the result that human powers to achieve excellence, and human conceptions of the ends and goods involved, are systematically extended. (MacIntyre, 187)

Two types of goods associated with the *practice* of honorable entrepreneurship are external and internal. External goods of material success take the form of profit, wealth and status, while internal goods are virtues of entrepreneurial excellence developed and used in the extended social order to acquire external goods. The roads to material success and virtue are the same for honorable entrepreneurs but, as Adam Smith observed, many successful people achieve their ends through "flattery and falsehood" rather than "merit and abilities" (Smith, 63). Entrepreneurs who are genuinely honorable may or may not achieve their external ends, but they always apply practical reasoning to cultivate virtues of courage, prudence, truth and justice as the means of pursuing these ends.

Earning profit in an extended social order requires entrepreneurial excellence in a continual search for better ways of satisfying consumer demands, and for more efficient methods of supplying products and services. Israel Kirzner has written about prudential entrepreneurial qualities that can result in the external good of profit, while increasing the community's wealth by offering better products, and transforming resources in new and useful ways. Entrepreneurs are "calculating agents" who are "*alert to opportunities*" that are "just around the corner" and "that may turn up." They recognize opportunities that others don't see because they know "when to obtain information (or other resources) and how to deploy it" (Kirzner, 7–8).

If Aristotelian virtue is defined as *an acquired human quality the possession and exercise of which tends to enable us to achieve those goods which are internal to practices . . .*" (MacIntyre, 191), then acquiring virtues in the *practice* of entrepreneurship entails achieving excellence in the application of talents required for acquisition of external goods in an extended social order, and also knowing and exercising those internal qualities that strengthen or preserve the institutions upon which this order depends. Honorable entrepreneurs satisfy the unmet needs of a community by practicing standards of excellence that have fostered human flourishing since before the time of Aristotle. In the *practice* of entrepreneurship both the internal good of virtue and the external good of honor are barred to those entrepreneurs who may be technically astute in their business decisions but who don't adhere to standards and principles necessary for perpetuation of the extended social order.

Thus, honorable entrepreneurs aggressively pursue profit while embracing the virtues of character that they practice in accordance with their conscience and abilities. In societies where obedience is the most important civic virtue, the private virtues wither though lack of use. People who are not free to make the right choices soon lose their moral sensibility. Entrepreneurs in open societies are free to experiment, discover their sometimes hidden talents, and learn to make choices that benefit themselves *and* the community at large.

CONCLUSION

We see in Rasselas someone who was at first unhappy because he did not have the freedom to pursue and discover his own happiness. With his escape from the happy valley we also see that freedom alone was not enough for Rasselas to achieve happiness. The knowledge he acquired from Imlac and through a systematic study of different ways of living created intellectual virtue, but he never used it to exercise virtues of character that can produce happiness. If Aristotle were to advise Rasselas, he would suggest that being happy requires a person to achieve a desired state "of being well and doing well in being well" (148–149). Lives studied by Rasselas seemed empty because he was only studying and not living them. Rasselas was, in effect, hooked up again to the "experience machine," this time outside the happy valley.

In Johnson's Cairo and elsewhere today, the interests of honorable entrepreneurs are guided and constrained by a constellation of material and nonmaterial factors. Their self-interest is informed by scientific and artistic interests and is sometimes animated by a fellow feeling described thusly:

> "How selfish soever man may be supposed, there are evidently some principles in his nature, which interest him in the fortune of others, and render their happiness necessary to him, though he derives nothing from it except the pleasure of seeing it." (Smith, 9)

Self-interest can be the self-interest of a researcher who discovers the cure for a virulent disease; the self-interest of a philanthropist who spends her previously accumulated riches helping people in need; and the self-interest of a businessman who enriches himself by making shoes affordable for the poor.

In the search for better ways of serving others, entrepreneurs have generally flourished when they have been free to pursue their ends. When freedom and personal enterprise are limited, opportunities for self-improvement are diminished, hopes for living a *choice of life* are dashed, and the ability to serve others is sharply curtailed. While freedom enables entrepreneurs to pursue material success and happiness, there is no guarantee that either of these ends will be attained. Accepting the risk of being compensated for how well other members of society are served creates the possibility of significant loss even when working long hours with exceptional skill and knowledge. What freedom provides is a chance for entrepreneurs to take risks if they choose, live their lives to the fullest, and pursue happiness as they perceive it. They can develop the business they have dreamed of, and create the kind of person they want to be.

Through the centuries, while some entrepreneurs have lived the life of Adam Smith's poor man's son, others have achieved wealth *and* happiness, and have better served their fellow man by creating new forms of business, discovering better ways of relocating things in time and space, and unlocking and transforming the world's hidden resources. Entrepreneurs fortunate to *live* their lives in a society characterized by "law in the sense of abstract rules," encounter physical and moral challenges threatening their firms and the extended social order that they are most likely to overcome by practicing those inner qualities known as virtues.

REFERENCES

Aristotle. 1973. *Nicomachean Ethics* in *Introduction to Aristotle*. Edited with a general introduction and introductions to the particular works by Richard McKeon. Chicago: University of Chicago Press. Second Edition Revised and Enlarged.

Belloc, Hilaire. 1926. "On Rasselas," *Short Talks with the Dead and Others*. London: Sheed & Ward, 173–83.

Hayek, F. A. 1988. *The Fatal Conceit: The Errors of Socialism*. Volume 1 of the Collected Works of F. A. Hayek. Edited by W. W. Bartley III. Chicago: The University of Chicago Press.

Johnson, Samuel. 1759. *The History of Rasselas Prince of Abissinia*. New York: Oxford University Press, Inc. 2009.

Kirzner, Israel. 1979. *Perception, Opportunity, and Profit: Studies in the Theory of Entrepreneurship*. Chicago: University of Chicago Press.

MacIntyre, Alasdair. 1981. *After Virtue*. Notre Dame: Notre Dame Press. Third Edition, 2007.

Mises, Ludwig von. 1927. *Liberalism in the Classical Tradition*. Translator Ralph Raico. Preface to the Third Edition by Bettina Bien Greaves. Foreword by Louis M. Spadaro. San Francisco: Cobden Press. 1985.

———. 1936. *Socialism: An Economic and Sociological Analysis*. Translated by J. Kahane. Indianapolis: Liberty Fund, Inc. 1981.

Nozick, Robert. 1974. *Anarchy, State, and Utopia*. New York: Basic Books, Inc.

Smith, Adam. 1759. *The Theory of Moral Sentiments*. Edited by D. D. Raphael and A. L. Macfie. Indianapolis: Liberty Classics Edition. 1982.

Tocqueville, Alexis de. 1835 and 1840. *Democracy in America*. Translator George Lawrence. Edited by J. P. Mayer. Garden City, New York: Anchor Books. Doubleday & Company, Inc. 1969.

Chapter 6

The Rime of the Neoclassical Economist

The Economist's Failure at Spreading the Passion of Capitalism

Derek K. Yonai

Many in the Capitalism movement[1] (Movement) have held economics on high as the science to convince people of the virtue of Capitalism and its necessary connection to dignified human flourishing. Thus far, the Economic Freedom of the United States, as measured by the Fraser Institute, has been on a downward trend for more than a decade. Nevertheless, some in the Movement have argued that better economic education is necessary to turn the tide. However, a science without passion, devoid of what makes us human, fails to convince or persuade.

Much like the authors of the Romantic Era, we must return to nature and find what moves us in our souls to animate our economic presentation to others. Only then will our economic poetry find an open and receptive ear. Then we will be able to persuade others about the convictions we have about the connection between Capitalism and human flourishing.

THE RHETORICAL PROBLEM

The main problem of convincing others about the value of Capitalism is neoclassical economics.[2] Deirdre McCloskey argues in *The Bourgeois Virtues* that economics by becoming value free has eroded its ability to defend Capitalism and that we need to return to reuniting Capitalism with the bourgeois virtues that underpin it. While not directly on point with McCloskey, this essay argues that neoclassical economics has lost the rhetorical battle, regardless of how many expanding production possibility curves we shove down the throats of the young and eager students in our courses. Just because someone is captive does not mean they will care what we tell them.

The reason we fail regularly is because neoclassical economists elevate as our John Galt, Mr. Maximum Utility, or Max U as McCloskey likes to call it.[3] Max U, the neoclassical economist's hero, is a sad thing. It cares not about love, friendship, ignorance, or things that make us human. Rather, Max U is a sociopath, it is "[i]mpulsive, manipulative, shallow"; it is a social moron (McCloskey 2006, 135, 136). The cold sterility of treating human beings as all knowing utility maximizers, squeezing every util out of each act, fails to capture the richness of human existence; reducing joy to mere utility does not dignify human beings but denigrates them. To this extent, Max U is a robot—a thing—not a human, much less a shining example of what ought to inspire the soul.

Not only is the neoclassical economists hero lacking, their implied audience is far from a being that warms one's heart. The usual implied audience of the economists is "cold-blooded, desiccated, uninvolved" (McCloskey 1990, 138). While not being as harsh as McCloskey, economists write for other economists. This is reinforced by their choice of a language that few understand, formal mathematics. Having a robot for one's hero and writing to other robots will not likely convince human beings with hopes and dreams that your path to human flourishing is correct. After all, how can one discuss human flourishing if one never deals with humans?

Neoclassical economists lack rhetorical oomph because they fail to address or examine human beings. As such, their arguments, valid though they may be, will fail to resonate with the non-robotic, namely all other human beings. Sometimes, being right doesn't matter if no one is convinced.

BACK TO THE ROMANTICS AND RHETORIC

Typically people characterize the Romantic Era as a movement wanting to return to nature and the natural world. The usual Romantic motif was moving away from pure cold hard reason and back to the more intuitive, natural, and internal. The Romantics typically held that the nature helped reveal truth. As such, they argued that humans can understand more than by purely quantifying the world. Their poetry conveys feeling, passion, and emotion. Their works move the soul in a way that neoclassical economics never can—regardless of its statistical significance or elegant mathematical models.

William Wordsworth's *Preface to Lyrical Ballads* (*Ballads*) discusses the role of the Romantic poet, and we can contrast that with the role the neoclassical economist has failed to play in celebrating human flourishing through Capitalism. Wordsworth begins *Ballads* by defining for us what the poet is. Wordsworth writes:

> He is a man speaking to men . . . who has a greater knowledge of human nature . . . than are supposed to be common among mankind . . . delighting to contemplate similar volitions and passions as manifested in the goings-on of the universe. . . . To these qualities he has added a disposition to be affected more than other men by absent things as if they were present. . . ." (Wordsworth, 1993 [1802], 147)

To Wordsworth, a poet is an expert of human nature who ponders and wants to understand the workings of the world. The poet also is one who is more inclined to see the inner connectedness of the universe, those "absent things" that are not present or obvious. Wordsworth's description of the poet could be mistaken for what economists are supposed to be. The economist, the expert of understanding human action, possesses knowledge and a methodology that allows us to better understand human social coordination. As economists, we ponder how human beings dovetail their plans with each other without having an all-knowing central planner just as Wordsworth's poet contemplates "the goings-on of the universe." Perhaps more striking, the economist, like Wordworth's poet, possesses the disposition to see the invisible hand, what other men would consider to be "absent things."

The poet according to Wordsworth "considers man and the objects that surround him as acting and re-acting upon each other, so as to produce an infinite complexity of pain and pleasure; he considers man in his own nature and in his ordinary life as contemplating this with a certain quantity of immediate knowledge. . . ." (*Ibid.*, 149).

Much like the poet, the economist attempts to understand mankind and the social order around us. The social order that the economist tries to explain is a complex and interdependent feedback mechanism that mirrors what the poet attempts to explain. However, this is where the common elements of the poet and neoclassical economist diverge.

The poet's task is not only to explain the world and its complexity; the poet humanizes this knowledge for other people. "The man of science seeks truth as a remote and unknown benefactor; he cherishes and loves it in solitude: the poet, singing a song in which all human beings join with him, rejoices in the presence of truth as our visible friend and hourly companion" (*Ibid.*). For Wordsworth, poetry "is the impassioned expression which is in the countenance of all science" (*Ibid.*). The poet reconnects the discoveries of science with the human condition; he imparts love, passion, and hope. "Poetry is the first and last of all knowledge . . . the poet . . . will be ready to follow the steps of the man of science . . . carrying sensation into the midst of the objects of the science itself" (*Ibid.*, 150). The poet "aid[s] the transfiguration" of science to flesh and blood (*Ibid.*).

Unfortunately, the neoclassical economist fails to humanize the knowledge of the invisible hand guiding us to the best of all worlds. Rather the economist keeps the promise of markets to herself by using the formal and obscure language of formal mathematics. Even as late as 1970, Wassily Leontief, in his presidential address to the American Economics Association, pleaded with economists to explain the impact of their work to people (Leontief 1971, 7). He saw what Wordsworth accused the man of science of doing, relishing their knowledge in solitude. Leontief complained, "[u]ncritical enthusiasm for mathematical formulation tends often to conceal the ephemeral substantive content of the argument behind a formidable front of algebraic signs" (*Ibid*, 1–2). The neoclassical economist builds models for the sake of building models. The economist has become an intellectual Rain Man who is content with creating generation after "generation of *idiots savants*, brilliant at esoteric mathematics yet innocent of actual economic life" (Kuttner 1985, 77). Even as late as 1999, Daniel Klein argued, in *What do Economists Contribute*, that the economist can contribute the most by helping the public understand the economic world around them and must take a greater role in public discourse (Klein 1999, 4–6).

The divergence between the role of the poet and the economist stems from a differing mental conception of their audience. The poet's audience, as Wordsworth alluded to earlier, is other people. Wordsworth writes:

> But poets do not write for poets alone, but for men. Unless therefore we are advocates for that admiration which depends upon ignorance, and that pleasure which arise from hearing what we do not understand, the poet must descend from this supposed height, and, in order to excite rational sympathy, he must express himself as other men express themselves. (Wordsworth, 1993 [1802], 151)

The poet does not undertake the task of humanizing the world purely for the sake of other poets. The poet comes down from the loftiness of the intellectual spire and shares the passion and excitement of the world with all human beings because that is the only way to stir the inner passions of the public. This differs from economists who merely write for themselves and by doing so share nothing with other human beings unless the public rises to the loftiness of the intellectual. As McCloskey puts it, economists only make kelly green golfing shoes for other economists who also make and peddle kelly green golfing shoes (McCloskey, 1995, 411).

As such, the implied audience colors the language used by the poet and the economist. The Romantics were known for elevating the commonplace that also includes the language they used in their writing. "The poet writes under one restriction only, namely, that of the necessity of giving immediate pleasure to a human being possessed of that information which may be expected from him, not as a lawyer, a physician, or a mariner, an astronomer or a natural philosopher, but as a man" (Wordsworth, 1802/1993, 148). The poet must write in a way that removes the jargon and the elevated sense of pompousness to communicate plainly and simply to another person. "The poet thinks and feels in the spirit of the passions of men. How, then, can his language differ in any material degree from that of all other men who feel vividly and see clearly" (*Ibid.*, 151)? Under this guide, many Romantics wrote commonly and plainly rather than in the over produced language that preceded them.

Contrasting this with neoclassical economists, we find that they do not write plainly or commonly for the common man. Even in an interdisciplinary field like law and economics where one would expect economists to write for legal professionals, we find that economists continue to write to themselves in their own obscure language. Of 246 law and economics articles examined, 90 required a working knowledge of calculus and 129 required a working knowledge of econometrics to understand them (Yonai, 2014, 16). Once overlapping articles, requiring both knowledge of calculus and econometrics, were removed only fifty-five (or 22.4%) of the surveyed articles could be read by a high functioning lay reader (*Ibid.*, 16). Economists fail to convince, not because of a lack of significance but because of a lack of being relevant to the common man.

In addition to the failure of being able to move the passions of humans, an additional problem of diverging from the poet's sense of attempting to communicate the profound to the common man using everyday language is that economists purposefully lose the ability to engage in deep thought, or as Wordsworth puts it, "thought long and deeply." Samuel Coleridge describes deep thinking as "attainable only by a man of deep feeling, and all truths is a species of revelation . . . a metaphysical solution that does not tell you something in the heart is grievously to be suspected as apocryphal" (Coleridge 1801). If the thing a person is attempting to explain does not move the listener, there must be something missing. Unfortunately, the economists' mode of explanation, while complex and technical, lacks the ability to move the audience because the analysis is entirely superficial.

Klein accuses economists of this very thing in his book *Knowledge and Coordination* and argues that this failure "lends itself to interventionist thinking" (Klein, 2012, 145). Klein argues that what economists have done is flatten knowledge, judgment, and wisdom down to purely information. By information, Klein means "the facts as seen through the working interpretation" (*Ibid.*, 145). For Klein, information only represents how we interpret the facts we encounter; it does not tell us why mentally interpreting those facts in that particular way is useful. As such, we may treat the same facts differently based on how we interpret them into information using our mental models. Knowledge, on the other hand, "is judgment, our taking stock in an interpretation and by acting on it" (*Ibid.*, 147). By making human behavior nothing more than a maximization problem based on information, neoclassical economists have flattened knowledge and judgment away (*Ibid.*, 148). As such, it leads to an overestimation of one's expertise, "a hubris common in self-styled scientists and do-gooders," because it is no longer about having the right judgment rather just having the right information (*Ibid.*).[4] The problem is that mere information fails to provide an understanding how to interpret it and use it.

If economists became more like the Romantics, they could, once again, be the advocates of a science that enables human flourishing and freedom. If economists practiced better economic poetry by understanding better their audience, they could move the souls of men toward a better understanding and reception of Capitalism. They would accomplish this by using language that is common to man, use language that stirs the noble emotion of people and help provide the deep thinking behind the power of voluntary economic markets. They would be able to turn base information back into the knowledge, judgment, and interpretation that was at the core of the moral philosophy called economics.

THE RIME OF THE ANCIENT MARINER AS AN ALLEGORY TO THE NEOCLASSICAL ECONOMIST

Often one thinks of Coleridge's *The Rime of the Ancient Mariner* as merely a poem of a fallen crazed man roaming the earth unburdening himself by confessing his sins of destroying nature. Some make the argument that it is a cautionary tale of not taking nature and the natural world seriously. Given the original draft was published in Wordsworth's *Lyrical Ballads*, one may interpret the poem as a warning or allegory to neoclassical economists given our discussion above.

We meet the Ancient Mariner stopping a wedding guest and confessing what happened at sea. The Ancient Mariner begins by describing how the journey began and how his ship was blown by a storm toward the South Pole. An albatross, a good omen to sailors, appeared; the sailors fed it and the albatross flew around the ship keeping company with the men. As the albatross did this, the winds changed and the ship began to return north away from the ice. The sailors believed in the connection between the albatross and the change in their luck; they appreciated the unquantifiable connection between the natural world and their flourishing because of the good omen.

The Ancient Mariner shot the albatross with his crossbow; killing the omen of good luck and effectively denying the natural world and the metaphysical connection between the albatross and the ship's good fortune. Neoclassical economists have shot their own albatross by removing the human condition through their creation and elevation of McCloskey's Max U. Neoclassical economists have turned their back on the natural state of man as a limited, error-prone creation by adopting the assumption of perfect information in their competitive equilibrium analysis. They have denied taking humans for what we are and instead substituted a robot that is all knowing and coldly calculating. By doing so, they severed the tie with being able to communicate the richness of our profession to other people. By creating Max U and taking him out of the real world, he is not relatable by human beings.

On the ship, the Ancient Mariner's shipmates yelled at him for killing the sign of good luck that "made the breeze to blow" (Coleridge, 1993 [1798], 333). The ship was now motionless, "day after day, / We stuck, nor breath nor motion" (*Ibid.*). They were cursed and had "[w]ater, water, everywhere / Nor any drop to drink" (*Ibid.*). As a form of penance to apologize for wronging nature, the sailors strung the albatross around the Ancient Mariner's neck. Neoclassical economists, by invoking the all-knowing Max U, created a static world where time plays little function and dynamic interaction ceases to exist. By dehumanizing Max U by removing him from his natural state, the neoclassical economist has killed the thing that made "the breeze blow" in economic analysis, human learning, and continual improvement. We are now stuck with static models where Max U moves from equilibrium to equilibrium instantly with instantaneous epiphany regarding changes in the environment. This leads to a world where we have social interactions around us to examine but the neoclassical economist has none of it because her static model does not allow for it. For example, we have the role of the entrepreneur who gap fills our limited knowledge of what people want but the entrepreneur does not exist in the neoclassical economist's neat robotic world because those gaps are instantly filled with perfect information. Social action everywhere and not a drop to examine.

Over time, the crew dies leaving only the Ancient Mariner behind. Much like neoclassical economics, it is not a social science in so far as it is an atomistic science studying the world through the lenses of Max U. Neoclassical economics discusses what is best for Max U. It does not address how Max U interacts with other people and the felt Smithian sympathies between people. It addresses the needs wants and desires of Max U and where others fit into Max U's utility function. It is not a social world but a world where others merely serve as a means to Max U's ends. To this extent, the neoclassical economists have accomplished what the Ancient Mariner accomplished; they killed off the rest of the crew and created a lone isolated atomistic individual.

Over time, the Ancient Mariner began to feel, emote love, and prayed. The albatross was released from his neck. He was told by a spirit, "The man hath penance done, and penance more will do" (*Ibid.*, 341). As part of the eternal penance, the Ancient Mariner roams the world telling the tale of why we need to love and respect the natural world. The Ancient Mariner realized the folly of ignoring nature and the natural world; he felt the pain of assuming a position above natural reality. He felt love; he did penance and continues to do penance. The question is whether neoclassical economists will ever have Max U's analytical heart of stone feel love. Will neoclassical economists remove Max U from his sociopathic altar and begin, again, to discuss the ability of flawed humans to coordinate with each other in spite of our limitations?

This part of the neoclassical economist's tale has yet to be written. Deirdre McCloskey has for decades argued that neoclassical economists need to address human beings. She has argued that our cold rational science only takes us so far and that a return to bringing virtue back into economic analysis will help make economists the defender of the morality of Capitalism and voluntary cooperation (see generally, McCloskey, 2006).

Likewise, Daniel Klein has argued that the proper role of the economist is to explain the world to other people. That the real purpose of economists is not to create models for the sake of building models, rather economists must engage the world so people can make better choices using better judgment. We need to return to our profession's original purpose, discover knowledge that is useful in improving the world. Recently, Klein has argued against the flattening of knowledge by economists and inspires us to return to a deeper way of thinking about social interaction (see generally, Klein, 2012).

McCloskey and Klein have taken up the sins of their discipline. Until neoclassical economists begin to acknowledge their sins and follow in McCloskey and Klein's shoes by engaging real people using words, themes, and issues that move the hearts of people, they will never be a sufficient defender of Capitalism. So is all hope lost?

ECONOMICS FOR REAL PEOPLE

Hope is not lost on the economics profession. While neoclassical economists have killed the albatross and condemned their endeavor to the motionless sea, we may be able to salvage the economics discipline from a sentence of being unable to defend Capitalism. Austrian economists tend to shy away from the mentality of using formal mathematics for the sake of looking scientific. They also keep human beings human and, like the Romantics, elevate our limitations to something to be celebrated. Because of these things, Austrian economists have been successful in explaining Capitalism to others without falling into the trappings of being a mere ideologue.

Austrian economists tend to focus more on getting the narrative right rather than showing off fancy mathematics.[5] Mises argues that mathematics fails to add to the economic analysis (Mises, 1996 [1949], 333). Modern Austrians, like Peter Boettke, understand that the mathematics is a tool of analysis rather than the purpose of the economic endeavor (Boettke, 1996).[6] Given this mental starting point, Austrians are more apt to speak the same language as the common person. They are more likely to use language to communicate the complex and dynamic processes of the market, which makes it more likely to resonate with the layperson.

Austrians understand that economics is social and that society matters. Unlike the neoclassical economist, the Austrian begins with the reconciliation of studying the individual but contextualizing her in the social world. In "Individualism: True and False," Hayek argues that true individualism, "it is primarily a *theory* of society, an attempt to understand the forces which determine the social life of man . . ." (Hayek, 1948/1980, 6). For Hayek, people are naturally in a social order rather than the atomistic world of the neoclassical or Ancient Mariner (*Ibid.*). Like the shipmates of the Ancient Mariner, Hayek understands the value in social conventions and other social norms that appear "unintelligible and irrational" (*Ibid.*, 22). Hayek argues that, "the individual, in participating in the social process, must be ready and willing to adjust himself to changes and to submit to conventions which are not the result of intelligent design" (*Ibid.*). The Austrian social approach to the individual humanizes the economic actor in a way that people can relate to given their life experiences. This provides an in road to moving the passion of the public in a way that neoclassical economics cannot.

As part of humanizing the economic actor by contextualizing him in a social setting, the Austrians take the Romantic approach of celebrating the lowly or weak by focusing on our human limitations rather than creating the soulless robot of Max U with perfect information. Rather than assuming away our human frailties of limited knowledge, the Austrians use it as the foundation for their market process approach. By doing so, they take a preconceived weakness and raise it up as why voluntary markets exist. Instead of assuming away the problem by granting omniscience to the economic actor, Hayek points out that, "before we can explain why people commit mistakes, we must first explain why they should ever be right" (*Ibid.*, 34). In this remark, Hayek points out that if we take human beings for what we are, limited in nature, why is it we should ever coordinate our activities in the market at all? We should not shake our fist when the perfect world outcome fails to materialize but wonder how we transcend our limitations and create so much coordination; we should appreciate and understand the powerful nature of how we create such a powerful outcome that works more often than not. By embracing our weaknesses, Austrians can explain how prices evolved to communicate subjective local knowledge from person to person regardless of language differences or distance in geography; how people can provide for others that they do not know. Austrians are also able to more robustly discuss the powerful role the entrepreneur plays in solving knowledge deficiencies in society by discovering opportunities to improve the lives of others in society. Much like the Romantics, Austrians, by embracing humanity as it is, are able to move the soul of the public by demonstrating the sheer power of voluntary social cooperation.

The Austrians' adoption of the rhetorical tools of the Romantics, though not by design, may explain why their students and practitioners are some of the most outspoken advocates of Capitalism. This kind of self-selection is not the result of Austrian economics being ideological driven, as accused by some. Austrians only "assess the efficacy of the means chosen to satisfy stated ends" which does not involve "the importation of values" (Boettke, 2001, 11). The reason, one can conclude, for the self-selection is that not only is their intellect moved by the logic of human action but also their heart by seeing more clearly the beauty of the social mechanisms that evolved over time to allow us to transcend poverty and enhance social cooperation.

CONCLUSION

Neoclassical economics, with its hero of Max U, fails to inspire people to understand or defend Capitalism. The notion of having more people understand economics and thereby improving the ability to educate people about the power of the market is misleading. If by that we mean teach people more about neoclassical economics, this endeavor will continue to fail. As the Romantics understood, science without the humanizing passion of a poet leaves it cold and sterile. People will not understand or appreciate the awe that the new science brings to understanding the natural world. Economists need to stir people's passions if they want to convince others about the dignity, virtue, and morality of Capitalism. Perhaps, they need to step back and take a lesson from the Austrians and humanize economics back into the social science it was meant to be.

NOTES

1. Sometimes it is referred to as the free enterprise movement, the liberty movement, or the free market movement.
2. For a fuller discussion of the inherent communication problems of economists talking to themselves rather than communicating to others, see Yonai (2014).
3. I said "it" because, as we'll see, Max U is hardly human.
4. Even Adam Smith acknowledged that information is not sufficient to form judgment or knowledge because a person may be "unfit to judge even though he was fully informed" (Smith, 1976/1776, 266).

5. This has to do with the fact that Austrians tend to analyze processes rather than static end states. Mathematics lends itself to static equilibrium analysis rather than the subjective process approach followed by Austrians.

6. There is nothing "wrong" with using mathematics in economic analysis but it must be done so properly.

REFERENCES

Boettke, P. J. 1996. What is Wrong with Neoclassical Economics (And What Is Still Wrong With Austrian Economics). In *Beyond Neoclassical Economics*. Edited by F. E. Foldvary. Northampton, Massachusetts: Edward Elgar Publishing.

Boettke, P. J. 2001. *Calculation and Coordination*. New York: Routledge.

Coleridge, S. T. 1993 [1798]. The Rime of the Ancient Mariner. In *The Norton Anthology of English Literature* (vol. 2). Edited by M. H. A. e. al. New York: W.W. Norton & Co.

Coleridge, S. T. 1801. [Letter to T. Poole].

Hayek, F. A. 1980 [1948]. Individualism: True and False *Individualism and Economic Order*. Chicago: University of Chicago Press.

Hayek, F. A. 1980 [1948]. Economics and Knowledge *Individualism and Economic Order*. Chicago: University of Chicago Press.

Klein, D. (Ed.). 1999. *What Do Economists Contribute*. New York: NYU Press.

———. 2012. *Knowledge and Coordination*. New York: Oxford University Press.

Kuttner, R. 1985. The Poverty of Economics. *The Atlantic Monthly, Feb. 1985*.

Leontief, W. 1971. Theoretical Assumptions and Nonobserved Facts. *The American Economic Review, 61*: 1–7.

McCloskey, D. N. 1989. Formalism in Economics, Rhetorically Speaking. *Ricerche Economiche, 43*: 57–75.

———. 1995. Kelly Green Golf Shoes and the Intellectual Range from M to N. *Eastern Economic Journal, 21*(3): 411–414.

———. 1990. *If You're So Smart: The narrative of Economic Expertise*. Chicago: University of Chicago Press.

———. 2006. *The Bourgeois Virtues: Ethics for an Age of Commerce*. Chicago: University of Chicago Press.

Mises, L. v. 1996 [1949]. *Human Action* (4th Revised Edition ed.). San Francisco, California: Fox & Wilkes.

Smith, A. 1976 [1776]. *An Inquiry into the Nature and Causes of the Wealth of Nations*. Oxford: Oxford University Press.

Wordsworth, W. 1993 [1802]. Preface to *Lyrical Ballads*. In *The Norton Anthology of English Literature* (vol. 2). Edited by M. H. A. e. al. New York: W.W. Norton & Co.

Yonai, D. K. 2014. I'm a Lawyer, Not an Economist: A plea for plain language law and economics. *Interdisciplinary Journal of Economics and Business Law, 3*(4): 8–37.

Chapter 7

Elizabeth Gaskell's *North and South*

Industrial Energy Versus "The Idiocies of Rural Life"

Paul A. Cantor

Most people view the nineteenth century as a bleak period in the economic history of England. According to the common narrative, eighteenth-century England was a largely rural and agricultural nation—"England's green and pleasant land," in William Blake's famous words. Then along came the Industrial Revolution to blight the pristine English landscape with coal pits, smoke-belching factories, and railroads cutting up the countryside. People left their happy open-air life on farms, and found themselves working long hours in crowded, unsafe, and unhealthy factories, run by greedy capitalist bosses, who mercilessly exploited their employees. This view of nineteenth-century England can be supported by some historical facts, but it has gained its widespread currency largely through the power of literature.[1] Romantic poets, especially William Wordsworth, created indelible images of the beauty of nature uncontaminated by technology, and celebrated the spiritual power of the English countryside.[2] Victorian novelists had an even greater impact on the popular imagination with their chronicles of the horrors of urban life. Charles Dickens was the single most important figure in shaping the popular image of industrialized England—an image that in its broad outlines survives to this day, endlessly recycled in films and television shows.

A rare exception in Victorian literature to the seemingly relentless—and one-sided—critique of industrialism is Elizabeth Gaskell's 1854 novel *North and South*. As if she had deliberately set out to redress the balance and tell the other side of the story for once, Gaskell takes a fresh look at mid-nineteenth-century Britain and asks some basic questions: Is farm life truly the paradise portrayed in Romantic poetry? And is factory life the pure hell portrayed in Victorian novels? In the course of exploring these questions, Gaskell gives one of the few sympathetic portraits in nineteenth-century literature of the new world of capitalism.

Gaskell's title refers to the regions that constituted the two poles of economic life in nineteenth-century Britain—the industrial, capitalist North and the agricultural, semi-feudal South. The novel is largely set in Milton-Northern, a fictionalized Manchester—the city that epitomized all the economic and technological developments associated with the Industrial Revolution. Manchester was the center of the cotton trade, and thus of the main industry—clothing manufacture—that made Britain the greatest economic power of the nineteenth century. Manchester was ground zero for the rising power of the middle class and the birthplace of Manchester liberalism—the intellectual and political movement that called for parliamentary reform, free trade, and laissez-faire capitalism (or at least the end of government monopolies and other mercantilist restrictions on manufacturing and commerce). Gaskell juxtaposes the forward-looking North, the vanguard of economic progress, with the backward-looking South, the bastion of rural counties still largely devoted to agriculture, and presided over by the country squires familiar to us from the novels of Henry Fielding and Jane Austen. The genius of Gaskell's novel is that she has a character from the South move to the North, thereby allowing the novelist to dramatize the clash between these two different worlds in the mind of a perceptive and intelligent woman.

Margaret Hale, a young, upper-class gentlewoman from a family fallen on economic hard times, moves to Milton-Northern with her father and mother in order to better their fortunes. Margaret is at first repelled by what she sees in the industrial city, especially when she compares it with the idyllic, rural conditions she remembers from her earlier life. But *North and South* is a kind of Bildungsroman in economics. As Margaret gets to know Milton-Northern and its people better, especially the cotton factory owner John Thornton (with whom she falls in love), she comes to appreciate the benefits of the new industrialism, and also is forced to acknowledge the deficiencies of her beloved rural world. *North and South* is not an autobiographical novel. Gaskell's personal background was very different from Margaret Hale's. Still, the novel does reflect Gaskell's own experience in moving to Manchester. She, too, initially disliked the city. In fact, her first novel, *Mary Barton*, portrayed the city's factory owners in a bad light. Gaskell had many doubts about economic developments in the nineteenth century and cannot be classified as a dogmatic advocate of capitalism, in the mold of Harriet Martineau. Nevertheless, Gaskell was a keen observer of the social scene, and, as a committed realist, she was determined to set the record straight about Manchester/Milton-Northern. To her credit, she did not allow her prejudices against the industrial world to blind her to the realities of genuine economic progress in nineteenth-century Britain.

As critics have noted, *North and South* offers a peculiar variant of the plot of Jane Austen's *Pride and Prejudice* (Uglow, 2004, 605). Upper-class

Margaret must overcome her initial biases against the middle-class factory owner Thornton in order to achieve romantic happiness (just as he must overcome his middle-class prejudice against Margaret as a member of the upper class). In short, the typical romance plot of the nineteenth-century novel (especially its interest in marriages cutting across class lines) allows Gaskell to create a dialogue between the classes in Britain and to explore the relative merits and demerits of the industrialized North and the agricultural South.

North and South contains many of the elements of the typical anticapitalist novel. In Margaret's first view of Milton, the city is covered by the obligatory urban smog:

> For several miles before they reached Milton, they saw a deep lead-coloured cloud hanging over the horizon. . . . Nearer to the town, the air had a faint taste and smell of smoke. . . . Here and there a great oblong many-windowed factory stood up, . . . puffing out black "unparliamentary" smoke. . . . They had to stop constantly; great loaded lorries blocked up the not over-wide thoroughfares. (Gaskell 1995, 60)

Between the air pollution and the gridlocked traffic, Milton embodies everything that repelled people in the emerging urban landscapes of nineteenth-century Britain. Gaskell adds noise pollution to the toxic mix with her description of "an immense many-windowed mill, whence proceeded the continual clash of machinery and the long groaning roar of the steam-engine, enough to deafen those who lived within the enclosure" (111). No wonder that, from the beginning, Margaret "had a repugnance to the idea of a manufacturing town" (60).

Margaret's initial distaste for the North goes beyond its ugly and unsalubrious characteristics. Margaret despises the commercial spirit of the North. Early in the story, she contemptuously dismisses the idea of visiting certain friends of the family because of their connections with the business world: "Are those the Gormans who made their fortune in trade at Southampton? Oh! I'm glad we don't visit them. I don't like shoppy people" (20). Margaret's mother, who was secretly hoping that her daughter might recoup the family's fortunes by marrying "a young and handsome Mr Gorman," rebukes her class prejudice: "You must not be so fastidious" (20). In her reply, Margaret reveals how deep her upper-class prejudices run: "I call mine a very comprehensive taste; I like all people whose occupations have to do with land; I like soldiers and sailors, and the three learned professions. . . . I'm sure you don't want me to admire butchers and bakers, and candlestick-makers, do you, mamma?" (20). When her mother points out that "the Gormans were neither butchers nor bakers, but very respectable coach-builders," Margaret remains adamantly aristocratic: "Coach-building is a trade all the same, and I think a much more useless one than that of butchers and bakers" (20).

Margaret's automatic rejection of "shoppy people" shows how prejudiced she is against all forms of middle-class money making. At the beginning of the novel, she is a captive of the values of the landed gentry, who respect only people who have inherited wealth, not those who have made it by producing goods to please the public. The positive side of this snobbery is the principle of *noblesse oblige*. In the spirit of the country squire, Margaret believes that she and her family are obligated to assist the poor people in their neighborhood. In leaving the South for the North, Margaret regrets that she and her family will no longer be able to come to the aid of their neighbors: "By the time the frost had set in, they should be far away from Helstone. Old Simon's rheumatism might be bad and his eyesight worse; there would be no one to go and read to him, and comfort him with little porringers of broth and good red flannel: or if there was, it would be a stranger, and the old man would watch in vain for her" (42). This is what the South represents for Margaret: a world in which people care for each other, and in particular the rich help the poor. Note the emphasis on personal ties in Margaret's view. The aid to Old Simon must come from her specifically, not from a stranger. There is something paternalistic about Margaret's sense of mission—she assumes that she is superior to the people she aids; Old Simon will be helpless without her. But this is still paternalism at its best. However condescending Margaret may be to the poor, she genuinely comes to their aid.

In the early pages of the novel, Gaskell may seem to be simply upholding the cause of the South against the North. But there are signs from the beginning that *North and South* is not going to be a one-sided polemic against capitalism. Living for a time in London and faced with an importunate suitor (Henry Lennox), Margaret starts speaking with fondness about her native village Helstone: "There is the church and a few houses near it on the green—cottages, rather—with roses growing all over them" (13). This is too much for the urban sophisticate Lennox, who interrupts: "And flowering all the year round, especially at Christmas—make your picture complete" (13). Detecting the sarcasm, Margaret insists that she is not overidealizing her hometown: "I am not making a picture. I am trying to describe Helstone as it really is" (13). Lennox recognizes his mistake, and backs off, but he cannot help further registering his skepticism: "I am penitent. . . . Only it really sounded like a village in a tale rather than in real life" (14). Even while Margaret keeps defending Helstone, she admits to the literary quality of her description: "All the other places in England that I have seen seem so hard and prosaic-looking. . . . Helstone is like a village in a poem—in one of Tennyson's poems" (14). In the course of *North and South*, Margaret will come to understand that her view of Helstone is indeed poetic, and that means it is a literary myth. In the realistic spirit of the novel, Gaskell will undercut the idealizing tendency of Romantic poetry.

Accordingly, Gaskell builds ambiguity into the scene in which the Hales first encounter the North and Margaret begins to reflect on how it differs from the South. The Hales approach Milton—by railroad, of course—via a small seaside resort:

> The next afternoon, about twenty miles from Milton-Northern, they entered on the little branch railway that led to Heston. . . . It had a character of its own, . . . different from the little bathing-places in the south of England. . . . To use a Scotch word, every thing looked more "purposelike." . . . The people in the streets, although on pleasure bent, had yet a busy mind. The colours looked grayer—more enduring, not so gay and pretty. . . . In such towns in the south of England, Margaret had seen the shopmen, when not employed in their business, lounging a little at their doors, enjoying the fresh air, and the look up and down the street. Here, if they had any leisure from customers, they made themselves business in the shop. (59)

Here the South seems at first more attractive than the North. The North is "grayer" and lacks the "gay and pretty" colors of the South. In the South, people can enjoy "the fresh air." In the North, everything is a matter of business; the people are governed by the principle of utility in all aspects of their lives. But not every detail in the passage counts against the North. From the beginning, Margaret senses a kind of energy in the North that is lacking in the South. While the Southerners are "lounging," the Northerners always maintain a "busy mind." As she gets to know the North better, Margaret learns to appreciate its dynamism and develops a respect for the commitment to hard work in Milton.

In a scene Gaskell added to the book version created out of the original serialized installments of *North and South*, she makes a point of showing the change in Margaret's opinions by having her return to the South after getting to know the North. Her arrival in the South seems carefully designed to counterpoint her earlier arrival in the North. At first, Margaret is happy to see "the old south country-towns and hamlets sleeping in the warm light of the pure sun, which gave a yet ruddier colour to their tiled roofs, so different to the cold slates of the north" (375). But soon Gaskell reveals that Margaret has developed a northerner's distaste for laziness:

> There were few people about at the stations, it almost seemed as if they were too lazily content to wish to travel; none of the bustle and stir that Margaret had noticed in her two journeys on the London and North-Western line. . . . As to the constant going to and fro of busy trades-people it would always be widely different from the northern lines. Here a spectator or two stood lounging at nearly every station, with his hands in his pockets, so absorbed in the simple act of watching, that it made the travellers wonder what he would find to do when the train whirled away. (375)

Having grown used to the dynamic pace of life in the North, Margaret is now disappointed by the static quality of life in the South.

Margaret's education in the ways of the North mainly results from her encounters with John Thornton. As the owner of a cotton factory, he represents the new spirit of capitalist enterprise in the North, specifically the ability to plan large-scale economic projects that create new products and new wealth. As Thornton tells Margaret: "I won't deny that I am proud of belonging to a town . . . the necessities of which will give birth to such grandeur of conception. I would rather be a man toiling, suffering—nay, failing and successless—here, than lead a dull prosperous life in the old worn grooves of what you call more aristocratic society down in the South, with the slow days of careless ease" (82). Here we see Gaskell displaying her remarkable skill as a novelist, giving voice to a viewpoint that was at first alien and perhaps even incomprehensible to her—the perspective of a middle-class entrepreneur. To Thornton, the South is mired in the past and resistant to all progress, while the North represents the wave of the future.

Upset by the aspersions cast on her beloved South, Margaret at first vehemently rejects Thornton's views:

> You do not know anything about the South. If there is less adventure or less progress . . . from the gambling spirit of trade, which seems requisite to force out those wonderful inventions, there is less suffering also. I see men here going about in the streets who look ground down by some pinching sorrow or care. . . . Now, in the South we have our poor, but there is not that terrible expression in the countenances of a sullen sense of injustice. (82)

Thornton shoots back: "And may I say you do not know the North?" (82). In the initial failure of both sides to understand each other, we see the fundamental opposition of the book played out. In these exchanges, Gaskell succeeds in giving *North and South* the genuinely dialogic character that M. M. Bakhtin sees as characteristic of the novel as a genre (Bakhtin, 1981).

North and South is indeed a novel, not an economic treatise, and so it is love that proves to be the most powerful force in Margaret's education. As she grows to respect, to admire, and finally to love Thornton, Margaret becomes more and more open to his perspective. Finally, toward the end of the story, she is ready to champion the North against the South in a debate with her father's friend, Mr. Bell. Bell is shocked by the way Margaret has gone over to the North's side: "Hear this daughter of yours, Hale! Her residence in Milton has quite corrupted her. She's a democrat, a red republican" (323). Just as the spirited Margaret originally stood her ground against Thornton, she now forcefully speaks in favor of his northern capitalist values: "Papa, it's all because I'm standing up for the progress of commerce. Mr Bell would have had it keep still at exchanging wild-beast skins for acorns" (323). Margaret can see the necessity and value of leaving a primitive world of barter to enter a fully modern market economy. It is now her turn to hear from Mr. Bell the objection she once made to Thornton about "the gambling spirit of trade," as her father's friend tells her: "I'm tired of this bustle. Everybody rushing over everybody, in their hurry to get rich" (323). Margaret's father comes to her defense with an effective rebuke to his friend: "It is not every one who can sit comfortably in a set of college rooms, and let his riches grow without any exertion of his own. No doubt there is many a man here who would be thankful if his property would increase as yours has done, without his taking any trouble upon it" (323). Of course the upper classes defend the status quo. It is easy to criticize money making if one already has plenty of it and never had to work for it.

By this point in the novel, Gaskell has turned its initial values on their head. *North and South* begins with Margaret's aristocratic contempt for money-making and a celebration of what we would call a leisure class, lifted above the mundane and mercenary concerns of the middle class. Margaret's experience in the commercial world of Milton has taught her the value, even the moral value, of hard work and struggle. She has come to look up to a self-made man like Thornton, who earned every penny he ever made. In a retrospective moment, Margaret recalls with shame her earlier contempt for Thornton as one of those "shoppy people" she grew up despising:

> Her cheeks burnt as she recollected how proudly she had implied an objection to trade (in the early days of their acquaintance), because it too often led to the deceit of passing off inferior for superior goods. . . . She remembered Mr Thornton's look of calm disdain, as in few words he gave her to understand that, in the great scheme of commerce, all dishonourable ways of acting were sure to prove injurious in the long run, and that, testing such actions simply according to the poor standard of success, there was folly and not wisdom in all such, and every kind of deceit in trade. (296)

Thornton is a good teacher in economics. He correctly explains to Margaret the way in which free markets are self-correcting and self-policing. Since a merchant's good name—specifically his reputation for business probity—is essential to his continued success, every form of fraud in business practices can lead only to short-term gains and long-term losses.

Thornton is not Margaret's only teacher in economics. She also learns from the lower-class figures she meets in Milton, especially Nicholas Higgins and his daughter Bessy. At first Margaret is put off by the attitude of the northern workers she encounters. They are not deferential enough to her; they fail to treat her with the respect she thinks a woman of her upper-class status deserves, respect that she is accustomed to receiving from poor people in the South (72). Gradually Margaret learns that she is dealing with what economists would call a tradeoff between North and South. If the northern workers do not pay her sufficient respect, the reason is their spiritedness. They have a sense of their own dignity and have learned to stand up for what they perceive to be their rights. By contrast, the southern laborers show proper reverence for their social betters, but only because they are dispirited and downtrodden. They have come to accept their lower status. No doubt Old Simon gave Margaret all the deference she wanted precisely because he had grown so dependent on her aid. What Margaret at first finds objectionable in the northern workers—their "sullen sense of injustice" (82)—is actually a positive sign. They care about the justice of their situation, as shown by their willingness to go on strike, even when it threatens their daily livelihood.

Learning about the Milton cotton mill strike is central to Margaret's education in the differences between North and South. As Margaret tells Higgins: "where I come from I never heard of a strike" (132). Margaret cannot understand why workers would risk losing their livelihood—and their ability to feed their families—for the sake of a higher wage. In yet another expression of regional incomprehension, Higgins tries to figure out why the southerners would *not* go on strike, and concludes that they must be a feckless lot:

> I know nought of your ways down South. I have heard they're a pack of spiritless, down-trodden men; welly clemmed [almost starved] to death; too much dazed wi' clemming to know when they're put upon. Now it's not so here. We known when we're put upon; we'en too much blood in us to stand it. We just take our hands fro' our looms, and say, "Yo' may clem us, but yo'll not put upon us, my masters!" and be danged to 'em, they shan't this time! (132–33)

The strike once again illustrates the dynamism of the North, as opposed to the passivity of the South.

Up to this point in the novel, Margaret has been championing the South, but her encounter with Higgins and his daughter about the strike becomes a turning point in her education. Thus far she has been free to indulge in her nostalgia for the South because it has not affected anyone else. But suddenly Margaret finds that her idealizing of the South may be misleading Bessy Higgins. Having listened to Margaret's florid praise of the South, Bessy exclaims: "I wish I lived down South" (133). Margaret feels compelled to correct any false impressions she may have created in Bessy: "There's a deal to bear there. . . . There are sorrows to bear everywhere. There is very hard bodily labour to be gone through, with very little food to give strength" (133). Finally Margaret says something bad about the South and soon she is deconstructing the agrarian myth she herself has been clinging to. Bessy makes the obvious reply to Margaret's questioning of the southern paradise: "But it's out of doors. . . . And away from the endless, endless noise, and sickening heat" (133). This is the idyllic image of farm labor we have become used to in the modern world; how can anything be bad if "it's out of doors"? But Margaret has news for Bessy about working outdoors on a farm: "It's sometimes in heavy rain, and sometimes in bitter cold. A young person can stand it; but an old man gets racked with rheumatism, and bent and withered before his time; yet he must just work on the same, or else go to the workhouse" (133).

In correcting the southern agrarian myth, Gaskell answers a question that has long bothered me: If the new urban life of the nineteenth century was so horrible and rural life was so attractive, why did so many people choose to leave the farms for the cities? After all, no one forced them to do so. There was no Maoist Great Leap Forward in nineteenth-century Britain, with the government commanding higher steel production from its citizens at the point of a gun. In fact, halfway into the nineteenth century, government policy in Britain heavily favored the agricultural sector, especially the Corn Laws, which, by placing high tariffs on imported grain, subsidized domestic farm production. This policy was only to be expected in a country in which the agricultural interests were heavily overrepresented in Parliament, while the manufacturing interests were woefully underrepresented. The series of Reform Bills was designed precisely to correct this injustice. At the beginning of the nineteenth century, Manchester (even though it was growing into a large city) did not have a single representative in Parliament. It is no accident that the parliamentary reform movement was centered in Manchester, and, once the city was granted representatives, its MPs (chiefly Richard Cobden and John Bright) led the fight to repeal the Corn Laws. Contrary to popular opinion today, for the first decades of the nineteenth century, the British government was largely in the hands of, not the manufacturing interests, but the agricultural interests (chiefly the great aristocratic landowners, who of course dominated the then still-powerful House of Lords, and were even well represented in the House of Commons).

Thus one must assume that the vast increase in England's urban population in the nineteenth century was largely a voluntary development, and reflected widespread discontent with rural life. When people compare life in industrial cities like Manchester in the nineteenth century to life today, they are of course appalled by how primitive and poor the living conditions were. But that is not the choice that people living in the 1800s faced—they did not have the option of living in the twenty-first century. They were choosing between life in the cities and life on the farms, and there were many reasons they preferred the former to the latter. Today we idealize farm life; indeed "life on the farm" is a persistent urban fantasy. City dwellers tend to imagine farm work on the model of gardening, and picture it almost as an outdoor hobby, an activity pleasant in itself. In fact, real farm labor is backbreaking work, even today. That is why farm workers are often immigrants who cannot find any other form of work. Today most people who have viable alternatives do not choose farm labor as their occupation, even though the mechanization of agriculture has made it much less physically demanding than it was in the nineteenth century. Living in the age of tractors, we find it hard to imagine how much effort it took to plough a field in Gaskell's day. If nothing else, farm workers had to contend with the notoriously bad English weather, as Gaskell emphasizes in *North and South*. For a fuller sense of how miserable farm conditions were in the nineteenth century, one should read Thomas Hardy's novels, especially *Tess of the D'Urbervilles*.

In an effort to counterbalance novelistic portraits of the horrors of urban life, Gaskell keeps coming back to the horrors of rural life in *North and South*. It is not just that farm work is backbreaking; it is also in Gaskell's view soul-destroying. Margaret is repeatedly reminded that she has misled her northern friends with her romanticized images of the bucolic South. Late in the novel, Higgins, like his daughter earlier, gets it in his head to follow Margaret's advice and journey south: "[Margaret] has often talked grand o' the South, and the ways down there. Now I dunnot know how far off it is, but I've been thinking if I could get 'em down theer, where food is cheap and wages good, and all the folk, rich and poor, master and man, friendly like; yo' could, may be, help me to work" (299).

Higgins has been taken in by Margaret's talk of the paternalistic ways of the South, where supposedly people care for each other. Troubled by the way Higgins has taken her claims for the South at face value, Margaret is quick to point out how low his wages as a farm hand would be—"nine shillings a week; may be ten, at the outside" (299). She reiterates what she told Bessy about the debilitating physical conditions of farm work: "You would have to be out all weathers. It would kill you with rheumatism" (299). Above all, Margaret emphasizes the stupefying effect of farm labor:

> I owe it to you—since it's my way of talking that has set you off on this idea—to put it all clear before you. You could not bear the dullness of the life; you don't know what it is; it would eat you away like rust. Those that have lived there all their lives, are used to soaking in the stagnant waters. They labour on, from day to day, in the great solitude of streaming fields—never speaking or lifting up their poor, bent, downcast heads. The hard spade-work robs their brain of life; the sameness of their toil deadens their imagination; they don't care to meet to talk over thoughts and speculations, even of the weakest, wildest kind, after their work is done; they go home brutishly tired, poor creatures! caring for nothing but food and rest. You would not stir them up into any companionship, which you get in a town as plentiful as the air you breathe, whether it be good or bad. (299)

This passage provides an effective counterweight to all the literary depictions of the way factory life reduced workers to unthinking machines. Margaret points out that farm work is dull and repetitive too, and, unlike factory work, it tends to occur in isolation, thus foreclosing the social possibilities urban life creates. In this critique of farm life, Gaskell finds unlikely allies in Karl Marx and Friedrich Engels. In their *Communist Manifesto*, they celebrate the bourgeoisie's achievement in making the city triumph over the country: "The bourgeois has subjected the country to the towns. It has created enormous cities, has greatly increased the urban population as compared with the rural, and has thus rescued a considerable part of the population from the idiocies of rural life" (Feuer, 1959, 11).

Gaskell keeps challenging our stereotypes of industrial and agricultural life. Perhaps the most surprising reversal of perspectives in *North and South* involves an issue most people would regard as unambiguous and settled: women working in factories. This practice is generally regarded today as one of the most obvious evils of the Industrial Revolution, and people think of the legislation that banned women from factory work as progressive. But once again Gaskell shows that there are two sides to any question. What looks like protection of women from exploitation can just as well be viewed as a restriction of their freedom of contract and indeed discrimination against their right to work.[3] Given our stereotypes of the Industrial Revolution, it comes as a surprise when first reading *North and South* that Gaskell does not offer the sort of scene of disgruntled laborers trudging to and from factory work familiar to us from such films as Fritz Lang's *Metropolis* or Charlie Chaplin's *Modern Times*. Instead, Gaskell pictures the Milton workers embodying the energy she sees everywhere in the North: "In the back streets around them there were many mills, out of which poured streams of men and women two or three times a day. . . . They came rushing along, with bold, fearless faces, and loud laughs and jests, particularly aimed at all those who appeared to be above them in rank or station" (72).

We do not expect to find industrial workers in the nineteenth century portrayed as laughing, especially not women, whom we think of as being compelled to work in factories against their will. But Gaskell has a story to tell quite different from what we are used to in Victorian narratives. We begin to get a clue as to what is going on when we learn that the Hales, newly settled in Milton and intent on maintaining their genteel status, are having a surprisingly hard time finding domestic help. They cannot hire young women to aid their old servant Dixon: "They could hear of no girl to assist her; all were at work in the factories" (69). Our reaction today is to wonder why in the world women would prefer factory work to domestic service. With visions of television series such as *Upstairs, Downstairs* and *Downton Abbey* in our heads, we assume that being a servant is surely preferable to working in a factory. But Gaskell gives us a different understanding when Margaret runs into "the difficulty of meeting with any one in a manufacturing town who did not prefer the better wages and greater independence of working in a mill" (71).

Like most human beings throughout history, the women of Milton are faced with a very limited range of options when it comes to choosing an occupation. It would be wonderful if they had the choice of being software engineers, or airline pilots, or investigative journalists, but the prejudices and restricted educational opportunities of their time severely curtail their employment possibilities. Basically they are faced with working as servants or in factories, and here the choice is not as clear-cut as we suppose today. As Gaskell points out, factory work offers "better wages and greater independence." In domestic positions, much of the compensation comes in the form of room and board, thus leaving the employee with very little disposable income. Moreover, any service position involves a good deal of servitude, of deference to one's master. By contrast, in factory work one gets one's whole compensation in the form of wages, which can be spent as one sees fit. Moreover, in factory work, the hours are long but they are finite, and one gets to go home at the end of the workday. One can put a healthy distance between one's home and one's job—a possibility denied to servants whose workplace *is* their home (or rather *not* their home, but their master's).

Faced with all these facts, some people today might still imagine that they would have chosen domestic service over factory work. But Gaskell shows that many women in her day made the opposite decision. In any case, her point is that women should be allowed to make the decision for themselves; they should not be banned from working in factories because the government pretends to know better than they do what is good for them. We may be initially puzzled by Gaskell picturing the factory workers "with bold, fearless faces, and loud laughs and jests," but this image is consistent with what she shows throughout *North and South*—that the capitalist way of life in the North is breeding a new spirit of freedom and independence—even among the lower classes.

In short, we today may find much that is attractive in the survivals of the old feudal world in England's South. We think it charming to see servants showing proper deference to their masters, and masters showing concern for the welfare of their servants. This is the paternalism of the feudal order, but, as we have seen, it has its dark side in the form of the master's condescension to those beneath him, and their passive subservience. In her surprising image of the happy factory women, Gaskell is suggesting that there is something healthy and spiritually liberating in the new employer-employee contractual relationships of a modern, capitalist economy. Thornton is the master of his employees during the hours they work for him, but that is the full extent of his mastery, as he points out with pride: "I choose to be the unquestioned and irresponsible master of my hands. During the hours that they labour for me. But those hours past, our relation ceases; and then comes in the same respect for their independence that I myself exact" (124). One might wish that Thornton would care more about the whole of his employees' lives, but there is something to be said for his granting them a realm of freedom and independence. Unlike a paternalistic master, he does not try to meddle in all aspects of his workers' existence, and instead he gives them space to lead their lives as they see fit. At the beginning, Margaret is troubled by the lack of personal ties in the North, but she learns that the impersonality of the market has its benefits. It means that people are no longer subject to the paternalistic intrusions into their private lives that the spirit of feudalism endorses.

The issue between feudalism and capitalism is neatly illustrated when Thornton, out of good will but also good business sense, provides a sort of co-op dining facility for his workers. Ever the upper-class paternalist, Mr. Bells asks Thornton: "Do you taste each dish as it goes in, in virtue of your office?" (353). In the spirit of *noblesse oblige*, Bell believes that Thornton's superiority to his workers obligates him to monitor their food intake, no doubt to make sure it is what is best for them. But Thornton rejects the paternalistic role of the aristocrat, and instead respects the judgment of the market, which is to say, the expressed wishes of his workers as consumers: "I was very scrupulous, at first, in confining myself to the mere purchasing part, and even in that I rather obeyed the men's orders, conveyed through the housekeeper, than went by my own judgment. At one time, the beef was too large, at another the mutton was not fat enough. I think they saw how careful I was to leave them free, and not to intrude my own ideas upon them" (353). Thornton cares less about the fat content of his workers' diet than their right to choose their own menu. For him, the company dining room is a matter of freedom for the workers, not an occasion for him to demonstrate his superiority as their master.

By the time Gaskell is through exploring the many ramifications of the North-South divide in nineteenth-century Britain, she succeeds in showing exactly what is at stake in the conflict. The South offers an apparently peaceful and stable way of life, but another way of describing that situation is: economic and social stagnation. The upper classes acknowledge their duty to take care of the lower classes. But the price the poor pay for their security is that they must defer to the upper classes as their betters and accept their subordinate position in an essentially static society that makes no allowance for social mobility or economic progress. The dynamic North offers little in the way of job security, and subjects everyone to the vicissitudes and fluctuations of a modern economy. But by the same token, the new capitalist system does deliver the goods, and can make the northern poor seem rich by comparison with their southern counterparts. Above all, the northerners develop a sense of independence in all ranks, and the workers take pleasure in making fun of their betters—because they do not believe that they are really better.

In short, Gaskell refuses to condemn capitalism root-and-branch, as many of its critics in the nineteenth century did, but she still is troubled by some of the new order's effects. Unlike Harriet Martineau, Gaskell is not simply in favor of free markets. In fact, her ideal in *North and South* seems to be some kind of synthesis of the old and the new orders. That is the point of her use of the traditional marriage plot. The union of Margaret Hale and John Thornton symbolizes the synthesis Gaskell would like to see come about. Margaret has learned to appreciate the values Thornton stands for, and his understanding of economics basically triumphs in the course of the novel. But Gaskell hopes that Margaret will temper Thornton's hard-headed business sense with some of her aristocratic virtues, including the attitude of *noblesse oblige*. Having been humbled by business reversals in the course of the story, Thornton is prepared to moderate his conflicts with his workers, and indeed getting to know employces like Higgins allows him to appreciate their perspective better. The mill cafeteria is a good symbol of the kind of reconciliation between the classes Gaskell would like to see occur in strife-torn Milton. Thornton is able to show his good will toward his workers without going too far outside his purely economic relation to them, and the eating place becomes the site for further communication between master and workers. Gaskell's hope is for some form of "capitalism with a human face."

Still, even if we cannot describe Gaskell as the Milton Friedman of the Victorian novel, she stands out among her fellow authors as one of the few who had anything good to say about capitalism, and she deserves credit for her careful observation of the new—and beneficial—social dynamics of a free market system. What is most striking is the fact that Gaskell champions capitalism precisely as a woman. Far from complaining that the industrial system exploits women, she celebrates the way it allows them the freedom to work in factories. For Gaskell, capitalism is an equal opportunity employer. She rejects treating women paternalistically and trying to shield them from the new challenges of a market economy. Gaskell champions the freedom and independence of women, and she sees their cause better served by the new factory system. She would rather see women work alongside men in factories than continue their traditional subordinate role as domestic servants.[4]

Gaskell had a special reason for believing that capitalism furthers the cause of women by allowing them to compete with men—the nineteenth-century market economy had been very good to her. With little beyond her writing talent working in her favor, Gaskell became one of the most commercially successful and critically acclaimed novelists of Victorian

Britain. Her first novel, *Mary Barton*, sold well and caught the attention of the publishing industry. To be sure, there were still prejudices against women being professional authors, which led Gaskell to have *Mary Barton* published anonymously. But insiders knew who had written the novel, and canny publishers soon were seeking her out. Charles Dickens, who sensed a potential rival in the author of *Mary Barton*, secured her services on his side by engaging her to write for his own magazine. *North and South* was originally published in serial form in Dickens' *Household Words*. Dickens and Gaskell had their differences—artistic and ideological—but as long as Dickens thought that Gaskell would help to sell copies of his magazine, he published her.[5] That is how capitalism operates. Dickens did not have to like Elizabeth Gaskell; he did not have to set out to promote the cause of women novelists out of the generosity of his heart or his commitment to gender equality. All that mattered to Dickens was the bottom line, and business considerations dictated that he publish Gaskell's work, whatever her sex. The lesson was apparently not lost on Gaskell. Like the women of Milton, she got to do the same job as men—in her case, writing novels. All she wanted was to be able to compete on an equal basis with male authors, and it was the world of commercial publishing in Victorian Britain that gave her that opportunity.

Gaskell's case was not isolated. To be sure, other women were troubled by the stigma still attached to female professional authors. That is why Mary Ann Evans wrote under the pseudonym of George Eliot, and the Brontë sisters—Charlotte, Emily, and Anne—published under the sexually ambiguous names of Currer, Ellis, and Acton Bell. But they did still publish, and in fact women came to dominate the market for fiction in Victorian Britain, much to the dismay and consternation of many male authors. Most people view capitalism as standing in the way of artistic progress. In fact, it was under the capitalist regime of Victorian publishing that women made their first great artistic breakthrough—it provided their first opportunity to play a major and indeed dominant role in any artistic movement in history. Under traditional forms of artistic patronage—royal, aristocratic, and ecclesiastical—women had been held back for centuries and achieved only intermittent and isolated successes. Only the undiscriminating capitalist marketplace—supposedly lacking taste and refinement—chose not to discriminate against women in publishing, and thereby tapped into a deep source of new literary talent, leading to an unprecedented flourishing of the novel in nineteenth-century Britain. Evidently Gaskell was grateful to British capitalism for providing her big opportunity. In the end, it is not Gaskell's support for capitalism that is surprising. The real puzzle is why her fellow female authors generally failed to share her gratitude to the new market economy for making them rich and famous. But at least *North and South* stands as a literary monument to the economic and social benefits of nineteenth-century capitalism and especially its achievement on behalf of women's rights.

NOTES

1. For the way historians have treated the Industrial Revolution, see Hayek (1954), especially the essays by Ashton and Hutt. For a concise and sympathetic history of the Industrial Revolution, see Ashton (1969). For a discussion of sympathetic treatments of industry in nineteenth-century British literature, see Bizup (2003).

2. For a fuller discussion of the Romantics' attitude toward nature and technology, see Cantor (1993).

3. For discussion of Gaskell's idea that capitalism furthered the cause of women's rights, and other cases of female authors in the Victorian period adopting this position, see Zlotnick (1998).

4. Gaskell's concern for women's right to work explains another aspect of her thought that most modern readers would find surprising—her hostility to labor unions, which she presents as tyrannizing over their members, indeed as greater tyrants than factory owners ever were to workers (154, 229). In Gaskell's day, the male-dominated labor unions led the fight in Parliament to ban women from working in factories, ostensibly out of humanitarian concerns, but really out of a desire to restrict the supply of labor and thereby to prop up wage rates for men.

5. For the professional relationship between Gaskell and Dickens, and the way *North and South* and his novel *Hard Times* enter into a dialogue with each other, see Meckier (1987, 46–92). Meckier points out that Dickens eventually "blamed a decline in sales of his periodical *Household Words* on Mrs. Gaskell's 'divided, wearisome' novel" (288n27).

REFERENCES

Ashton, T. S. 1969. *The Industrial Revolution*. London: Oxford.

Bakhtin, M. M. 1981. *The Dialogic Imagination: Four Essays*. Translated by Caryl Emerson and Michael Holquist. Austin: University of Texas Press.

Bizup, Joseph. 2003. *Manufacturing Culture: Vindications of Early Victorian Industry*. Charlottesville: University of Virginia Press.

Cantor, Paul A. 1993. "Romanticism and Technology: Satanic Verses and Satanic Mills." In *Technology in the Western Political Tradition*. Edited by Arthur M. Melzer, Jerry Weinberger, and M. Richard Zinman. Ithaca, New York: Cornell University Press. 109–28.

Feuer, Lewis S., ed. 1959. *Basic Writings on Politics and Philosophy: Karl Marx and Friedrich Engels*. Garden City, New York: Doubleday.

Gaskell, Elizabeth. 1995. *North and South*. Harmondsworth, United Kingdom: Penguin.

Hayek, Friedrich, ed. 1954. *Capitalism and the Historians*. Chicago: University of Chicago Press.
Meckier, Jerome. 1987. *Hidden Rivalries in Victorian Fiction: Dickens, Realism, and Revaluation*. Lexington: University Press of Kentucky.
Uglow, Jenny. 2004. Article on Elizabeth Cleghorn Gaskell. *Oxford Dictionary of National Biography*. Edited by H. C. G. Matthew and Brian Harrison. Oxford: Oxford University Press. vol. 21.
Zlotnick, Susan. 1998. *Women, Writing, and the Industrial Revolution*. Baltimore, Maryland: Johns Hopkins University Press.

Chapter 8

Where Have You Gone, Horatio Alger

A Long Gone Literary Hero and the Bourgeois Virtues

Amy Willis

"I want to grow up 'spectable. But I don't know where to go."

Horatio Alger, *Ragged Dick*, 72

A Google search for "success stories" yields well over twenty-six million results. Indeed success stories seem an indelible part of the American popular culture experience. Most results take the searcher to stories of business success. Searching for "personal success stories" takes one into the realm of the how-to manual. Personal success further breaks down to include entries on weight loss, personal financial planning, dating and relationship advice, et cetera. Although "success stories" are not anything new, in earlier days they comprised a more uniform genre, specifically, more often the story of a particular individual, be he real or fictitious. Personal success in these stories seemed a natural combination of the moral and financial. For example, one of the first "best-sellers" in America[1] was *The Autobiography of Benjamin Franklin*, explicitly penned by the author to provide insight into how to live a rich and full life. It is also regarded as the first true-life account of the American Dream.[2] The following century would produce a similar icon of the success story, Horatio Alger. Over one hundred novels (in addition to a handful of non-fiction works) poured forth from Alger's pen, and the author's name became synonymous with the American Dream. And in our own century, we hear these icons recalled while longing for a renewed appreciation of the virtues they exude. The "success stories" of Horatio Alger can be seen as tales of the morality of capitalism. Why their allure is no longer what it once was is another question altogether.

Horatio Alger's stories remain icons of our shared cultural experience, yet his stories no longer have the readership they once enjoyed. One might think

Alger would have withered away earlier under the various storms of criticism he and his works have been subject to over the years. Although he wrote well over one hundred young adult novels, they did not become "best-sellers" until the early 1900s, after Alger's death[3]. Nonetheless, Alger was well known in his day, and was able to earn a living by his pen. And Alger's name appears on nearly every list of the most influential children's authors of the nineteenth century. Alger first published two books, one an adult novel and one a volume of satirical poetry, neither of which met with much commercial success. His first juvenile novel, *Frank's Campaign*, brought him his first taste of critical accomplishment, and shortly thereafter he moved to New York to focus full-time on his writing. One of the first institutions Alger became acquainted with was the Newsboys Lodging House. The Newsboys Lodging House would become a lifelong haunt of the author, and its influence on his fiction is undeniable, particularly in thinking of Alger's first best-selling, and still best-known, series of novels, beginning with the story of the aspirational young bootblack Richard Hunter in *Ragged Dick* (1868). Indeed, this volume so surpasses Alger's others both in sales figures and general renown, and its formula is so similar to that of his other novels, *Ragged Dick* will be the source of illustrative examples herein.

Alger's novels have received harsh criticism on several fronts. Literary critics have been particularly virulent in their condemnation of Alger as an author. Accusations of stock characterization, repetitious and formulaic plots, and stilted dialogue are as numerous as Alger's own novels. Alger's novels enjoyed their greatest popularity a decade or so after his death in 1899. But by the 1920s and '30s, Alger's novels began to lose their popular appeal, even though his name would live on. The 1940s and '50s saw the beginnings of cultural battles over what to "make "of Alger, battles which would rage through the 1970s. Alger novels acquired the reputation of beings "rags to *riches*" stories, implying that the young hero invariably turns tycoon, tempting many to criticize their purported materialistic tone. But Alger's stories are better classified as "rags to *respectability*." "The Alger stories were never about the fabulous few who rose from poverty to great riches; they were, at best, tales of a much more accessible ascent from rags to respectability. His nonpareils do not wax wealthy so much as they grow reputable, leaving the promiscuity of the streets for the propriety of a desk job."[4] Unfortunately, ". . . his earliest novels which conclude as the moral hero grasps the bottom rung of the ladder of respectability were rarely reprinted, and some publishers abridged others by deleting as many as seven of the original chapters, often those in which the hero performs virtuous deeds for which he is later rewarded."[5] Gary Scharnhorst argues that Alger's work was "editorially reinvented" toward Progressive Era ends, casting Alger heroes as mini Robber Barons. Yet Alger boys, particularly in these earlier novels, showed their readers that despite what many saw as the Robber Baron's stifling influence on the prospects of the many, one could still manage to find their own personal success. Importantly, this success would come as a result of the boys' characters, which were morally superior to those of the "tycoons" of the day. According to one Alger commentator, "Alger's heroes succeeded . . . because they are good, not because they have sharper fangs and longer claws than anyone else."[6] Rather than being agents of (capitalistic) exploitation, these boys are also chivalrous and live by a rather strict code that would never allow them to visit harm on those who are weaker. In many stories, such as *Ragged Dick*, well before the end of the story (and when he attains a position of financial independence and responsibility), the young protagonist has taken an even younger waif under his wing. One can see Alger's young heroes as emblematic of a certain cultural ethos, one much like that Deirdre McCloskey suggests took hold in eighteenth and nineteenth centuries in the West. Yet somehow, "Whereas in his own time Alger was credited with inventing a moral hero who became modestly successful, during the early years of this century he seemed to have invented a successful hero who was modestly moral."[7]

Criticism aside, Alger's stories *have* maintained a reputation as being stories of upward mobility. Though we could quibble over the details, as well as the "spin," in terms of comparison a more pertinent question might be, how do we tell stories of success? Alger's stories suggest the *process* of striving toward virtue is perhaps more important than either where the individual currently stands or ends. Part of the Alger "formula" is allowing us to witness the incrementally improving virtue of one exceptional boy among many. And these virtues, though never explicitly named by Alger, seem very much like those listed by McCloskey in her path-breaking economic history tour-de-force, *The Bourgeois Virtues*. When we meet young Dick, he has yet to achieve many of what we have come to be known as the bourgeois virtues; we are offered a glimpse into the world of nineteenth-century New York street boys generally. Alger none too subtly suggests that many of these urchins are undeserving of our sympathy, and that even the story's hero is replete with faults. But some, like Dick, are of a different- and better- character. Dick has a difficult time waking on the first morning we witness, the result of having spent the previous evening at the Old Bowery, leaving him penniless (again) as well. Cases of alcohol abuse are hinted at; many of the street boys have a taste for beer, and as we meet an expanding cast of characters, we learn several have found themselves on the street as a result of abuse suffered at the hand of alcoholic guardians. We quickly learn of Dick's aspiration for temperance. But extravagance, Alger tells us, is "the mother" of all Dick's faults. "However much he managed to earn during the day, all was generally spent before morning,"[8] on extravagances such as the Old Bowery, gambling halls, and (inappropriately) magnanimously treating the other boys to oyster stew. Dick also had the bad habit of smoking, a fault compounded by his taste for expensive tobacco, which he was also quick to treat his companions to.

But despite these faults, Dick also possesses great stores of hopeful enterprise at the beginning of the novel. Alger tells us early on that, ". . . in the boot-blacking business, as well as in higher avocations, the same rule prevails, that energy and industry are rewarded, and indolence suffers."[9] Whether shining shoes, giving tours of the City, or later working as an office boy, Dick is the first to arrive and the last to quit, and he never shies away from an opportunity. Honesty is another bourgeois virtue we see in Dick right away, when he connects with the gentleman, Mr. Greyson, who will ultimately become his greatest patron. Greyson had not the proper change for a shine, and tossed Dick a coin too great. Dick promised the gentlemen he would bring him the change once he obtained it, as Greyson did not have time to wait. Skeptical, Greyson gives Dick the address of his office. The next day, Dick arrives at Greyson's door with the change, and Greyson asks him who has taught him such honesty. "Nobody," said Dick. "But it's mean to cheat and steal. I've always knowed that."[10] It is as a result of this encounter that Greyson takes young Dick under his wing, offering him a position in his office. Dick's resolution is another virtue he possesses in great stores throughout the story. Shortly after the incident with Greyson, Dick finds a greater opportunity for the day than shoe-shining when he overhears a conversation between a Mr. Whitney and his nephew, Frank. Frank is stopping in New York on his way to boarding school to visit with his uncle, who had planned to show him the sights of the city. But his business matters are pressing, and Mr. Whitney finds himself unavailable, so Dick quickly suggests himself for the task. Whitney agrees, and Dick and Frank spend an enjoyable day together, and Dick is mightily impressed with the respectability of his new customer. Dick is told by his new companion Frank, that to become respectable, one must not only work hard, but "work right." Frank recognizes Dick's resolution when he says, "You began in the right way when you determined never to steal, or do anything mean or dishonorable, however strongly tempted to do so."[11] Love and affection, like so many of the virtues, also need to be learned on the road to respectability, a fact which does not escape Dick. Having been set on the path to self-improvement by the Whitneys (even if only unconsciously), Frank takes in a younger boot-black, Fosdick, when Dick realizes he cannot afford a suitable supper or a place to stay that night. Dick agrees to take him on as a roommate if Fosdick will teach him to read, demonstrating love, but also prudence, a skill that would later serve him well in the market.

Another mechanism Alger employs to illustrate this process of becoming virtuous is highlighting contrary examples, and in a violent confrontation with one such character, we witness Dick's stores of courage. The principal foil in *Ragged Dick* is Mickey Maguire. We meet this unsavory character just after Dick has settled into his new lodging and is on his way out to open his first bank account. Because Dick cannot tolerate his old suit of clothes, he ventures forth in one acquired from Frank Whitney. Maguire, the leader of a gang of ruffians, ". . . was democratic in his tastes, and had a jealous hatred of those who wore good clothes and kept their faces clean. He called it putting on airs, and resented the implied superiority."[12] When Mickey turns upon Dick, accusing him of these airs, Dick offers a wonderfully positive-sum retort, "Well, what's the odds if I am? Does it hurt you any?"[13] Dick recognizes that life is not a zero-sum game, that his measure of success in no way impedes Maguire's potential. Maguire, clearly a zero-sum thinker, takes aim, literally, at our protagonist, who must defend himself not only to protect his investment (his suit), but also his bourgeois honor. Maguire's physical attack is clearly unjust, although Alger takes pains to suggest that Dick's physical response is wholly justified. When the scrabble is broken up by the police, Maguire also quickly accuses Dick of having turned to violence first, another breach of justice. We see that sorts like Maguire, while certainly mean, are also profoundly untrustworthy. Trust, as we learn from McCloskey and the economic literature at large, is a fundamental component of a bourgeois market society, as repeat interactions and contractual relationships seldom fare well in the absence of trust.

The ability of any individual to attain respectability and independence seems never to have been in doubt in Alger's characters; their actions suggest this as a very solid assumption. Alger takes many opportunities to remind the reader, through Dick, that origins are of little consequence, and that respectability, not riches *per se*, is his ultimate criterion of success. At the end of his outing with Frank Whitney, for example, Frank and Dick are discussing several of New York's prominent citizens. When Dick opines that he likely will never become mayor, Frank replies, "No, probably not, but you may rise in some other way. A good many distinguished men have once been poor boys. There's hope for you, Dick, if you'll try. . . . If you'll try to be somebody, and grow up into a respectable member of society, you will. You may not become rich,— it isn't everybody that becomes rich you know,—but you can obtain a good position, and be respected."[14]

So what may we deduce to have been Alger's authorial intent? There is little that seems to be *auto*-biographical in Alger's fiction, although much is arguably somewhat biographical. In creating amalgams of the young boys he came to know through the Newsboys Lodging House for example, Alger may have been trying to teach his young readers a worthwhile collection of virtues. Regardless of the specific question of form, we hear similar calls for this sort of virtue-success story today. Deirdre McCloskey argued in her famous 1994 *American Scholar* article that, "A modern society needs poetry and history and movies about bourgeois virtue: integrity, honesty, trustworthiness, enterprise, humor, respect, modesty, consideration, responsibility, prudence, thrift, affection, self-possession."[15] So success stories are *necessarily* stories of virtue. They are stories that can and *should* be told. And they should be told because they are not simply morality tales; they are tales of the virtues of capitalism as well as the virtues of the individual. Alger evokes nostalgia similar to that found in McCloskey's *Bourgeois Virtues*, the first volume of her "apologia to capitalism. "In it, she opines the lost belief that commerce breeds ethics (a term she uses interchangeably with morality). It is easy to sympathize with her lament that ". . . the assaults on . . . capitalism . . . [have] made an impossible Best into the enemy of an actual Good."[16] McCloskey skillfully describes how capitalism has brought unprecedented economic growth to the world. She writes of the triple revolutions in politics (largely interpreted as the triumph of democracy over totalitarianism), population, and prosperity over the past two centuries in particular. She also asserts that capitalism and its concomitant virtues were appreciated, or at least not excoriated, by those who reaped its benefits until the mid-nineteenth century (coincidentally, the time in which Alger begins writing).

The stories of Horatio Alger support McCloskey's claim that ". . . modern capitalism does not need to be offset to be good."[17] McCloskey asserts that the more common thinking about the relationship between the market and virtues is that virtues support the market. Though she does not disagree with this, she says that, more importantly, the *market supports the virtues*. To the extent that this is true, then one cannot compose a true story of success that does not simultaneously revere the market. For this reason, Alger's novels also ought to be read as tales of the virtues of the market. One should read them as stories of capitalism; the virtues that the Alger boys exhibit are the same that help markets to function peacefully and prosperously, and the situations in which they find themselves and avail themselves of would not be possible under a system other than capitalism. By capitalism, McCloskey means "merely private property and free labor without central planning, regulated by the rule of law and by an ethical consensus."[18] She does not mean the endless pursuit and act of consumption. In fact, she argues that the "vulgar" pursuit of consumption is more characteristic of pre- and anticapitalist societies. Rather than enabling people to focus their efforts toward consumption, McCloskey says it enables them to focus on purpose. As a result, capitalism has produced the best the world has to offer—the best people, the best arts, the best products, and so on. This, of course, is counter to what most intellectuals since 1848[19] have hypothesized. McCloskey is stymied by this, as ". . . we all take happily what the market gives—polite, accommodating, energetic, enterprising, risk-taking, trustworthy people,"[20] people very much like Ragged Dick and his many counterparts. McCloskey argues that as markets have expanded through history, greater and greater virtue is made possible and promoted, and to a wider sphere of the populace.

McCloskey argues that markets support morals (and vice versa), and that the key ingredient for making this happen is human freedom. Freedom bloomed in commercially minded places as a result of their inhabitants' fear of oppressive governments. Persons in these sorts of places (Amsterdam in 1568, London in 1689, and Philadelphia in 1776 are examples she cites[21]) believed in the Lockean concept of self-ownership. This, McCloskey argues, is a very modern freedom, differentiated from ancient freedom whose focal point was the collective. Rather than the right to participate in politics, the modern freedom offered individuals the right to pursue their own interests as they saw fit. Of what use would Ragged Dick, looking first for ways to elevate himself from poverty, have for the ancient freedom? Interest in political life may come in time, as it did with boys in some other Alger stories. But by enabling people to seek the "useful," markets allow the individual to rise, and also to take others with him. "It's the Bourgeois Deal: leave me alone to buy low and sell high, and in the long run I'll make *you* rich."[22]

So *Ragged Dick* (and most of Alger's other novels) are positive portrayals of markets and capitalism. But why is it equally important that we recognize these stories exemplify the bourgeois virtues? McCloskey believes that we have come to doubt the virtues of capitalism as a result of two phenomena: the first is an error of reduction, and the second is an act of opposition to capitalism by the clerisy. The roots of what McCloskey terms an error of reduction lie in the Enlightenment. The Enlightenment gave us tremendous insight into the ways human markets and societies function, but in some ways, too much. Economists in particular McCloskey faults for reducing all the virtues into one: prudence. Prudence is indeed important, and certainly in part how our Dick was able to attain measures of success. But were prudence the only virtue in these stories, how boring they would be! Were these characters "prudence only," or simply utility maximizers, we would see none of the tales' human drama, an essential feature of their appeal. Frank Whitney would not give Ragged Dick a suit of clothes, let alone carry on a lengthy correspondence with him from boarding school through the rest of the story. Frank Whitney, as well as Ragged Dick, are clearly more than the sum of their prudent parts. These are things that make their lives better and fuller, although not necessarily (fiscally) richer. They are also things the characters would not be *able* to do unless and until they had become (again, financially) self-sufficient. McCloskey's point about purpose is crucial here. Poor people the world over crave the material fruits of capitalism *first*. Rightly so. But then, the individual freedom they are afforded by free markets and limited states enables, and maybe even encourages them, to seek the *spiritual* fruits next. What is a virtue to McCloskey? "A 'virtue' is a habit of the heart, a stable disposition, a settled state of character, a durable, educated characteristic of someone to exercise her will to be good."[23] She calls for a more Aristotelian (than Platonic) approach to living a life of excellence, one in search of many potential "goods" as opposed to a unitary Idea of the Good. This can account for the multiple and varying objectives of the Alger boys. McCloskey quotes Aristotle, who said, "We shall better understand the nature of the ethical character if we examine its qualities one by one."[24]

Another important part of McCloskey's project is to explain why the clerisy ("the theoreticians and followers of theoreticians . . . the opinion makers and opinion takers"[25]) seems to have turned against capitalism. This attack is the second reason she believes we have come to doubt the bourgeois virtues. McCloskey claims that the clerisy has done perhaps irreparable damage to the reputation of capitalism, and hers is an attempt at rectification. McCloskey describes the history of this disavowal in tremendous detail, too much to recount herein. But if we take as an assumption that such a disavowal did occur, Alger's novels may serve as additional evidence of her claim. Alger has been accused by the clerisy of presenting an impossible dream that is ultimately harmful to their readers insofar as their stories promote false hope. How could young readers expect the same sorts of opportunities would open themselves to them, the critics argued, even were they to strive assiduously for virtue? Alger's name is today more often associated with "the Horatio Alger myth." Those who advance the "myth" would deny that honesty and industry, indeed any of the bourgeois virtues, are a guarantor of success. This accusation of disingenuousness was leveled even during Alger's lifetime, although it gained much more traction some decades after his death. Alger, as well as many other writers of juvenile fiction, such as his contemporaries Oliver Optic and Harry Castlemon, even found their works banned in public libraries, as debate over the merits of their "sensationalism" raged. The Fletcher Free Library, in Burlington, Vermont, lauded itself in its Annual Report printed in the *Library Journal* in 1881 on the "wise innovation" of its trustees in removing such books from their shelves. The Young Men's Association of Buffalo, New York, urged censorship of Alger, Optic, and company on several grounds in the March 1882 *Library Journal*. They claimed such works were lacking in any artistic merit, but more importantly were "cultivating unwholesome falsities of sentiment and mischievously misrepresenting the honest realities of life."[26] Was the world as painted in Alger's novels truly only imaginary, or did he offer accurate portrayals of life in nineteenth-century America? If the former, then according to C. Bradley Thompson, "Alger was irrelevant in his own time and, more importantly, . . . is certainly irrelevant to ours."[27] While McCloskey does not answer this question specifically in relation to Alger, one might assume she would answer that Alger's novels reflected reality more often than not. She may, like others, point out that certain elements of the nineteenth-century economy were conspicuously absent. Thompson argues that Alger's portrayal is on the whole historically true, and suggests that the very durability of Alger's name and stories suggests those who argue otherwise have an incorrect understanding of nineteenth-century American history.

One can also find evidence of the attack of clerisy in references to Alger in twentieth-century literature. It is interesting that while Alger's works have received very little direct scholarly attention, they seem to have had tremendous indirect influence. "It seems that, whereas the Alger formula was frequently employed in the fiction of the period, Alger himself had not yet acquired symbolic status as the progenitor of the American success myth."[28] In Thomas Wolfe's *Look Homeward Angel*, for example, Alger receives significant mention. Wolfe describes his hero as an assiduous reader of Alger novels, buoyed by their optimism, yet Wolfe is identifying with "the Horatio Alger myth," not the actual stories. Of his hero, Wolfe says, "At the library he ravaged the shelves of boys; books, going unweariedly through all the infinite monotony of the Algers . . . He gloated over the fat money-getting of these books (a motif . . . that has never been sufficiently recognized)."[29] His hero's goal is "no fortune under $250,000," a sum far beyond that ever achieved by an Alger hero. Another eminent figure in American literature, Stephen Crane, parodied Alger's plots in his (1899) short story "A Self-Made Man: An Example of Success That Anyone Can Follow." Nathaniel West's 1934 novel, *A Cool Million*, did the same, and even more directly, borrowing character names and profiles, as well as plot lines. Similarly, William Dean Howells, in *The Minister's Charge*, mirrored Alger's (1875) *The Young Outlaw* and (1876) *Sam's Chance*, purporting to write a more realistic version of the story. Yet Howells's ending is decidedly un-Alger-like. It has even been suggested that no less than F. Scott Fitzgerald parodied Alger's *Jed the Poor-House Boy* in the sixth chapter of *The Great Gatsby*. Alger's influence on characters in other works *not* satirizing his own has also been noted. Theodore Dreiser's villainous *Financier*, Frank Algernon Cowperwood, was apparently named quite literally—not an Alger hero. That the clerisy took the effort it did to comment as such may automatically recommend these as stories of capitalism.

McCloskey considers virtually all of us to be a member of the bourgeoisie at one level or another, as are such caricatures as Algernon Cowperwood. "Yes, we are bourgeois, we educated folk, not aristocratic or proletarian. We are businesspeople or bureaucrats, not kings or peasants."[30] Yet while we all inhabit it, somehow self-loathing has become one of the defining characteristics of the bourgeoisie. McCloskey notes that this became particularly apparent in the post-World War II era, which may help us situate such success-story protagonists as Dick. Dick is pleased with himself at the end of his journey. Is his pleasure the result of having attained a greater degree of moral perfection, or at having attained a comfortable (financial) station in life? McCloskey would argue that these are inseparable. And why shouldn't they be? One may need to be able to operate within the market context in order to attain this virtue. Why, then, are members of the bourgeoisie today so unable to experience this same simple pleasure? Perhaps the more appropriate question is how to disengage the clerisy's attack on capitalism. A central part of McCloskey's argument, and one too frequently left unacknowledged by classical liberals, is that not all consequences of markets are desirable. She points to examples of things undesirable yet still produced and sold, and acknowledges that there will always exist bad (un-virtuous) actors in the market. Yet she holds that attributing *a*morality to markets is still inappropriate. "We must in our moralizing not mistake human failing for specifically capitalist failing."[31] One is reminded of the early picture of our hero Dick- drunken, lazy, and profligate, but with limitless potential which he is ultimately able to overcome. McCloskey assumes man to be fallen, an assumption which does a great deal of heavy lifting in her analysis. Given this assumption, she necessarily compares how man will behave within different institutional contexts. "If capitalism is to be blamed for systemic evils, then it is also to be given credit for systemic goods, compared not with an imaginary ideal but with actually existing alternatives."[32] Greed, for example, is a vice McCloskey accepts (although not as a defining characteristic of capitalism). Greed, being inherent in all men, will rear its ugly head in a capitalist economy as well as a socialist economy. But there are characteristics of the latter type of system that make the incidence of greed higher. Greed, like any other vice (or virtue) is not endogenous to any system. Certain systems elicit more or less of any given virtue or vice. McCloskey also, as noted earlier, finds it easy to prove that capitalism enriches its citizens. Thus, we can read Dick's financial independence as made possible by capitalism. But for McCloskey, *Ragged Dick* should qualify as a success story *only* because it is *also* a morality tale. The latter is the more significant legacy of capitalism: ". . . had capitalism not enriched the world by a cent nonetheless its bourgeois, antifeudal virtues would have *made us better people* [emphasis added] than in the world we have lost. As a system it has been good for us."[33]

If capitalism has been good for us, an assertion with which few, if any, of us would disagree, then it is likely that its celebratory success stories are good for us as well. By extolling the interconnectedness of virtues and the market, these stories help us imagine the possibilities of capitalism. Do we still tell such stories today? McCloskey leaves us with what might be construed as an optimistic prediction: ". . . during the late twentieth century capitalism and its bourgeois virtues resumed their triumphs."[34] Would this imply a resurgence of "Influence Writings" in the style of Alger? If so, at whom would such offerings be directed? Should we look to the self-help aisle, or the young adult section, for example? A search for similar exemplars today might be worth effort. And if these stories are not yet written, what form should they take? And who is (or should be) writing them? These are questions that we should put on the table, and consider seriously. Because, as McCloskey cautions, capitalism needs defenders, even, or perhaps especially, among the young.

NOTES

1. Most credit Thomas Paine's *Common Sense* with being the very first American best-seller.
2. The phrase "American Dream" is believed to have been first used in James Truslow Adams's 1931 *The Epic of America*. A freelance author of popular American history books, Adams described the American dream as "that dream of a land in which life should be better and richer and fuller for everyone, with opportunity for each according to ability or achievement. It is a difficult dream for the European upper classes to interpret adequately, and too many of us ourselves have grown weary and mistrustful of it. It is not a dream of motor cars and high wages merely, but a dream of social order in which each man and each woman shall be able to attain to the fullest stature of which they are innately capable, and be recognized by others for what they are, regardless of the fortuitous circumstances of birth or position" (Adams, p. 404).
3. Alger died July 18, 1899. His first juvenile book, *Frank's Campaign*, was published in 1865, although he had several poems and short stories published dating back to 1849. His only best-selling novels published during his lifetime were released in the brief period from 1868 to 1871. Only a few of his works were first published posthumously, and these at his designation by Edward Stratemeyer, who later gained fame for the creation of several popular children's series, including Tom Swift, the Hardy Boys, and Nancy Drew.
4. Zuckerman, p. 198.
5. Scharnhorst, "Demythologizing Alger," p. 186.
6. Zuckerman, p. 197.
7. Scharnhorst, pp. 186–187.
8. Alger, p. 6.
9. Alger, p. 8.
10. Alger, p. 72.
11. Alger, p. 40.
12. Alger, p. 64.
13. Alger, p. 66.
14. Alger, p. 31.
15. McCloskey, *American Scholar*, p. 180.
16. McCloskey, p. 2.
17. McCloskey, *The Bourgeois Virtues*, p. 1.
18. McCloskey, *The Bourgeois Virtues*, p. 14.

19. 1848 is a significant turning point for McCloskey in her analysis, as it marks the point at which, for all intents and purposes, capitalism had in practice triumphed. It also marks the point at which the European clerisy became antibourgeois and began to bemoan the system that had so nourished them.

20. McCloskey, *American Scholar*, p. 181.

21. McCloskey, *The Bourgeois Virtues*, p. 38.

22. McCloskey, *The Bourgeois Virtues*, p. 53.

23. McCloskey, *The Bourgeois Virtues*, p. 64.

24. McCloskey, *The Bourgeois Virtues*, p. 65.

25. McCloskey, *The Bourgeois Virtues*, p. 5.

26. Hoeller, p. 162.

27. Thompson, p. 277.

28. Scharnhorst, "Demythologizing Alger," p. 188.

29. Wolfe, p. 84.

30. McCloskey, *The Bourgeois Virtues*, p. 68.

31. McCloskey, *The Bourgeois Virtues*, p. 29.

32. McCloskey, *The Bourgeois Virtues*, p. 29.

33. McCloskey, *The Bourgeois Virtues*, pp. 29–30.

34. McCloskey, *The Bourgeois Virtues*, p. 11.

REFERENCES

Adams, James Truswell. 1931. *The Epic of America*. Boston: Little, Brown, and Company.

Alger, Horatio Jr. 1985. *Ragged Dick and Struggling Upward*. New York: Viking Penguin Inc.

Franklin, Benjamin. 1993. *The Autobiography of Benjamin Franklin*. Boston: Bedford Books.

Gardner, Ralph D. 1978. *Horatio Alger, or the American Hero Era*. New York: Arco Publishing Company, Inc.

Lawrence, D. H. *Studies in Classic American Literature* (online at http://www.toqonline.com/blog/lawrence-on-franklin/).

Nackenoff, Carol. 1994. *The Fictional Republic: Horatio Alger and American Political Discourse*. New York: Oxford University Press.

McClelland, David C. 1976. *The Achieving Society*. New York: John Wiley and Sons, Inc.

McCloskey, Deirdre. 1994. "Bourgeois Virtue." *American Scholar*, 63(2): 177–91.

McCloskey, Deirdre. 2006. *The Bourgeois Virtues: Ethics for an Age of Commerce*. Chicago: University of Chicago Press.

Sarachek, Bernard. 1978. "American Entrepreneurs and the Horatio Alger Myth. "*The Journal of Economic History*, 38: 439–56.

Scharnhorst, Gary. 2007. "Demythologizing Alger," *Ragged Dick Norton Critical Edition*. New York: W.W. Norton & Company.

Scharnhorst, Gary. 1985. *The Lost Life of Horatio Alger, Jr.* Bloomington: Indiana University Press.
Seelye John. 1965. "Who Was Horatio? The Alger Myth and American Scholarship." *American Quarterly*, 17(4): 749–56.
Thompson, C. Bradley. 1997. Review [untitled] of *The Fictional Republic* by Carol Nackanoff. *The Journal of Politics*, 59(1): 275–77.
Wolfe, Thomas. 1957. *Look Homeward Angel.* New York: Scribner.
Young, Arthur P. 2009. "Horatio Alger, Jr.—Juvenile Writer, Enduring Icon, and Collectible Author." Keynote address presented at the Snyder Book Collecting Contest, University of Kansas, April 10.
Zuckerman, Michael. 1972. "The Nursery Tales of Horatio Alger." *American Quarterly*, 24(2): 191–209.

Chapter 9

Crony Capitalism in *The Gilded Age* by Twain and Warner and Its Relevance for Today

Michelle Albert Vachris[1]

INTRODUCTION

The Gilded Age, A Tale of Today by Mark Twain and Charles Dudley Warner tells the story of crony capitalism in the United States after the Civil War. The novel is Twain's only coauthored novel and was inspired by a challenge from Twain's and Warner's wives to write a better novel than the ones they had been reading. The plot is a thinly veiled account of actual "backroom deals, sexual intrigue, and high-powered deception" from that era and is the book that gave "The Gilded Age" its name.[2]

This chapter describes how *The Gilded Age* can be used in undergraduate courses to teach about crony capitalism. The Public Choice framework is used to analyze themes in the novel and guidance as to how the novel could be incorporated into an undergraduate upper level field course in Public Choice, Public Sector Economics or US Economic History.

USING LITERATURE TO TEACH ECONOMICS

There is a growing body of work that describes and encourages the use of literature to teach economics, and more economics conferences are including sessions on economics and literature. Bohanon and Vachris (2012) survey over forty articles in economics journals that either use the tools of economics to analyze specific works of literature or that describe how to incorporate literature into the teaching of economics. They also provide an overview of literature *written* by economists and students for the purpose of teaching and learning economics.

Why use literature to teach economics? Research into learning behavior, such as Bransford et al. (2000), demonstrates that students, especially students in introductory courses, learn best from memorable storytelling. Such stories abound in literature and can increase student's ability to understand the formal models presented in class. In addition to the potential for increasing student learning, the use of literature in the economics curriculum can support the interdisciplinary and integrative goals of a liberal education.

Cowen (2008) argues that novels and social science models have similar structures and uses and therefore complement one another. When economists use models we begin by describing our initial assumptions and setting out propositions about how exogenous variables influence certain endogenous variables, for example by outlining utility or production functions. After setting the model's initial equilibrium, we then introduce a shock to the system by changing one of the exogenous variables (e.g., increasing the price of a substitute good). We then perform comparative statics analysis to trace through the effects of this shock as the model adjusts to a new equilibrium. Models are judged not by how realistic they are, but rather by whether they are internally consistent and have empirically predictive power.

Some novels, according to Cowen (2008), follow this comparative static pattern. Authors begin by describing the initial state of the characters' lives and their environments. This initial equilibrium is then disturbed by some event that changes the lives of the characters. For example in *The Gilded Age,* main character Laura Hawkins goes to Washington, DC, to become a lobbyist in an attempt to persuade the federal government into buying her family's land. The rest of the novel describes the results of this shock to the system. Novels, then, can be seen as informal models that "use a stylized setting to show how one set of causes lead to particular effects, working through a mechanism of some generality" (Cowen, 2008, 11). These informal models are similar to the models used by economists "before the mathematization of the economics profession" (*Ibid.*).

Despite the potential gains from trade between literature and economics, a very small proportion of instruction time in economics classes is reportedly spent on examples from literature. Watts and Schaur (2011) provide results from surveys of economic instruction that include a question on how much class time is spent on references to literature/drama/music. The survey results are reported for Principles courses, Intermediate Theory courses, Statistics and Econometrics courses and Upper Level Field courses. Not surprisingly, the median response for Statistics and Econometrics courses in each of the surveys was no class time devoted to literature/drama/music.[3] At the Principles level, the median time reported was stable at 6 percent for the 2000, 2005, and 2010 surveys. Both the Intermediate Theory courses and Upper Level Field courses have seen slight increases in the use of such references. For the Intermediate Theory courses, the median increased from 0 percent in 2000 and 2005 to 6 percent in 2010, and for the Upper Level Field courses, the median increased from 0 percent in 2000 to 6 percent in 2005 and 2010. Analysis of the mean data reported by Watts and Schaur (2011) also show increases in the use of literature/drama/music, especially in the Principles and Upper Level Field courses. Most of the recent gains are in upper level field courses, and the rest of this chapter describes how parts of the novel, *The Gilded Age*, can illustrate economic concepts in these types of courses.

PUBLIC CHOICE THEMES IN *THE GILDED AGE*

The novel *The Gilded Age, A Tale of Today* by Mark Twain and Charles Dudley Warner provides three story lines that offer illustrations of public choice theory in action. The first story line, attributed to Twain, involves the poverty-stricken Hawkins family's attempts to become rich from the sale of a plot of undeveloped land in Tennessee. The second story line, attributed to Warner, describes the quest for riches by two upper class men, Philip Sterling and Henry Brierly. A subplot interwoven into these two main story lines involves Senator Dilworthy who manages the backroom deals behind both efforts. Public choice topics such as rent-seeking and incentives of politicians are well illustrated.

The various pieces of legislation introduced by Senator Dilworthy can be analyzed using the format that Caplan (2007) describes in his piece about how the events in the novel *Atlas Shrugged* parallel public choice theory. Caplan explains that each of the pieces of legislation in *Atlas Shrugged* has the following components: (1) a public-interest rationale; (2) supportive interest groups with a hidden financial agenda; and (3) negative consequences for the general public. These components are also found in the bills introduced in *The Gilded Age*.

Silas "Si" Hawkins, the patriarch of the Hawkins family, holds title to 75,000 acres of land in East Tennessee and imagines that this purchase is an investment for his and his family's future. He foresees many possible fortunes arising from this land. The land is about twenty miles from a river where he expects steamboats to come and stimulate the local economy and he holds a similar expectation about the as-yet-to-be built railroad. These high hopes lead him to reject offer after offer to take the land off his hands, much to the dismay of his long suffering wife. The lessons in public choice begin once the Hawkins' adopted daughter, Laura, goes to Washington to pursue the latest scheme—petitioning the federal government to fund the development of Knobs Industrial University on the land.[4]

Laura is invited to Washington by the Senate sponsor of the bill, Senator Dilworthy, who employs her brother (coincidentally named Washington). She is accompanied on her journey by Colonel Sellers, a longtime family friend, a "flamboyant backwoods speculator and loudmouth opportunist" (Powers, introduction, xxvi) who has enticed Si Hawkins over the years with many get-rich-quick schemes.[5] Signs of crony capitalism appear at the very start of the journey, as Laura and Colonel Sellers travel using tickets provided to Senator Dilworthy for free by the railroad companies.

Once in Washington, Laura, with her beauty and charm, quickly becomes the "reigning belle" of the town (Twain and Warner, 235) and a powerful lobbying force under the Senator's tutelage. In true public choice colors, Senator Dilworthy instructs Laura on the importance of cloaking private interests in public interest terms:

> Don't misunderstand me, Laura. I don't deny that it is for the interest of us all that this bill should go through, and it will. I have no concealments from you. But I have one principle in my public life, which I should like you to keep in mind; it has always been my guide. I never push a private interest if it is not justified and ennobled by some larger public good. (p. 259)

The proposed bill would fund the purchase of the Hawkins' land and the founding and building of Knobs Industrial University which would then provide much needed education to transform the unskilled labor of the South into the skilled labor needed for industrialization. The student population targeted by this new university would be the newly freed Negroes. The Representative reporting the bill from committee predicts, "In five years the increase in local wealth would not only reimburse the government for the outlay in this appropriation, but pour untold wealth into the treasury" (p. 329). The land, itself, was described as being rich in natural resources, including coal and metals for mining instruction (though no evidence is actually provided for the existence of such resources).

A moral foundation is also woven into the arguments for the bill as follows: "God had given us the care of these colored millions. What account should we render to Him of our stewardship? We had made them free. Should we leave them ignorant?" (p. 329). That this richly endowed land had never been developed before is interpreted as "providence" that it was "consecrated for some great use" (p. 329) as opposed to evidence that the land was worthless.

The combination of private interest with moral arguments is reminiscent of Yandle's (1983) account of the strange political bedfellows of "bootleggers and Baptists."[6] Yandle explains how the prohibition against selling alcohol on Sundays would be supported by both Baptists (who are against drinking on moral grounds) and bootleggers (who would profit from the lack of competition on Sundays). When such disparate groups support a regulation, it is difficult for that regulation to be dismantled by the political process. Bootleggers and Baptists come together in *A Gilded Age* to promote the development of the Hawkins' land.

The public choice theory of the brokering function that politicians play in the provision of government regulation and policy is prevalent in the novel. The excerpt that most captures the corruption in voting from the Knobs Industrial University storyline is chapter 42, in which Laura meets with Representative Trollop, who opposes the House bill. Once she convinces Trollop that she has information about his past improper behavior, he agrees to promote her bill. Laura then explains the *quid pro quo.*

> [T]hese gentlemen are to vote and work for the bill, simply out of love for the negro–and out of pure generosity I have put in a relative of each as a member of the University incorporation. They will handle a million or so of money, officially, but will receive no salaries.–A larger number of statesmen are to vote and work for the bill—also out of love for the negro—gentlemen of but moderate influence, these—and out of pure generosity I am to see that relatives of theirs have positions in the University, *with* salaries, and good one, too. You will vote and work for the bill, from mere affection for the negro, and I desire to testify my gratitude becomingly. Make free choice. Have you any friend whom you would like to present with a salaried or unsalaried position in our institution? (p. 309)

Ironically, despite Laura's lobbying abilities, the bill ultimately loses all support once Dilworthy is accused of paying a bribe to keep his Senate appointment. The Hawkins never realize a fortune from their land.

The secondary plot line involving the speculative pursuits of Henry Brierly also contains lessons about crony capitalism. In this storyline, Colonel Sellers plays a larger role. He works with Henry to try to get Congress to appropriate funds for a project that would make the river running through his land in Missouri navigable enough for steamship traffic. Senator Dilworthy introduces the petition from the citizenry "with the remark that he knew, personally, the signers of it, that they were men interested, it was true, in the improvement of the country, but he believed without any selfish motive" (pp. 166–67). The race card is played, yet again, in that "[i]t pleased him to see upon the roll the names of many colored citizens, and it must rejoice every friend of humanity to know that this lately emancipated race were intelligently taking part in the development of the resources of their native land" (p. 167).

The appropriation of $200,000 is passed and work begins on the project. Workers are hired and supplies bought—on credit backed by the promise of the appropriated funds.

> Beautiful credit! The foundation of modern society. Who shall say that this is not the golden age of mutual trust, of unlimited reliance upon human promises? That is a peculiar condition of society which enables a whole nation to instantly recognize point and meaning in the familiar newspaper anecdote, which puts into the mouth of a distinguished speculator in lands and mines this remark:—"I wasn't worth a cent two years ago, and now I owe a million dollars." (p. 192)

No appropriated funds ever reach the project and the workers eventually turn into a mob that runs Henry out of town. Henry meets with the president of the company financing the project to obtain the funds, only to realize that the whole project is nothing but a house of cards. Chapter 28 includes the following description of where the initial appropriation went.

> Why the—matter is simple enough. A Congressional appropriation costs money. Just reflect, for instance—a majority of the House Committee, say $10,000 apiece—$40,000; a majority of the Senate Committee, the same each—say $40,000; a little extra to one or two chairman of one or two such committees, say $10,000 each—$20,000; and there's $100,000 of the money gone, to begin with. Then, seven male lobbyists, at $3,000 each—$21,000; one female lobbyist, $10,000; a high moral Congressman or Senator here and there—the high moral ones cost more, because they give tone to a measure—say ten of these at $3,000 each, is $30,000; then a lot of small-fry country members who won't vote for anything whatever without pay—say twenty at $500 apiece, is $10,000; a lot of dinners to members—say $10,000 altogether; lot of jimcracks for Congressmen's wives and children—those go a long way—you can't spend too much money in that line—well, those things cost in a lump, say $10,000—along there somewhere; and then comes your printed documents—your maps, your tinted engravings, your pamphlets, your illuminated show cards, your advertisements in a hundred and fifty papers at ever so much a line—because you've got to keep the papers all light or you are gone up, you know. Oh, my dear sir, printing bills are destruction itself. Ours so far amount to—let me see—10; 52; 22; 13;—and then there's 11; 14; 33— well, never mind the details, the total in clean numbers foots up $118,254.42 thus far! (pp. 204–205)

In other words, the initial appropriation was merely seed money to buy off enough votes for future appropriations.

The subplot of Senator Dilworthy and the bribe includes a scathing description of influence peddling in politics. Indeed, Dilworthy's character is based on real-life Senator Samuel Pomeroy who was removed from office in 1912 after offering a bribe to a state legislator to support his bid for reelection.[7] (Remember that prior to the passage of the 17th amendment to the US Constitution, state legislatures elected US senators.) In the novel, Dilworthy offers $7,000 (the same sum as Pomeroy) to state legislator, Mr. Noble, to guarantee support for reelection. During the investigative hearings about the incident, described in chapter 59, Dilworthy is somehow able to turn the tables on Mr. Noble. Dilworthy learns of the accusation and immediately demands an investigation . . . into Mr. Noble for attacking the reputation of a US senator! Noble testifies that he received the bribe from Dilworthy, to which an investigative committee member exclaims,

> *At last*, Mr. Chairman, this shameless person has arrived at the point. This is sufficient and conclusive. By his own confession he has received a bribe, and did it deliberately. This is a grave offense, and cannot be passed over in silence, sir. By the terms of our instructions we can now proceed to mete out to him such punishment as is meet for one who has maliciously brought disrespect upon a Senator of the United States. (p. 433)

In Dilworthy's account of the incident, he describes how he merely gave the cash to Noble to deliver to a friend of his who was borrowing the money from Dilworthy to start a bank. No receipts or borrowing agreement were necessary, of course. The Committee ends up setting Mr. Noble free and letting the whole matter drop.

The inability of the legislature to police itself is covered more generally in chapter 51 where Colonel Sellers explains to Washington Hawkins that the vote of their land bill will be delayed because Congress begins each session by making a show of cleansing itself. No one is ever actually expelled from the legislature, of course. Voter's short term memory is illustrated by the fact that no one gets upset at the lack of expulsions because "the proceedings drag on so long that the country is sick and tired of it" (p. 377).

In contrast to these examples of rent-seeking and corruption, the novel also contains a counter-example of honest-to-goodness capitalism in action in the case of Philip Sterling's eventual success at finding coal. For most of the novel, however, Philip, like his partner Henry, is described as follows:

> There are many young men like him in American society, of his age, opportunities, education and abilities, who have really been educated for nothing and have let themselves drift, in the hope that they will find somehow, and by some sudden turn of good luck, the golden road to fortune. . . . He saw people, all around him, poor yesterday, rich to-day, who had come into sudden opulence by some means which they could not have classified among any of the regular occupations of life. (p. 369)

Eventually, however, Philip develops surveying skills and work habits that lead him away from wealth redistribution toward the production of wealth. While Henry fakes learning enough surveying skills to participate in the various land deals, Philip actually learns the trade. He dedicates himself to finding ore in the land owned by the family of the woman he loves, and ultimately "[t]he mine turned out even better than was at first hoped, and would, if judiciously managed, be a fortune to them all" (p. 462). That the novel ends with Philip's success, both in business and in love, is a moral statement against crony capitalism.

USING *THE GILDED AGE* IN THE CLASSROOM

Any of the excerpts described above could be used in the teaching of Public Choice topics such as rent-seeking, politicians as vote-maximizing brokers, voter rational ignorance, and crony capitalism. One way to incorporate literature into the teaching of upper level economics courses is to have the students read the novel over the semester and to hold several discussion days as they progress through the novel. Students can use the public choice model to analyze the various bills proposed in the novel using questions like those listed below.

From full novel:

1. Explain the public interest rationale for the Knobs Industrial University bill. Which interest groups with a hidden a financial agenda would benefit by the passage of the bill? What might be some of the negative consequences for the general public and unintended consequences of the bill?
2. Explain the public interest rationale for the Appropriation for Improving the Navigation of the Columbus River. Which interest groups with a hidden a financial agenda would benefit by the passage of the bill? What might be some of the negative consequences for the general public and unintended consequences of the bill?
3. Describe examples of rent-seeking in the various get-rich-quick schemes undertaken by Col. Sellers.
4. Describe examples of the brokering function that politicians play in the market for votes.

Rather than reading the whole novel, students can be assigned to read certain chapters that stand alone, such as chapters 28, 42, 51 and 59 described above. These excerpts and associated questions listed below can be used as homework assignments or exam questions.[8]

From specific excerpts:

5. Chapter 28: Use Henry's meeting with the President of the Navigation Company to explain the brokering function that politicians play in the market for votes.
6. Chapter 42: Use Laura's meeting with Mr. Trollop to explain the brokering function that politicians play in the market for votes.

7. Chapter 51: Find examples of principal-agent problems between politicians and voters in Col. Sellers' explanation of how Congress pretends to police itself.
8. Chapter 59: Use the theory of voter rational ignorance to explain how Sen. Dilworthy gets away with making a bribe.

THE GILDED AGE AND ITS RELEVANCE FOR TODAY

The Gilded Age can be used to illustrate specific Public Choice topics as outlined above, but the novel can also be used to help students understand parallels between today's economy and the roots of the Progressive Era, perhaps in a course on US Economic history.

Two opposite narratives exist that portend to explain the rise of Progressive legislation in the United States during the late 1800s and early 1900s. The first narrative explains that as the US economy industrialized and as improvements in transportation, especially the railways, expanded the reach of markets there were increased economies of scale which led to the concentration of power in various industries. Large Trusts were created which were headed by "Robber Barons" who used their economic power to exert power in the political realm. The political influence of the "Robber Barons" led to policies that favored big business over the working man. The concentration of economic power also led to vast income inequalities. Legislation of the Progressive era, as early as the Interstate Commerce Act of 1887 and the Sherman Antitrust Act of 1890, was the result of widespread popular outcry against the crony capitalism of the day. Increased regulation was in the public interest to control the excesses of laissez-faire capitalism.

Another narrative holds that much of the Progressive era legislation was determined by private as opposed to public interests. Specifically, regulation of big business was supported by small, inefficient businesses that could not compete with the larger companies. Increased regulation led to a cozy relationship between government and business as Stigler's (1971) "capture theory" of regulation would predict. Once the government had favors to hand out, crony capitalism resulted.

Which came first, the chicken (political power) or the egg (economic power)? A similar discussion is happening today with regard to the causes of the recent financial crisis. One narrative, favored by the Occupy Wall Street movement, argues that economic power is the root of the problem. Big business, especially banks, used their economic power to lobby for deregulation and once they got too big to fail, used that power to obtain bailouts. Their obvious solution is to increase regulation to prevent another crisis and to use income redistribution to level the playing field.

Smith and Yandle (2014) explain that the Occupy protests missed a great opportunity to expose the Bootlegger and Baptist pattern of cronyism. Yes, their protests showed some vague discontent with the "vast plunder of public coffers by well-organized Bootleggers," but "they routinely misdiagnosed it as a symptom of 'free-market' policies run amok" (73). Smith and Yandle (2014) conclude on a more positive note, hoping that improved communication through vast social media networks can increase our ability "to expose the Bootleggers—and embarrass the Baptists for supporting them" (176) thus leading to less crony capitalism overall.

A Public Choice explanation for the recent financial crisis centers on political power as the root cause. The potential existence of political favors invites rent-seeking as those who cannot compete in the economic sphere instead resort to obtaining market share though the political sphere. Those who can, compete, those who cannot, rent-seek. The solution here is to restrict the power of government so that there are no rents available to seek.

While novels set in historical times are usually not unbiased accounts of actual events, it so happens that *The Gilded Age* includes characters based on real persons and includes some pretty close descriptions of the scandals of the day. More importantly, reading and discussing a novel such as *The Gilded Age* in a course covering US Economic History is a way to introduce students to the cultural context of the events of the era. As McCloskey (2010) addresses, cultural context and rhetoric of the day are essential for understanding and explaining underlying economic trends.

To which narrative about the rise of the Progressive movement (and the recent financial crisis) in the United States would Twain and Dudley likely have subscribed? While not trained in Public Choice Economics, they certainly seemed skeptical of the political process in general, so they would probably not see re-regulation as the preferred path. As Colonel Sellers states "in a free country like ours, where any man can run for Congress and anybody can vote for him, you can't expect immortal purity all the time—it ain't in nature . . . Even in these days, when people growl so much and the newspapers are so out of patience, there is still a very respectable minority of honest men in Congress" (375–76).

NOTES

1. Christopher Newport University—Newport News, VA.
2. Powers, Introduction, xviii.
3. Nonetheless, a set of Econometrics Haiku is presented by Keisuke Hirano at: http://www.u.arizona.edu/~hirano/haiku.html.
4. Laura's character is based on "the ranking femme fatale of the time, Laura D. Fair" (Powers, Introduction, xxi).

5. Colonel Sellers' character is patterned after Twain's mother's cousin and the land speculations have roots in Twain's actual life (Powers, Introduction, xxiii).
6. Indeed, the quote "Politics makes strange bedfellows" is attributed to Charles Dudley Warner.
7. US Senate, Reference. "The Gilded Age."
8. Additional assignments are available from the author upon request.

REFERENCES

Bohanon, Cecil and Michelle Albert Vachris, (2012). "Economics and Literature: the Gains from Trade." In Hoyt, Gail and KimMarie McGoldrick (Ed.), *The International Handbook on Teaching and Learning Economics*. Aldershot: Edward Elgar Press. pp. 223–33.

Bransford, J. D., A. L. Brown and R. R. Cocking (2000). *How People Learn: Brain, Mind, Experience, and School: Expanded Edition*, Washington, DC: National Academy Press.

Caplan, Bryan. (2007), "*Atlas Shrugged* and public choice: The obvious parallels," in E. Younkins (ed.), *Ayn Rand's* Atlas Shrugged*: A Philosophical and Literary Companion*, Burlington, VT, US and Aldershot, UK: Ashgate, pp. 215–24.

Cowen, Tyler. (2008), "Is a novel a model?," in S. J. Peart and D. Levy (eds.), *The Street Porter and the Philosopher: Conversations on Analytical Egalitarianism*, Ann Arbor, MI: The University of Michigan Press, pp. 319–37.

McCloskey, Deirdre. (2010), *The Bourgeois Dignity: Why Economics Can't Explain the Modern World.* University of Chicago Press.

Smith, Adam C. and Bruce Yandle. (2014), *Bootleggers and Baptists: How Economic Forces and Moral Persuasion Interact to Shape Regulatory Politics*. Washington, DC: Cato Institute.

Stigler, George, J. (1971). "The theory of economic regulation," *The Bell Journal of Economics and Management Science* 2(1): 3–21.

Twain, Mark and Charles Dudley Warner (2006). *The Gilded Age*. With introduction by Ron Powers. New York: The Modern Library.

US Senate. Reference. "The Gilded Age." http://www.senate.gov/reference/reference_item/gilded_age.htm

Watts, Michael. and Georg Schaur. (2011). "Teaching and Assessment Methods in Undergraduate Economics: A Fourth National Quinquennial Survey," *Journal of Economic Education* 42(3): 294–309.

Yandle, Bruce. (1983). "Bootleggers and Baptists—The Education of a Regulatory Economist." *Regulation* May/June: 12–16.

Chapter 10

Henrik Ibsen's *An Enemy of the People*

Cynthia Hunter

The short play *An Enemy of the People* (original Norwegian title: *En folkefiende*) was written in 1882 by Norwegian playwright Henrik Ibsen. Although the play has many comedic elements, its underlying themes address complex sociopolitical issues that are both relevant and timeless.

The main character, Dr. Thomas Stockmann, is a man who is remains true to his ideals despite overwhelming odds. He is a complete innocent who has no interest in manipulating information for economic or political causes, and he clings to his ideas as though they are his moral obligation. The play examines whether such individual innocence is sustainable in a modern society.

While the doctor is concerned with morality and science and not with economics or politics, his brother, Peter, is concerned with staying in power. Peter has risen successfully through the political hierarchy of a small forest town. He is now the mayor and chief of police of the town, which is known for its therapeutic hot springs. As such, he was able to use his influence to secure a lucrative position for his brother.

Prior to being appointed to the position, Dr. Stockmann lived a very poor existence in the countryside, but he now enjoys a very comfortable lifestyle as medical officer of the baths, along with his wife, two sons, and a daughter. He and Peter have worked together to establish and promote the springs, and the town's economy depends on them.

The doctor takes his responsibilities very seriously, and he is disturbed that his recommendations during the construction of the baths were not heeded. Shortcuts were taken, and he is concerned that the purity and safety of the baths may have been compromised.

The mayor is unwilling to address any issues with the baths because of the potential political repercussions. He fears that acknowledging the need for any changes to the baths would be tantamount to admitting that he made mistakes. He knows the majority of voters are afraid of risk, and, accordingly, they might be inclined to oust him for past mistakes.

The relations between the brothers raise important questions about personal integrity, morality and idealism. Nevertheless, they are somewhat secondary to the underlying theme of the play, which, in many ways, is a criticism of democracy.

Many of the characters in the play claim to be "freethinkers," but most of them are very concerned with politics. Unlike Dr. Stockmann, few of them stick by their claims when the political tide is against them. Their combined interactions beg the question of what "freethinking" actually means in a closely knit democracy.

Ibsen depicts how most leaders of society are afraid to do the right thing because they are concerned for their own welfare. In a democratic society, the leaders are at the mercy of the people. If the leaders are unpopular, they may be unseated; therefore their actions are bound by the tyranny of the majority.

At the same time, the play depicts how leaders can manipulate their constituents and use the power of the majority to achieve their own ends. The idea and threat of the majority keeps leaders from acting honestly because they pander to what will trend well with the people. Thus, it is Ibsen's perception that the majority does not truly rule because they are only privy to information that their leaders choose to reveal.

As the play opens, the mayor comes to the Stockmann house, along with the editor of the town's newspaper, Mr. Hovstad. Mrs. Stockmann is entertaining dinner guests, and Dr. Stockmann is not at home, but the two insist on waiting for him. When the doctor returns, the Mayor asks to speak with him privately and tells him that rumors are being circulated that the baths are contaminated.

Dr. Stockmann tells the Mayor that he suspects the rumors are true. He is angry because his orders were not carried out in the beginning, and now the health and welfare of town, as well as his reputation, are at risk. He declares that it is his civic duty to protect and inform the public. This leads to an argument between the brothers. Dr. Stockmann contends that, in a democratic society, the truth should always be revealed to the public and should never be altered for political reasons.

The mayor is aggravated, and he tells Dr. Stockmann that the public should not be informed of the situation because it would destroy the town's economy, He tells the doctor he should think more of how to function within a society and less as an individual, and accuses him of being disrespectful of authority.

As they argue, there is a knock at the door. The doctor's daughter, Petra, delivers the report on the water analysis to her father. Stockmann reads it immediately and discovers that, indeed, the baths are infected with a deadly disease. He vows he will instruct the town to repair or close the baths.

The Mayor does not believe the report. He declares he will refuse to close the baths because it will cause the financial ruin of the town.

Mr. Hovstad tells Dr. Stockmann that he is willing to print an article in *The People's Herald*, and let the story unfold immediately.

As the second act begins, the doctor has sent an official report on the pollution of the baths to his brother, the mayor. The mayor returns the report with a note stating that he will come by the doctor's house to speak with him.

When the mayor arrives, he announces his displeasure that the doctor conducted the investigation without telling him. He believes the report is exaggerated and says he is not convinced there is a problem. To make the suggested repairs would be very expensive and would take at least two years. The loss of income from the baths for that length of time would be catastrophic to the town's economy. He insists that nothing about the baths' pollution must reach the public, although he concedes that the board might be willing to make some changes in a few years.

Dr. Stockmann is outraged. He says that he will not submit to fraud, and that the *People's Herald* will support him and print a story about it. The mayor reminds him that it was he who secured the doctor's appointment, and that the doctor owes him for getting him a job. He basically admits that he expected to control the doctor in exchange for his employment. He tells the doctor he is out of control, and that he will lose his job if he does not cooperate.

The brothers continue to argue about who is ultimately responsible for the baths. Dr. Stockmann asserts that if his original plan had been followed, there would not be a problem. The mayor insists that, as an employee, the doctor has no individual rights, and that he must submit to authority. He commands the doctor to make a public announcement that, upon further review, his findings were proven false.

After the mayor leaves, Mrs. Stockmann tries to convince her husband to remember his family. She has practical concerns and fears the family will suffer if her husband opposes his brother. Their daughter, Petra, interjects, urging her father to stand for what he knows is right. Dr. Stockmann explains that he will never be able to look his sons in the eyes if he bows to the mayor's demands.

The next morning, Morten Kiil, Mrs. Stockmann's father, stops by. He has come to congratulate his son-in-law on his discovery. He assumes the doctor's report is some kind of joke or a political maneuver designed as revenge for the harassment his company has received from the town council. He is delighted that Dr. Stockmann's report is creating conflict among the town's authorities. He does not believe the bacteria in the baths is harmful, and he encourages Dr. Stockmann to go ahead and "pull their legs." At this point, he doesn't understand the consequences the discovery might have on his tanneries, which are implicated in the pollution of the baths.

Later, Hovstad, the editor, and Aslaksen, the printer of the newspaper, also stop by the house to congratulate the doctor and extend their gratitude. Hovstad and the doctor go to speak in private, and Hovstad tells the doctor that he hopes to use the information about the pollution of the baths to attack the town's conservative leadership. The doctor agrees with him politically, but he is hesitant to attack the town's leadership, acknowledging that it is made up of the most qualified men, including his own brother.

Mr. Aslaksen is also the chairman of the powerful Homeowners Association. He assures Dr. Stockmann that he can count on their support, as well as that of the Temperance Society. Aslaksen emphasizes that he does not want to upset the town's leaders, but he that he would be in favor of organizing a moderate demonstration to show support for repairing the baths. Dr. Stockmann tells him that won't be necessary because he is convinced the board of directors of the baths will approve the needed repairs.

Though Dr. Stockmann is heartened by Mr. Aslaksen's support, Hovstad deems that his approach is cowardly. He expects the issue of repairing the baths will be a heated and controversial one. Dr. Stockmann is confused, believing it unthinkable that anyone would be in opposition to making the required repairs to the baths. Nevertheless, he tells Hovstad that if the mayor refuses to make changes to the water system, the editor can print the doctor's entire report in the paper. The editor leaves, and Dr. Stockmann tells his family that he is very proud to have support of the "solid majority."

As Act III opens, Hovstad (the editor) and Billing (the sub editor) are at the newspaper office discussing the potential outcomes of publishing Dr. Stockmann's article. They seem to be ready to attack the reputation of the town government and expose corruption within the privileged classes.

When Dr. Stockmann appears and authorizes them to release the article, however, everyone in the office suddenly comprehends the larger meaning of that action. They begin to question the merits of exposing the town government and destroying the reputation of the baths. There is a mounting realization that printing the article will do more harm than good and will not help the situation.

There is a sudden and complete shift of opinions, and the paper now plans to support the mayor. They resolve to print a statement from the mayor, endorsing the baths and claiming how good they are. Dr. Stockmann is exasperated. He decides he must call a town meeting to inform the townspeople that the baths are contaminated.

Mrs. Stockmann fears her husband is being overly zealous, and that he is risking his reputation. She is obviously concerned for her family's welfare, and she fears there will be repercussions for her husband's radical decision. Nevertheless, she reluctantly supports him.

Act IV is set in a large hall in Captain Horster's house, where the town meeting is underway. A large crowd has gathered and the family, the mayor, Aslaksen, and Hovstad are present. Billing is there to cover the meeting for the paper. Aslaksen is elected to serve as a moderator.

The crowd reacts as Dr. Stockmann enters the hall. Some are applauding and some are jeering. Aslaksen fears that the situation may get out of hand. He moves that a chairman be appointed, and he is quickly elected to moderate the proceedings.

The mayor immediately moves that Dr. Stockmann should not be allowed to read his report or talk about the baths. He and Aslaksen collaborate to convince the crowd that the doctor is out to harm the town's best interests, and the motion passes.

Dr. Stockmann is angry. Since he is not to be permitted to speak about the pollution in the baths, he begins to speak about the pollution in the town government. He talks of how he conceptualized the spa project to help the people. As he became more involved, he says, he realized the "colossal stupidity of the authorities."

Aslaksen tries to quiet him, but he continues. He talks about his brother's failures as mayor, but goes on to say that the authorities are entirely to blame. The worst enemy, he says, is the majority. The crowd reacts wildly and angrily. Aslaksen urges the doctor to retract his comments, but will not relent. The doctor says that the majority is made up of stupid people.

He states that intelligent, freethinking people are in the minority, and that morality and freethinking go hand in hand. The doctor sums up by saying that his message will be heard, and he will write to newspapers in other towns. He insists that the idea of the common, uncultured majority ruling on complex and progressive issues is outdated.

The townspeople feel insulted by these accusations and anger starts growing in the room. By the end of the meeting, the town has rebelled as a mob against Dr. Stockmann.

Aslaksen moves that Dr. Stockmann be declared an enemy of the people and banished from the town. This act represents the climax of the play, as the men who were having dinner at Dr. Stockmann's house in the first act are publicly denouncing him, and he is denouncing them.

By the next morning (Act V), the town has turned against the Stockmann family. Peter comes to the house with a letter from the board of directors of the baths, terminating Dr. Stockmann's contract. He also has a resolution from the householders association stating that no one should hire Dr. Stockmann in the town again. The mayor insinuates that the doctor's actions were merely a scheme to inherit more of Morten Kiil's money. He advises him to leave town for a few months.

Soon, Kiil, himself, arrives to give credence to the mayor's point of view. Kiil declares that he has just bought an interest in the bath business, suggesting that, because his tannery is causing all the contamination, his son-in-law will back off. The inference is that Dr. Stockmann will let the issue go, now that his family's money is also in jeopardy, if he continues this battle.

In rage and disappointment, Dr. Stockmann's first reaction is to take his family and go abroad. But, when the townspeople break his windows and make sinister threats and offers, he comes to realize there is no independent thought in the town.

He sees that the people have become pawns in the politicians' game, and so he refuses Morten Kiil's suggestions and ignores Peter's advice to leave town. In defiance and anger, he decides to stay and devote himself to educating the citizens to participate in the political process. He realizes he has alienated everyone and that he is standing alone. He decides he will embrace his fate and stay true to his principles. He will be "the enemy of the people" if that is what it takes to do what is right.

The question remains as to whether Dr. Stockmann acted righteously or foolishly. His decision to stay and keep fighting will certainly make life difficult for him and his family and will doubtless do little to change the status quo.

REFERENCE

Ibsen, Henrik. [1882] 1999. *An Enemy of the People*. Minneola, New York: Dover.

Chapter 11

William Dean Howells' Work Ethic in *The Rise of Silas Lapham*[1]

Zennure Köseman

> We accept and welcome, therefore, as conditions to which we must accommodate ourselves, great inequality of environment, the concentration of business, industrial and commercial, in the hands of a few, and the law of competition between these, as being not only beneficial, but essential for the future progress of the race.
>
> Andrew Carnegie, "The Gospel of Wealth" (16)

The popularity of the self-made man who becomes rich through pursuing the path of hard work and strife is a theme in most American fictional works. Especially after the advent of industrialization, with the accumulation of financial wealth, the self-made man becomes an important person to study. After this period, individuals achieved success more often through reliance on others and the acceptance of social values that conflict with self-identity. A pivotal book showing this literary turn is in the *The Rise of Silas Lapham*, a highly influential fictional work of the Gilded Age.[2] Howells emphasizes that as individuals gain social improvement in their lives, their moral values demise. For Howells, the destruction of ethical values implies that achievement through moral perfection and self-reliance is rewarded in material perspectives. In the Gilded Age, Americans' pursuit of success is substantially about material accumulation rather than the development of moral values.

This transformation of the means and the meaning of success in American literature is notable first through an analysis of autobiographies, self-help books, popular essays and novels. Success, meant as moral perfection through early American Republic, was redefined in the post-Civil War era, when the acquisition of success meant material wealth by the means of chance. In the new era of mass culture and industrialization of the Gilded Age and the Progressive Period, as Timothy M. Roberts also remarks in his *Commentary*

Foreword for Köseman's *From the Way to Wealth to the Gospel of Wealth,* the redefinition of the acquisition of achievement meant heightened social status of material prosperity achieved through dependence on others, rather than self-reliance.[3]

The continuity in the success ethic is reflected in some critical sources, one of which is Richard Weiss's *The American Myth of Success*. Weiss expresses that the persistence of success theme never ends, but it goes on in different meanings according to men's world views:

> Many myths in the nineteenth century have withered and disappeared, [but] the myth of success, however, continues to flourish. Conveyed in a massive literature, it stands as one of the most enduring expressions of American popular ideals. I do not use the word myth to imply something entirely false. Rather, I mean to connote a complex of profoundly held attitudes and values which condition the way men view the world and understand their experience. However inaccurate as a description of American society, the success myth reflects what millions believe that society is or ought to be. (1969, 3–4)

The success myth, as Weiss underlines, continues, but became redefined—in materialistic achievement in the Gilded Age and the Progressive Era. William Dean Howells is critical of the change in social life and gives an ironic title for his realist fictional work. *The Rise of Silas Lapham* title suggests Silas Lapham's moral rise which is contradictory to his material accumulation. Howells reflects the success story of rags-to-riches and portrays his protagonist, Silas Lapham, as a man who pursues moral redemption, although it brings about financial destruction.

Eyal Naveh picks up on this theme. He states in his essay, "The Transformation of 'Rags to Riches' Stories" that the protagonist starts his life in poverty in his new environment after leaving his rural background. According to Naveh, individuals strive hard in tremendous hard work, honesty, integrity and self-reliance to acquire monetary accumulation. In this striving hard, businessmen are the essential individuals who long for moral virtues sustained through self-reliance in their "rags-to-riches" background. However, the acquisition of "moral conduct and reward of virtue" is most of the time an illusion in the economic and social life of the Gilded Age. As Naveh states, success

> is reflected in the perception of opportunities for upward mobility that existed in America's free and democratic society based on abundant physical resources, entrepreneurial spirit, laissez faire economy, and audacious individual initiative. As a common cultural discourse, the stories' main function was to give meaning to the American experience rather than to reflect or contradict the reality of American life. (1991, 60–61)

Here, there is a man who is in search for moral perfection. However, due to his materialist living circumstances, he just criticizes the individuals surrounding him. Signifying the moral perfection to acquire success as defined by Benjamin Franklin, James Fennimore Cooper, Ralph Waldo Emerson, Henry David Thoreau, and Frederick Douglass in early American literary history, Silas Lapham sacrifices his social achievement in his business world for moral improvement (Köseman, 2013: 9). This indicates that William Dean Howells has a retrospection for self-improvement through moral perception in this fictional work. Thus, Howells is a social critic who uses literary context in detail to show the attitudes and behaviors of individuals in their social settings.

Unlike the early American writers who consider success as the moral perfection through self-reliance, the writers of the Gilded Age and the Progressive Era reformulate it as the accumulation of prosperity by means of the reliance on others by the turn of the twentieth century. The period was reflected by the realist and the naturalist genres that portray the moral corruption and the acceptance of social values that conflicted with self-identity. However, although Silas Lapham is a person who cares for moral perfection, in *The Rise of Silas Lapham*, he is also the main character depending on others to have social acceptance in society. His wife, his daughters, and the members of Boston's upper middle class society, the Coreys, are the group of people on whom he depends to acquire success. For him, his house in Beacon Street is a means of social improvement in society. His wife, Persis Lapham also thinks of Boston Brahmin aristocratic families as a means to acquire success. Moreover, important to the Lapham family, the Coreys respect them, as much as their house is well decorated and well-furnished. Lapham always respects his wife's decisions, because she thinks of Lapham as a witty and clever person (Köseman, 2013, 117). He manifests how he is proud of his wife and her pivotal role in his social and materialistic rise:

> Lapham was proud of his wife, and when he married her it had been a rise in life for him. For a while he stood in awe of his good fortune, but this could not last, and he simply remained supremely satisfied with it. The girl who had taught school with a clear head and a strong hand was not afraid of work; she encouraged and helped him from the first, and bore her full share of the common burden. She had health, and she did not worry his life out with peevish complaints and vagaries; she had sense and principle, and in their simple lot she did what was wise and right. (Howells, 1965, 44)

In addition to his wife, Lapham aims to receive the favor of Boston Brahmin society by participating in its clubs, dinners and meetings. This signifies a social rise through financial success for Lapham. Lapham's diving into different social activities hints at becoming a socially accepted individual in urban life, even though pursuing such leisure activities contradicts with the old means of achievement by means of self-reliance. However, he relies on some others in order to be a successful man in his work life.

In the course of the novel, Lapham is pleased with being a self-made man, and is content with his position in life. His self-assurance is the reason for his business success. As the narrator reveals:

> Lapham had the pride which comes of self-making, and he would not openly lower his crest to the young fellow he had taken into his business. He was going to be obviously master in his own place to everyone; and during the hours of business he did nothing to distinguish Corey from the half-dozen other clerks and book-keepers in the outer office, but he was not silent about the fact that Bromfield Corey's son had taken a fancy to come to him. (1965, 98–99)

This quotation indicates that he is content with all that he has done in his work life. He becomes proud when some people such as Bromfield Corey's son come to visit him in his house. Actually, what he wants to do is to direct other individuals in his work rather than be directed by the others. He intends to control them in their living circumstances.

The scholar Francis Albert Berces signifies that Lapham is proud of being a self-made man: "Because Lapham is a self-made man who respects hard work, his choices favor what he thinks is best for himself. He is, to be sure, a likable and basically charitable but crude man who is proud of his prosperity and eager to boast." (1970, 200). Although for Lapham life is based on the principles of integrity, honesty, justice and perseverance, financial prosperity is much more significant when the aim is to rise socially. His pride in his wealth signifies that for Lapham the meaning of success is ultimately dependent on financial terms. Yet, Lapham shares an Emersonian optimism implying that success can be reached through self-reliance. Lapham says:

> My wife was at me all the time to take a partner—somebody with capital; but I couldn't seem to bear the idea. That paint was like my own blood to me. To have anybody else concerned in it was like—well, I don't know what. I saw it was the thing to do; but I tried to fight it off, and I tried to joke it off. (1965, 15)

Lapham knows that perseverance, diligence, patience and determination will make him a successful paint manufacturer. Devoting himself to material achievement by means of hard work, Lapham implies that he will struggle for his paint business whatever the conditions are:

> Simple, clear, bold, and straightforward in mind and action, Colonel Silas Lapham, with prompt comprehensiveness and a never-failing business sagacity, is, in the best sense of that much-abused term, one of nature's noblemen, to the last inch of his five eleven and a half. His life affords an example of

single-minded application and unwavering perseverance, which our young business men would do well to emulate. There is nothing showy or meretricious about the man. He believes in mineral paint; and he puts his heart and soul into it. He makes it a religion; though we would not imply that is his religion. Colonel Lapham is a regular attendant at the Rev. Dr. Langworthy's church. (1965, 19)

Thus, Lapham pursues an Emersonian attitude in his business life despite the competitiveness of the industrial world. However, what is distinctive is his evaluation of his success as gaining financial wealth via hard work. This indicates that he is in between the wish for moral achievement through attaining self-reliance and the wish for material accumulation by depending on others. Yet, material prosperity is a longing for Lapham in his work life especially when he goes bankrupt. In the early sections of *The Rise of Silas Lapham*, success for Lapham meant having material and social prowess. For him, accumulation of wealth was the main path toward upward mobility. A well-built house decorated with ornaments was the indication of his willingness to achieve materialistic success. Such a house would also lead to his acceptance by the other rich families in Boston. According to Lapham, the quantity and the quality of the possessed materials were the indication for social acceptance as well as social improvement in society:

When the spring opened Colonel Lapham showed that he had been in earnest about building on to the New Land. His idea of a house was a brown-stone front, four stories high, and a French roof with an air-chamber above. Inside, there was to be a reception-room on the street and a dining room-back. The parlours were to be on the second floor, and finished in black walnut or party-coloured paint. The chambers were to be on the three floors above, front and rear, with side-rooms over the front door. Black walnut was to be used everywhere except in the attic, which was to be painted and grained to look like black walnut. The whole was to be very high studded, and there were to be handsome cornices and elaborate center-pieces throughout, except, again, in the attic. (36)

In addition to Silas Lapham, Mr. Corey, a wealthy businessman in the novel, also defines success as the possession of money because it "buys position at once"; it is the "romance" and "poetry" of the age. Moreover, "It's the thing that strikes the imagination" (1965, 58).

Howells' novel clearly expresses that making money dominated Americans' outlook in the 1880s. Richard Weiss in *The American Myth of Success* emphasizes, "men were consumed by the passion for wealth. The love of money dominated their soul such as Lapham's. This influence implies that the historical and social evaluation of earning money was the only end in life for the businessmen of the Gilded Age. Success meant to be "the amount of money earned in the business world" (Weiss, 1969, 104). The novel, then, characterizes the main features of the Gilded Age in which financial growth, rapid improvement of railroads, factories, banks, mines, manufacturing and other enterprises created both investment and employment opportunities. In this period, technological progress through the rise of rich industrialists and financiers such as Cornelius Vanderbilt, John D. Rockefeller, Andrew Carnegie, Henry Flagler, and J. P. Morgan became dominant in business life. During this period, government promoted economic growth by giving manufacturers money, land and resources. In this way, the government regulated industrial activity. Moreover, in the Gilded Age, the entrepreneurs flourished. Their admirers referred to them as the "captains of industry" while their foes called them as "robber barons" because of their overpowering and unethical financial manipulations (Divine, 1984, 517). In *The Rise of the Silas Lapham*, Howells refers to the features of this age by portraying the Coreys and the Rogers as representative of robber barons whose only goal is money. These businessmen aim at social rising and financial wealth through devaluing spiritual and ethical behavior in society. The industrialists, the new "rugged individualists" of thc Gilded Age interpret success as "the gaining of money and position" not through pursuing the morality of the maxims of "Poor Richard" but through pursuing the greediness of personal interests as the Coreys and the Rogers do (*RSL* 98).[4] As Robert Wiebe in his *The Search for Order* indicates, the bureaucratic values of the prosperous families and entrepreneurs such as the Coreys and the Rogers are the reason for the change in social order:

> The new middle class supplied the largest body of adherents to bureaucratic thought. Leaders in a major social reorganization, these men and women required values suitable to their new sense of location. More simply, they were the ones who thought that way. From an urban vantage point, they quite literally saw that impersonal life in flux which they could understand most readily as the interaction of groups—their relation with others. In the city people daily felt the need for continuity and regularity. These were the natural values of the trade associations and somewhat later of the craft unions as well. (1967, 153)

In *The Rise of Silas Lapham*, then, individuals such as the Coreys and the Rogers are representative of the people who disregard the old moral values. The novel is, in fact, an actual representation of life in this era. "It [is] a combination of method (realism in physical detail and fact) and intent (the authorial effort to present lives as they were really lived)" (Hough, 1977, 54). *The Rise of Silas Lapham* exposes the reality of the immoral business world, as well as materialistic ruin. Robert Lee Hough explains in his article "William Dean Howells: *The Rise of Silas Lapham*" that

> the book has the *sine quo non* of realistic fiction: the texture of life. This quality is an accumulative thing; it comes to the reader through detail, speech, incident,

and characterization. At the end, most readers feel that they can accept Howells' characters as "real" people and that the author is seriously interested in what happens to real people. Howells may be weak in places, but he does not cheat. In fact, if Howells, in a few passages, seems to us overly concerned about the morality of literature, it reveals that we have lost something of the idealism and high purpose that he held for fiction. (1977, 61)

The emergence of realism as an outcome of the loss of idealism implies that whereas in the romantic period the basis of the achievement was moral perfection, in Lapham's world of 1885, it turned out to be the accumulation of wealth. However, although Howells considers the principles of truth and equality in his concept of realism, real-life circumstances contradict with what Howells desires. "Real events experienced by real people" becomes the subject matter of *The Rise of Silas Lapham* in which Lapham experiences material ruin because of the rugged individualism of the period (Boardman, 1967, 45–46). Howells indicates that individuals' wish for material ethos in his time cause them to become socially and morally corrupt. As Nettels also argues, "The ruling idea of his criticism is that fiction is justified by its realism, its truth to actual life that the illusion of reality depends upon 'the faithful, almost photographic delineation of actual life.' His materialism is the 'truthful treatment of material'" (1988, 63). Thus, what Howells does in the novel is to present a "slice of life" in which individuals become morally corrupted because of the desire for financial gain.

Lapham's world is late nineteenth-century Boston where he experiences his success and failure in the business world. What makes the novel realistic is the existence of evil in society which causes his decline. At a moment of crisis at a dinner party, Lapham finds the opportunity to make a correct choice in his life through his withdrawal from pursuit of materialistic prosperity, and his renewed search for moral perfection (Pizer, 1984, 265). Thus, Lapham gives up his scramble after money, embraces his morality and leads his life by keeping his virtues. Rather than desiring to be a rich man in possessions, he prefers to be a morally wealthy man. This implies that although Lapham considered the attainment of monetary wealth as success before the dinner party, he came to evaluate success as moral perfection after that. Lapham's initiation of this spiritual enrichment amidst financial interests symbolizes Howells' own consideration of the dangers in society. As Robert W. Schneider explains, Howells was "one of the members of the older generation who, during his long and productive life, came face to face with many of the problems of an industrializing America" (1965, 19). Through Lapham in *The Rise of Silas Lapham*, Howells exposes the problems of industrialization. For instance, as an ordinary man Lapham acquires success through his own efforts in poverty, but loses all his possessions in life because of being cheated by the Rogers (Bell, 1993, 31). Success in such a society, in this sense, meant to accumulate money and power even through illegal ways, as the Rogers did. As Henry Bamford Parkes explains, money became the main avenue to success during the age of industrialism:

> With the transformation of the pioneer into the businessman, money became the principal symbol of success and the main object of ambition . . . The business classes sought to prove their strength by the conquest of money, as their ancestors had done by the conquest of the wilderness and judged each other in monetary terms. (1959, 260)

Here, the domination of money in the industrial world is the main theme. The conquest of the material terms become noteworthy in social lives much more than anything else. Moral perfection is less significant than the success of material accumulation, because it became as a loss most of the time.

James Truslow Adams in his monumental literary study *The Epic of America* states that America is a "land of dreams" and "promises" (1931, 214). Adams explains that, "There has been also the American dream, that dream of a land in which life should be better and richer and fuller for every man, with opportunity for each according to his ability or achievement. It is a difficult dream for the European upper classes to interpret adequately, and too many of us ourselves lave grown weary and mistrustful of it" (1931, 404).

Adams, here, refers to men like Silas Lapham who strive hard to acquire success in their rags-to-riches life stories. Adams also indicates that most opportunity pursuers become skeptical of it as they become unsuccessful in their business and social lives. They lose their self-reliance for achievement because they experience it only as a dream. What they have to do turns out to be reliance on others rather than self-reliance for monetary accumulation.

CONCLUSION

Silas Lapham expresses the significance of money in his life when he expresses that he becomes pleased with being accepted by the others who are prominent individuals in their social environment. This indicates that Lapham is basically after monetary wealth to acquire success although he has a retrospection for moral perfection to attain social improvement in his life. Lapham's longing for moral prosperity in his work life, despite his desire for accumulation of money is a cue that there has been a tension between moral virtues and material prosperity, a tension that began to emerge by the end of the nineteenth century in an industrializing America. Lapham is proud that people around him pay attention to him because of his accumulation of wealth and social status. Interest in social ascendancy and monetary prosperity emphasizes how secular values dominated the American mind of the 1880s.

NOTES

1. This article basically generates from one chapter of Köseman's PhD. Dissertation entitled as "From The Way of Wealth to the Gospel of Wealth."
2. The Gilded Age (1875–1889) is basically known as a period in which there is historically the new wave of immigrants as a result of industrial growth and accumulation of wealth in the upper-class Americans who employ the newcomers. Striving hard to acquire success in business life and the industrial world is the most important characteristic of this period.
3. Köseman underlines in detail the change in the meaning and the means of success through analyzing several literary works of different periods in her book.
4. *The Rise of Silas Lapham* is hereafter abbreviated as *RSL* in parenthetical documentation.

REFERENCES

Adams, James Truslow. 1931. *The Epic of America*. Boston: Little, Brown, and Company.

Bell, Michael Davitt. 1993. *The Problem of American Realism: Studies in the Cultural History of a Literary Idea*. Chicago: The University of Chicago Press.

Berces, Francis Albert. 1970. "Mimesis, Morality and *The Rise of Silas Lapham*." *American Quarterly*, vol. 22. no. 2. Part 1. (Summer): 190–202.

Boardman, Arthur. 1967. "Social Point of View in the Novels of William Dean Howells." *American Literature*, vol. 39. no. 1. (March): 42–59.

Carnegie, Andrew. 1962. "Introduction" (1896) and "The Gospel of Wealth" (1889). *The Gospel of Wealth and Other Timely Essays*. (1900). Cambridge: The Belknap Press of Harvard University Press: 3–50.

Divine, Robert A. 1984.*American Past and Present*. Illinois: Scott, Foresman and Company,

Hough, Robert Lee. 1977. "William Dean Howells: *The Rise of Silas Lapham*." *The Voice of America Forum Lectures: The American Novel*. Washington, D.C.: United States Information Agency: 53–63.

Howells, William Dean. (1885). 1965. *The Rise of Silas Lapham*. New York: Harper & Row, Publishers.

Koseman, Zennure. 2013. *From the Way to Wealth to the Gospel of Wealth: The Transformation in the Concept of Success in American Literature*. Palo Alto, California: Academica Press.

Naveh, Eyal. 1991. "The Transformation of 'Rags to Riches' Stories; Business Biographies of Success in the Progressive Era and the 1920s." *American Studies International*, vol. 29. No: 1. (April): 60–80.

Nettels, Elsa. 1988. "Realism and Dialect." *Language, Race, and Social Class in Howells's America*. Lexington: The University Press of Kentucky: 62–71.

Parkes, Henry Bamford. 1959. *The American Experience*. New York: Random House.

Pizer, Donald. 1984. *Realism and Naturalism in Nineteenth-Century American Literature*. Carbondale: Southern Illinois University.

Schneider, Robert W. 1965. *Five Novelists of the Progressive Era*. New York: Columbia University Press.

Weiss, Richard. 1969. *The American Myth of Success: From Horatio Alger to Norman Vincent Peale*. New York: Basic Books.

Wiebe, H. Robert. 1967. *The Search for Order: 1877–1920*. New York: Hill and Wang.

Chapter 12

Capitalism Contra Ethics

William Dean Howells and the Moral Ambivalence of Business

Michael Spindler

William Dean Howells was a prolific author who in the late nineteenth and early twentieth centuries attained the status of "the Dean of American Letters."[1] A later generation including H. L. Mencken and Van Wyck Brooks was iconoclastic toward his writings, and his reputation since has suffered various ups and downs as different critical perspectives have been applied to his work.[2] The consensus, however, is that his major two novels are *The Rise of Silas Lapham* (1885) and *A Hazard of New Fortunes* (1890), and in these he explored and dramatized the tensions that had come into play between leading an ethical life and success in business. Was it possible to follow the good in one's actions as well as the profitable, or in the world of competitive capitalism was there an irreconcilable conflict between the two?

Howells was born in the frontier town of Martins Ferry, Ohio, in 1837 and grew up in the preindustrial handicraft economy, even spending a year in a log cabin. From the agricultural society around him he absorbed the values of democracy and egalitarianism, and from his father, a Swedenborgian, he absorbed a strong moral absolutism. As a result of this paternal influence he never lost the conviction that Christian principle and good works save and that self-concern and love of worldly things damn (Cady 1956, 21, 34). "Morality," he wrote in 1891, "penetrates all things, it is the soul of all things" (Kirk, 1959, 42). And despite the commanding position he later achieved in the Eastern literary establishment as a major novelist, he never lost his identification with the frontier and the West. All his life he regarded himself as a "Buckeye," a boy from Ohio (Cady, 1956, 92).

These two main strands in his make-up clearly determine many of the attitudes represented in his fiction. *The Rise of Silas Lapham*, in particular, expresses Howells' nostalgic view of the ante-bellum agrarian era as a morally superior age, as well as his confidence in the power of its characteristic

Protestant and democratic values to survive in the face of rapid economic change. Lapham's development from freeholder into industrial capitalist represents in microcosm both the transformation of the national economy in the late nineteenth century and the persistence of the older ideological frameworks. Howells' protagonist is the embodiment of Jeffersonian individualism and the Protestant ethic, and the novel presents a commercial and social milieu in which these traditional codes of behavior are tested and ultimately vindicated.

The Protestant ethic emphasized the spiritual duty to one's worldly calling, and Lapham shares with some of the real-life entrepreneurs of the time that attitude, identified by Weber and Tawney, of business as sacrament (Weber [1930] 1971, Tawney [1926] 1938). His wife charges him with having made his paint his god, and, as an exchange with Tom Corey reveals, his faith in his product is quasi-religious in tone: "It's the best paint in God's universe," he said, with the solemnity of prayer. "It's the best in the market," said Corey (Howells, [1885] 1963, 45). This Protestant view of business arose out of and endorsed the behavior demanded by a period of primitive capital accumulation. On the one hand it exhorted an intense industry, and on the other, an ascetic compulsion to save, two traits Howells exemplifies in his character. Lapham is extremely hard-working, arriving at his office in the morning before his employees and taking no summer holiday, and his lifestyle is very modest. Until he is tempted to social emulation he conforms closely to Weber's ideal type of entrepreneur who "avoids ostentation and unnecessary expenditure as well as conscious enjoyment of his power" and whose manner of life is "distinguished by a certain ascetic tendency" (1971, 71). Even after he and his wife have become wealthy and have moved to Boston their lives are still characterized by a combination of asceticism and capital accumulation. "Their first years there," Howells writes, "were given to careful getting on Lapham's part, and careful saving on his wife's" (1963, 25). This combination eventually produces an embarrassing growth of personal wealth: "Suddenly the money began to come so abundantly that she need not save; and then they did not know what to do with it" (1963, 25). This financial surplus could be absorbed by reinvestment, but a general business depression proscribes that option, or by consumption, but that is inhibited by the old habits of worldly asceticism.

One honorific way the business millionaires evolved for absorbing their huge money surpluses was the adoption of an aristocratic lifestyle based on the hired services of butlers, footmen, chambermaids, cooks and so on, but Howells does not wish the reader to imagine the Laphams capable of abandoning their erstwhile simplicity; they "had not yet thought of spending their superfluity on servants who could be rung for" (152). Instead, he shows Lapham indulging in another form of conspicuous consumption and class awareness, namely the construction in Boston's fashionable Back Bay area of a mansion which will impress his pecuniary strength and social standing upon the community.

The egalitarian Lapham has been oblivious to issues of status until he becomes acquainted with the Coreys, an aristocratic family who represent the traditional Boston elite. Through them Howells implies that the old Boston merchant class has lost economic leadership to the industrial manufacturer and now in addition fears the loss of social leadership. "The suddenly rich are on a level with any of us nowadays," Bromfield Corey observes regretfully, and continues "Money buys position at once" (60). "Snobbery," Lionel Trilling observed, "is pride in status without pride in function," and Howells invidiously contrasts the pride in status of the functionless Coreys (Bromfield Corey is a dilettante artist) with the homely pride in function of Lapham (Trilling, 1970, 212). If the Coreys and their class are guilty of a snobbish aloofness toward the parvenus, Lapham, Howells illustrates, also has all the arrogant faith of the bourgeois in the power of money to buy him whatever he wishes. His contact with the Coreys alerts him to the niceties of stratification in the Boston hierarchy and to the necessity of consolidating his financial success by establishing himself and his family in Society. Constructing the Beacon Street mansion is his first gesture in that direction.

He is elated at the acceptance into the Boston elite which a dinner invitation from the Coreys implies, and the dinner itself provides a fine comedy of manners as we observe the gauche Laphams clumsily negotiating a path through all the unspoken proprieties of a Society occasion. Tom Corey, having been exposed to the more egalitarian West, has a more open and democratic outlook than his family. He recognizes Lapham's essentially fine nature, courts his daughters, and goes to work for him, so restoring that active participation in economic life which his "India Merchant" grandfather had enjoyed but which his father had lost. It was necessary, Howells, implies, for the Boston Brahmins to revivify their class by allying themselves with the new business forces in America. For Lapham, however, his association with the Coreys and his financial pride tempt him toward the abandonment of two major elements of agrarian ideology.

First, he attempts a transition from the Protestant scheme of modest living to a tentatively asserted scheme of conspicuous consumption. Secondly, he deserts his erstwhile egalitarianism by identifying himself with the rigid and snobbish hierarchy of the Boston Brahmins: "He had always said that he did not care what a man's family was, but the presence of the young Corey as an applicant to him for employment, as his guest, as the possible suitor to his daughter, was one of the sweetest flavors that he had yet tasted in his success" (85). The "moral" of the novel as summarized by Howells at the end refers not only to the main developments of the business plot but also to these ideological desertions: "Adversity had so far been his friend that it had taken from him all hope of the social success for which people crawl and truckle, and restored him, through failure and doubt and heartache, the manhood which prosperity had so nearly stolen from him" (330). Lapham, influenced by the Coreys' regard, had begun to "crawl and truckle" for social success and to prejudice his "manhood" by abandoning his modest lifestyle and democratic frontier outlook. After he has lost his mansion, so symbolic of his social rise, and becomes bankrupt, he no longer takes a snobbish pride in the Corey connection: "Neither he nor his wife thought now that their daughter was marrying a Corey; they thought only that she was giving herself to the man who loved her" (330). Their reversal of fortune thus leads not only to the resumption of a frugal, agrarian way of life, but also to the reassertion of egalitarian humane values.

Other ideological issues also play their part in the thematic structure of the novel but these are more closely integrated with the central ethical dilemma of the business plot.[3] In his characterization of Lapham Howells fused his own moral absolutism with the moral integrity demanded by the two dominant value systems of the early nineteenth century—Jeffersonian individualism with its premise of self-restraint, and Protestantism with its emphasis on the scrutiny of all actions for their ethical implications. Yankee Silas Lapham is steeped in Christian ethics (but not religion) and is endowed with an acutely moral conscience. One of the functions of the romantic sub-plot in which the Laphams agonize over the correct course to adopt in regard to Tom's proposal to Penelope is to emphasize the centrality of ethical considerations to their lives.[4] Existence for Silas Lapham, as for Howells, we are made aware is inescapably moral. He is independent in his judgment, self-reliant in his actions, and guided by his "underlying principles" (297). There is, however, a stain on his otherwise spotless record, one ethically dubious act, a sin, to which he later attributes his downfall.

One of the major drivers of economic activity, as Adam Smith famously noted, is self-interest, but this is also one of the key threats to moral rectitude. And Lapham once allowed his own gain to overcome his scruples, for he forced his former partner, Milton K. Rogers, out of the business so he could reap all the profits himself. His conscience is only slightly uneasy over this maneuver which he justifies as common business practice, but his wife sensitizes him to its moral dubiousness, and in an effort to rectify his previous selfishness he makes some large loans to Rogers. Then, various developments characteristic of the late-nineteenth-century commercial world force Lapham—and here we clearly see Howells' realist strategy of grounding his fiction in the actual processes and complexities of contemporary society—to the point of yielding to amoral self-interest once again. The novel's business plot, therefore, dramatizes the difficulty of maintaining a proper equilibrium between self-interest and moral scruple, a balance central to Jeffersonian individualism, against the corrupting pressures of the Gilded Age.

The stock market, a significant factor in post-bellum finance capitalism, tempts Lapham to speculate in stocks and shares, and he finds himself caught up in the dynamic of the accumulation of capital. His wife remarks, "Seems as if the more money he got, the more he wanted to get" (138). When other matters are already pressing him he begins to make heavy losses on his investments, and consequently reverts to his earlier moral stance on speculation: "I always felt the way I said about it—that it wan't any better than gambling, and I say so now. It's like betting on the turn of a card" (274).

Further, Lapham is shown caught in a crisis of overproduction. American industry grew so rapidly in the 1870s and 1880s that its productive capacity repeatedly outstripped demand, resulting in the periodic closure of factories and economic slumps. "The market's overstocked. It's glutted. There wan't anything to do but shut *down*," he tells his wife after closing his paint factory (265). In order to raise demand American businessmen expanded into foreign markets and this is represented in the novel by Lapham's hiring Tom Corey in preparation for entering the Latin American market. But with the current downturn in business Lapham is caught with a great deal of his capital tied up in its commodity form in unsold stocks of paint. Much of his capital is also tied up in his new Beacon Street mansion and when it burns down he is unable to realize a fraction of his investment so that his urge to self-aggrandizement also contributes to his downfall. The fire, of course, is a heavily contrived development which too obviously plays its role in the theme of retribution and a return to simplicity.[5]

Many firms in the 1880s sought to avoid price competition by forming combinations or "trusts." And Howells places Lapham in this context by showing him attempting to set up a "trust" with some West Virginia manufacturers. However, for this he requires a large amount of ready capital which thanks to the stock market losses, the slump, and the mansion he does not possess. When he tries to raise it from bankers and associates he discovers that in the late-nineteenth-century business world moral scrupulosity and fairness are not reciprocated. A good name is no longer sufficient to secure credit. Instead, there is a merciless spirit of Social Darwinism abroad: "He had not found other men so very liberal or faithful with him; a good many of them appeared to have combined to hunt him down" (284). Howells does not elucidate the details of Lapham's commercial transactions during his financial collapse, as Dreiser does of Cowperwood's in *The Financier* (1912), for his purpose is not to focus on the processes of economic failure themselves but on the moral quandary into which his entrepreneur is driven by the threat of bankruptcy.

Lapham could sell some mills he owns out West but he knows they're worthless and he is righteously indignant when Rogers suggests he unload them on to some naïve English buyers: "And do you think that I am going to steal these men's money to help you plunder somebody in a new scheme?" (296). But financial pressures bear more and more heavily on him, bringing him face to face with ruin and causing him to waver in his resolution. The individualistic urge of economic self-interest, the intensely competitive business milieu, and the desire to preserve his social success all war with his refusal to act unethically and bring on an acute crisis of moral decision. This is intensified by the English agents' connivance in the deal and Rogers' offer to take responsibility for the transaction on himself. Having skillfully sketched in the cumulative pressures, Howells brings his protagonist to a moment of great trial: "He walked out into the night air every pulse throbbing with the strong temptation. . . . It was for him alone to commit this rascality—if it was a rascality—or not" (301). Howells has also been at pains to emphasize Lapham's isolation at this crucial time. Alienated from members of his own class by their pursuit of unrestrained self-interest, from the Boston Brahmins by their snobbish aloofness, and from his wife by her unjust suspicions of his infidelity, he is thrown back on his Protestant capacity for self-communion and the strength of his "underlying principles."

This time, resisting the lure of self-interest and material gain, he keeps steadfast to those principles and retains his moral integrity. He turns the deal down so precipitating his bankruptcy and, a poor but purified man, he returns to the Vermont homestead, where, improbably, not even the stigma of debt follows him. There is a strong note of cultural nostalgia in Howells' image of the Laphams' return to "the day of small things" as Persis describes their reversal of fortune. There, on the farm, far from the complex moral pressures associated with industrial capitalism, the simple lifestyle and values of the agrarian era live on and are validated by Lapham's prescriptive example. For Mr Sewell he provides a "moral spectacle" and he has been restored, Howells assure us, to that "manhood which his prosperity had so nearly stolen from him" (335). There is thus a double meaning in the title: his "rise" though initially social, is ultimately ethical.[6] Material success and moral integrity, Howells suggests, were unable to coexist in the 1870s and 1880s and the only *right* way to act in business was to obey the traditional dictates of the Protestant ethic and Jeffersonian individualism.

Howells was unequivocal about the didactic purpose of writing. "No conscientious man," he wrote, "can now set about painting an image of life without perpetual question of the verity of his work, and without feeling bound to distinguish so clearly that no reader of his may be misled between what is right and what is wrong, and what is noble and what is base, what is health and what is perdition, in the actions and the characters he portrays" (Kirk, 1959, 48–49). *The Rise of Silas Lapham* is thus a morality tale for the Gilded Age, demonstrating the triumph of ethical principle over business expediency and holding up the Yankee paint manufacturer as an *exemplum* of the good and noble, of how indeed all entrepreneurs ought to behave.

Fortunately, Howells was not only a moralist but also a realist in his fiction, and his quality of light irony, his humane sympathy, and his fine capacity for realizing scene and character based on sharp observation of everyday detail and a scrupulous attention to the individual idiom of personal speech mean that the novel rises far above the drily schematic. Yet, though he emphasized the importance of realism in the novel and was America's foremost practitioner of it at the time, he failed to consider how his didactic intention might compromise or even contradict realism's requirement of accurate representation. The first question we ought to ask of a book, he said, is "Is it true?—true to the motives, the impulses, the principles that shape the life of actual men and women?" (Kirk, 1959, 49). So, is the novel "true" as an image of business life? Is it true to the "motives" and "principles" of actual entrepreneurs in the late nineteenth century?

On the basis of broad historical evidence the answer can only be in the negative. This was, after all, the era of the graphically termed "Robber Barons" who grabbed so much of the new land's wealth and established unassailable monopolistic positions by the most ruthless means.[7] Business morality was kept distinctly separate from personal morality, and such a dilemma as Lapham agonized over never disturbed for a moment even the most scrupulous of the entrepreneurs. The climactic decisions of their lives were not moral but material and practical, related to concrete problems of manufacture, transport, expansion, and finance. The harsh realities of competitive business life exist only in the wings in the novel and Howells' ethical and domestic focus succeeds in softening and humanizing, and so mystifying, the rampant industrial capitalism which demanded a more "warts and all" presentation than the pioneer of American realism could bring himself to provide.[8]

As a product of frontier society and its ideologies, Howells tended to analyze social situations at this point in his life in warmly optimistic and individualistic terms. "Our novelists," he observed approvingly, "therefore, concern themselves with the more smiling aspects of life, which are the more American, and seek the universal in the individual rather than the social interests" (Kirk, 1959, 62). This attitude lies behind the relative absence in the novel of any sense of Lapham's belonging to a class composed of similarly situated people with common interests and under common threat from the growing labor militancy of the day. The one or two hints about the manufacturer's relationship with his workers imply he is a paternalistic employer and his visit to Zerilla's dingy home offers only the briefest glimpse of life "on the other side of the tracks." Howells was later to demonstrate a greater awareness of the class basis of society, but in *Silas Lapham* his image of American capitalism is naïve, indicating that he did not understand the impersonal economic forces that held sway within it. His criticism of laissez-faire capitalism is a moral and not a social one, a perspective that allowed him to make the issues in the book clear within his own terms but which prevented him from correlating those issues more closely with the central social and business conflicts of his day.

He did, however, modify his viewpoint to accommodate historical change, his own observation of industrial conditions, and a growing awareness of social injustice. He later adopted a socialist and collectivist stance and by his next important novel, *A Hazard of New Fortunes* (1890), his critique had broadened to include a social as well as moral dimension. This novel is his most ambitious, presenting, as Pizer remarks, an "extraordinary breadth," and Howells' enlargement of perspective is evident in his treatment of the entrepreneur figure, Jacob Dryfoos (Pizer, 2013, 1). He, like Lapham, begins economic life as an independent farmer with all the traditional virtues, including "hard-headed practical commonsense," "intense individualism," and the "conservative good citizenship, which had been his chief moral experience" (Howells, [1890] 1965, 233–34). Industrial change suddenly intrudes upon the stable agrarian pattern in the form of natural gas found beneath his land, and against his better judgment Dryfoos sells his farm for the huge sum offered. Initially, his loss of occupation and the meaning it gave his life leaves him disconsolate, but then he discovers speculation and with seemingly inexhaustible luck rapidly turns his thousands into millions.

Uprooting themselves from Indiana, he and his family vainly try to adapt themselves to the lifestyle of the nouveaux riches in New York. This marks a significant choice of setting for Howells, reflecting his awareness of New York's growing status as a metropolitan economic centre. The Dryfoos' mansion and the artifacts in it, "whose costliness was too evident," testify to their tasteless conspicuous consumption. Dryfoos, it is indicated, may drive a hard bargain but he never swindles or double-crosses, and once again Howells paints his fictional representative of a late-nineteenth-century entrepreneur as essentially a virtuous man. The transformation from Midwest farmer to Wall-Street speculator has, however, had its costs, and here, as in the previous novel, Howells implicitly equates farmstead simplicity with moral integrity and urban wealth and sophistication with moral decay. "He must have undergone a moral deterioration, an atrophy of the generous instincts," Basil March remarks of old Dryfoos, "and I don't see why it shouldn't have reached his mental make-up. He has sharpened, but he has narrowed; his sagacity has turned into suspicion, his caution to meanness, his courage to ferocity. . . . I am not very proud when I realise that such a man and his experience are the ideal and ambition of most Americans" (199). Howells was addressing an audience that took the entrepreneur for its model and hero and so he tries to define critically that spiritual impoverishment, that cultural barrenness, which results from the loss of productive function and the monomaniacal pursuit of money.

By the time of *Hazard* Howells had come to appreciate the role of social forces. Through Basil March, the novel's liberal centre of consciousness, he expresses the proviso that character is partly to blame for the faults of laissez-faire capitalism but also acknowledges that "conditions *make* character" (396). The moral judgment on Dryfoos is therefore softened by the consideration that he is more the passive victim of industrial and social change than its dynamic hero. Far from it being he who has made the money, it is the money which has made him, and Howells' portraiture generates pity rather than condemnation. Dryfoos becomes conscious of the loss which his sudden riches brought in their train but unlike Lapham—and here we see a sterner, less retrospective vision at work—he cannot, any more than American society at large, return to the old agrarian way: "We *can't* go back!" shouted the old man fiercely. "There's no farm any more to go back to. The fields is full of gas wells and oil wells and hell holes generally; the house is tore down, and the barn's goin" (207–8). It sounds like the agonized cry of a whole culture that has just awoken to the relentless irreversibility of the industrial changes it has embraced and to the irrecoverable loss of the homestead republic with its democratic and moral virtues.[9] In his earlier portrait of the entrepreneur Howells was concerned to demonstrate the continuing relevance of the traditional moral and democratic values to the age of big business, but in *Hazard* his confidence in this agrarian ideology's durability and adequacy is considerably qualified and he succeeds in communicating (in spite of himself perhaps) its insufficiency in a society of plutocrat and proletarian.

For it was while he was writing *The Rise of Silas Lapham* in his new Beacon Street home in Boston that he became increasingly aware of the disparities in wealth which gave the lie to that egalitarianism on which his confidence was based. Simply to be alone in the relative comfort of his huge empty house on the water's edge in August made him feel guilty. "How unequally things are divided in this world," he wrote to his father, "While these beautiful airy wholesome houses are uninhabited, thousands upon thousands of poor creatures are stifling in wretched barracks in the city here, whole families in one room. I wonder that men are so patient with society as they are" (Cady, 1956, 244–45). His social conscience was further sensitized by two developments. First, there was the trial and execution in an atmosphere of hate and hysteria and on the basis of spurious evidence of some anarchists for their alleged part in the 1886 Chicago Haymarket Riot. Secondly, there was his first-hand experience of industrial conditions when in February 1887 he visited factories in Lowell, Massachusetts. He was shocked by what he saw there and used the experience in *Annie Kilburn* (1888) in which he condemned laboring conditions and false, middle-class philanthropy.[10]

Howells was familiar with the ideas of the American social critic, Henry George, who in *Progress and Poverty* (1879) had questioned traditional American confidence in the virtues of American society, and he also knew the ideas of Marx as predigested for the American public by Laurence Gronlund, author of *The Co-operative Commonwealth* (1884). Tolstoy, too, became a spiritual as well as a literary influence. Increasingly, his intimate correspondence focused on the problems of contemporary American society and expressed a critical attitude. He was becoming radicalized. He announced to Henry James,

> I should hardly like to trust pen and ink with all the audacity of my social ideas, but after fifty years of optimistic content with "civilisation" and its ability to come out right in the end, I now abhor it, and feel that it is coming out all wrong in the end, unless it bases itself anew on a real equality. Meantime, I wear a fur-lined overcoat and live in all the luxury my money can buy. (Cady, 1958, 91)[11]

He was thus caught in the contradictions of the humane liberal who, though he might feel sympathy for the poor, could never express solidarity with them since his own financial and class position by no means coincided with theirs. Howells was both Ohio democrat and dean of American letters and the egalitarian thrust of his social thought coexisted uneasily with the income and social success that he enjoyed. So hand in hand with his moral indignation at the poverty produced by industrial capitalism there walked a guilty acknowledgment of his egotistic indulgence. *A Hazard of New Fortunes* is a much broader, more comprehensive representation of the conflict between ethics and business than *The Rise of Silas Lapham* because as well as portraying the entrepreneur figure it explores and dramatizes these ambivalences of social life, these contradictions which contemporary circumstances forced upon the humane middle-class liberal and the weak compromises that usually resulted.

In 1888 Howells moved from Boston to New York and he begins the novel with a similar migration by the Marches. They leave the comparatively protected milieu of the older cultural centre for the teeming heterogeneity of the economic capital, and through their reactions of bewilderment and disillusion Howells presents his own sense of social change and class conflict. New York better represented the new social and ethical context created by industrialization and urbanization, and Howells, both fascinated and repelled by the city, could draw upon his own fresh experience for striking realistic detail and perceptive psychological response. The Marches' middle-class sentiments, then, provide the novel's controlling perspective, but they are brought into relief, redefined and measured, against several other ideological positions embodied in appropriately conceived characters.

Jacob Dryfoos, the entrepreneur figure already mentioned, totally accepts the "dog eat dog" basis of laissez-faire capitalism and has nothing but contempt for the workers. Fulkerson is a more humane but nevertheless complacent apologist for the status quo. "One of those Americans," Howells tells us, jibing at the shallow optimism which he had found inadequate, "whose habitual conception of life is unalloyed prosperity" (Howells, [1890] 1965, 80). Ranged as a battery of representative critical viewpoints upon the class system are: the Christian Socialism of Conrad Dryfoos who prefers the rigors of charity work to the luxurious entertainments of his class; the patriarchalism of Colonel Woodburn who compares the cash-nexus callousness of the industrial North unfavorably with the feudal relations of a romanticized antebellum South; and the socialism of the old German, Lindau, who in the most cogent critique presented in the novel points to capitalism and big business as the real cause of mass poverty and the corruption of the ideals contained in the Declaration of Independence:

> Dere *iss* no Ameriga any more. You start here free and brafe, and you glaim for efery man the righdt to life, liperty, and de bursuit of habbiness. And where haf you ented? No man that vorks vith his hands among you hass the liperty to bursue his habbiness. He iss the slafe of some richer man, some gompany, some gorporation, dat rindts him down to the least he can lif on, and rops him of the marchin of his earnings that he might pe habby on.

The republic, he says, is "bought oap by monobolies, and ron by drusts and gompanies, and railroadts and oil gompanies" (285–86).

Edwin H. Cady regards Lindau as a fanatic and idealist committed to an "irrational philosophy of violence" (1958, 105), but such a view, heavily ideological in itself, distorts Howells' presentation. Nowhere in the novel, through direct or reported speech, does Howells show Lindau advocating the destruction of life or property or calling for violent revolution. It is the *tone* of his arguments that is violent, not their content. The sentiments put into his mouth were shared, after all, in part by that gentlemanly Anglophile, Henry James, whose views, though more measured in their expression, still directed their critical thrust at the same objects. He remarks in *The American Scene* (1907),

> You are as constantly reminded, no doubt, that these rises in enjoyed value shrink and dwindle under the icy breath of Trusts and the weight of the new remorseless monopolies that operated as no madnesses of ancient personal power thrilling us on the historic page ever operated. . . . There is such a thing, in the United States, it is hence to be inferred, as freedom to grow up to be blighted, and it may be the only freedom in store for the smaller fry of future generations. (James, 1968, 136–37)

Howells' solitary stand in defense of the Chicago anarchists had taught him that the conservative prejudices of a large section of the American public, including his friends, required undermining and not reinforcement. In the light of the Haymarket affair any characterization of a left-wing opponent of laissez-faire capitalism as a bomb-throwing hothead would have seemed reprehensible to Howells since it was upon such vicious caricature that a conscienceless repression had based itself. Consequently, Howells takes pains to portray Lindau as a highly cultured, patriotic (he is an injured veteran of the American Civil War), compassionate and justly embittered man. However, he was also aware of the limitations of his audience, and he knew that such socialistic views could not be put forward in the novel unless they were at least formally, if not polemically, countered. The process of emasculating Lindau's subversive critique is accomplished first by the careful rendering of the German accent, which emphasizes his foreignness, and secondly, by the Marches' evasion or complacent rejection of his arguments.[12]

For the Marches represent the liberal centre, halfway between the callous Social Darwinism of Dryfoos senior and the socialism of Lindau. Basil March, humane, observant, critical, is, in the Jamesian phrase, "the centre of revelation" of the novel, and the story charts his deepening unease as his traditional ideology of Jeffersonian individualism and egalitarianism is forced to come to terms with the brute realities and inequalities of urban-industrial America. On his arrival New York seems a personal, hospitable place. The familiar hotels and restaurants welcome him and his wife and reception clerks and waiters remember their names. Their initial image of the city is thus inevitably colored by their financial and class security, and they do not suffer the dispiriting anonymity which is often the newcomer's fate. Though the city teems with thousands of immigrants, these do not threaten the Bostonian Marches with "dispossession" of their Americanness as they would with Henry James (James, 1968, 86). Rather, the Marches relish the sights and sounds of the ethnically diverse neighborhoods. To them the immigrants are so "picturesque" and "gay," an exclusively aesthetic appreciation that denies the human reality of poverty. "I don't find so much misery in New York," Basil announces complacently to his wife (50). Gradually, Howells displaces this bland view of the city by showing how a growing acquaintance with the suffering of the poor deepens and humanizes the Marches' response.

To appreciate fully the mild and possibly self-deprecatory irony with which Howells depicts the Marches' accommodation to an uncomfortable social awareness we must recall a telling sociological detail, namely that they receive an unearned income of two thousand dollars from stocks together with an unspecified rent from their Boston house. The average working wage at this time was one dollar fifteen cents a day or about four hundred dollars annually, assuming a full year's work. Howells, therefore, means us to recognize that the Marches are relatively well-off and that they belong in a moderate way to the propertied class. As sensitive, humane people they may come to have sympathy for the poor, but they could never, as Lindau does, express solidarity with them since to do so would clash with their own class and material interests. This tension between altruism and egoism in which the Marches are caught and the shifts they adopt in order to resolve or evade its contradictions provide the novel's central ideological issues.

As prosperous citizens of the republic, the Marches are convinced of the essential rightness of the American social system and they cling to its ideology of individualism and egalitarianism. Lindau tries to expose that ideology to them as false consciousness in the light of contemporary conditions, but they resist his criticisms, preferring the security of their reassuring middle-class values. It alarmed Mrs March "to hear American democracy denounced as a shuffling evasion" and to be told that "there was not equality of opportunity in America," and Basil dismisses Lindau's ideas as "false" even though he himself recognizes the loss of the old egalitarian society and the rise of an aristocracy in fact if not in name (262, 249). It is part of Howells' irony that despite March's growing perception of the arrogance of the nouveaux riches and the undeserved suffering of the urban poor, he does not shift his ideological stance until his own material prospects and middle-class lifestyle are threatened by the collapse of the journal. The sudden possibility of himself having to struggle in a hostile society inclines him to a much more cynical view of American civilization: "Someone always has you by the throat, unless you have someone else in *your* grip." He has arrived at Jacob Dryfoos's conception of society as Darwinian struggle, but unlike Dryfoos he finds such a state of affairs reprehensible for the individual corruption it entails: "So we go on, pushing and pulling, climbing and crawling, thrusting aside and trampling underfoot; lying, cheating, stealing; and when we get to the end, covered with blood and dirt and sin and shame, and look back over the way we've come . . . I don't think the prospect can be pleasing" (395–96).

March tends to think of society largely in moral categories and sees capitalists and entrepreneurs naively in individual ethical terms as men of good will or ill will. He criticizes Jacob Dryfoos for his moral decay but not for his social parasitism as a speculator on Wall Street, and he seems unable to see (as Howells seems unable) that membership of the propertied class inevitably involves the selfishness of living off others' work. Yet, in the compromises of viewpoint Basil is forced into, Howells does present a half-hearted adoption of social determinism.

In the moralist-individualist perspective derived from Protestantism the blame for conditions lies not with the social structure but with personal character. Mrs March propounds this view, but her husband, while partly agreeing, also significantly qualifies it: "We can't put it all on conditions;

we must put some of blame on character. But conditions *make* character; and people are greedy and foolish, and wish to have and to shine, because having and shining are held up to them by civilisation as the chief good of life" (396–97). This mild determinism with its insight into the conditioning to which individual values and behavior are subject represents the farthest point of the Marches' education into the real basis of the new socioeconomic order. Toward the novel's close there is a retreat from the understanding gained and the book's conclusion is marked by a conservative reassertion of the continuing reality of American democracy and egalitarianism as Lindau's views are finally dismissed as "wrong" (409).

A Hazard of New Fortunes, then, like *The Rise of Silas Lapham*, represents the testing of a traditional ideology against the complex contemporary situation and the eventual validation of that ideology. Unconvincingly, Christian moralism and middle-class values (and middle-class income) are left secure at the end so that the novel's departing note is one of comfort and reassurance. It is to the climactic strike scene that we have to look for any audacity in Howells' presentation of the ugly, morally ambivalent aspects of business.

In the year he moved to New York Howells came face to face with the war between capital and labor when a serious traction strike was called. The dispute lasted for months and erupted into violence when the company brought in strike-breakers and every car had to be guarded by police. Howells uses this conflict to bring his plot to a dramatic head and provide a focal event around which the main characters' contrasting social perspectives are brought into relief. Basil March, petty-bourgeois intellectual, stands on the side-lines and becomes a "philosophical observer" of the struggle; Jacob Dryfoos, millionaire speculator, is not so detached, regarding the strikers as a "pack of dirty, worthless whelps" who deserve to be shot; and Conrad, his Christian-Socialist son, believes they have "a righteous cause, though they go the wrong way to help themselves" (378, 380). Even this gentle assertion of support is too much for the speculator embittered at his son's class betrayal and he hits him, causing a wound on the temple. Subsequently, Conrad comes upon a violent scene in which strikers are being attacked by the police and there sees Lindau about to be clubbed to the ground. As he moves to the old man's rescue he is shot through the heart, and Basil March (by one of those strained coincidences to which Howells occasionally resorts) finds the bodies of the two men lying together on the sidewalk. It is an intense and emotive passage of social drama, and a close reading reveals how Howells uses certain details to manipulate our feelings against the police and by implication in favor of Lindau and the strikers.

Firstly, he emphasizes the brutality of the police when they attack the strikers: "Conrad could see how they struck them under the rims of their hats; the blows on their skulls sounded as if they had fallen on stone" (383).

Secondly, he reminds us of Lindau's age and patriarchal dignity just before the old German becomes a target, and of his infirmity and self-sacrifice during the Civil War when he throws up his arm to protect himself and Conrad sees "the empty sleeve dangle in the air, over the stump of his wrist" (383). Conrad, it seems, is shot by a policeman. This is left unclear, but since the bullet came from a tramcar which had police guards it is a plausible deduction. The specific and general culpability of the police is further confirmed by Conrad's perception on immediately being shot of the policeman who is clubbing Lindau. His face "was not bad, nor cruel; it was like the face of a statue, fixed, perdurable; a mere image of irresponsible and involuntary authority" (384). In one remarkable moment of insight Howells succinctly conveys the petrifaction of the human responses and the abdication of moral responsibility—the pejorative tone of that "irresponsible" is forceful—the dehumanization in short that the policeman has undergone during his metamorphosis from individual to "authority."

Howells thus makes it plain that Conrad and Lindau are both victims of police repression, a repression that is associated in two ways with the ruling class.[13] Before being clubbed into silence the indomitable old socialist accuses the police of being the partisan agents of the bosses, and physical violence as an aspect of authority is embodied directly before the strike passage in Jacob Dryfoos, arrogant millionaire. Why does Howells have Dryfoos hit his son? It seems unlikely that a writer of his mature artistry would have engineered the incident solely to exploit some coffin-side sentimentality later. The wounding works to prefigure the mortal wounding by the police, and the authoritarian father's blow against his son's opposition is the dramatic equivalent of the ruling class's violence against those who threatened its domination.[14] That Dryfoos himself is an indirect victim of that violence is, of course, an irony calculated to enforce the pacifist point that those who advocate the use of brute force against others may themselves come to suffer by it. "I should hardly like to trust pen and ink with all the audacity of my social ideas," Howells wrote, and he seems to be conveying dramatically here what he dare not have made explicit. Interpreted in this way, *A Hazard of New Fortunes* reveals more tensions in its attitudes than are superficially apparent. The novel also demonstrates how bravely Howells represented in fictional terms the ideological contradictions and moral ambivalences generated by late-nineteenth-century capitalism.

NOTES

1. See Crowley (1999) for an exposition of his "ascension to glory as an exemplar of the American Victorian ethos."

2. Crowley (1999, 102–103); for a succinct summary of Howells criticism over the decades see Rubin 2008. Rubin comments on his ambivalent status: "Among canonical American writers Howells continues to attract both significant interest and intriguing indifference," 2.

3. See Pizer (1993), "The Ethical Unity of *The Rise of Silas Lapham*," in Cady and Budd (1993, 65–70).

4. Pizer (1993) points out the parallelism between the two plots: "The thematic similarity in the two plots is that both involve a principle of morality which requires that the individual determine correct action by reference to the common good rather than an individual need" (Cady and Budd, 1993, 66). G. Thomas Tanselle, "The Architecture of *The Rise of Silas Lapham*" in Cady and Budd (1993, 104–31), also stresses the close interrelationship between the two plots and the structural symmetry of the novel.

5. It thus constitutes a counterexample to the argument for the artistry of the novel which Tanselle (1993), makes in "The Architecture of the *The Rise of Silas Lapham*" in Cady and Budd (1993, 104–31). Bennett (1959) also points to "the incredible patchwork of coincidence which Howells is forced to employ to satisfy his own dicta," 187.

6. As Pizer 1993 points out: "The main plot of *The Rise of Silas Lapham* concerns Silas's financial fall and moral rise," Cady and Budd (1993, 65).

7. I am invoking here, of course, Matthew Josephson, *The Robber Barons: The Great American Capitalists 1861–1901* (1934, reprinted London, Eyre and Spottiswode: 1962)

8. As S. Foster (1978) remarks in "W. D. Howells: *The Rise of Silas Lapham*," in Williams 1978, Howells "embraces ethical idealism which risks being destructive of Realism" (176).

9. Rubin (2008) after listing all the social changes in late-nineteenth-century America comments on the "nostalgic sense of loss, alienation, and discontinuity" these had brought about, 4.

10. Howells stood alone among prominent Americans in publicly defending the anarchists and in petitioning the governor of Illinois for their death sentences to be commuted (Cady 1958, 64, 79–80).

11. Quoted in Cady 1958, 91. See George Warren Arms, "Further Enquiry into Howells' Socialism," *Science and Society*, 3 (1939), 245–48. Parrington (1930) pointed out how radical Howells was for his era and argued that he was "the first distinguished American man of letters to espouse Marxist socialism," 156.

12. Kaplan (1988) makes a perceptive point about Lindau's language: "In the figure of Lindau, Howells questions one of his own fundamental assumptions about realism: that all Americans speak a common language—the language "we all know"—which stems from and refers to the shared social reality," 58. Nettels (1988) also notes, "Finally, dialect prevents Lindau, who voices many of Howells's convictions . . . from appearing to be Howells's spokesman," 95. There is no space here to go into the origins of the Lindau figure or his various aspects, but see Bauch (2008), and Darda (2014).

13. Cady (1958) thinks otherwise: "It's Lindau who is the immediate precipitating agent of Conrad Dryfoos' death; and he dies too, victim also of his irrational

philosophy of violence" (105). This is a misreading both of Howells' presentation of Lindau and of the police violence.

14. Kaplan (1988) points out how Howells suspends the narrative concerning the strike to intercalate the scene from earlier in the day between Dryfoos and his children, thus enforcing the parallelism: "This splicing of scenes forces the reader to experience the confrontation between Dryfoos and his children in the midest of the violence on the city streets," 60.

REFERENCES

Arms, George Warren. 1939. Further Enquiry into Howells' Socialism. *Science and Society*, 3: 245–48.

Barton, Cyril. 2007. Howells's Rhetoric of Realism: The Economy of Pain(t) and Social Complicity in *The Rise of Silas Lapham* and *The Minister's Charge. Studies in American Fiction*, 29, no. 2 (Autumn): 159–87.

Bauch, Jonathan. 2008. Public German, Private Jew: The Secret Identity of Berthold Lindau in Howells' *A Hazard of New Fortunes. American Literary Realism*, 41, no. 1 (Fall): 14–34.

Bennett, George N. 1959. *William Dean Howells: The Development of a Novelist.* Norman: University of Oklahoma Press.

Cady, Edwin H. 1956. *The Road to Realism: The Early Years 1837–1885 of William Dean Howells*. Syracuse, New York: Syracuse University Press.

———. 1958. *The Realist at War: The Mature Years 1885–1920 of William Dean Howells*. Syracuse, New York: Syracuse University Press.

Cady, Edwin H. and Cady, Norma C. (eds.). 1983. *Critical Essays on W. D. Howells 1866–1920* . Boston, Massachusetts: G. K. Hall & Co.

Cady, Edwin H. and Budd, Louis J. (eds.). 1993. *On Howells: The Best from American Literature*. Durham, North Carolina and London: Duke University Press.

Crowley, John W. 1999. *The Dean of American Letters: The Late Career of William Dean Howells*. Amherst: University of Massachusetts Press.

Darda, Joseph. 2014. The Sacrificial Enterprise: Negotiating Mutilation in W. D. Howells' *A Hazard of New Fortunes. American Literary Realism*, 46, no. 3 (Spring): 210–29.

Hamilton, Geordie. 2009. Rethinking the Politics of American Realism through the Narrative Form and Moral Rhetoric of W. D. Howells' *The Rise of Silas Lapham. American Literary Realism*, 42, no. 1 (Fall): 13–35.

Harman, Charles. 1997. *A Hazard of New Fortunes* and the Reproduction of Liberalism. *Studies in American Fiction*, 25, no. 2 (Autumn): 183–95.

Howells, William Dean. [1885] 1963. *The Rise of Silas Lapham*. New York: Signet.

———. [1890] 1965. *A Hazard of New Fortunes*. Oxford, United Kingdom: Oxford University Press.

James, Henry. [1907] 1968. *The American Scene*. London: Hart-Davis.

Kaplan, Amy. 1988. *The Social Construction of American Realism*. Chicago, Illinois and London: University of Chicago Press.

Kirk, Clara and Rudolf (eds.). 1959. *Criticism and Fiction and Other Essays.* New York: New York University Press.

Kohler, Michelle. 2014. Some Glittering Nondescript Vertebrate: The Provocative Style of Realism in Howells' *A Hazard of New Fortunes. American Literary Realism*, 46, no. 3 (Spring): 189–209.

Nettels, Elsa. 1988. *Language, Race, and Social Class in Howells's America.* Lexington: University of Kentucky Press.

Parrington, V. L. 1930. *Main Currents in American Thought: An Interpretation of American Literature from the Beginning to 1920 Vol. 3.* New York: Harcourt, Brace & Company.

Pizer, Donald. 2013. W. D. Howells' *A Hazard of New Fortunes*: A Mostly Formalist Reading. *American Literary Realism*, 46, no. 1 (Fall): 1–11.

Raczkowski, Christopher. 2008. The Sublime Train of Sight in *A Hazard of New Fortunes. Studies in the Novel*, 40, no. 3 (Fall): 285–307.

Rubin, Lance. 2008. *William Dean Howells and the American Memory Crisis.* Amherst, New York: Cambria Press.

Tawney, R. H. [1926] 1975. *Religion and the Rise of Capitalism.* Harmondsworth: Penguin.

Trilling, Lionel. [1951] 1870. *The Liberal Imagination: Essays on Literature and Society.* Harmondsworth, United Kingdom: Penguin.

Weber, Max. [1930] 1971. *The Protestant Ethic and the Spirit of Capitalism*, translated by Talcott Parsons. London: Allen and Unwin.

Williams, D. A. (ed.). 1978. *The Monster in the Mirror: Studies in Nineteenth-Century Realism.* Oxford, United Kingdom: Oxford University Press.

Young, Arlene. 1992. The Triumph of Irony in *The Rise of Silas Lapham. Studies in American Fiction*, 20, no. 1 (Spring): 45–55.

Chapter 13

The Panic of '93

The Literary Response

Stephen Cox

Remembering his early days on America's Great Plains, an Episcopal bishop described "a remarkable and most critical summer":

> Hot winds from the south blew for weeks at a time. No rain nor even cloud came to shield the crops. The thermometer ranged from one hundred to one hundred and fifteen degrees, Fahrenheit, in the shade. The air was filled with a fine, impalpable dust, which made the sun look dark red like a ball of fire. The wheat and oats were dried up before they ripened. The corn everywhere turned white and dead when two or three feet high. As the people expressed it, "the crops were fired." Pigs and chickens wandered miles from home in search of food, and many of them starved to death. The wild sunflowers, dwarfed by the drought, were gathered for feed and fuel. In August and early autumn, thousands . . . left and moved away. It was a sad sight to see them wending their way slowly over the prairies, homeless and broken-hearted. . . . I traveled twenty-five miles in Holt County [Nebraska] without passing an inhabited house where before all the land had been occupied.

A fellow churchman provided this memory of that place and time:

> Vacant buildings could be seen in almost every direction. This in itself was bad enough, but when we began to realize that the whole country was in the grip of a financial panic, things began to look very serious indeed. . . . [O]ftentimes we labored from early morning until late at night, giving out all kinds of help to the needy. Many of them came long distances over the bleak prairies to ask for sufficient food for themselves and their families for another week.

When did these things happen? Reading the two passages I just quoted, people answer immediately, "the 1930s," "the Great Depression," "the dustbowl of the 1930s." But they're wrong. What the clergymen recalled was not the 1930s but the 1890s (Graves, 1911, 134–35; Beecher, 1950, 51–52). They remembered a time of distress that was almost as bad, by common economic measurements, as that of the 1930s, and perhaps even worse, given the lower level of material culture that had existed beforehand. Yet few contemporary Americans include that time in their vision of history.

This period of economic depression is often called the Panic of '93 or the Crash of '93, after the financial failure that initiated it. It was accompanied by agricultural failure in the central states and by a political struggle so dramatic that one of the era's major political figures, Secretary of the Treasury John G. Carlisle, a man not given to overstatement, said of it: "There has never been a time since the close of the civil war and the settlement of the questions growing out of it when passion and prejudice exerted such a powerful influence in controlling the action of the people upon political and economic questions" (Carlisle, 1895, 4).

If that comment seems quaintly exaggerated, consider the matter-of-fact remark of Allan Nevins, a leading historian of the mid-twentieth century, who had no ideological interest in overstating the troubles of the 1890s or understating those of his own time. He says of the early 1890s, "Probably never before or since in American history have the times been so completely out of joint for so many millions of producers" (Nevins 1932, 590). Nevins' judgment is emphasized by the year of its publication—one of the worst years of the depression of the 1930s. Since then, however, the depression of the 1890s has vanished almost completely from popular memory.

Such vanishings and forgettings are important; they can tell us a good deal about the history of what Americans imagine their history has been—what they think occurred, why they think it occurred, and why they think it was significant or not. This chapter is about authors who experienced the depression of the 1890s, and what they came to think of it, to the degree that they did continue to think of it. In a work of this kind, there can be no question of scientific sampling or scholarly completeness. Only a few authors can be considered, and my focus is on writers of poetry and fiction, who are sometimes, but not always, a literate society's most influential providers of images of the past. My special interest is in writers whose ideological involvements might have made them especially concerned with the events of the 1890s.

The results of my investigation came as a surprise to me. They may surprise other people as well, people who were also nurtured on the idea that a great depression is by its nature a crucial event, fraught with compelling meanings. That is not the message projected by the authors I examine here.

The depression of the 1890s began in May 1893, with sharp declines in industrial stocks. Soon banks were calling in loans, suspending payments in cash, and discovering that they were unable to meet their obligations. By the end of the year, there were 554 bank failures nationwide (Hoffmann, 1970, 58). Deprived of credit, and of cash to meet their payrolls, factories and commercial enterprises began to close. By the middle of 1894, 192 railroad companies were in receivership. Investment shrank; new construction dwindled; wage earnings declined (63, 24–33, 258–63). Unemployment climbed toward 20 percent; crowds of destitute people wandered the streets of commercial cities.[1] To meet a crisis of gold withdrawals from the Treasury, President Grover Cleveland pushed currency reform through Congress; nevertheless, four issues of government bonds were required to raise enough money to stabilize the gold reserve.

In 1894, jobless workmen, rallying in support of various relief proposals, stole trains on Western railways and headed them toward Washington to demand that jobs be made for them. Soon afterward, the American Railway Union added to the distress by going on strike in sympathy with workers striking the Pullman sleeping-car company, which had responded to reduced revenues by reducing wages (without reducing rents in its company town [Nevins, 1932, 611–12]). As rail traffic neared paralysis, Cleveland used force to ensure that the mails went through. After serious violence, particularly in Chicago, the hub of rail transportation, the strike was broken.

The causes of the Panic were varied and complex. Many of the nation's railroads—traditional subjects of government regulation, subsidy, and bribe-farming—were corrupt, mismanaged, and overextended. America's trading partners in Europe, Asia, and Australia were suffering from their own financial instabilities, or disasters, which reduced the total amount of world buying, lowered world prices, and contracted world investments. The failure of the Australian economy and the near collapse of Baring's Bank, an investor in the debts of the Argentine government, had an especially bad effect on American financial confidence. For many years, improvements in mass production had been lowering prices of American manufactured goods. At the same time, advancements in farm productivity and agricultural expansion in what today would be called developing countries were multiplying the world's stock of food and reducing the price of American farm exports. This was a particularly inconvenient trend for farmers who had gone into debt in their attempt to colonize the hot, dry lands of the western prairies, places where a series of wet years was yielding to a series of dry, exhausting ones, resulting in the terrible scenes described in the passages I quoted in my introduction.

One non-agricultural commodity was especially troublesome—silver. The price of silver had been greatly reduced by the opening of large silver mines in the Western United States and by currency reforms undertaken by foreign governments. Most commercial nations had changed from a silver standard to a gold standard. In 1893, India, the largest remaining silver economy, abandoned coinage of silver. America, however, was constrained to faithfulness by the Bland-Allison Act of 1878 and the Sherman Silver Purchase Act of 1890, two successive means of subsidizing mine operators and their employees. The Sherman Act required the federal government to buy immense amounts of silver every year, paying for its purchases with notes redeemable in gold as well as silver. Most people redeemed them in gold.

The contemporary fiction was that one ounce of gold was equal to sixteen ounces of silver. Such a ratio could never have been successfully fixed, because all commodity prices fluctuate, and gold and silver are commodities. One to sixteen was an echo of the relationship established in 1834, by a reform Act of the Jackson administration. In the 1890s, according to both friends and foes of Free Silver, a gold dollar was actually worth about thirty-two silver dollars (Harvey, 1894, 35; Carlisle, 1895, 24). This meant that people could go to the Treasury window and, in effect, exchange a silver dollar for a gold dollar, worth about twice as much. That is what they did, and that is one reason the Treasury's gold reserves sank, during the Crash, below the one hundred million dollars regarded as essential.

This was the crisis that confronted Cleveland soon after he took office in March 1893. He courageously induced Congress to repeal the Sherman Silver Purchase Act, which had many political friends. Later, he mobilized the big banks to float the bond issues needed to replenish American gold reserves. He thus permanently alienated the large portion of his party that claimed to represent miners, farmers, and debtors of all kinds, people who looked to silver as a means of employment, a means of paying their debts in cheap money, or a means of raising the (nominal) price of their labor and the commodities they produced. (They were not equally concerned about increased prices of the commodities they purchased.)

The solution they favored was Free Silver: "the free and unlimited coinage of silver at the ratio of 16 to 1." It became the most popular economic nostrum in American history; to contemporaries, it was "by far the most important question that has been presented for the consideration of the American people during this generation" (Carlisle, 1895, 6). The idea was that anyone with silver should be empowered to bring it to the mints and have it "coined, at the public expense, into silver dollars, at the ratio of 16 to 1 with gold—that is, that sixteen pounds of silver shall be considered equal in value to one pound of gold, and the weights of the coins shall be adjusted accordingly," notwithstanding the higher market value of gold, and that "all the people of the United States shall be compelled by law to receive them as dollars of full value" (23–24). Proponents of Free Silver were reluctant to regard this as inflation. They believed that the nation's money supply had been contracting since 1873, when the government ended the fiat-money system of the Civil War period and (briefly) demonetized silver. Free Silver was therefore an antidote to deflation. Books and pamphlets, such as the engagingly written and immensely popular *Coin's Financial School*, argued that it was the total quantity of money that made commodity values and prosperity increase. Further, when silver was "free," its price would rise to the designated relationship of 16 to 1 with gold (Harvey, 1894, 70, 83, 95–113, 27–38).

To President Cleveland, a hard-money Democrat, these ideas were palpable nonsense, nonsense even worse than the Republicans' standard proposal to raise wages and prices by raising the protective tariff. His reward for fiscal common sense was the most demeaning rebuke ever delivered by an American political party to the man it had elected president. In July 1896, the Democrats met in convention in Chicago, repudiated Cleveland's policies, endorsed Free Silver, and nominated for the presidency a critic of Cleveland whom virtually no one but himself had regarded as a serious contender, thirty-six-year-old William Jennings Bryan. The young lawyer from Nebraska was selected after rousing the convention to frenzy by a speech advocating Free Silver. It is known as the Cross of Gold speech, because of its final lines, concerning the promoters of the gold standard: "Having behind us the commercial interests and the laboring interests and all the toiling masses, we shall answer their demands for a gold standard by saying to them, you shall not press down upon the brow of labor this crown of thorns. You shall not crucify mankind upon a cross of gold" (Bryan, 1896, 234).

Following an exceptionally vigorous campaign, Bryan lost to the Republican nominee, William McKinley, a recent governor of Ohio. Bryan is remembered today, when he is remembered at all, not as the brilliant populist and Progressive, but as the pompous fundamentalist of the play and movie *Inherit the Wind* (1955, 1960)—good evidence that even such dramatic events as his crusade for the presidency drop out of popular memory if no one is interested in portraying them dramatically. People who have heard of Bryan picture him as a bloated bigot, not as a crusader for Progressive causes.

Free Silver, the Cross of Gold, and the Boy Orator of the Platte were not the only phenomena of the nineties that vanished in clouds of amnesia. Still more dramatic and more fated to be forgotten were the mass demonstrations of 1894—the strike of the railroad workers and the protest movements of the unemployed. It is possible that the strike faded from memory because it was just one of many temporarily disruptive labor actions in American history. But the actions of the unemployed were a different matter. They were events so colorful, so appealing to human sympathy, so satisfying to the human desire for theater, yet so quickly lost to memory that in writing about them four decades later, Rose Wilder Lane thought it necessary to assure her readers that "it is all in the files of old newspapers, for those who do not remember those days" (Lane, 1936, 34).

Let's survey this spectacle. In late 1893, Jacob Coxey, a wealthy businessman of Massillon, Ohio, became aware that his ideas about political economy were suddenly solidifying into two legislative proposals and an idea of how to get them enacted. One proposal was that the federal government should provide road-building jobs to anyone who wanted them, financing the project with fiat money—"legal tender"—which, Coxey claimed, was the only authentic kind of money. (Coxey named his son Legal Tender.) The other was that the federal government should provide no-interest loans to local governments that wanted to employ jobless people on public works projects. In exchange for their promise to pay off the bonds in twenty-five years, these governments would receive the value of the bonds in fiat money.[2] Coxey's method of persuading Congress to enact his proposals was a march of unemployed men from Massillon to Washington, where Coxey would deliver a speech on the Capitol steps. That, he thought, should do it.

The Coxeyite pilgrimage was America's first "petition in boots," and the very rare instance of a "march on Washington" that was actually a *march* on Washington. The Commonweal of Christ, otherwise known as Coxey's Army, paraded out of Massillon on Easter, 1894, with about 120 marchers and more than a third as many journalists; it arrived at the Capitol, on schedule, on May 1, with about 300–400 marchers, about the same number of policemen ready to confront them at the Capitol, and many times more people watching them (Schwantes, 1985, 10, 45–46, 178). Publicity had already spread to the far West, where other armies, some of them larger than Coxey's, had begun forming among the unemployed. These too set out for Washington, walking when they had to but preferring to steal or "borrow" trains.

Despite their unorthodox methods, these men were not armies of brigands or vandals. People understood that; the armies were generally treated well by the towns on their way—although hospitality was commonly exhausted by the first army that came along. The pilgrims learned that they could expect assistance from two types of people: those who supported them (a dwindling number), and those who wanted to get rid of them. Railroad officials, judges, and federal marshals were seldom sympathetic.

The journeys of these Western armies involved locomotive chases, mass detentions, near starvations, weird feats of skill, weirder feats of demagoguery, games of wits among marchers, cops, politicians, and railwaymen, the spontaneous construction of miniature republics with their own generals, cabals, and revolutions, their own treasons and heroic displays of loyalty. About these stories, there is nothing more to be desired, except success. Few of the Western pilgrims managed to reach Washington. Coxey himself was arrested at the Capitol for demonstrating on the grounds and *walking on the grass*. The remnants of his army retired into the world beyond newsprint. It had been, nevertheless, an epic performance.

In 1932, two distant imitations of Coxey's Army materialized in Washington. One was a demonstration led by a Roman Catholic priest, James R. Cox, in favor of public works for the unemployed and various other economic programs. Inevitably nicknamed "Cox's Army," it "marched" to Washington in trucks. It was many times larger than the force commanded by Jacob Coxey, but like the original, it has vanished from popular memory. The second was the Bonus March of military veterans demanding payment of an award from Congress. This was also much larger than Coxey's effort, and it used various means of transportation: trucks and trains, provided gratuitously by railroads and state governments, and private motor vehicles (Daniels, 1971, 68, 79–85, 182–83). Despite its deficiency in the romance of the open road, this "march" has lingered at the edges of the mythos of the Great Depression, presumably because President Hoover used force to remove marchers who refused the offer of railway tickets to go home, thereby contributing to his reputation as the man who needed to be replaced by Franklin Roosevelt.

Today, no story of the hard times of the 1890s is remembered even as well as the Bonus March. Whether popular narratives about the New Deal and "the greatest generation" are true or not, they are broadly accepted, compelling myths, capable of rousing passions and motivating behavior.[3] They are constantly used by politicians to do just that. No one exploits the 1890s in that way.

The reason is matter for speculation. At the end of this chapter, I will introduce my own speculative ideas. My main job, however, is to sample the range of historical perspectives that developed in the absence of any dominant myth of the 1890s. Among the authors I am about to consider, differences in psychology, political ideas, and literary approaches come through clearly. Yet these people had one thing in common: they declined to see anything of crucial and lasting importance in the events of the 1890s.

The most extravagant treatment of these events, by anyone recognizable as an important author, has to be that of Vachel Lindsay. A dedicated (he would say a consecrated) myth-maker, Lindsay momentarily adopted William Jennings Bryan as the apotheosis of the great Midwest. He sang of Bryan,

> Candidate for president who sketched a silver Zion,
> The one American Poet who could sing outdoors,
> He brought in tides of wonder, of unprecedented splendor,
> Wild roses from the plains, that made hearts tender,
> All the funny circus silks
> Of politics unfurled,
> Bartlett pears of romance that were honey at the cores,
> And torchlights down the street, to the end of the world.

Lindsay's poem, written in 1919, narrates Bryan's practical defeat and proclaims his spiritual victory. Essentially an elegy, it ends by envisioning its hero as "Gone to join the shadows . . . / Where the kings and the slaves and the troubadours rest." Mythically, Bryan had passed to his reward. Literally, he was still alive. So, of course, was the poet, although he pictures his innocence as having ended with Bryan's electoral misfortune: "Defeat of my boyhood, defeat of my dream." But the poem is not simply an elegy; it is also a satire in which Bryan's opponents, McKinley and his campaign manager, Mark Hanna ("low-browed Hanna"), are rendered as comic-book politicians "who climbed every greasy pole, and slipped through every crack" ("Bryan, Bryan, Bryan, Bryan," Lindsay, 1984, 343, 348–49).

And those people won. Oddly, however, there is no sense that all this wickedness had any consequence, beyond the asserted death of the poet's youth (which had a way of returning, whenever he wrote a poem); no sense that the election, or the depression it was supposed to remedy, was any more serious than any other tremor among the people in Lindsay's superb folk dramas. Nothing appeared to have changed.

An author of very different character was Hamlin Garland, a story writer noted for his treatment of the hardships of farm life on the Great Plains, hardships made vivid for him by the struggles of his own family. For Garland, everything was serious, and stayed that way. Garland was actively involved in the radical movements of the nineties. He was a spokesman for populism, writing for it and touring the Plains to agitate for it. In his memoir of his early life, *A Son of the Middle Border,* the distress of his father and mother, struggling to maintain their farm in South Dakota, spreads across the chapters like a malignant haze—"this barren, empty, laborious life on the plain" (Garland, 1917, 373). Nearing the end of the book, one realizes that one is also nearing 1893, that fateful year, and that there is every reason to expect an account of the Panic and its aftermath. Surely, one thinks, those things will be treated in detail and with appropriate emphasis. Yet the climax of the book is, of all things, the Chicago World's Fair, America's grandest exposition of its own material progress.

Ironically, the Fair and the Panic began together, in mid-1893, but the irony is lost on Garland. He describes the wonders of the Fair; he describes his insistence that his parents visit the Fair and enjoy it; he believes that they did enjoy it, in a way. But, as he sees, they preferred the Thanksgiving that followed, a Thanksgiving full of "squashes and turnips and cranberry sauce and pumpkin pie and mince pie," and a twenty-pound turkey. Earlier, he has lamented the low price of agricultural products; now, he enjoys the low prices paid by consumers such as himself. His sole reference to the Panic is a curious comment that "the nation [was] on its way back to prosperity," which at Thanksgiving 1893 it assuredly was not. His parents' new-found comforts had been created by his own ability to sell his literary skill in the capitalist marketplace—a marketplace that easily accommodated *The Arena,* a radical journal that warmly welcomed his work. This irony, too, goes unnoticed. Success is accepted as perfectly natural. It is as if, despite his economic theories, he had always expected things to work out that way (421, 464–65).

Theodore Dreiser's reminiscences of 1893 are almost as unconcerned with the significance of the Panic, and they also provide a lengthy account of pleasant days at the Fair; the Panic arrives as an afterthought, occasioned by Dreiser's attempts to help two of his numerous siblings find jobs. He himself was working as a journalist, but, he explains, he "had forgotten, or did not know, or the fact did not make a sufficiently sharp impression on me, that this was a panic year (1893) and that there were hundreds of thousands of men out of work, the country over. Indeed, trade was at a standstill, or nearly so" (Dreiser, 1922, 314).

Dreiser, who would later become a communist, regrets his lack of economic awareness: "it had been my first experience of a panic and should have made a deep impression on me had I been of a practical turn." Yet "experience of a panic" seems more generic than specific; indeed, Dreiser still has trouble saying what went on back then. "There were," he regrets to say, "to be hard times for a year or more." Actually, the hard times lasted four or five times longer than a year, but that detail has vanished from his recollection (314, 315). He remembers '93 as just another panic, just another piece of evidence for his developing opinion that no matter what political events take place, "the condition of the average man" will be "about as it ha[s] been before" (370). There appears to have been nothing special about the economic disaster of the 1890s, nothing he needs to pay much attention to. When his story gets to 1894, he briefly mentions Coxey and "his 'hobo' army, at that time moving toward Washington to petition congress against the doings of the trusts" (406). But trusts weren't Coxey's issue; Dreiser just assumes that they would have been.

Unlike Dreiser, Edgar Lee Masters, whose *Spoon River Anthology* (1915) established him as the great elegiac poet of a tragic Midwest, was an activist for Bryan. According to Masters' memoir, *Across Spoon River*, he was present at the Democratic convention in Chicago and heard the Cross of Gold speech. It made him feel that "a new life had come to [him] as to the Democracy [the Democratic Party]." So committed did he become to Bryan's cause that he called Bryan's defeat by the Republicans "the great disaster that had come to the country." He tried to believe, with his friend Vachel Lindsay and with John Peter Altgeld, the Progressive governor of Illinois, that Bryan had been defeated by corrupt means (Masters, 1936, 209, 277, 213, 218).

Yet in Masters' memoir, as in Garland's, the disaster appears unreal, whether one means by "disaster" the crash of '93 or the crash of Bryan in '96. Masters offers some statements of opposition to Republican policies, at home and abroad—as well as a memorable tribute to Theodore Roosevelt, a much more charming acquaintance than Bryan, though a political enemy—but he offers no evidence of post-electoral devastation. The hard times of the 1890s present themselves in an historical aside: "The depression of the period was now making itself felt in Chicago, as well as over the country, and banks were beginning to close their doors" (380–81, 177). Seemingly, the big event of '93 wasn't the panic and depression, but, again, the "wonders" of the World's Fair. Only when Masters has reached the point in his narrative when the summer of the Fair is almost over—and when financial institutions have been collapsing, all over the country, for several months—does he note that "in Chicago we heard of the panic, and Congress was in special session reforming the currency"; that is, repealing the Sherman Silver Purchase Act (168, 171). The sound of the collapse is heard from afar, and vanishes. In *Spoon River* the sound is even softer. That work says much of interest about banks and money and small-town financial oppression, yet nothing about a great disaster. It is haunted by populist attitudes, but not by the ghosts of '93 or '96.

No one could present a starker contrast to Masters and Garland—stalwartly middle class and Middle Western—than Jack London, the West Coast adventurer from the underclass who tried to combine his faith in socialism with his Nietzschean contempt for the creatures of society. In 1906, London was a successful author preparing for a two-year voyage to the South Pacific in his own vessel, *Snark*, and writing of his experiences as a hobo in the 1890s. His tales of life as a tramp, published in 1907 as *The Road*, include a story of his travels with the Coxeyite army led by Charles T. Kelly.

Kelly's army started in California and headed for Washington. London met it in Iowa and abandoned it when it reached the Mississippi. There was no ideological disagreement; he was just tired of being involved. At approximately the same time he was writing *The Road*, London wrote *The Iron Heel* (1908), a grim work of alternative history describing the American people's imminent enslavement by big business and glorifying popular revolts, real and imagined. In this 90,000-word socialist tract I can identify no reference to the depression of the 1890s, beyond a general allusion to "many bitter strikes" that had once been "curbed" in Chicago (London, 1982, 525). Neither is there any reference to the politics or the economic problems of the time in London's account of Kelly's army. It provides no indication of why Kelly was leading an army across the continent; indeed, it represents the army as composed entirely of "hoboes" and "tramps."

Thorough research on the protest armies has demonstrated that they were precisely what they claimed to be, bodies of unemployed workers, skilled and unskilled. They attempted to exclude hoboes and tramps (McMurry, 1968, 49–61, 187–89, 232–34; Schwantes, 1985, 261–66). London doesn't try to explain such non-hobo behavior, but his text describes a well-organized group that enjoyed religious services and other respectable diversions (London, 1982, 289). He, it seems, was one of the army's few actual tramps, romping across the countryside stealing supplies that were meant for his comrades. The kind of events celebrated in his tall tales could happen in any period, any social climate; they are as perennially adolescent as the events in *Tom Sawyer*, although not as charming. Dispelling any sense that something bad was happening to the country, London indicates that for him (and in this story, he is the only one who counts) everything ended well and profitably. Picturing a return to the scene of his "hobo" days, he says: "Last year, while on a lecturing trip, I rode into Des Moines in a Pullman—I don't mean a 'side-door Pullman [a boxcar],' but the real thing" (289). Complacency could be no more complacent. No one would consider London's recollections a story of historical disruption, or even of historical change. From his point of view, there have always been hoboes.

One can discern, at certain points, an unexpected similarity between the recollections of Jack London, proponent of socialism, and the recollections of Rose Wilder Lane, proponent of libertarianism. Neither discerns in the troubles of the 1890s the type of episode that a president of the 1930s called "a rendezvous with destiny" (Franklin Roosevelt, 1936).

Lane, a journalist and novelist and the daughter and collaborator of the enduringly popular Laura Ingalls Wilder, had the ability to tell a good yarn, even in works that were meant to be nonfiction. She also had the ability to enter into her neighbors' ideas, no matter how fictional she thought they were. In the introductory chapter of her fine collection of stories, *Old Home Town*, she tries to recreate America as it appeared to people in her youth. Looking into her girlhood memories, she summons images of "Coxey's Army, 60,000 strong," which

> captured whole railroad divisions in the west and marched footsore from the Mississippi to Washington; when banks failed everywhere and everywhere farm mortgages were foreclosed; when Federal troops guarded government buildings against the mobs and on all the mid-western roads long caravans of covered wagons were crawling east, west, north, south, filled with hungry families, driven by men desperately seeking food, desperately eager to work twelve hours a day for scraps of food—after that Panic, in the years of poverty that seemed unending . . . white and yellow flowers became symbols of fanaticism. To me, a yellow aster still stands for the hated gold standard; the white aster means William Jennings Bryan, whose free coinage of silver would have taken us back to prosperity. But Bryan was defeated by the soulless corporations and our country was forever ruined. (Lane, 1935, 8–9)

The passage has its share of factual errors. Coxey's Army started in Ohio, not at the Mississippi or further west; none of the sympathizing armies numbered more than 2,000 men at any point, and the total was only about 10,000, of whom few ever made it to Washington; there were no mobs requiring troops to guard government buildings (McMurry, 1968, 176, 242).[4] The passage also contains some ironies, unannounced and unexplained, but obvious still. Silver, Lane suggests, ventriloquizing her neighbors, "would have taken us back to prosperity"; yet she regards both the silver and the golden flowers as "symbols of fanaticism." Her emphasis falls on the supposed disaster of Bryan's defeat; yet elsewhere in the chapter there is nothing to indicate that any "country" has been "ruined." The chapter is concerned almost exclusively with the regularities of normal life. In the 1890s, ordinary America was so much poorer in material goods than it was in the 1930s that she needs to describe its hardships in great detail, just to make them plausible; but despite its lack of comforts, that America was still as homey as an old home town could be. No ruins are sighted.

Almost thirty years later, in 1962, Lane returned to her memories of the 1890s. The occasion was the writing of an introduction to her mother's diary of the family's trek from South Dakota, where their farm had failed, to Missouri, where a new farm would become at least marginally successful. Lane sets the scene in this way:

> For seven years there had been too little rain. The prairies were dust. . . . Crop after crop failed. Again and again the barren land must be mortgaged, for taxes and food and next year's seed. The agony of hope ended when there was no harvest and no more credit, no money to pay interest and taxes; the banker took the land. Then the bank failed.
>
> In the seventh year a mysterious catastrophe was world-wide. All banks failed. From coast to coast the factories shut down, and business ceased. This was a Panic. (Lane, 1962, 1)

With similar exaggeration ("*all* banks failed") Lane describes "Coxey's Armies of unemployed" coming "all the way from California," "seizing the railroad trains" and "running them full speed, open throttle, hell-for-leather toward Washington. . . . In all the cities Federal troops were guarding the Government's buildings" (2). Lane is dramatizing, in fact grossly overdramatizing, what happened. But irony asserts itself again: when she puts the events of the nineties in a different perspective, they lose their drama—or their uniqueness, at any rate. The truth, it appears, is that Americans were used to that kind of thing: "Everyone knew about Panics. . . . A Panic was nothing new to Grandpa, he had seen them before; this one was no worse than usual, he said, and nothing like as bad as the wartime. Now we were all safe in our beds, nobody was rampaging but Coxey's armies" (1).

Lane was a child of six in 1893, and the narrative reads like the dream of a child, a child who awakes from panic to discover that she has always been safe. In the last paragraph of her introduction to *Old Home Town*, she characterized its "time and place" as "remote" and "fantastic to us now" (Lane, 1935, 25). In her introduction to her mother's diary, what she says about the political and economic crisis increases the impression of dreamlike remoteness. Was it a fantasy, after all?

In 1936, Lane had written another account of the nineties. It appears in "Credo," a manifesto of her maturing political ideas, which explores her emergence from what she presents as socialist and communist fantasies into the clear light of individualism. "Credo" was published in the favorite magazine of middle-class, middlebrow, Middle Western Americans, *The Saturday Evening Post.* As Lane knew, many of her readers had been present for the events she discusses. She apparently assumed that, once they were reminded, they would share her impressions of the Panic, the better to follow her argument about the larger shape of American history.

"Credo" touches on some leading features of the nineties—agricultural distress, bank failures, factory shut-downs, mortgage defaults, a populace embittered by government subsidies awarded to railroads that the populace had originally wanted the government to subsidize. It offers Lane's habitually exaggerated story of Coxey's armies, insisting that they "terrorized smaller cities and towns" and "demoralized" railway traffic: "East of the Mississippi dispatchers cleared all trains off their divisions" (Lane, 1936, 34). That didn't happen. But her emphasis is on something that did happen: "Meanwhile most families went on living undramatically, as they always do. . . . No one starved. Someone in America will always divide food with the desperately hungry" (34).

Once more, Lane acknowledges and intensifies the drama of the nineties, only to place it in a broader, anti-dramatic narrative. In what she says about the agitation for Free Silver, one notices two contrasting points of view—one close, one distant. Writing from the first perspective, that of an emotionally engaged observer, she describes Bryan's campaign as "the fiercest political battle in the history of the republic" and maintains that his attempt to redistribute wealth by means of inflation was beaten at the polls by "the narrowest margin" (34). Actually, he was beaten by fifty-one to forty-six and seven-tenths percent in the popular vote, a substantial defeat in an American presidential election, although to put it in that way would diminish the immediate dramatic effect: Lane's exaggeration shows how his defeat might have looked at the moment. But that snapshot is just one picture in a sequence. Lane is heading toward her own political point of view, which involves a comparison between the depression of the 1890s and the depression of the 1930s. Seen close, the events of the nineties appear climactically significant to the nation's history; but when she backs away, puts them in a frame that includes both the hard times of 1896 and the hard times of 1936, she finds continuity, normality, and a type of optimism.

The optimism comes from noticing certain facts, facts that can best be seen by comparing one snapshot with another. It is clear, from the first snapshot, that the silver people failed in their attempt to distribute wealth by means of inflation. Bryan lost. But later views suggest something else—something general, yet also clear and distinct, about the pattern of American history. Since 1896, Lane says, "wealth has so increasingly been created and distributed that today, harassed as we are by personal anxieties and seriously alarmed by the public debt, few Americans would refuse help from public funds to any family as destitute of proper food, clothing, shelter, medical care and financial safety as the majority of American families were then"—in the 1890s. Progress has been so certain that Americans no longer notice it. We are "so accustomed" to its manifestations that "we do not see them" (34).

Lane clinches her point by turning to events of the 1930s that people without historical perspective might regard as crucial and climactic: the protest armies marching on Washington, the agricultural refugees abandoning the plains states. In *The Grapes of Wrath* (novel, 1939; film, 1940) John Steinbeck would read an apocalyptic message in the sufferings of the Joad family, fleeing Oklahoma in their ramshackle car. Lane finds a different meaning. The protest armies and the refugee movements had happened before, in the 1890s; there was no reason to be surprised by them. They were not a portent of revolution—although something had changed since the last great depression:

> Twenty-five years ago, the automobile was a rich man's prerogative; it still is, everywhere but here. In America, the anarchy of individualism had so distributed automobiles that California is overwhelmed by scores of thousands of penniless families arriving in them, and hunger marchers do not march but travel in trucks. And these people should have automobiles; that is my point. They should have them, and individualism has somehow, without plan or any such definite purpose, seen to it that they do have them. (34)

In 1915, Vachel Lindsay had unconsciously provided corroboration of Lane's view of history as an account of real things, not just the claims that authors and politicians make about real things. In a poem lauding Bryan as the foe of "the corporation magnate," he pictured the great man visiting a country town:

> When Bryan speaks, the town's a hive.
> From miles around, the autos drive. ("When Bryan Speaks," Lindsay, 1984, 284)

Strangely, with no help from Bryan, the people whom he fought to save from financial extinction now come to political meetings in private automobiles, and no one, not even Bryan's eulogist, thinks that is at all remarkable.

Novelist and literary critic Isabel Paterson, a sometime friend of Lane and born in the same year, was an earlier, more extensive, and more disciplined contributor to libertarian ideas. But her perspective on the events of the 1890s was similar to Lane's, and so was her reason for providing it: dismay at the notion that the depression of the 1930s was by its nature an historic turning point, an event so extraordinary as to require the extraordinary government response that was represented by the New Deal.

In the 1890s, the girl who became Isabel Paterson was one member of a large and impoverished family migrating around the American and Canadian West, where she was forcibly acquainted with economic realities. As a young adult, she worked in the offices of lawyers and bankers; she learned the difference between bad investments and good ones, and the normal way of dealing with businesses that made too many bad investments. The normal way was: liquidate the assets; start again. In 1931, she had no trouble applying this common knowledge to the business conditions of the day. There was nothing pleasant about the prospect of liquidation, but when she compared the current condition of the country with its condition in the 1890s, she was reassured. Writing to Burton Rascoe, a friend and fellow critic, she argued against the idea that a revolution was about to happen. No, she said, history was taking its accustomed course:

> This country experienced bankruptcy in the nineties. Part of the loss was borne by foreign bondholders. That part of the situation is now reversed. It is a much worse bankruptcy. But that is all it is, all it promises to be as yet. The bankers have discredited themselves, and failed to organize the machinery they meant to. They are shown up, and the "control" cannot operate because it is a receivership, which nobody is willing to accept. All that anyone will accept is the old political arrangement after liquidation. . . . There is no particular *kind* of new order that people *want*. You and I, who are in the main representative, do not want revolution; we really want "normalcy." Cut the losses, and go on. (Paterson, 1931)

Paterson was wrong: a kind of revolution had begun—the transformation of America into a welfare state managed by a central government. That concept of the state, which in the 1890s had been scorned as "paternalism" by everyone except the populists and socialists (and not all of them), was now realizing itself in some measure in the Hoover administration, which felt called upon to treat the current depression with more active remedies than the Cleveland and McKinley administrations had ever imagined. The goal for Herbert Hoover, as for his successor, Franklin Roosevelt, was to prevent liquidation, to rescue the banks and the mortgage holders, to save institutions and individuals from the consequences of bad investments, and in so doing to keep prices, including the price of wages, as high as they had been before the crash. But that was the statesmen's view of "normalcy," not Paterson's. If, she believed, "the public credit" had not been used "to keep bankrupt banks and businesses afloat . . . then all the unsound, badly managed institutions would long since have been liquidated, the half-wits who brought them to bankruptcy would be out and discredited, and abler men would have taken over" (Paterson, 1933b).

What the experience of the 1890s suggested to her was that the government should "do nothing at all, let nature take her course, let it all go." If this were allowed to happen, "then we might pick up the pieces, individually" (Paterson, 1932b). That would be truly "a new deal": cards laid out afresh, by an impartial dealer, and picked up by people who could play a decent game. That new deal would be "out of the same deck" that Americans had always used (Paterson, 1933a). It was a fair approximation of what happened in the nineties: the national government maintained sound money; it did not try to redeem all losses, much less to reconstruct the economy on new foundations.

From Paterson's point of view, the idea that government could and must do those things was new, strange, intellectually outrageous, historically *abnormal*. For her, the 1890s were not significant in themselves; they were an unfortunate part of the normal course of human affairs. And although the course of America in the 1930s was something like the opposite of what she desired, she would insist on her idea of a naturally developing economy, with decentralized risks and rewards, for the rest of her life.[5]

Willa Cather, the great interpreter of the American Plains, was reluctant to issue political statements of any kind, in print or in private; but when she did indicate her political views, she often connected them with the experience of the 1890s.[6] One of her most explicit statements was elicited by an invitation from *The Nation* to write an article about her home state, Nebraska. In this work, she gives special attention to the crisis of the nineties. Her approach is essentially the same as that of Paterson and Lane: when you see hard times in historical perspective, they are nothing that requires a new political economy; common experience and common sense will do. Recalling "the years 1893–1897," she says,

> These years of trial, as everyone now realizes, had a salutary effect upon the new State. They winnowed out the settlers with a purpose from the drifting malcontents who are ever seeking a land where man does not live by the sweat of his brow. The slack farmer moved on. Superfluous banks failed, and money lenders who drove hard bargains with desperate men came to grief. (Cather, 1923, 238)

So complete was the victory of the hard workers and right thinkers that "the 'hard times' of twenty-five years ago . . . are already forgotten." They don't "mean" very much, she says (238). The observation isn't a sign of smugness: Cather's own finances were never secure, and during most of her life they were barely adequate.

Common sense . . . but common sense is not evenly distributed. Cather had written about that aspect of the nineties (and every other period) in the first of her novels that she regarded as a success, *O Pioneers!* (1913). The story in that book begins in Nebraska in the 1880s, when pioneer farmers were already fleeing the place: their Eastern methods weren't right for the land, and their Old World conception that wealth is inherent in land and labor was terribly wrong. What the land needed, to make it valuable, was ways of saving labor—ways of farming that were different from the ordinary conception. "The right thing," says Cather's hero, the young Alexandra Bergson, "is usually what everybody don't do" (Cather, 1987, 172).

Alexandra convinces her brothers to use innovative methods of farming their land. The result is that they succeed while their neighbors fail. By the standards of their place and time, they grow rich, so rich that no mention is made of the great depression of the 1890s. Its absence is indicative of Cather's individualist economic ideas: while others were giving up and leaving Nebraska, like the refugees recalled at the beginning of this chapter, Alexandra was investing her time, money, and common sense in ways that paid off. For her, there is no depression.

There is, however, the political agitation that attended the depression. Alexandra's brother Lou, whom she has enriched by shrewd investments, is a vigorous anti-plutocrat. Like Jacob Coxey, he has done very well in the economic system he denounces, but he envies those who have done even better and looks forward to the possibility that Bryan's electoral defeat will be attended by a massive vengeance. "We gave Wall Street a scare in ninety-six," he "bluster[s]," "and we're fixing another to hand them." He accuses a visitor from the East of representing "a tame lot" of people: "If you had any nerve you'd get together and march down to Wall Street and blow it up. Dynamite it, I mean." Alexandra's neighbor, Frank Shabata, also envies the rich, reveling in scandalous stories about their vices. He, consequently, is one of "the political agitators of the county" (192, 210). Given Cather's analysis of his envy and frustrated vanity, it is not surprising that he ends up a murderer. Envy has already murdered his common sense.

Of course, Cather is not equating Bryanism with the impulse to murder. She knew Bryan, and she was genuinely, and generously, interested in him as a person (Cather, 1970). His partisans in *O Pioneers!* embody human qualities more permanent, and more unfortunate, than the craze for Free Silver. That is why one can understand *O Pioneers!* (though incompletely) even if one knows nothing about politics in the 1890s. From Cather's point of view, as from Paterson's and Lane's, the logic of human life does not change, cannot be "revolutionized." If, through some failure of perspective, one comes to believe it can be changed, by "dynamite" or other methods, the results are likely to be regrettable.

This is an idea suggested by the most considerable work of art inspired by Free Silver, the election of 1896, and all the rest of it—Cather's story "Two Friends." It was written in spring, 1931, in the midst of the Great Depression, but it isn't about financial collapse; it is about the destructive political impulses called forth by it. As in *O Pioneers!,* the depression is never mentioned, although Bryan's movement is. His campaign is the event that transforms vital, organic relationships into relationships of negation, denial, and sterility.

"Two Friends" is set in a town like Red Cloud, Nebraska, where Cather grew up. The great men of the town are Mr. Dillon, a banker, and Mr. Trueman, a cattleman. They are of opposite character, religion, party allegiance, and moral philosophy, yet the narrator—a woman of Cather's generation—remembers their friendship as the symbol of a mysterious harmony, the measure of social and psychological stability. When they sat and talked together, she recalls, "they seemed like two bodies held steady by some law of balance, an unconscious relation like that between the earth and the moon" (Cather, 1992, 688). Each man has made his own investments, in his own way, including investments in friendship; but each has chosen the other as his complement—until Dillon visits Chicago and hears Bryan's Cross of Gold speech.

He returns with the idea that "we've found a great leader in this country, and a great orator." "Great windbag!" Trueman retorts. "Sounds like a schoolboy had written it. Absolutely nothing back of it but an unsound theory." When Dillon announces that now "the under dog is going to have a chance," Trueman rebukes him: "That's no way for a banker to talk." Trueman's commonsensical view is that "a banker ha[s] no business to commit himself to a scatter-brained financial policy which would destroy credit" (685–87).

No one can doubt that this is Cather's view as well. Dillon never comes up with a plausible argument for the idea that Free Silver will "remedy" "the miseries and inequalities of the world," yet it is not only plausible but obvious that this is no way for a banker to talk. The narrator says that she—a callow adolescent—was impressed by Dillon's ideas, then felt otherwise; her zeal "to free humanity from the cross of gold had cooled." And while Trueman just continues being himself, a deliberate, undemonstrative conservative, Dillon becomes an agitator, driving "about the country convincing the farmers" and organizing "the Bryan Club and the Bryan Ladies' Quartette" (686–87). Cather could be very sarcastic about such things as ladies' quartettes. The righteous cause hasn't elevated Dillon morally or intellectually; on the contrary, it has made him less than himself. It soon destroys his friendship with Trueman, the only man he really values. Their quarrel devastates both their lives. It damages the narrator's sense of stability and even of "truth" (690).

"Two Friends" is an important exploration of the way in which political illusions prey on their hosts. (Perhaps that is why it has never been popular with modern, politically engaged critics.) It is also a memorable evocation of the time when people such as Dillon predicted that "the cornfields would show [high finance] a thing or two" (686). That demonstration never took place. The moment passed, and Cather's nostalgic narration emphasizes that it was only a moment. Normal life continued. Except for the incident in which Trueman startles the town by removing his deposits from Dillon's bank, what one sees of economic activity in "Two Friends" is buying and selling and investing in the normal, imperfect way, without regard to crises of high finance or the agitation to eliminate them. In this sense, Cather implies, there was nothing special about the 1890s. Possibly she also implies that there was nothing special about the 1930s, unless the "agitators" had their way.

In the modern world, economic distress is a field perennially rich in illusion and the language of illusion. The assumption is that hard times are not to be endured but to be conquered—an admirable expectation, but one that is impossible to fulfill with anything like the completeness commonly demanded. Already it was illusion that spoke with the tongues of Lou Bergson and Mr. Dillon, of the Coxeyites and Bryanites. Even before Bryan's campaign for the presidency, his paper, the *Omaha World-Herald*, proclaimed that "civilization itself [was] at stake" in the fight for Free Silver (Nevins, 1932, 657). During the Coxeyite adventure, Russell Scott Osborn, Secretary of State of Kansas, a populist, projected this illusion of the future:

> [T]here will be no overt act until the next election, then, simultaneous with the returns, flames will shoot into the air from the Atlantic to the Pacific and every palatial residence be destroyed in the uprising of the people. Woe unto them who have sought to stay this tide of the past six months. The farmers are preparing for this; they are selling a horse or a cow and buying Winchesters, and the mechanics are doing the same. (McMurry, 1968, 274)

A large book could be compiled, consisting entirely of unbalanced statements from the Panic period. But as soon as the nineties were over, the illusion passed and the statements were forgotten. None of it was enshrined in American myth. As Lane said, you have to look it up in old newspaper files. Even the astonishing speech of Theodore Roosevelt, delivered in 1912 when he was campaigning for president as an apocalyptic visionary in the manner of the populists, has been forgotten; the speech in which he said, "We stand at Armageddon, and we battle for the Lord," never made it into America's mythic memory (Theodore Roosevelt, 1912). It was once his most famous speech, by far; but now he has no famous speeches.

What did remain in memory, at least in part, was Franklin Roosevelt's first inaugural address (1933): "We have nothing to fear but fear itself. . . ." Having delivered that exhortation, Roosevelt assumed the mantle of Bryan and blamed the depression on "unscrupulous money changers" who had finally "fled from their high seats in the temple of our civilization." Continuing in this prophetic vein,[7] he spoke of "the unprecedented task before us" and of "an unprecedented demand and need for undelayed action." He called for "broad Executive power to wage a war against the emergency, as great as the power that would be given to me if we were in fact invaded by a foreign foe" (Franklin Roosevelt, 1933).

This speech, delivered at a low point in the depression of the 1930s, presents a curious contrast to the first inaugural address of William McKinley, delivered at a low point in the depression of the 1890s. That earlier speech is a plodding oration, far beneath the speaker's intellectual capabilities; it actually contains the words "business conditions are not the most promising." McKinley calls for the preservation of American institutions, for reduction of the national debt, for "the severest economy . . . in every branch of the Government at all times," and for the maintenance of a sound currency—ordinary desiderata in a nineteenth-century presidential address. "Most of our financial laws," McKinley says, "are the outgrowth of experience and trial, and should not be amended without investigation and demonstration of the wisdom of the proposed changes. We must be both 'sure we are right' and 'make haste slowly'" (McKinley, 1897).

This is the way to normalize a depression and send it on its way, not to establish it as a metaphysical ultimate or a turning point of history. Here is no mention of an unprecedented emergency, no hint of a grand conspiracy to defraud the public, and certainly no talk, as there would be in the 1990s, of a "greatest generation" courageously confronting the greatest of human problems.

Had earlier depressions made an indelible mark on American memory, more notice might have been paid to the fact that the depression of 1929 to 1940 (approximately) lasted longer than any of the others—twice as long as the depression of 1893 to 1898 (approximately)—and that it was ended, not by the dynamic actions of a political hero, but by the advent of a world war, in which the United States was the only great and undevastated industrial power. As conservatives and libertarians have frequently noticed, the federal government actually prolonged the depression by its many dramatic interventions in the economy and by the anxiety they produced among investors. In the 1931to 1938 period, America suffered six very rare years of "negative" private investment—strong evidence that, as Paterson said, "The volunteer fire department is usually about as bad as the fire" (Higgs, 1997, 566–67; Paterson, 1932a).[8]

Franklin Roosevelt's imaginative writing was undoubtedly important in enshrining the depression of the 1930s as *the* economic crisis of America. Books and movies such as *The Grapes of Wrath* were important as well. But it took more than books and movies and the occasional prestigious speech.

Shrines are institutions. They need many people, preferably salaried people, to build and maintain them.

This chapter began with a mystery: Why has the depression of the nineties been forgotten, while the depression of the thirties survives and thrives in popular memory? Every year that distances us from the thirties deepens that mystery. The Crash of 1929 will soon be ninety years in the past, with the Crash of 1893 only thirty-six years behind it; yet the spotlight continues shining brightly on the hard times of the 1930s, while the hard times of the 1890s are visited only by explorers with special flashlights.

Here are two speculative solutions to the mystery. The first is fairly easy to identify and perhaps to adopt: The depression of the 1930s became the Great Depression because it was preceded by the great advancements in material culture that were emphasized by Rose Wilder Lane in her account of the two depressions. Having experienced such marvelous improvements in the years leading up to 1929, Americans then experienced, in their sudden deprivation, the pathos and surprise that increase the power of myth.

The other solution is more complicated and may be more difficult to accept: The depression of the 1890s, unlike the depression of the 1930s, had virtually no paid staff to keep thoughts of it alive. It had only dying memories, and a few literary artists such as the ones I have sampled, whose contribution was mainly to suggest that, when one looked back on it, it didn't seem particularly important. But that wasn't the case with the depression of the 1930s.

A notable difference between pre- and post-1930s America is the virtual absence, before the 1930s, of permanent, well-organized national policy groups, the kind that spend professional time and talent projecting ideas, explanatory narratives, and historical myths, sometimes with considerable imaginative force. The older America had political parties, more or less organized, depending on the era; but these bodies had little or no national organization outside of Congress. Should one of the parties win the White House, it could rely on a political staff of insignificant size, employed directly by the president, and little more. In the early nineteenth century, the winning party, like its opposition, boasted a set of newspapers commissioned and subsidized to maintain its line; but newspapers subject to party discipline almost vanished in the later nineteenth century, when innovations in printing made it possible and desirable to appeal to a mass audience. Newspapers now made their money on advertising, not on party patronage. Few were house organs in the old sense.

Three reasonably coherent and well-funded national political organizations existed in the nineteenth century. One was the Grand Army of the Republic, a fraternal organization of northern Civil War veterans that prolonged and enhanced the mythos of that war, and did it successfully enough to secure veterans' benefits that by the 1890s may have amounted to 43 percent of federal expenditures (Daniels, 1971, 11). A second was the web of advocacy groups that promoted abolition. They gathered strong influence in a relatively short time, but they were never united on a strategy or even on the world picture they wanted to present. Mainly, they were groups of Protestant church people, operating at a time when none of the large Protestant denominations could be accused of having a central office or a central political vision. The third national organization overlapped strongly with the churches, and with the abolition movement, but it achieved its own national staff and lobbying force. This was the campaign for Prohibition, which was an economic and social nostrum as well as a religious and moral one.

From such precedents, and from many other sources, institutional and intellectual, potent social welfare organizations developed in the twentieth century: Social Gospel societies and missions, sharing ideas and staffs with local churches and national denominations; academic institutions for social research and the training of social workers; professionally organized labor groups; associations of economists and agricultural experts with Progressive visions. When Franklin Roosevelt set out to cure the Great Depression, he knew where to turn for professional help. The established idea of the welfare professionals was that economic problems demanded a permanent institutional solution and specifically a governmental one (Cox, 2014, 105–27).

This was quite a different idea from that of most intellectual and political leaders of the 1890s. President Cleveland fought the depression by promoting sound money and keeping labor unions from stopping traffic on the railroads. Welfare was provided by local churches, local individuals, and (often) by local governments. There was no federal welfare establishment, and practically no one dreamed of any. When Cleveland wanted to project an historical vision—such as the idea that Free Silver would be a disastrous break from American financial traditions—he encouraged his secretary of the treasury to deliver a series of learned speeches on the topic (Nevins, 1932, 680; Carlisle, 1895). The unpopular president's mail shrank "till it was less than that of an ordinary business man" (Nevins, 1932, 674).

Nothing could be more different from the world of government set spinning by the depression of the 1930s. One of the New Deal's recovery programs was the Division of Subsistence Homesteads, the institutional embodiment of a nostrum almost as peculiar as Free Silver: the idea that economic "imbalances" can be cured by the creation of very small farms, these farms to be provided by the government, fully equipped, to "homesteaders" returning from "over-populated" cities to "the land." (A large part of Franklin Roosevelt's First Inaugural was devoted to the imaginary problem of "the overbalance of population in our industrial centers.") In a single year, the Division grew from seven employees (four of them part-time) to more than 300, with another 1850 associates. The Resettlement Administration, the agency that sometimes included and supervised the Division of Subsistence Homesteads, boasted more than 13,000 employees (Maloney, 2011, 154, 155, 158). That was just one hive of activity; there were hundreds more.

Organizations always imply an ideology; in the modern word, they are usually funded to make the ideology explicit. If the idea of Free Silver had been supported by 13,000 paid employees, it might have made a more permanent impression on the American psyche. As things went, Resettlement was lost amid a host of other institutionalizations of paternalistic ideas; when it passed away, no one noticed. But paternalism did not pass away. It is the full-time occupation of a thousand governmental agencies that are with us now.

What is the story, the myth, that justifies their existence? Certainly it is not the story of a great depression—the depression of the 1890s—that came and went, affected less by government than by the decisions, good or bad, of individual people acting in the marketplace. It is, instead, the story of a great depression—the depression of the 1930s—that required the creation of a giant welfare state. The story gives life to the state; the state gives life to the story. No other stories need be told.

NOTES

1. Unemployment statistics and estimates were too crude, in the 1890s, to allow anything like a precise statement, then or now. Charles Hoffmann (1970, 97–112) reviews the problem, helpfully but not with perfect cogency, and proposes a 15–20 percent non-agricultural unemployment rate. Readers may judge how much progress is made by mathematical reprocessing of the incomplete data (Romer, 1986).
2. For the proposals, Coxey's process of thought, and his view of legal tender, see Schwantes (1985, 37); McMurry (1968, 291, 301–303).
3. On the nature and importance of myth, see Cox (2003).
4. It was observed that there were about six times more tramps on the road than Coxeyites (McMurry, 1968, 242).
5. On Paterson's life and works, see Cox (2004).
6. See Cox (2009) for an examination of Cather's political and economic views throughout her literary career.
7. Roosevelt's immediate source was the story of Christ and the money changers: Matthew 21, Mark 11, Luke 19, John 2.
8. Roosevelt's war-related willingness to reduce the volatility and aggressiveness of the New Deal appears to have been essential to producing economic recovery (Higgs, 1997, 579–80).

REFERENCES

Beecher, George Allen. 1950. *A Bishop of the Great Plains*. Philadelphia: Church Historical Society.

Bryan, William Jennings. 1896. Address to the Democratic National Convention. *Official Proceedings of the Democratic National Convention . . . Reported for the Convention by Edward B. Dickinson, Official Stenographer.* Logansport, Indiana: Wilson, Humphreys & Co.

Carlisle, John G. 1895. *The Free Coinage of Silver.* N. p., n. pub.

Cather, Willa. 1923. Nebraska: the end of the first cycle. *The Nation* 117 (Sept. 5): 236–38.

———. 1970. The personal side of William Jennings Bryan [1900]. In *The World and the Parish: Willa Cather's Articles and Reviews, 1893–1902.* Edited by William M. Curtin. Lincoln: University of Nebraska Press, 782–89.

———. 1987. *Early Novels and Stories.* New York: The Library of America.

———. 1992. *Stories, Poems, and Other Writings.* New York: The Library of America.

Cox, Stephen. 2003. The *Titanic* and the art of myth. *Critical Review* 15, nos. 3–4: 403–34.

———. 2004. *The Woman and the Dynamo: Isabel Paterson and the Idea of America.* New Brunswick, New Jersey: Transaction Publishers.

———. 2009. Cather's capitalism. In *Literature and the Economics of Liberty: Spontaneous Order in Culture.* Edited by Paul A. Cantor and Stephen Cox. Auburn, Alabama: Ludwig von Mises Institute, 323–70.

———. 2014. *American Christianity: The Continuing Revolution.* Austin: University of Texas Press.

Daniels, Roger. 1971. *The Bonus March: An Episode of the Great Depression.* Westport, Connecticut: Greenwood.

Dreiser, Theodore. 1922. *A Book About Myself.* New York: Boni & Livewright.

Garland, Hamlin. 1917. *A Son of the Middle Border.* New York: Macmillan.

Graves, Anson Rogers. 1911. *The Farmer Boy Who Became a Bishop.* Akron, Ohio: New Werner Company.

Harvey, William Hope. 1894. *Coin's Financial School.* Chicago: Coin Publishing Company.

Higgs, Robert. 1997. Regime uncertainty: Why the Great Depression lasted so long and why prosperity resumed after the war. *Independent Review* 1 (Spring): 561–90.

Hoffmann, Charles. 1970. *The Depression of the Nineties: An Economic History.* Westport, Connecticut: Greenwood.

Lane, Rose Wilder. 1935. *Old Home Town.* New York: Longmans, Green.

———. 1936. Credo. *The Saturday Evening Post* 208 (March 7): 5–7, 30–31, 34–35.

———. 1962. Setting. *On the Way Home: The Diary of a Trip from South Dakota to Mansfield, Missouri, in 1894*, by Laura Ingalls Wilder. New York: Harper & Row, 1–13, 75–101.

Lindsay, Vachel. 1984. *The Poetry of Vachel Lindsay.* Edited by Dennis Camp. Peoria: Spoon River Poetry Press.

London, Jack. 1982. *Novels and Social Writings.* New York: Library of America.

Maloney, C. J. 2011. *Back to the Land: Arthurdale, FDR's New Deal, and the Costs of Economic Planning.* Hoboken, New Jersey: John Wiley & Sons.

Masters, Edgar Lee. 1936. *Across Spoon River: An Autobiography.* New York: Farrar & Rinehart.

McKinley, William. 1897. First Inaugural Address. The American Presidency Project http://www.presidency.ucsb.edu/ws/index.php?pid=25827.
McMurry, Donald L. 1968. *Coxey's Army: A Study of the Industrial Army Movement of 1894.* Second ed. Seattle: University of Washington Press.
Nevins, Allan. 1932. *Grover Cleveland: A Study in Courage*. New York: Dodd, Mead & Company.
Paterson, Isabel. 1931. Letter. To Burton Rascoe. December. Rare Book and Manuscript Library, University of Pennsylvania.
———. 1932a. Turns with a book worm. *New York Herald Tribune "Books,"* April 10.
———. 1932b. Letter. To Garreta Busey. July 16. Herbert Hoover Presidential Library and Museum.
———. 1933a. Turns with a book worm. *New York Herald Tribune "Books,"* January 29.
———. 1933b. Letter. To Lillian Fischer. March 4. Manuscripts and Archives Division, The New York Public Library, Astor, Lenox, and Tilden Foundations.
Romer, Cristina. 1986. Spurious volatility in historical unemployment data. *Journal of Political Economy* 94, no. 1 (February): 1–37.
Roosevelt, Franklin D. 1933. First Inaugural Address. The American Presidency Project http://www.presidency.ucsb.edu/ws/index.php?pid=14473.
———. 1936. Acceptance Speech for the Renomination for the Presidency. The American Presidency Project http://www.presidency.ucsb.edu/ws/?pid=15314.
Roosevelt, Theodore. 1912. Speech, Progressive Party Convention, August 6. *Almanac of Theodore Roosevelt.* http://www.theodore-roosevelt.com.
Schwantes, Carlos A. 1985. *Coxey's Army: An American Odyssey.* Lincoln: University of Nebraska Press.
Williams, R. Hal. 2010. *Realigning America: McKinley, Bryan, and the Remarkable Election of 1896.* Lawrence: University Press of Kansas.

Chapter 14

Heroism Redefined

Integrating Mind and Emotion in Calumet "K"

Virginia Murr

Heroes typically rise above obstacles with unusual skill, courage, and perseverance, thereby saving the day when lives and fortunes hang in the balance. They are men and women who act when nobody else acts; they are just in their execution of their heroic deeds, and they hold firm standards for themselves and others. Heroes are the human ideal in action. On their way to triumph, most literary heroes experience a simultaneous internal struggle—a struggle that must be overcome as the last hurdle to achieving final victory. Charles Bannon, the protagonist of Ayn Rand's favorite novel, *Calumet "K,"* closely follows this heroic ideal. As the superintendent for a construction company, Bannon saves the day with purposeful action, a keen sense of justice, an unyielding sense of integrity, and a persistent dedication to accepting reality at face value.

In spite of Bannon's heroic actions, he persistently struggles with personal decisions, friendships, and romantic love. These struggles, evident throughout *Calumet "K,"* are a result of Bannon's view that emotions are inherently irrational and, therefore, detrimental to a successful life. Disconnected from his emotions, Bannon is left to unconsciously navigate the emotional terrain of his life. This is where Bannon diverges from the typical heroic figure in that the resolution of Bannon's mind-emotion dichotomy doesn't occur until after the triumphant action. This change of structure implies that the highest ideal is not the heroic completion of the grain elevator since Bannon possesses the very traits that enable him to achieve this success from the outset. Rather, the highest heroic ideal lies in the triumph that follows. Thus, Bannon's true heroic achievement—his final victory—comes when he begins to integrate his emotions with his conscious mind.

Charles Bannon is unfamiliar with failure. On the contrary, he is the man who MacBride and Co. call when they are in a bind because he "made a business of rising to emergencies" (8–9). Not only is he a man of action, as Ayn Rand states in her introduction to the 1967 reprint of *Calumet "K,"* Bannon "is an *efficacious* man; a man able to deal with reality" who faces challenges directly, figures out how to deal with them, and then produces the desired results (iii). A freight company refuses to carry his materials? Bannon enlists the aid of local farmers to haul the loads to a barge instead. A parasitic walking delegate from the union threatens to instigate a strike unless Bannon pays for "protection"? Bannon enables the uncorrupt union leader to catch the walking delegate at his own game. Need to construct a belt gallery Christmas Day in order to make up for months of lost time? Bannon offers the employees a free, all-you-can eat dinner to those who voluntarily work—then he keeps his promise. Through these and innumerable other unhesitant actions, Bannon shows his unfailing dedication to purposive action.

In addition to his skill and willingness to act, Bannon also maintains a keen sense of justice. This virtue is an integral part of Bannon's character. As long as people are upfront and honest with him, he will give them the same. If the men need something while on the job and the request is reasonable as pertains to getting the job done, Bannon will get them what they need because it is a just request. When he needs the men to work after their shift has ended, he tells Pete to offer "the men double pay, and tell them that any man can go home that wants to, right now, but if they say they'll stay, they've got to see it through" (69). Bannon views this exchange of value for value as just because both parties benefit. Simultaneously, when there is an imbalance in an exchange, Bannon demands justice. For example, after Bannon refuses to pay "protection," the walking delegate, Grady, attempts to instigate a strike. Appalled by Grady's actions, Bannon calls the union representatives to his office and informs them:

> To-night he's ordered a strike. He calls himself your representative, but he acted on his own responsibility. Now, I am going to talk plain to you. I came here to build this elevator, and I'm going to do it. I propose to treat you men fair and square. If you think you ain't treated right, you send an honest man to this office, and I'll talk with him. But I'm through with Grady. I won't have him here at all. If you send him around again, I'll throw him off the job. (256)

Another virtue vital to Bannon's character is his impenetrable integrity. So true to his word is Bannon that his bosses, co-workers, and laborers know that regardless of how impossible or complicated a situation may seem, "[I]t would be done if Bannon said so" (115). Even when Bannon figures out early on that a Clique is attempting to monopolize the wheat industry and a successful businessman suggests that Bannon could profit enormously from delaying the job, Bannon scoffs at the idea: "I see . . . All I'd have to do would be to buy all the wheat I could get trusted for and then hold back the job a little. And while I was at it, I might just as well make a clean job and walk off with the payroll. . . . I'd look pretty, wouldn't I, going to MacBride with my tail between my legs, telling him that the job was too much for me and I couldn't get it done on time" (64).

It is this thorough dedication to his core principles that makes Bannon the grounding force of the project. Not only does Bannon inherently refuse to take advantage of the situation, which would simultaneously financially harm the customer, destroy his boss's contract with the customer, harm the hundreds of workers depending on their jobs for an income, and severely undercut his integrity, but the entire suggestion is so far outside of Bannon's principles that the idea is ludicrous to him.

The one consistent thread that ties Bannon's actions, sense of justice, and integrity, is his overt dedication to reason. When trying to explain to Peterson why waiting for supplies that were two weeks behind schedule is a problem, Peterson takes offense. Bannon replies: "It's facts, that's all. . . . Maybe you think somebody up in the sky is going to hand you down a present of two extra weeks so the lost time won't count. That would be all right, only it ain't very likely to happen" (33). Bannon deals with reality as it is—not as he wishes it were. Bannon needs this foundation in reality in order to accept problems as they arise, to take appropriate action, to evaluate when a transaction is just or not, and to be able to identify the standard by which he assesses his own character. In other words, Bannon's fierce dedication to reality is the premise that gives rise to the heroic virtues through which he is able to save the day by constructing the grain elevator before the highly anticipated delivery of wheat on January 1.

> And then in a moment the straining hawsers were hauling cars up into the house. The seals were broken the doors rolled back, and the wheat came pouring out. The shovellers clambered into the cars and the steam power shovels helped the torrent along. It fell through the gratings, into steal tanks, and then the tireless metal cups carried it up, up, up, 'way to the top of the building. And then it came tumbling down again; down into garners, and down again into the great weighing hoppers, and recognized and registered and marketable at last, part of the load that was to bury the Clique that had braved it out of sight of all but their creditors, it went streaming down the spouts into bins. (320–21)

In this triumphant moment, Bannon effectively becomes the hero of *Calumet "K."* However, this triumph is only half of Bannon's heroic journey. Bannon's personal life isn't nearly as successful as his professional success might suggest. More to the point, Bannon's personal life can justly be viewed as a complete failure since he doesn't have one. The unfortunate result of

Bannon's near-zealous dedication to his professional life is that he doesn't know what to do with himself outside of work. He is indecisive about his personal desires; he has no friends outside of work; he has no romantic relationship to speak of.

Bannon's struggles with his personal life are a direct result of his rejection of emotion. In Bannon's experience, the unrelenting use of reason is good because it is vital to business success. On the other hand, emotion is bad because it is detrimental to business success. When the walking delegate, Grady, holds up the work for no other reason than to instigate dissension among the workers: "Bannon was angry. He stood looking at Grady with snapping eyes, and his hands closed into knotted fists. But Bannon knew the power of the unions, and he knew that a rash step now might destroy all hope of completing the elevator" (96). Had Bannon acted upon his anger, he would have fed the union's power and created further tension on the jobsite. The message is clear: Bannon must suppress his subconscious, emotive reactions if he wants to be successful. Over time, Bannon's habitual, conscious suppression of emotion leads him to unconsciously repress emotion as well.

With his emotions detached from his conscious mind, Bannon has very little access to the information in his subconscious mind. Without such information, Bannon is unable to understand himself. An example of this occurs right after Bannon rids the jobsite of the walking delegate. Instead of feeling happy along with everyone else, Bannon becomes irritable and concerned that things are running smoothly. Unable to grasp why he's snapping at people when they aren't doing anything wrong, he asks Hilda to tell him what is wrong with him (266). Bannon's confusion exists because without a conscious connection to his emotions, he cannot introspect. According to Ayn Rand, "Without a ruthlessly honest commitment to introspection—to the conceptual identification of your inner states—you will not discover what you feel, what arouses the feeling, and whether your feeling is an appropriate response to the facts of reality, or a mistaken response, or a vicious illusion produced by years of self-deception" (Rand, 1984, 17). Bannon's lack of emotional understanding, therefore, leaves him wandering aimlessly, unable to identify what he feels or why.

Bannon's inability to introspect also leaves him unable to identify his personal desires. At one point, Bannon tells Hilda he is thinking about taking his vacation "up on the St. Lawrence" because the people there "know how to enjoy life—it isn't all grime and sweat and making money" (216–17). Later, Bannon starts contemplating his vacation again. This time, however, he tells Hilda: "I rather think now I'll start on the third for Montreal. I'm telling you a secret, you know. I'm not going to let Brown or MacBride know where I'll be. And if I can pick up some good pictures of the river, I'll send them to you. I'll get one of the Montmorency Falls, if I can. They're great in winter" (298).

Bannon again changes his mind again and proposes to Hilda that they both go up to the St. Lawrence (304–5). Without a connection to his emotions, Bannon is missing important data that can only be established by his subconscious mind. This missing data handicaps his understanding of anything he desires outside of the work environment, which leaves him indecisive and insecure about personal matters.

Bannon's struggle with personal relationships is another consequence of his lack of introspection. Living a life largely of solitude, Bannon travels from job to job with little sustained social interaction. Bannon makes attempts at friendly overtures toward a few work colleagues. For instance, Bannon has known his superior, Fred Brown, for more than a decade and it is evident that Bannon likes Brown on a more casual level than simply boss-employee. Bannon's letters to Brown are much less formal than they are to the main boss, MacBride. In one letter, Bannon jokes in a post script: "I guess we'd better set fire to the whole damn thing and collect the insurance and skip" (18). Rather than signing these letters with the more formal "C. H. Bannon," he signs letters to Brown with "Bannon" and his post scripts with an even less formal "C. B." or "C."

However, even these minor attempts at expressing friendly feelings toward Brown create a struggle for Bannon. This struggle is first exposed when Bannon explains to Peterson that he had only taken one vacation in his twelve years of working for MacBride—and that vacation was with Brown: "Well, [Brown] came 'round and saw I was feeling pretty tired, so he asked me to knock off for a week and go fishing with him. I did and it was the hardest work I ever tackled . . . I worked like a horse for about a half a day and then I gave up. Told Brown I'd take a duplex car-puller along next time I tackled that kind of a job, and I went back to the elevator" (12–13). Not only does this half-day vacation enunciate Bannon's discomfort in attempting to enjoy life outside of work, it clearly shows that even though he feels friendly toward Brown, he is uncomfortable with those feelings.

Bannon's discomfort with Brown manifests as a result of Bannon's difficulty with accurately interpreting the friendly exchanges between them. At a previous job he performed for MacBride, Bannon lost his hat. At that time, he jokingly told Brown that he owed him a hat—a silk hat—to replace the one he lost. Bannon frequently nudges Brown with this joke in the letters he writes to Brown while on the Calumet job. Yet when Bannon receives a silk hat from Brown on Christmas Eve, Bannon's responds with confusion: "Wouldn't I look silly in a thing like that, though? I'd rather wear an ordinary length of stovepipe. That'd be durable, anyway. I wonder what Brown sent it for. I thought he knew a joke when he saw one" (279). Without access to the feelings that cause him to desire friendship, Bannon's relationship with Brown is doomed to remain quasi-personal.[1]

If we define love as "the highest of emotions. . . . [It is] the expression of one's values, the greatest reward you can earn for the moral qualities you have achieved in your character and person, the emotional price paid by one man for the joy he receives from the virtues of another" (Ayn Rand, 1963, 147), it is little wonder that Bannon has a tougher time navigating this more complex emotion than he does navigating his desire for friendship. Bannon is disconnected from the very thing required of him in a romantic relationship—emotion. As deeply repressed as his emotions may be, those emotions are still within him.[2] And Bannon, without deliberation or understanding, still acts on those emotions when he meets his clerk, Hilda.

The first day he meets Hilda, Bannon offers to walk her back to her boarding house. This is an extraordinary gesture from a man who must be forced to leave the job site in order to sleep. Unlike any other situation or any other person, Hilda's presence "took Bannon far away from this environment of railroad tracks and lumber piles" (87). She distracted him from the one thing he loved—the sole purpose of his life—his work. After working with Hilda for a while, Bannon spontaneously decides to take Hilda out on the job to show her the construction in progress (143). Since Bannon's reactions to Hilda are so out of the ordinary for him, it would be appropriate for him to ask himself such questions as "Why am I distracted by Hilda?" "Why do I feel the need to show Hilda the frame of the cupola we are building?" For those with a basic understanding of human emotion and relationships, these questions may seem fairly simple to answer. This is not the case for Bannon, however. On the contrary, Bannon doesn't even stop long enough to consider these questions.

Even though Bannon condemns emotion as irrational, Bannon has developed an astute and impersonal understanding of other's emotions since their emotional reactions give him cues about how to interact with them in order to encourage efficiency and production. When a laborer is feeling underappreciated, Bannon consciously senses it and is able to offer him the appreciation needed to inspire his best efforts. When Bannon observes that the general mood among the laborers is tense, he responds by inspiring respect and calm. Yet, even this well-developed understanding of other people's emotions is stunted with Hilda because her feelings, like his, are personal rather than professional. Their emotions have entered territory long detached from Bannon's conscious mind. When Hilda is too embarrassed to ask Bannon to visit her and her brother, Max, after she speaks with an injured workman on behalf of the company, "Bannon was a little puzzled. His eyes rested on her for a moment, and then, without understanding why, he suddenly knew that she had meant to ask him to see her after the visit, and that the new personal something in their relationship had flashed a warning" (230). Thus, a fundamental part of Bannon feels a connection to Hilda, but he is unable to identify what that feeling is or why it exists.

Commensurate with his heroic status, over the course of the story Bannon starts an internal progression of incrementally opening his conscious mind to his emotions. Nathaniel Branden refers to this coming into awareness as *noticing*—"Noticing the feelings in my body. Noticing my emotions during an encounter with someone. Noticing patterns in my behavior that may not be serving me. Noticing what excites me and what drains me" (Branden, 1995, 80). Bannon's noticing begins when he realizes that there is a difference in tone in his conversation with Hilda, when the discussion has become personal (217). Even after an exciting and full day focused on the job, Bannon can feel when his discussion with Hilda again takes on a personal tone (295). Eventually, the strength and persistence of Hilda's impact on him causes Bannon to ask Hilda to accompany him on vacation because he doesn't "want to go anywhere alone" (305). After his request, he waits, "fists knotted tightly, and a peculiar expression on his face almost as if he were smiling, but it came from a part of his nature that had never before got to the surface" (305). Bannon is now face-to-face with himself.

Bannon has many truths to unearth about himself—truths that have been there all along. One truth that Bannon will unearth as he continues noticing his emotions is that he is a man of action. While this reality about Bannon is evident to those closest to him, it is not evident to Bannon. So when he asks Hilda what is wrong with him since he doesn't understand why he is acting irritably on a day that everything is running smoothly, Hilda accurately responds:

> You're tired out, of course, if you don't have enough to occupy your mind, you don't know it. The trouble to-day is that everything is going too smoothly. You weren't a bit afraid yesterday that the elevator wouldn't be done on time. That was because you thought there was going to be a strike. And if just now the elevator should catch fire, or anything, you'd feel all right about it again. (267)

Yet Bannon, in an attempt to describe what would bring him pleasure in life, suggests that he wants to get away from the action.

> Time don't count with [a farmer]. . . . I'd like to be that way myself; never do anything till to-morrow. I'm going to turn farmer some day. Once I get this job done, I'd like to see the man who can hurry me. I'll say to MacBride: "I'm willing to work on nice, quiet, easy little jobs that never have to be finished. I'll want to sit at the desk and whittle most of the time. But if you ever try to put me on a rush job I'll quit and buy a small farm." (126)

The difference is drastic between Bannon's subconscious desires (as noted by Hilda) and what he consciously believes he wants. The reality is that

Bannon's job provides him with joy—joy in productive action, overcoming challenges, and achieving his goals. Even though Bannon is emotionally unaware of it, he confirms this joy with his following assessment: "A good many people think there's nothing in this kind of work but just sawing wood and making money for somebody up in Minneapolis. But it isn't that way. It's pretty, and sometimes it's exciting; and things happen every little while that are interesting enough to tell to anybody, if people only knew it" (152). Bannon loves his work. To tell himself anything else can only mean that there is a breach in his self-knowledge.

Another vital truth that Bannon will unearth during his noticing is that he is drawn to people who hold similar values to his own.[3] The clearest way to understand *how* Bannon is drawn to people is by looking at how he assesses them. Bannon has liked Peterson for years, but one day "Peterson, coatless and hatless as usual, with sleeves rolled up was at work with the men, swinging a hammer here, impatiently shouldering a bundle of planks there. And Bannon saw more clearly what he had known before, that Peterson was a good man when kept within his limitations" (120). What makes Peterson a "good man" in Bannon's mind, therefore, is not how nice or generous he can be. Rather, Bannon concludes that Peterson is a "good man" because, when held to his limitations, Peterson shows himself to be skilled, driven, and dedicated to achieving a goal. All of these qualities fit well with Bannon's own, core principles.

Bannon judges his love interest, Hilda, in much the same way. Hilda piques Bannon's interest when she drops by the office the night before she was to begin her job with Bannon (86). Bannon also finds himself pleased that, from her first day on the job, Hilda shows interest in the entire project, not just her role as clerk (112). With these qualities as well as her aptitude as clerk, Bannon assesses Hilda as "first class" not long after meeting her (116). Bannon later confirms his initial assessment of Hilda when he discovers that, like himself, Hilda finds aesthetic pleasure in the elevator even as it is being constructed (195). Hilda even refuses to take time off when it is offered on Christmas night because she is so anxious to see the completion of the belt gallery (294). So many of Hilda's qualities are harmonious with Bannon's principles, it is little wonder that his emotive reaction to Hilda was strong enough to get him to take notice of his normally repressed emotions.

While noticing his emotions is an important step for Bannon, these truths about his authentic self only become available to Bannon's awareness when he begins to fully integrate his mind and emotions. The moment of this internal victory comes during the belated Christmas dinner Bannon holds for the laborers shortly after the construction of the grain elevator is completed. In the midst of decorating the hall, Bannon discusses his new project with Hilda.

> He told her, a few words at a time, of the new work Mr. MacBride had assigned to him, and in his enthusiasm he gave her a little idea of what it would mean to him, this opportunity to build an elevator the like of which had never been seen in the country before, and which would be watched by engineers from New York to San Francisco. He told her, too, something about the work, how it had been discovered that piles could be made of concrete and driven into the ground with a pile driver, and that neither beams nor girders—none of the timbers, in fact—were needed in this new construction. He was nearly through with it, and still he did not notice the uncertain expression in her eyes. It was not until she asked in a faltering undertone, "When are you going to begin?" that it came to him. . . . He had forgotten all about the vacation and the St. Lawrence trip. (341–42)

The only way for Bannon to have forgotten something as important as the trip he had planned to take with Hilda to the St. Lawrence is if the thing that got him to forget—the new job—is more valuable to him. Thus, Bannon's new practice of integrating his emotion with his mind lets him understand that his vacation is less valuable to him than the job. On the other hand, it also lets him understand that, regardless of where he goes, he wants Hilda with him. Without missing a beat, Bannon asks Hilda to go with him to the new job (342).

Bannon's successful construction of the grain elevator against multiple forces actively trying to stop him would typically be seen as heroic—and indeed, it is. Yet Bannon is this "hero" from the beginning of *Calumet "K."* No growth or development is necessary for Bannon to be successful in his professional life. All he needs to do in order to save the day is to continue to be himself. On the contrary, at the beginning of *Calumet "K,"* Bannon's personal life is blatantly unsuccessful. Isolated from personal relationships and unable to enjoy the fruits of his labor because of his strictly disciplined, Stoic approach to emotion, Bannon is not capable of being a hero to himself.[4] Herein lies the redefinition of heroism in *Calumet "K."* In order to be a complete hero, Bannon must not simply be a hero to others, he must also become a hero to himself. This requires Bannon to overcome the cavernous divide he has created between his emotions and his conscious mind. Once Bannon allows his conscious mind access to his emotions and the information they provide, he opens the path to a successful personal life.

NOTES

1. Aristotle's *Nicomachean Ethics* directly addresses the importance of friendships to just individuals. "Between friends there is no need for justice, but people who are just still need the quality of friendship; and indeed friendliness is considered to be

justice in the fullest sense. It is not only a necessary thing but a splendid one" (Book VIII, Chapter 1).

2. In his essay "The Unconscious," written in 1915, Sigmund Freud concurs that repression does not erase emotion. "Psychoanalysis has taught us that the essence of the process of repression lies, not in abrogating or annihilating the ideational presentation of an instinct, but in withholding it from becoming conscious" (Freud, 2008).

3. See Aristotle's *Nicomachean Ethics* for the notion that rational people are happiest developing friendships with people who are "good and like in virtue" (Book, VIII, Chapter 4).

4. The Stoic approach to emotion is well stated in Seneca's epistle CXVL: "The question has often been raised whether it is better to have moderate emotions, or none at all. Philosophers of our school reject the emotions; the Peripatetics keep them in check. I, however, do not understand how any half-way disease can be either wholesome or helpful."

REFERENCES

Aristotle. 2009. *Nicomachean Ethics.* Revised edition. Edited by Lesley Brown. Translated by David Ross. Oxford: Oxford University Press.

Branden, Nathaniel. 2008. *The Psychology of Romantic Love: Romantic Love in an Anti-romantic Age.* New York: Penguin Group.

———. 1995 [1994]. *The Six Pillars of Self-esteem.* Reprint edition. New York: Bantam.

Freud, Sigmund. 2008 [1915]. "The Unconscious," *General Psychological Theory: Papers on Metapsychology.* New York: Simon and Schuster, 109–46.

Merwin, Samuel and Henry Kitchell Webster. 1993 [1967/1901]. *Calumet "K."* Reprint edition. Oceanside, California: Second Renaissance Books.

Rand, Ayn. 1963. *For the New Intellectual.* New York: Signet.

———. 1984. "Philosophical Detection," *Philosophy: Who Needs It.* Reissue edition. New York: Signet, 12–22.

Seneca, Lucius Annaeus. 1917–25. *Moral Epistles.* Vol. III. Translated by Richard M. Gummere. Cambridge, Massachusetts: Harvard University Press.

Chapter 15

Women's Work

Edna Ferber, Emma McChesney, and the Portrait of the American Businesswoman

Sarah Skwire

We have a tendency to think of the great age of American business fiction as the mid-twentieth century. With novels like *Revolutionary Road* (1961), *What Makes Sammy Run?* (1941), *The Embezzler* (1966), *The Hucksters* (1946), and *The Man in the Grey Flannel Suit* (1955), mid-century American business fiction heavily populates any list of top recommended novels for businesspeople. Right behind the mid-century fiction in popularity is the business novel of the 1980s. Exemplified by Tom Wolfe's *Bonfire of the Vanities* (1987) these novels tangled with the boom times and big scandals of the 80s, just as the earlier novels wrangled with post-war business and prosperity.

But there is a less often discussed era of business fiction that is prior to both of these. In the 1910s and 1920s, spurred on by the massive growth of industrial work and immigrant labor in the United States and by the growth of women's rights movements, stories in The *Saturday Evening Post,* The *New Yorker*, and other newly stylish periodical were the voice of this now-neglected era of business fictions. And one of the masters of the form was Edna Ferber.

Ferber, who won a Pulitzer for her novel *So Big* and is best known as the author of *Showboat* and *Giant*, had her first real writing successes with a series of business short stories for *American Magazine* between 1911 and 1913. The stories were later collected into three volumes: *Roast Beef Medium; Personality Plus;* and *Emma McChesney and Co.* They feature the business adventures of Emma McChesney, a traveling saleswoman for the T.A. Buck Featherloom Company's line of petticoats. Ferber's stories are a vivid depiction of early twentieth-century business life, and her choice of a divorced mother as her main character also allows her to explore the way the era's changing sexual politics affected the business world.

But aside from their historical usefulness and charm, Ferber's stories offer us the chance to consider an early and extended depiction of the characteristics of the successful businessperson, and to do so in light of more contemporary depictions like Deirdre McCloskey's bourgeois virtues, Israel Kirzner's entrepreneurial instincts, and Michael Novak's idea of business as a calling.

"MORALS DON'T FIGURE WITH A MAN ON THE ROAD": EMMA MCCHESNEY'S BOURGEOIS VIRTUES

As the daughter of a mid-western storekeeper, Edna Ferber had daily opportunities to study markets and their participants. The stories produced by that study suggest that she would have agreed with the astute and provocative observations of the economist Deirdre McCloskey who makes a persuasive case in her book *The Bourgeois Virtues* that a market system not only requires virtues to be possessed by those who participate in the system, it also produces virtues as they participate. From the very first Emma McChesney story, it is clear that—without McCloskey's historical framework or economic expertise—Ferber is arguing the same thing.

We are introduced to Mrs. McChesney in the story "Roast Beef, Medium" named for the tedious, but digestively undisruptive dinner relied upon by the "drummer" or traveling salesperson of the early 1910s. She is dining alone and reading the trade journal *Dry Goods Review* when another young drummer insists on joining her at her table. He begins to try to chat her up, refusing to believe that she could possibly be a competitor, "throwing her a languishing look" and begging her come out with him, "take in all the nickel shows, and then see if we can't drown our sorrows . . ." (Ferber, 1913, 6). While Emma appears to take him up on his offer, when they find themselves seated alone on a park bench and he kisses her, her real objective becomes clear. First, she informs him that she is not quite what he thinks. "I was married when I was eighteen, and stayed married eight years. I've had my divorce ten years, and my boy is seventeen years old" (Ferber, 1913, 8). Far from the young, blonde, and innocent creature he expects, Emma is an experienced adult, a businesswoman, and the mother of a son not much older than her hopeful swain. And in response to his attempted seduction—and the discovery that he's not just a wolf, but a married wolf—Emma reads him a sermon.

> You remember what I told you about old stagers, and the roast beef diet? Well that applies right through life. It's all very well to trifle with the little side-dishes at first, but there comes a time when you've got to quit fooling with the minced chicken, and the imitation lamb chops of this world, and settle down to plain, everyday, roast beef medium. That other stuff may tickle your palate for a while, but sooner or later it will turn on you and ruin your moral digestion. (Ferber, 1913, 10)

It is, in other words, a sermon on temperance. McCloskey has pointed to temperance as one of the four most important bourgeois virtues, noting that bourgeois temperance is not only "the Temperance to save and accumulate, of course. But it is also the temperance to educate oneself in business and in life, to listen to the customer humbly, to resist the temptations to cheat, to ask quietly whether there might a compromise here" (McCloskey, 2007, 507). Emma's sexual and dietary temperance help her to avoid the many temptations of life on the road, and surely assist her in becoming a successful salesperson.

This temperance is all the more important because Emma is not just a traveling salesperson, of course. She is a traveling sales*woman.* And she is a traveling saleswoman in 1911, when a woman traveling alone was considered fairly shocking, and a woman traveling alone for business was nearly unheard of. As a result of such cultural contexts, Emma's morals are far more scrutinized and far more vulnerable to rumor and traduction than those of her male competitors. In the story, "Simply Skirts" for example, Emma's nemesis, Ed Meyers, is, as ever, out to steal Emma's position as the Midwestern sales representative for Featherloom. Meyers comes to visit T. A. Buck, Jr., who will inherit the T. A. Buck Featherloom Company from his father and is shaking things up around the office. After some general insults to the mere idea of women as successful drummers, Meyer's gets down to the real topic of conversation.

> I want to say to you that McChesney's giving this firm a black eye. Morals don't figure with a man on the road, but when a woman breaks into this game, she's got to be on the level. . . . Why last summer I had it from the clerk of the hotel in that town that she ran around all day with a woman named LeHaye, Blanche Le Haye, of an aggregation of bum burlesquers . . . And say, for a whole month there, she had a tough young kid traveling with her that she called her son. Oh, she's queering your line all right. (Ferber, 1913, 48)

We know, of course, that Emma's morals are unimpeachable. The only question is whether T. A. Junior, the new, soon-to-be boss will agree. After he questions Emma about whether the young man she claimed was her son was really her lover, he suggests that he might be thinking about letting Meyers have her sales territory. Emma reacts with a dismay that is only furthered when he then suggests that she should "have dinner with me to-night, will you? And we'll take a run out in the country somewhere. It's warm, even for March. I'll bring along a fur coat for you. H'm?" (Ferber, 1913, 51).

We have seen, in "Roast Beef Medium," how briskly Emma dispenses with the importunities of youthful suitors. But we may, for a moment, worry about what this divorced working mother will do to keep her job.

What she does is give T.A. Junior a very blunt earful.

> Let's get down to cases. If I let you make love to me, I keep my job. Is that it? . . . Don't embarrass yourself. I just want to tell you that before I'd accept your auto ride I'd open a little fancy art good and needlework store in Menominee, Michigan, and get out the newest things in Hardanger work and Egyptian embroidery. And that's my notion of zero in occupation. Besides, no plain, everyday workingwoman could enjoy herself in your car because her conscience wouldn't let her. She'd be thinking all the time how she was depriving some poor, hard-working chorus girl of her legitimate pastime. (Ferber, 1913, 51)

T.A. Junior, completely humbled, admits that he had been testing the veracity of Meyers's rumors, assuming that Emma would fall for his seduction, and thinking he would fire her. Exercising her temperance yet again, Emma avoids getting angry. She politely informs him that his new petticoat design is an unsellable disaster, and steps back into her office, personal and professional morals as unstained as ever. Her choice to discuss business rather than to argue demonstrates prudence, which McCloskey calls "The leading bourgeois virtue" and defines as "the Prudence to buy low and sell high . . . But it is also the prudence to trade rather than invade, to calculate the consequences, to pursue the good with competence" (McCloskey, 2007, 507). Emma McChesney pursues the good, as she does everything else, with competence.

As Emma's son grows older, there are further lessons in the bourgeois virtues for the readers of Ferber's stories. When Emma bumps into her son Jock chatting up a salesgirl—as Emma has been chatted up so often and so tediously over the years—on a day when he is supposed to be in class she questions him about his current practices. "Jock, I've been earning close to six thousand a year . . . Just how much money have I been providing you with?" (Ferber, 1913, 25).

Discovering that it has been "quite a lot" and that much of it has gone to "clothes, and tobacco, and then flowers and cabs for the skirts—girls, I mean" (Ferber, 1913, 25). Emma decides it is time for a serious talk with her son. "Your mother is a working woman, Jock. You don't like that idea, do you? But you don't mind spending the money that the working woman provides you with, do you? I'm earning a man's salary. But Jock, you oughtn't to be willing to live on it" (Ferber, 1913, 26).

The bourgeois virtues require the proper training up of the younger generation. But they are not to be trained up to be unworking aristocrats. They are to be trained up to become bourgeois producers like their parents. The virtue of justice, which in the bourgeois manifests primarily as an insistence on respect for honestly acquired private property "is also the justice to pay willingly for good work, to honor labor, to break down privilege, to value people for what they can do rather than for who they are, to view success without envy"

(McCloskey, 2007, 508). And these are lessons that Emma works to teach her son. He can honor her labor by not wasting her money. He can break down privilege by not pressing his attentions on shopgirls, and he can learn to view success without envy by taking his mother's success as a goal for his own career, rather than merely leeching off it.

Emma's lessons for Jock continue in "The Man Within Him" when various challenges Jock faces as the newest ad-man at Berg and Shriner, Inc., have him feeling frustrated and stalled. Offered the chance to work around these frustrations unethically, Jock is sorely tempted. When Emma hears her son dismissing business ethics as "something that sounds all right, Mother—in the story books" (Ferber, 1914, 103), she is horrified and lets him know it. This time, her lecture nearly isn't enough, and Jock nearly goes astray. His good home training does not desert him, though, and by the end of the story his ethical near-violation has turned into an opportunity to display the solid bourgeois principles he learned from his mother.

But one of the finest examples of the bourgeois virtues at work in Ferber's writing is in "Underneath the High Cut Vest," a story where Emma does uncharacteristically little selling. Taken ill in a small town in Minnesota, Emma finds herself living in a small local hotel, attended by local doctors and a visiting nurse, and stuck there for her convalescence as well. During that time, as Emma fluctuates between feverish hallucinations and lonely despair:

> the local members of the U.C.T (United Commercial Travelers) sent roses enough to tax every vase and wash-pitcher that the hotel could muster, and asked their wives to call at the hotel and see what they could do. . . . Every travelling man who stopped at the little hotel on his way to Minneapolis added to the heaped-up offerings at Emma McChesney's shrine. Books and magazines assumed the proportions of a library. One could see the hand of T.A. Buck, Junior, in the cases of mineral water, quarts of wine, cunning cordials and tiny bottles of liqueur that stood in convivial rows on the closet shelf and floor. (Ferber, 1913, 55)

Emma's illness is, at last, the chance for the people around her to display their own virtues as they take care of her. Displayed in full here are the bourgeois versions of love and faith: ". . . the Love to take care of one's own, yes. But it is also a bourgeois love to care for employees and partners and colleagues and customers and fellow citizens . . . the Faith to honor one's community of business" (McCloskey, 2007, 508). McChesney's fellow businesspeople—bound by nothing greater than the loose ties of the bourgeois ethic and some small town kindness—rush to provide her with aid and with comfort. Even her nemesis Ed Meyers stops by to keep her company for a few minutes.

"Underneath the High Cut Vest" reminds us, I think, that Emma McChesney is an exceptionally good and particularly virtuous businessperson, but not that she is an exception. Her bourgeois virtues flourish, but they can only do so in a business world where they are—for the most part—shared virtues. It is true that young salesmen, old competitors, new bosses, and adolescent sons need occasional instructive reminders of the importance of upholding the code of virtues that is so easily forgotten, but Emma McChesney, as this story reminds her and us, is not alone.

"HURRAY FOR THE HUNCH!": EMMA MCCHESNEY'S ENTREPRENEURIAL INSTINCTS

But the bourgeois virtues, powerful though they are, are not the only important aspects of Emma McChesney's character. Indeed, her character would surely become tedious if every one of Ferber's stories starred Emma giving another lecture to yet another lamb who had strayed from the path of virtue. Emma is a virtuous bourgeois businesswoman. But let us never forget that the accent should fall on the last word in that phrase.

For many readers, Emma will be at her most entrancing when she is at her most entrepreneurial. It is worth noting that among economists, business schools, and lay-people "entrepreneurial" is something of a vexed term, with a range of differing meaning of greater and lesser precision and detail. What I mean by "entrepreneurial" for the purposes of this essay is essentially what the economist Israel Kirzner said in 2008 in revisiting a discussion he had opened in 1973 in *Competition and Entrepreneurship*.

> Casual observation surely confirms Schumpeter's insights into entrepreneurial creativity. Anecdotal evidence surely abounds to assure us that in real world capitalism change often, if not always, begins with entrepreneurial outside-the-box thinking regarding newly invented products, newly devised production techniques, and innovative penetration into hitherto untapped market territories. At the same time it is equally apparent that some entrepreneurial profit is indeed attributable to alert awareness of already-occurred changes in consumer preferences, changes in the availability of already-in-use resources, and the like. Apparently, there must be scope for both a creative ("Schumpeterian") entrepreneur (one who generates pure profit) and a "passive," alert ("Kirznerian") entrepreneur (one who snuffs out given profit opportunities by promptly exploiting them). (Kirzner, 2008, 7)

It is this combination of the creative entrepreneur, who makes his or her own new opportunities, and the alert entrepreneur, who finds ways to embrace the opportunities that already exist, that is at the core of Edna Ferber's portrait of Emma McChesney.

We see this combination of creativity and alertness at work over and over again in Ferber's stories. In "Knee-Deep in Knickers" the creative element is at the forefront. A year after the death of its founder, the T.A. Buck Featherloom Petticoat company is having a very bad year. Emma explains the problem thusly: "And they call that thing a petticoat! Why fifteen years ago the material in this skirt wouldn't have made even a fair sized sleeve" (Ferber, 1913, 74). And not only that, according to Emma, women are scarcely bothering with petticoats anymore at all! The Featherloom company is in grave danger of becoming manufacturers of sartorial buggy whips.

Happily, Emma refuses to allow her company to be the loser in a corporate game of musical chairs. Emma has made many attempts to save the fuller petticoat. She has persuaded the press to run "think-pieces" on the coming (fictional) trend for fuller skirts. She has invented a fringed petticoat called the "Carmencita" that failed to sell. And, in a glorious example of Bruce Yandle's Baptists and Bootleggers theory she even tries to enlist the Municipal Purity League in support of fuller skirts, and is thwarted only when competitors can prove that hoop skirts, poorly handled, can be even more revealing.

Having exhausted all those possibilities, Emma's creative entrepreneurship kicks in. She suggests that the company produce a full line of knickers for women to wear under the more form-fitting skirts, as well as a line of pajamas for women as well. In order to persuade her shocked business partner, T.A. Buck, Junior, that the line will sell and isn't too scandalous for the company, she has it modeled for him by a young woman, whose enthusiastic response to the new styles is evidence that Emma's creativity has allied with her knowledge of her customers to produce a winning asset for the company.

Emma provides a similar boost for the company two years later in "Hoops, my Dear." Here she revisits the continued trend for form-fitting skirts and realizes that, by now, women must be growing tired of them. And so she disappears into the workshop.

> Emma McChesney Buck always vigorously disclaimed any knowledge of that dreamy-eyed damsel known as Inspiration. T.A. Buck, her husband-partner, accused her of being on intimate terms with the lady. So did the adoring office staff of the T.A. Buck Featherloom Petticoat Company. Out in the workshop itself, the designers and cutters, those jealous artists of the pencil, shears, and yardstick, looked on in awed admiration on those rare occasions when the feminine member of the business took the scissors in her firm what hands and slashed boldly into a shimmering length of petticoat-silk. When she put down the great shears, there lay on the table the detached parts of that which the appreciative and experienced eyes of the crafts man knew to be a new and original variation of that elastic garment known as the underskirt. (Ferber, 1915, 69)

What she creates is a new hoop skirt. "A Skirt that billowed and flared and flounced and spread in a great, graceful circle—a skirt strangely light for all its fullness—a skirt like, and yet, somehow unlike those garments seen in ancient copies of Godey's Lady Book" (Ferber, 1915, 73). Again, Emma's male partner is doubtful, but Emma knows her customers. They are ready for something new, something different, and something that will give some mobility to the increasing number of women who were working, or playing sports, or enjoying the outdoors in these years on the cusp of the Roaring 20s. Yet again, it takes some hard work and a clever campaign, but the skirt is a success, and Emma can call herself the "Lincoln of the skirt trade . . . literally freeing my sisters from the shackles that have bound their ankles for five years" (Ferber, 1915, 76).

Such creativity is hard work, however, and even the indomitable Emma finds herself doubting her abilities every now and again. In "Dictated but Not Read" her son Jock has become an advertising man, and works hard to persuade Emma that the Featherloom company needs a real advertising campaign. Emma is unpersuaded until she joins him for lunch and asks to look at the dessert tray before she orders. Jock notes:

> You've proved my point . . . about advertising. Don't you see that what applies to pastry applies to petticoats? You didn't think of French pastry until he suggested it to you—advertised it, really. And then you wanted a picture of them. You wanted to know what they looked like before buying. That's all there is to advertising. Telling people about a thing, making 'em want it, and showing 'em how it will look when they have it. (Ferber, 1914, 75)

Persuaded, but also struck by the fear that she is suddenly aging out of the modern ways of doing business, Emma agrees to let Jock's company create a new and modern advertising campaign.

It is a disaster.

Emma then rewrites the campaign, using what F. A Hayek has called the "the knowledge of the particular circumstances of time and place" (Hayek, 1945) and what we might call the voice of experience. She takes the conversations she has had on the road selling skirts, and the women she has known who buy these skirts, and writes a campaign to appeal to them. "It isn't classic advertising. It isn't scientific. It isn't even what they call psychological, I suppose. But it's human. And it's going to reach that great, big, solid, safe, spot-cash mass known as the middle class" (Ferber, 1914, 88). It is a creative use of what Emma already knows to be true, and it sells.

But perhaps the most classically entrepreneurial moment for Emma is one where her creativity combines with her alertness. In "Broadway to Buenos Aires" she notices that her nemesis, Ed Meyers, has purchased a tropic-weight suit, and surmises that he is going to try to open up the South American market. But Emma is not merely guessing. She has been studying the South American market for a while, talking to women who have been there, noticing that Argentinian women love to dress well, realizing that the only petticoats for sale in Argentina are English. "You know what that means. An English woman chooses a petticoat like she does a husband—for life. It isn't only a garment. It's built like a tent. If once I can introduce the T.A. Buck Featherloom petticoat and knickerbocker into sunny South American, they'll use those English and German petticoats for linoleum floor coverings" (Ferber, 1915, 5). The opportunity has been sighted, and Emma is ready. She boards the next available boat to Argentina and prepares to put to work all her "alertness to present and future price patterns, alertness to new technological possibilities, and alertness to possible future patterns of demand (Kirzner, 2008, 11).

When she finds that the owner of the finest shop in Buenos Aires is a fellow passenger, she must not only be alert, she must be creative, particularly when she discovers that he dislikes women in business. Her solution is to bet him that she can produce a business woman that is just as charming as she is. Naturally, she does. He is won over. And the T.A. Buck company wins the first foothold in the South American market.

Emma, in these stories, is what Kirzner has described as "Mises's *homo agens* . . . endowed not only with the propensity to pursue goals efficiently, once ends and means are clearly identified, but also with the drive and alertness needed to identify which ends to strive for and which means are available" (Kirzner, 1973, 27). She is a triumph.

"THIS IS MY BUSY DAY": EMMA MCCHESNEY AND BUSINESS AS A CALLING

Michael Novak's *Business as a Calling: Work and the Examined Life* encourages readers to think of business as a field to which one can be called—much as clergy are called to serve God in a congregation, or artists are called to serve their art. Engaging in business, he argues, is not merely, or even primarily, about the money one earns. It is about the passion that draws one to the task. Novak writes of callings:

> At least four points should now be clear about callings in general and those in business in particular. First, each calling is unique to each individual. . . . Each of us is as unique in our calling as we are in being made in the image of God. . . . Second, a calling . . . requires talent. Another precondition is love—not just love of the final product but . . . long hours, frustrations, small steps forward, struggles; unless these too are welcomed with a certain joy, the claim to being called has a hollow ring. Third a true calling reveals its presence by the

> enjoyment and sense of renewed energies its practice yields to us. A fourth truth about callings is also apparent; they are not usually easy to discover. . . . Experiments, painful setbacks, false hopes, discernment, prayer, and much patience are often required before the light goes on. (Novak, 1996, 34–35)

Ferber's Emma McChesney stories are tales of a woman who enters the business world from necessity and discovers her true calling. Emma arrives in the offices of the T.A. Buck Featherloom Petticoat Company as a young mother, "divorced, penniless, refusing support from the man she had married eight years before" (Ferber, 1913, 62). Steadily, she works her way up the chain of command, "from stenographer to head stenographer, from head stenographer to inside saleswoman, from that to a minor road territory, and finally to the position of traveling representative through the coveted Middle Western territory" (Ferber, 1913, 62–63).

Again and again, Ferber's stories focus on the moments when Emma realizes the power of her calling in the face of the "long hours, frustrations, small steps forward, struggles" and other challenges Novak outlines. In "Representing T.A. Buck" we find Emma dealing with the ordinary annoyances of the average business trip—bad hotel service, cheeky clerks, buyers who think she might be interested in more than business, and so on. As she walks back to her hotel she finds herself "watching the women hurrying by, intent on the purchase of their Sunday dinners" (Ferber, 1913, 14), and she begins to long for the domesticity she has had to forgo in order to support herself and her son. "She wanted to go in and poke her fingers in the ribs of a broiler. She wanted to order wildly of sweet potatoes and vegetables, and soup bones, and apples for pies. She ached to turn back her sleeves and don a blue-and-white checked apron and roll out noodles" (Ferber, 1913, 15).

Emma's longing only increases when she stops into the hotel parlor and hears a fellow traveler playing Mendelssohn's *Spring Song*. Enormously moved by the performance, she compliments his playing. He reveals that he is also a traveling salesman, and he shares his own frustrations over his lost dream of being a concert pianist. After a long conversation he comes to a decision:

> 'I'm through,' he said. 'I quit tonight. I've got my own life to live. Here, will you shake on it? I'll quit if you will. You're a born housekeeper. You don't belong on the road any more than I do, It's now or never. And it's going to be now with me. . . . By the way . . . what's your line?'
>
> 'Petticoats. I'm out for A.A.Buck's Featherloom Skirts. What's yours?'
>
> 'Suffering cats!' shouted the fat man. 'D'you mean to tell me that you're the fellow who sold that bill to Blum, of the Novelty Cloak and Suit concern, and spoiled a sale for me?'

> ". . . Oh now, don't give me that bunk. You've got a good little seller, all right, but that guaranty don't hold water any more than the petticoat contains silk" (Ferber, 1913, 18).

And just that quickly, all the halcyon dreams of domestic bliss and artistic satisfaction evaporate. When they both realize they are supposed to head to De Kalb the next morning, they wish each other well, and race to see who can get to DeKalb first to make the sale.

Several stories in these collections follow this same pattern, and it is one familiar to any working woman or man. A worn-out Emma toys with leaving the business world for the traditionally feminine sphere and discovers, even as she considers the change, that the world of business is where her calling is. Ferber's work in these tales is clever and pointed. Just as the twenty-first-century reader (and surely just as the early twentieth-century devoted businessperson) is getting ready to throw up her hands at Emma's idealized daydream of sweet domesticity, Emma herself realizes that the dream is only a dream, and a fairly unsatisfying one at that. What she loves best is making a big sale, creating a new product, and beating a competitor to the finish line. Ferber manages to convey the divided desires of any working parent with a heavy travel schedule, while never denigrating either the domestic sphere or the business world. And Emma always chooses the latter.

Emma states her choices even more emphatically when other people tell her that she ought to make that change for the domestic. At the end of "Underneath the High-Cut Vest" (discussed above) as Emma begins to recover from her long illness, her son swears she will never have to go out on the road again. Emma's response? "Um-m-m-m—ye-ee-es . . . pull out that big sample case to the side of my bed. The newest Fall Featherlooms are in it, and somehow, I've just a whimsy notion that I'd like to look 'em over" (Ferber, 1913, 61). In "Knee Deep in Knickers" Emma—newly made a partner in the company—has just innovatively redesigned the firm's Spring line. When she offers to go on the road to sell the new line, she is told by her boss, "I won't have you fighting with buyers, taking their insults, kowtowing to them, salving them. It—it isn't woman's work" (Ferber, 1913, 61). Her response is one that every businesswoman ought to memorize as part of her MBA.

> Don't argue, please. If it's no work for a woman, then I suppose it follows that I'm unwomanly. For ten years I traveled this country selling T.A. Buck's Featherloom Petticoats. My first trip on the road I was in the twenties—and pretty too. I'm a woman of thirty-seven now. I'll never forget that first trip—the heartbreaks, the insults I endured, the disappointments, the humiliation, until they understood that I meant business—strictly business. I'm tired of hearing you men say that this and that and the other isn't women's work. Any work is woman's work that women can do well. I've given the ten best years of my life

> to this firm. Next to my boy at school it's the biggest thing in my life. Sometimes it swamps even him. Don't come to me with that sort of talk . . . This is my busy day. (Ferber, 1913, 83)

Notice that here Ferber isn't shy about allowing Emma—whom we know adores her son—to admit that sometimes her love for the business overwhelms even that personal affection.

Indeed, when Emma marries for a second time, she marries T.A. Buck, Junior—but only after they discover they can compete equally in the marketplace. On the way to their honeymoon, Emma nearly misses a train in order to catch up with a buyer and ask him to wait until she returns from her honeymoon to place his orders for the seasons. When her new husband expresses some mild dismay, Emma notes, "I've only been your wife for a week. But I've been Featherloom petticoats for over fifteen years. It's a habit" (Ferber, 1915, 51).

The first real test the newly married pair face in their marriage is when they decide that Emma should stay home for three months, just to see how she likes a life of leisure. At the end of those three months, they will compare notes and decide whether their like their married life better when they are business partners as well. The experiment goes well for a while, and Emma happily restocks her wardrobe, reads, and attends conferences. By the second month she is bored. In the third month she runs into a former employee of hers, who is now also a married lady of leisure. They share their mutual pleasure in their happy marriages and their mutual boredom with their lives of domesticity. That night, Emma returns home to tell her husband that she might have been a homebody if she "hadn't been obliged to get out and hustle. But it's too late to learn now. Besides I don't want to" (Ferber, 1915, 66). Happily, he doesn't want that either. "I've missed my business partner every minute for three months. All the time we've been going to those fool dinners and all that kind of thing, I've been bursting to talks skirts to you. I—say Emma, Adler's designed a new model . . . but there's something wrong with it. I can't put my finger on the flaw, but—" (Ferber, 1915, 66).

When you have a calling, it brings you renewed energies and resources, as Novak says. Emma is really only herself when she is working. And her husband—because he is a good partner—is happiest when she is most herself. They spend the next two hours working on a new design, and Emma returns to the office the next day.

The significance of seeing Emma's love for business as a calling becomes particularly important when seen in the context of Ferber's 1917 novel, *Fanny Herself*. More autobiographical than the Emma McChesney stories, Ferber's *Fanny Herself* is the story of a young Jewish girl growing up in Wisconsin as the daughter of a widowed shopkeeper. Fanny and her mother keep up her father's store, and Fanny turns out to have a talent for business, but not a calling. Much of the novel is taken up with Fanny's decision to pursue her talent for business in order to support her brother's music career, while she neglects her talent for drawing. The triumphant moment of the novel comes when Fanny realizes that ignoring her calling has led her to become an incomplete and unhappy person. She finds a way to make a business out of her art, and is able to fulfill both her calling and her need for money. Emma McChesney has done that her whole life.

Emma is no cut-out caricature. She is a fully realized human being. She has a son she adores. She has friends and colleagues. She has a happy second marriage. She has dreams and desires. And she has a calling that is at least as important as all of those things. And her bourgeois virtues and entrepreneurial instincts combine with the strength of her calling to make her a model portrait of a business women from the previous, or any, century.

REFERENCES

Ferber, Edna. [1913] 2008. *Roast Beef Medium.* The Echo Library: Teddington.

———. [1914] 2002. *Personality Plus.* Urbana and Chicago: University of Illinois Press.

———. [1915] 2009. *Emma McChesney & Co.* Lexington, Kentucky: Valde Books.

———. [1917] 2012. *Fanny Herself.* Teddington, United Kingdom: The Echo Library.

Hayek, F. A. 1945. "The Use of Knowledge in Society." *The American Economic Review*, vol. 35, no. 4. 519–30.

Kirzner, Israel. [1973] 2013. *Competition and Entrepreneurship.* Eds. Peter Boettke and Frederic Indianapolis, Indiana: Sautet. Liberty Fund.

———. 2008. "The Alert and Creative Entrepreneur: A Clarification." *IFN Working Paper No. 760.* Research Institute of Industrial Economics.

Novak, Michael. 1996. *Business as a Calling.* New York: Free Press.

Chapter 16

The Great Gatsby

A Commentary on the Wealthy in America of the 1920s

Gary Wolfram

The Great Gatsby is a semi-autobiographical novel by F. Scot Fitzgerald. Written in 1925 it depicts life in New York in 1922, the early part of the "Roaring Twenties." While a story of a failed romance, it provides Fitzgerald's commentary on upper income America as the country moved out of the shadow of World War I and into the light of a fast-growing American economy.

The main character, who serves as narrator, is Nick Carraway. As he explains in the first pages of the novel, Nick comes from a prominent Midwestern family. He graduated from Yale, served in World War I, and returning to the "Middle West" and having found life slow and unappealing, moved to New York to learn the bond business.

Nick is able to secure an old bungalow in the area of Long Island known as West Egg. West Egg is directly across the bay from East Egg. West Egg is where the newly rich live, while East Egg is where those who are from prominent families live. Nick's old bungalow happens to be next door to a massive mansion occupied by Jay Gatsby.

Nick is able to mix with both worlds as he is a Yale graduate and the cousin of Daisy Buchanan, who is married to Tom Buchanan. Tom went to Yale with Nick and comes from a prominent family. When Nick becomes a friend and confident of Gatsby he is able to be immersed in both the world of East Egg and of West Egg, allowing him to provide commentary about the culture of those who are the established rich and those who have recently become rich.

The Great Gatsby, while set among the wealthy of New York, does not offer an uplifting view of how the 1920s was an era of innovation and wealth is created out of risk-taking and hard work. One is more reminded of the "parable of the carriage" from Edward Bellamy's *Looking Backward* (1888), where the wealthy get that way mostly out of happenstance.

The period of the 1920s was an era of innovation in every aspect of American life. Innovations in film, radio, music, dance, and architecture expanded the intellectual breadth of everyone. Innovations in technology, such as the discovery of penicillin and the production of household items such as vacuum cleaners and electric irons resulted in improvements in the standard of living for all. The automobile became available for ordinary household use. But there is no acknowledgment of this in the novel. The focus is on the decadent lifestyle of both the old wealth and the newly wealthy.

It is not clear what anyone in the novel does to obtain their lifestyle, other than Nick, who works for a bond dealer, and Jordan Baker, a love interest of Nick's, who is a professional golfer. Tom has old money and thus is an inhabitant of East Egg. Gatsby is a mysterious character who is suspected of being, and turns out to be, a bootlegger and is perhaps involved in illegal bond deals.

In Fitzgerald's presentation there are no entrepreneurs. Even Jordan, who at least is a professional athlete, turns out to have gotten her big break by cheating. There is one person who has made his money through starting a legal business and that is Dan Cody. Gatsby had returned to his Midwestern roots as a decorated veteran of The War, seeking a route to wealth so he could marry Daisy. She, being of a connected family, could not bring herself to marry someone who was yet to have a fortune.

Gatsby had attended "the small Lutheran college of St. Olaf's in southern Minnesota." It is clear in Fitzgerald's view that this is not a route to wealth. To enter the realm of the wealthy one must have connections to the elite. One must attend one of the Ivy League schools to accomplish this.

Discouraged by the slow path to finding a way to gain Daisy through a small Midwestern college, and despising his job as a janitor that paid his way through, Gatsby returned to Lake Superior. As luck (which is how the rich get rich) would have it, Dan Cody's yacht comes into port. Cody takes the young Gatsby under his wing and comes to rely on him. Cody had in fact become wealthy by working and taking risk in a legal profession—mining.

As Fitzgerald puts it, Dan Cody was "a product of the Nevada silver fields," and his investment in copper fields made him "many times a millionaire (90)." Thus, the one person who might have been seen as an entrepreneur was wealthy because he engaged in an in industry where one might, as the expression goes, "strike it rich." One becomes wealthy in the world of *The Great Gatsby* by luck, by coming from wealth, or as Tom Buchanan put it: "A lot of these newly rich people are just big bootleggers, you know" (97).

The wealthy, whether old wealth or new wealth, are not portrayed in a positive light. They are primarily concerned with pursuing an opulent lifestyle and indifferent at best to the needs and feelings of those who are not in their inner circle.

Gatsby attempts to enter the realm of the old wealth, and thus win back Daisy, by hosting extravagant parties every Saturday. Crowds of people attend, most of whom have no idea who Gatsby is, and would not recognize him if they met in the drawing room. The people are not there because they are friends of Gatsby, or because they enjoy his company. They are there to be seen with other wealthy individuals in the hopes of moving up the social ladder to East Egg society.

Daisy had cast Gatsby aside when she tired of waiting for him to return to her with enough wealth to sustain the lifestyle she sought. Instead she married Tom Buchanan, who can provide her with old wealth. When Gatsby is able to get Daisy to come over to his place, he begins an affair with her. She admits to loving him, but when Gatsby attempts to get her to confront Tom and leave him, he realizes she is not going to do so, and remarks to Nick that "Her voice is full of money" (107). In the end, she deserts Gatsby and doesn't even attend his funeral as she and Tom leave without a forwarding address once Gatsby is killed.

Tom is the quintessential old family, Yale graduate, who gets everything he wants, including Daisy. He believes that the only way Gatsby could have attained a fortune was by being a bootlegger. He takes the wife of the one poor working class person in the novel, Wilson, as a mistress with no regard for the effect this will have on her husband. Wilson services Tom's car and believes that Tom comes by as a business relation, when in fact Tom is there to meet up with Wilson's wife.

It is clear that Tom uses Wilson's wife for nothing other than pleasure. When in the climactic scene she is killed by Daisy driving Gatsby's car, while Tom shows some emotion (Nick hears a sob and sees tears running down Tom's face) his main concern is to make sure Wilson knows the yellow car was not his.

Upon Gatsby's death at the hand of Wilson, who wrongly believes Gatsby was driving the car that killed Wilson's wife, Nick has trouble getting anyone to attend the funeral. None of those who attended the parties at Gatsby's house could be bothered to come. Tom and Daisy have left, probably to ensure no further investigation into the accident occurs. Gatsby's business partner, Wolfsheim, "cannot get mixed up in the thing" (151).

The Great Gatsby paints a picture that wealth in the capitalist system is based either on privilege or luck. Those who are wealthy are self-absorbed individuals that use other people for their own benefit or pleasure. The lifestyle is decadent and provides nothing of value to the rest of humanity.

This can partly be explained by Fitzgerald's life. He also grew up partly in the Midwest, attended an Ivy League school (Princeton), was a veteran of

World War I and fell in love with a social matron of the South (Zelda). She refused to marry him at first because he was not wealthy enough. Fitzgerald was able to marry her when his first novel became an instant success and he was able to support Zelda's lifestyle.

For Fitzgerald, it does appear that wealth comes from luck and privilege as that was his main experience. Yet the 1920s was an era of economic advancement after the recovery from the recession of 1920–21. Lowered marginal tax rates created incentives to take on the risk of innovation. The expansion of the use of electricity and the assembly line were but one part of the improved standard of living that occurred, not just for the rich, but also for the middle class. Radios, washing machines, and automobiles became affordable for more than just the extremely wealthy.

Since it is a system of voluntary exchange, one becomes wealthy in a market system by pleasing others. As Adam Smith (1776, 261) pointed out: "Give me that which I want and you shall have this which you want is the meaning of every such offer, and it is in this manner that we obtain from one another the far greater part of those good offices which we stand in need of." In order to get resources, including labor, producers must pay the owner of the resource the value of that resource in its next-best alternative (what economists call opportunity cost). Then they must use those resources to produce something that consumers value even more or go out of business. You cannot pay one hundred dollars for resources and produce things that consumers are only willing to pay ninety dollars for.

Entrepreneurs must constantly figure out what consumers want, and even what the consumers don't know that they are going to want. Few of us twenty years ago knew we would want to download an app for our smart phone. Those who are successful in pleasing large numbers of people, Steve Jobs, Bill Gates, Mark Zuckerberg, in our era or Andrew Carnegie, John D. Rockefeller, and Henry Ford, of Fitzgerald's era, will become very wealthy.

While there are some who do become wealthy through luck, and undoubtedly one way to get wealthy is to inherit wealth, the majority of billionaires on the Forbes 400 wealthiest people were self-made. The newly rich are just as wealthy as the old rich and today are likely to be more known than old wealth. About a quarter of the Forbes 400 are in the technology sector where they are able to please billions of people worldwide.

The workers in a market economy are not like Wilson, a hard-working, hard-scrabble man taken advantage of by the wealthy. As Mises (1927) argued, in about the same time that Fitzgerald was writing, market capitalism is the only system capable of creating wealth for the masses. It is the masses who gain from the advancements made possible by the innovation driven by the incentives of markets. The wealthy, rather than taking advantage of the workers, have every incentive to make them more productive through training and by adding capital. This improves the productivity of labor and results in a higher standard of living for all.

Robert Rector (2011), in his survey of poor households in the United States, found that 80 percent have air conditioning, three-fourths have a car or truck and greater than two-thirds have more than two rooms per person. The Fraser Institute's *Economic Freedom of the World 2014 Annual Report* finds that the income earned by the poorest 10 percent of the population is nine times higher in countries that rank in the top quartile of economic freedom than in countries that are in the bottom quartile (2014).

Those who see the world from Fitzgerald's view are likely to demand public policy that is harmful to the very people they would like to help. If the wealthy got that way through birth, luck, or "bootlegging," then taxing the rich and redistributing it to the rest of us is a reasonable thing to do and will not result in less production. But again as Mises noted (66), taxing the rich and redistributing the income will result in less production and a lower standard of living. One cannot tax the existing rich without reducing the incentives for those who aspire to work hard, innovate and become rich. Less innovation harms the lower and middle classes since they are the greatest beneficiaries of innovation.

The picture of the wealthy drawn by Fitzgerald is driven by his own unique personal experience. It is perhaps a case of what Sherlock Holmes would say is seeing but failing to observe. Unfortunately, the belief that the wealthy are uncaring, decadent individuals who gained their wealth through luck, cheating, or accident of birth can lead to public policy that harms the poor and middle class. Perhaps it is time to write the next novel: *The Great Bill Gates*.

REFERENCES

Bellamy, Edward. [1888] 2009. *Looking Backward 2000–1887*. Oxford: Oxford University Press.

Carlyle, Erin. 2013. "How Self-Made Forbes 400 Billionaires earned their Money." http://forbes.com/sites/erincarlyle/2013/09/18/how-self-made-forbes-400-billionaires-earned-their-money.

Fitzgerald, F. Scott. [1925] 2004. *The Great Gatsby*. New York: Scribner.

Gwartney, J., R. Lawson, and J. Hall. 2014. *Economic Freedom of the World 2014 Annual Report*. The Fraser Institute.

Mises, Ludwig von. [1927] 2010. *Liberalism*. Auburn, Alabama: Ludwig von Mises Institute.

Rector, Robert and Rachel Sheffield. 2011. *Understanding Poverty in the United States*. Washington, DC: The Heritage Foundation.

Smith, Adam. [1776] 2013. *An Inquiry into the Nature and Causes of the Wealth of Nation*. Indianapolis, Indiana: Liberty Fund.

Chapter 17

Steinbeck's Perspectives on Capitalism

From The Grapes of Wrath *to* East of Eden

Mimi Reisel Gladstein

Winston Churchill is often quoted as having remarked that being a liberal when one is young demonstrates a good heart while being conservative when one is older shows a good brain. This observation about age and political persuasion can easily be applied to Steinbeck's thinking about business.[1] His hostility to some of the methods and manipulations of capitalism in his early career, particularly in *The Grapes of Wrath,* won him some popularity and status in communist Russia and a reputation as an advocate for the worker. But, although his novels of the 1930s often show how the worker is abused by the capitalist system, by the time he was a world-renowned and comfortably fixed author, there is a decided change in his perspective.

In the 1930s, often called the "Red" decade because of the preponderance of left-leaning intellectuals and artists, John Steinbeck and his wife Carol, who was actually a registered member of the Communist Party, were well-acquainted with not only members of the John Reed Club, but also the Young Communist League. Many of these young people were part of a group that gathered at the Carmel, California, home of Lincoln Steffens and Ella Winter. It was there that Steinbeck met individuals associated with some of the agricultural workers' strikes and got information that he used in writing *In Dubious Battle.*[2] In addition, among the guests were such leftist luminaries as Anna Louise Strong and Mike Gold. Strong, who settled in Communist China in her final years, was a friend of Zhou Enlai. As a journalist she had written in support of the communist movements in both the Soviet Union and People's Republic of China. After the publication of *The Grapes of Wrath,* Strong was to make a special visit to Steinbeck, expecting that he would be amenable to her politically. Steinbeck, unlike his wife Carol, did not want to be identified with any political group. "He hated to be branded or categorized, and above all, he feared being labeled forever as a social-political writer. He was particularly wary of attempts by the Marxists to adopt and use him" (Benson, 424). Helen Hosmer, who arranged the meeting for Strong, remembers how resistant Steinbeck was and Strong's disappointment after the meeting.

Of course, *The Grapes of Wrath* was a very strong indictment of not only big business, but also law enforcement, political powers, and others who did their bidding. Steinbeck's condemnation of the way the California big growers manipulate and play the workers is one among many of his indictments of big business in the book. He writes about a technique used to insure that wages will be kept low and that there will be an abundance of workers. Steinbeck explains how thousands of flyers are produced and disseminated, so that more workers than are needed will appear. When, the Joads make it to California after a harrowing trip across the desert, a young man in the Hooverville laughs at Tom's explanation that they have come because of a handbill they saw that says they need people to work the crops. The man explains the economics of the situation: "They say they's three hundred thousan' us folks here, an' I bet ever' dam'fam'ly seen them hand'bills" (254). When there are more workers than work, the growers can pay lower wages. In one of his narrative chapters Steinbeck explains that if there was work for one man, ten men fought for it. As the migrants become more desperate and hungry, they bid against each for who will do the job for the cheapest price. As the narrator explains: "This was good, for wages went down and prices stayed up. The great owners were glad and they sent out more handbills, to bring more people in" (294).

Later in the novel, Steinbeck illustrates another way the owners maintain labor cost control. When the Joad family arrives at the Hooper Ranch to pick peaches they have to pass through a gauntlet of people picketing, trying to let them know that once their picketing stops, the price the pickers are being paid will drop. With the whole family picking at a price of 5 cents a box, the Joads are barely able to earn enough for dinner. Having eaten, Tom leaves the compound to try to find out what the people outside are shouting about. He finds Jim Casy with a group of men and Casy explains it to him: "This here's a strike" (398). He tells Tom that originally workers were paid 5 cents a box of picked peaches, but then, when a surplus of workers showed up, the company dropped the price to 2 ½ cents. It is only because of the strike that they are now being paid 5 cents, but Casy tells Tom that as soon as they are able to clear out the strikers, the price will drop again. Casy encourages Tom to get the people inside to join the strikers because: ". . . jus' the minute they ain't strikebreakin' they won't get no five" (399). Casy proves prophetic and he is murdered by vigilantes for his efforts to help the workers. In this and other sections of the novel Steinbeck shows how the police, vigilantes, and other locals help the California agricultural barons control and take advantage of the workers.

In the novel, Steinbeck expresses a variety of concerns about the evils of capitalism, big business in particular. This is often in one of his inter-chapters where the narrator addresses the reader directly: he explains how the small landowners, because of growing debt, will eventually be bought out by the big holdings or fall into the hands of the bank. The traditional family farm is being turned into agribusiness. Carey McWilliams's *Factories in the Field,* published the same year as *The Grapes of Wrath* is a non-fiction validation of Steinbeck's depiction of the California agricultural situation.

But, perhaps the most potent scenes are about how food is destroyed while people starve. Steinbeck presents a scenario where in order to keep prices up, all the surplus fruits are dumped on the ground, squirted with kerosene and burned while a million hungry people are on the roads. He calls it "a crime . . . that goes beyond denunciation" (363). Potatoes are dumped in the rivers and guards are placed on the banks so that the hungry people cannot get at them. Pigs are slaughtered, covered with quicklime and buried, rather than used to feed the starving.

All through the book Steinbeck highlights the virtues of the collective, the "we" over the "I." In Chapter Seventeen, he writes "In the evening a strange thing happened: the twenty families became one family, the children were the children of all" (200). When Ma cooks a stew for the family, although there is barely enough, she allows the hungry children to clean out the pot. In the final part of the novel, Tom leaves the family to devote himself to continuing Casy's mission of trying to organize the workers, as he tells Ma, "An I been wondering if all our folks got together an' yelled, like them fellas yelled . . ." (435).

Steinbeck's reputation as sympathetic to the workers was not garnered by a single book. Prior to writing *The Grapes of Wrath,* his portrayal of the loneliness of the migrant worker was a key theme in *Of Mice and Men.* The boss/owner of the farm is not portrayed as a bad fellow or one who oppresses his workers, although prejudice against Blacks and the perils of the elderly handicapped are underscored in the portrayals of Crooks, the Negro stable buck, and Candy, the old swamper who has lost his hand. But, though the boss is not a bad man, the same cannot be said about his son, Curley. *In Dubious Battle* is definitely an exploration of how the worker is abused and manipulated by not only the owners, but also by those who present themselves as there to help them.[3] Mac and Jim join the workers in order to help organize the strike, but mostly because they want the workers to join their cause, identified as the Party "assaulted by the beast of Capitalism" (21). They are willing to use any edge they can develop or take advantage of, be it when Mac delivers a baby, the grandchild of one of the strikers, or when Joy's dead body is used to stir the emotions of the strikers. It was *The Grapes of Wrath,* however, that cemented Steinbeck's reputation as an opponent of capitalism and for that he often found himself in danger. Wartzman opines that next to Salman Rushdie, who had a *fatwa* put on his head, Steinbeck suffered the most threats for what he wrote.[4] One story is that Steinbeck was warned not to be alone in a room with a woman as there was a plot for one to yell "rape" so as to sully his reputation. Steinbeck was condemned not only by the powers that be in California, but also in the statehouse in Oklahoma. Oklahomans were insulted by the image of the "Okie."[5]

Notwithstanding Steinbeck's actual beliefs and behavior, he was so strongly associated with leftist causes that when World War II came about, he had to fight his government in order to serve it.[6] A sad byproduct of his perceived politics was that what might have been Steinbeck's helpful suggestions were ignored. In one case, because of his interest in marine biology and the work he had done in that field with his friend Ed Ricketts, they attempted to contribute to the war effort against Japan. The idea was to use the work of Japanese scientists, who wrote in English, to map the environment around the Pacific islands that the military would have to conquer on the way to Japan. Japanese zoologists explored and wrote about the depth, tide, currents, reefs and other particulars of the coasts of those islands. Steinbeck describes the government reaction as a "fiasco" and "comic opera."[7] In short, because J. Edgar Hoover had categorized Steinbeck as a Communist, his ideas were ignored. Sadly, Steinbeck wondered about the possible casualties that resulted from his ideas being discarded.

Steinbeck was in his thirties during the 1930s, married to his first wife, when he wrote what are sometimes referred to as his proletariat novels, the chronicling of the travails of the working man. *The Grapes of Wrath* catapulted him to international fame and some financial security. Thus, his personal and professional situations were greatly changed by the time he began writing what would be published as *East of Eden*.[8] Rather than living in California, where so many of his early works were set, he was now a New Yorker. No longer a young man, he was a father, married to his third and final wife. Steinbeck was fifty years old when *East of Eden* was published, and the novel is many things, but one above all. He wrote, both in the journal he kept while writing the novel and in his narrative chapters where Steinbeck addresses the reader directly: "We have only one story. All novels, all poetry, are built on the never-ending contest in ourselves of good and evil" (477). For this purpose, Steinbeck chose the archetypal story of Adam and Eve and Cain and Abel. And, as would be expected, most critical response is focused on that premise. However, notwithstanding this main theme, a few commentators have also found other topics for their exploration, such as analyses of his presentation of dysfunctional families and his misogynistic portrayal of women.[9]

East of Eden was a best-seller, and has inspired both a film and a TV adaptation. The main Cain and Abel sibling rivalry is also a controlling metaphor for a book of critical essays titled *The Betrayal of Brotherhood in the Works of John Steinbeck: Cain Sign.* This collection includes an address to the 1990 Steinbeck Festival in Salinas by one of the sons the book was addressed to, John Steinbeck IV. Titled "Adam's Wound" the speech presented a meditation on the effect of the novel on him and his brother. Interestingly enough, what is conspicuously absent in this and most other studies of John Steinbeck's works is attention to the subject of business or capitalism in *East of Eden.* Whereas one can understand why the topic of business might be absent from articles gathered under the rubric of the betrayal of brotherhood in the works of Steinbeck, its absence in other anthologies is not so easily explained. For example, *East of Eden* does not figure as a topic for any of the essays in *A Political Companion to John Steinbeck.* About the most significant point made about it in that volume is that it "received perhaps the highest imprimatur in modern American Publishing when it was chosen as an Oprah's Book Club selection in 2003, with the host declaring that it was possibly the best novel she had ever read" (Stow, 9). In John Timmerman's book, tellingly titled *Searching for Eden: John Steinbeck's Ethical Career*, whereas Timmerman discusses many of the ethical issues presented in *East of Eden*, focusing on the dilemmas of choice between good and evil, nowhere does he mention anything about the ethics of capital.

East of Eden is an unusual novel in that it not only tells the story of three generations of the fictional Trask family, it also includes interactions between these fictional characters and John Steinbeck's actual family. Starting with Adam Trask's arrival in California, Steinbeck's maternal grandfather, Samuel Hamilton, plays an important role. Samuel Hamilton is presented as an independent workman, a well-digger and a good one, for even before Adam meets Samuel, he is told "He knows more about water than anybody around here. He's a water witch and a well-digger too. . . . He's put down half the wells in this part of the valley" (158). In the journal kept as he was writing the novel, Steinbeck wants to make sure that he is correct about the business costs of digging a well. He goes so far as to figure out that Samuel charged 50 cents a foot for digging a well, and that was the equivalent to a half day's pay then. Given inflation and changing values, Steinbeck concludes that it would be feasible that his well-digging would be profitable. In addition to Samuel Hamilton, other members of the Steinbeck family also appear, mostly later in the book as when the author himself peaks out from behind a door of the family home on Central Avenue as his mother opens it for Adam Trask.[10] Whereas *The Grapes of Wrath* grew out of fact-gathering and reporting, *East of Eden* is a very personal work. In a letter to Toby Street, he called it a work he had been "practicing for all my life" (1975, 408). And it is just that subjective aspect, the importance of the work to him personally that makes the attitudes Steinbeck conveys in it about business that much more significant.[11]

Adam Trask as entrepreneur is a key plot point in this part of the story. Adam has moved to town from the farm and Lee, the Chinese American man who has helped him raise his sons and keep his household, has returned to be with the family. An interesting fact here is that Lee had wanted to go into business for himself, to open a Bookstore in San Francisco. He does not return because he is unsuccessful in business; he returns because he is lonely. As the family settles into town, Adam finds himself with nothing to do and he tells Lee, "I think I'll go into business" (496). The year is 1915 and Adam's interest in refrigeration leads him to think it might be used to transport produce from California to the East Coast. He explains to Lee about an article he read: ". . . they've dug up a mastodon in Siberia. Been in the ice thousands of years. And the meat's still good" (496). Unfortunately, it does not work out as planned and thus sets up the situation for his son Cal to go into business.

We feel sympathy for Adam and his loss, and from our perspective today, we realize that the problem was not so much with the validity of the business idea and more about bad luck and/or the fact that Adam was a bit ahead of his time. In this part of the novel, it is Will Hamilton, Steinbeck's uncle, who is his main representative of business people in his family. In fact, he remembers his Uncle Will as the go-to person in the whole area: "Nearly every business proposition in the country came sooner or later to Will Hamilton's attention" (497). When Adam comes to Will with his idea, Will tells him to forget about it and explains why: "People in the East aren't used to vegetables in the winter. They wouldn't buy them. You get your cars stuck on a siding and you'll lost the shipment" (501). This, of course, is exactly what happens. First, a snow slide keeps the rail cars stuck for two days and then confusion about the order lets the cars sit for five more days in Chicago. By the time the carloads of lettuce arrive in New York, there is a sizeable mess. Notwithstanding the negative outcome, what is mentioned in the novel, but also demonstrated in the film, is the joy of setting up the business. The text notes Adam's untapped energy and how since everything was so new, everything had to be improvised. Steinbeck's narrator even finds humor in the situation: "Everyone gave advice but no one helped" (502–3). In the film, Cal, played by James Dean, even finds a way of improving the assembly line. The scene is one of zest and high energy.

As Will Hamilton is Steinbeck's main positive presentation of a capitalist in the novel, being that in his narrative introduction Will is described as "a very substantial businessman" (497), Steinbeck's choices in this characterization are significant. Steinbeck has Will counsel Adam Trask about not only what is wrong with his business proposition, but advise him what kind of business he should go into. He points out that there is a war going on in Europe and he anticipates that although President Wilson has promised to keep the United States out of it, he does not trust Wilson. If the United States does get into the war, there will be a need for imperishable foods such as rice, corn, wheat and beans. Will advises Adam to plant beans on his farm, explaining that if he wants to turn a profit, he should plant beans. This idea, however, does not interest Adam.

Thus a situation is set up whereby Adam's son Cal, who wants to make up for his father's loss when Adam does not take Will's advice, goes to Will Hamilton for guidance on how to make money. Here, again, Steinbeck's characterization of his businessman Uncle is one of positive appreciation. He presents a man who enjoys what he does, even the simple things like taking pleasure in the movement that goes on outside the glass cage that is his office at the automobile agency.

Steinbeck creates a most unusual situation for a novel. He has his real-life uncle go into business with his fictional protagonist. Will offers Cal a partnership, but he does it in such a way that Cal understands his responsibilities. He does not "give" him anything but an opportunity. He insists that Cal put money into the venture and he will not loan Cal that money. Of course, Steinbeck has conveniently set the situation up so that Lee, since he did not open his bookstore, has $5,000 to offer Cal. Will carefully explains the economics of the business to Cal. Using Adam Trask's tenant farmer Rantani as an example, he theorizes that he is a good farmer and can put five hundred acres under cultivation. He proposes that he and Cal guarantee Rantani five cents a pound for beans and give him a seed loan to plant them. When Cal counters that the market for beans is only three cents, Will explains that he has a contract with the British Purchasing Agency that will pay them ten cents a pound or more (552). Therefore, Rantani will make a profit and so will they.

Of significance here is that Steinbeck the man is writing of an uncle whose inner life he cannot have known and, if there are bits and pieces of fact in this portrayal, they were probably provided by remembrances of both he and his sister. Everyone knows how unreliable old family stories are. Different members of the family shape them in different ways. Therefore, the fact that he presents a three dimensional man, a businessman of character and one who plays a crucial role in aiding the fictional character who is the novel's final protagonist—Steinbeck's Cain figure who represents all of us—is noteworthy.

A major part of the Cain and Abel rivalry occurs when both brothers make an offering to God and God accepts Abel's offering of the firstling of his flock, but not Cain's fruit of the ground, one and not the other. The jealousy causes Cain to rise up against his brother and slay him.[12] In Steinbeck's version the initial jealousy because of the way a father favors the gift of one brother above the other is in the story of Charles and Adam Trask. In this first iteration of the Cain and Able paradigm in the novel, Charles actually tries to kill Adam. Charles explains his jealousy is because Cyrus, their father, preferred Adam. To illustrate, he cites Cyrus's attitude toward the different gifts the boys had given him. Charles states: "He liked everything you brought him . . . He didn't like anything I gave him" (72). He tells Adam about how he worked to earn money to buy his father a pocketknife, which Cyrus left in his bureau drawer, while the pup that did not cost Adam a thing was at Cyrus's funeral. In the final section of the novel, the gift offering happens when Cal goes into business to get a gift of $15,000 to pay back his father for the loss in the lettuce venture. Adam rejects it explaining that since he is on the draft board and sends boys out to die, he cannot profit off of the war. Not only does he reject Cal's gift, but he suggests to him that he might be more like his brother, thus plunging the knife further into the wound—favoring one son over the other. This, of course, sets up the final Cain and Abel plot parallel. In this case, Cal does not try to kill his brother, but instead hurts Aron by showing him the truth, taking him to see their mother who is the madam of a notorious whorehouse. In a reversal of the Biblical archetype however, in this case, instead of Cain/Cal striking Abel, it is Abel/Aron who "cut him down with a fist like a whip" 648). Nonetheless, Aron cannot handle the truth and enlists, because, as one of the recruiters suggests, "Maybe he is running away from himself" (626). Eventually, this does result in Aron's death. Although the character of Adam rejects making any profit on the war, the narrator/Steinbeck is clearly in understanding of and sympathetic with the business man during wartime. He states: ". . . it is natural for a man whose life function is the making of money to make money out of the war. No one blamed a man for that. . . . " (594). He adds the fact that some of that money is used to buy war bonds.

In this final section of the novel, Steinbeck's sympathies are clearly with Cal, the Cain figure. Aron has become increasingly self-absorbed. Even Abra, who is in love with him, points out: "He just seems to think only about himself" (571). Aron takes the lettuce failure harder than anyone else, seeing it as a humiliation. He wants to get out of town and thus takes his high school exams early so he can go away to Stanford. Cal, who sees himself as the inferior son, always trying to win his father's favor, realizes at this juncture why his father favors Aron. Aron's beautiful blond, angelic looks echo Cathy's and resonate for Adam. The fact that Adam has never gotten over his love for Kate is verified when, although she shot him and deserted the children, when he is told of her death, he weeps and cries out, "Oh my poor darling."

A focal point of the novel is the interpretation of the Hebrew word "timshel," which is God's instruction to Cain. Steinbeck even had Pat Covici, his editor, research the word. Covici questioned Dr. Louis Ginzberg of the Jewish Theological Seminary. Steinbeck had read different translations, some seeing it as a commandment—"thou shall," others as a choice, "thou mayest" triumph over evil. In keeping with the Hebrew scholars, Steinbeck uses it as meaning that God told Cain that he had a choice. He even has Samuel, Adam, and Lee discuss the variant translations. In the final scene of the novel, Adam, who has had a stroke, garners the strength to help free his son Cal from guilt. He makes the effort to utter the word "timshel." Thus the novel ends on a glimmer of hope. Cal and Abra are a couple and have Adam's blessing.

It is not my purpose here to suggest that commerce or capitalism are a main focus of this novel. But, it certainly is telling that in this most personal of works, Steinbeck chose to highlight Will Hamilton, his businessman uncle, and create a protagonist, Cal, who ends up with the main fictional heroine of the work, a sort of happily ever after ending.[13] It is also interesting that in his portrayal of his uncle, he has him empathize with Cal. He, like Cal, has felt that his father favored his siblings. In short, neither business nor businessmen are portrayed in a negative light. The wrath seems to have cooled considerably by the time Steinbeck wrote *East of Eden.*

NOTES

1. I am well aware that there is some debate about whether or not Churchill actually said this or some variation thereof. Nevertheless, it has been widely attributed to him.

2. Although there were many women who played key roles in both putting Steinbeck in touch with strike leaders and in working on the strike, they are inexplicably absent from his fictional portrayal. See my essay on "Missing Women."

3. Jackson Benson quotes Steinbeck as saying that in the writing of *In Dubious Battle* he was not so much interested in writing about the strike or ranting about oppression, as the underlying conditions that are demonstrated (646).

4. He carried a pistol as among other threats, a man who pointed a gun at him told him that he better stop writing or else (1).

5. Ironically, the citizens of Oklahoma did not understand that for Steinbeck, the Joads were heroic figures.

6. James H. Meredith and I detail the incongruities of his situation in "Patriotic Ironies: John Steinbeck's Wartime Service to His Country" in *A Political Companion to John Steinbeck,* Eds. Cyrus Ernesto Zirakzadeh and Simon Stow, University Press of Kentucky, (2013, 293–310).

7. Steinbeck recounts the story in "About Ed Ricketts," published as an Appendix to *The Log from the Sea of Cortez.*

8. Originally the book was to be titled *The Salinas Valley.*

9. Cathy Ames has drawn particular attention as perhaps the most villainous female character in American Literature. It has proved a plum role for actresses: Jo Van Fleet won the 1955 Academy Award for Best Supporting Actress for the film version and Jane Seymour won a Golden Globe for her portrayal in the television version.

10. The house is still there and is open to the public. It features a restaurant and a gift shop where one can even purchase a Steinbeck family recipe book.

11. Given my argument about Steinbeck's especially personal connection with this book, I will focus my case on Part Four, which is where the major part of the stories of both Steinbeck's family and the Trasks are told.

12. This archetypal story of sibling rivalry has fascinated writers over the century. In Lord Byron's *Cain*, he has Cain logically explain that he could not have known that striking Abel would kill him as there had been no death in their world before this.

13. John IV told of the conflict between him and his brother Thom as to who their father meant to get the girl—Abra.

REFERENCES

Benson, Jackson J. *The True Adventures of John Steinbeck, Writer.* New York: The Viking Press, 1984.

Gladstein, Mimi Reisel. "Missing Women: The Inexplicable Disparity Between Women in Steinbeck's Life and Those in His Fiction," *The Steinbeck Question: New Essays in Criticism.* ed. Donald R. Noble, Troy, N.Y: The Whitston Publishing Company, 1993, 84–98.

Gladstein, Mimi R. and James H. Meredith. "Patriotic Ironies: John Steinbeck's Wartime Service to His Country," *A Political Companion to John Steinbeck.* Eds. Cyrus Ernesto Zirakzadeh and Simon Stow. Lexington: University of Kentucky Press, 2013, 293–310.

Steinbeck, John. *The Grapes Of Wrath.* New York: The Viking Press. 1939.

———. *In Dubious Battle.*

———. "Appendix: About Ed Ricketts," *The Log from the Sea of Cortez,* New York: Penguin Books, 1951, 225–74.

———. *East of Eden.* New York: The Viking Press. 1952.

———. *Journal of a Novel: The "East of Eden" Letters.* New York: Penguin Books. 1969.

———. *Steinbeck: A Life in Letters.* Eds. Elaine Steinbeck and Robert Wallsten. New York: The Viking Press. 1975.

Stow, Simon. "The Dangerous Ambivalence of John Steinbeck," *A Political Companion to John Steinbeck,* Eds. Cyrus Ernesto Zirakzadeh and Simon Stow, University Press of Kentucky, 2013, 8–16.

Wartzman, Rick. "John Steinbeck in the 1930s: Living Under the Gun," *A Political Companion to John Steinbeck,* Eds. Cyrus Ernesto Zirakzadeh and Simon Stow, University Press of Kentucky.

Chapter 18

Ayn Rand, *Atlas Shrugged*, and Libertarianism

Walter E. Block

Ayn Rand has had a love-hate relationship with libertarians. On the one hand, she was one of the most influential writers in the libertarian movement.[1] On the other, she reviled and demeaned libertarians, dismissing them as "hippies of the right."[2] Her intellectual followers were, if anything, even more vicious in their revulsion of the libertarian freedom philosophy.[3]

I, in turn, also have a love-hate relationship with the Objectivists, the philosophical system created by Ayn Rand. In section II of this chapter, I shall relate my own autobiographical experience with this movement. Section III is devoted to an analysis of the issue of accepting government subsidies, with a little help from my favorite character in Atlas Shrugged, Ragnar Danneskjold. The purpose of section IV is to comment on Charles Murray's reaction to Ayn Rand. I conclude in section V.

A PERSONAL HISTORY

I was born in Brooklyn, New York in 1941 and lived there until 1979, when I was thirty-eight years old. My parents were Jewish, and in our neighborhood the political views of everyone ranged from left-liberal on the right, all the way to Marxism and then Communism on the left. Sad to say, I fully imbibed this perspective. I went to Madison High School in Brooklyn[4] from 1955 to 1959 and then enrolled in Brooklyn College, where I majored in philosophy. 'twas there that I first met Miss Ayn Rand.[5] She came to Brooklyn College to lecture on her Objectivism, and I came there to boo and hiss at her, since she favored laissez faire capitalism, and "everyone" knew that the result of that economic system would be immiseration, sweat shops, exploitation of labor, outright starvation and even slavery. She was a fascist, and I wasn't going to let her get away with spewing forth her intellectual filth.

Well, she spoke, and I booed and hissed her, along with several hundred other outraged students. At the end of this presentation, an announcement was made by the Brooklyn College Ayn Rand study group that had invited her to campus that there was to be a luncheon in her honor, and that all were invited, whether we agreed with her or not. I didn't get in my fair share of hissing at her, so I went to this gathering. There was a long table with about fifty people on each side of it, with Miss Rand sitting at the head of it, surrounded by her chief followers such as Barbara and Nathaniel Branden, Alan Greenspan, Leonard Piekoff. I was relegated to the foot of the table, way at the other end. I turned to my neighbor and challenged him to a debate between socialism and capitalism. He said that he really didn't know all that much about this issue, but that the people at the other end of the table sure did. Chutzpanick that I was then, I walked over there and stuck my head in between Ayn's and Nathan's and said there was someone who wanted to debate socialism versus capitalism. They asked who it was, and I said, me. Mr. Branden was very kind, gentle and courteous with me. He said he would sit at the other end of the table with me and discuss these issues if I agreed to two conditions. One was that we would not allow the conversation to lapse after merely one go around; we would continue it until we reached some sort of understanding. And, second, I would promise to read two books he would recommend to me.[6] I agreed, and we talked that day. So much for the end of my hate relationship.

I followed this up with about six to eight visits to his and Ayn's home in Manhattan. There, again, I also met people such as Barbara Branden, Alan Greenspan, Leonard Piekoff. I read the two books. I was converted to the one true faith: I was now a supporter of laissez faire capitalism. This was my love episode with Objectivism. I was inspired by *Atlas Shrugged* and given intellectual ammunition by *Economics in One Lesson*. I started going to the Nathaniel Branden Institute lectures in Manhattan. And here began the third chapter in my love-hate relationship.

I passionately loved the economics they were supporting. To think that the market has self-organizing principles and that no government intervention could improve it, was a thing of beauty.[7] I was enchanted. But they also talked, incessantly about metaphysics, epistemology, aesthetics, and all sorts of other issues that did not really interest me. That was not so bad. More than just a little disquieting was their assertion that romantic music[8] was objectively better than anything else.[9] I was a subjectivist on matters of this sort. I thought *de gustibus non disputandum*. But what really turned me off was the cultishness. If Ayn Rand were asked a question such as, "On page 304 of *Atlas* you said thus and such, could you please elaborate on that?" it would be met with smiles and effusive responses. But, if the questioner gave a challenge of the sort "On page 304 of *Atlas* you said thus and such, but on page 567 you said something else, and I sense a contradiction between the two statements," she would turn livid, expel the questioner from the meeting, and say he would be taken off the mailing list of NBI. When I first heard that sort of thing I was astounded. This, surely, is no way to run an intellectual seminar. So, I would stop attending NBI meetings. But, my love-hate relationship was still in force. I knew no other free enterprisers other than the Objectivists. Everyone else was by now a disgusting pinko or a downright red. So I engaged in an approach avoidance behavior. I would leave NBI in disgust, only to return, tail between my legs. Not a happy time.

Later on, when I was enrolled in the PhD program at Columbia University, one of my fellow students, Larry Moss, and his then roommate Jerry Woloz, forced, enticed, compelled, demanded, that I meet Murray Rothbard. They made the mistake of saying he was a libertarian anarchist. I was still enough of a Randroid to be completely put off by such a statement. So I resisted meeting Murray for several months. Finally, finally, Larry and Jerry frog-marched me to Murray's house, and the rest, as they say, is history. Murray converted me to anarcho-capitalism in about five minutes.[10] I had found my intellectual home, and never looked back.

But, I still have great fondness, and, yes, even love, for Ayn Rand and Nathaniel Branden who together showed me the intellectual and ethical morass of socialism and mixed economy government interventionism. Were it not for them, gulp, I might have gone, horrors, the Bernie Sanders route.

ACCEPTING GOVERNMENT SUBSIDIES

Should a libertarian who opposes government intervention into the economy, subsidies to business, welfare, rent control, socialized medicine, bailouts, etc.,—in a word, socialism—yet avail himself of the "benefits" of these programs.

No. This would be unwise, at least on pragmatic grounds, since political, economic and philosophical illiterates will accuse you of "hypocrisy."

But what about as a matter of principle? Then, yes, for there is nothing in the free enterprise ethic which precludes such a choice. The capitalist system is strictly one of voluntarism; no one may initiate force against those not themselves guilty of such uncivilized behavior. All of these government initiatives, in contrast, are coercive: they compel innocent people to finance programs that they would either eschew entirely were they free to choose, or would purchase instead on the free market. True, in a democracy, economic interventionism is supported by the electorate. But for the libertarian, this is just tyranny of the majority. Hitler, after all, came to power through the ballot box; yet this certainly gives no imprimatur to what he did. If the majority desire socialist programs, let them do this on their own account. Why force the minority to take part?

When a man is forced to pay for socialized medicine against his will, it is as if the money for this purpose is being stolen from him. If he avails himself of this program by seeing a statist doctor, he is only getting back what was taken from him by force. If a publisher is compelled to pay taxes part of which go to subsidize magazines, again the same principle applies, he may accept the largesse of the government. This is but the return of stolen funds. But more. Even a Martian (who never paid any taxes whatsoever) could arrive on earth and still be justified in utilizing government programs. They are predicated upon stolen money after all, and the worst possible result would be for the thieves to keep their ill-gotten gains. The best scenario would be for the Martian, like Ragnar Danneskjold in Ayn Rand's (1957) novel "*Atlas Shrugged*" to return this stolen money to the long-suffering tax payer.

Suppose all pizza parlors were required to pay a special "oven tax" whereupon Washington, DC, then gave ("free of charge") to all members of this industry an oven in which to bake pies. If a family restaurant, purveyor of "arch-conservative" pizzas, refused to accept this government "benefit" they would put themselves at a severe competitive disadvantage vis-à-vis all their competitors who went along with the game.

Critics of this perspective would say to libertarians:

> Aha, you oppose agricultural subsidies? Therefore, do not eat eggs nor drink milk. You oppose socialized medicine? Then, lest you be considered a hypocrite, do not consult a doctor when sick. You favor privatization of roads and highways? This means you must sit at home and not venture out onto the public streets. You think the U.S. Post Office ought to be privatized? This requires you not to mail letters. You don't like paying payroll taxes? Then quit your job.

These pundits do not understand the most basic premise of the free market philosophy: voluntarism. Imagine if they were writing under the old U.S.S.R. economic system. What a field day they would have had, then, at the expense of any libertarians suffering under the yoke of Communism. Since the Soviets commandeered virtually the entire economy, they could have hurled the charge of hypocrisy to anyone who opposed even the slightest aspect of this evil system–and wanted to remain alive. Too bad, from their perspective, that the present government has not Sovietized the entire economy. Then, according to their lights, adamant and logically consistent libertarians would be forced to die off.

U.S. Supreme Court Justice Robert Jackson (1949) said that the Constitution is not a suicide pact. Well, neither is the libertarian philosophy, despite the efforts of some to paint adherents of this view into that corner. If the liberals wish to see some real hypocrisy in action, they have only to look to the luxury car driving egalitarians in their midst.

ON CHARLES MURRAY

Charles Murray (2010) asks "Why Ayn Rand Books Still Sell So Well" and says it is because:

> "Rand expressed the glory of human achievement. She tapped into the delight a human being ought to feel at watching another member of our species doing things superbly well. The scenes in *The Fountainhead* in which the hero, Howard Roark, realizes his visions of architectural truth are brilliant evocations of human creativity at work. But I also loved scenes like the one in 'Atlas Shrugged' when protagonist Dagny Taggart is in the cab of the locomotive on the first run on the John Galt line, going at record speed, and glances at the engineer: 'He sat slumped forward a little, relaxed, one hand resting lightly on the throttle as if by chance; but his eyes were fixed on the track ahead. He had the ease of an expert, so confident that it seemed casual, but it was the ease of a tremendous concentration, the concentration on one's task that has the ruthlessness of an absolute.' That's a heroic vision of a blue-collar worker doing his job. There are many others. Critics often accuse Rand of portraying a few geniuses as the only people worth valuing. That's not what I took away from her. I saw her celebrating people who did their work well and condemning people who settled for less, in great endeavors or small; celebrating those who took responsibility for their lives, and condemning those who did not. That sounded right to me in 1960 and still sounds right in 2010."
>
> "Second, Ayn Rand portrayed a world I wanted to live in, not because I would be rich or powerful in it, but because it consisted of people I wanted to be around. As conditions deteriorate in 'Atlas Shrugged,' the first person to quit in disgust at Hank Rearden's steel mill is Tom Colby, head of the company union: 'For ten years, he had heard himself denounced throughout the country, because his was a "company union" and because he had never engaged in a violent conflict with the management. This was true; no conflict had ever been necessary; Rearden paid a higher wage scale than any union scale in the country, for which he demanded—and got—the best labor force to be found anywhere.'"
>
> "That's not a world of selfishness or greed. It's a world of cooperation and mutual benefit through the pursuit of self-interest, enabling satisfying lives not only for the Hank Reardens of the world but for factory workers. I still want to live there."
>
> ". . . In scene after scene, Rand shows what such a community would be like, and it does not consist of isolated individualists holding one another at arm's length. Individualists, yes, but ones who have fun in one another's company, care about one another, and care for one another—not out of obligation, but out of mutual respect and spontaneous affection."

I first read Atlas Shrugged when I was in my early twenties. I have read it again every decade without fail. Each time I learn more and more from it, get more and more out of it.[11] I assign it as a required reading in my introductory economics courses. To say that I am a fan of this book would be a gigantic understatement. I think it is *the* best novel ever written.[12]

I use Murray's (2010) as a jumping off point for this section of the paper since I greatly admire him, his courage (Murray, 1984; Herrnstein and Murray, 1994) and his appreciation of Rand (1957). However, I would quarrel with several aspects of what I quote from him above. He says: "That's not a world of selfishness or greed." No, I say, that *is* a world of selfishness and greed, but, in the immortal words of Gordon Gekko "Greed is good."[13] This, at least, is the message I get from Smith (1776) and his "invisible hand":

> "But the annual revenue of every society is always precisely equal to the exchangeable value of the whole annual produce of its industry, or rather is precisely the same thing with that exchangeable value. As every individual, therefore, endeavours as much as he can both to employ his capital in the support of domestic industry, and so to direct that industry that its produce may be of the greatest value; every individual necessarily labours to render the annual revenue of the society as great as he can. He generally, indeed, neither intends to promote the public interest, nor knows how much he is promoting it. By preferring the support of domestic to that of foreign industry, he intends only his own security; and by directing that industry in such a manner as its produce may be of the greatest value, he intends only his own gain, and he is in this, as in many other cases, led by an invisible hand to promote an end which was no part of his intention. Nor is it always the worse for the society that it was no part of it. By pursuing his own interest he frequently promotes that of the society more effectually than when he really intends to promote it. I have never known much good done by those who affected to trade for the public good. It is an affectation, indeed, not very common among merchants, and very few words need be employed in dissuading them from it."

The point I take away from the "invisible hand" is that greed, magically, is turned into something good, e.g., cooperation (Childs, 1977; Diamond, 1987; Flew, 1987; Garrison, 1985; Smith, 1776). The entrepreneur does not intend to promote anything like the "public good," or, even, to help other people. He only wants to selfishly, earn money.[14] But, through the "magic of the marketplace" or, what is the same thing, the "invisible hand," this goal of his is made compatible with helping other people. For, the only way he can earn wealth under laissez faire capitalism, is by making other people offers they see as beneficial to themselves. So, paradoxically to many, "greed is good." The more money a man has made, honestly that is,[15] the greater has been his contribution to society.

Consider in this regard the following exchange[16] from Atlas Shrugged:

Hank Rearden: "Inasmuch as the formula of Rearden Metal is my own personal secret, and in view of the fact that the Metal costs much less to produce than you boys can imagine, I expect to skin the public to the tune of a profit of twenty-five per cent in the next few years."

Boy: "What do you mean, skin the public, Mr. Rearden?" asked the boy. "If it's true, as I've read in your ads, that your Metal will last three times longer than any other and at half the price, wouldn't the public be getting a bargain?"

Rearden: "Oh, have you noticed that?"

Let us focus on the phrase "skin the public." If this is not selfishness, incarnate, then nothing is. Of course, Rand's excellent command of economic theory will not allow her to end the discussion on that note. She knows full well that on the market, under the rules of the free enterprise system, *both* parties to any and all exchanges must expect to benefit, otherwise there would be no deal. So, of course those who purchase Rearden Metal "get a bargain." But that fact cannot be allowed to undermine the claim that Rearden was indeed "skinning the public" and that at least one of the underpinnings of such an arrangement would be greed. Rearden, of course, could have *given away* his discovery to all and sundry. That would not have been greedy. But he did not. Instead, he allowed greed to enter into his deliberations.

I gently chide Murray (2010) and also Rand (1957) herself, for pulling punches as far as unionism is concerned. The former highlights a member of organized labor: "As conditions deteriorate in 'Atlas Shrugged,' the first person to quit in disgust at Hank Rearden's steel mill is Tom Colby, head of the company union." To be sure, it cannot be denied, that there is nothing per se wrong with labor organizations, whether company unions or not, as long as they confine themselves to threatening and/or actually engaging in mass quits. After all, if a single individual cannot quit, he is a slave. The overwhelming objection to that "curious institution" is that its victims could not leave. They were compelled to stay. But if one person quits a job, his fellow workers to not thereby lose their rights to engage in the same behavior. Therefore, a mass quit is justified under libertarian law.[17] However, apart from company unions of course there are no such organizations, without exception, that limit themselves in this manner. They all threaten and engage in violence during "strikes": they use physical force to prevent raw materials from entering the factory, finished products from leaving it, and intimidate replacement workers the boss dares to hire in their stead.[18] And, if they do not engage in such acts on their own accounts, they rely, depend upon, favor, benefit from, support, labor legislation that accomplishes these same ends. The employer is forced to "bargain fairly" with unionized workers, when he would vastly prefer to fire them all, and hire a different labor force.

Murray might object that he was only focusing positive attention on a company union, which necessarily forebears from restricting entry. True. But why compliment even these kinds of labor organizations? Did Rearden Steel really need a union in the first place? Not hardly, since he "*paid a higher wage scale than any union scale in the country, for which he demanded—and got—the best labor force to be found anywhere.*" But even if this company paid *lower* wages, as long as they were voluntarily agreed upon, there would be nothing untoward about such a situation, as implied by this statement of his.

CONCLUSION

I shall never forget my numerous meetings with Ayn Rand. She had the most piercing eyes I have ever witnessed. She fairly sparkled with brilliance. She and her chief lieutenant, Nathaniel Brandon, were instrumental in turning me toward the path of promoting liberty. I shall always be grateful. Yes, she had personal flaws. I cannot agree with all of her opinions (Block, 2003). She was far too harsh to us libertarians. However, I can never think of her without breaking out into a huge smile.

NOTES

1. Doherty (2007) very correctly mentions her in this regard along with Milton Friedman, Friedrich Hayek, Ludwig von Mises and Murray N. Rothbard.

2. She (1971) stated: "For the record, I shall repeat what I have said many times before: I do not join or endorse any political group or movement. More specifically, I disapprove of, disagree with, and have no connection with, the latest aberration of some conservatives, the so-called hippies of the right, who attempt to snare the younger or more careless ones of my readers by claiming simultaneously (sic) to be followers of my philosophy and advocates of anarchism. Anyone offering such a combination confesses his inability to understand either. Anarchism is the most irrational, anti-intellectual notion ever spun by the concrete-bound, context-dropping, whim-worshiping fringe of the collectivist movement, where it properly belongs." So disgusted with libertarians was she that she could not even bring herself to mention the dread "L" word in this rejection of them.

3. See for example Schwartz (1986). For a rejoinder, see Block (2003).

4. Another person who fully imbibed the political economic philosophy then prevailing in this geographical area was Bernie Sanders, an acquaintance of mine and

a fellow member of our high school track team. He is now a Senator from Vermont, running for the presidency of the U.S. and a leading "progressive."

5. Bless her, so to speak; she always insisted upon "Miss Rand," rejecting the politically correct "Ms." appellation.

6. They were Rand (1957) and Hazlitt (1946).

7. In a previous version of this essay, the following words appeared: "I passionately loved the economics they were supporting. To think that the market has self-organizing principles and that no government intervention could improve it, nay, would necessarily worsen it, was a thing of beauty." But upon further reflection, I was then in error with regards to these words: "nay, would necessarily worsen it. . ." The point is, whenever the government acts, it benefits some (the bureaucrats, the crony capitalists, etc.) and violates the rights of others (taxpayers, those worsened by regulations). So, some gain, others lose. Since interpersonal comparisons of utility are invalid, it is impossible to say that on net balance government intervention "worsens" anything. All we can say that is necessarily true is that it can never be shown that the state improves economic welfare.

8. Brahms, Chopin, Liszt, Schumann, Berlioz, Rachmaninoff, Bruckner.

9. My favorites then, and now, were and are Bach, Mozart, Handel, Vivaldi, Beethoven.

10. Austrian economics took a bit longer. I was a student of logical positivist Chicagoan Gary Becker, and I simply couldn't get my mind around the idea of the synthetic a priori: a statement that was necessarily true and yet related to the real world, e.g., not a tautology. I also had a vested interest in my studies at Columbia in neoclassical economics.

11. I have never read the 100 page or so Galt's speech section of this book. A moral failing on my part? I think not. My assessment is that the economics of the Objectivists are inspiring, uplifting, magnificent. The rest of it I can do without.

12. My second and third favorites are Potok (1967, 1969) Hey, I *told* you this paper would be autobiographical.

13. https://www.youtube.com/watch?v=PF_iorX_MAw.

14. Typically, of course, not only for himself but for his family, friends, charity, whatever.

15. If he "earns" it though a bailout, or a tariff protection, he is part of the crony capitalist system, not the laissez faire version, and Rand would never in a million years champion him. Indeed, Atlas is replete with disdain for people like that, for example Jim Taggart and other villains.

16. Source: http://en.wikiquote.org/wiki/Atlas_Shrugged.

17. Early antitrust laws and judicial decisions made such behavior illegal on grounds of so-called "restraint of trade."

18. These are called "scabs" by members of these employees associations. Why this is not part of "hate speech," on the lines of the "N" word for black people, or the "K" word for Jews, is not that much of a mystery. It is because the powers that be, at least on the left side of the aisle, themselves hate and denigrate replacement workers who they see as exploiters working as junior partners for the bosses. Whereas they see African Americans and Jews as downtrodden victims.

REFERENCES

Block, Walter E. 2003. "Libertarianism vs. Objectivism; A Response to Peter Schwartz," *Reason Papers*, vol. 26, Summer, 39–62; http://www.reasonpapers.com/pdf/26/rp_26_4.pdf.

Childs, Roy A., Jr. 1977. "The invisible hand strikes back." In *The Journal of Libertarian Studies*, vol. 1, no. 1, Winter, 23–34.

Diamond, Jr., Arthur M. 1987." The Intergenerational Invisible Hand: A Comment on Sartorius's "Government Regulation and Intergenerational Justice." In *The Journal of Libertarian Studies*, vol. 8, no. 2, Summer, 269–74.

Doherty, Brian. 2007. *Radicals for Capitalism*. New York, New York: Public Affairs

Flew, Anthony. 1987. "Social Science: Making Visible the Invisible Hands." In *The Journal of Libertarian Studies*, vol. 8, no. 2, Summer, 197–212 .

Garrison, Roger W. 1985. "Intertemporal Coordination and the Invisible Hand: An Austrian Perspective on the Keynesian Vision." In *History of Political Economy*, vol. 17, no. 2 (Summer), 309–21.

Hazlitt, Henry. 2008 [1946]. *Economics in One Lesson*. Auburn, Alabama: Mises Institute; http://mises.org/books/economics_in_one_lesson_hazlitt.pdf; https://www.google.com/#q=amanda+billyrock+economics+in+one+lesson.

Herrnstein, Richard J. and Murray, Charles. 1994. *The Bell Curve: Intelligence and Class Structure in American Life*. New York: The Free Press.

Jackson, Robert H. 1949. *Terminiello v. Chicago*, 337 U.S. 1, no. 272. http://scholar.google.com/scholar_case?case=2189837708321658845&q=terminiello+v.+chicago+(1949)&hl=en&as_sdt=8000006&as_vis=1.

Murray, Charles. 2010. "Who is Ayn Rand? A review of Goddess of the Market: Ayn Rand and the American Right by Jennifer Burns." In *Claremont Review of Books*. vol. X, Number 2, Spring; http://www.claremont.org/article/who-is-ayn-rand/#.VNAgwE90yM8.

Murray, Charles. 1984. *Losing Ground: American Social Policy from 1950 to 1980*. New York: Basic Books.

Potok, Chaim. 1967. *The Chosen*. New York: Simon and Schuster.

Potok, Chaim. 1969. *The Promise*. New York: Simon and Schuster.

Rand, Ayn. 1957. *Atlas Shrugged*. New York: Random House.

Rand, Ayn. 1971. "Libertarians." The Objectivist, September, 1;http://aynrandlexicon.com/lexicon/libertarians.html.

Schwartz, Peter. 1986. "Libertarianism: the Perversion of Liberty," New York: The Intellectual Activist; a condensed version of this work appeared in "Ayn Rand, The Voice of Reason: Essays in Objectivist Theory." Edited by Leonard Peikoff. New York: New American Library, 1988, 311–33.

Smith, Adam. [1776] 1979. *An Inquiry into the Nature and Causes of the Wealth of Nations*. Indianapolis, Indiana: Liberty Fund; B.IV, Ch.2, Of Restraints upon the Importation from Foreign Countries in paragraph IV.2.9.

Chapter 19

The Freedom Gradient in Ayn Rand's Novels

Andrew Bernstein

The focus of Ayn Rand's fiction is the importance of values in human life. An individual's personal values—whether education, career, friendship, romantic love, children and family, any and all of them, or something entirely different—provide meaning to his/her life.

But a significant degree of political freedom is required to seek one's values—or, alternatively stated, to engage in the pursuit of happiness. If individual rights are respected and upheld, one is at liberty to pursue one's cherished dreams; conversely, if one's life belongs to the state, then one's values are dictated by the state, and dissent brings punishment swift, certain, and often terminal.

Rand, therefore, shows profound concern for the political-economic principles of the societies in which her characters reside. If, by contrast, she were in the modernist school of literature, telling stories in which characters, riddled with ennui, slouched purposelessly about, valueless, aimless, seeking no goal and pursuing no attainment, then politics would be irrelevant; one could idle as fulsomely under freedom as in a dictatorship; a spineless individual's dysfunctional family could spiritually crush him with equal facility regardless whether or not his rights are upheld by the legal system.

But an individual of significant moral strength—an Ayn Rand hero—to take action leading to achievement of goals worthy and arduous, requires freedom to take such steps. For a Howard Roark or a Dagny Taggart, it is vital that his/her rights are recognized, respected, and protected by the legal system. Political realities to such a person—fictitious or in real-life—are, in fact, a difference maker.

Observe the societies presented in Rand's four novels: Two are totalitarian states—in *We The Living* and in *Anthem;* a third is on the cusp of becoming one—in *Atlas Shrugged;* and the fourth is a mixed economy leaning toward freedom—in *The Fountainhead.* Therefore, the struggles of her differing protagonists to achieve values are necessarily different—as are the respective outcomes of those struggles.

Scan the freedom gradient from worst to best.

In *Anthem,* the entirety of planet Earth is an inveterate totalitarian state. The Communists, Fascists, or some hybrid of the two have seized control of human society, have converted the globe into a single, unified collectivist dictatorship, and did so an unspecified number of decades in the past. Society has been thoroughly collectivized. The state controls not merely the bodies of its citizens, compelling them to toil for the people; but more insidiously, their minds—all first-person singular pronouns have been expunged from the language. Men cannot even think of themselves as individuals; even if referring to themselves alone, a solitary unit, outside the presence of other human beings, they necessarily think of themselves as "we." The word "I" is an "Unmentionable Word" in this society; discovering and speaking it is the sole crime punishable by death. The collectivists have utterly stifled the independent mind, making progress impossible, regress certain, and a second dark age—mirroring that of the past—a grim reality.

We The Living is set during the early years of the Soviet Union, a society recently collectivized by the Communists, who now consolidate their power; but for centuries prior a land ruled by a brutal absolute monarchy, a nation that, throughout its history, has had but scant experience of political-economic freedom. The Communists, fighting remorseless and unrelenting class warfare, persecute members of the former bourgeoisie, above all, those who had been aristocrats. An individual has no right to his/her own life, and persons are condemned to hard labor in Siberian gulags—a death sentence—for disagreement with the State. The borders are closed to emigration—so those who yearn for freedom cannot gain it elsewhere. Collectivists here—in contrast to the social rulers in *Anthem*—have not had sufficient time to consolidate power, to suppress freethinking minds, or to expunge first-person singular pronouns from the language. A dark age, although looming, is not yet reality.

Atlas Shrugged, written in the 1950s, is set in an America of an unspecified future. The rest of the world has been swallowed by Communism; only America remains a mixed economy, still featuring a precarious remnant of individual rights and private property. The society slides precipitously toward full collectivization—totalitarianism is one severe crisis and no more than several years away—but, throughout most of the story's action, is not yet present. Further, America's collapse into statism is abetted by a mysterious disappearance of its leading minds, a brain drain that is as frightening as it is inexplicable. Nobody seems to know where the country's top minds are going. In their absence, vital social institutions—schools, the economy, the arts, science—egregiously devolve, giving the power-craving politicos pretext to seize increasing rights-violating authority; in their absence, there are none to speak out against escalating despotism.

The Fountainhead, set in America between the world wars of the twentieth century, features a mixed economy still possessing significant elements of freedom. Although in the 1930s—in real life and in the universe of the novel—collectivist dictatorships subjugate large portions of Europe, in America individual citizens retain most of the fundamental rights upheld by the nation's Founders. Freedom of speech, freedom of religion, the right to private property, the right to earn and retain profit, the right to emigrate, and others are all upheld by the legal system. The universe of *The Fountainhead* presents a society and economy vastly freer than that exhibited in any of her other novels. The result is that a quest for significant values undertaken by any rational, determined man or woman is confronted by no insuperable governmental impediments.

In brief: The society of *Anthem* is a long-established, deeply entrenched totalitarian state of unquestioned authority; of *We The Living* is a dictatorship recently imposed and still consolidating power; of *Atlas Shrugged* is a near dictatorship about to take the last fateful steps and expunge all elements of individual rights; of *The Fountainhead* is a mixed economy still leaning toward freedom, but with an intellectual figure of significant social power—Ellsworth Toohey—pushing it inexorably toward collectivism.

One important question Rand addresses in these stories is: For an independent individual to pursue and attain significant values in these differing societies, what types of actions are necessary? What steps are inescapable? What forms of opposition will he/she confront?

Study the stories one at a time.

In *Anthem,* Equality's goal to be a scientist *within the parameters of the collectivist state* is doomed. The rulers crush his aspirations at every turn. They deny him entry to the Home of the Scholars; they relegate him to the lowliest of menial tasks, that of street sweeper—and do so because they recognize his superlative intelligence; they will terminate both his light and his life. A man of great intelligence is a potential threat; a man who deploys that intelligence independently is a severe danger. Like the "Saint of the Pyre," who is burned alive for re-discovering and speaking the Unmentionable Word, "I," Equality, if he remains in this society, will be executed by the state.

Equality's only chance, therefore, lies outside the collectivist state. He has but two options: He may escape—or he may rebel. In the event, he does both. When the dictators make clear they will execute him for the "crime" of thinking and functioning autonomously—and worse, that they will destroy his re-invented electric light—he breaks out of the makeshift courthouse, bolts through the empty streets, and plunges into the uncharted wilderness.

The rulers, afraid to enter the primeval forest, and convinced the transgressor will be devoured by wild beasts, let him go.

He is joined there by the woman he loves, who likewise escapes—together they find remnants of an earlier freer period—including a former private residence containing books, from which they learn much, especially regarding the power of electricity. Armed with electricity, a force far beyond the ken of the Dark Age rulers, they will convert their house into a fortress, then steal into town to liberate those most independent, who will join them in re-establishing a free society. In time, word of their achievements will spread and lead to a mass exodus from the collectivists' brutally suppressive, primitive world and to the shining city on the hill founded by Equality and his lover.

The all-encompassing power of the state is a double-edge sword, hindering and endangering Equality's quest for scientific advance, to be sure, but at the same time, it curtails the rulers' ability to effectively oppose him. The stifling of mankind's finest minds, the brutally imposed requirement to kowtow to the people, the harsh penalties meted out to autonomous thinkers, have resulted necessarily in a stagnant, collapsed, utterly backward society akin to dark age Europe, and for the same reason. Accustomed to nothing but decades of blind obedience, intellectually unequipped to confront a brilliant thinker and his advances—facing electric light with candle, and, in effect, machine guns with bow and arrow—the dictatorial rulers have little chance to prevail.

A fully collectivist world, with no free society from which to beg, borrow, or steal ideas, devolves rapidly to primitivism. Brute force (as Ragnar Danneskjold in *Atlas Shrugged* teaches the collectivists) will necessarily succumb before the vastly greater power of mind plus force.

In *We The Living,* Kira Argounova and especially Leo Kovalensky—like Equality—have no chance to fulfill their respective dreams within the confines of the totalitarian state. Leo is the especial target of the Communist dictatorship. He is an aristocrat—the son of Admiral Kovalensky, executed by the Communists for "counter-revolutionary" activities—and he is a dashing, gay-spirited, brilliant young man, who openly, recklessly mocks Communism, its principles, its policies, its practices. He is in his twenties during the course of the story; his life expectancy, in this society, can be measured perhaps in years—but not in decades. The field of philosophy, his love, is closed to him; only Marxists may enter this profession; those critical of socialist principles are thankful to retain their lives, and may bid definitive farewell to all hopes of a career. When he contracts tuberculosis, the doors of every state sanitarium are slammed vigorously in his face; he is to be left to die; his life is saved only by Kira, his lover, sleeping secretly with a Communist, thereby raising funds sufficient to send him to one of the few private hospitals remaining in the early years of the Soviet Union.

Kira, daughter of a factory owner, common law wife of an aristocrat, individualist, and outspoken critic of Communism, is likewise doomed in this society, her dream of being an engineer crushed by the state when—despite her brilliant mind and great potential—she is expelled from school.

When Leo, the last of her major values, is morally and spiritually broken by the totalitarian state, there is nothing for her in the Soviet Union but unrelieved misery. The only hope lies in escape to the West, where, living in freedom she can pursue a career of engineering and, presumably, love again. She and Leo, in the past, had tried defection, but caught, were fortunate to emerge with their lives. This time Kira is not so fortunate. She is shot and killed as she attempts to cross the Finnish frontier—cold-bloodedly murdered in an impassioned quest for freedom.

A relatively young totalitarian state, one nation in a wider world where freedom still exists, is unable to impose a virulent collectivism that crushes all autonomous functioning. Defiant spirits, in this society, still exist. But this absence of full collectivization, for the heroes, is as much a double-edged sword as is its presence in the universe of *Anthem.* Soviet society has not collapsed into unrelieved primitivism. With the mind not yet fully repressed, and with contact preserved with a freer West, there still exist some elements of art, of science, and of technology.

Because of these, Kira and Leo have some limited access to telephones, radios, automobiles, electric light, and twentieth-century medicine—conveniences denied to Equality. But the State likewise has access to these technologies—and to guns, cannons, and trucks, as well. Related, the rulers of the nascent dictatorship have extensive experience dealing with independent thinkers left over from the country's slightly freer past; they have not been lulled into lethargy by multiple consecutive decades of mindless obedience to their every dictate; they are vigilantly suppressive of such "counter-revolutionaries" as Leo Kovalensky. Escape—and/or revolution—in an infant dictatorship are undertakings significantly more arduous and vastly more dangerous than under a collectivist regime in its dotage.

The stories of *Atlas Shrugged* and *The Fountainhead* are Rand's only ones set in the United States—and in an America recognizable to her twentieth-century readers. Although one society possesses vastly more pronounced elements of freedom and fewer of statism than the other, they are both nevertheless mixed economies. In *Atlas Shrugged,* however, the elements of freedom are imminently to be effaced, replaced by the type of collectivist dictatorship depicted in *We The Living.*

The freedom of thought and action possessed by Dagny Taggart and Hank Rearden throughout much of *Atlas Shrugged* vastly exceeds that not only of Equality but of Kira and Leo, as well. They can and do speak out against the growing despotism of the state; they run their businesses (and in Rearden's case, owns his) with a degree of autonomy diminishing but real; they own and enjoy their wealth; they choose their friends, their lover—each other—and the use of their time. The state depicted here equals in despotism that shown in *We The Living* only near the end of the story's extended development; it never approximates the brutal, blanket suppressiveness of the regime presented in *Anthem.*

Because of this, the heroes can reach spectacular intellectual and practical achievements: Rearden revolutionizes the field of metallurgy with the invention of Rearden Metal, an alloy as superior to steel as is steel to iron. Dagny builds the John Galt Line, saving for the moment the great industrial enterprises of Colorado. Above all, behind the scenes, unobserved for a full two-thirds of the story by the narrators and, consequently, by the reader, stands the imposing figure of John Galt. Even the attenuated freedom of America's mixed economy is sufficient for Galt to reach exalted successes: He not only invents a motor based on a revolutionary theory of energy, one that will transform industrial society—but even more revolutionary, he identifies previously unrecognized moral and philosophic principles enabling him to prostrate the incipient collectivist dictatorship before its noxious presence is fully established. Throughout most of the story, Galt is sufficiently free to covertly travel the breadth of the country, speak to leading disaffected thinkers, and persuade them to join the mind on strike.

The success of Galt's strike leads to two important, related developments: The first is that it hastens the collapse into primitivism of America's socialist dictatorship. The leading thinkers are suppressed not over a period of years or decades, leading to society's inexorable but gradual descent into the abyss; rather, they are removed before the dictators consolidate power. The effects of this brain drain are experienced before the imposition of blanket statism: Philosophy devolves into arrant skepticism—the arts are practiced exclusively by talentless hacks—science is taken over by men seeking political power not cognitive advance—technological and medical development cease—the railroads collapse—the steel industry collapses—agriculture collapses—all of this even before Dagny Taggart and Hank Rearden join the strike.

The second consequence is the providing of safe haven for mankind's best—those who choose to fully cultivate and deploy their intelligence. Throughout history and across the globe, independent thinkers have been at the mercy of brutes. They have been tortured, beheaded, burned, forced to drink poison, and savagely persecuted in a variety of other forms. Galt's strike definitively ends this. Galt's Gulch is a refuge for the intellect, haven of the mind, safe port from the centuries-old storm of oppression unleashed on mankind's noblest benefactors. Here, the mind is free; here, the mind flourishes; here, the mind nurtures advance in every cognitive field. Here civilization exists. When the dictatorship collapses but a short interval into its full inception, the men of the mind return to the world. Unencumbered by dictatorial impediment, they will rebuild it quickly.

The strike of the men of the mind, in bringing down the collectivist dictatorship, is a form of revolution. In effect, it constitutes a revolution of omission, rather than of commission. Rather than taking oppositional action *against* the state, it withdraws supportive action *from* the state. In largest part, the strike is designed to provide a free enclave for mankind's thinkers; but it additionally seeks to bring down the wider dictatorship and restore freedom to America.

Observe an important similarity with *Anthem* and *We The Living:* In all three novels, the heroes seek escape from a repressive state. In the society of *Atlas Shrugged*, its tenuous, soon-to-be-extinguished element of intellectual-political-economic freedom is sufficient for the thinkers to escape, and to accomplish in practice that which Equality aspires to: They create a free society, an impregnable fortress of the mind from which individual liberty will radiate out into the wider world.

Howard Roark, in *The Fountainhead,* stands alone among Ayn Rand's heroes in confronting no dictatorial regime. He struggles forward against the entrenched architectural standards of a conservative society—principles uncritically held by compliant, conforming private individuals and institutions—but it is only at story's climax that he confronts the legal, rights-crushing power of the state. He creates brilliant plans for an innovative, government-built housing project—but the enterprise is controlled by Ellsworth Toohey, a Marxist social worker-power luster, to whom Roark represents the individualist devil—the sole payment Roark requests is the building be constructed in exact specification with his design—he is not paid—for Toohey and other government bureaucrats permit his brilliant design to be adulterated, and the building thereby stripped of artistic integrity.

What is Roark to do? He has no recourse to the courts, because he cannot sue the government. He does what he must—he blows up the building—first ensuring there is no one present—then turns himself in, stands trial, and speaks loudly, brilliantly, passionately for the rights of an individual to his own mind, his own work, his own life. He is heard. He is acquitted. He is vindicated. A private businessman purchases the property from the U.S. government, and hires Roark to build the housing project exactly as he originally designed it.

Roark lives and triumphs in a fictitious version of America's mixed economy of the 1920s and 1930s—the freest society, by far, in any of Ayn Rand's novels. Roark needs neither to escape nor bring down the regime. He can succeed in his field and on his terms in the largely free society he currently inhabits.

Toohey, knowing that in a relatively free society he is powerless to stop Roark and other individualists, seeks to extirpate all vestiges of American freedom. In the Communist dictatorship Toohey lusts to impose, he, as intellectual advisor behind the throne, can incarcerate, enslave, and/or execute the Roarks of the world. Toohey, in the freer America of *The Fountainhead,* attempts to obtrude upon her citizens a dictatorial regime akin to that of *We The Living;* perhaps, in time, even that of *Anthem.*

It is of interest to note that the societies of *The Fountainhead* and of *We The Living* are reasonably accurate portrayals of societies extant in Ayn Rand's lifetime, both of which she experienced first-hand; whereas the societies depicted in *Atlas Shrugged* and, especially, in *Anthem* are fictitious projections of where America and the world would end if the collectivist trends of Rand's lifetime continued.

Rand's passionate interest, as noted, was to examine the role of values in human life. The political-economic system under which an individual lives plays a critical role in deciding the outcome of his/her pursuit of values. Therefore, Rand's fictional corpus can be understood as a study of the indispensable role played by political-economic liberty in the quest for man's earthly fulfillment.

REFERENCES

Rand, Ayn. [1957] 1996. *Atlas Shrugged.* New York: Signet.
Rand, Ayn. [1961] 1999. *Anthem.* New York: Plume.
Rand, Ayn. [1943] 1996. *The Fountainhead.* New York: Signet.
Rand, Ayn. [1936] 1996. *We the Living.* New York: New American Library.

Chapter 20

Identity, Professional Ethics, and Substantive Style in *The Fountainhead*

William Kline

INTRODUCTION

At first glance, *The Fountainhead* is an awful book on business ethics. The protagonist, Howard Roark, doesn't listen to clients. He passes up lucrative deals and refuses to network in order to get contracts. The few offers he does get he's likely to refuse because he does not get his own way; he doesn't compromise an inch. *The Fountainhead* reads like a manual on how not to do business. As for ethics, Roark is a self-proclaimed egoist. The reason he doesn't listen to others is he simply doesn't care, not for them or their opinions. Even when he helps design a home for the poor he does so only out of his own interest in solving certain architectural puzzles. A total unwillingness to compromise combined with a "me first" attitude seems like a recipe for business and ethical disaster, and many interpret it that way. This popular interpretation is wrong. A profession can be part of one's identity and, as such, following your business calling is every bit as important as any other such endeavor. *The Fountainhead* is a powerful vision of both business and ethics. Business can be an art embodying the substantive style of the professional. Substantive style comprises the integrated character traits that embody skill, virtue, aesthetics and mindset. The content of this style is determined both through personal ethics and the nature of the profession one chooses. In this regard, *The Fountainhead* makes the argument that intermediary institutions like professional standards are crucial for flourishing lives within capitalism. In turn, capitalism's defense in *The Fountainhead* is that it allows for multiple such styles. Business ethics, far from being an oxymoron or ad hoc list of rules, helps us to flourish within a market economy by mapping out the different substantive styles required by different professions; enabling us to consciously choose how we work and live.

IDENTITY AND BUSINESS

People seem to understand the importance of identity when it comes to religion and/or sexuality, but they almost never acknowledge it with business. John Stuart Mill in "On Liberty" discusses the importance of liberty for finding truth and meaning in experiments in living. His arguments go beyond simple utility. Living free and choosing your own path is essentially human. A theme we even find in his essay "Utilitarianism" where he tells us it is better to be Socrates dissatisfied than a pig satisfied (Mill, 1985, 264).

Separating someone from their beliefs or loved ones is an exceptionally cruel act that strikes at the foundation of our humanity. Oddly, though, he also tells us that the "principle of free trade" and the principle of liberty rest on different grounds and that the principle of individual liberty is not involved in the doctrine of Free Trade" (1991, 105). We also find this in his *Principles of Political Economy (*858–59), where he holds that there are many exceptions in economics (871), while almost none in the sphere of personal liberty (859). Personal liberty and economics liberty are entirely different and the latter can be interfered with for almost any utilitarian reason. Mill's only possible argument, which he never explicitly gives, is that money and commerce are fungible and hence cannot have the same deep meaning as either truth or experiments in living. *The Fountainhead* shows that Mill's distinction is much too facile.

Howard Roark always wanted to be an architect. It's an essential part of who he is.

It is the limit case, but one that needs to be made: Business is not always something separable from identity. If it were always separable, then commercial activity would be fungible and one choice would be as good as any other. If, however, the choice of career can be like the choice of a spouse this has real moral implications. Separating Roark from architecture would be cruel for precisely the same reasons as not allowing someone to marry the person of their choice. Given the reasons some choose to marry, it may even be worse to interfere with a person's choice of profession.

Roark does more than talk about how important architecture is. He does not simply fall in love with it and stare into its eyes. He structures his life around it. He easily puts in the 10,000 hours Malcolm Gladwell talks about for success (2008). His work experience exhibits Flow as identified by Mihaly Csiksentmihalyi (2008). Roark *is* an architect because he *does* architecture and he does it because it is who he is. It is not difficult to find real-life examples of this behavior. The Beatles' early years in Hamburg are one example.[1] Reading Chef Gordan Ramsey's autobiography provides another example (Ramsey, 2007). Howard Roark may be fictional, but how hard he works because his work means so much to him, is not. There is no principled argument for separating business from identity and any reason given for such a separation could be applied to any area of life. If who we are guides what we do which in turn also influences who we are, then how we approach business says something about who we are and want to be just like any other human endeavor.

You could argue that Roark is actually an artist and this is importantly different from just doing business. The artistic muse lies deep within the artist's psyche driving them to create their vision with a passion and dedication few of us really ever experience. This, it could be argued, is what separates art from business. It could be argued that by conflating the two Rand makes it look like business is central to our lives when, in fact, it is art that holds this place and Rand is engaging in a fallacy of composition. There are two limitations, though, with this type of argument.

First, it takes money to pursue creative activities. In a market economy, pursuing art often requires selling art. Clients are paying clients and, as such, a significant portion of the artist's activity rests on the necessity of earning money. Even in a nonmarket system, the artist would still need to gain money either from wealthy patrons or the government. The question is about the source of the funding, not the need for funding. Second, problem with the "artistic muse vs. business golem" argument is that it posits making money as a mindless, and hence virtueless, activity. We will consider both in order.

"THE MARKET"

The Fountainhead does not primarily argue against taking money from the government. Roark works on Cortland with only a minor polemic on how he does not understand the logic of subsidized housing. He then proceeds to design it. The main point with Cortland is the danger of having a single benefactor, public or private. Those who completely depend upon Wynand, he often destroys. Keating takes Ellsworth Toohey's attentions as a God send and comes to depend on them, only to find Toohey withdrawing them later with disastrous consequences. Relying solely on government favors has the same effect on the State Science Institute in Atlas Shrugged. Putting all your eggs in one funding source basket jeopardizes the independence which is required to form an identity through creative thought and action.

One could counter argue that putting all your eggs in the market does the same thing. We should be careful, though, not to reify "the market." First, there is no single market that governs everything. In the world there are many, many markets that interact with each other and individuals. Second, "the market" is shorthand for a system that allows and protects individuals making deals among themselves. "The Market" does not pay Roark, individuals who are interested in his work pay him. These individuals operate within a framework where they are free to contract with him, and he with them. He is free to reach any individual, or group of individuals, within this system. He is also free to walk away from them. Each client is a single funder within a sea of other such independent clients. This is what allows Roark to diversify his clients within his niche. Depending on any one source of income would threaten the creative freedom he so values and it is the market that allows for this diversity. And this is not just fiction. What Roark does with many projects including the Enright House, and Monadnock Valley, the famous Welsh architect Clough Williams-Ellis does with the village/resort of Portmeirion.

From the beginning, Clough Williams-Ellis relied on markets for his masterpiece: The Village of Portmeirion. Williams-Ellis lacked the funds to build the entire project immediately out of his own pocket. He tells us that while he has had some very compliant clients in the past, none have been so complaint as to let him do whatever he wanted and this is why Williams-Ellis eschews one or a few wealthy donors as the source of funding for Portmeirion (2014, 14). Instead, from the beginning, he envisions a project with a "vivifying principle, a use, a job, that would make and keep it viable" (13) and by viable, he means profitable. His reasoning is something that could come straight out of *The Fountainhead.* "I must have my own tune, so I alone must pay the piper . . . Therefore the thing had to be so devised that it would not only pay adequate interest on my small initial investment, but soon begin to accumulate reserves for further capital expenditures on expansion and improvement" (15). His great work of architecture would need a business model that was equal to the project. Broad commercial interest in his project is what would give him the most freedom to create his own artistic vision.

In *The Fountainhead*, this dependence on customers is initially bad news for both Mallory and Roark since most do not seem to want the art either has to offer. The difference between the two is that Roark is confident he will find and build his market, Mallory has all but given up until Roark finds him. There is a real strength in *The Fountainhead* here, for while free interactions within a market are what enables these artists to pursue their passion it is anything but an easy course. It almost destroys Mallory and forces Roark briefly out of the profession and into working in a quarry. "The Market" is not a quick fix, it requires hard work, and even then there is no guarantee of success as is shown in the character of Henry Cameron. Cameron was talented, had worked hard and built a customer base. Changes in time, to his working team, and even to his temperament led him to lose his clientele and he finishes his working life redesigning garages from a garret of an office, going to live with his sister after his health fails him. Critics of Rand who accuse her of a Panglossian view of the market have simply not read the book.

This deep criticism of the market is often overlooked by detractors and fans alike. *The Fountainhead* is about the ultimate human flourishing that can be achieved by following your own path according to your own lights. It's when you choose the Road Less Travelled for your own reasons and revel in that choice. But, through both the machinations of Ellsworth Toohey and Gail Wynand's Banner we see Rand's opinion of most market actors: They are short-sighted sheep who have no thoughts of their own. In the background of the book that gives Roark the stark contrast he needs to make Rand's point, is an almost entire population succumbing to J.K. Galbraith's "dependence effect" and Thorstein Veblen's "conspicuous consumption." This is mighty ironic since she would vigorously argue against both of these economists, yet the cattle she portrays as market actors in *The Fountainhead* exhibit exactly these thoughtless tendencies and the market caters to their banality.

Rand does not have some primrose notion of what the market is, *The Fountainhead* acknowledges the down side of markets and leads to the one argument in favor of the market that she has: The market allows the best to succeed in a manner that allows them to keep the greatest amount of independence of thought and action. It does not guarantee success, and it is not the only system that allows great minds to succeed. But the argument of *The Fountainhead* is that it is the only system that maximizes both success rates and independence.

THE MONEY

In market economies people want money and getting money does not always require being virtuous. Rand recognizes this problem. In *The Fountainhead* Roark's foil is Peter Keating, and Peter makes a great deal of money simply copying the work of others or getting others to outright do his work. He eventually gets his comeuppance, but a host of other copycat architects do just fine in the book. Independent rational thinking is not a necessary requirement for the individual to make money in the market. The same goes for groups of business people. Rand portrays corporate Boards of Directors in both *The Fountainhead* and Atlas Shrugged as mindless masses trying to avoid responsibility. Certainly these are not the people responsible for creative success, yet they still do financially well for themselves.

Rand never portrays the money changing part of business itself as the *sine qua non* of substantive style. Nor is getting rich the purpose of business. "Getting ahead" is something Peter Keating worries about. Money does influence integrity, but in *The Fountainhead* it consistently does so in a bad way. Steven Mallory carves cherubs to afford his hovel. Heaps of money are thrown at Roark and he struggles to decline commissions he badly needs.

Wynand uses money to degrade mistresses and to corrupt those who appear virtuous like Dwight Carson. In *The Fountainhead*, having money be the driving force for your motivation is much the same as a quest for power: it makes you a second-hander.

If money or power is your primary motivation, then you will do the same as Wynand does and publish lurid stories of fallen women instead of stories about scientists. You will act like Peter Keating and sell your wife for a lucrative and high profile development. The argument of *The Fountainhead* here is subtle, but important. Getting money does not always require independent thought and action. It doesn't even always require virtue. Luck and graft are two ways money can be made as well with Keating exhibiting the former and Wynand some of the latter. It is rather the point that making money can be part of substantive style, virtue, and individual judgment. It is this very possibility that is denied by so many. Forget Marx, no less than steel magnate Andrew Carnegie (1901) thought that business was an amoral activity that had to, more or less, be atoned for by philanthropic efforts. *The Fountainhead* is not a statistical study, it is a hypothetical argument of how making money can be an integral part of a virtuous life and hence part of one's identity. If Rand cannot show even hypothetically how this is possible, then the argument is lost at the start.

We are given one example of someone taking an identity from more traditional business in *The Fountainhead.* Kent Lansing is the person who helps Roark get the Cortland Hotel commission. He prides himself on being the middleman in deal making. He makes connections, he persuades, and gets people to invest in the best options possible. As such, he metaphorically stands for a wide range of merchant and finance activity that directs resources from less to more valued uses. He revels in his skill as a "middle man." Of course, he admits that most of those he deals with do not take the same joy from their work and do not have independent ideas on which business deals to pursue. He does, though, and he takes his measure of success form his ability to seal these deals.

Likewise, Roark does not take money as the measure of his success. In fact, we see Roark sacrificing income in order to redo projects in order to get them right. He never views "making money" and success as something separate from doing the work. In wanting money and fame Keating makes this distinction and it is why Keating doesn't really care how the job is done as long as it gets him money and fame. This is why Keating is always worried about what others think since it is their opinion that yields the returns he wants. For Roark, doing business is doing the work to the best of his ability, this is his business model. Roark's substantive style fundamentally involves honesty, integrity, independence, dependability and a host of other virtues that are all directly tied to the job at hand. This exemplifies a point business ethicist

Robert Solomon repeatedly makes: "Business is not "just business." It is not self-contained, with its own rationale, its own rules, its own reason for being. It is essentially, a part of human life and human community" (Solomon, 1999, 37). Roark's business model is almost invisible because it is entirely integrated with the rest of his life. Roark's life is actually his greatest work of art.

THE BEAUTIFUL (AND THE UGLY)

We do not need to prove that making money is always the pinnacle of human effort in order to show it can be quite important for identity and meaning. If we had to argue in this manner then Peter Keating's lackluster paintings toward the end of the book would serve as proof that Art really isn't that important to the artist or society. Nobody does that with bad art, we should start refraining from doing the same with unexceptional business deals.

Focusing on the lackluster in business taints all of business with the view that it is just a "grubbing" activity involving no skill and certainly no élan. Business ethicist Robert Solomon wisely calls our attention to how language and conceptual models frame our view of business. "How we do business—and what business does to us—has everything to do with how we think about business, talk about business, conceive of business, practice business" (1999, xxii). If we think of business a certain way, those within the field have a tendency to act that way and those outside the field tend to treat it that way thus having a mutually reinforcing effect on both business actions and business regulation. This is one reason books like *The Fountainhead* are so important. They write about business as it is and can be in aspirational, even aesthetic, language.

The Fountainhead, and later Atlas Shrugged, undoubtedly use aesthetics as part of the moral critique of both unethical and unexceptional behavior. Her vision of Romantic art is behind much of her descriptive prose and it is neither aesthetically nor morally neutral (Rand, 1971). Rand's descriptions of how Boards of Directors evade responsibility is an argument that these people are not engaging in business, but the argument is carried out aesthetically. Their actions, contrasted with the protagonists', are ugly and low. A sight that makes you want to turn your head. Often Roark has to force himself to look at these people while trying to do business with them. Some ethicists may resist the claim that this has anything to do with ethics. Certainly, the relationship between ethics and aesthetics needs more attention than we can give it here, but one thought is worth considering.

Philosophers like David Hume argue that our moral sensibilities are awakened more strongly the closer a person or event is to us. Pictures are one way this is done. Photos can alert people to moral horrors around the world. Judgments made while looking at these pictures involve a description of what happened and some standard as to why it is wrong. In addition to whatever ethical rules I use to judge such things, one further element impinges upon my judgment to make the scene even sadder: the thought of the beauty that could have been. It's an aesthetic judgment, but it is also a vision of flourishing of the scene on its own terms. Here the aesthetic component is integral to the moral judgment. If philosopher's like Hume are correct, one reason contiguity affects us so greatly is because it engages our notions of beauty. The same happens in writing

We find environmentalists like John Muir engaging in aesthetic critique as well as social critics like Patrick Geddes and Upton Sinclair. Dickens certainly employs descriptions of ugliness to critique industrial England. We find Rand doing the same in *The Fountainhead.* We see Roark respecting the landscape and building in harmony with it. This is not to make Rand a modern environmentalist, but it strongly suggests that the beauty of the physical world is part of the moral equation in *The Fountainhead*, and it is what makes her work powerful.

In *The Fountainhead*, the beauty of business comes through in people exercising their professional skills and capacities to their limits. Competent professionals comport themselves well. Roark, Dagny, and Wynand are beautiful in more than their looks. It is in their gait, tastes, conversation, and discretion. Roark's is an ascetic aesthetic. There is no clutter in his life as there is none in his mind. Wynand's is lavish and rich. Rand describes him as looking aristocratic and his trappings reinforce that. Ellsworth Toohey has a certain beauty to him. Even as one of the major antagonists, he uses his abilities to the utmost and he has a style to match.

This suggests something about Rand's view of business in *The Fountainhead.* It is the "doing" of a profession that constitutes the most important part of business. The standard of good business is a combination of the talents of the individual and the demands of the profession. It is a substantive style based on being not seeming. This is why while Toohey is Roark's enemy, it is Peter Keating who is Roark's opposite. Peter just seems. There is nothing real behind his success. He definitely does not want to do architecture and gets others to do it for him whenever he can. He never exercises his own judgment, wastes his talent and thereby wastes himself: the ultimate sin.

Business ethicist Robert Solomon might as well be talking about Keating when he discusses the "Chameleon." "The chameleon displays a . . . lack of integrity in his or her total absence of not only principles but goals as well, unless we want to accept "fit in and do whatever seems to please other people" as some sort of purpose in life" (Solomon, 1999, 41). The chameleon has no integrity (42). And, according to Solomon, without integrity there is no "self" (96). The source of flourishing is self-directed effort focused on self-chosen goals.

ETHICS

It is this primacy of beginning with the self that probably garners the largest popular and academic misgivings about *The Fountainhead.* One example in popular culture of this misgiving is expressed in the movie Dirty Dancing where one of the more sleazy characters, Robby, produces a copy, which gets a close-up, and says for the protagonist, of the movie, "Baby," to read it. Robby then states that "Some people matter and some people don't": his summary of the main message. In Academic circles, Robby's synopsis is taken as broadly correct and what we need is not to encourage emphasis on the self, but emphasis on the wants and needs of others. We need smarter Peter Keatings. In business ethics this takes the form of Stakeholder theory.

"Simply put, a stakeholder is any group or individual who can affect, or is affected by, the achievement of a corporation's purpose. Stakeholders include employees, customers, suppliers, stockholders, banks, environmentalists, government and other groups who can help or hurt the corporation" (Freeman vi, 2010). There is a rough distinction in the literature between management and normative stakeholder theory.[2] The former is offered as a pragmatic heuristic for doing good business. The latter is proposed as the way business ethically ought to be done. Normative stakeholder, theory, though, is actually ethically neutral. Its "normative core" is empty. How businesses ought to ethically operate depends on which ethical theory to choose to fill this normative core. R. Edward Freeman (1997) offers several moral theories that could serve as this core including pragmatic liberalism, the Doctrine of Fair Contracts, Feminist Standpoint Theory and Ecological principles. Looking at the normative cores he cites, not a single one focuses primarily on the business at hand. People, and their varying states of well-being are the direct data to be considered and adjusted to accordingly. This does not mean you cannot decide against some of those interests, only that you have considered them and decided to intentionally favor other stakeholder interests.

The primary job of the manager is to satisfy stakeholders and the way to do this is by considering their wants/needs first. Only after we have considered every stakeholder group can we then come up with an ethical plan for business implementation. Ideally, the manager's job is to satisfy, or at least not anger, stakeholders. It is the manager's job not to adversely impact their interests and, when possible, promote their interests. The manager does, the stakeholder receives. Furthermore, in addition to this responsibility the manager has discretionary authority to bring these states about. The manager *can* make you feel better or the manager *can* make you feel worse. It is the manager's job to make good states come about in the stakeholders and avoid causing bad states in these same stakeholders. Where only direct intention to do good for others counts as moral action, business becomes a vehicle for serving this version of common good and not an institution to produce a good or service for trade (Kline, 2006).

Alternatively *The Fountainhead* offers a vision where, within certain general rules, people should pursue their own interests and goals. These rules will consist of the rights to property, life, contract, and a body of rules prohibiting harm to others. In this respect, Rand follows a venerable line of economists and philosophers including Adam Smith, John Locke, John Stuart Mill, and Robert Nozick. Within this framework of "side constraints" your task is to do the best you can, or want, to do. You may make choices that help others, like giving them a job. You may makes choices that hurt their interests, like firing them. Within this framework, each agent is in charge of their own substantive style from choosing their profession to choosing how they will pursue that profession. It is within this framework that each individual fountainhead pursues their own goals.

From the perspective of business ethics, though, there is a huge gap between side constraints. This gap includes both the personal question of "what should I do with my time?" and the follow up question of what I should do once I have made that decision. Classical Liberal and Libertarian political theory has no answer or even guidance to this question (Rasmussen and Den Uyl, 2005). What *The Fountainhead* brings to the table is that the answer to the first question should be tied to the second via professional ethics.

The profession is the repository of professional practices and lessons learned over the years. Roark learns from Stanton, Henry Cameron, and even while working for Guy Francon. Roark does learn from others. Professional standards are not formed in social isolation. They are formulated concomitantly with suppliers, employees and customers. Guiding and focusing self-interest through the lens of the profession is how Roark actually serves others even though others are not his primary intentional concern. His primary concern is the profession: the purpose and art of architecture.

Roark's primary argument is not that he should be free of all rules. That is the kind of argument Guss Webb makes. Roark argues throughout the book that professional ethics ought to be tied to the work of the profession. The scope of this work is determined by the problems and tasks the profession claims to address. Concomitantly, you ought to decide to engage in that profession where you want to do that type of work. This is what channels self-interest in *The Fountainhead.* This love of the profession is why Cameron teaches Roark. He sees in Roark this same devotion and hence, teaching Roark *is* advancing the profession. It is only after they work together in this common bond that Cameron and Roark begin to have a real personal attachment. In the first instance it is not a sympathy for others that channels self-interest. In *The Fountainhead*, it is not an "enlightened" self-interest that somehow calculates the long range benefits of not harming others. We never see Roark calculating what the rest of his life would look like if he made a decision. All of his decisions are surprisingly in the moment, including his first attempt to establish his own practice. Professional ethics for Roark is not an additional *ad hoc* layer of how to be good to others. Rather it is a practice integrated with serving the client by considering the nature of the good or service being offered and the problem being solved. Roark identifies so fully with the profession that personal integrity, for Roark, is professional integrity.

Much attention is given to Roark's refusing to change a façade or cornice for a client when this would get him a job. Roark argues that by focusing solely on facades of the past the profession has quit being true to itself. Every critique of every building Roark and Dominique invoke involves something that discomforts and inconveniences the owners in favor of a façade done for the sake of putting the judgment of those long dead ahead of your own. According to Roark, the proper rules of architecture take account of all those elements, from the building costs to how the sun light hits a room. If his clients want to violate those principles he does reject them. His love of the building and work of art trump these types of requests. He rejects them on the basis of a personal integrity dedicated to the professional ethics of architecture not, as critics claim, a personal integrity to an ad hoc list of requirements he has determined in a selfish vacuum.

It is not just about the facades, though, it is about the types of clients Roark thinks he should work with. Remember, Roark gets burned at least twice from choosing the wrong client. These types of clients do not even like these old facades. Where Roark gets hurt they do not even like his architectural style. Personally liking something would at least be an individual preference. At least Peter is trying to get something he thinks he wants: fame. It's the only desire Peter can come up with that seems to be his own, and this perception of at least some goal is probably Roark's soft spot for Peter. Roark's other potential clients, though, never even muster this much of a desire. Rather they want a certain style because everyone else says they should want that style, and those recommending that style do so because yet others say that should be the style. It's not that these patrons have bad taste, it's that they have no taste. They bow to an amorphous opinion that no one really holds but everyone accepts for the sake of satisfying others. In rejecting these clients Roark is not refusing to serve a client. There is no client.

Contrast these instances of rejection to when Roark has no problem designing for the client. Austen Heller, the gas station, Gail Wynand, Monadnock Valley all explicitly include consideration for the client. Heller's library is specially placed. The gas station is well lit and easy to access. Roark explicitly incorporates privacy into Monadnock Valley because that is the commodity those clients will want, and Wynand's house gets consideration of a single guest room and the site Wynand loves so much. In every single case, the direct desires, preferences, and judgments of the client concerns Roark, but it concerns him as part of the architectural problem. By considering the problem first he serves his client.

The problem is always the function the building and that function directly includes what the clients want from the building. The form of the building is the solution to that problem. This isn't just a view about architecture, it's a statement about business. The problem comes first and must be solved within the rules of the market, Professional ethics further defines better and worse solutions to the problem. This includes practical matters like engineering and not just people's feelings and interests. Finally, individual talent will determine how well any given individual meets these benchmarks.

There is no doubt that Rand writes to show that Roark's way of solving problems is the best both aesthetically, ethically, and even self-interestedly. Yet, there are a plurality of differing views in *The Fountainhead* concerning the nature of Architecture. Roark never tries to convince other architects that they should all be designing like him. He never argues with the other architects at Kiki's parties. He never considers it his duty to convert everyone to his way of thinking. He certainly never advocates for a licensing structure that would mandate his style as the only legal way to get a license. For someone so passionate about architecture, he has a decidedly live and let live attitude toward both clients and competitors.

This plurality of methods and people is important for understanding both the book and the business ethics within. Most people seem to read the book and focus only on Roark. They then take away the meaning that the book represents a "my way or the highway" theme and that this is what capitalism is about. Rather, the book represents Roark's way as the best way, but not the only way. Others are free to seek their paths and pay the price. Roark pays the price for his views several times and so do other architects in the book. Gordon Prescott loses Heller because of his belief that all styles must be mixed. Holcombe loses anyone who doesn't want Renaissance. For *The Fountainhead*, capitalism isn't about doing things one way, rather it's about choosing one of many ways and being prepared to pay the price for that choice, and not just in terms of money.

CONCLUSION

In the best of the tradition of virtue ethics, Rand is arguing that Roark's set of virtues is the true way to flourish. This also separates *The Fountainhead* from Atlas Shrugged. In the latter, all those not adopting the philosophical viewpoint of John Galt are doomed to perish. In *The Fountainhead* it is only those who totally abandon their self through total lack of integrity that perish, if not physically then psychologically. We see this with Catherine Halsey as well as Keating. The one mystery is Gail Wynand. Wynand is devastated at the end of the book because of his central second-hander lust for power. Roark believes that Wynand exhibited enough integrity to survive this blow, but we never hear from Wynand again. However, whatever his mental states, behind the scenes he arranges for his life's monument to be built by Roark: The tallest skyscraper in New York. This is definitely a nobler outcome for him than painting pictures that elicit only pity from Roark. Even for Wynand there is some redemption. Keating is the only architect we see trying to satisfy everyone; he is the only one who exhibits absolutely no integrity and in the end is the worst loser.

Through *The Fountainhead* we are given captivating examples of how business can be part of one's larger identity. The phrase I have used is "substantive style": a way of doing and being that incorporates talent, ethics, self-chosen goals, and how we go about enacting them. It includes both our aesthetic judgment and our aesthetic presence in the world. It is meant to be telling that Keating can't use his own judgment to even choose the furniture for his own apartment. Keating knows this at some level, and he also knows the reason why he does this: choosing a substantive style involves costs. It will cost you money, some people may not like you. You will lose some clients to competitors. Without it, though, you lose yourself.

Roark, on the other hand, chooses a substantive style opposite of Keating. Roark loves doing architecture including the engineering and all the smaller bits Keating never learns. To say, though, that Roark's identity is tied to architecture means that he also identifies with the professional ethics of architecture. As we see in *The Fountainhead*, there are different conceptions of professional ethics and adopting any of them entails certain costs. Importantly, professional ethics fills in the gaps left by classical liberal political and market institutions. Professional ethics provides a guide of how to live and, as such, is one of the subjects of choice when deciding on which profession to pursue. As such, professional ethics is an experiment in ways to live and ought to be protected just as jealously in the market as Mill defends it in other spheres of life.

The characters in the novel are free to experiment with these different styles because they operate within a market. But, *The Fountainhead* is not about monetary profit maximizing, it is very much about business and the moral importance of business activity within one's life. This conception of business deserves attention since business is often thought of as an amoral aspect of life when, rather, it is integral to human flourishing (Kline, 2008).

The problem is that many forget the importance of formal institutions like property and mediating institutions like professional ethics. These formal and cultural institutions focus self-interest on problem solving that actually helps people, even though the direct object of the actor's attention, and intention, may be anything but the final receiver of the good or service. In championing a focus on the problems and self-chosen goals of the business person, we see that the book stands as a counterargument against what is now commonly called "stakeholder theory." Serving others in business is not about prostituting one's self to any customer who comes along, it is about cultivating your product or service within a market in order to flourish. This includes determining who your market segment is, and is not. As Peter Keating demonstrates, trying to be something for everyone is the true guide to business and personal disaster.

The Fountainhead is a good primer for business ethics precisely because it emphasizes that choices must be made and that these choices have a cost in money, opportunity, and psychological well-being. We should not make these choices as if they are in isolation from the rest of our life. Robert Frost realized that choosing one path necessarily means leaving other paths behind. "The Road not Taken" reflects with a sigh on the opportunity costs of choice. In contrast, *The Fountainhead* focuses on the joy of choosing a path, even in business, and is a fine example of how business ethics can have both meaning and beauty as a result of your own chosen substantive style.

NOTES

1. When Paul McCartney stated that he did not wish to be singing "She Loves You" at 30, he realized this relationship and both how his work and identity had been evolving.
2. Actually there can be up to nine different forms that stakeholder theory can take, but this rough distinction captures most of them and is fine for our purposes here. See Joseph Heath (2014).

REFERENCES

Carnegie, Andrew. 1901. *The Gospel of Wealth and other Timely Essays*. New York: The Century Company.

Csikszentmihalyi, Mihaly. [1990] 2008. *Flow: The psychology of optimal experience*. New York: Harper Perennial Modern Classics.

Freeman, R. Edward. [1984] 2010. *Strategic Management: A Stakeholder Approach*. Cambridge: Cambridge University Press.

Freeman, R. Edward. 1997. A stakeholder theory of the modern corporation. In *Ethical Theory and Business* 5th edition. Edited by Tom Beauchamp and Norman Bowie. Upper Saddle River: Prentice Hall.

Frost, Robert. 1916. The Road not Taken. In *Mountain Interval*. New York: Henry Holt and Company.

Galbraith, J. K. 1958. *The Affluent Society*. Boston: Houghton Mifflin.

Gladwell, Malcolm. 2008. *Outliers*. New York: Little Brown and Company.

Heath, Joseph and Norman Wayne. 2014. Stakeholder theory, corporate governance, and public management. In *Morality, Competition, and the Firm: The Market Failures Approach to Business*. Oxford: Oxford University Press.

Kline, William. 2006. Business ethics from the internal point of view, *Journal of Business Ethics* 64, no. 1 (March): 57–67.

———. 2008. Flourishing through trade. In *Reading Rasmussen and Den Uyl: Critical Essays on Norms of Liberty*. Edited by Aeon J. Skoble. Lexington Books.

Mill, John Stuart. 1985. Utilitarianism. *The Collected Works of John Stuart Mill, Volume X—Essays on Ethics, Religion, and Society*. Edited by John M. Robson, Introduction by F.E.L. Priestley. London: Routledge and Kegan Paul. 258–302. http://oll.libertyfund.org/titles/241.

———. 1991. On liberty. In *Mill, On Liberty and Other Essays*. Edited by John Gray. Oxford: Oxford University Press.

———. 2004. *Principles of Political Economy*. Amherst, N.Y.: Prometheus Books.

Rasmussen, Douglas and Den Uyl, Douglas. 2005. *The Norms of Liberty: a Perfectionist Basis for Non-Perfectionist Politics*. University Park: The Pennsylvania State University Press.

Ramsey, Gordon. 2007. *Roasting in Hell's Kitchen: Temper Tantrums, F Words, and the Pursuit of Perfection*. New York: William Morrow Paperbacks.

Rand, Ayn. 1943. *The Fountainhead*. New York: New American Library.

———. 1971. *The Romantic Manifesto: A Philosophy of Literature*. New York: New American Library.

Solomon, Robert C. 1999. *A Better Way to Think About Business: How Personal Integrity Leads to Corporate Success*. Oxford: Oxford University Press.

Veblen, Thorstein. 1899. *The Theory of the Leisure Class*, New York, Macmillan.

Williams-Ellis, Clough. 2014. *Portmeirion, the Place and Its Meaning, revised edition.* Portmeirion, Wales: Portmeirion Shops, Ltd.

Chapter 21

Business in Ayn Rand's *Atlas Shrugged*

Edward W. Younkins

Atlas Shrugged is very much a novel about business and the individuals located in the world of business. Businesspeople have always been among *Atlas Shrugged*'s most ardent admirers. They are thrilled to find a novel that understands, respects, and recognizes the value of what they do. In *Atlas Shrugged*, Rand clearly celebrated businesses from the industrial era (such as railroads, steel mills, and coal mines) that were dominant in America during her lifetime. In addition to championing industrial processes and producers in the novel, she also embraces the potential of future new technologies such as Galt's motor, which would supply "the cleanest, swiftest, cheapest means of motion ever devised" (Rand, 1957, 289).

Instead of heavy industries, today's leading-edge companies and emerging technologies include: software and information technology, biotechnology, logistics, social networks, telecommunications, photonics, nanotechnology, and so on. Despite this, the fundamental principles and virtues for business success in today's industries are the same as the ones illustrated in *Atlas Shrugged*. Readers can learn these from Rand's business heroes and learn what not to do from her business villains. In *Atlas Shrugged*, Rand provides crucial insights into business and especially the connections between business and the virtues.

The purpose of this article is to provide a description of Rand's treatment of business and businesspeople in *Atlas Shrugged*. The first section of this paper discusses how this novel illustrates that wealth and profit are products of the human mind and that they are created by adding value to the world through the production of desirable and needed products and services. The following section compares, at a general level, the worldviews, motivations, strategies, and tactics of the business heroes and villains in *Atlas Shrugged*. The next part takes a detailed look at the novel's main producer-protagonists

Dagny Taggart and Hank Rearden. This is followed by a section that provides snapshot portraits of other *Atlas Shrugged* characters embedded in the business world. The last part of this essay is devoted to a discussion of how *Atlas Shrugged* is being used in college and university business courses.

WEALTH CREATION, PROFIT, AND THE MOTIVE POWER OF THE HUMAN MIND

Wealth in the form of goods and services is created when individuals recombine and rearrange the potential resources that comprise the world. Something does not become a resource until its possible uses are discovered and developed. Wealth increases when someone conceives of and produces a more valuable configuration of the earth's substances. Although abeyant resources or raw materials are finite, the human mind, through ingenuity and creativity, is able to continually increase the wealth of the world (Simon, 1996). Profits are a person's reward for wealth creation. The core of business is wealth creation through the offering of desirable goods and services.

Entrepreneurs create wealth by offering what is perceived to be a more valuable combination of resources than the combination that existed previously. Profits are an entrepreneur's reward for increasing the wealth of individuals in society. The entrepreneur does not profit at the expense of others. Rather, he gains because the product of his actions is judged to be worth more than what existed before his undertaking. *Atlas Shrugged* portrays wealth creators as able, rational, and visionary individuals who pursue their goals persistently in the face of obstacles and adversities.

In the Valley, Ellis Wyatt says to Dagny:

> What's wealth but the means of expanding one's life? There's two ways one can do it: either by producing more or by producing it faster. And that's what I'm doing: I'm manufacturing time. . . . I'm producing everything I need. I'm working to improve my methods, and every hour I save is an hour added to my life. . . . That's the savings account I'm hoarding. . . . Wealth, Dagny? What greater wealth is there than to own your own life and to spend it on growing? (Rand, 1957, 721–22)

To be successful, entrepreneurs must objectively perceive reality and rationally process and evaluate information. They must detect information gaps between consumer wants and needs and the potential of a new but as yet undeveloped product or service to meet those wants and needs. They must anticipate new markets and consumers' future wants and needs, learn from competitors' successes and failures, accumulate capital for their projects, acquire the needed resources, coordinate numerous activities and employee skills, and take risks by trading present and known values for resources that only promise a potential future value. Profit is payment for the entrepreneur's thought, vision, initiative, determination, efficiency, risk-taking, and effectiveness.

Atlas Shrugged illustrates that the profit-and-loss system in a voluntaristic society is just and moral. A person's wealth under capitalism depends upon his productive achievements and the choice of others to recognize them. When pursuing profits, one must appeal to the interests of others. Profits indicate that a businessperson has pleased his fellow consumers by using resources to produce a product or render a service at costs below the value that people place upon the product or service. The firm making profits is using resources in a manner that satisfies what people want and need. Losses indicate that a businessperson has failed to deal with his fellow consumers efficiently.

This exchange takes place at a press conference when Hank Rearden is asked about his profit motive for building the John Galt Line with Rearden Metal. Rearden states:

> "Inasmuch as the formula of Rearden Metal is my own personal secret, and in view of the fact that the Metal costs much less to produce than you boys can imagine, I expect to skin the public to the tune of twenty-five per cent in the next few years."
>
> "What do you mean, skin the public, Mr. Rearden?" asked the boy. "If it's true, as I've read in your ads, that your Metal will last three times longer than any other and at half the price, wouldn't the public be getting a bargain?"
>
> "Oh, have you noticed that?" said Rearden. (235)

In *Discovery, Capitalism, and Distributive Justice* (1989), Israel Kirzner explains that before a profit opportunity is discovered it cannot be said to have existed in any economically intelligible and meaningful sense. The discoverer, who creates an opportunity and brings something into existence, is justly entitled to it. The discovery of the possibility that a certain act would be worthwhile actually created the opportunity's existence. It follows that the discovering entrepreneur is entitled to the profit he has created. The following exchange between James Taggart and Cherryl Brooks reflects this insight. Jim says:

> "Rearden. He didn't invent smelting and chemistry and air compression. He couldn't have invented his Metal but for thousands and thousands of other people. *His* Metal!
>
> Why does he think that it's his? Why does he think that it's his invention? Everybody uses the work of everybody else. Nobody ever invents anything." (262)

> The puzzled Cherryl responds: "But the iron ore and all those other things were there all the time. Why didn't anybody else make that Metal, but Mr. Rearden did?" (262)

When Eugene Lawson, past president of the Community National Board of Madison boasts that he has never made a profit in his entire life, Dagny solemnly responds: "Mr. Lawson, I think that I should let you know that of all the statements a man can make, *that* is the one I consider most despicable" (313).

Hank Rearden tells the judges at his trial:

> "I work for nothing but my own profit—which I make by selling a product they need to men who are willing and able to buy it. I do not produce it for their benefit at the expense of mine, and they do not buy it for my benefit at the expense of theirs; I do not sacrifice my interests to them nor do they sacrifice theirs to me; we deal as equals by mutual consent to mutual advantage—and I am proud of every penny that I have earned in this manner." (480)

Rand illustrates in *Atlas Shrugged* that the mind is the root cause of wealth and profit. It is the skilled thinkers and doers who create and maintain wealth and promote prosperity. Even inherited wealth requires entrepreneurship for it to be retained. In *Atlas Shrugged* the passionate and productive prime movers include Hank Rearden, Dagny Taggart, Ken Danagger, Ellis Wyatt, Midas Mulligan, Dan Conway, and Andrew Stockton, among others.

For example, Hank Rearden has the vision to foresee the possible future value, uses, and benefits of a new metal alloy that will take him ten years to invent and bring to market. He wants to make real his dream of developing a revolutionary metal that is stronger and lighter than steel. He is well-prepared and motivated to take on this pursuit. Beginning as a teenager, Rearden held various jobs in steel-related businesses. Eventually, he owned and operated ore, coal, limestone, and steel businesses. Not only does Rearden Metal enable Hank to earn his desired profits, its use in railroad tracks enables the John Galt Line to earn more profits by running faster and hauling more freight at lower costs to Colorado's industrial shippers who themselves, as a result, also earn greater amounts of income. These industrialists are able to expand their operations, purchase more resources, hire more employees, build more products that benefit their customers, and make greater profits—the rewards for wealth creation.

Bradley (2011) has commented that energy is at the center of business life in *Atlas Shrugged.* To begin with there are John Galt's revolutionary motor, Ellis Wyatt's oil fields, Ken Danagger's coal mines, Taggart Transcontinental and the Phoenix-Durango's railroads, Hammond and Nielson's automobile factories, Roger Marsh's electrical appliance company, Andrew Stockton's foundry, Dwight Sanders's airplane factory, and so on. In addition, the book portrays an energy planning agency (i.e., the Bureau of Economic Planning and Control), government intervention with energy, oil shortages, gasoline shortages, electricity blackouts, energy rationing, conservation edicts, an Industrial Efficiency Award, public utility regulation, common carrier regulation, etc.).

In discussing the importance of locomotives, Eddie Willers says to John Galt who is disguised as a railroad worker: "Motive power—you can't imagine how important that is. That's the heart of everything . . . What are you smiling at?" (Rand, 1957, 63). The next paragraph, which begins a new chapter reads: "Motive power—thought Dagny, looking up at the Taggart Building in the twilight—was its first need; motive power, to keep that building standing, to keep it immovable. It did not rest on piles driven into granite; it rested on the engines that rolled across a continent" (64).

Entering the motor room of the locomotive during the initial run of the John Galt Line, Dagny contemplates what the engines depend upon:

> They *are* alive she thought, because they are the physical shape of the action of a living power—of the mind that had been able to grasp the whole of this complexity, to set its purpose, to give it form. For an instant, it seemed to her that the motors were transparent and she was seeing the net of their nervous system. It was a net of connections, more intricate, more crucial than all of their wires and circuits: the rational connections made by that human mind which had fashioned any one part of them for the first time.
>
> They are alive, she thought, their soul operates them by remote control. Their soul is in every man who has the capacity to equal this achievement. Should the soul vanish from the earth, the motors would stop because *that* is the power which kept them going—the power of a living mind—the power of thought and choice and purpose. (246)

Through her characters, Rand illustrates that human reason, insight, choice, creativity, and motivated action are the keys to productivity and wealth creation. Human beings have the intelligence to discern new possibilities, to discover the earth's productive potential, and to realize their creative insights through their persistent efforts.

PRODUCERS VERSUS LOOTERS: A CONFLICT OF VISIONS

Not only is *Atlas Shrugged* a novel about philosophy, politics, and economics, it is also very much a novel about business and businesspeople. Not only does much of its action takes place in commercial settings, many of its protagonists and antagonists are situated in business establishments.[1] While many of the novel's heroes run businesses, a number of its villains also do so. Of course, Rand distinctly differentiates between businesspersons and those who merely are referred to as such because they are associated with a business. Not every person who is referred to as a businessperson is an authentic businessperson. Many of the inauthentic businesspeople do not understand that reality is an absolute and that rationality is needed to deal with reality.[2]

At a general level, we have the producers and the looters. *Atlas Shrugged* follows the effects of the battle of the thinkers and producers versus the predators and parasites across the entire economy and over a long period of time. The clash is between those who do business by voluntary trade and profit through their initiative and productive ability and those who operate through force and fraud and "profit" by means of political power.

Atlas Shrugged illustrates that business *qua* business serves those who wish to trade and does not make use of coercion. When a failed or faltering business is rescued by a government handout, it is no longer a genuine business. Likewise, when businesspersons obtain results outside the market framework by receiving special privileges granted by the government, they forfeit their status as legitimate businesspersons. These special privileges include bailouts, price supports, subsidized loans, trade protection, resource privileges, grants of monopoly, etc.

The thinkers and doers are rationally purposeful, are dedicated to their work, achieve their goals through their initiative, thought, and action, concentrate on continual improvement, innovation, and on earning their profits, understand that earned wealth is the effect of an entrepreneur's moral status, and despise mediocrity and collectivism. *Atlas Shrugged* makes clear that, because life requires the production of values, legitimate entrepreneurial actions are morally proper. Rand's heroes flourish and find happiness in producing what others value.[3]

In contrast, the looters attack reason, are reactive to outside forces, advocate the morality of altruism, profit by dealing with dishonest politicians, avoid rationality and productivity by utilizing pressure groups and political pull to exploit the wealth created by the prime movers, and wrongly believe that they will gain moral status and self-esteem through such expropriation. The looter businessmen fear genuine competition and surrender their independence, resourcefulness, and creativity for the protection of government regulation. These crony capitalists gain their results outside the marketplace by running to the government for special privileges that protect them from open competition. They tend to be supporters of government planning, spending, regulation, and redistribution.

Both the producers and the looters want to obtain money but there is a critical difference between their methods for doing so. The prime movers make money by creating products and offering services that their customers need and want to make their lives better. The looters' goal is to gain money, the result of production, via government force and/or altruism. They believe that money is meaningful no matter how it is obtained. The non-creators are content with money acquired through corruption, dishonesty, backhanded deals, and altruism.

An example of crony capitalism or crony statism in *Atlas Shrugged* is the arrangement between James Taggart and Orren Boyle through which the "Anti-dog-eat-dog rule" and the "Equalization of Opportunity Bill" come about. Taggart employs Boyle to use his connections to get the National Alliance of Railroads to adopt the Anti-dog-eat-dog rule to destroy Taggart's chief competitor in Colorado, Dan Conway's outstanding Phoenix-Durango Railroad. In return, Boyle gets Taggart to use his political connections in Washington to divest Hank Rearden of his ore mines through the passage of the Equalization of Opportunity Bill. Rearden is forced to give up his iron and coal businesses in order to provide business opportunities for his struggling competitors. Ideas such as "social responsibility" and "public interest" are used to sell the propriety of both of these decrees to the public. Many businesspeople in the real world operate in the same manner as rent-seekers, James Taggart and Orren Boyle, running to their political connections rather than by being productive, efficient, and innovative.

Dagny is angry and disgusted at the unethical and undeserved liquidation of Dan Conway's Phoenix-Durango Railroad through a vote of the members of the National Alliance of Railroads. Unlike her brother, she would never consider making money through the unjust destruction of a competitor. She runs to Conway and urges him to fight them, but he declines. The only way that she would like to put the Phoenix-Durango out of business is through honest competition by providing the best railroad service in Colorado.

While in Galt's Gulch, composer Richard Halley tells Dagny that legitimate entrepreneurs are examples of a human being's highest creative spirit:

> "Whether it's a symphony or a coal mine, all work is an act of creating and comes from the same source: from an inviolate capacity to see through one's own eyes—which means: the capacity to see, to connect and to make what had not been seen, connected, and made before. That shinning vision which they talk about as belonging to the authors of symphonies and novels—what do they think is the driving faculty of men who discover how to use oil, how to run a mine, how to build an electric motor? That sacred fire which is said to burn within musicians and poets—what do they suppose moves an industrialist to defy the whole world for the sake of his new metal, as the inventors of the airplane, the builders of the railroads, the discoverers of new germs or new continents have done through all the ages?" (782–83)

In his speech, John Galt discusses the nature of authentic businesspeople:

> "I have called out on strike the kind of martyrs who had never deserted you before. I have given them the weapon they had lacked, the knowledge of their own moral value. I have taught them that the world is ours, whenever we choose to claim it, by virtue and grace of the fact that ours is the Morality of Life. They, the great victims who had produced are the wonder of humanity's brief summer, they, the industrialists, the conquerors of matter, had not discovered the nature of their right. They had known that theirs was the power. I taught them that theirs was the glory." (1051)

In his "Money Speech," Francisco states:

> "To the glory of mankind there was, for the first and only time in history, a *county of money*— and I have no higher, more reverent tribute to pay to America, for this means: a country of reason, justice, freedom, production, achievement. For the first time, man's mind and money were set free, and there were no fortunes-by-conquest, but only fortunes by work, and instead of swordsmen and slaves, there appeared the real maker of wealth, the greatest worker, the highest type of human being—this self-made man—the American industrialist." (414)

Atlas Shrugged offers profound insights regarding the virtues that lead to morality and success in business. A case can be made that virtues should serve as a foundation for achieving a firm's goals, values and purposes. Virtues, as rational moral principles, need to be integrated with a company's vision, culture, and climate. Rand's novel demonstrates the presence or the absence of these principles in the lives of the various characters. They include rationality, honesty, justice, independence, integrity, productiveness, and pride.[4]

Morality in business entails objectively recognizing individual rights by treating customers, employees, creditors, shareholders, and others as autonomous rational individuals with their specific goals and desires. Justice is the virtue of granting to each individual that which he objectively deserves. A virtuous businessperson must make certain that customers get what they pay for and needs to hire the most talented employees and reward them for what they achieve. In addition, specific contractual agreements with creditors and others must be respected. Also, managers are the employees of the stockholders and have a contractual, fiduciary, and moral responsibility to fulfill their wishes. They have the obligation to use the shareholders' money for specifically authorized projects that are in the shareholder's interest. In *Atlas Shrugged*, the business protagonists are just in their business relations with their actual and potential employees, suppliers, business partners, customers, competitors, and other parties. They discriminate based only on performance, ability, and character.

The notion advanced by the looters in *Atlas Shrugged* that the producers should have a social conscience and an obligation to produce for society is similar to today's expectation that businesses have a social responsibility. At his trial, Hank Rearden goes out of his way not to apologize for his income and his wealth. He recognizes that a firm's social responsibility is to respect the natural rights of individuals while earning profits for the owners of a business. There is no special morality for businesses. The pursuit and earning of profit does not require moral absolution through social responsibility. There is no justified reason for an honest entrepreneur to be ashamed of his profession, to feel guilty about his earnings, or to think that he needs to "give back" in order to earn respect.

Atlas Shrugged demonstrates that production metaphysically precedes consumption and that productiveness is a virtue. We must produce before we can consume. It is production that originates demand for other products and services. Rationality and self-interest are prerequisites of production. A legitimate entrepreneur's actions are morally proper because life requires the production of values. The self-actualizing rational producer in *Atlas Shrugged* is the visible hand in markets. It is businesspeople, entrepreneurs, and industrialists who are prime movers in the economy. In *Atlas Shrugged,* Hank Rearden is the exemplar of a virtuous and productive businessman.

THE PRIMARY PRODUCER-PROTAGONISTS: DAGNY TAGGART AND HANK REARDEN

Achiever and creator, Dagny Taggart, the intellectual equal of Ayn Rand's male heroes, is perhaps the strongest female protagonist in Western literature. Free of inner conflict, she is passionately creative and comfortable with respect to her fundamental relationship to existence. She is a model of synthesis, unity, and mind-body integration. Dagny personifies the values of independence, individualism, purpose, and self-actualization.

Dagny is an engineer and the operating vice-president of a transcontinental railroad, who deals with every industry and every policy of the looters. Because of her integrating context, she has contact with every industry, thus permitting the reader to see the total scope of modern industrial civilization.

Dagny, like Hank Rearden, is a self-initiator who goes by her own judgments and is the motive power of her own happiness. Unlike Rearden, she does not feel guilty for her achievements. Dagny is a purposeful, strong, and passionately creative embodiment of mind body unity. She understands that the world both lives because of the work of the prime movers and then hates them for it. The parasites both need the creators and despise them at the same time. They desire to exploit the creators and then make them take blame for their actions. Dagny realizes that it is because producers are concerned with nature and reason that they are able to create within the reality of an objective and knowable universe. According to Dagny, "the sight of an achievement was the greatest gift a human being could offer to others" (237). She knows that material production is an expression of man's highest aspect and defining characteristic—his reasoning and creative mind. It is the mind that enables individuals to deal with physical reality.

Dagny recognizes that the creators are wrongly expected by many people to feel guilty for their virtues. Of course, the creators are guilty only of not claiming their moral value and virtues. Dagny chooses romantic partners who affirm her positive sense of life, which involves the integration of values, including love and sex. She understands that love is an emotional response, as are friendship and admiration, when one encounters a person who embodies his or her values. Dagny's romances with Francisco, Rearden, and Galt exemplify what a relationship between two integrated and self-actualized persons can be. Her relationships illustrate that sex is the supreme form of admiration of one human being for another and that the values of one's mind are connected to the actions of one's body.

Although Dagny is a paragon of mind-body integration, she does not fully understand the world's situation and is conflicted because of this lack of knowledge. Salmieri (2007)[5] notes that Dagny thinks that the strikers are "giving up." Although she realizes that it is wrong to live and work under the rule of the looters, she also believes that it is immoral and dishonorable to surrender the world to them. She views quitting as a form of resignation or capitulation. Dagny does not want to give up Taggart Transcontinental but does not realize that by staying in the world she is giving the looters the means to enslave her. By remaining in the world she is sanctioning her enemies' moral code. Her willingness to continue to fight the looters in the world indicates that she does not completely understand the full value of herself and of the other producers. Dagny also does not totally comprehend that it is at root a battle of very different philosophical premises.

At one point in the novel, Dagny is on a "mini-strike" of herself when Directive 10-289 is passed. The Taggart Tunnel Disaster is an effect of this directive and of Dagny's absence. She is not there to advise regarding the situation. The disaster is the effect of the mind's absence and thus concretizes the novel's theme of the importance of the mind in human existence.

Salmieri explains that for most of the story Dagny wrongly believes that the looters love their lives and that they want to live. We could say that she is on the "wrong track." She thinks that she can make them see the truth and that she can win the battle. Dagny does not want to abandon the greatness of the world of the producers. Throughout Part Three of the novel she progressively comes to realize that the irrational looters are indifferent, purposeless, and do not value their lives. This begins to become apparent to her when she meets with Mr. Thompson and the other looter-politicians. At that point, she is on the verge of understanding that the strike is required by the nature of existence and is thus the embodiment of rational egoism. She and the other heroes will ultimately realize that the looters' irrational doctrines are not errors of knowledge but instead are conscious breaches of morality.

Throughout most of the novel, Dagny believes she is right to go on in a world that she does not fully understand that is somehow stopping her from achieving her values. She needed to check her premises. She did not comprehend that Taggart Transcontinental and other great enterprises are only values in a certain context and that the required context of freedom no longer existed in the looters' world. She ultimately realizes that the looters do not value her products or those of the other producers. By the end of the story, she understands what motivates the looters. At the close of the novel she understands the contradictions in her principles and the need to go on strike. She realizes that there is no chance of winning by staying in the world of the looters. Dagny recognizes that justice cannot be attained by submitting to injustice.

Dagny has a fuller and more explicit conception of morality than Rearden does and is more morally consistent than he is. Her error is that she does not fully understand the looters' moral code and motives. Although she sees Rearden's moral error, she is blind to her own. She understands that the looters' policies have the effect of keeping the men of the mind from functioning at their best but she does not grasp that such obstruction is, in fact, their intention. This is an intention that they desire to hide even from themselves. It is inconceivable to Dagny that the looters actually want to destroy the creators. Their motive becomes fully clear to her when they want to torture and/or kill Galt rather than to switch course and rescue themselves. It becomes apparent to her that she must quit when she realizes that the looters do not desire to live and that they are motivated by hatred for Galt and the other prime movers, for themselves, and for existence. Prior to this point she believed that the looters would eventually comprehend the uselessness of their policies and would concede. Because she thought that they were rational and that they wanted to live, she fought to save Taggart Transcontinental and to force the looters to give up (Wright, 2007).[6]

Hank Rearden, a great industrialist who, despite accepting the mind-body dichotomy, is the primary human instantiation of Atlas in *Atlas Shrugged*. He is a master of reality whose erroneous surface ideas do not corrupt his essential character and subconscious in terms of his psycho-epistemology. Although Rearden's words and ideas sanction an unearned guilt, his actions belie his words. Down deep he does not believe the notion of the mind-body split. His error is the inconsistent application of rational principles in different aspects of his life.

Rearden is a self-made man who is devoted to productive work and achievement. In the beginning of the novel his existence is schizophrenic and compartmentalized with a most satisfying work life and a bad family life. Hank works passionately and enthusiastically and then feels guilty about it.

His family members, especially his nihilist wife Lillian, desire to destroy his greatness and do all they can to make him feel guilty for his productivity, work ethic, and rational achievement. As a result, Rearden feels a guilty sense of obligation toward his family and attempts to atone, in an altruistic sense, to their many accusations.

Hank and the other industrialists are the worst victims of the conventionally accepted altruist-collectivist philosophy. It is the mistaken sanction by the men of ability that paves the way for the parasites and statist looters who want the creators to produce for the world and then to suffer for doing so. A moral code based on altruism and the idea of a mind-body split holds the creators guilty because of their greatest virtues. This moral code is used as a weapon against Rearden who does penance by sentencing himself to many years of selfless service to his family and to the looters. Once Rearden and the other producers gain an understanding of the looters' evil and of the importance of their own morality, they will attain the sense that life is about accomplishment and joy rather than about suffering and disaster.

Not only is he a constant victim of the looters, his relatives, and his associates, Hank also views his passion for Dagny Taggart as animalistic and degrading. When Rearden finds himself desiring Dagny, his split-self experiences a meltdown. Riddled with guilt, Hank is worried about his wife and his lack of virtue. He considers his forced love for his wife to be virtuous and thinks that his authentic love for Dagny is wrong and a guilty pleasure. Early in the novel, Hank has concluded that sex is purely physical, degrading, lustful, sinful, and of no spiritual meaning. Although Rearden himself as a very sexual being, he regards sex as a lower bodily urge.

For a great part of the novel, Rearden experiences an internal civil war between the principles of the creators in his work and the principles of the looters and moochers in the rest of his life. Hank desperately needs to import to his personal life the same principles that he uses in his productive life. It is under the tutelage of Francisco and Dagny that Rearden slowly awakens to the truth, understands the motives of the looters and of his family, and realizes his own virtues and values. They assist Hank in integrating his productivity and sexual desire with each other and with his self-worth.

Salmieri explains that throughout the novel Rearden comprehends more deeply and progressively the causes of, and interrelationships between, the various problems he faces in his personal life and work life. The story of his liberation from guilt is one in which many strands and threads of his new realizations are woven together. For example, he sees the connection between the guilt surrounding the sale of Rearden Metal to Ken Danagger and the guilt associated with his affair with Dagny. Throughout the novel, the connection between economics and romance becomes ever more explicit. By the end of the story he understands the evil of the idea of the mind-body dichotomy. Rearden's discussion with Francisco at James and Cherryl's wedding reception aids in Rearden's liberation from guilt. Francisco introduces a more philosophical perspective to Rearden and to the readers when he tells Rearden that he is willing to bear too much suffering. This talk gives Rearden a moral sanction and leads him to realize that he has been guilty in accepting a wrong moral code and of giving the looters and his family a moral sanction based on that wrong code of morality. He comes to understand that he should not accept condemnation from a false moral code. Rearden learns from Francisco that the guilt is his own because he has been willing to bear punishment for what were really his virtues. Hank voices at his trial what he has learned:

> "I am earning my own living, as every honest man must. I refuse to accept as guilt the fact of my own existence and the fact that I must work in order to support it. I refuse to accept as guilt the fact that I am able to do it and do it well. I refuse to accept as guilt the fact that I am able to do it better than most people—the fact that my work is of greater value than the work of my neighbors and that more men are willing to pay me. I refuse to apologize for my ability—I refuse to apologize for my success—I refuse to apologize for my money." (Rand, 1957, 480)

Throughout much of the novel, Rearden needs to absolve himself of his unearned and undeserved moral guilt that had damaged his moral estimate of himself and of his capability for self-esteem. He needed to attain a belief in his own morality and in his right to self-esteem. His limited tacit approval of the ethics of altruism was behind his failure to comprehend the role and existence of moral values and ideals in his life (Wright, 2007).

Hank Rearden's decision to go on strike takes a long time to develop. Until his discussion with Tinky Holloway and the other looters regarding the proposed Steel Unification Plan, Rearden had thought that the looters would ultimately be rational. During this encounter the looters make irrational claims on Rearden to produce for them. Under the Steel Unification Plan, Rearden will go bankrupt no matter what his output happens to be and Orren Boyle's Associated Steel will receive the majority of Rearden's profits. After the confrontation, Rearden drives back to his mills, happens upon the dying Wet Nurse, is saved by Francisco (disguised as worker "Frank Adams"), and listens to Galt's logic as delivered to him by Francisco. In the next chapter, "The Concerto of Deliverance," Rearden disappears to Mulligan's Valley. Now seeing the truth, he recognizes that he must give up the world in order to save it.

By understanding morality and himself in terms of the metaphysical principle of mind body integration, Hank is freed from the self-sacrifice ethics that underpin his servitude. It is Rearden's inner conflict that drives the plot and it is his liberation from his mistaken premises and ultimate conscious acceptance of his subconscious Objectivist premises that resolve the conflict. In the end, he no longer feels guilty for his greatest virtues.

Wright (2007) explains that Dagny and Rearden's misjudgment is that they consider evil to be powerless and view the looters' policies as self-defeating. They do not understand for much of the story that these are impotent unless they are empowered by the good (i.e., by themselves and the other creators). It is only the producers' toleration and tacit acceptance of the looters' moral code that makes the devastating results possible. The producers had allowed their enemies to write the moral code. Before Dagny and Rearden can effectively battle their enemies, they must come to understand how they are complicit in their own victimization. Irrational (i.e., evil) people and their schemes can only succeed if they are helped and supported by rational (i.e., good) individuals. Actually, Rearden accepts this conflict only in his personal life and Dagny does not accept it at all. However, she believes that the looters have made an error, but will come around if only she can show them the invalidity of their beliefs through her productive achievements.

Atlas Shrugged demonstrates that the greater a person's productive ability, the greater are the penalties he endures in the form of regulations, controls, and the expropriation and redistribution of his earned wealth. This evil, however, is made possible only by the sanction of the victims. By accepting an unearned guilt—not for their vices but for their virtues—the achievers have acquiesced in the political theft of their minds' products. *Atlas Shrugged* shows the creators being sacrificed to the parasites and also dramatizes that the irrational looters need the assistance of rational people in order to "succeed." The moral code of self-sacrifice is used against and accepted by many of the creators who are made to feel guilt for their achievements and wealth. This is the "sanction of the victim" moral principle. The fact that Galt understands this principle and that Dagny and Rearden fail to comprehend it, establishes the major plot conflict in the story. In order to fight the altruist foundation of statist political economy, the men of the mind will need to withdraw their sanction.

Rearden, Dagny, and the other prime movers suffer spiritually and begin to view life as a mental weight and weary load rather than as a joy. Rearden's spiritual suffering runs deeper than Dagny's. Rearden lacks an explicit awareness of objective morality that Dagny possesses. He is open to attack because in his conscious beliefs he is oblivious to correct morality. Whereas Dagny never questions her right to her own happiness and self-esteem, Rearden does question his right to them. This destroys him spiritually and produces the foundation for his material exploitation. His partial acceptance of altruism despiritualizes his pursuit of happiness and his capacity for self-esteem. Rearden does not explicitly realize that he is operating by a moral code in his work life. Of course, he does so implicitly. His work life epitomizes morality as it leads to production, life, and life-enhancing values. Although he was proud of his thinking and acting, he did not explicitly identify these as moral and virtuous. He failed to identify the source of his pride as a moral value and as morally justified (Wright, 2007).

OTHER BUSINESS CHARACTERS

Francisco d'Anconia inherited the world's largest copper mining company that has been in his family since the days of the Spanish Empire. A man of tremendous ability and intelligence, he is purposeful, courageous, benevolent, and enthusiastic. Francisco admires productive work and money making and is dedicated to d'Anconia Copper. As a young man his stated goal was to be worthy of what he had inherited by expanding the already massive d'Anconia Copper empire. Francisco is the first person to join John Galt's strike when he sees that the majority of people had abandoned reason. Although he is connected to the strikers in Galt's Gulch, he remains in the outside world in order to recruit additional strikers and to accelerate the fall of the anti-reason and anti-life world. As President of d'Anconia Copper, Francisco deliberately, gradually, and systematically destroys his own company that is under threat of nationalization. By doing so he also helps to bring down the looter American businessmen who invested in his company, contributes to the destruction of other industrial concerns, and deprives people of benefiting from the accomplishments of his ancestors. This ironic character poses as a profligate playboy in order to camouflage his real purposes and essential nature.

Eddie Willers is Dagny's dedicated, indispensable, competent, and diligent chief assistant. His title is special assistant to the vice-president of Operation of Taggart Transcontinental. Attached to the company, he is loyal to it and to Dagny. Eddie admires the achievements of productive geniuses such as Hank Rearden, Ellis Wyatt, and others. He is not a genius but he is rational, realistic, and highly moral. He always wanted to do "Whatever is right" (Rand, 1957, 6). Eddie is John Galt's unwitting accomplice revealing information to Galt who is disguised as a common track worker in the employee cafeteria.

Dan Conway is the middle-aged owner and president of the Phoenix-Durango Railroad in Colorado. He built what was once a tiny railroad into the dominant railroad in the Southwest and Taggart Transcontinental's chief competitor in Colorado. His railroad supplies superior freight service to his commercial customers. This prompts James Taggart to conspire to get the

National Alliance of Railroads, a private association, to pass the Anti-dog-eat-dog rule, which puts the Phoenix-Durango out of business. He does not want to fight, accepts his defeat, and retires to his ranch in Arizona. Although Conway loves what he does, he does not protest being sacrificed because of the majority vote of the association members. Dagny urges him to fight but he declines. Conway explains that, although he does not think that it is right that he be sacrificed, he promised to obey the majority and, therefore, has no right to object. He has been taught to obey a moral code that makes him a willing victim. He says:

> "Dagny, the whole world's in a terrible state right now. I don't know what's wrong with it, but something's very wrong. Men have to get together and find a way out. But who's to decide which way to take unless it's the majority? I guess that's the only fair way of deciding; I don't see any other. I suppose somebody's got to be sacrificed. If it turns out to be me, I have no right to complain." (78)

Later, Conway does take somewhat of a stand when he refuses to sell his Colorado railroad to James Taggart.

Ellis Wyatt is the most productive of Colorado's industrialists. The young, quick-tempered, and innovative entrepreneur devises a method for extracting oil from shale rock, thus creating an economic boom in Colorado. His production of oil from shale is eerily similar to today's fracking. Wyatt's oil enables other industrialists to run their machinery effectively and efficiently. Wyatt's company is the pillar of Colorado's economy. When the destructive Colorado Directives force the state's profitable firms to share the suffering by redistributing their earnings, Ellis Wyatt is prompted to quit. In an act of defiance Wyatt sets fire to his wells resulting in "Wyatt's Torch" and disappears. He left behind a board nailed to a post containing a hand written note stating "I am leaving it as I found it. Take over. It's yours" (336). These directives also put other companies out of business and destroyed the Rio Norte Line. The Colorado Directives precipitated the retirement and disappearance of many productive and competent Colorado industrialists including Andrew Stockton (foundry), Laurence Hammond and Ted Neilson (automobiles), Dwight Sanders (airplanes), and Roger Marsh (electrical appliances), among others. Of the above productive individuals, Stockton is the only one that does the same work in Mulligan's Valley as he did in the outside world.

Ken Danagger is a no-nonsense, prototypical self-made coal producer and friend of Hank Rearden. He began as a coal miner and advanced to become owner of Danagger Coal in Pennsylvania. He and Hank make a private agreement to circumvent legal restrictions on the amount of Rearden Metal that could be sold to one individual. Danagger and Rearden are indicted and charged with subverting government orders when Rearden sells an illegal amount of his metal to Danagger. He joins the strike after listening to the logic of the "destroyer" (Galt) just before Rearden's trial.

Financier Midas Mulligan was the owner of Mulligan Bank and was the richest man in the world. As a realist, he only makes loans to people who he judges will pay them back with adequate interest. He can tell whether or not a person is a good risk or not by judging his character, productive ability, and record. Mulligan joins the strike when a court orders him to grant a loan to the undeserving president of Amalgamated Service Corporation, Lee Hunsacker. Mulligan purchases a remote valley in the Colorado Rockies. This valley becomes Galt's Gulch where the able and competent "men of the mind" gather. Midas runs a bank in Galt's Gulch where all transactions must be made in gold.

Tony, the Wet Nurse, is a young man just out of college who is assigned by Washington bureaucrats to be Deputy Director of Distribution at Rearden's mills to enforce government policies. He began as a cynic who was taught nothing except moral relativism by his professors. He does not believe that there are any absolutes. Throughout the novel, he learns about values, comes to admire and respect Hank Rearden for his morality and productiveness, and recognizes the looters' evil. He asks Hank for a job and Rearden tells him that he would hire him gladly and at once but that he cannot because of the looters' restrictions. Hearing that from Rearden is what really matters to the Wet Nurse. Ultimately, he loses his life while protecting Rearden's mills.

Mr. Ward is the decent, hardworking president of Ward Harvester Company, a small, solid firm that has been in his family for four generations. When Orren Boyle's Associated Steel fails to deliver the steel that he needs he goes to see Hank Rearden desperately in need of help. His company will go out of business if he does not get the required materials. He and Hank share the same values and virtues. Mr. Ward greatly needs to obtain some Rearden Metal to keep his business running. In order to do so he is willing to sell at a loss and to pay Rearden anything that he asks. Rearden responds positively to Mr. Ward's request. In the middle of Hank's quest to find the extra metal that Ward requires, Gwen Ives informs Rearden that the Equalization of Opportunity Bill had just passed. The shocked Mr. Ward gets up to leave and Rearden tells him to stay while they complete their deal. Rearden says: "We had business to transact, didn't we? . . . Mr. Ward what is it that the foulest bastards on earth denounce us for, among other things? Oh yes, for our motto of 'Business as usual.' Well—business as usual, Mr. Ward" (212).

Gwen Ives is Hank Rearden's efficient, professional, and loyal secretary. She and Dagny Taggart are the only two working women in business in *Atlas Shrugged* whom we see performing good work. She understands the evil of the looters' ideology and breaks down in tears when she learns about the passing of the Equalization of Opportunity Bill. When Rearden retires and disappears, he advises her to leave the firm and make a run for it, which she does.

Dick McNamara of Cleveland is the competent contractor who completed the San Sebastián Line for Taggart Transcontinental. Dagny initially lines up the reliable contractor to lay the new Rearden Metal track for the Rio Norte (i.e., John Galt) line. He is one of the best contractors in the country and gets his projects done right and on time.

Unfortunately, despite a thriving business, he walks out. He is one the first of Dagny's business associates to vanish mysteriously. Forced to find a replacement contractor, Dagny hires Ben Nealy. Nealy sees no role for intelligence in human accomplishments, does not exert much effort, is disorganized, is reluctant to make decisions, and requires constant instruction from Dagny. He expresses the erroneous Marxist belief that only physical labor creates value: "Muscles, Miss Taggart . . . muscles—that's all it takes to build anything in the world" (162).

James Taggart is the primary business villain in *Atlas Shrugged.* He epitomizes the looters' unreason, is reluctant to depend upon his own business judgments and fears and dislikes business people who do rely upon their own evaluations. James frequently takes credit for Dagny's decisions and relies on her to get him out of trouble. In addition, in his efforts to gain wealth, he tries to ride on Francisco's intelligence. He is anti-effort and wants the unearned. James is a parasite and a whim-worshipper who manipulates and deceives people in order to fake self-esteem to himself. Also, he is afraid that he will be held responsible for anything. Taggart has a strong sense of inferiority and needs to feel superior. Jim does not possess the skills, energy, and ability required for legitimate business success. Down deep he finds his self-deception ridiculed by the existence of individuals with real ability, values, and virtues. He obtains money by using his political connections to garner subsidies or to get regulations passed that stifle his competitors. He thinks that by gaining wealth in that manner he will achieve moral status and self-esteem. James spends most of his time on public relations, cultivating friendships and knowing the people who make things possible rather than being concerned with facts and reality. He would rather deal with his friends than those who are best suited to produce the desired results. For example, Jim deals with Orren Boyle who will either deliver the product late or not at all. He rationalizes to others and to himself that he is motivated by his altruistic love for others and his dutiful concern for social justice. By the end of the novel, he realizes that he is actually a nihilist operating on a death premise and that he wants to destroy the good because it is good.

Orren Boyle is a friend of James Taggart and owner of Associated Steel. He started with $100,000 of his own and obtained government loans in the amount of $200,000,000 to purchase a number of struggling steel firms that he merged into Associated Steel. In *Atlas Shrugged*, he uses his political connections and a too-big-to-fail argument to obtain even more help from the government. Boyle runs his company badly; he is either late fulfilling his orders or does not deliver the product at all, and measures his company's success based on its popularity. He is disdainful of efficiency monopolies and dominant producers, says that private property is a trusteeship for benefit of society as a whole, and contends that he wants everyone to have a fair chance of getting iron ore. He says that he wants to pass the Equalization of Opportunity Bill in order to preserve the steel industry "as a whole." The collectivist philosophy that he espouses portrays a world in which no one can survive at the same time that others fail. This implies that all firms participate in a process that should yield equal benefits to all. Of course, his real goal is to divest Hank Rearden of his ore mines and have them turned over to Paul Larkin who would give Associated Steel the first opportunity to purchase the ore.

Both James Taggart and Orren Boyle are at war with reality. They are postmodern "businessmen" who think that they can create the reality that they desire merely by wanting it, thinking it, and persuading others to share in a narrative that supports their desires. They believe that social reality creates its own reality and that they can control reality by having the right political connections, the appropriate public relations strategies, and enough people having the desired opinion about them and their companies.

The Starnes heirs (Eric, Gerald, and Ivy) bankrupt the Twentieth Century Motor Company with their socialist scheme in which the employees as a group voted to determine the needs of each employee as well as the production expected of each worker based on an evaluation of his ability. They considered their father, Jed Starnes, to be an evil man who cared for nothing but money and business. Their plan was based on the principle of selflessness and required men to be motivated by love for their brothers rather than by personal gain. In effect, they put into practice the Marxist slogan "From each according to his ability, to each according to his need." They believed that the fulfillment of the needs of others is a person's greatest moral imperative. It follows that it is the inability to create value that merits rewards, rather than the ability to create value. When the plan failed, Ivy complained that it was defeated by greed and maintained that the plan was a noble idea but that human nature was not good enough for it.

Lee Hunsacker had been the incompetent president of Amalgamated Service Corporation which had taken over the Twentieth Century Motor Company. Midas Mulligan refused to grant Hunsacker a loan because of his past record of failures. Feeling that he was entitled, he brought suit against Mulligan under a law that said that people were not allowed to discriminate against anyone in a matter involving that person's livelihood. After Judge

Narragansett instructed the jury to bring in a verdict for Mulligan, Hunsacker appealed the verdict, which was reversed by a higher court. Both Mulligan and Narragansett disappeared shortly thereafter. Eventually, Hunsacker was able to get a loan from the "banker with a heart," Eugene Lawson of the Community National Bank who had collectivist, humanitarian loan policies. Predictably, Amalgamated went bankrupt.

Paul Larkin is a weak, unsuccessful businessman who acts like he is Hank Rearden's friend. He is actually in on the deal that strips Hank of his iron ore and coal mines. In fact, when the Equalization of Opportunity Bill is passed he takes possession of Rearden's ore mines and tells Hank that he will always consider the ore mines to belong to Rearden. Of course, this is untrue and Larkin gives Orren Boyle the initial opportunity to get the ore.

ATLAS SHRUGGED IN THE BUSINESS SCHOOL

Novels, as well as plays and films, are excellent teaching tools for communicating ideas to students. A well-constructed and compelling story can engage students and make a subject more vital to them. Fiction provides students with interesting material that does not seem like hard work. The result is that novels tend to have greater teaching power and more appeal to students than articles, textbooks, or case studies. Because students are apt to enjoy reading fiction, it is likely that they may grasp ideas quicker and better than when more conventional teaching methods are used. For many people, pure theory is not as exciting as a good story.

A compelling and relevant story stays in one's memory. Graduate and undergraduate business students have grounds for paying attention to novels concerning the business world. Many graduate business students are already in the world of entrepreneurship, manufacturing, and finance and undergraduate business students aspire to soon be in the corporate world. Novels can provide examples of challenges that a student may one day confront. It is no wonder that business novels connect with such students and work their way into the students' thinking.

Novels can come close to mirroring reality and are able to illuminate the full context of a situation. Novels about business describe life as lived in the world of commerce. Situations in novels can be more realistic than the hypothetical examples postulated in articles, case studies, or lectures. A novel can provide a superb background from which to view business. A well-written novel about business can pose complex questions and deepen a student's capacity for critical thinking. Such a novel can bring management problems and issues of business ethics to life by contextualizing organizational and moral questions and dilemmas. Ultimately, one's character may be influenced by reading fiction. This pedagogical method may stimulate the moral cognition and insight of the reader. Some narratives have the potential to open one's eyes with respect to what is really important.

Unfortunately, most novels are not representative of the real business world. It can safely be said that businesspeople have not fared well in novels on the whole. The literary culture is often unflattering in its depictions of businesspeople and capitalism, has attacked business and industry for destroying an old communal order based on equality, laments the capitalist preoccupation with material success, and abhors the dominance of large organizations in people's lives. Many novels go so far as to portray the businesspeople with hostility and derision.

Fortunately, there is at least one novel—Rand's *Atlas Shrugged*—that portrays the entrepreneur in a positive manner by emphasizing the essential moral nature of business and the legitimacy of people engaged in business, showing us the energy and fortitude of the diligent men and women of commerce, and the value of the entrepreneur as wealth creator and promoter of economic progress. *Atlas Shrugged* depicts the businessperson's role as potentially heroic. *Atlas Shrugged* shows the business hero as a determined, creative, and independent thinker who follows an idea to its accomplishment. Rand's novel dramatizes the positive qualities of the business by illustrating the victory of individualism over collectivism, portraying successful businesspeople as noble and attractive, and by characterizing business careers as at least as honorable as careers in other professions, if not more so.

Atlas Shrugged is now being taught in colleges and universities in a variety of courses. It is being used in the classroom to study the moral foundations of capitalism and commerce and related topics in philosophy, economics, free enterprise, management, business, and other areas.[7] For example, due to the tireless efforts of John Allison, former CEO and Chairman of BB&T Bank, there are now nearly seventy programs at institutions of higher learning that use *Atlas Shrugged* in their classes. This novel provides an excellent base for teaching issues in business, business ethics, economics, and political and economic philosophy. The use of *Atlas Shrugged* aids in moving between abstract principles and realistic business examples. The novel serves as a link between philosophical concepts and the practical aspects of business and illustrates that philosophy is accessible and important to people in general and to business people in particular.

Atlas Shrugged fosters a spirited exchange of ideas among students in the classroom as many students respond strongly and positively to this novel and its heroes. The novel presents the pursuit of profit as thoroughly moral, makes the discussion of capitalism intellectually legitimate, provides a powerful critique of socialism and challenges the prevailing beliefs of our culture. Students are impressed with *Atlas Shrugged*'s prophetic nature. It portrays the United States economy collapsing due to government intervention and regulation, politicians placing the blame on capitalism and free market, and the government countering with ever more controls that further the crisis. Government intervention is shown to discourage innovation and risk-taking, and the novel portrays how regulations in a mixed economy are made with political interest groups lobbying the government, which grants favors to those who have the most votes, political pull, or influence.

I use *Atlas Shrugged* to help undergraduate business students better understand the philosophical, moral, and economic concepts underlying business and capitalism. I incorporate Rand's novel into my "Conceptual Foundations of Business" course at Wheeling Jesuit University. In the class, students take turns leading discussions on all thirty chapters of Rand's 1,168-page novel.[8] During class discussions, students cite specific scenes and passages and their accompanying page numbers. During the last five class sessions I deliver detailed and in-depth lectures on *Atlas Shrugged.* The final exam consists of an essay exam on the novel.

My book, *Capitalism and Commerce*, provides a discussion of the philosophical, moral, and economic foundations upon which a capitalistic society is constructed. Rand's novel becomes the vehicle for the incarnation of these ideas—bringing abstract philosophy to life through character and plot.

The novel shows students in this course that the only way for man to survive in society is through reason and voluntary trade. *Atlas Shrugged* focuses on the positive and shows students what it takes to achieve genuine business success and how to create value.

Like Aristotle, Rand maintains an agent-centered approach to morality and focuses on the character traits that distinguish a good person. Reading *Atlas Shrugged* prompts students to think about what makes up a good life. Rand's business protagonists are shown to live by correct principles and acquire pertinent character traits. The villains in the novel show what happens when people hold incorrect principles and fail to cultivate indispensable virtues.

Some discussions in class revolve around virtues such as rationality, independence, integrity, justice, honesty, productiveness, and pride. The novel's characters are analyzed to see if these are absent or present in them. The novel teaches students that there are traits that correlate with business success and success in life. These include independent vision or foresight, an active mind, competence, confidence, personal or egoistic passion, a drive to action, the love of ability in others, and above all, having virtues.

Atlas Shrugged presents a thought-provoking portrait of entrepreneurs who won't allow politicians to kick them around anymore. The novel presents steel-makers, railroad tycoons, and bankers as heroes—the problem-solvers, producers, and thinkers. If Rand were writing today, she would likely be including software designers, builders of telecommunications networks, and those who work with photovoltaics, cryogenics, aerogels, biochips, radio-wave lighting, microelectromechanical systems, quantum chips, shape-memory metals, and so on.

The class discussion of heroes in *Atlas Shrugged* leads to comparisons with real-life business leaders such as Bill Gates, Ken Iverson, Jack Welch, Sam Walton, Steve Jobs, Thomas Edison, Michael Dell, Michael Eisner, Edwin Land, Henry Ford, Walt Disney, Roberto Goizueta, Fred Smith, Ginni Rometty, Marissa Mayer, Meg Whitman, Denise Morrison, and Sheryl Sandberg. The class dialogue centers around the character traits, principles, decisions, and actions of these individuals.

In my course, I use the novel to show that there are good and bad businesspeople, and that they don't always act virtuously. There are two types of businesspeople. There are those who lobby government for special privileges, make unethical deals, and engage in fraud and corrupt activities. In addition, there are the real producers who succeed or fail on their own. Rand's book illustrates what it takes to attain authentic business success and how to create value.

In a tribute article to the "money-making personality," Rand ([1963] 2011, 68–70) draws a contrast between mindful people of independent judgment who make money and the mindless socially dependent looters who appropriate it:

> The Money-*Maker* is the discoverer who translates his discovery into material goods. In an industrial society with a complex division of labor, it may be one man or a partnership of two: the scientist who discovers new knowledge and the *entrepreneur*—the businessman—who discovers how to use that knowledge, how to organize material resources and human labor into an enterprise producing marketable goods.
>
> The Money-*Appropriator* is an entirely different type of man. He is essentially non-Creative— and his basic goal is to acquire an unearned share of the wealth created by others. He seeks to get rich, not by conquering nature, but by manipulating men, not by intellectual effort, but by social maneuvering. He does not produce, he redistributes: he merely switches the wealth already in existence from the pockets of its owners to his own.
>
> The Money-Appropriator may become a politician—or a businessman who "cuts corners"—or that destructive product of a "mixed economy": the businessman who grows rich by means of government favors, such as special privileges, subsidies, franchises; that is, grows rich by means of *legalized force* . . .
>
> The Money-Maker, above all else, is the originator and innovator. The trait most signally absent from his character is *resignation*, the passive acceptance of the given, the known, the established, the *status quo*. He never says: "What was

good enough for my grandfather is good enough for me." He says: "What was good enough for me yesterday will not be good enough tomorrow."

He does not sit waiting for "a break" or for somebody to give him a chance. He makes and takes his own chances. He never whines, "I couldn't help it!"—he can, and does . . .

The man who will never make money has an "employee mentality," even in an executive's job; he tries to get away with a minimum of effort, as if any exertion were an imposition; and when he fails to take the proper action, he cries: "But nobody told me to!"

The Money-Maker has an "employer mentality," even when he is only an office boy—which is why he does not remain an office boy for long. In any job he holds, he is committed to a maximum of effort; he learns everything he can about the business, much more than his job requires. He never needs to be told—even when confronting a situation outside his usual duties. These are the reasons why he rises from office boy to company president . . .

It is only the Money-Appropriator who lives and acts short-range, never looking beyond the immediate moment. The Money-Maker lives, thinks and acts long-range. Having complete confidence in his own judgment, he has complete confidence in the future, and only long-range projects can hold his interest. To a Money-Maker, as well as to an artist, work is not a painful duty or a necessary evil, but a way of life; to him, productive activity is the essence, the meaning and the enjoyment of existence; it is the state of being alive.

Rand's business protagonists are independent, rational, and committed to the facts of reality, to the judgment of their own minds, and to attaining their own flourishing and happiness. Each one thinks for himself, actualizes his potential, and views himself as capable of dealing with life's challenges and as deserving of achieving success and happiness. *Atlas Shrugged* makes a case that the legitimate businessperson is a befitting symbol of a free society.

Atlas Shrugged also recounts the rise of "businessmen" who seek "profit" by currying favor with dishonest politicians. They refrain from rationality and productivity by using their political pull and pressure groups to rob the producers. Rand condemns those who would loot the individuals who create human progress and prosperity.

Government intervention discourages innovation and risk-taking and obstructs the process of wealth-creation. In *Atlas Shrugged*, the producers' minds are shackled by government policies. Lacking the freedom to create, compete, and earn wealth, the independent thinkers withdraw from society. This is Rand's recommended response to the bureaucratic assault of the entrepreneurial spirit.

Atlas Shrugged delineates government intervention as the great enemy of the entrepreneur. Rand details how government intervention into private markets produces costs and consequences more harmful than the targeted problem itself. Socialistic bureaucrats attempt to protect men from their own minds and tend to think only of intended, primary, and immediate results while ignoring unintended, ancillary, and long-term ones. Government-produced impediments to a free society are shown to include taxation, protectionism, antitrust laws, government regulation, social welfare programs, monetary inflation, and more.

Atlas Shrugged is a great story that helps students to understand the nature of the world in which they live. It illustrates that only a free society is compatible with human nature and the world and that capitalism works because it is in accordance with reality. Capitalism is shown to be the only moral social system because it protects the human mind, the primary means of human survival and flourishing. *Atlas Shrugged* is a powerful tool to educate, persuade, and convert people to a just and proper political and economic order that is a true reflection of human nature and the world properly understood.

ACKNOWLEDGMENTS

I would like to thank the following individuals for their useful comments and suggestions for improving and clarifying the ideas that appear in this article: Walter Block, Sam Bostaph, Rob Bradley, Stephen Cox, Erik Dent, Stephen Hicks, Jerry Kirkpatrick, William Kline, Allen Mendenhall, Jomana Papillo, John Parnell, Chris Matthew Sciabarra, Fred Seddon, Brian Simpson, Gennady Stolyarov, Michelle Vachris, and Gary Wolfram.

NOTES

First published in *The Journal of Ayn Rand Studies*. 15 no. 2, 2015. 157–184.

1. In *Atlas Shrugged*, Ayn Rand assigns names of individual owners to companies operated by legitimate producer businesses and collectivist sounding names to companies run by inauthentic looter businessmen. Among those companies in the first category are Rearden Steel, Taggart Transcontinental, Wyatt Oil, d'Anconia Copper, Danagger Coal, and so on. Examples of firms in the second category are: Associated Steel, Amalgamated Switch and Signal, and United Locomotive Works. The men who have attached their names to their companies ultimately became strikers during the course of the story.

2. Luskin and Greta (2011) introduce readers to real-life business heroes who have lived their lives like *Atlas Shrugged*'s fictional heroes and the scoundrels who have lived like Rand's fictional villains. For example, on the business hero side the book presents: John Allison as John Galt, Bill Gates as Hank Rearden, and T.J. Rodgers as Francisco d'Anconia. On the business villain side the authors cite Angelo Mozilo as Jim Taggart and Barney Frank as Wesley Mouch, who is a politician who meddles in the economy rather than actually working in the business world.

3. See Locke (2000), Rand in Ralston (2000), Locke (2009), and Ghate (2009) for excellent discussions of businesspeople as heroes and prime movers.

4. Ayn Rand's Objectivist virtues as a basis for morality and success in business are discussed in depth in Greiner and Kinni (2001), Woiceshyn (2012), and Younkins 2012.

5. Salmieri's (2009) essay is Mayhew (2009) is based on his (2007) audio course.

6. A great deal of the material found in Wright's 2007 audio course can also be found in his 2009 article in Mayhew (2009).

7. Several recent articles have discussed how *Atlas Shrugged* can be integrated into college economics courses. See Boettke (2005, 2007), Kent and Hamilton (2011), and Chamlee-Wright (2011).

8. I have my students read the entire text of *Atlas Shrugged* in my "Conceptual Foundations of Business" course. Some faculty members at various institutions choose to selectively assign portions of it to their students. For example, Michelle A. Vachris (2007) of Christopher Newport University assigns pages to be read and typed answers to discussion questions to be brought to class and used as the basis for class discussions in her "The American Economy in Literature" course. Here is a summary of her page assignments and related discussion questions: (1) Who benefits and who is hurt by the Anti-dog-eat-dog Rule? What are some possible unintended consequences? (74–88); (2) Who benefits and who is hurt by the Equalization of Opportunity Bill? What are some possible unintended consequences? (130–36, 217–18, 270–71); (3) How does Galt's motor work? What would be the economic effects of such an invention? (287–91); (4) Who benefits and who is hurt by the Fair Share Law? What are some possible unintended consequences? (298–99, 360–67, 499–500); (5) In Francisco d'Anconia's "Money Speech": What are the roles of money and profit? Find examples that illustrate the differences between the voluntary nature of the market and the coercive nature of government (409–15); (6) Find examples of self-interest versus the public good (475–84); (7) Who benefits and who is hurt by Directive Number 10-289? What are some possible unintended consequences? (535–49); (8) Compare and contrast the two different views of why the Twentieth Century Motor Company failed (321–24; 660–72); (9) Explain the role that self-interest has in the market economy (701–61); and (10) Find examples of capitalism versus collectivism in terms of their views about prices, profit, and property rights (1009–69).

REFERENCES

Boettke, Peter J. 2005. Teaching economics through Ayn Rand: How the economy is like a novel, and how the novel can teach us about economics. *The Journal of Ayn Rand Studies* 6, no. 2 (Spring): 445–65.

———. 2007. The economics of *Atlas Shrugged*. In Younkins 2007, 179–87.

Bradley, Robert Jr. 2011. *Atlas Shrugged*: Its philosophy and energy implications. Online at: http://www.masterresource.org/2011/04/atlas-shrugged-and-energy-i/.

Chamlee-Wright, Emily. 2011. Cultivating the economic imagination with *Atlas Shrugged*. *Journal of Economics and Financial Education* 10, no. 2 (Fall): 41–53.

Ghate, Debi. 2009. The businessesmen's crucial role: Material men of the mind. In Mayhew 2009, 299–316.

Ghate, Debi and Richard E. Ralston, eds. 2011. *Why Businessmen Need Philosophy*. New York: New American Library.

Greiner, Donna and Theodore Kinni. 2001. *Ayn Rand and Business*. New York: Texere.

Kent, Calvin A. and Paul Hamilton. 2011. Inclusion of *Atlas Shrugged* in economics classes. *The Journal of Private Enterprise* 26, no. 2: 143–59.

Kirzner, Israel M. 1989. *Discovery, Capitalism, and Distributive Justice*. Chicago: University of Chicago.

Locke, Edwin A. 2000. *The Prime Movers*. New York: AMACOM.

———. 2009. The traits of business heroes. In Mayhew 2009, 317–34.

Luskin, Donald L. and Andrew Greta. 2011. *I am John Galt*. Hoboken, New Jersey: John Wiley and Sons.

Mayhew, Robert, ed. 2009. *Essays on Ayn Rand's "Atlas Shrugged."* Lanham, Maryland: Lexington Books.

Rand, Ayn. 1957. *Atlas Shrugged*. New York: Random House.

———. [1963] 2011. The money-making personality. In Ghate and Ralston 2011, 67–74.

Salmieri, Gregory. 2007. *Atlas Shrugged as A Work of Philosophy*. Four audio lectures. New Milford, Connecticut: Second Renaissance Books.

———. 2009. Discovering Atlantis: *Atlas Shrugged's* demonstration of a new moral philosophy. In Mayhew 2009, 397–452.

Simon, Julian 1996. *The Ultimate Resource 2*. Princeton: Princeton University Press.

Vachris, Michelle A. 2007. Economics lessons in literature. *Virginia Economic Journal* 12, no. 1: 23–32.

Woiceshyn, Jaana. 2012. *How to be Profitable and Moral: A Rational Egoist Approach to Business*. Lanham, Maryland: Hamilton Books.

Wright, Darryl. 2007. *Ayn Rand's Ethics from "The Fountainhead" to "Atlas Shrugged."* Two audio lectures. New Milford, Connecticut: Second Renaissance Books.

———. 2009. Ethics: From *The Fountainhead* to *Atlas Shrugged*. In Mayhew 2009, 253–73.

Younkins, Edward W. 2002. *Capitalism and Commerce: Conceptual Foundations of Free Enterprise*. Lanham, MD: Lexington Books.

———, ed. 2007. *Ayn Rand's "Atlas Shrugged": A Philosophical and Literary Companion*. Aldershot, England: Ashgate.

———. 2012. Ayn Rand's Objectivist virtues as the foundation of morality and success in business. *The Journal of Ayn Rand Studies* 12, no. 2 (December): 237–62.

Chapter 22

Business as an Agent of Human Progress in *Time Will Run Back*, *Methuselah's Children*, and *The Transhumanist Wager*[1]

Gennady Stolyarov II

The structures and incentives of businesses can be harnessed in order to achieve breakthroughs that dramatically improve the human condition. Works of fiction that explore the impact of business on technological and societal progress feature strong protagonists who are able to use the businesses under their control in order to change the world. Peter Uldanov in Henry Hazlitt's *Time Will Run Back* (1951) incrementally reintroduces elements of free enterprise to rejuvenate a stagnant and impoverished one-world socialist dystopia. The Howard Families in Robert A. Heinlein's science-fiction novel *Methuselah's Children* (1958) maintain a financial enterprise to reward life-extension research and encourage practices that create a small population of supercentenarians in the twenty-second century. In Zoltan Istvan's novel *The Transhumanist Wager* (2013), a science-fiction work about a possible near future, the protagonist, Jethro Knights, creates a commercially oriented seasteading nation, Transhumania, where the world's top innovators are invited to perform research on life extension and many other emerging technologies, in the hopes of achieving major breakthroughs and implementing Jethro's vision of a transhumanist world that transcends age-old human limitations. This article explores the methods used and goals pursued by the protagonists in *Time Will Run Back*, *Methuselah's Children*, and *The Transhumanist Wager* to achieve their visions of a better world through the avenues that the operation of businesses provides.

TIME WILL RUN BACK: UNLEASHING BUSINESS TO IMPROVE THE HUMAN CONDITION

The free-market economist, journalist, and editor Henry Hazlitt wrote his novel *The Great Idea* in 1951; the book was re-released under the title *Time Will Run Back* in 1966 in order to emphasize the rediscovery of the lost ideas of free-market capitalism by the novel's protagonists. In addition to being the most rigorous work of fiction available for the teaching of economic ideas, *Time Will Run Back* highlights the role of business in taking a society from a condition of destitution, misery, and brutality to one of widespread prosperity, progress, and personal fulfillment.

The novel's hero, Peter Uldanov, is the son of Stalenin, the dictator of Wonworld—a socialist dystopia that, in the year 2100 (282 A.M.—After Marx) spans the entire globe. Peter, raised away from politics by his mother, has not been indoctrinated into Wonworld's ideology of totalitarian central planning of all aspects of its citizens' lives. While completely new to politics, Peter is highly intelligent and an accomplished pianist and mathematician. Stalenin is dying and, out of paternal affection, seeks to engineer Peter's succession. Peter is intellectually honest and is perplexed at the widespread poverty, famines, and shortages of Wonworld, as well as the constant climate of terror in which its subjects live—even though the regime claims to have "liberated" them from oppression by the capitalists of old. Peter attempts to introduce a series of reforms to allow criticism of the government and free elections, but his goal of achieving human liberation fails to take hold so long as the economy remains completely centrally planned. Peter's nemesis is Stalenin's second-in-command Bolshekov, who zealously defends the system of command and control while he is the main agent of torture, execution, and mismanagement within it. Peter enlists the assistance of Thomas Jefferson Adams—the third-highest official in Wonworld. Adams is disillusioned with the socialist system and gropes for alternatives but, like Peter, does not have the benefit of the lessons of history—since any works of literature, economics, philosophy, and political theory that disagreed with Marxism-Leninism were purged after Wonworld's establishment a century earlier. Adams has become cynical by observing decades of attempted "reforms" within Wonworld, which tinkered with specific policies and plans but never challenged the overarching fact of total central planning. Peter, as an outsider with a fresh perspective, is more willing to overhaul the system's most fundamental features. In the genuine search for greater prosperity and more humane treatment for Wonworld's population, he begins to dismantle the socialist system piece by piece, at first without even recognizing that this is the effect of his actions.

Much of the novel depicts Peter and Adams groping toward a system of incrementally freer markets and greater individual liberty as they discuss possible reforms and attempt to understand both their direct and secondary, unintended consequences. As a result of their stepwise sequence of liberalizations, Peter and Adams inadvertently rediscover the old system of capitalism that Wonworld sought to stamp out. Adams often acts as a foil to Peter, proposing modified central plans or mixed-economy systems and attempting to posit the arguments made by inflationists and protectionists that emerge as milder obstacles to liberalization once private property, money, and decentralized economic planning by individuals are restored. Peter, however, is sufficiently wise to be able to perceive the secondary consequences of these proposals and to consistently espouse and act in favor of unhampered individual economic liberty.

Peter's first successful reform is to permit people to exchange ration coupons which they were allocated for various specific commodities. Previously, each citizen of Wonworld received ration coupons that were limited to his personal use, and there was no way to realize any value from coupons for goods that the individual did not wish to personally consume. Initially, the citizens of Wonworld—terrorized for generations—are reluctant to exchange coupons for fear of being tricked into showing disloyalty, but after a few months of encouragement by Peter's government, exchanges begin to occur:

> At first individuals or families merely exchanged ration tickets with other persons or families living in the same room with them. Then in the same house. Then in the same neighborhood or factory. The rates at which the ration tickets exchanged was a matter of special bargaining in each case. They at first revealed no describable pattern whatever. In one tenement or barracks someone would be exchanging, say, one shirt coupon for five bread coupons; next door one shirt coupon might exchange for fifteen bread coupons.
>
> But gradually a distinct pattern began to take form. The man who had exchanged his shirt coupon for five bread coupons would learn that he could have got fifteen bread coupons from someone else; the man who had given up fifteen bread coupons for one shirt coupon would learn that he might have got a shirt coupon for only five bread coupons. So people began to "shop around," as they called it, each trying to get the highest bid for what he had to offer, each trying to get the greatest number of the coupons he desired for the coupons with which he was willing to part. The result, after a surprisingly short time, was that a uniform rate of exchange prevailed at any given moment between one type of coupon and another. (Hazlitt, 1966, 103)

This reform inaugurates a price system, which facilitates rational planning by individuals and the effective allocation of goods to their most highly valued uses. It also leads to the emergence of markets where large volumes of exchanges can take place:

> Then another striking thing happened. People had at first shopped around from house to house and street to street, trying to get the best rate in the kind of coupons they valued most for the kind of coupons they valued least. But soon people anxious to trade their coupons took to meeting regularly at certain places where they had previously discovered that they found the most other traders and bidders and could get the best rates in the quickest time. These meeting points, which people took to calling coupon "markets," tended to become fewer and larger.
>
> Two principal "markets" gradually established themselves in Moscow, one in Engels Square and the other at the foot of Death-to-Trotsky Street. Here large crowds, composed in turn of smaller groups, gathered on the sidewalk and spread into the street. They were made up of shouting and gesticulating persons, each holding up a coupon or sheet of coupons, each asking how much he was bid, say, in beer coupons for his shirt coupon, or offering his shirt coupon for, say, twelve beer coupons, and asking whether he had any takers. (Hazlitt, 1966, 103–4)

As markets take hold, professional brokers emerge to handle large numbers of transactions for ordinary people in exchange for a percentage of ration coupons. The brokers quickly become adept at spotting and eliminating discrepancies among exchange rates between any two types of coupons:

> Their competitive bids and offers continued until the relationships were ironed out, so that no further profit was possible for anybody as a result of a discrepancy. For the same reason, Peter found, the ratios of exchange in the market at Engels Square were never far out of line for more than a very short period with the ratios of exchange on Death-to-Trotsky Street; for a set of brokers were always running back and forth between the two markets, or sending messengers, and trying to profit from the least discrepancy that arose between the markets in the exchanges or quotations.
>
> A special name—"arbitrage business"—sprang up for this sort of transaction. Its effect was to unify, or to universalize, price relationships among markets between which this freedom of arbitrage existed. (Hazlitt 1966, 105)

By allowing free exchange and permitting private entrepreneurs to take advantage of arbitrage opportunities, Peter enables a solution to emerge for Wonworld's previously intractable problem of how to make the best use of scarce resources to fulfill as many human needs as possible. Peter recognizes that, even though the adjustments to prices that guide this process of rational resource allocation may appear automatic, they are in fact the effect of the actions of businesspeople seeking to earn a profit:

> They took place solely because there was an alert group of people ready to seize upon the slightest discrepancy to make a transaction profitable to themselves.

> It was precisely the constant alertness and the constant initiative of these specialists that prevented any but the most minute and short-lived discrepancies from occurring. (Hazlitt, 1966, 105)

Allowing free exchange of ration tickets leads to the spontaneous emergence of a monetary system as exchange rates begin to be quoted in terms of only a few leading types of coupons and eventually only in terms of cigarette coupons. These are superseded by packages of cigarettes themselves, which are in turn eventually replaced by gold.

The power struggle between Peter and Bolshekov escalates until Bolshekov engineers Stalenin's assassination and seizes power in Wonworld. Peter and Adams flee to North America, assisted by their loyal Air Force, and establish their own country—Freeworld—where Peter's economic reforms continue. Private ownership of land and capital goods is introduced, and large factories are privatized through the issuance of transferable shares to their workers, entitling them to receive a percentage of the profits from the enterprise. This greatly raises the incentives for production, responsibility, and prudent management of resources, as the newly empowered citizens inform Peter:

> When he asked one of these new peasant-proprietors about his changed attitude, his explanation was simple: "The more work I and my family put into the farm, the better off we are. Our work is no longer offset by the laziness and carelessness of others. On the other hand, we can no longer sit back and hope that others will make up for what we fail to do. Everything depends on ourselves."
>
> Another farmer-owner put it this way: "The greater the crop we raise this year, the better off my family will be. But we also have to think of next year and the year after that, so we can't take any risk of exhausting the soil. Every improvement I put into the farm, whether into the soil or into the buildings, is mine; I reap the fruits of it. But there is something that to me is more important still. I am building this for my family; I am increasing the security of my family; I will have something fine to turn over to my children after I am gone. I don't know how I can explain it to you, Your Highness, but since my family has owned this land for *itself,* and feels secure in its right and title to *stay* here undisturbed, we feel not only that the farm belongs to us but that we belong to the farm. It is a part of us, and we are a part of it. It works for us, and we work for it. It produces for us, and we produce for it. You may think it is just a thing, but it seems as alive as any of us, and we love it and care for it as if it were a part of ourselves." (Hazlitt, 1966, 131)

The ability of individuals to own and run their business and earn a profit turns Freeworld into an economic powerhouse. Whereas Wonworld had, for a century, remained at the level of technological advancement approximately resembling that of 1918–1938, Freeworld becomes a haven for invention, the benefits of which disseminate rapidly to the population. Freeworld's development appears to rapidly catch up to the condition of Hazlitt's 1950s and 1960s America:

> Constant and bewildering improvements were being made in household conveniences, in fluorescent lighting, in radiant heating, in air-conditioning, in vacuum cleaners, in clothes-washing machines, in dishwashing machines, in a thousand new structural and decorative materials. Great forward leaps were now taken in radio. There was talk of the development, in the laboratories, of the wireless transmission, not merely of music and voices, but of the living and moving image of objects and people.
>
> Hundreds of new improvements, individually sometimes slight but cumulatively enormous, were being made in all sorts of transportation—in automobiles and railroads, in ships and airplanes. Inventors even talked of a new device to be called "jet-propulsion," which would not only eliminate propellers but bring speeds rivaling that of sound itself.
>
> In medicine, marvelous new anesthetics and new lifesaving drugs were constantly being discovered . . .
>
> "In our new economic system, Adams," said Peter, "we seem to have developed hundreds of thousands of individual centers of initiative which spontaneously co-operate with each other. We have made more material progress in the last four years, more industrial and scientific progress, than Wonworld made in a century." (Hazlitt, 1966, 153)

Instead of dreading work and needing to be terrorized into toil, the people begin to welcome and yearn for productive innovation:

> Peter was struck by the startling change that had come over the whole spirit of the people. They worked with an energy and zeal infinitely greater than anything they had shown before. Peter now found people everywhere who regarded their work as a pleasure, a hobby, an exciting adventure. They were constantly thinking of improvements, devising new gadgets, dreaming of new processes that would cut costs of production, or new inventions and new products that consumers might want. (Hazlitt, 1966, 139)

Peter explains to Adams that this "is precisely what economic liberty does. It *releases* human energy" (Hazlitt, 1966, 139). Whereas, previously, only the Central Planning Board could decide how to direct resources,

> Now *everybody* can plan. Now everybody is a center of planning. The worker can plan to shift to another employer or another line of production where the rewards are higher. He can plan to train himself in a new skill that pays better. And anybody who can save or borrow capital, or who can get the co-operation

> of other workers or offer them more attractive terms of employment than before, can start a new enterprise, make a new product, fill a new need. And this puts a quality of adventure and excitement into most people's lives that was never there before. In Wonworld, in effect, only the Dictator himself could originate or initiate: everybody else simply carried out his orders. But in Freeworld *anybody* can originate or initiate. And because he can, he does. (Hazlitt, 1966, 139)

Hazlitt frequently emphasizes the connection between the economic empowerment that freedom in business offers and the resulting surge in the quality of life and daily experience—a sense of responsibility, opportunity, self-direction, and the ability to chart one's own future that permeates an economy where individuals are their own economic masters. While under central planning, no progress occurs unless initiated by the exceptionally rare enlightened rulers at the top, in a free market every businessman and worker can be an agent of human progress. Peter observes that a free-market system is meritocratic and tends to reward contributions to human well-being: "Everyone tends to be rewarded by the consumers to the extent that he has contributed to the needs of the consumers. In other words, free competition tends to give to labor what labor creates, to the owners of money and capital goods what their capital creates, and to enterprisers what their co-ordinating function creates" (Hazlitt, 1966, 139). Adams responds that, to the extent a free-market system is able to achieve this, "no group would have the right to complain. You would have achieved an economic paradise" (Hazlitt, 1966, 139). In a later discussion, Peter notes that the profits realized by business-people in a free-market system cannot be maintained on the whole except in a growing economy where consumers are increasingly better off; a free-market system cannot be called a profit system "in a declining or even in a stationary economy. It is, of course, a profit-*seeking* system" (Hazlitt, 1966, 150), but the search for profit in a free economy will only succeed if human needs are fulfilled by the entrepreneur in the process.

Cultural and esthetic progress, too, are facilitated by the actions of Freeworld's entrepreneurs. Hazlitt points out that "it was not merely in material progress that Freeworld achieved such amazing triumphs. No less striking were the new dignity and breadth that individual freedom brought about in the whole cultural and spiritual life of the Western Hemisphere" (Hazlitt, 1966, 155). By contrast with Wonworld's regime-monopolized "art" designed to praise the ruling ideology, the outpouring of creativity and variety in Freeworld "showed itself in novels and plays, in criticism and poetry, in painting, sculpture and architecture, in political and economic thinking, in most sciences, in philosophy and religion" (Hazlitt, 1966, 155). Even though freedom in artistic production results in catering "to the presumed tastes of a mass public; and the bulk of what was produced was vulgar and cheap"

(Hazlitt, 1966, 155), there also emerges the opportunity for some artists to pursue lasting greatness:

> What counted, as Peter quickly saw, was that each writer and each artist was now liberated from abject subservience to the state, to the political ruling clique. He was now free to select his *own* public. He did not *need* to cater to a nebulous "mass demand." He could, if he wished, write, build, think, compose or paint for a definite cultivated group, or for his fellow specialists, or for a few kindred spirits wherever they could be found. And plays did have a way of finding their own special audience, and periodicals and books of finding their own special readers.
>
> In contrast with the drabness, monotony, and dreariness of Wonworld, the cultural and spiritual life of Freeworld was full of infinite variety, flavor, and adventure. (Hazlitt, 1966, 155)

The intellectual honesty of Peter Uldanov enables him to transform the role of inadvertent world dictator to that of guardian of individual freedom. Freeworld overcomes Bolshekov's Wonworld in a largely bloodless military campaign, due to Freeworld's overwhelming superiority in production and the eagerness of Wonworld's citizens to throw off Bolshekov's totalitarian rule. At the novel's end, Peter decides to hold free elections and subject his own position to the people's approval. Running against the mixed-economy "Third Way" advocate Wang Ching-li, Peter narrowly wins the election and becomes the first President of Freeworld, even though his preference would be to devote his time to playing Mozart. Peter has the wisdom to unleash the productive forces of free enterprise and then to step aside, except in maintaining a system that punishes aggression, protects private property, and provides a reliable rule of law. The ending of *Time Will Run Back* is a happy one, but it is made possible by one key tremendously fortunate and unlikely circumstance—the ability of a fundamentally decent person to find himself in a position of vast political power, whose use he deliberately restrains and channels toward liberalization instead of perpetuating the abuses of the old system. Peter is, in effect, a "philosopher-king" who reasons his way toward free-market capitalism, unleashing private business to bring about massive human progress. Without such an individual, Wonworld could have lingered in misery, stagnation, and even decline for centuries. In our world, however, where the vestiges of free enterprise and the history of economic thought are much stronger, we do not need to rediscover sound economic principles from whole cloth, so perhaps existing societies could eventually muddle through toward freer economies, even though no philosopher-kings are to be found. Hazlitt gave us Peter Uldanov's story to enable us to understand which reforms and institutions can improve the human condition, and which can only degrade it.

METHUSELAH'S CHILDREN: BUSINESS AND THE VIRTUOUS CYCLE OF PROGRESS

Methuselah's Children is a pioneering science-fiction novel by Robert A. Heinlein, remarkable for its favorable treatment of greatly extended lifespans several decades before the era of biotechnology and the advent of the transhumanist and life-extension movements. Moreover, *Methuselah's Children* presents important insights regarding the virtuous cycle of improvement that occurs when a business structure is deliberately oriented toward catalyzing both technological progress and increased length and quality of human life.

Originally published as a series in the July, August, and September 1941 issues of *Astounding Science Fiction* magazine, *Methuselah's Children* was released as a full-fledged novel in 1958. Exceptionally long-lived humans—the members of the Howard Families—are the novel's protagonists and are portrayed in a favorable light, as the novel chronicles their escape from persecution in a society where most people continue to live lives of conventional duration and falsely believe the Howard Families to possess a means to artificially engineer extended lifespans. In fact, the Howard Families' exceptional longevity is genetic—a legacy of generations of selective breeding.

The Howard Families' origin dates to the nineteenth century and is made possible by the success of a businessman—Ira Howard—who dreamed of overcoming death but who himself was cursed with premature senescence, dying in 1873 at the age of 48. In spite of his tremendous business acumen as a grocer for the gold miners of San Francisco in 1849 and as a seller of provisions for Union troops during the Civil War, he could not purchase longer life for himself. Instead, he bequeathed his fortune for the prolongation of lifespans. The administrators of his estate found a way to pursue this aim via the cultivation of reproduction among individuals genetically predisposed toward longevity (Heinlein, 1958, 141).

Ira Howard applied his business fortune and business expertise to create a foundation and trust for the purpose of lengthening human life, enabling a small fraction of humankind to become supercentenarians over the course of generations. Officially, the Howard Foundation is "an openly chartered non-profit corporation" (Heinlein, 1958, 6). The Foundation's strategy is to provide financial support and a strong social network for its beneficiaries, while avoiding public notice and adhering to the legal constraints of the eras through which the Foundation prevails. In a conversation in 1874 with medical student and future beneficiary Ira Johnson, a lawyer for the Foundation explains that, in order to avoid legal prohibitions, the Foundation does not form official contracts with those whom it supports, and contracts would not be enforceable in any event. However, if Ira Johnson *happened* to marry a woman on the list provided to him, then the Howard Foundation would voluntarily bestow wealth upon their progeny (Heinlein 1958, 6).

Methuselah's Children is set on Earth during the twenty-second century, in the largely peaceful and rights-respecting society of The Covenant. Generations of selective breeding by that time had, by then, raised the life expectancy of members of the Howard Families past 150 years. The Howard Families had hitherto kept their existence a secret from the broader population through periodic reinventions of individual members' public identities, an effort in which the Foundation was instrumental. By a practice called the Masquerade, members of the Families periodically faked their own deaths and then constructed new lives in different locations with the financial assistance of the Howard Foundation (Heinlein, 1958, 8).

During the more tolerant era of The Covenant, the Howard Families decide to attempt a gradual disclosure of their exceptional lifespans. Part of the motivation is to benefit the progress of humankind, as explained by Foundation trustee Justin Foote: "the Families as a group had learned many things through our researches in the bio-sciences, things which could be of great benefit to our poor short-lived brethren. We needed freedom to help them" (Heinlein, 1958, 9).

The Howard Families decide to reveal 10 percent of their membership and observe the reaction, but their estimation of their fellow humans' tolerance is far too generous. Their plan backfires: the general public becomes falsely convinced that the Howard Families possess a biotechnological secret that could rejuvenate anyone and are withholding it from the remainder of humanity. All of the civil liberties afforded by The Covenant fall by the wayside as the masses clamor for the Howard Families to be detained so that their secret could be extracted from them by force.

Administrator Slayton Ford, who is sympathetic to the Howard Families, nonetheless feels compelled to authorize their arrest due to public pressure, while secretly assisting with the Families' plan to escape to another world. This plan is the brainchild of Lazarus Long—a member of the Families and a recurring Heinlein protagonist memorable for his inventiveness, wit, practicality, and self-reliance. Lazarus Long—named Woodrow Wilson Smith at birth—is a space adventurer and rugged individualist who has stayed away from the Families but reveals himself to be their oldest member at an age of at least 241 years. By the rules of the Foundation, which reward longevity with authority, this gives him a leadership position. Lazarus manages to sway the initially reluctant membership of the Families with the rhetorical assistance of more forward-thinking trustees such as Zaccur Barstow. Barstow points out that it is precisely because of the Families' accumulated wealth and ability to use business and commerce to their advantage that Lazarus's plan might succeed. Barstow suggests that cosmic exploration is the destiny of people of exceptional longevity, and that the assets of the Howard Families would enable them to purchase or construct a spaceship suitable to that purpose (Heinlein, 1958, 47).

The wealth accumulated through Ira Howard's business and preserved over the course of centuries enables the Howard Families to purchase the small spaceship *Chili,* which becomes an instrument to take control of the larger ship *New Frontiers* with Administrator Ford's clandestine assistance. An interesting conversation regarding the economic effects of longer lifespans occurs between Lazarus and Joseph McFee, who sells him the *Chili.* McFee posits that uncertainty about the cause of the Howard Families' longevity has resulted in a disruption to many individuals' ability to engage in economic planning:

> Never saw such a dull market. Some days you can't turn an honest credit." McFee frowned. "You know what the trouble is? Well, I'll tell you—it's this Howard Families commotion. Nobody wants to risk any money until he knows where he stands. How can a man make plans when he doesn't know whether to plan for ten years or a hundred? You mark my words: if the administration manages to sweat the secret loose from those babies, you'll see the biggest boom in long-term investments ever. But if not well, long-term holdings won't be worth a peso a dozen and there will be an eat-drink-and-be-merry craze that will make the Reconstruction look like a tea party. (Heinlein, 1958, 72–73)

Through McFee, Heinlein illustrates an important insight regarding the impact of lifespan-related expectations on economic behavior. Longer anticipated lifespans extend people's time horizons and render them more willing to undertake long-term projects and investments, out of the recognition of a high probability of personal benefit from such undertakings. On the other hand, anticipation of short lives and imminent mortality engenders a "live for today" attitude where prudent, long-term planning falls by the wayside, and actions that sustain and drive forward human civilization are neglected. Longer lifespans tend to result in a lower rate of time preference—the degree by which present satisfactions are preferred to future satisfactions.[2] With longer time horizons available to people, remoter future satisfactions can be conceived of and worked toward. Such work generates numerous ancillary benefits along the way for oneself and others—in terms of both material well-being and cultivation of the virtues and habits conducive to an actualized, fulfilling life. Therefore, extending human lifespans ought to bring about more businesses that focus on long-term human well-being and are comfortable with realizing profits over many decades or centuries, whereas short lifespans drive a mentality of focusing on immediate profits only, without regard for longer-term consequences of business decisions.

Through the engineering and navigational abilities of Andrew "Slipstick" Libby, another member of the Howard Families, the long-lived protagonists manage to use faster-than-light travel to escape the Solar System together with Administrator Ford, who defects to them at the last moment. While the Howard Foundation made the Families' exodus possible, it also rendered itself obsolete in the process. Once the Families are underway on their journey, Justin Foote explains the need for a new decision-making structure to emerge. He states that the trustees of the Howard Foundation no longer legally exist, because their primary duties were to manage the interactions of the Howard Families vis-à-vis the broader human society. According to Foote, now that this relationship with broader society had been severed, the Howard Foundation has lost its reason for existence and needs to give way to new methods of organization (Heinlein, 1958, 99).

From its formation to its dissolution, the Howard Foundation embodies some of the noblest and most admirable qualities possible for a business structure. It prioritizes its mission of promoting longer lifespans and the well-being of its members over its structural survival as an organization. It acts genuinely to protect and empower its beneficiaries—the Howard Families—enabling them to transcend the need for the Foundation's existence and to form a new organizational structure. The Howard Families utilize Ford's administrative skills to coordinate the effort of the *New Frontiers*' interstellar journey and the formation of colonies on two successive planets, where the Howard Families coexist with two friendly but utterly non-individualistic species—the Jockaira and the Little People. In most respects apart from coordinating the logistics of the voyage and the initial settlement phase, the new administration adopts a hands-off, libertarian approach toward the colonists' time allocation and life choices—enabling many of the settlers to lead lives of ease and leisure on the second world of the Little People, where there are abundant resources for all. However, Lazarus cannot accept this as a permanent condition, as his human ambition and desire for challenge are not fulfilled. Furthermore, even though they possess exceptional longevity, members of the Howard Families are still mortal and still face the prospect of losing their individual existences either through death or through voluntary sublimation into the group-mind structures of the Little People—which still destroys individual personality and self-awareness. Lazarus convinces the majority of the settlers that, in order to strive for more than contentment and to have the potential to achieve further progress, they must endeavor to return to Earth.

On Earth, seventy-five years have passed since the Howard Families' exodus. Human society has become far more enlightened in the meantime, and the Howard Families are no longer perceived as public enemies to be persecuted, but rather as admirable early pioneers in life extension and interstellar exploration. Driven by the impression that there was a "secret" to super-longevity, human scientists independently achieved through biotechnology the same results that the Howard Families attained through selective breeding. In a society where everyone possesses life expectancies of over a century and a half, the Howard Families cease to be outliers or targets for envy and suspicion. Ultimately, Ira Howard's plan to greatly lengthen human lifespans is realized for the entirety of humankind. The Howard Foundation's efforts led the remainder of humanity to view super-longevity to be attainable for all. This perception motivated massive research efforts to this goal after the Howard Families' exodus. This result illustrates the ability of a business organization oriented toward human progress to achieve transformation of the wider society, even if explicitly focused on a much narrower subset thereof. A businessman who seeks to catalyze technological progress and create a better future can achieve a wider scope of success by setting an example of what is possible and inspiring others to pursue similar outcomes.

Upon returning to Earth, Lazarus Long and Andrew Libby discuss business plans to explore further reaches of the galaxy—facilitating the expansion of human settlement there—while enabling Lazarus and Libby to lead an enjoyable lifestyle free of significant material limitations. Lazarus suggests that he and Libby found a real-estate business and lay claim to newly explored areas of the galaxy. Libby inquires how they would acquire funds. Lazarus responds:

> I'll set up a parent corporation, while I'm about it, with a loose enough charter to let us do anything we want to do. There will be daughter corporations for various purposes and we'll unload the minor interest in each . . . (Heinlein, 1958, 181)

When Libby objects that this would involve too much work, Lazarus replies that he would simply hire a person with legal and accounting expertise, such as Justin Foote, to manage the day-to-day affairs of the business, while Lazarus and Libby remain able to lead lives they enjoy.

What leads Lazarus to formulate such a far-reaching vision—in terms of both space and time—for a combination of business and unending personal adventure? It is precisely the emerging ability, at the novel's conclusion, of human scientists to artificially extend lifespans even beyond the Howard Families' typical life expectancies. Lazarus remarks, "I didn't start planning our real estate venture till I heard about this new process. It gave me a new perspective. I find myself thinking about thousands of years—and I never used to worry about anything further ahead than a week from next Wednesday" (Heinlein, 1958, 182). Here, too, Heinlein illustrates the tremendous incentive that lengthened lifespans provide for long-term thinking and planning, enabling people to accomplish, experience, and create on a grand scale instead of remaining mired in the immediately accessible.

Methuselah's Children offers an insightful vision of the positive feedback loop between progress-oriented business structures and the attainment of longer, better lives. Through establishing the Howard Foundation, Ira Howard set in motion a chain of events that resulted in super-longevity for all humans and ambitious efforts at interstellar exploration and colonization. The fruits of this effort—incentives for long-term thinking—motivate Lazarus Long to initiate business ventures of his own for the purpose of pushing further outward the boundaries of human ability and expansion. Heinlein concludes the novel with Lazarus's statement of unending ambition: "Yes, maybe [the universe is] just one colossal big joke, with no point to it. [. . .] But I can tell you this, Andy, whatever the answers are, here's one monkey that's going to keep on climbing, and looking around him to see what he can see, as long as the tree holds out" (Heinlein, 1958, 183). This never-ending aspiration for discovery and improvement ought to motivate real-world businesspeople and humans in general to continually seek out ways in which they can apply their skill sets to expand the boundaries of possibility in any endeavor that advances human well-being.

THE TRANSHUMANIST WAGER: THE BUSINESSMAN AS RADICAL REVOLUTIONARY

Zoltan Istvan's 2013 science-fiction novel *The Transhumanist Wager* portrays how a combination of business enterprises, united to achieve a philosophical goal, can transform the world. The novel's protagonist, Jethro Knights, develops a wide-ranging business enterprise that simultaneously operates as its own country—Transhumania—and withstands a military offensive from the combined navies of the world powers. Transhumania then serves as the platform from which Jethro's vision of transhumanism—the transcendence of age-old human limitations through science and technology—can spread throughout the world and become universally adopted.

The Transhumanist Wager takes place in a near-future world where economic malaise, resurgent Luddite sentiments, and labyrinthine political barriers to technological innovation have resulted in a climate of stagnation. Jethro Knights endeavors to change all this, knowing that the status quo will eventually result in his own death. He takes a highly principled, completely uncompromising, and often militant approach toward achieving his goal: indefinite life extension through science and technology. Jethro endeavors to avoid death through any rational means possible, while simultaneously striving to become the "omnipotender"—"an unyielding individual whose central aim is to contend for as much power and advancement as he could achieve, and whose immediate goal is to transcend his human biological limitations in order to reach a permanent sentience" (Istvan, 2013, 33). As a college student, Jethro formulates his philosophical system of Teleological Egocentric Functionalism (TEF), which he later explains to an audience of fellow transhumanists:

> Teleological—because it is every advanced individual's inherent design and desired destiny to evolve. Egocentric—because it is based on each of our selfish individual desires, which are of the foremost importance. Functional—because it will only be rational and consequential. And not fair, nor humanitarian, nor altruistic, nor muddled with unreachable mammalian niceties. The philosophy is essential because it doesn't allow for passive failure. It doesn't allow transhumanists to live in delusion while our precious years of existence pass. (Istvan, 2013, 84)

Jethro circumnavigates the world on his sailboat and works as a journalist in conflict-ridden areas, with the aim of learning as much as possible about the world. Upon returning to the United States, Jethro founds the activist organization Transhuman Citizen, which aims to promote emerging technologies—particularly biotechnological research into indefinite life extension. He must also to foil the increasingly violent and destructive attacks against cutting-edge scientists and research centers by Christian fundamentalist terrorists spearheaded by the Neo-Luddite Reverend Belinas. The Redeem Church, headed by Belinas, has no qualms about hiring thugs to brutally murder transhumanist scientists. At the same time, Belinas maintains a façade of public respectability and functions as a high-profile "moral leader." He influences public opinion and prominent politicians—including Jethro's former college classmate Senator Gregory Michaelson—to despise radical technological progress and crack down on transhumanist research through prohibitions and force. After Jethro's wife and unborn child are murdered by Belinas's henchmen and Transhuman Citizen rapidly loses support due to Belinas's political and public-relations war, Jethro's dream seems to be on the verge of total collapse. Jethro's only opportunity for a turnaround arrives in the form of the Russian oil tycoon Frederich Vilimich.

Vilimich is not the ideal rights-respecting free-market capitalist; his rise to power during the chaotic post-Soviet era is marred by the suspicious death of a general with whom he illegally seized a large number of bankrupt oil companies. Vilimich has high business acumen and recognizes the benefits of using the best technology available: "Against the opinion of many people—including the general—Vilimich used every ruble of the company's booming earnings to acquire the most technologically advanced oil extraction equipment available. Within a few years, the company quadrupled its oil output and became a dominant player in the worldwide energy field" (Istvan, 2013, 174).

Vilimich can be capricious and tyrannical but understands economic incentives and is ruthless about harnessing them to fulfill his objectives:

> He was loathed by his own people for never giving one ruble to charity. He treated his workers poorly compared with other large oil companies, but paid them better. Governments feared him for his habit of impetuously shutting down his oil pipeline for days at a time, thus creating worldwide spikes in energy prices. Some said he did it just to amuse himself; others insisted he just wanted higher oil prices; still others grumbled that he just wanted to remind people who was in control. (Istvan, 2013, 175)

Vilimich is a tragic figure; all joy had left his life when his wife and son were murdered by terrorists two decades earlier. Vilimich dedicates his time and his vast oil fortune to repeated, unsuccessful attempts to bring them back from the dead. Vilimich's redeeming quality is his understanding and embrace of the necessity of radical technological progress: "Vilimich was a believer in change via technology. It had always been a natural instinct for him" (Istvan, 2013, 176). Upon learning of the concerted worldwide crackdown against Transhuman Citizen, Vilimich's reaction is to sympathize with Jethro: "The world was afraid of evolution, Vilimich told himself, shaking his head in frustration. His grueling but successful battle against colon cancer reminded him that life was not open-ended" (Istvan, 2013, 175). Vilimich realizes that some of his previous, mystical attempts to revive his family could not possibly have worked; "however, advanced scientific technology, hard work, and wits most certainly could. They were the exact same things he had used to create his sprawling oil empire" (Istvan, 2013, 176).

Vilimich initially approaches Jethro with the aim to redirect Jethro's quest for biological immortality toward bringing back the dead instead. He tells Jethro, "I can give you billions of dollars for exactly that mission. We can build a nation of scientists to accomplish it. It may not follow the pure transhuman and immortality quests you wanted, but it's close enough" (Istvan, 2013, 179). Not even Vilimich's billions, however, can redirect Jethro from his overarching plan for transforming the world in the pursuit of indefinite life extension, as outlined in his TEF Manifesto. Jethro points out that biological life extension for the living is a far more realistic and proximately achievable goal than reviving the dead. He replies to Vilimich, "What you want is just not even on the transhuman timeline right now. And it would be irresponsible to dedicate more than only a fraction of transhuman resources to it at a moment when the real goals of the movement are, literally, on the verge of collapse; when the longevity of our own lifespans are so immediately threatened" (Istvan, 2013, 180). A clash of personalities ensues. Jethro attempts to reason with Vilimich: "But your money could be used for more practical and possible goals, for near-term successes like your own immediate health and longevity. Then, at some later point, you could consider tackling the monumental task of bringing back the dead. What you want is not even reasonable just yet" (Istvan, 2013, 180). To this Vilimich responds, "I didn't get to be so successful because I was always reasonable" (Istvan, 2013, 180). Both Vilimich and Jethro have lost their families to violence. However, unlike Jethro, who seeks to base his decisions on an overarching "machine-like" rationality, Vilimich is driven by his passionate obsession with bringing back his loved ones above all. Both men are stubborn and unyielding, and their initial meeting ends in an impasse.

However, four days later, Vilimich becomes swayed to give Jethro 10 billion dollars—half of Vilimich's stake in Calico Oil—unconditionally. Vilimich sees much of himself in Jethro's intransigence and single-mindedness, and his reversal makes all the difference for Jethro. Immediately, Jethro undertakes an elaborate scheme to conceal the money from the world's governments, which would have expropriated it:

> The next morning, in a rented private jet, Jethro flew around the world to Vanuatu, Singapore, Lebanon, Panama, Maldives, Djibouti, and Switzerland. He spent two weeks establishing bank accounts for various pop-up companies and corporations in out-of-the-way places, acting as the sole manager. He made up odd business names like Antidy Enterprises, Amerigon LLC, and Dumcros Inc. The money was wired in small, varying portions to all his hidden accounts belonging to the companies so it could never be frozen, tracked, or calculated by the NFSA [National Future Security Agency—a US federal agency established to crack down on transhumanist research] or anyone else on the planet. Even the Phoenix Bank president wasn't aware of the account names or numbers, as third-party escrow accounts were used to hide and deflect all traceable sources. Jethro sent secondary codes and addresses to Mr. Vilimich, as the only other person capable of locating the money. But even *he* wasn't allowed to know everything or control anything. On every account, there was a different company, a different address, a different identification number, a different mission statement. The ten billion dollars was split in a hundred different ways, all with digital tentacles that led only to Jethro Knights.
>
> When the money was safe, he emailed Vilimich:
>
> *Dear Mr. Vilimich,*
>
> *Thank you. The money is safe and being put to good use for the right reasons. I'll be in touch as the transhuman mission progresses. Furthermore, you have my pledge that I will not forget that picture in your pocket.*
>
> *Jethro Knights* (Istvan, 2013, 184)

What Jethro does with Vilimich's money is nothing short of revolutionary. He endeavors to construct an independent community of cutting-edge scientists—Transhumania—on a floating platform—a seastead—in international waters, away from any country's jurisdiction. Jethro fabricates the appearance of Transhuman Citizen's continued decline, so as to trick the anti-transhumanist politicians and religious leaders into thinking that their victory against Jethro is imminent. In secret, Jethro reaches out to architect Rachel Burton, who pioneered many concepts for futuristic structures but is frustrated at the lack of interest in ambitious architectural projects due to the ongoing economic and technological stagnation in mainstream societies. Although the acerbic Burton is initially wary of Jethro, she becomes elated when he explains his vision to her:

> A floating city should shield transhumanists and the people I need away from those forces, giving me certain worldwide legal protections. The city will have to be built to house approximately 10,000 scientists and their immediate families. You'll have to build up, because I want most of the city open for creating green spaces, jungles, and parks—so people like living there. Actually, so they *love* living there. These will be very picky people, some of the smartest in the world. They'll want the best of everything, and they deserve it. I want them to be enthralled with every bit of their new home. I want the city big enough to have an airport for passenger jets, but small enough to comfortably ride a bike around in twenty minutes. I want to build the most modern metropolis on the planet, a utopia for transhumanists and their research. (Istvan, 2013, 192)

Unlike Vilimich, who pays his workers well but treats them poorly, Jethro is more focused on the quality of his employees' lives. He understands the importance of employee motivation and creating a rewarding work environment and the opportunity for fulfilling personal lives outside of the workplace. Because Jethro must attract the best and brightest in order to have a hope of realizing his goal of living indefinitely, he needs to give these creative minds the best possible quality of life in order to entice them to come to Transhumania.

The platform and infrastructure for Transhumania—dominated by three towering skyscrapers—are assembled in Liberia at Burton's recommendation. She outlines the geopolitical and economic considerations behind this choice: "West Africa is far off the radar screen for the rest of the world, so hopefully, there won't be any troublesome interruptions by the media or the NFSA. Besides, Liberia has cheap labor, good weather, and lots of beach space to launch this puppy. It's going to be at least ten soccer fields long, you know. We're going to need lots and lots of space" (Istvan, 2013, 193). The construction effort is a massive project—requiring an "army of 15,000 workers" to labor for five months (Istvan, 2013, 193). Jethro is a hands-on project manager who spends much time at the construction site and gets involved in the details of the plan for the seastead, as well as the means by which it is assembled. Jethro hires an international team of workers and, with the help of a multilingual foreman, sets up a work rotation to facilitate uninterrupted construction: "The work was endless: Twenty-four hours a day, there was a symphony of hammering, drilling, welding, grinding, and shouting. There was no break from the movement; sprawling bodies and their machines zipped tirelessly around the platform. The sheer creation process was a marvel to behold" (Istvan, 2013, 195).

As Transhumania nears completion, Jethro travels throughout the world to clandestinely invite leading scientists to live there. Jethro becomes an expert presenter:

> Jethro mastered his task of pitching the spectacular possibilities of the transhuman nation to his chosen candidates. His invitation to share in the rebirth of the transhuman mission and its life extension goals was compelling, exciting, and novel. Part of his presentation was done in 3D modeling on a holographic screen that shot out of his laptop computer. The state-of-the-art technology Burton's company provided was impressively futuristic. (Istvan, 2013, 196)

Jethro promises the candidate scientists that they will live in "The most modern buildings in the world. Every luxury and convenience you can imagine: spas, five-star restaurants, botanical gardens, farmers' markets, an entertainment plaza, a world-class performing arts center. Then over there would be your offices and laboratories. No expense spared on your research equipment. The most sophisticated on the planet—I guarantee it" (Istvan, 2013, 196–197). Furthermore, Jethro emphasizes the tremendous freedom that scientists would have to pursue their research in the absence of political restraints: "Once scientists arrived there, he promised hassle-free lives from bossy governments and others that disapprove of transhumanist ways. The United Nations decreed three decades ago that rules and ownership 200 miles away from any land masses on the planet do not exist" (Istvan, 2013, 197). Jethro grasps the essential harmony of interests between a well-run business and its employees, and therefore does not forget about providing generous pay and benefits, as well as creating a family-friendly living environment on Transhumania:

> Additionally, he promised the scientists amazing salaries, stellar healthcare, and citizenship to Transhumania if people desired. For their children, there would be competitive schools, sports groups, piano tutors, French classes, tennis lessons, and swim teams. Dozens of varied restaurants and cafes would serve organic,

> sustainable, and cruelty-free foods. Coffee shops, juice bars, and drinking pubs would be ubiquitous. Movie theaters, art galleries, fitness centers, libraries, science and technology museums, and shopping centers would dot the city. Innovative designers would set up furniture and clothing outlets, including those that created products and garments with the latest intelligent materials capable of bio-monitoring the body. Whatever you wanted or needed, no matter how far-fetched; it would all be there. Jethro laid out the promise of an ideal, advanced society, the chance to belong to a country with everything going for it. (Istvan, 2013, 197)

Jethro's hiring policy is enlightened and meritocratic with regard to avoiding any prejudice based on attributes irrelevant to a person's ability to get the job done. However, Jethro is also unforgiving of sub-optimal performance and ruthless about preventing or suppressing any possible behavior or institution that would get in the way of the fulfillment of his overarching vision for Transhumania. Moreover, Jethro—unlike a principled libertarian—does not brook significant ideological dissent in his country:

> His hiring policy was simple. He didn't give a damn where you came from, or what color you were, or with whom you had sex, or what gender you were, or if you had disabilities, or whether you were a criminal or not. But if you were hired for a position, and you failed to meet the goals assigned to you, or if you hindered other hires from meeting the goals assigned to them, then you would be fired and forced off Transhumania at once. There were no labor unions allowed. No workers' compensation. No welfare. No freebies. In short, there was no pity, or even pretense at pity. There was just usefulness—or not. And if you didn't like it, or didn't agree with it, then you didn't belong on Transhumania. Every contract of every scientist who wanted to join bore this severe language, as well as their consensual agreement to uphold the [tenets] of the *TEF Manifesto* and the core mission of transhumanism. (Istvan, 2013, 197)

Because Jethro acts not only as the head of a vast business but also as the leader of a *de facto* independent city-state, it is not clear whether his behavior is consistent with respect for individual rights. On the one hand, every arrangement into which Transhumania's residents enter is a freely chosen contract. On the other hand, they lose every association with Transhumania if they fail to adhere to Jethro's demanding terms. They not merely lose their jobs, but they may no longer live or own property on Transhumania. Ultimately, Jethro facilitates comfortable lifestyles and offers abundant economic incentives not out of a devotion to individual freedom *per se*, but out of a recognition that a considerable allowance for economic liberty (though constrained by Jethro's overarching purpose) would be the most conducive to rapid technological innovation and the eventual discovery of a means to reverse biological senescence and live indefinitely.

In spite of the severity of some of Jethro's terms, the scientists who come to work on Transhumania know what they are getting into. Many come willingly after being inspired by a speech filled with Jethro's characteristic militant, uncompromising rhetoric:

> After so many years of being professionally stifled, intellectually muted, and socially ostracized, many transhuman entrepreneurs and scientists of the world cheered. While the speech was worded stronger than they themselves would have delivered, they respected Jethro Knights' unwillingness to compromise the transhuman mission. They valued his promotion of the determined and accomplished individual. They applauded his hero's journey to reverse the falling fortunes of the immortality quest. They especially appreciated the face-slapping of religion, human mediocrity, and overbearing government. Modern society was at a tipping point of such cowardly self-delusion and democratic self-sacrifice that someone needed to stand up and fight for what everyone wanted and admitted secretly to themselves: *I want to reach a place of true power and security that can't be snatched from me at the world's whim.* (Istvan, 2013, 203)

Vilimich is pleased with his investment and sends Jethro a one-line note, "*Thanks for punching the world for me*"—to which Jethro replies, "*Thanks for giving me muscles to do so*" (Istvan, 2013, 203). Through this exchange, Istvan illustrates the indispensability of these two visionary, intransigent men's business partnership to making Transhumania possible.

Jethro raises the incentives for coming to Transhumania by offering each researcher "a tax-free million dollar signing bonus. It was more money than many had accumulated in decades of work. If they brought approved colleagues from their fields with them, an additional hundred thousand dollars was given. The main obligations of those who joined the transhuman nation included staying their full five-year term and reaching reasonable performance goals in their work" (Istvan, 2013, 203). Jethro also creates the possibility of owning real estate: "One-, two-, three-, and four-bedroom residences were sold at enticing prices. Jethro made it cheaper to own than to rent, and most people opted to buy upon arriving. It replenished the cash Transhumania needed for actual research and city operations" (Istvan, 2013, 204). Jethro understands that ownership of private property (limited though it may be by the requirement to adhere to the TEF Manifesto) gives the owner a powerful incentive to strive for the economic progress of the community where the property is located. By turning his employees into stakeholders of Transhumania, he not only enhances Transhumania's revenue stream but also turns his scientists into more motivated, dedicated producers and innovators. Essentially, Jethro utilizes the principles of running a successful start-up technology firm and applies them to an entire small country: "Jethro ran the entire nation as if it were an aggressive, expanding technology company racing to bring an incredible invention to market. Every scientist had stock in its success, in the urgency of its mission. The result was a hiring domino effect. Soon, hundreds of scientists were showing up weekly to make tours of Transhumania and to sign contracts" (Istvan, 2013, 204).

Jethro succeeds in cultivating a motivated, even inspired, workforce, with a prevailing "can-do" ethos:

> Problems occurred, but they were quickly worked out for the most part. These were not people who complained about a broken hot shower or a bad Internet connection. These were professionals of the highest order, and they were all building the nation together. They fixed things themselves, went out of their way to improve operations, and helped one another when they could. These citizens were people of action, of doing—and doing it right. (Istvan, 2013, 205)

Jethro is also able to vastly improve his scientists' quality of life by restoring their sense that an amazing future can be created through their own work:

> Many scientists commented they felt like graduate students again—when the world was something miraculous to believe in, when anything was still possible, when the next great discovery or the next great technological leap was perhaps just months away. [. . .]At night, many of them looked at the stars from the windows of their skyscrapers and felt as if they had arrived on a remarkable new planet. They were never happier or more productive, or bound with a greater sense of drive. (Istvan, 2013, 205)

In his discussion of the incentives and outcomes found in Transhumania, Istvan illustrates that the best-run businesses will not only generate economic value but will also inspire employees with the prospect of improving the human condition and creating a better world. Even though Jethro's methods of sweeping aside all opposition are questionable, his goals of overcoming disease, lengthening lifespans without limit, and producing life-improving technological advances on all fronts are clearly some of the most admirable aims for any enterprise.

Five years after Transhumania's founding, a major breakthrough enables the goal of indefinite lifespans to approach fruition. Jethro's colleague, the scientist Preston Langmore announces that "The new cell-like substance that we've developed has so many applications. The manipulation of its DNA, controlled by our nanobots, will bring unprecedented changes to human life in the next decade, perhaps even in the next few years. We will begin our ascent to a truly immortal life form, full of all the benefits of what it means to be a transhuman being" (Istvan, 2013, 222).

But the obstacles to the realization of Jethro's dream do not cease once Transhumania becomes economically and scientifically successful. Jethro recognizes that anti-transhumanist organizations and governments will not simply allow Transhumanian research to continue in peace. Therefore, he devotes a third of Transhumania's budget to defense. Transhumania's vast revenues enable the construction of a missile shield, four megasonic airplanes, and ten combat robots, as well as the world's most advanced cyberwarfare infrastructure. Shortly after Transhumania's defensive capabilities are deployed, Belinas orchestrates Jethro's kidnapping and torture. However, Jethro's colleagues manage to locate the compound where he is held hostage, and one of the Transhumanian combat robots destroys Belinas's thugs and kills Belinas himself. Jethro is freed, and Belinas's crimes are broadly publicized, to the shame of the world's governments. However, too many politicians and military leaders have become personally vested in attempting to seize Transhumania's scientific and economic production for themselves, and it is too late to stop them from mobilizing their combined navies in an assault on Transhumania. Jethro's hackers manage to cripple most of the invaders' missile-guidance systems, causing the nations' fleets to destroy one another. Only some extremely obsolete Russian missiles, whose use Jethro did not anticipate, manage to inflict moderate damage. Within twenty-four hours, the ingenuity of Transhumania's scientists enables them to anticipate these missiles and effectively defend against them as well. By creating the world's freest and most innovative economy, Jethro enabled the creation of the ample resources needed to resist those who would stand in the way of his ambition.

Having defeated the combined might of the world's navies, Jethro considers it impossible for Transhumania to peacefully coexist with the political status quo. Now that he possesses the technological means to easily outmaneuver and foil any nation's military, Jethro is able to occupy much of the world after destroying all of the major religious and political monuments of traditional human societies. This is where Jethro crosses the line from justifiable self-defense of his society and into aggression against the rest of humanity—becoming an authoritarian world dictator in his quest to be the omnipotender. What distinguishes Jethro's rule from historical totalitarianism is his instrumental use of free-market policies and incentives to facilitate technological and economic growth—but, again, only insofar as this serves his overarching goal of transforming the human condition along the path outlined in the TEF Manifesto. Jethro's approach to the population of Earth is more utilitarian than based on any absolute, inviolate concept of individual rights; Jethro will recognize a semblance of personal freedom, but only for those who are useful to his broad ambition of turning humanity into a rapidly advancing, transhuman species. Those who cast their lot with Jethro during the early days of Transhumania are, on the other hand, rewarded with unprecedented power. Jethro urges his Transhumanian colleagues to renew their contracts and oversee vast swaths of the transhumanist-dominated Earth:

> You will have a choice, of course, to do as you desire and go where you like, and take the wealth you've earned. Nevertheless, in the best interest of the transhuman mission, I feel it expedient to appoint you as interim leaders of your birth nations and its major cities. Many of you will also oversee massive new science projects that only the resources of individual continents can foster. Others of you will be asked to found and build new universities and educational institutes, some of which will become the largest, most populated learning centers in the world.
>
> It is my hope that in your new appointments, you will seed and cultivate a surplus of amazing new transhuman projects to fruition for us all. As incentive to accept these new duties asked of you, your compensation packages will be staggering. I aim to make each and every one of you—as well as all other citizens on Transhumania—some of the richest and most powerful people in the world. (Istvan, 2013, 231)

In effect, Jethro takes the meritocracy he established in Transhumania and transposes it onto the wider world, turning the best and brightest into world leaders and fulfilling the age-old dream of some thinkers to put enlightened "philosopher-kings" in charge of human society. Jethro explicitly announces that the entire world will become Transhumania writ large:

> Earth, and human habitation of it, will be redesigned. It will no longer be many different countries with different cultures on different continents, but one committed transhuman alliance. It will be transformed into one global civilization bound to advancing science—one great transhuman planet. There will be no more sovereign nations, only Transhumania. Our transhuman goals will be the same as before; there will just be a lot more people working towards them, and a lot more resources to help us achieve success. (Istvan, 2013, 231)

With all of the Earth's resources at his disposal, Jethro continues his quest to overcome disease and death, and by the novel's end it appears that he is successful. Jethro is even able to be cryonically frozen and subsequently revived. He begins to venture into the possibility raised by Vilimich of eventually recovering deceased loved ones—but this quest remains unconcluded, and Istvan leaves the question of its feasibility as open-ended.

The Transhumanist Wager is a story about the clever use of a vast business structure and carefully crafted economic incentives to achieve the most revolutionary transformation of humankind conceivable: a revolution against contemporary societies and in favor of a global culture committed to rapid technological progress and the defeat of death above all. Jethro Knights is more of a utilitarian than a libertarian, and his choice of means eventually departs starkly from principled libertarianism, since a consistent respect for the individual rights of all people, including those whom one considers deeply hostile to one's vision of progress, must ultimately clash with the desire to become an "omnipotender" and achieve as much power as possible. However, during the stage in which Jethro uses free-market policies and innovative business management as instruments toward the attainment of his vision, he is able to create an admirable and inspiring model for human progress.

CONCLUSION

Henry Hazlitt's *Time Will Run Back,* Robert Heinlein's *Methuselah's Children,* and Zoltan Istvan's *The Transhumanist Wager* each portray a different path by which business enterprises can dramatically improve the human condition, catalyzing paradigm shifts in the societies around them. Far from being concerned solely with immediate profits or meeting quarterly earnings goals, the entrepreneurs depicted in these novels endeavor to thrive despite political persecution and manage to escape and overcome outright dystopias.

Among these three novels, *Methuselah's Children* shows the tamest business-based route to reform. For centuries the Howard Foundation aims not to transform the broader society, but rather to protect its own beneficiaries and encourage incrementally greater longevity with each subsequent selectively bred generation. The Howard Families adapt to existing legal and cultural climates and prefer keeping a low profile to instigating a revolution. But even their mild outreach to the general public—motivated by the hope for acceptance and the desire to share their knowledge with the world—brings upon them the full force of the supposedly enlightened and rights-respecting society of The Covenant. Rather than fight, the Howard Families choose to escape and pursue their vision of the good life apart from the rest of humanity. Yet the very existence of this remarkable group and its members' extraordinary lifespans fuels major changes for humanity during the seventy-five years of the Howard Families' voyage. By remaining steadfast to its purpose of protecting its members, the Howard Foundation shows humankind that radical life extension is possible, and Ira Howard's goal is attained for the remainder of humanity, whose pursuit of extended longevity cannot be stopped once society is confronted with its reality.

The path of incremental and experimental—but principled—reform through the use of business is illustrated in *Time Will Run Back*. Even though Peter Uldanov does not intend to embark on a capitalist world revolution, he nonetheless achieves this outcome over the course of eight years due to his intellectual honesty, lack of indoctrination, and willingness to consistently follow valid insights to their logical conclusions. Peter discovers the universality of the human drive to start small and, later, large enterprises and produce goods and services that sustain and enhance human well-being.

Once Peter begins to undo Wonworld's climate of perpetual terror and micro-regimentation, his citizens use every iota of freedom to engage in mutually beneficial commerce that allows scarce resources to be devoted to their most highly valued uses. Peter, too, must escape political persecution at the hands of Bolshekov, but, unlike the Howard Families, he does not have the luxury of completely distancing himself from his nemesis. Instead, he must form a competing bulwark against Wonworld's tyranny and, through the superiority in production that free enterprise makes possible, overthrow the socialist dystopia completely. Where Wonworld experienced a century of technological stagnation, Peter's Freeworld is able to quickly regain lost ground and experience an acceleration of advancement similar to the one that occurred in the post-World War II period during which Hazlitt wrote *Time Will Run Back*. Because human creativity and initiative were liberated through free-market reforms, the novel ends with a promise of open-ended progress and a future of ever-expanding human flourishing.

The most explicitly revolutionary use of business as a transformative tool is found in *The Transhumanist Wager*. Jethro Knights conceives Transhumania specifically as a haven for technological innovation that would lead to the attainment of indefinite lifespans and rapid, unprecedented progress in every field of science and technology. Transhumania is an incubator for Jethro's vision of a united transhumanist Earth, ruled by a meritocratic elite and completely guided by the philosophy of Teleological Egocentric Functionalism. Like Lazarus Long and the Howard Families, Jethro finds it necessary to escape wider human society because of political persecution, and, like them, he plans an eventual return. He returns, however, without the intent to re-integrate into human society and pursue what Lazarus Long considers to be a universal human striving for ceaseless improvement. Rather, Jethro considers unaltered humanity to be essentially lost to the reactionary influences of Neo-Luddism, religious fundamentalism, and entrenched political and cronyist special interests. Jethro's goal in returning to the broader world is a swift occupation and transformation of both the Earth and humankind in Jethro's image.

Jethro's path is, in many respects, the opposite of Peter Uldanov's. Peter begins as an inadvertent world dictator and sequentially relinquishes political power in a well-intentioned, pragmatic desire to foster his subjects' prosperity. Along the way, Peter discovers the moral principles of the free market and becomes a consistent, rights-respecting minarchist libertarian—a transformation that impels him to relinquish absolute power and seek validation through a free and fair election. Jethro, on the other hand, begins as a private citizen and brilliant entrepreneurial businessman who deliberately implements many free-market incentives but, all along, strives to become the omnipotender—and ends up in the role of world dictator where Peter began. The two men are at polar opposites when it comes to militancy. Peter hesitates even to wage defensive war against Bolshekov and questions the propriety of bringing about the deaths of even those who carry out repeated, failed assassination attempts against him and Adams. Jethro does not hesitate to sweep aside his opposition using massive force—as he does when he obliterates the world's religious and political monuments in an effort to erase the lingering influence of traditional mindsets and compel all humankind to enter the transhumanist age. Jethro's war against the world is intended to "shock and awe" governments and populations into unconditional and largely bloodless surrender—but this approach cannot avoid some innocent casualties. Jethro will probably not create Wonworld, because he still understands the role of economic incentives and individual initiative in enabling radical technological progress to come about. However, the benefits of the progress Jethro seeks to cultivate will still be disseminated in a controlled fashion—only to those whom Jethro considers useful to his overall goal of becoming as powerful and advanced as possible. Therefore, Jethro's global Transhumania will not be Freeworld, either.

All three novels raise important questions for us, as human society in the early twenty-first century stands on the cusp of major advances in biotechnology, nanotechnology, robotics, artificial intelligence, space travel, and hopefully radical life extension. However, reactionary political and cultural forces continue to inflict massive suffering worldwide through brutal warfare, sweeping surveillance and humiliation of innocent people, policies that instill terror in the name of fighting terror, and labyrinthine obstacles to progress established by protectionist lobbying on behalf of politically connected special interests. Indeed, our status quo resembles the long, tense stagnation against which Jethro revolts to a greater extent than either the largely rights-respecting society of The Covenant or the totalitarian regimentation of Wonworld. But can the way toward a brighter future—paved by the next generation of life-improving technologies—be devised through an approach that does not exhibit Jethro's militancy or precipitate massive conflict? Time will tell whether humankind will successfully pursue such a peaceful, principled path of radical but universally benevolent advancement. But whatever this path might entail, it is doubtless that the trailblazers on it will be the innovative businessmen and entrepreneurs of the future, without whom the development, preservation, and dissemination of new technologies would not be possible.

NOTES

1. Portions of *The Transhumanist Wager* reprinted by permission of the author and Futurity Imagine Media LLC.

2. The concept of time preference was extensively elucidated by the renowned Austrian economist Ludwig von Mises (1881–1973). For a concise overview of this idea, see "Austrian Economics and Time Preference" (Stolyarov, 2005).

REFERENCES

Hazlitt, Henry. [1966] 2007. *Time Will Run Back.* New York: Arlington House. Ludwig von Mises Institute. Available at http://library.freecapitalists.org/books/Henry%20Hazlitt/Time%20Will%20Run%20Back.pdf. Accessed December 13, 2014.

Heinlein, Robert A. [1958] 2005. *Revolt in 2100 & Methuselah's Children.* New York: Baen.

Istvan, Zoltan. 2013. *The Transhumanist Wager.* San Bernardino: Futurity Imagine Media LLC.

Stolyarov II, G. 2005. "Austrian Economics and Time Preference." *The Rational Argumentator,* Issue XLII. Available at http://rationalargumentator.com/issue42/austriantimepreference.html. Accessed December 11, 2014.

Chapter 23

Rabbit in the Showroom

Healthy, Wealthy, and No Place Left to Run

Carl S. Horner

Although Rabbit Angstrom luxuriates in the power and masculinity that he commands as front man and co-owner of Springer Motors, he shudders in John Updike's ([1981] 1982) *Rabbit Is Rich* at the face that he sees in mirrors, the "shadowy presence" of the blue-suited businessman "looking overweight and dangerous" and jarring his inner being like someone whom he somehow does not wish to know. "Jesus," an alien spirit whispers inwardly. "It is himself" (283–84).

Here is a man who dreads considerably more than merely growing old and dying. The greater anguish, as his wife puts it for him, is "the fear that tomorrow will be the same as yesterday" (331), the fear that the little boy is dying inside the businessman, for even though Rabbit owns one quarter of the business that he manages and thus enjoys liberties of which non-vested employees could only dream, he must silence his boyish impulse for freedom and new adventure in order to satisfy the practical needs of his customers, staff, and profit and loss sheets. Knowing and confessing that he is not naturally suited to the risks and challenges of auto sales—that he has beaten corporate Darwinism only by marrying the boss's daughter—and yet transfixed by money, a house with location-location-location, the plush greens and fairways of country club golf, and new cars, for which he knows that he could qualify in no other way, Harry Angstrom deliberately conditions himself to the cost-effective, do-or-die mentality of the American corporate psychostructure.

"The face far behind him" of an impatient and disorderly boy, living always in the present tense, taking in specs in an endless transience of experience, all new and all made up, "exists in his present face like the chrome bones of a grille within the full front view of a car and its fenders" (4). Ruth finds the transformation into the mainstream world of money and clocks appalling and dishonest, reminding Rabbit when they meet for the first time after twelve years that by nature he used to run from enclosure. "My eyes are watery because they can't stand looking at you. A regular Brewer sharpie. A dealer. The kind of person you used to hate, remember?" (415).

But while Rabbit "avoids mirrors" (4) and confrontations with people like Ruth who see him for what he has really become, he is by no means blind to his contradiction. In a tremendous revelation, voiced during a game of tennis in the Poconos, Rabbit thinks: "What has he done . . . with this life of his more than half over?" People including his mother and old basketball coach had seen "something special," something very vibrant and creative in him as a boy. He had certainly felt it, and even Ruth had seen it, although she did not trust or understand his eruptive energy. She had also seen "it winking out" (129).

In what George Searles (1985) identifies as our "occupational malaise" (91), Harry Angstrom compromises the best of his spiritual creativity for "pernicious materialism," nearly guaranteeing his "moral dissolution" (84) as he ensnares himself in "the hideous cultural vulgarity" (28) that he once so passionately eschewed. Although Rabbit sees "that to be rich is to be robbed, to be rich is to be poor," he remains lost in "the murk" (351) of his new comforts. Time washes us away, and our inner-most possibilities can yellow and die like Rabbit's childhood basketball moments entombed under glass. For all but the most recent years of his adult life, Rabbit "had kicked against death," but spinning in the opportunities that would enthrone him at Springer Motors, "he gave in and went to work" (129).

Now at the age of forty-six and seven, caught in the whirlpool of American meritocracy, his economic power source, "he sees his life as just beginning, on clear ground at last, now that he has a margin of resources, and the stifled terror that always made him restless has dulled down. He wants less. Freedom, that he always thought was outward motion, turns out to be this inner dwindling" (89). Insisting that he is healthy and happy for the first time in his life since childhood, "in these middle years it is so clear to him that he will never run"—never run from his Toyota dealership and never run again from his wife, "the keystone of his wealth" (426).

How many businessmen trade the best of their boyish impulse for fortune-making potential in a country that places its highest premium on urban success and the material wealth that proves it? "How can you respect the world when you see it's being run by a bunch of kids turned old?" is a popular joke at Rotary luncheons, but the joke is painfully true of the American corporate psyche. "The thing about those Rotarians," Rabbit thinks, "if you knew them as kids you can't stop seeing the kid in them, dressed up in fat and baldness and money like a cardboard tuxedo in a play for high school assembly" (255). Businessmen do not mature or even outgrow boyish tendencies as much as they learn to discipline, suppress, or kill inner direction in order not to collide with the successful competition, productivity, and profit that give and take life in our commercial universe. As Rabbit puts it, "life, just as we first thought, is playing grownup" (232).

The truth about nepotism in American business is that the son, nephew, or son-in-law does not always start at the loading dock and work from the ground floor up the chain-of-command in order to learn all operations of the company as well as any employee. Too often the relative, with or without appropriate ability, immediately assumes some kind of executive leadership. Upon the death of his patron, he also rises to the presidency, if not ownership. Although, as Ma Springer is quick to point out, Rabbit had no prior experience in sales and was even a questionable candidate for account work in the minds of some company advisors, shortly after Rabbit was terminated in the dying linotype business, Fred Springer brought his son-in-law into the dealership as senior sales representative. And then, perhaps sensing in his heart condition the inevitability of an early death, he deliberately groomed the neophyte for the position as front man. Rabbit agrees that luck and not merely talent or goal-oriented hard work seriously influences the American urban success story. "The great thing about the dead," he says, not meaning to sound insensitive about Springer's coronary, is that "they make space" (3).

Nelson complains that his father has not earned his terrific "happiness"—that he does not deserve his position in business and the good fortune that has swept over him like a fairy wind. "He doesn't know anything the way Charlie does," he insists to Melanie, who can do little to ease Nelson's tension over what he sees as his father's parasitic attitude in business. "What did he ever do, to build up the lot? My granddad was grubbing his way up while my father wasn't doing anything but being a lousy husband to my mother. That's all he's done to deserve all this money: be too lazy and shiftless to leave my mother like he wanted to." The second generation of stewardship does not have the business acumen of Fred Springer. "He *is* bad," Nelson persists, "really bad. He doesn't know what's up, and he doesn't *care*. . . . My grandfather used to have a performance board but Dad's let it drop. You can tell Charlie thinks Dad's really lazy and sloppy" (121–24).

Although Rabbit learns how adequately to manage his inventory for profit, he represses nightmare memories about the "hard" expectations of "long hours" at the lot and Old Man Springer's "grinding" focus on "performance guidelines and washout profits and customer servicing." Feeling in the old days that he was expected "to fill some big skin that Springer spent all his time and energy imagining," Rabbit now claims that skin to be his own little kingdom "to stand around in loosely" (3).

With less than natural business mentality, Rabbit survives in auto sales luckily because of the kind of dealership that he manages. First, Fred Springer paid off the mortgage on his physical plant before he died. And second, the product sells itself, given the existing fuel crisis and the growing reputation of the Toyota Celica, Corolla, and Tercel for gas mileage and dependability. "Read *Consumer Reports*, April issue. That's all he has to tell the people when they come in. And come in they do, the people out there are getting frantic, they know the great American ride is ending. Gas lines at ninety-nine point nine cents a gallon and ninety percent of the stations to be closed for the weekend" (1).

Typically, only a wizard of account work gets rich in the auto industry, but with the law of supply and demand including product, price, and service favoring the seller, Rabbit wins by default, having only to be available for a canned presentation and a test drive in order to get the contract. "Ah, this isn't selling," laments Charlie, who loses motivation more by shrinking risk and challenge than by his progressive heart disease. "It's like supermarkets now: it's shelf-stacking, and ringing it out at the register" (207). Even so, Dale Carnegie and in a more limited sense Horatio Alger, Jr., would have predicted survival and success for Charlie and not for Rabbit in order-taking sales, given Rabbit's aversion at times to grub for the highest profit.[1]

Although he responds with appropriate aggression during his son's wedding reception in his effort to talk Reverend Campbell out of his Opel and into a new Tercel, this aggression is never consistent, never even predictable, as if it is the forced by-product of Rabbit's adaptation to his work. "The world runs on push," Rabbit knows, but that is not the Angstrom Ethic that undergirded even his participation and odd success in basketball: "Rabbit's feeling has been that if it doesn't happen by itself it's not worth making happen" (380).

While Rabbit has neither the "creativity" nor the "drive" that would suit him to car sales, he does not run Fred Springer's dealership "into the ground" (140), as Nelson so vehemently claims.[2] As lucky as he is to have inherited management responsibilities of an order-taking business, he does respond naturally and therefore fluently to the public relations necessary in his industry. Rabbit has always loved to be the cynosure of attention, and as front man for his company, business is like playing basketball again, "a center of sorts, where he had been a forward." The visibility and often need and appreciation and love that this company "star and spearpoint" senses in his routine public contact reincarnate a boyhood pulse effectively rewarded by the kind of "airiness" that he feels about his work and "the nod he gets from the community," a community "that had overlooked him like dirt ever since high school" (2–3).

In the breakdown of the American Dream, Harold C. Angstrom emerges not by the Grace, persistence, and thrift of the colonial Puritan, and not by the pluck of the Alger hero, but by doing nothing, nothing but buying the winning ticket for the state lottery or spinning Vanna White's Wheel of Fortune to claim his wife, "his stubborn prize" (426), and dealership. Indeed, we witness a man whose corporate life all but falls into place like the events late at night in a dream, a man now "having money to float in" (4) and beginning to see "that life can be lived selectively, as one chooses from a menu, or picks a polished fruit from a bowl" (127).[3] But what is he doing, his sister asks, "to feed the inner man?" (240).

In *John Updike's Novels*, Donald Greiner (1984) writes that while middle age and economic comfort have forced Harry Angstrom "to readjust his sights closer to earth" (92), Rabbit "still longs for a world without ruts" (85), still "senses his need for a quest" (91), still refuses to believe in less than "the possibility of new territories, the glow of affirmation" (99). Even with the obvious "decline of his spiritual aspirations" (93), and with the "shrinking inner spaces" (96) that come with the limits that years and adult responsibilities have imposed upon him, in "Rabbit's urge to say 'yes' to life," in "his inarticulate yet intuitive feeling that around the next corner or down the next fairway or in the next baby," there still "exists a possibility for grace despite the hardness of the heart" (98). After all, Greiner contends, "what makes Harry 'Rabbit' is his refusal to be pinned down" (92).[4]

But while it is true that he still quests for freedom and new adventure, perhaps most hopefully during his Caribbean retreat, as long as he continues to spearpoint an auto dealership as conservatively structured even as Springer Motors, Rabbit faces the certainty of enclosure. Harry Angstrom cannot leave the firm, says Charlie who knows that he "can sell anywhere" (252) but that luck has given the boss his only potency in American culture and business. Rabbit may always keep an eye on the exit lights (as instinctively he must), but as long as he wants to glisten with the lights of corporate health and wealth, Harold C. Angstrom is his own "Fortune's hostage" (437) trapped at the helm of his inherited kingdom, trapped upright and grinning in his coffin, his showroom—with no place left to run.

NOTES

First published in Carl S. Horner, *The Boy inside the American Businessman*. Latham, MD: University Press of America, 1992.

1. Since no one at Springer Motors is as qualified to sell cars as Charlie, given not only his highly seasoned knowledge of the company but also his actual gift for account work, it is ironic, indeed, that Rabbit and even Jake and Rudy will outlast him both in the auto industry and at the Springer dealership. Entropy in Updike's intuition relates to corporate Darwinism. First, this born salesman is literally running

out of energy, depending some days on nitroglycerine for even marginal strength, in the wake of his terminal heart condition. And second, while he used to be effective at "kissing Springer's ass" (85) in order to insulate himself from Bessie's expectations for his personal life, he can no longer defuse her negative feeling about him. "I never liked that about Charlie, that he was unwilling to get married," Ma Springer confesses as she explains why Nelson will replace Charlie and not more sensible candidates, either Rudy or Jake. "It bothered Fred, too, I know" (249). All the fresh-cut flowers, business contacts, and revenue in Brewer cannot save Charlie when he finally rubs this "tough" but irrational Toyota queen the wrong way over Nelson's live-in friend. "If you want to know what I think cooked my goose," he tells Rabbit, "it was that trip with Melanie" (251–52).

2. Nelson at times reflects the wheeler-dealer mentality of his grandfather, but he subverts his suitability for the auto industry with highly "negative thinking" (229), insisting to his father that "money is shit" (157)—a violation of the first law of business—and never ceasing to "knock the product" (325) that Springer Motors is franchised to sell. Not only is he impractical, unreliable, naturally unfriendly, and "overanxious as a salesman" (141)—the consensus at least of Melanie, Rabbit, and Charlie—but also as he thinks about the dealership with its redundant little Toyotas, wishing that they were old convertibles with character and style, "his stomach sinks" from a childhood anguish "of being in the wrong place" (309). In the showroom, he cannot escape "feeling idiotic" (305) about routine customer relations as if thrust upon "a stage where he hasn't quite learned the lines yet" (337).

3. Donald Greiner (1984) argues that "the American dream goes sour" for Rabbit, "with the bad taste of advancing age and aimless youth" (84). However, within Updike's ironic multiplicity of beating corporate Darwinism, as the country supposedly runs out of gasoline, suffering from the economic crisis of the decade, oil companies realize windfall profits, and Rabbit, the son of a common laborer, rises above his class, complete with his upper-middle class income and own home in Penn Park.

4. In his second book, *Adultery in the American Novel: Updike, James, and Hawthorne*, Greiner (1985) contradicts his thought that Rabbit's granddaughter distracts his fear of mortality: "Looking at his granddaughter . . . he sees another nail in his coffin" (105). Updike ends his novel with caution, with the binding resources of wealth: "Fortune's hostage, heart's desire, a granddaughter. His. Another nail in his coffin. His" (437), and yet despite Updike's nailing Rabbit down, Jeff Campbell (1984) argues in "Light on Your Fur: Regeneration in Updike's *Rabbit Is Rich*" that "new shoots" (12), including his granddaughter, suggest "a counter-force to entropy" in Rabbit's life, "an interrelationship of imaginative self and objective world that offers regeneration in spite of a continuing energy shortage" (11). Given "yes—but" (8) exposure, which to some extent Campbell compares to the paradigm of Kierkegaard, Rabbit can see his granddaughter in a light other than death: "The new baby is what Rabbit has been waiting for, his heart's desire, a hostage to fortune—and she is his, she can belong to no one else in quite the same way. Her presence does not change the outward reality of the empty house where he is bound to take a fall, nor does she reverse the aging process—she is another nail in his coffin, another sign of his moving closer to his own eventual death. Rabbit is running down. All things run

down. But there is another light besides that of the perceptively cooling sun. There is a Rabbit-light on one's fur that affirms the real presence of an audacious, unique human personality. . . . and the real presence of his granddaughter affirms the reality and renewability of human selfhood" (13).

REFERENCES

Campbell, Jeff H. 1984. Light on your fur: Regeneration in Updike's *Rabbit Is Rich*. *Lamar Journal of the Humanities* 10, no. 1 (Winter): 7–13.

Greiner, Donald J. 1985. *Adultery in the American Novel: Updike, James, and Hawthorne*. Columbia, South Carolina: University of South Carolina Press.

———. 1984. *John Updike's Novels*. Athens, Ohio: Ohio University Press.

Searles, George J. 1985. *The Fiction of Philip Roth and John Updike*. Carbondale, Illinois: Southern Illinois University Press.

Updike, John. [1981] 1982. *Rabbit Is Rich*. New York: Fawcett-Ballantine.

Chapter 24

Roger Rueff's *Hospitality Suite*

Theodore N. Pauls

Upon initial consideration, Roger Rueff's *Hospitality Suite* would seem to be most appropriately compared and contrasted with Industrial Marketing or Organizational Behavior. It is, after all, a play for which the premise is a trade show for industrial lubricants. Intentional or not, the playwright chose a product, a location, and a setting each of which lacks much hedonic allure.

For the product, Rueff did not make a selection for which most of the general population could relate. He chose industrial lubricants. Not any lubricants; industrial lubricants. The adjective "industrial" conjures up images of massive machinery and mills in rust-belt cities. The detailed application for this product is foreign to most, existing only in imagination.

The location, Wichita, Kansas, an industrial mecca and a great city in its own right, does not offer the same glamour and glitz often associated with national conventions and trades shows. To be sure, Wichita is largely associated with the aircraft industry and would certainly be the place of choice for an aviation convention. But remember, the play's product is industrial lubricants, not aviation lubricants. Just as aviation lubricants may have distracted from the neutrality of the author's intent, the same may be said of more common national convention sites such as Las Vegas, Dallas, Miami, or New Orleans.

With all that Wichita does have to offer, Rueff chose a mid-tier hotel for the setting. His description of the room is very predictable and ordinary: a non-stylish sofa and matching chair, bland commercial grade tables, and matching lamps. It is exactly the type of room one would expect in a Holiday Inn. It is exactly the ordinary and relatively mundane combination of the hotel, city, and convention that draws this author to use this play as a guide for applying consumer behavior principles. It is the characters and their interests, interaction, and outcomes that makes *Hospitality Suite* so applicable to the study of consumer behavior, occasionally with the unique approach of examining it from the supplier's perspective. The purpose of this chapter is to examine how the play may be used for examples of select concepts and applications of consumer behavior. Not intended to be collectively exhaustive, this chapter cites some of the play's many opportunities for consumer behavior applications. Additionally, most of the concepts are not defined as they may be in a consumer behavior text but rather highlighted as examples of textbook terms. This intentional omission will aid in readers' synthesis and integration of concept and application.

Consider the three primary, almost exclusive, personalities of the play's characters; Larry, an aggressive, demanding, and often times crass salesman who is willing to do almost anything to meet the CEO of the largest customers at the convention. In complete contrast is Bob, a young, recent research graduate who sees the good in everyone and whose mission, it seems, is to serve more as a missionary than as a salesman. He wishes Larry would be more like him because his life, although not nearly as experienced, is cleaner and more Christ-like. Finally, there is Phil, an intermediary to Larry's boisterous, callous, demeanor and Bob's cleanly lived, saintly character. These three characters are easily personified into the Freudian System of *Id*, primarily pleasure at any cost, *Superego*, the conscience and the good, and the *Ego*, mediating between the id and superego. The scenario repeats itself throughout the play. For example, early in the play Larry expands in depth on his preference for women in business suits. In turn, he inquires what women wear that Bob finds desirable. Bob explains that he is married and therefore does not look at other women. Larry immediately interrogates Bob with the blunt question "Are you gay?" causing Phil to intervene with a scolding "Larry!"

Early in the play, before Larry enters, Phil and Bob are engaged in small talk. Innocently, Bob inquires what magazine Phil is reading, Phil answers "Penthouse." Phil offers to share the magazine with Bob when he is finished, but Bob politely but curtly answers that he does not because he does not read those types of magazines. When Phil asks Larry if he is "one of those who believes that magazines like this should not be published, Bob responds, "I'm the type of person who believes they shouldn't be purchased." In doing so, Bob demonstrates the principle of *desacralization*, that what in his opinion should remain *sacred* has become profane, the basis for the objection to pornography. Phil commends Bob for his clever reply to which Bob replies he was not trying to be clever. It is that impromptu, natural response that leads Phil to suggest Bob may have a career in marketing. The conclusion is based on the concept of *modeling* in which behavior is based on the imitation of others. Soon after this exchange Larry enters the scene for the first time.

Upon entering the suite, Larry immediately expresses dissatisfaction with the choice of rooms, drawing attention to the fact that it is too small, not the type of suite that is expected for hospitality. He further expresses concern over the choice of hors d'oeuvres, comparing his suite's cheese balls, sliced carrot sticks, and celery sticks to the competition's jumbo shrimp, French cheeses, puffed pastries, and oysters on the half shell. Based on both *cultural norms*, both *enacted* and *crescive*, Larry believes that the unsatisfactory nature of his surroundings will *transfer meaning* to an unsatisfactory *perception of product quality*. The *semantic meaning* suggests that shrimp and oysters are more symbolically associated with success than are celery sticks and cheese balls. The *customer expectations* will not fall into a zone of acceptance if Larry is correct.

In an attempt to overcome the shortcomings, Phil retorts that the room is high in the hotel, on the twenty-sixth floor, and that the view from that height is enough to impress the customers. Larry's response indicates that because it is Wichita, Kansas, it does not matter if "we're on the first floor or the five-hundredth floor, it all looks the same." In doing so, Larry addresses the concept of customer *perception* and more specifically *sensory thresholds*. To Larry, there is no benefit to having a room on a higher floor because no *differential threshold* exists, no visual distinction is made among floors' heights. In the same sense, Larry had addressed the noticeable difference between what was being served between the two competing suites on adjacent floors. Again, the hors d'oeuvres would easily exceed the *absolute threshold* and therefore give a much more favorable company image to the potential customers.

After completing his side-stage and quiet telephone call with his wife, Bob enters the conversation by suggesting the room and its' amenities look acceptable. Larry introduces himself to Bob who apologizes that he had been on the phone. Even though he had been engaged in his own conversation and therefore unable to eavesdrop, Larry uncannily suggests correctly to Bob that the conversation with his wife had focused on furniture. Further, Larry is able to tell Bob, nearly line for line, how the conversation about furniture unfolded: It began with his wife suggesting she found some furniture, asking what Bob thought, and how Bob's response would be that he'd like to see it first. Bob is impressed but also curious as to how Larry could know such things. Larry explains that "it's what we all tell our wives, Bob. It's what every man since Adam has told his wife when she said she's found a piece of furniture. It's instinct. Salmon swim upstream to spawn. Birds fly south in the winter. Once every four years, lemmings throw themselves off a cliff. And we, as husbands, tell our wives we're not sure we can afford it right now when they talk about furniture." This is an example of a learned behavioral *script*. On a broader scale, it is an example of *predictive behavior*, the backbone of consumer behavior.

Later in the same conversation, the topic turns to what each person's *role* is at the convention. (Ironically, *role theory* is often explained as the behavior one would undertake in a play!) When Bob is initially told that he is there to represent Research Technical Support, Larry confounds the role by telling Bob that "If you want to know the truth, bob, nobody is really here. You think you see people walking around up and down the halls? You don't. What you see is a functions." In an effort to alleviate Bob's confusion, Phil enters with "What Larry means, Bob, is that there's a certain detachment that takes place at these things. If you look at it from the standpoint of why we're here, what we are is more important than who we are." After a brief exchange about the impersonality of such a viewpoint, Larry further explains each of the three men's functions. This conversation offers an excellent opportunity to examine and understand elementary principles of *multiple selves* and *role identity*.

Eventually, the three characters begin to address the single most important account for which they should all be prospecting. In a complete and perhaps sarcastic turnaround from his previous attack on the unimpressive suite, Larry pantomimes the behavior of the person to whom they must appeal. Larry suggests that this customer will enter the room and be stunned by its aesthetic appeal and "so overwhelmed with the fact that he's on the twenty-sixth floor, overlooking all of Wichita, Kansas, like some ancient king surveying his fiefdom." Larry's description of the king is based on a *Jungian archetype*. He knows that mental image he paints will be similar for both Bob and Phil despite their different backgrounds.

The three characters banter about with small talk until Phil leaves to go downstairs to purchase cigarettes. Once he exits, Bob and Larry are left alone for the first time. They continue with small talk and in due course the topic begins to focus on Phil in his absence. Larry explains to Bob that Phil has changed over the last few years. "He used to be the real manic-depressive type. One day, he'd be riding in the clouds. The world was a beautiful place, and he was just happy to be here. The next day, you wouldn't even know you were talking to the same person. He'd walk around looking like somebody'd let the air out of him. You got the impression that, at any moment, he might pull out a gun and shoot himself. Even then, he was real personable." This description of Phil exposes deeper levels of *multiple selves*. This expanded scene offers an applicable example of one person's *self-concept* and *self-esteem*. Phil's *ideal self* and his *actual self* are incongruent. He wants come across as being personable while inside he's feeling discontent. He understands that the relationship he has with others will create their opinions of who he is. This *symbolic interactionism* is part of Phil's *impression management*, controlling what others think of him. The two continue to talk until Phil returns then conclude Act One by going to get dinner, discussing the plan to return for a successful evening as they leave.

Act Two opens with an unidentified man leaving the hospitality suite, the last visitor to do so. Only two of the three main characters are in the room,

Larry being absent. When Larry does appear, he explains that he had been looking for the client whom they had most aggressively sought but for which they had been unsuccessful. Larry and Phil are at a loss as to how this client may have eluded them. It is Larry, however, that seems more concerned and relentless is determining how they missed him, questioning whether or not he even showed. Bob suggests that they can simply schedule an appointment to meet with him, to which Larry replies "You don't schedule appointments with this guy, Bob. He's the president. He refers you to his people." This single line introduces the concept of *decision making*, remotely addressing *decision roles* of *initiator*, *gatekeeper*, *user*, *influencer*, and *buyer*. When Bob asks why they shouldn't just get in touch with the "people," Larry continues "There are people in this world, Bob, in positions of authority who shouldn't be." At this point Larry is addressing levels of *power sources* these individual decision makers may have: *referent power, information power, legitimate power, expert power, and reward power.* Referring to these authoritative people, he goes on to say "(They) get in bed with somebody. A certain supplier, let's say. And who refuse to get out, no matter what. You come at them with something demonstrably superior to what they're using." Larry is making an appeal to helping the customer realize *opportunity recognition*, *problem recognition*, and *need recognition*. Larry concludes "They say . . . 'we are not in the mood to try anything new'. Completely discounting the fact that they're losing money hand over fist because of all the equipment failures and whatnot that you could prevent, if they would let you. Nobody wants to change things, Bob." Larry 's comments incorporate two separate theories, *expectancy theory* on which the salesperson is relying as a motivator and *consistency theory*, and more accurately *denial* and *ignoring* in this case, from the perspective of the customer. Larry also directly uses the *theory of trying* in his explanation to Bob.

Feeling defeated, Larry questions Bob on whether he thinks this is something he would want to do as a living having just experienced Larry's tirade. Bob replies that it was interesting, but questions if there are always so many people. Larry explains "It just seemed like a lot of people, Bob. Because the room's so damn small." This example related to the effect of *contrast* suggests that the smaller room may actually have been beneficial from the perspective of *interpretation of arousal* and *crowd density*, making it that much more interesting and attractive to observers. Soon after this exchange, the dramatic revelation occurs that their primary customer target had in fact been in the room under a false identity. Bob, unaware of who the customer was, had been the only one of the three to talk to him. He did so at length which concerned the other two immensely, but certainly Larry more so than Phil.

Bob's conversation with Fuller, the principal target customer's president, focused on personal subjects, primarily dogs Fuller had owned and religion.

Larry inquired whether Bob had been supportive or contradictory in his conversation about religion with Fuller. Upon hearing that the conversation amiable, Larry explains to Bob in great detail the value of remaining in good face with the customer. Throughout this explanation, Larry is simultaneously detailing the *consistency principle* through seeking out others with whom we share values and beliefs and *balance theory*, in this case Fuller's *triad* beliefs of Bob, his views, and his company.

Because of the missed opportunity to speak with Fuller, the three try to decide what course of action should be taken. By accident, Phil discovers that Fuller had invited Bob to another gathering later in the evening. Larry suggests that they all go but Bob relays that it by invitation only and that they might anger Fuller (more *balance theory*) if they were to all go. Phil agrees that they should send Bob by himself but with very strict instructions on how to conduct himself. Because Bob had already established rapport with Fuller, Phil's recommendation to send him alone is based on the principles of *source effect*, *source credibility*, and *source attractiveness*. Further concluding that by Fuller extending a personal invitation to Bob, he must value something about Bob. This premise supports the *exchange theory* so important to salesperson effectiveness and to the purchasing process as a whole. The dyadic relationship and interaction styles between Fuller and Bob is the only connection on which the three salesmen can rely. As such, Bob is off to find Fuller while the other two helplessly wait, never leaving the hospitality suite.

Old friends, Phil and Larry spend the late night engaged in more personal, reflective conversation. Through the conversation Larry learns that Phil is beginning to consider a different line of work. Larry exclaims "Something other than marketing?" as if no other option is a reasonable choice. In justifying his thought process, Phil offers that Bob may be a good replacement partner for Larry. Through an extremely reflective monologue, Phil describes a childhood dream that is leading him to believe his life's work may lie elsewhere. This reflection and the suggestion of Bob as a replacement for Phil are closely aligned with the *divesting* of his useful career in marketing sales. Through offering Bob as a replacement, Phil essentially places himself in a position of *transition place ritual*. By preparing himself to follow some other calling, some dream, he undergoes a personal *ritual cleansing*. None of this is satisfactory to Larry, who seems interested not only Phil's future but his own potentially disrupted career as well. The conversation continues briefly until Bob returns from his rendezvous with Fuller.

Larry leads the inquisition about the meeting's success only to discover that Bob had not followed the sales pitch as he had been instructed, but rather discussed Jesus Christ instead. In an attempt to recover any of his quickly fading hope, Larry asks "What, exactly, did you say about Jesus, Bob? Did you mention, perhaps, what line of industrial lubricants Jesus would've endorsed?" Larry understands the power of a good endorsement but is shortsighted in his application of *match-up hypothesis*. Through further discussion, Larry draws out that it was Bob, not Fuller, who had led the discussion on Jesus rather than industrial lubricants. At this point it becomes clear that Bob is more interested in eternal salvation than short-term sales. Larry contends "We're here to sell lubricants, Bob, Industrial lubricants. We're not here to save souls." Larry attacks the *attitude* and *belief* that the most important thing about this trip is to talk about Jesus and God, that there are bigger things at issue, a discrepancy that has for the duration of the play been leading Larry and Bob on different courses. Realizing that the two will not agree, Larry makes plans to meet the two in the morning then leaves. When Bob says to Phil that he'll be going, too, Phil stops him for one final lesson and serves for one final time as the mediating *ego* between Larry and Bob.

> The man who left the room. Moments ago. Is a very good friend of mine. Now. You ask yourself why. Is it because I've known him a long time? There are many people, Bob, I have known for quite a long time. Some of them, I wouldn't let wipe my dog's ass. Others, I could take or leave. They don't matter to me, irrespective of how long I've known them. But Larry matters very much. The reason being, I trust him. I know I can trust him. He's honest.

Bob questions whether Larry is honest or just blunt. Phil responds that it's honesty. He goes on . . .

> to have honesty means to have the potential—the potential—to see things in a certain light (*perception*). To attain frankness, which you can apply or not at your discretion. It does not mean to grab ahold of some standard and wave it around. To impose your vision of right and wrong on everything that crosses your path. No one respects that.

In this lesson Phil encapsulates much of what marketing and consumer behavior is about: Understanding and valuing customer needs over personal expectations and desires as well as corporate needs and objectives. Understanding that people come from many different experiential backgrounds, and that finding an acceptable working medium of those backgrounds takes considerable effort. The play ends with a call to the room from an unidentified caller. Hearing only one side of the conversation, the audience concludes (*Gestalt principal*) that the caller is Larry, asking to speak with Bob and answering the deepest of questions that Phil had asked earlier. In the final line, Phil answers back.

REFERENCES

Rueff, Roger. 1992. *Hospitality Suite*. Transcend Press.

Soloman, M. 2015. *Consumer Behavior: Buying, Having, and Being* (11th ed.). India: Prentice Hall.

Chapter 25

Writing, Money, Markets, Slavery, and Unintended Consequences at the Beginning of History

Samuel R. Delany's Return to Nevèrÿon[1]

Jeff Riggenbach

Samuel R. Delany was born on April Fools' Day 1942 in Harlem, New York City. He grew up there, the son of an undertaker, attending private schools until 1956, when he entered the Bronx High School of Science as a freshman. After graduation, he spent a single semester at City College before dropping out to pursue a career as a writer. His first novel, written when he was nineteen, was published when he was twenty. Over the next seven years, he published another six novels—all of them, like his first, works of either fantasy or science fiction. Then he took nearly half a decade off, publishing nothing but a handful of award-winning short stories, while he devoted himself to his first undeniably major work, the controversial novel *Dhalgren*, which first saw print early in 1975. Four years later, in 1979, he published the first volume of his second major work, the four-volume Return to Nevèrÿon, a novel in the form of eleven closely interrelated "tales," varying in length from around 20 pages ("The Tale of Small Sarg") to nearly 300 pages (*Neveryóna*).

It is significant that both of these works are centered in and around cities. The action of *Dhalgren* takes place entirely in the Midwestern city of Bellona, which was once populated by hundreds of thousands, but now, after some sort of disaster (the nature of which is never revealed) is almost completely deserted and home to no more than 2,000 or so persons. The action of Return to Nevèrÿon takes place largely (though not entirely) within the city limits of the prehistoric metropolis of Kolhari at a time when money, writing, and a number of other things we now regard as parts of the foundation of civilization had only recently been invented and when civilization itself was a new and still very fragile and tenuous excrescence on human society.

I call this central interest in the city as a human habitation in Delany's major works "significant" because, as Jane Jacobs has observed "it is in cities that new goods and services are first created. Even innovations created specifically for farming depend directly upon earlier developments of city work. For example, McCormick's first horse-drawn reaper was a tremendous innovation for farm work; here was a machine that replaced hand implements and supple, complex hand movements. Although this idea and the device to carry it out were new to farm work, the same idea and devices similar in principle were already commonly used in industrial work. Nor could McCormick have manufactured the reaper if other industrial tools had not already been developed. The industrial revolution occurred first in cities and later in agriculture" (Jacobs, 1969, 9).

Both *Dhalgren* and Return to Nevèrÿon (which latter I will sometimes call the Nevèrÿon Quartet) concern themselves with the issue of order in human society. *Dhalgren* explores the kinds of what Friedrich A. Hayek has called "spontaneous order" that come into being in a society reduced to "chaos," that is to say, a society freed from rulers of any kind (Hayek, 1960, 159–61). Return to Nevèrÿon concerns itself with more narrowly economic questions, focusing on the spontaneous order of the marketplace and the kinds of unintended consequences that can emerge after the adoption within it of new kinds of economic policies and behaviors.

As a case in point, consider writing. In *Tales of Nevèrÿon*, the first volume of Delany's Nevèrÿon Quartet, we are introduced early on to Norema, a young girl growing up in what might well be described as provincial Nevèrÿon (she has never been to Kolhari, the only true city in her world). She is sent to "school" by her parents, where she studies under the tutelage of "Old Venn," a local woman of legendary acumen who has traveled widely and even spent time in Kolhari. Old Venn teaches her pupils

> the marks Venn could make on pieces of dried vegetable fiber (that you could unroll from the reeds that grew in the swamps across the hill): some marks were for animals, some for fish, some for numbers, and some for ideas; and some were for words (Norema's own contribution to the system, with which Venn was appropriately impressed) . . . Marks in red clay meant one thing. The same mark in black charcoal meant something else. You could use Venn's system, or make up a new one with your friends. (Delany, 1979, 84)

Venn tells her students,

> "I did not invent this system. I only learned it—when I was in Nevèrÿon [the original name of Kolhari]. And I modified it, even as you have done. And do you know what it was invented for there? The control of slaves. If you can write down a woman's or a man's name, you can write down all sorts of things next to

that name, about the amount of work they do, the time it takes for them to do it, about their methods, their attitudes, and you can compare all this very carefully with what you have written about others. If you do this, you can maneuver your own dealings with them in ways that will soon control them; and very soon you will have the control over your fellows that is slavery." (85)

Norema is suitably impressed by this speech.

And Norema thought about her father's ship yard, where there was an old man who came to work some days and not others and about whom her father always complained: If I wrote down his name, Norema thought, and made one mark for every day he came to work and another for every day he failed to come, if after a month I showed them to my father, and said, yes, here, my father's grumbling would turn to open anger, and he would tell him to go away, not to come back, that he was not worth the time, the food, the shelter, and the man would go away and perhaps die . . . And Norema felt strange and powerful and frightened. (85)

In the second volume of Delany's Nevèrÿon Quartet, the novel-length tale *Neveryóna*, another literate provincial teenager, a girl called Pryn, accepts an appointment as accountant to a provincial brewer. It's not long before she notices that there are many "shirkers" among the laborers employed by the brewery, most noticeably among those who work in the smaller of the company's two cooling caves. Pryn has been "assigned . . .among her accounting duties to keep count on the comparative number of scum barrels that came out of the auxiliary cave and out of the main cave." The workers in both caves "skim the fluffy scum" off the "wide, wooden, first-fermentation settling troughs foaming over the floor." Each "scum-filled barrel" is "finally rolled out" and placed "in a clearing by an oak grove." There they stand "till local farmers, driving up," cart "them off for fertilizer" (Delany, 1983, 278–79).

This job of loading the scum in barrels and taking it outside to be picked up by local farmers is what occupies the laborers in both cooling caves during the period right after each day's break for lunch. And during this time, "the main cooling cavern was a fury of after-lunch activity, with mule carts and paddle cleaners and troops of skimmers and barrel stackers and barrel-rollers." And "anyone passing the half-closed gate of the auxiliary cave heard such a racket knocking and banging within, that they'd surely think twice as much work was taking place inside as in the bustle out here" (279).

But, as Pryn soon discovers for herself, that passerby would have been fooled. When she starts writing down the actual production of the two cooling caves she discovers that "each day the main cave produced between forty and fifty barrels of yellow-green gunk," while the auxiliary cave, which "could easily have filled twelve or thirteen," usually produced only two or three. The knocking and banging was "all acoustics." It was a way of covering up what was really an "hour's sham work—a sham that seemed to have grown without conspiracy." You might say that it was a "spontaneous order," an order that had never been planned by anyone, but which had evolved out of the motives and decisions of each of the workers in the smaller cave, most of whom "were old . . . sick . . . new or inexperienced." They wanted to give the impression that they were working and working hard, but it was all theatre, all a sham (279–81).

Pryn never consciously thinks about the "power" that the ability to write about their on-the-job performance gives her over the workers at the brewery—as Norema had done with regard to her ability to write about the workers in her father's shipyard. But where Norema simply tries to steer clear of employment opportunities that would put her in such a position of power, Pryn chooses to make adjustments in the figures she presents to her employer. "Who am I to commit myself to a truth so far from what is expected?" she asks herself before she begins "to adjust that 'two' up to a 'six,' a 'seven,' or an 'eight'" (280–81).

As the brewery accountant, Pryn keeps all sorts of written records. "Bushels of barley, barrels of beer; names of fields, numbers of workers; names of workers, numbers of barrels; names of customers, numbers of orders; comments on qualities of rope, quantities of carrots, amounts of crockery for the eating hall, numbers of pruning hooks for the orchards" (280). And, of course, the amounts of money that change hands in the course of the brewery's various business transactions. Her literacy gives Pryn a natural advantage when it comes to keeping track of the money that passes through her office, for the ability to read is intimately connected with the ability to count and record the values of coins.

Marc Shell, in his extraordinarily useful book *The Economy of Literature*, points out that "coins were the first widely circulating publications or impressions in history" (Shell, 1978, 64). And evidence of this ancient connection between writing and specie remains in our language to this day. If a writer comes up with a new and novel way of characterizing some thing or event, we say that writer has "coined" a word or phrase. Words symbolize ideas, thoughts, concepts. Coins (or, later, paper bills) symbolize goods and services—economic values. Languages and economies are both spontaneous orders, orders that are the results of human action but not of human design.

Peter N. Ure, writing nearly a century ago in *The Origin of Tyranny*, ventured the opinion that "the seventh and sixth centuries B.C. constitute from many points of view one of the most momentous periods in the whole of the world's history." For, he wrote, "it was at the opening of this epoch that the Greeks or their half Hellenized neighbors the Lydians brought about perhaps the most epoch-making revolution in the whole history of commerce by the invention of a metal coinage like those that are still in circulation throughout the civilized world" (Ure, 1922, 1). Shell, writing much more recently, in his book *Money, Language & Thought*, agrees, stating that coined money was first widely circulated "in the sixth and seventh centuries BC" (Shell, 1982, 171). But the human beings who began using money in their business transactions back in that day—how did they regard this new invention?

In "The Tale of Potters & Dragons," the fourth of the eleven tales that make up Return to Nevèrÿon, Zwon, an old potter who owns and operates his business near the busy Kolhari waterfront decides to send his young apprentice, Bayle, on a journey south. Bayle's mission is to negotiate a contract that will give his employer exclusive license to import an increasingly popular children's toy, manufactured in the south, into Kolhari. Zwon provides his apprentice with all that he'll need for the trip, including a small sum of money. And along with the coins, he gives young Bayle a kind of pep talk on what he sees as the many and manifest virtues of this only recently invented medium of exchange. "Think of the people it connects!" he exclaims to Bayle.

> "It makes all of us one, as if we were fingers a-jut off a single palm: myself, a common pot spinner, a drudger forty years in this poor waterfront shop in this poor port city; a noble gentleman like Lord Aldamir [the aristocrat who owns the trees that supply the rubber for the toys, as well as the works that transform that rubber into finished products], once an intimate, you may be sure, of the Child Empress herself (whose reign—" The knuckles came up from knee to forehead, and the wrinkled eyes dropped to the shards about the floor—"is fine and fecund); and even that taciturn giant of a messenger who approached me with that distant lord's ingenuous plan; and the children who will buy the little treasures, bounce them, prattle over them, trade and treasure them. It is as though we are all rendered heart, bone, liver, and lights of a single creature. Money—" and his eyes rose as high at the name of the exchange commodity as they had dropped low at mention of the Empress—"is what allows it all to be. Yes, though others argue, I'm convinced it's an entirely good thing. Ah, my boy, I can remember back when it was all trade. A pot went out; eggs came in. Another pot; barley this time. Another pot; goat's milk. But suppose I wanted cheese when there was only butter available? Suppose someone with butter needed grain but had more than enough pots? Oh, those were perilous times—and perilous in ways that money, which can be saved, stored, spent wisely or foolishly, and doesn't go bad like eggs or butter, has abolished. But that was fifty years ago and need not worry a young head like yours."

The old man pauses, perhaps for breath. Then he repeats himself, presumably for emphasis.

> "All of us, a lord, a lord's man, an enterprising and successful artisan with a will to expand his business, and the little children whose joyous laughter gilds the city from the alleys of the Spur to the gardens of Sellese—the web of money makes us all one!" (Delany, 1979, 163)

It isn't long, however (only a few weeks, in fact), before Zwon trades in his earlier exuberance for a far more skeptical, even gloomy, outlook. "Madame," he says to Madame Keyne, a wealthy businesswoman with whom he is discussing a possible joint venture, "I have come seriously to question the whole concept of money, and the system of profit and wages by which it works." He explains that he "sent my assistant, on a boat, to the south—with *very* little money, madame; certainly not what anyone would call a great deal." The assistant, young Bayle, "was to be away for a week. And I have not seen him now for three months. And that, madame, is money for you!"

Zwon is convinced that Bayle has "absconded with my meager funds," and that this painful outcome was an unintended and unforeseen consequence of the transition in recent years from a barter economy to a money economy.

> "After all," [he says] "under the old system, when we paid in kind, if you took a poor apprentice into your house and rewarded him with a meal from your table, a bed in your store, the shelter of your own roof, and the tutelage of your craft, then your apprentice was essentially as rich as you were, having his share of all that supplied the quality of your life. But if you take the same poor apprentice and pay him with money—pay him with the *pittance* of money one pays an apprentice—all you do is emphasize his poverty by your riches. How can one expect even a good boy to remain honest under such abuse and insult?" (210–11)

As it happens, the old potter has jumped to an incorrect conclusion; his apprentice has not, in fact, "absconded" with his employer's "meager funds." But, as Madame Keyne reminds Zwon, whether he did or didn't is really neither here nor there. "What must be foremost in our mind is that we shall be henceforth joined in a money-making scheme all in the glorious and innocent here and now—not in the bad dreams and errors of a disastrous past. Money, old potter, money—believe me, I am convinced that it is the greatest invention in the history of mankind and, for all your doubts, an entirely good thing" (213).

If Madame Keyne's venture in partnership with Zwon the old potter is not the very least of the capitalist acts she initiates or continues in Delany's Nevèrÿon Quartet, it is certainly far from the largest. For that title must by rights belong to her ambitious plan to build a New Market for Kolhari. At some point between the fifth and sixth tales in the series, she has bought up and demolished all the run down houses and apartment buildings that once made up one of Kolhari's poorest neighborhoods and is now, in the sixth tale, the novel-length *Neveryóna*, in the process of building her New Market, only one street over from the city's Old Market. Her project, which, today, we would speak of in such terms as "slum clearance" and "urban renewal," is looked at in almost exactly that way by its mastermind. "The Old Market in the Spur," she tells Pryn at one point (Pryn is visiting Kolhari for a few weeks before traveling to the south of Nevèrÿon, where, though she doesn't know it yet, she will find employment in the provincial brewery), "has become merely a quaint and archaic metaphor for commerce, whereas really to know the life and pulse of this city, one must lose and make a fortune or two in the New Market—don't you think?" (Delany, 1983, 94).

Not everyone agrees with Madame Keyne's view of the Old Market, however. And one of the most prominent of the dissenters is her creator, Samuel R. Delany, who told an interviewer in 1988 that "the Old Market, the 'original' Kolhari market," which is seen by Madame Keyne and others of her persuasion as probably "the market, the node, the occurrence around which Kolhari initially grew up, till finally the city itself outstripped it, leaving it a sort of economic memory and a site of barter/nostalgia," is in fact much more than that and is not to be so cavalierly and simplistically brushed off. He points out that the Old Market is "still. . .a reliable map of the city, the nation, the world which it serves, however inefficient and shoddy its goods." For the Old Market has grown up "as a natural and original response to the imminent and unauthorized play of profit and loss, collectivity and common good" in "the city that it at once causes, grounds, and exists as a fundamental mirror of" (Delany, 1994, 130).

"The New Market," on the other hand, "is constructed in Nevèrÿon because Madame Keyne and people like her have noticed ways in which the Old Market works—and are trying to abstract those principles, to improve on them, and to set them to work at greater intensity, over a greater range, at a manufactured site, in order to control loss, profit, capital in particular, and power in general." The New Market thus "grows. . .from a conscious realization of, from an active pursuit after the principles of, profit and loss and exploitation of collective need." For Delany, "the two markets are. . .profoundly different places." Friedrich Hayek would probably say the same thing, though he would use different terminology. He would say, doubtless, that the Old Market was a spontaneous order, while the New Market was a centrally planned imitation of the spontaneous order one street over. Moreover, Hayek would likely have said that the planners behind this imitation were guilty of "the fatal conceit" of believing that markets can be planned and centrally managed in an efficient and profitable manner (Hayek, 1988, *passim*).

One of Delany's points about the Old Market—that it is "a reliable map of the city, the nation, the world which it serves," that it is "a fundamental mirror of" the society in which it exists—is also expressed by the man whom I would call the main character of the Nevèrÿon Quartet, the onetime-slave-turned-slave-revolt-leader, Gorgik. The afternoon before Madame Keyne's conversation with Pryn, Gorgik gives Pryn a guided tour of Kolhari's Old Market, along with much detailed commentary. Gorgik asks rhetorically, "Do certain country markets necessarily secrete cities about themselves? Must a nation raise markets, and cities around them?" (Delany, 1983, 52) Whatever the answers to those questions might be, he tells Pryn, the Old Market of Kolhari is "only a particularly recomplicated inscription of the nation around it." What he means by this is that the Old Market is surrounded by neighborhoods in which one can find all the various ethnic groups that make up Nevèrÿon itself, while, in the Old Market, one can find all the characteristic handicrafts traditional to those ethnic groups.

I have called Gorgik the main character in Return to Nevèrÿon, for, as Delany himself told an interviewer in 1994, "the background tale that holds them [the eleven tales that make up Return to Nevèrÿon] all together is that a green-eyed black man called Gorgik is himself taken. . .as a slave when he is sixteen. Over the course of the series, which covers some thirty-five years, Gorgik gains his freedom, foments a slave revolt, finally manages to be appointed a minister of state, from which position, after much work, he eventually abolishes slavery from the land" (Delany, 1999, 118).

Gorgik himself would probably not have taken credit for the abolition of slavery in Nevèrÿon. As he candidly admits in "The Tale of Fog & Granite," when speaking to the princess who is the chief funder of his slave rebellion, "We all know what drives slavery from the land: a new farming technique, a more efficient yam stick, the spread of minted coin, some imperceptible warming of the very earth itself over fifty years, or an equally unpredictable increase in the rainfall, yielding the greater affluence that makes slavery impracticable and paid labor more profitable" (Delany, 1985, 127).

At one time—at the beginning of the first tale, in which Gorgik, age sixteen, was enslaved—slavery accounted for nearly a third of all economic output in Nevèrÿon (Delany, 1987, 169). By the time, some thirty-five years later, when he finally succeeded in legally abolishing it, the factors he had listed in his conversation with his financial backer had already brought about a sharp decline in its usage. This is often, even typically, the case with political movements to abolish types of behavior which have come to be associated with an earlier, less civilized period in a nation's history. The economist Steven Horwitz has noted, in this regard, that

> it is worth asking why it has come to be the conventional wisdom that the laws ended child labor. It likely reflects our evolutionary and intellectual biases that lead us to think we directly control more of the social world than we really can. It is easier, as well as morally more self-satisfying, to believe that we intentionally made something unpleasant go away through taking a stand against it than that underlying processes we do not control were responsible. In addition, it does seem to be a trend that laws against behavior that we find to be morally reprehensible remnants of an unenlightened past tend to get passed when the practices in question have mostly disappeared, making the few examples still in existence all the more reprehensible. This was certainly true of the heightened

> focus on child labor as the declining need for children's incomes spread downward through the middle class. Even in our own time, think of the ways in which cigarette smoking has been the target of increasingly heavy-handed regulation even though smoking rates have been on an ongoing decline for decades, largely independent of laws limiting or prohibiting the activity. It also is easier to legislate against a practice whose economic necessity or desirability has long passed for most people. (Horwitz, 274)

Delany has described the four volumes of Return to Nevèrÿon as an attempt to tell a compelling story set against the background of a land that is "on the brink of civilization," a land based on "what can, most safely, still be imagined about the transition from a barter economy to a money economy" (Delany, 1977, 197). In his Nevèrÿon Quartet, he has accomplished this with a deftness and skill that should make this work an object of great interest to anyone interested in the portrayal of capitalism and commerce in imaginative literature.

NOTE

1. Return to Nevèrÿon is quoted in the pages that follow by permission of the author, Samuel R. Delany.

REFERENCES

Delany, Samuel R. 1977. *The Jewel-Hinged Jaw: Notes on the Language of Science Fiction*. New York: Berkley Publishing.

———. [1979] 1994. *Tales of Nevèrÿon*. Hanover, New Hampshire: Wesleyan University Press.

———. [1983] 1993. *Neveryóna*. Hanover, New Hampshire: Wesleyan University Press.

———. [1985] 1994. *Flight from Nevèrÿon*. Hanover, New Hampshire: Wesleyan University Press.

———. [1987] 1994. *Return to Nevèrÿon*. Hanover, New Hampshire: Wesleyan University Press.

———. 1994. *Silent Interviews on Language, Race, Sex, Science Fiction, and Some Comics: A Collection of Written Interviews*. Hanover, New Hampshire: Wesleyan University Press.

———. 1999. *Shorter Views: Queer Thoughts & the Politics of the Paraliterary*. Hanover, New Hampshire: Wesleyan University Press.

Hayek, Friedrich A. 1960. *The Constitution of Liberty*. Chicago: University of Chicago Press.

———. 1988. *The Fatal Conceit: The Errors of Socialism*. Chicago: University of Chicago Press.

Horwitz, Steven. 2015. *Hayek's Modern Family: Classical Liberalism and the Evolution of Social Institutions*. New York: Palgrave Macmillan.
Jacobs, Jane. 1969. *The Economy of Cities*. New York: Random House.
Shell, Marc. 1978. *The Economy of Literature*. Baltimore, Maryland: Johns Hopkins University Press.
———. 1982. *Money, Language and Thought: Literary and Philosophic Economies from the Medieval to the Modern Era*. Berkeley: University of California Press.
Ure, Peter N. 1922. *The Origin of Tyranny*. Cambridge, United Kingdom: Cambridge University Press.

Chapter 26

"We Do Not Sow"

The Economics and Politics of A Song of Ice and Fire

Matthew McCaffrey and Carmen Elena Dorobăţ

The wonderful thing about engrossing fantasy worlds is that they can seem more familiar to us than real ones. In fact, this very trait is what makes the fantasy genre one of the most effective for communicating lessons about human life and society. As C.S. Lewis put it,

> At all ages, if [fantasy] is used well by the author and meets the right reader, it has the same power: to generalize while remaining concrete, to present in palpable form not concepts or even experiences but whole classes of experience, and to throw off irrelevancies. But at its best it can do more; it can give us experiences we have never had and thus, instead of "commenting on life," can add to it. (Lewis, 1956)

Readers of George R.R. Martin's fantasy epic *A Song of Ice and Fire* will surely agree. Spanning five books, with two more yet to be published, the series establishes and explores a world of immense depth and richness, not the least part of which is its human detail. For Martin, just as for J.R.R. Tolkien, the conventions of fantasy are less important than how people react to them (Kaveney, 2000). In fact, Martin agrees with William Faulkner that the "human heart in conflict with itself" is a central theme for worthwhile writing in any genre (Farley, 2011). This focus on the human element is what makes his story appear timeless and universal.

At a time when book series of enormous scope and detail are ubiquitous, Martin's world provides far more than conventional swords-and-sorcery fiction: it also offers a searching account of economic and political relations in human society. The saga uses its fantasy setting to explore numerous social problems and to dramatize important questions about power, conflict, and the state. However, in contrast to novels like *Nineteen Eighty-Four* or *Atlas*

Shrugged, *A Song of Ice and Fire* is not dystopian or overtly didactic; instead, the underlying themes are just that—underlying. This in no way reduces the power of the narrative, and if anything, enhances it. The story is personal and human, capturing first the reader's imagination and empathy, and then, more subtly, her intellect. In this sense it brings Lewis's remark about the power of fantasy to life.

The aim of this essay is to consider the economic and political implications of Martin's fantastic but realistic epic. It is impossible in a short chapter to mention every point of interest in the series, which is currently almost four times the length of *Atlas Shrugged.* Instead, we explore only a small number of ideas about political economy, society, and the state that underlie the central story and provide much of its structure.[1] The discussion will be intelligible to those who have read Martin's books or watched their television adaptation *Game of Thrones*, but also, we hope, for readers altogether unfamiliar with the series (although naturally, many characters and personal or political relationships cannot be explained in detail). For those who have not read the books, we hope our essay will provide the impetus to take them up.

"WE DO NOT SOW": THE ORIGIN AND GROWTH OF STATES

Before exploring the story in more detail, we should mention the broader geopolitical context in which it takes place. The narrative conjures an enormous world consisting of two major continents and a number of smaller islands. These spaces are populated by numerous cultures that vary widely in terms of social norms, forms of government, and levels of economic development.

For example, on the continent of Westeros—where the bulk of the story takes place—societies are similar to medieval European states, especially feudal monarchies (Vallier, 2014). In fact, Martin seems to use the fantasy setting to reimagine Europe's past. Westeros is clearly modeled on England during the War of the Roses (c. 1455–1487), and Westerosi conflicts contain numerous parallels to those between the houses of Lancaster and York that arose from the social and financial turmoil following the Hundred Years' War. Just like these historical powers, the seven major kingdoms of Westeros are each ruled by a great House seeking to further its own ambitions, while nominally pledging fealty to the king.

The eastern continent, on the other hand, is populated by a mixture of nomadic tribes and aristocratic city-states—similar to twelfth-century Venice, Genoa, and Milan—dubbed "free cities." This is a misnomer though, as all of the free cities (except for Braavos) engage in slave ownership and trade. More importantly, nowhere in *A Song of Ice and Fire* is there a region resembling an industrial economy, much less one with a significant degree of economic and social freedom. As a result, the books generally depict a world of poverty and stagnation ruled by institutions hostile to economic development, usually command economies of some sort.

By contrasting different social groups within an overarching narrative about political power, Martin's world illustrates key ideas about its (and our) institutions, especially those directly responsible for organizing and controlling society. As the first volume—titled *A Game of Thrones*—indicates, the series is fundamentally about power and the dangers of wielding it. However, "it does not celebrate power and the powerful but challenges and interrogates them" (Carpenter, 2012). Questions about the nature of political power and the relations between rulers and ruled thus provide the background for much of the storyline. The narrative points naturally then to the institution of the state, which represents the greatest concentration of power in society. Much of the story deals directly or indirectly with states and their relation to society at large, especially their economic interactions.

To explore these themes, we first draw on Franz Oppenheimer's famous distinction between the *economic* and the *political* means of acquiring property and organizing society. Simply put, the economic means consists in peaceful cooperation and trade, while the political involves the forcible redistribution of wealth (Oppenheimer, 1926, 24–27). States represent the *organization of the political means*, and when considered in light of Oppenheimer's dichotomy, are economically no different from organized groups of bandits.[2]

Martin hints at this very point throughout the novels, but the insight shines through with special beauty in a conversation between two characters, the smuggler Davos Seaworth and his acquaintance, the pirate Salladhor Saan. Saan is renowned as "a smuggler . . . as well as a trader, a banker, a notorious pirate, and the self-styled Prince of the Narrow Sea." Pondering this dubious résumé, Davos concludes, "*When a pirate grows rich enough, they make him a prince*" (Martin, 2011b, 138). This brief comment bears a striking similarity to a passage from St. Augustine's *City of God*:

> It was a pertinent and true answer which was made to Alexander the Great by a pirate whom he had seized. When the king asked him what he meant by infesting the sea, the pirate defiantly replied: "The same as you do when you infest the whole world; but because I do it with a little ship I am called a robber, and because you do it with a great fleet, you are an emperor." (Augustine, 1998, 146)[3]

Both anecdotes suggest the difference between plunder and public finance is a matter of degree, not of kind. In practice, the distinction usually rests on a rhetorical trick that masks the pirate's self-interest with the politician's proclaimed public interest. But in terms of their economic effects, plunder and government activity both reduce welfare and hinder social cooperation.

Ideas about the foundations of political power appear throughout the novels, so we now consider further examples from two different societies: the Dothraki tribes and the Ironmen of House Greyjoy. The Dothraki horselords are probably the simplest of Martin's societies in terms of their technological and economic development. The Dothraki are comprised of a series of independent tribes, each formed around a single leader who unites his group by dint of martial prowess.[4] They are essentially nomadic, although they do regard the region of Vaes Dothrak as kind of capital city and spiritual home to which they bring the spoils of war. However, they do not engage in trade, use money, or accumulate capital, obtaining whatever wealth they have either through conquest or as bribes from potential targets. In fact, the only permanent structures in the city of Vaes Dothrak are constructed by foreign slaves using plundered materials (Martin, 2011a, 374–75, 377–78). In Oppenheimer's terms, Dothraki society is based entirely on the political means. Importantly though, these means are not organized, and there is no Dothraki state as such.

At the same time, the lack of Dothraki economic and political development can be attributed to their refusal to engage in the division of labor, and consequently to adopt a medium of exchange. For human societies to survive and thrive, they require liberty, property, and sound money: "Abolish all, or even one, of these institutions and human society disintegrates amid a congeries of isolated household economies and predatory tribes" (Salerno 1990, 50). This observation accurately characterizes the Dothraki—their tribes are basically examples of military socialism, and because successful war making is virtually their only goal, they fail to encourage either further political development or economic progress. In other words, the Dothraki "roving bandits" have not yet become "stationary bandits." With no institutions to encourage economic growth, they lack a consistent source of surplus to use as the basis for a permanent state. The step toward the kind of systematic, long-term redistribution of wealth characteristic of modern forms of government is one the Dothraki are either unable or unwilling to take. This results in political stasis, where militaristic values prevent the emergence of market activity.

A further stage of political development is evident in the Iron Islands. The population of this area, known as the "Ironmen," is a society of Viking-like warriors ruled by House Greyjoy. Geographically separated from the more developed parts of Westeros, they are nonetheless a more close-knit society than the Dothraki. Yet the Ironmen find themselves increasingly out of place in a realm where piracy and rebellion are ruthlessly suppressed—and replaced—by a central monarch. In addition, they scorn social cooperation, especially market exchange, which they derisively refer to as "paying the gold price." Wealth is only admirable if it is acquired through violence and plunder, which the Ironmen call "paying the iron price" (2011b, 166–67).

In such a society, where cooperation is penalized and violence rewarded, it is unsurprising that talent and productive capacity are directed almost entirely toward the latter (Baumol, 1990).

Instead of participating in the division of labor and exchange, the Ironmen dream of returning their anachronistic culture to a past age where simple, brutal strength was sufficient to overawe their neighbors and provide the plunder needed to support their parasitic way of life. Their overtly predatory form of social organization is thus another powerful depiction of the political means, which are summarized perfectly in the Greyjoy family words: "We Do Not Sow" (Martin, 2011a, 796). That is, rather than sow and thereby reap a just reward, the Ironmen choose instead to pillage the fruits of what others have sown.[5]

THE GAME OF THRONES IS A GAME OF COINS

However, in more developed states, as economic relations become more complex, simple violence and plunder are replaced by organized, formal systems of government and public finance. Large parts of Martin's novels involve the struggle to rule the Seven Kingdoms of Westeros, and the wartime setting allows numerous characters to ponder the economic state of the realm. In particular, the series excels in dramatizing the political logic that drives states to war and economic disaster. The narrative thus adds a literary spin to economic theory, which tells us that the essential characteristics of states make them prone to economic and social conflict, war making, and imperialism (Salerno, 2008). More specifically, government intervention tends to waste or destroy resources, creating domestic economic problems. War and conquest are then used as means to acquire new resources and distract the populace from the effects of poor economic policy. What's more, this process tends to perpetuate itself, as governments rarely learn hard lessons about the limits of their power, and frequently struggle to avoid the consequences of bad decisions by making even worse ones. Thus, conflict breeds conflict.

Yet wars are costly, and require a consistent (actually, increasing) stream of resources in order to finance. The problem of war is therefore inextricably linked with the practice of public finance. Importantly, this fact helps explain why states take the form of geographically defined economic monopolies. Charles Tilly, for instance, argues that the nation state emerged when it became necessary for rulers to concentrate and exploit private wealth on a scale large enough to pay for increasingly expensive military campaigns (Tilly, 1990). To that end, states establish exclusive privileges over taxation, borrowing, and money creation, which constitute their major revenue sources. Each of these policies is exploited to finance war, and as we shall see, because they become difficult to justify publicly, states increasingly resort to less visible forms of finance such as inflation.

We witness this drama of public finance play out through the eyes of one of series' main characters, Tyrion Lannister, who briefly takes on the role of Master of Coin (i.e., finance minister) to the Seven Kingdoms. Tyrion's plans, as well as those of his predecessor Lord Petyr Baelish—another central character—shed light on the crown's financial habits, and implicitly, those of real-world governments. The bulk of the crown's financial schemes are actually set in motion by Baelish, also known as "Littlefinger," who is the quintessential political entrepreneur. He controls a large network of crown businesses, keeping the finances of the realm afloat while increasing his own wealth and power. Tyrion, acting as narrator, paints a vivid portrait of Littlefinger:

> King Robert had been a prodigious spender. A man like Petyr Baelish, who had a gift for rubbing two golden dragons together to breed a third, was invaluable to [the crown]. Littlefinger's rise had been arrow-swift. Within three years of his coming to court, he was master of coin and a member of the small council, and today the crown's revenues were ten times what they had been under his beleaguered predecessor . . . though the crown's debts had grown vast as well. A master juggler was Petyr Baelish . . .
>
> He did not simply collect the gold and lock it in a treasure vault, no. He paid the king's debts in promises, and put the king's gold to work. He bought wagons, shops, ships, houses. He bought grain when it was plentiful and sold bread when it was scarce. He bought wool from the north and linen from the south and lace from Lys, stored it, moved it, dyed it, sold it. The golden dragons bred and multiplied, and Littlefinger lent them out and brought them home with hatchlings. (Martin, 2011b, 247–48)

Littlefinger's remarkable political power is acquired without force of arms, revealing the truth in Tyrion's warning that, "A coin is as dangerous as a sword in the wrong hands" (Martin, 2011c, 264), which might as well be the motto of the many characters that play the game of thrones. More importantly, Baelish also reveals how, in the context of government administration, petty corruption thrives and evolves into a grander network of political dealings. Just as in the real world, control of the state treasury enables the subversion of the economic and legal system: "[I]n the process, [Baelish] moved his own men into place. The Keepers of the Keys were his, all four. The King's Counter and the King's Scales were men he'd named. The officers in charge of all three mints. Harbormasters, tax farmers, customs sergeants, wool factors, toll collectors, pursers, wine factors; nine of every ten belonged to Littlefinger" (Martin, 2011b, 248).

There is an analogy here between monetary theory and political theory. In economic terms, money is never neutral—the effects of new money creation ripple outward, beginning with the first receivers of new money, who usually enjoy close connections with money producers such as central banks. Likewise, power over money production is never neutral either, because it also creates a complex web of political exchanges and dependencies, as Littlefinger's experience illustrates. It is no surprise then that when the northern region of Westeros rises in rebellion, its lords quickly set about negotiating for the privilege of coining new money (Martin, 2011b, 226). We now explore how the different forms of public finance work in practice.

TAXATION

When the reader is introduced to Westeros, before the outbreak of war, the crown is already heavily in debt, and its financial situation only deteriorates over the course of five novels. The crown's first remedy to its troubles is taxation, the most basic tool of public finance. But to meet the rising costs of war, new and creative taxes have to be introduced. One such is a tax on prostitution in the capital (Martin, 2011c, 526), King's Landing, which is even disguised as a means to "improve the morals of the city"! A shrewder idea is to tax refugees fleeing from war to the safety of the capital:

> It was no secret that King Robert had left the crown vastly in debt . . . "Lord Littlefinger always finds a way, my lord. He has imposed a tax on those wishing to enter the city."
>
> "Yes, that would work," Tyrion said, thinking, *Clever. Clever and cruel.* Tens of thousands had fled the fighting for the supposed safety of King's Landing. He had seen them on the kingsroad, troupes of mothers and children and anxious fathers who had gazed on his horses and wagons with covetous eyes. Once they reached the city they would doubtless pay over all they had to put those high comforting walls between them and the war. (Martin, 2011b, 57–58)

Once the major fighting subsides, other taxes emerge, such as a license to sell within King's Landing (Martin, 2011d, 272). However, facing continued political strife, these imposts prove to be only half-measures. Because taxes are relatively direct and obvious to those obliged to pay them, they are also politically unpopular. Even the nobility of Westeros are prepared to resist further demands on their incomes, and it is suggested that, "half the lords in the realm could not tell taxation from tyranny and would bolt to the nearest usurper in a heartbeat if it would save them a clipped copper" (Martin, 2012, 481). The solution then is to find subtler means of obtaining funds, either through borrowing to postpone immediate taxation, or by hiding taxation with inflation.

BORROWING

Finding its treasuries increasingly difficult to replenish, the crown also relies on borrowing. In fact, at the outset of the story, King Robert has already established a habit of overspending that his creditors are only too happy to oblige. The most important of the domestic financiers is House Lannister.[6] However, as Robert dies and the realm descends into chaos, the Lannisters become increasingly unwilling or unable to lend gold to the crown, and the royal treasury turns to foreign banks in order to finance the war effort.[7] The ensuing relationship between the crown and its creditors helps highlight two important ideas: first, borrowing is only a temporary solution to fiscal problems, and second, financial assistance comes at a price, namely, political influence.

The first point is relatively straightforward: debts must be repaid with interest, and borrowing therefore involves a tradeoff between present and future consumption, as well as between higher taxes now and higher taxes later. However, this lesson is rarely if ever learned by governments, and the fictional rulers of Westeros are no exception. The narrative returns frequently to the problem of the crown's heavy borrowing and the increasing pressure it faces to make good on its obligations. Predictably, as the size of its debts increases, the prospect of repayment diminishes. As already mentioned, the tax base of Westeros declines considerably over the course of the series, leaving little means for the treasury to escape the debt spiral (except possibly inflation; however, Westeros' use of metallic currency and the high standards of foreign lenders do place some limitations on this means of finance).

When they begin to believe the Lannister government cannot pay its debts, its creditors naturally turn to those who will: the crown's political enemies. This leads to the second point: those who control the purse strings of the realm thereby acquire political power. The most obvious case is House Lannister, whose patriarch, Tywin Lannister, uses his role as financier to become Hand of the King—and effective ruler of the Seven Kingdoms. After his death, the crown turns increasingly to the Iron Bank of Braavos for additional funds. Yet the Iron Bank eventually starts to doubt the willingness or ability of its debtors to repay their loans, and offers its services to usurpers with better reputations for fair dealing. Thus, although it is a foreign institution, the Iron Bank becomes a key political player in Westeros, and its support may prove decisive in the final volumes of the series.

INFLATION

Last but not least is the inflationary expansion of the money supply. When it becomes difficult to pay in coin, people on all sides of the war begin using paper promises of repayment instead. These promises are rightly regarded as worthless, and are generally used only by the strong as an excuse for stealing resources from the weak (Martin, 2011b, 139, 378; 2011c, 185, 541; 2011d, 85). But the widespread practice hints, perhaps, at a process of inflation through the use of money substitutes, e.g., treasury certificates not covered by resources in the vaults.

Inflation as such is never explicitly discussed by the narrators or other characters, but the story does include several references to the practice of "coin clipping" in Westeros (Martin, 2011b, 241; 2012, 481). What is more, there are also hints that Lord Baelish, known as a "wizard of coin" (Martin, 2011c, 259), is behind the inflationary scheme. Consider further the above remark that Littlefinger's "golden dragons bred and multiplied, and [he] lent them out and brought them home with hatchlings." The "hatchlings" appear at first glance to be the profit and interest Lord Baelish earns through his political ventures.

However, Martin also indicates Baelish is clipping coins. For instance, "rubbing two golden dragons together to breed a third" may be symbolic of the historical practice of "sweating" coins to whittle down their metallic content. And the fact that Littlefinger controls the official counts, scales, and mints places him in an ideal position to alter the coinage as he sees fit. One character even remarks "Gold . . . Littlefinger mints the stuff from goldenrod, I vow" (Martin, 2011d, 273). Tyrion Lannister is more explicit, claiming that the royal family's gold "is dug from the ground," while "Littlefinger's gold is made from thin air, with a snap of his fingers" (Martin, 2011c, 264). There are strong implications then that Littlefinger is debasing the coinage in order to artificially increase the money supply and sustain the public debt.

"OURS IS THE FURY": THE RHETORIC OF POWER IN WESTEROS

Political institutions in Westeros do not then inspire much hope for good governance or the transition to a developed market economy. Indeed, how could they, given that ideas about liberty and commerce are almost completely lacking in the Seven Kingdoms? This absence of any market ideology—much less a liberal one—deserves some additional explanation. To better understand the economic stasis, let us consider some of the distinctly illiberal ideas prominent in Westeros and how they support existing political organizations, while also preventing the emergence of market institutions.

Although there are many ways to think about this problem, we focus on the importance of rhetoric, which is frequently emphasized in Martin's saga. Throughout the story, it becomes clear that the ways people speak about institutions are just as important in shaping society as the institutions themselves. Language helps form ideology, and if language is heavily biased against liberal ideas, it is likely institutions will be too.[8] In particular, the rhetoric of power can tell us a good deal about the kind of political values people hold, and whether they are likely to change. With this in mind, we turn to the ideological prejudice against liberal ideas and institutions that is revealed through the rhetoric of the ruling class of Westeros.

The most obvious forms of rhetoric used in *A Song of Ice and Fire* are the "words" of the noble houses of Westeros. These words are "family mottoes, touchstones, [and] prayers of sorts" (Martin, 2011a, 21). They are invoked as sources of counsel and comfort, and although each mantra is specific to a certain family, they often conceal universal insights about the world of *A Song of Ice and Fire*. As mentioned above, the words of some houses, such as the Greyjoys, clearly reflect the primacy of the political over the economic means. Others, though not as explicit, are filled with allusions to political power and military might. Importantly, they rarely refer to peace and cooperation, let alone trade and commerce. House Targaryen promises its enemies "Fire and Blood," and the Baratheons boast "Ours is the Fury" (Martin, 2011a, 783–801). Still others are filled with contempt and disdain, especially for the "small folk," as the commoners are called. Words like "I Have no Rival," "Above the Rest," and "Touch Me Not" clearly distinguish rulers from ruled, reinforce caste distinctions between the nobility and the rest of the realm, and highlight the perpetual contest between noble families for political control (McCaffrey, 2013). The rhetoric of the nobles often reflects an ideology of violence and plunder that leaves no room for fundamental changes to the existing social order, or even marginal political improvements. The distinctly illiberal and vicious outlook of the nobility can be summed up in the common Valyrian saying "Valar Morghulis," or, "all men must die."

However, despite the bleak political outlook, there is some hopeful rhetoric in Westeros as well. It should not come as a surprise that the most apolitical words are found in the houses furthest from the capital city and its game of thrones. The words of the relatively isolated House Stark, for instance, warn that "Winter is Coming." This saying stresses the need to be patient, careful, and above all, prepared. In other words, lasting achievements require deferring gratification so as to survive difficult times—the worldview of capitalists and entrepreneurs more than politicians. It is no wonder then that the Starks are looked down on by other noble houses: they quietly but firmly remind the Seven Kingdoms that there are greater powers in the world than thrones. Taken literally, these powers are the forces of nature embodied in the inevitable return of winter. Metaphorically, the more significant forces—and perhaps harder ones to escape—are the laws of economics and their political consequences. In the words of Ludwig von Mises:

> Princes and democratic majorities are drunk with power. They must reluctantly admit that they are subject to the laws of nature. But they reject the very notion of economic law. Are they not the supreme legislators? Don't they have the power to crush every opponent? No war lord is prone to acknowledge any limits other than those imposed on him by a superior armed force . . . In fact, economic history is a long record of government policies that failed because they were designed with a bold disregard for the laws of economics. (Mises, 1998, 67)

Mises' observation nicely summarizes the root cause of the economic and social turmoil of Westeros, and its desperate need for liberal ideas. It also explains why any words (or peoples) supporting limitations on power are doomed to obscurity; after all, "Ours is the Fury" is a more attractive mantra to a warrior noble than, for example, the words of House Wydman: "Right Conquers Might" (McCaffrey, 2013).

Happily though, "all men must die" is not the only philosophy in *A Song of Ice and Fire*. As the story progresses, it is revealed that this saying is only the first part of an exchange: "All men must die" is countered with "Valar dohaeris," or, "all men must serve." These words represent the hope of Westeros, and indeed, of any world. If the philosophy of the nobility is that "all men must die," the philosophy of liberalism is that all human beings have a role to play in improving the lives of others. This is the essence of human cooperation and the division of labor, two sides of the same coin that represent the foundation of human society. Although the phrase is used in a very different way by the characters in the story, "all men must serve" captures the spirit of the marketplace, where each individual benefits by promoting the interests of others.

Unfortunately, if the words of the great houses of Westeros are any indication, serious progress is unlikely to occur unless it is forced on the established nobility via radical change in the political landscape. However, the as-yet-unpublished volumes of the series hold the promise of just such a social transformation. In the real world too, a change in ideology—from war and destruction to peace and free enterprise—is required for healthy economic and social progress.

MORMONT SHRUGGED

A Song of Ice and Fire often reads like a cautionary tale about the dangers of power. It hints at universal problems of government, but also warns of more specific hazards to human society. In concluding our study of Martin's fantasy world and its social and political implications, we realize, not without a touch of irony, that it holds no shortage of similarities with our own world.

The Seven Kingdoms are being consumed by endless warfare, increasing taxes, government debt, and reckless money creation, problems all-too-familiar in the twenty-first century, notwithstanding the prevalence of governments ostensibly superior to those of Westeros.

Yet while playing the game of thrones is complex and treacherous, the needs of society are deceptively simple. The truth is that peace, cooperation, and the freedom to prosper are vital conditions for human flourishing. At the same time, politics and the game of thrones have little in common with the liberal ideal of human progress. The characters and lives of George R.R. Martin's novels chronicle this all-too-human struggle between peace and war, good and evil, and progress and destruction, a struggle that lies at the heart of the entire series. This point is made eloquently in a conversation between the aspiring queen Daenerys Targaryen and her companion, the world-weary knight Ser Jorah Mormont. Daenerys believes the common people of the Seven Kingdoms are praying for a great and enlightened ruler to free them through force of arms (Martin, 2011a, 226). Mormont's reply is telling: "The common people pray for rain, healthy children, and a summer that never ends," Ser Jorah told her. "It is no matter to them if the high lords play their game of thrones, so long as they are left in peace." He gave a shrug. "They never are."

NOTES

1. Many of the ideas in this essay were first presented in a series of public writings (McCaffrey and Dorobăț, 2013a, 2013b; McCaffrey, 2013).
2. This categorization is by no means unique to Oppenheimer. For instance, Frédéric Bastiat expressed a similar view in his classic *The Law* (2007, 5–8, 13–15).
3. Augustine's remark is preceded by a discussion of what are essentially the political means:

> Justice removed, then, what are kingdoms but great bands of robbers? What are bands of robbers themselves but little kingdoms? The band itself is made up of men; it is governed by the authority of a ruler; it is bound together by a pact of association; and the loot is divided according to an agreed law. If, by the constant addition of desperate men, this scourge grows to such a size that it acquires territory, establishes a seat of government, occupies cities and subjugates peoples, it assumes the name of kingdom more openly. For this name is now manifestly conferred upon it not by the removal of greed, but by the addition of impunity. (Augustine, 1998, 145–46)

4. Prior to the events of the books, the Dothraki were a strictly male-dominated society.
5. The Greyjoy philosophy has so far proved disastrous for the Ironmen. In an attempt to control the Seven Kingdoms of Westeros, they have sacrificed several

leaders and largely exhausted their resources, all while making little in the way of strategic gains. This bleak outlook obliges them to venture far from their home region in search of dragons, which they believe will guarantee victory over their enemies. The lengths they go to preserve their way of life only show the folly of refusing to engage in economic cooperation.

6. Tyrion Lannister, who eventually becomes Master of Coin, is a member of this wealthy family. His appointment to public office hints at the network of personal and economic relationships—the "revolving door"—between governments and their economic partners.

7. The fact that the head of House Lannister, Tywin, refuses either to forgive the crown's massive debts or lend additional funds is odd, given that after King Robert's death, Tywin's grandchildren ascend to the throne, and his daughter becomes queen regent. In this situation, it would be natural for him to throw further financial support behind the crown, but he does not. One possible explanation is that the Lannisters' legendary supply of gold may be running dry. Whether this is the case or not, we can hope that Tywin's seemingly inconsistent behavior will be resolved in future books.

8. The most significant historical example of the influence of rhetoric is the industrial revolution. Some scholars argue that changes in the rhetoric of business and innovation were the primary causes of this unprecedented surge in economic development; in other words, when rhetoric improved—allowing and reflecting ideological changes—institutions followed suit (McCloskey, 2010).

REFERENCES

Augustine. 1998. *The City of God against the Pagans*. Translated by R.W. Dyson. Cambridge: Cambridge University Press.

Bastiat, Frédéric. 2007. *The Law*. Auburn, Alabama: Ludwig von Mises Institute.

Baumol, William J. 1990. "Entrepreneurship: Productive, Unproductive, and Destructive." *Journal of Political Economy*. 98(5): 893–919.

Carpenter, Charli. 2012. "Game of Thrones as Theory." *Foreign Affairs*. March 29. Available at: http://www.foreignaffairs.com/articles/137360/charli-carpenter/game-of-thrones-as-theory.

Farley, Christopher John. 2011. "'Game of Thrones' Author George R.R. Martin Spills the Secrets of 'A Dance with Dragons.'" *Wall Street Journal Online*. July 8. Available at: http://blogs.wsj.com/speakeasy/2011/07/08/game-of-thrones-author-george-r-r-martin-spills-the-secrets-of-a-dance-with-dragons/.

Kaveney, Roz. 2000. "A Storm Coming: An Interview with George R.R. Martin." *Amazon.co.uk*. Available at: http://www.amazon.co.uk/exec/obidos/tg/feature/-/49161/026–1281322–7450821. Lewis, C.S. 1956. "Sometimes Fairy Stories May Say Best What's to be Said." *New York Times*. November. 18: 310.

Martin, George R.R. 2012. *A Dance with Dragons, Part 2: After the Feast*. London: Harper Voyager.

———. 2011a. *A Game of Thrones*. London: Harper Voyager.

———. 2011b. *A Clash of Kings*. London: Harper Voyager.

———. 2011c. *A Storm of Swords, Part 1: Snow and Steel*. London: Harper Voyager.

———. 2011d. *A Storm of Swords, Part 2: Blood and Gold*. London: Harper Voyager.

McCaffrey, Matthew and Carmen Dorobăţ. 2013b. "The Economic Sense in *Game of Thrones*." *Mises Daily*, Jun. 7. Available at: http://www.mises.org/daily/6453/The-Economic-Sense-in-Game-of-Thrones.

McCaffrey, Matthew, and Carmen Dorobăţ. 2013a. "The Game of Thrones is a Game of Coins." *International Business Times*, Apr. 17. Available at: http://www.ibtimes.com/game-thrones-game-coins-1198543.

McCaffrey, Matthew. 2013. "Right Conquers Might: A Song of State and Society." *The Freeman*. Dec. 19. Available at: http://fee.org/freeman/detail/right-conquers-might.

McCloskey, Deirdre N. 2010. *Bourgeois Dignity: Why Economics Can't Explain the Modern World*. Chicago: University of Chicago Press.

Mises, Ludwig von. 1998 [1949]. *Human Action: The Scholar's Edition*. Auburn, Alabama: Ludwig von Mises Institute.

Oppenheimer, Franz. 1926. *The State: Its History and Development Viewed Sociologically*. New York: Vanguard Press.

Salerno, Joseph T. 2008. "Imperialism and the Logic of War Making." *Independent Review*. 12(3): 447–57.

———. 1990. "Postscript: Why a Socialist Economy is 'Impossible.'" In *Economic Calculation in the Socialist Commonwealth*. Auburn, AL: Ludwig von Mises Institute.

Vallier, Kevin. 2014. "The Iron Throne: A Feudal Monarchy with Diminishing Modern Power." Bleeding Heart Libertarians, Aug. 31. Available at: http://bleedingheart-libertarians.com/2014/08/the-iron-throne-a-feudal-monarchy-with-diminishing-modern-power/.

Chapter 27

Harry Potter and the Invisible Hand; or, the Virtue of Business That Is Not Serious

Heather King

Previous discussions of economics in the Harry Potter series have primarily focused on consumption and class, particularly noting ways in which consumption patterns signal "good" or "bad" characters, and the ways in which class is defined economically. There have been multiple, competing attempts to identify or label the economic structure in the books, with corresponding implications for the representation of business. Schulzke notes that "readers can find events or institutions to support both the conservative and the progressive interpretation." He observes that "some critics argue that the books include many capitalist themes" but points out that the "celebration of competition is counterbalanced by the books' glorification of generosity and the negative representation of elites" (2012, 113). Westman argues that Rowling creates a detailed version of "a late capitalist, global consumer culture" (2002, 306). But Adams describes the wizarding world as having "an economic system that William Morris would have approved of, with every shop run by owner-operator artisans" (2003, 5). Sterling-Folker and Folker probe this structure to ask why the magical economy so closely resembles contemporary "capitalist-market systems"; they note that if Ollivander's has really been in business since 382 B.C., the firm has weathered many different economic models during the course of history; why "replicate these historically specific forms of muggle economic exchange"? (2006, 107). On the other hand, Hall has suggested that the wizarding world presents "a society where there appears to be only one of everything: one school, one hospital, one bank, and most important, one Ministry. There is no competition in many areas, and the absence of competitive market pressure means changes and improvements come slowly, if at all" (2011, 289). Whether the capitalism on display is early or late, there is certainly buying and selling going on in the vividly described shops of Diagon Alley.

Gellis and others suggest that the economic system contributes to the meaning of the text; for her, the capitalist context highlights not a simple contrast of "'evil' Muggle materialism with a 'good' non-materialistic wizarding world," but the more complex comparison of "the individual's way of dealing with consumerism . . . not the act itself" (2005, 33). Westman also asserts that "Rowling's narrative, then, acknowledges the overwhelming desire to enter a system of capitalist exchange" by showing Harry's eagerness to buy and share luxuries with his friends: "the narrative also suggests that *consuming* that system's goods only pays off emotionally when items are needed or are given to others as gifts" (2002, 311). Others see the representation of the economy as doing cultural work on the reader. Rangwala suggests that the magical world offers not a "fantasy of production without labor" but a "specifically middle class sort of labor," that of a "typical professional managerial middle class subject" (2009, 129). Park, in general critical of the class structure in the books, notes that there is "a distinct difference drawn between those who inherited wealth and those who 'earned' it—a throwback to the Industrial Age and the rise of the modern middle class" (2003, 180). Absent from most of these discussions is what it means to be a producer in the system Rowling depicts. This essay focuses on how characters in the novels become producers in the economic system, and the moral implications of this agency. Through the characters of Fred and George, mischief makers in chief and successful entrepreneurs, Rowling presents a vision of business and commerce that strengthens communal bonds and that is associated with the chaotic, creative, and comedic forces that ultimately defeat the sinister, centrally controlling, Voldemort.

BUSINESS AS USUAL IN CHILDREN'S LITERATURE

Fred and George are noteworthy in part because the impulse to make money, whether strictly capitalist or not, frequently gets bad press in children's books.[1] To take one example, in *The Magician's Nephew*, the first of the Narnia books, Uncle Andrew confirms his corruption when the miraculous power of growth in Narnia gives him mercantile fantasies. Seeing a length of iron wrenched from a lamppost "grow" into a full-sized lamp post in the newly created Narnian soil, he begins to covetously ponder the use to which he could put this magic, exclaiming, "The commercial possibilities of this country are unbounded. Bring a few old bits of scrap iron here, bury 'em, and up they come as brand new railway engines, battleships, anything you please. They'll cost nothing, and I can sell 'em at full prices in England. I shall be a millionaire" (2000, 120). His fantasy of production without labor and the financial gain that would result is repugnant to the children, and scoffed at by Aslan; notably, the Narnian animals think *he's* the beast. More recently, *The Hunger Games* depicts a corrupt, decadent capital parasitically flourishing on the labor of the downtrodden districts, with all the cosmetic refinement of a decaying empire. And, of course, remember *The Lorax.*[2]

There are also plenty of examples in the Harry Potter series that align with the traditionally negative portrayal of business in children's literature[3]. The greed and materialism of the Durselys has gotten the most critical attention to date. Rangwala focuses on the Dursleys' relationship to consumerism, arguing that they "reinvest the fruits of Vernon's middle-class labor in consumer goods for their beloved son Dudley," whom she reads as "a caricatured child of late-capitalist permissiveness." She remarks that "Dudley's senseless consumerism—inscribed onto his enormous body—is without utility or purpose" (2009, 136). In a similar vein, Gellis contends that "what makes Harry's consumerism acceptable and Dudley's contemptible—is what they do with their purchases. Dudley uses his to hurt people and indifferently destroys his toys" (2005, 34). As is clear from Vernon's equating a man's worth with the kind of car he drives (1999, 3; 2000, 41), and the dinner party which begins book two, which was not a chance to break bread together but rather a carefully orchestrated attempt to close a deal, the Dursley's economic activity is pointlessly acquisitive and socially divisive.

The negative portrayal of business in the series is not limited to the Muggle world. Over the course of the series, business, which I'm defining loosely as the exchange of goods or services for money, becomes associated with betrayal, dishonesty, and abuse of power. The idea that the *Daily Prophet* "exists to sell itself" is a painful truth for Harry and Hermione and a passing jab by Rowling (2003, 567). Individuals are as suspect as companies. Robemaker Madame Malkin and wandmaker Olivander are both occasionally presented as ambiguous characters, as are the inn-keepers Madame Rosmerta—especially imperiused—and Aberforth. Florean Fortescue, the ice-cream parlor owner, is one of the only positive merchants, and considering the amount of ice-cream he gives away to Harry, he may not be a very savvy businessman. There are more sinister instances, as well. For example, the young Voldemort—still Tom Riddle at that point—works as an employee for Borgin and Burkes, the Dark Arts purveyors. His job is to collect objects, not produce anything new; Margaret Oakes suggests that "'obtainer' may be a more accurate term" for Riddle's position than "buyer" (2009, 152). The reactions of other wizards indicate the esteem in which such positions were held in the wizarding world: "what a waste . . . a brilliant young wizard like that, working in a shop," even though he was "no mere assistant" (2005, 432). Riddle's questionable techniques in obtaining items casts further disrepute on his line of work. The doting Hepzibah Smith thinks Riddle will be the exception to the rule and will enjoy the sight of Helga Hufflepuff's cup and Salzar

Slytherin's locket, because "you, Tom, you'll appreciate it for its history, not how many Galleons you can get for it" (2005, 435). When Tom kills her to obtain them, the reader is left with the impression that Burgin and Borkes would have been more upset by the fact that they didn't get the objects than the methods Riddle used.

Mundungus Fletcher adds to the negative portrayal of business within the books. Susan Hall points out that he is presented as barely human at first, being mistaken by Harry for a pile of rags as he slumps on the table, and "his nickname of 'Dung' gives a fairly clear hint of how the reader is supposed to regard him" (2003, 286). Dung's idea of "business" lands him in multiple confrontations. He is absent from his post guarding Harry the night the Dementors turn up in Little Whinging because he had a "business" deal he wanted to pursue. Arabella Figg is outraged that "He left! . . . Left to see someone about a batch of caludrons that fell off the back of a broom!" (2003, 20). The "back of the truck" allusion makes this an oddly humorous moment in the wake of a dementor attack, and the sneering tone against Dung's "business" remains consistent for the rest of the series. His feeble defense that "It . . . it was a very good business opportunity, see . . ." (2003, 23) is greeted with blows from Mrs. Figg. He's still singing the same song when Harry arrives at Number 12, Grimauld Place, claiming "'See, I wouldn't 'ave left,' said Mundungus, leaning forward, a pleading note in his voice, 'but I 'ad a business opportunity —"; he receives no answer from Harry for this attempt at exculpation (2003, 82). Molly Weasley tries, with limited success, to prevent Mundungus from sharing stories of double-dealing and graft with the twins, remarking "sharply" that "I don't think we need to hear any more of your business dealings, thank you very much, Mundungus," and adding "coldly" that "I don't know where you learned about right and wrong, Mundungus, but you seem to have missed a few crucial lessons" (2003, 86). Her distaste grows when Dung actually brings the questionable cauldrons to the house. She explodes, "WE ARE NOT RUNNING A HIDEOUT FOR STOLEN GOODS!" (2003, 107). In *The Half Blood Prince*, Dung's tricks are even more distasteful as Harry catches him peddling silver goblets stolen from Sirius' house after his death (2005, 245–47). If this is business, neither Harry nor the reader want any part of it.

Professor Horace Slughorn, despite having cultivated the persona of a man of leisure and luxury, is not above trying to make a profit off of opportunities that come his way, and this is also presented as less than admirable behavior. After having taken Felix Felicis, Harry lures Slughorn to the spider Aragog's funeral with the possibility of collecting the venom from his fangs: "seems an awful waste not to collect it . . . might get a hundred Galleons a pint. . . . To be frank, my salary is not large. . . ." Slughorn mutters disjointedly (2005, 481). Slughorn's greed gets the better of him, and he agrees to attend. When seated in Hagrid's hut, he notices the unicorn hair hanging from the ceiling, asking incredulously: "but my dear chap, do you know how much that's *worth*?" (2005, 486). Hagrid, of course, has never given this matter thought. As Slughorn sits in the room, Harry is aware that the sybaritic professor is looking "for more treasures that he might be able to convert into a plentiful supply of oak-matured mead, crystalized pineapple, and velvet smoking jackets" (2005, 486). When a tipsy Hagrid gives Slughorn an entire unicorn tail, Slughorn toasts him: "to friendship! To generosity! To ten Galleons a hair!," making clear that the personal and commercial priorities of this character are muddled. Through Riddle, Mundungus, and Slughorn, "business" is given connotations of deceit, crime, and selfishness.

FRED AND GEORGE: FUNNY BUSINESS

Against a background of "old money" wizarding families, the respectably down-at-heel, and the morally bankrupt, the entrepreneurial drive evinced by Fred and George Weasley is downright heroic, and rewarded with tremendous success. Hall describes them as "first class research wizards" but asserts that "such individuals are precisely that: individual, and few in number. There seems to be no framework within which their research endeavors can be recognized and rewarded" (2003, 281). She overlooks, however, the tremendous financial reward accorded them via the market. They win, and win big, through sustained entrepreneurial effort. Their "wheezes" are created through their skill at enchantments, and tested on their own bodies. Their chaos and comedy make them appealing representatives of the spontaneous order of a free market. The idea for this paper was born out of reading Adam Smith's 1759 *Theory of Moral Sentiments* (1982) and Hayek's 1949 *Individualism and the Economic Order* (1980). The twins seem to fit in this intellectual tradition. Specifically, they embody a kind of entrepreneurship that keeps alive the communal connotations of commerce, represented by the link between market innovation and humor. Hall reminds us of Bakhtin's "'laughing chorus' of the medieval marketplace," underscoring the possible connection between business, comedy, and rebellion (2011, 71). Fred and George's version of business fosters community rather than fragmenting it, emphasizing creativity and choice over planning and regulation.

In most accounts, Fred and George begin the series as typical—well, more accomplished than average—scapegraces. McEvoy and Boll both read the twins as trickster figures. Boll notes that "while the trickster figure is often depicted as a two-faced Janus, the Potter series relies on two identical faces, i.e., twins who, somewhat consequently, do not embody good and evil but share the values of the hero" (2011, 92). McEvoy articulates a portion of those values, noting that at the end of *Goblet of Fire*, the twins' "established role" is "to help people find relief from the trauma and misfortune to come" (2011, 219). Along these lines, Longster casts the twins in the role of jesters to Harry's prince, tracing the ways in which their humor is put to his service (2005). I contend that there is more to their personae than just tricksters or jesters: they are in fact important moral forces in the series, which Rowling signals through a variety of details. They are better able to bridge the magic and muggle worlds than most wizards, even using trade to do so; they are among the only men we see who are competent in romantic situations; they are recognized as being nearly unstoppable forces, capable of pulling off just about anything; and they are fiercely loyal and surprisingly kind.

True sons of Arthur Weasley, they are better able than most wizards to recognize and utilize ideas and practices from the Muggle world. They are able to open the door to Harry's room with a hairpin instead of wands, observing "a lot of wizards think it's a waste of time, knowing this sort of Muggle trick, . . . but we feel they're skills worth learning, even if they are a bit slow" (1999a, 26). In their successful joke shop, they carry Muggle novelty items as well: "'Muggle magic tricks! 'said Fred happily. . . . 'For freaks like Dad, you know, who love Muggle stuff. It's not a big earner, but we do fairly steady business, they're great novelties" (2005, 118). They are not strictly motivated by profit in selecting how they stock their store, targeting this niche market out of affection for their father as much as desire for profit. The ability to work between worlds shows not just their open-minded ingenuity, but also the way in which they are literally able to trade between the magic and muggle world in a manner that respects both. They repeatedly put this ability to Harry's service, particularly George, who is the kinder twin.[4] It is, after all, the twins who first recognize Harry on Platform 9 ¾, in the course of helping him lug his trunk onto the train, so there is a way in which they usher Harry into his magical peer group. The ecumenical attitude of the twins toward knowledge is an early sign that they are going to be innovative thinkers.

In a series with some cringe-worthy adolescent attempts at romance, the twins are surprisingly effective suitors. When Ron asks Fred who he is taking to the Yule Ball, Fred replies "promptly, without a trace of embarrassment" that he's taking Angelina, and proceeds to ask her in front of them, shouting "Oi! Angelina! Want to come to the ball with me?"; when this brash proposal meets with success and a "bit of a grin" from Angelina, Fred pronounces "There you go. Piece of cake" leaving Harry and Ron in open-mouthed wonder (2000, 394). In *Half-Blood Prince*, the twins head into the local town because "there's a very pretty girl working in the paper shop who thinks my card tricks are something marvelous . . . almost like real magic . . ." (2005, 328). They are the only wizards we read of knowingly pursuing a Muggle girl; most "mixed" relationships are in the tradition of "Bewitched," and feature a witch hiding her talent from her male partner. They also seem able to remain objective about their sister-in-law, Fleur Delacouer, a part-Veela who melts most men's brains with her beauty any time she enters a room. They possess confidence and self-command, and fare better in romantic entanglements than any of their peers.

The ability of the twins to pull off the impossible becomes a refrain in the series. They are described as "human bludgers" by Oliver Wood, implying both that it takes force to stop them and that their actions are likely to be unpredictable (1998, 169). In Book 2, when they bring Ron to rescue Harry from his imprisonment at the Dursley's, they are not just driving the get-away car. Ron's faith in his brothers' ability is clear when he responds to Harry's worry that they can't use magic to remove the bars from his window with a smile and the reassurance "you forget who I've got with me" (1999a, 25). Ginny repeats this sentiment later, in Book 5, when she remarks that "the thing about growing up with Fred and George . . . is that you sort of start thinking anything's possible if you've got enough nerve" (2003, 655). That ethos sums up the risk taking and optimism necessary for both entrepreneurial endeavor and for quixotic moral quests like standing up to Voldemort.

Discussions of Fred and George tend to focus on their mischief making, and miss out on their kindness. McEvoy declares that in making mischief, they "sometimes cross the line into maliciousness" (2011, 18–19). However, they are shown repeatedly to be concerned for others. As mentioned, they offer Harry help before they know who he is; that knowledge is the reward of their kindness. In *Chamber of Secrets*, when the Dobby-fied bludger is menacing Harry, the twins are his stalwart defenders not just in their role as Beaters, but also in their outrage at the pressure Oliver Wood is placing on Harry to win the game at such high personal risk. Fred tries to make light of Wood's win "or die trying" pep talk initially (1999a, 167), but when death suddenly seems a possible outcome because of the bewitched bludger, George is the one to call a time out, and the most outraged when he thinks Harry is being pressured to continue the game despite the obvious foul play: "This is all your fault," George said angrily to Wood. "'Get the Snitch or die trying,' what a stupid thing to tell him—" (1999a, 170). In *Prisoner of Azkaban*, when a dementor has caused Harry's collapse on the train, Fred and George are comforting voices against Malfoy's teasing. They expose Malfoy's own fearful response on the train, and they share their own fear of the dementors as well: "'I wasn't too happy myself, said George. They're horrible things, those dementors . . .' 'Sort of freeze your insides, don't they?' said Fred," "bracingly" telling Harry that everyone is bothered by the dementors' presence (1999b, 97). They offer similar comfort after Harry falls from his broom when dementors swarm the Quidditch field, telling him "there had to be one time you didn't get it" and "you're still the best Seeker we've ever had" (1999b, 180–81). In *Goblet of Fire*, when Harry's name emerges from the goblet, Fred and George do not hold a grudge—Fred questions how he did it, looking "half annoyed, half deeply impressed" and George exclaims "Brilliant!" (2000, 284). While Ron's jealousy gets the better of him, the twins are the ringleaders in throwing a party to celebrate Harry's selection. And when Harry sees his father and Sirius in the Pensieve, tormenting Snape, he "could not imagine Fred and George dangling someone upside down for the fun of it . . . not unless they really loathed them . . ." (2003, 653). The twins' efforts to make Harry and others feel better may occasionally be rough or clumsy, but they are repeatedly the first to offer a pat on the shoulder to those upset, unlike the other, selfish, businessmen depicted in the series.

The twins' moral stature is important to note, since in *The Goblet of Fire* the twins' entrepreneurial ambitions become part of the plot line. Their market aims work in concert with, rather than contrast to, their admirable qualities, which consequently redefines business as a positive activity. We learn from Ron and Ginny that the twins are trying to sell their joke inventions under the name of Weasleys' Wizarding Wheezes, complete with order forms and merchandise stocked in their room. Ron remarks "it was brilliant, I never knew they'd been inventing all that . . ." (2000, 55). Ginny adds that "we've been hearing explosions out of their room for ages, but we never thought they were actually *making* things" (2000, 55); together the siblings' account bears witness to the labor, skill, and perseverance involved in the boys' undertaking. When Mrs. Weasley confiscates the rest of the offending toffees, Fred shouts "We spent six months developing those!" (2000, 68). This is also the conversation in which we learn that the twins have declared a desire to go into business rather than following their father into the Ministry. Mrs. Weasley is particularly displeased with this goal, declaring they have "no ambition, unless you count making as much trouble as they possibly can," which irritates her all the more because "it's not as though they haven't got brains" (2000, 58, 59). At this point, business is not taken seriously as an ambition, nor an activity that requires intelligence.

The twins are also openly focused on raising money to make this dream come true. They bet their entire combined savings on the outcome of the Quidditch World Cup, which Matthews describes as "an act of courage and daring" (2005, 140). When defrauded by Ludo Bagman, they risk stooping to blackmail to try and recoup their loss, and Ron describes them as "obsessed with making money" (2000, 568). They don't want the money for consumer purposes, but because "they keep going on about how it's time to think about their future, and Dad can't help them, and they need gold to get started" with their joke shop (2000, 568). The twins' relationship to money is therefore different from the status-conscious Malfoys or Dursleys, or the disreputable Mundungus. They want the money to do something, to create.

Despite the worrisome conclusions to which Ron, Hermione, and Harry jump about the twins' efforts to get money, at the end of the novel their financial need becomes a way to redeem Harry's Triwizard winnings; a sort of spiritual money-laundering. On the way home for the summer holidays, after the stress and horror of the Triwizard Tournament and Cedric's death, knowing that Voldemort has returned, Harry chooses to give his 1,000 galleon prize to Fred and George, insisting that if they don't take it, he'll throw it away. This is, of course, an important reminder that Harry is above personal gain as all good heroes should be, but his charge to the twins also underscores the coming importance of their role as economic agents in the future books. He tells them, "You take it, and get inventing. It's for the joke shop. . . . I don't want [this money] and I don't need it. But I could do with a few laughs. We could all do with a few laughs. I've got a feeling we're going to need them more than usual before long" (2000, 733). This isn't just rent money—it demands activity: "get inventing." As Longster observes, this is one of the few times we see the twins silenced (2005, 120). Harry's other stipulation is that the twins buy Ron new dress robes (a promise they have kept by the start of the next book (2003, 164). The conclusion therefore emphasizes care for friends and family and entrepreneurial efforts as the countermovement to Voldemort's return.

In *The Order of the Phoenix*, Fred and George are more prominent figures, even read by McEvoy (2011) as the heroes of this book, and they seem to be blending business with political resistance. Consequently, their shenanigans begin to redefine how business is viewed in this series. They are clearly moving toward their entrepreneurial future, advertising for testers, and casually talking about their "market research," complete with clipboards (2003, 227). Fred has started spouting phrases like "Time is Galleons," or "business as usual," (2003, 68, 658), and ending conversations with pronouncements like "can't stand around chatting all day, we've got business to discuss" (2003, 183). Their plans for merchandise emphasize choice again and again. When describing the Skiving Snackboxes to Harry, Fred explains that they enable a student to skip class with a feigned illness, consume the antidote, and "pursue the leisure activity of your own choice" instead of spending time in an "unprofitable" manner (2003, 104). And they plan to "produce the products to fit the demand" once they find out what students want (2003, 227). They are free-market entrepreneurs.

They are also politically principled, acting for freedom more generally as well, specifically against Dolores Umbridge. Fred and George reveal how restrained they've been previously, explaining to Hermione that they no longer care about getting into trouble. She scoffs that they never have, but they reply that they have "always known where to draw the line," "always stopped short of causing real mayhem" (2003, 627). They announce that "we'd walk out right now if we weren't determined to do our bit for Dumbledore first," making clear that their rebellious antics are motivated by a moral and political commitment (2003, 627). Real "mayhem" is precisely what they plan to undermine Umbridge. As Castro notes, "Nothing hurts an established power figure more than being made to look ridiculous, and the history of resistance movements overflows with incidents where official repression was greeted with guerilla stunts dedicated to bringing that ridiculousness into sharp relief" (2005, 129). The twins are masters at such stunts. The fireworks and swamp they unleash in two separate rebellions shake her control, and it should be underscored that these incidents are made possible through their own products—their "jokes" have political power. The opposing elements of fire and water in their two massive pranks hints at the range of the twins' power. These antics significantly give the professors a chance to show their resistance too. Bealer notes that Fred and George create through chaos a subversive space for others to register resistance to Umbridge as well (2009). She observes that "in addition to drumming up business for their nascent joke shop, the number and variety of bewitched fireworks both result in chaos and . . . create a subversive space for the other professors" (2009, 182). I would like to underscore that commercial activity here is politically empowering for students and faculty alike, building community, staging resistance, and having a laugh all at the same time. Bealer further notes that "Fred and George explicitly align their innovative merchandise with anti-Umbridge resistance, offering markdowns to those who promise to use the products to further enrage and destabilize Umbridge" (2009, 183). Harry remarks that Fred and George's fireworks would "put Dr. Filibuster out of business, no problem" (2003, 633); in a series rife with puns, the conclusion the reader draws is that their fireworks are competitive in the market, and are a more effective means of political resistance than a "filibuster."

Having caused an effective ruckus, the twins then elude Umbridge's clutches, facing her "without the slightest sign of fear" (2003, 674), performing strong enough *Accio* spells to tear iron pegs out of the castle walls in freeing their brooms, and managing to get in a plug for their business by announcing their new premises. Then, in a scene familiar to anyone who has ever seen a western, the triumphant boys, mounted on their brooms, "wheeled about to tumultuous applause from the students below and sped out of the open front doors into the glorious sunset" (2003, 675). Their heroic status is clear even to Peeves, who salutes them. Again, their business ambitions are in line with their political aims.

The danger, of course, increases in book 6, but again, Fred and George refuse to cower in fear, and continue to combine humor, entrepreneurial endeavor, and political stances. As Hall notes, "the success of the Weasley twins and their joke shop is an ongoing demonstration of the revolutionary spirit of laughter in the face of oppression" (2003, 75). Mrs. Weasley explains to Harry what is happening in the market as Voldemort gains power: "odd things have been cropping up for sale everywhere, things that are supposed to guard against You-Know-Who and the Death Eaters" (2005, 84). But they are fake or dangerous most of the time: "in the main the perpetrators are just people like Mundungus Fletcher, who've never done an honest day's work in their lives and are taking advantage of how frightened everybody is, but every now and then something really nasty turns up" (2005, 85). It's clear that there are multiple market models on display in the series, and that they are not morally equal; also clear is that the "business" previously associated with Mundungus is not the same line of work in which the twins are engaged. We are assured via a conversation between Molly (who now realizes that the boys "have a flair" (2005, 88) for their chosen line of work) and Arthur Weasley that Fred and George would never stoop to false protection charms—pointing out both that unscrupulous vendors will spring up to capitalize on fear-based needs in the market place, and that the twins are not that kind of entrepreneur: "The boys wouldn't do anything like that now, not when people are desperate for protection!" (2005, 87). They seem to be doing well by doing good, since Ron calls his mother's assessment of the twins' having "a flair for business" an "understatement," declaring that "they're raking in the Galleons!" (2005, 96).

One key element in the depiction of the Weasley brothers' endeavors is that they are producers within the system. Their "wheezes" are created through their own skill at enchantments. Even Hermione is impressed; as she peruses their wares in their store, she remarks, "that really is extraordinary magic!" (2005, 117). And no less a judge than Professor Flitwick memorializes a "tiny patch" of the portable swamp they created because "it was a really good bit of magic" (2003, 848). This success doesn't come without investments of time and labor; as Mrs. Weasley explains, the twins are so busy with their joke shop, they've moved into the lodgings above it (2005, 88). There are other physical sacrifices too: Fred provides Hermione with a salve for the bruise on her eye, remarking "we had to find a decent bruise remover. We're testing most of our products on ourselves" (2005, 118). Since they have employees at this point, who even refer to them as Mr. Weasley, they presumably have other options for testers, but don't subject others to those rigors. And while they end book five in new dragon skin jackets, because "business is booming and we thought we'd treat ourselves" (2003, 867) they clearly do not let up on themselves in terms of creating and developing new products.

In fact, we see with Fred and George not just success but political courage in keeping with their school antics. Smith describes Fred and George making the turn from tricksters into "savvy businessmen who contribute to society," a transition all the more impressive since it occurs "during the dark times of Voldemort's second rise" (2012, 76). The first description of the shop is set in stark contrast to the depressed "poster-muffled shop fronts" and failed businesses on either side: "Fred and George's windows hit the eye like a firework display" (2005, 116). Of course, the firework simile is descriptive of the explosive advertising, but it also calls to mind the twins' previous political mayhem at Hogwarts, suggesting that they are still mixing business with resistance. The sign in the window of their shop, "Why are you worrying about You-Know-Who? You should be worrying about U-No-Poo—the Constipation Sensation that's Gripping the nation!" (2005, 116) is cheeky to the point of madness. Not only does it mock Voldemort—because it is "purple like those of the ministry," it is mocking that authority as well. Mrs. Weasley fears they are inviting retribution, but Harry and Ron see it as both funny and emboldening for others, terming it "brilliant" (2005, 116). The fact that the shop is "packed with customers" while Fortescue's ice cream parlor is boarded up indicates that others find the sign brilliant, too (2005, 116). As Harry had predicted at the end of book four, the need for laughter has grown desperate, and Fred and George courageously meet that need. Notice too that through a sign like this, they offer the laugh for free—you don't have to buy the product to laugh at the marketing—unlike those selling false protection charms. Their joke is a generous and courageous response to the darkening political culture.

Market demand and political resistance are even more entwined when the twins develop a line of Defense Against the Dark Arts products after they discover that the Ministry of Magic is using their Shield Hats to protect staff who can't cast effective shield charms. The demand is "massive" (2005, 119), and they develop the line because it is such a "money-spinner" (2005, 119), but this isn't mere exploitation of need, since the products are intended for the purpose of fighting the Death Eaters, and work.[5] As Matthews observes,

> the success of their pranks and the quality of their mischief is the clear result of hard work and application . . . they achieve success, the impact of which resounds far beyond the essentially trivial nature of the niche they have claimed as their own . . . They find themselves contributing to the commonweal in more significant ways than they ever imagined. They thought they were just opening a joke shop, but . . ., they have discovered that a joke shop can be a much more important weapon for resisting the forces of evil than anything else they could have done. (2005, 140–41)

Matthews' description evokes Hayek's remark that "the spontaneous collaboration of free men often creates things which are greater than their individual minds can ever fully comprehend" (1980, 7). They are innovative and effective businessmen, achieving admirable political ends in the course of making a profit.

Barrat summarizes "the fear of many critics of consumerism," as the danger "that a consumer culture eventually causes people to replace the pursuit of social capital with the pursuit of material capital," defining social capital as "the network of social relations, the underlying mutual trust on which they rest, and their eventual consolidation and institutionalization, which contribute to resilient, democratic, and ultimately functional societies" (2012, 151–50). There are multiple examples that the twins are able to combine social and material capital in their success. They insist that Harry cannot pay for their goods, since they are so deeply in his debt for their startup money, and they keep their word about buying Ron proper dress robes. This ethos continues They have given their mother a "midnight blue witch's hat glittering with what looked like tiny starlike diamonds, and a spectacular golden necklace" (2005, 339). These are real gifts, unlike what Westman describes as "the coerced exchanges" of the Dursleys. Westman sees Harry's pleasure in giving gifts "with no expectation of a gift in return," as suggesting that participating in a capitalist system of exchange is only satisfying "emotionally when items are needed or are given to others as gifts" (2002, 311). Fred and George are, I think, therefore part of the reformed consumer economy Westman traces in the series. Nor is that all: when Ron is accidentally poisoned, Fred and George visit him. They have brought him a large, wrapped present, which they had planned to surprise him with for his birthday in Hogsmeade. Fred mentions in passing that "we were thinking of buying Zonko's, . . . a Hogsmeade branch, you know, but a fat lot of good it'll do us if you lot aren't allowed out at weekends to buy our stuff anymore. . . . But never mind that now" (2005, 400). Fred's dismissal of his own business plans as of secondary importance to his brother's health makes clear that the twins' huge success has not gone to his head.[6]

As the gloom of *Deathly Hallows* opens, Fred and George are still a roaring success, roaring with laughter in the process. Their humor becomes more central than their entrepreneurial endeavors, but reminds us that they are both businessmen and family men. When George is wounded during the effort to transport Harry to the Burrow, his attempt at humor is moving, even when the jokes about his missing ear making him "saintlike" because "holey" aren't that good (at least in Fred's opinion). The humor of the twins, here, and perhaps always, is aimed at making people feel better, at forging and renewing bonds between family and friends. We certainly see laughter as curative; when Harry, Ron and Hermione listen to Fred on "Potterwatch" later, "for the first time in weeks and weeks, Harry was laughing; He could feel the weight of tension leaving him" (2007, 443). Fred is still poking fun—suggesting that Voldemort can "move faster than Severus Snape confronted with shampoo"—but also still tending to community, repeatedly speaking to the listeners as a group—"listen, people"—and ending with caution: "I never thought I'd hear myself say it, but safety first!" (2007, 444). The broadcast and the humor remind Harry, Ron, and Hermione that "other people were resisting Voldemort" too, and eases their sense of isolation (2007, 444).

As the DA and the Order assemble in the Room of Requirement prior to the Battle for Hogwarts, Fred and George are "cracking jokes for the benefit of those nearest"; Rowling's phrasing denotes that the jokes are being told for those who can hear them, but the connotation of actual benefit seems apt, too (2007, 583). And when Percy joins those pitching a desperate last stand, the twins are the first to accept him back. Percy splutters, unable to finish his apology, "'I was a fool, I was an idiot, I was a pompous prat, I was a- a- .' 'Ministry-loving, family-disowning, power-hungry moron'" Fred offers. When Percy accepts this, Fred's forgiveness is instant: "Well, you can't say fairer than that, said Fred, holding out his hand to Percy" (2007, 606). Their joking continues even during the fighting; George urges them to hurry to the scene of the battle "or all of the good Death Eaters'll be taken" (2007, 606), and Fred quips "nice night for it!" as Harry passes him in the midst of explosions (2007, 621).

The bond of humor is, of course, part of what makes Fred's death so poignant just pages later—Percy has become a real Weasley again, sending witty repartee along with his hexes as he duels the Minister of Magic, and Fred is in the midst of rejoicing that his brother has recovered his sense of humor when he is killed in an explosion. Percy blasts the Minister as he asks, "did I mention I'm resigning?" (2007, 636). Fred responds with "glee" to hear Percy joking, reverting to his family nickname of Perce, and reminiscing that "I don't think I've heard you joke since you were—", and then he's hit (2007, 636). The scene of Percy and Ron devastated by Fred's death is completed by the description of "the ghost of his last laugh still etched upon his face" (2007, 637). The implication, perhaps, is that he has gotten the last laugh; his brother has returned to the right side, and he leaves his family unified once more. His death is tragic, but not vain, his last smile one of fraternal bonding. McEvoy characterizes this as a fitting hero's death, asserting that "Fred dies as he lived, joyful and mischievous" (2011, 220).[7] Voldemort, Umbridge, and others who value relics over production, who oppress rather than collaborate, and who resist the human impulse to commerce with their kind, will ultimately be defeated by those who innovate, laugh, love, and exchange. What Rowling provides is perhaps neither strictly conservative or radical, but a reformed vision of how economic action is part of the human project, along with laughter and community. The twins are successful businessmen, and successful human beings at the same time. Rowling has redefined "business" as a human activity that unites and empowers people through chaos and humor.

NOTES

1. *Learning from the Left* recounts a longstanding tradition of reading and condemning "capitalist" values of conformity and materialism in mainstream children's literature: "By reaffirming the existing social order, much of the familiar children's literature of the twentieth century at least implicitly supports the individualistic values of capitalism" (Mickenberg, 2006, 7). In general, this study seems to conflate capitalists with corporations, which is a distinction I prefer to maintain.

2. Roald Dahl's *Charlie and the Chocolate Factory* offers some interesting departures from this anti-profit tradition. Willy Wonka is an innovative and successful businessman, and is described as saving rather than exploiting the oompa-loompas (though this is a matter for debate). He also intends to give away his company, rather than selling it for a profit. Of course, this would have to be balanced against Matilda's unscrupulous used-car-salesman father in Dahl's *Matilda*. Dahl seems to distinguish between types of entrepreneurship, rather than lumping them all together.

3 There are also a number of scholars who read capitalism as problematic in the series. See, for example, Farah Mendlesohn, "Crowning the King: Harry Potter and the Construction of Authority" (2002); Tammy Turner-Vorbek, "Pottermania: Good, Clean fun or Cultural Hegemony?" (2003); Lisa Giselle Anatol, "The Fallen Empire: Exploring Ethnic Otherness in the World of Harry Potter" (2003); and Susan Hall, "Marx, Magic, and Muggles: Class Conflict in Harry Potter's World" (2011). Edmund Kern provides a useful summary of the early stages of these arguments, and a counterargument: *The Wisdom of Harry Potter: What our Favorite Hero Teaches Us about Moral Choices* (2003).

4. It is George, for example, who sees "Harry's puzzled look" and explains what O.W.L.'s are (1999, 46), and who expresses anxiety for his parents' financial state repeatedly in book 2 (1999, 29, 44, 46).

5. Though since Draco manages to get a hold of some of the Peruvian Darkness Powder, clearly things can't be controlled—Ron thinks the twins need to screen their customers more carefully (HBP, 618). Free markets are not without risk.

6. It also suggests that, contrary to Hall's assertion, there is competition in the wizard economy, since expanding and buying out failed competitors seems a pretty common practice.

7. Phyllis Morris describes losing one of the twins as "an unparalleled depth of loss, disruption, horror," and quotes Rowling's rationale for killing Fred, because "he's slightly harder . . . funnier but also the crueler" and the death would be less expected (2009, 148).

REFERENCES

Adams, Richard. 2014. "Harry Potter and the Closet Conservative," in *The Voice of the Turtle* http://voice oftheturtle.org/printer/reviews/books/Richard_potter.shtml, accessed 9/24/2014.

Anatol, Giselle Liza (ed). 2003. *Reading Harry Potter: Critical Essays*. Westport, Connecticut: Praeger.

Anatol, Lisa Giselle. 2003. "The Fallen Empire: Exploring Ethnic Otherness in the World of Harry Potter." In *Reading Harry Potter: Critical Essays*. Edited by Lisa Giselle Anatol. Westport, Connecticut: Praeger.

Barrat, Bethany. 2012. *The Politics of Harry Potter*. London: Palgrave/MacMillan.

Bealer, Tracy. 2009. "(Dis)Order and the Phoenix: Love and Political Resistance in Harry Potter." In *Reading Harry Potter Again: New Critical Essays*. Edited by Lisa Anatol. Santa Barbara: ABC-CLIO.

Boll, Julia. 2011. "Harry Potter's Archetypal Journey." In *Heroism in the Harry Potter Series*. Edited by Katrin Berndt and Lena Steveker. Farnham, Surrey: Ashgate Publishing.

Bousquet, Marc. 2009. "Harry Potter, the War against Evil, and the Melodramatization of Public Culture." In *Critical Perspectives on Harry Potter* (second edition). Edited by Elizabeth E. Heilman. New York: Routledge.

Castro, Adam-Troy. "From Azkaban to Abu Ghraib: Fear and Fascism in Harry Potter and the Order of the Phoenix." In *Mapping the World of the Sorcerer's Apprentice: An Unauthorized Exploration of the Harry Potter Series Complete through Book Six.* Edited by Mercedes Lackey. Dallas, Texas: BenBella Books, Inc.

Gellis, Roberta. 2005. "The Dursleys as Social Commentary." In *Mapping the World of the Sorcerer's Apprentice: an Unauthorized Exploration of the Harry Potter Series Complete through Book Six.* Edited by Mercedes Lackey. Dallas, Texas: BenBella Books, Inc.

Hall, Jordana. 2011. "Embracing the Abject Other: The Carnival Imagery of *Harry Potter*." *Children's Literature in Education* 42:70–89.

Hall, Susan. 2003. "Harry Potter and the Rule of Law: The Central Weakness of Legal Concepts in the Wizard World." In *Reading Harry Potter: Critical Essays.* Edited by Liza Giselle Anatol. Westport, Connecticut: Praeger.

———. "Marx, Magic, and Muggles: Class Conflict in Harry Potter's World. In *Harry Potter and History*. Edited by Nancy Regin. Hoboken, New Jersey: John Wiley and Sons.

Hayek, Freidrich. 1980. *Individualism and Economic Order*. Chicago: University of Chicago Press.

Kern, Edmund M. 2003. *The Wisdom of Harry Potter: What Our Favorite Hero Teaches Us about Moral Choices*. Amherst, New York: Prometheus Books.

Lewis, C.S. 2000. *The Magician's Nephew*. New York: Harper Trophy.

Longster, Rebecca. 2005. "The Harlequins in the Weasley Twins: Jesters in the Court of Prince Harry (and J.K. Rowling)." In *Scholarly Studies in Harry Potter: Applying Academic Methods to a Popular Text*. Edited by Cynthia Hallett. Lewiston, New York: Edwin Mellen Press.

Matthews, Susan. 2005. "Ich Bin Ein Hufflepuff: Strategies for Variable Skill Management in J.K. Rowling's Harry Potter Novels." In *Mapping the World of the Sorcerer's Apprentice: an Unauthorized Exploration of the Harry Potter Series Complete through Book Six.* Edited by Mercedes Lackey. Dallas: BenBella Books, Inc.

McEvoy, Kathleen. 2011. "Heroism at the Margins." In *Heroism in the Harry Potter Series*. Edited by Katrin Berndt and Lena Steveker. Farnham, Surrey: Ashgate Publishing.

Mendleshon, Farah. 2002. "Crowning the King: Harry Potter and the Construction of Authority." In *The Ivory Tower and Harry Potter*. Edited by Lana Whited. Columbia: University of Missouri Press.

Mickenberg, Julia L. 2006. *Learning from the Left: Children's Literature, the Cold War, and Radical Politics in the United States*. Oxford: Oxford University Press.

Morris, Tom. 2006. *If Harry Potter Ran General Electric: Leadership Wisdom from the World of the Wizards*. New York: Currency Doubleday.

Morris, Phyllis. 2009. "From Gred and Forge to Fred and George: Character Transformation in Harry Potter." In *Harry Potter's World Wide Influence*. Edited by Diana Patterson. New Castle upon Tyne: Cambridge Scholars Publishing.

Oakes, Margaret. 2009. "Secret Domination or Civic Duty: The Source and Purpose of magical Power in Harry Potter." In *Reading Harry Potter Again: New Critical Essays*. Edited by Lisa Anatol. Santa Barbara: ABC-CLIO.

Ostry, Elaine. 2003. "Accepting Mudbloods: The Ambivalent Social Vision of J.K. Rowling's Fairy Tales." In *Reading Harry Potter: Critical Essays*. Edited by Liza Giselle Anatol. Westport, Connecticut: Praeger, 89–101.

Park, Julia. 2003. "Class and Socioeconomic Identity in Harry Potter's England" in *Reading Harry Potter: Critical Essays*. Edited by Giselle Liza Anatol. Westport, Connecticut: Praeger.

Rangwala, Shama. 2009. "A Marxist Inquiry into J.K. Rowlng's Harry Potter Series." In *Reading Harry Potter Again: New Critical Essays*. Edited by Lisa Anatol. Santa Barbara: ABC-CLIO.

Rowling, J. K. 1999a. *Harry Potter and the Chamber of Secrets*. New York: Arthur A. Levine.

———. 2000. *Harry Potter and the Goblet of Fire*. New York: Arthur A. Levine.

———. 2005. *Harry Potter and the Half-Blood Prince*. New York: Arthur A. Levine.

———. 2007. *Harry Potter and the Deathly Hallows*. New York: Arthur A. Levine.

———. 2003. *Harry Potter and the Order of the Phoenix*. New York:Arthur A. Levine.

———. 1998. *Harry Potter and the Sorcerer's Stone*. New York: A.A. Levine.

———. 1999b. *Harry Potter and the Prisoner of Azkaban*. New York: Arthur A. Levine.

Schulzke, Marcus. 2012. "Wizard's Justice and Elf Liberation: Politics and Political Activism in *Harry Potter*." In *J.K. Rowling: Harry Potter*. Edited by Cynthia J. Hallett and Peggy J. Huey. Houndmills: Palgrave Macmillan, 111–21.

Smith, Adam. 1982. *Theory of Moral Sentiments*. Indianapolis, Indiana: Liberty Fund, Inc.

Smith, Daniel. 2012. "'I suppose your parents will go hungry for a month to pay for that lot': Reciprocity, Recognition and Moral Worth in the Wizarding Economy." In *The Sociology of Harry Potter: 22 Enchanting Essays on the Wizarding World*. Edited by Jenn Sims. Hamden, Connecticut: Zossima Press.

Stephens, Rebecca. 2003. "Harry and Hierarchy: Book Banning as a Reaction to the Subversion of Authority." In *Reading Harry Potter: Critical Essays*. Edited by Giselle Liza Anatol. Westport, Connecticut: Praeger, 51–65.

Sterling-Folker, Jennifer and Brian Folker. 2006. "Conflict and the Nation-State: Magical Mirrors of Muggles and Refracted Images." In *Harry Potter and International Relations*. Edited by Daniel Nexon and Iver Neumann. Lanham, Maryland: Rowman and Littlefield Publishers.

Turner-Vorbeck, Tammy. 2003. "Pottermania: Good Clean Fun or Cultural Hegemony?" In *Harry Potter's World: Multidisciplinary Critical Perspectives*. Edited by Elizabeth Heilman. New York: RoutledgeFalmer.

Westman, Karin E. 2002. "Specters of Thatcherism: Contemporary Culture in J.K. Rowling's Harry Potter Series." In *The Ivory Tower and* Harry Potter. Edited by Lana Whited. Columbia: University of Missouri Press, 305–28.

Chapter 28

Race, Rules, and Real Estate in August Wilson's *Radio Golf*

Susan Love Brown

Business has often been the subject of American literature, being exposed more often than not for its downside and shortcomings. From the beginning, Americans have negotiated the rocky shores of capitalism and its place next to the political, legal, and social domains of American life. The African American presence has always been a part of this negotiation before and after the United States was born. African Americans have long been the keepers of history—the American memory—and have had to live with the contradiction (slavery in a country based on individual liberty) present from the beginning. Present from the beginning when the first Africans set foot in the new world along with Christopher Columbus, when they first arrived on British ships as indentured servants and finally slaves, when they settled the first legally all black town in Florida (Fort Mose), and when they built the northern cities and the southern plantations, these contradictions have acted as a maze that has had to be negotiated by blacks in order to survive. The story of the United States is the story of African Americans, but their perspective and experience has been lacking in literary representation. When he set about telling the story of African Americans, August Wilson wanted to create the drama of black experience from the black perspective. In his now classic address, *The Ground on Which I Stand*, he justified his mission:

> The term black or African American not only denotes race, it denotes condition, and carries with it the vestige of slavery and the social segregation and abuse of opportunity so vivid in our memory. That this abuse of opportunity and truncation of possibility is continuing and is so pervasive in our society in 1996 says much about who we are and much about the work that is necessary to alter our perceptions of each other and to effect meaningful prosperity for all. (2001)

Radio Golf is the last play in August Wilson's *Twentieth Century Cycle*, a series of plays that take place in each decade of the twentieth century, tracing the experiences of African Americans in American history. Taking place in 1997, *Radio Golf* explores the clash between past and present through the conflict between people of different generations and classes, each of whom, as an African American, has had a different experience of the world, especially the world of commerce. It is the only one of Wilson's plays that involves middle-class African Americans and their dilemmas. The play brings to the forefront the conflicts inherent in American society, stemming from the original failure to incorporate African Americans into the mainstream of American life. But it also addresses the dilemmas with which they have been left in trying to live their own lives.

The play exposes the losses that each character has endured and the irreconcilable differences that those losses have created. From an African American perspective, the play provides an explanation of the nature of losses caused by injustices, the role of commerce in aggravating these losses, and the ultimate irreconcilability of the past and the present when such contradictions exist. In the course of the play, the audience is exposed to the intersectionality of race, class, and gender within the African American experience, but it is also exposed to the problems generated when the relationship between politics and commerce becomes blurred.

Whether or not he intended it to be so, Wilson has constructed a scenario in which the fundamental principle of the rule of law (as justly conceived—and specifically property rights) comes into competition with the politics and commerce and often loses out to them. But before examining how Wilson constructs this scenario, it is necessary to meet the characters and their backgrounds and motivations.

Radio Golf presents two men and one woman who are from the African American middle class and two men from the African American working class, each of whom represents a unique perspective and set of goals that have to be achieved within the context of the present that the past has created. As we move through the events of the play, the complications created by the interaction of law, politics, and commerce illustrate how ambiguous life has become for African Americans at the turn of the century. *Radio Golf* brings into relief the entanglements that African Americans face and, in doing so, also brings into clear relief American society itself.

FIVE CHARACTERS IN SEARCH OF A FUTURE

Harmond Wilks, Roosevelt Hicks, Mame Wilks, Sterling Johnson, and Old Joe Barlow are the five characters whose lives are intertwined. The history of each character is a testament to the past and the clashes that it will create in the present. Harmond Wilks and Roosevelt Hicks are businessmen, partners, and best friends. At first they appear to have the same goals, but as the play develops, the distinction between them becomes evident. At the beginning of the play, this distinction is symbolized in the icons they choose to exhibit on the walls of their redevelopment office. Harmond puts up a poster of Martin Luther King, Jr., the martyred civil rights leader and moral icon of the black community during the civil rights era of the 1950s and 1960s. Roosevelt puts up a poster of Tiger Woods, the golf prodigy who took the world of golf by storm in 1997 based solely on his personal achievements. These iconic bookends come to have more meaning as the play proceeds. They represent, on the one hand, a history of struggle to gain full citizenship and, on the other hand, the monetary reward and fame that follows when one's abilities are fully realized. Harmond Wilks values the past and the African American history he hopes to reclaim through their redevelopment project. Roosevelt Hicks values personal achievement and longs for business success. Both men are also symbolized by their love of golf, but for Harmond the game symbolizes tradition as represented by the classic set of clubs that he values more than the car from which they are stolen. For Roosevelt, the game represents liberation and the chance to master his abilities.

Harmond Wilks has inherited the family real estate business that has boosted his family into the upper middle class, put him through college at Cornell and then law school, granted him a certain level of intellectual and aesthetic sophistication, and positioned him to become the first black mayor of Pittsburgh. Harmond Wilks had a twin brother, Raymond Wilks, who was a champion football player in high school, but who died in Vietnam while Harmond was at Cornell. Raymond wanted to go to Grambling State University to play football, but his father refused to pay for it. So Raymond joined the army to earn the money but was killed in Vietnam before he could realize his dream. Harmond, on the other hand, did just what his father asked, but speaks of becoming his own man as his brother was. Harmond's main dream is a nostalgic one—to restore the Hill and reclaim its history.

Roosevelt Hicks, who attended Cornell with Wilks, has become a vice president at Mellon Bank but chafes under the authority of his current boss and wants nothing more than to establish his independence from that institution and make his own way in the world. Apparently, upper management at Mellon had insisted on the promotion of Roosevelt to the vice presidency against the wishes of his current boss, who has not even ordered Roosevelt's new business cards. His love of golf represents his desire to master life and to feel the exhilaration that comes from doing so. Hicks makes a deal with a white businessman, Bernie Smith (who never appears in the play) to buy a black radio station, which can only be done if a minority person is involved, and although Harmond warns him about being used, it is clear that this is a way for Roosevelt to move beyond Mellon Bank and become part owner of his own business.

In pursuit of their goals, Harmond and Roosevelt will move from the domain of business into the world of law and politics through which they both hope to achieve their goals: Wilks to restore his cherished Hill District through his position as mayor and with it part of the African American past and Hicks to gain financial independence through the redevelopment project that will establish his own power to control his future and become a player in the business big leagues. Their success depends on their successfully negotiating the quicksand of law, politics, and crony capitalism that threatens to sink them and destroy the bond between them. As Wilks looks to the past, as symbolized by the poster of Martin Luther King, Jr. and his vintage set of golf clubs, Hicks looks to the future, as symbolized by the poster of Tiger Woods and his radio show, "Radio Golf." As the play begins, both are caught in the present, seeing only the "blue skies" ahead.

Mame Wilks, who has been married to Harmond for more than twenty years, is a public relations specialist handling Harmond's bid for mayor. As the play begins, she is being courted by the governor's office to handle all of its public relations, a job that would constitute her big break. Yet, we are given less history for Mame Wilks than for any of the four male characters. All we know of her is Harmond's love for her and the advice that she gives him, which seems very astute, but which he continually ignores. Even though the play takes place in 1997 and gender relations have somewhat improved, there is still the problem of women claiming their own history and identity and being taken seriously.

Sterling Johnson, a carpenter and former prison inmate, comes to the redevelopment office looking for work. He is good at what he does (at least according to him), but he is not a member of the union, his resume consisting of the actual work that he has done around the Hill. Of all the characters, he seems the most attuned to current realities. Although he has a history and has appeared as a character in previous Wilson plays, he also represents the black working class, which has been the subject of all of Wilson's plays before this one.[1] Sterling Johnson is a realist. He knows that the Hill is gone, never to be retrieved, as the past cannot be retrieved and tells this to Harmond Wilks. Sterling possesses much native wisdom, which he shares with Harmond Wilks and Roosevelt Hicks. He is a mirror that reflects aspects of both of these characters, but he also serves as a conscience for Harmond and a critic of Roosevelt.

Old Joseph Barlow is the oldest of the characters and functions as the community's historian.[2] He is the only one who remembers the distant past and chronicles it throughout the play. He has traveled throughout the country, served in battle on behalf of his country, and he remembers the way the Hill used to be—its businesses and its inhabitants. He is the catalyst who sets off the string of complications that will force Harmond and Roosevelt to confront their own motives. He will do so simply by insisting on his property rights—a foundational right inscribed in American culture. Yet, events will show that even such a foundational right is not beyond manipulation in the world of politics and commerce.

THE HILL DISTRICT INTO BEDFORD HILLS[3]

Radio Golf takes place in 1997 in Pittsburgh's Hill District, an African American neighborhood in which most of the characters have grown up. However, its current blight—low population, high crime, and lack of businesses—constitutes the opportunity by which Harmond, Roosevelt, and Mame hope to realize their goals. As we learn within the play itself, the neighborhood and its inhabitants have been subjected to a history of events that have resulted in the blight—events not unusual or unknown in the world beyond The Hill. For example, we learn from Old Joe Barlow that the Hill never enjoyed the amenities that other parts of Pittsburgh enjoyed, such as electric lights on its football field. As they move into the Bedford Redevelopment Office, Harmond Wilks and Roosevelt Hicks are forced to confront the past in ways they had not anticipated.

We learn right away that Harmond is going to locate his mayoral campaign office in the Hill District against Mame's advice, even though the small population of the Hill does not turn out to vote. "Politics is about symbolism," Harmond tells her (8). But he ignores her well-reasoned advice. Right away we learn the difference between Harmond and Roosevelt. While Harmond has a romantic notion about the Hill, Roosevelt has a negative one. He constantly keeps an eye on his car, calls the lower class inhabitants he encounters "niggers," and generally discounts as crazy the wisdom of Sterling Johnson and Old Joe Barlow.

The redevelopment plan calls for a shopping center with a Barnes & Noble, a Starbucks, and a Whole Foods, along with an apartment building with a roof-top garden, which we find out was Mame's idea. Roosevelt is proud of the architect's rendering of the development, but Harmond immediately finds fault with it. We discover that he intends to rename the twenty-year-old Model Cities Health Center after Sarah Degree, the first black registered nurse in Pittsburgh, "So we remember." But the name has remained unchanged in the rendering. In spite of arguments by Mame, Harmond gets on the phone to arrange to meet with the administrators to get the name changed, thus emphasizing the importance of African American history to him.

We learn that Harmond's decision to run for mayor is exciting people in many quarters because of his "idea about developing city commerce" (11). On the other hand, the Bedford Redevelopment project plans depend on getting five million dollars in federal money, which in turn depends on the city declaring the Hill blighted. We learn that the city council's approval may depend on Harmond's announcing his bid for mayor at the groundbreaking of the development and winning over the council. But Harmond is confident. He tells Hicks: "When I announce my candidacy at the groundbreaking ceremony next month you'll feel the ground shift and the wind will start blowing our way. Once the Party's behind me, all the city council will be in line to shake *my* hand. See how fast the Hill District's declared blighted then" (12).

While Roosevelt leaves the politics to Harmond, he is busy pursuing his own desire to introduce African American children to the game of golf by starting a golf camp. Describing his first time hitting a golf ball, he says, "I felt free. Truly free. For the first time . . . I felt something lift off me. Some weight I was carrying around and didn't know it. I felt like the world was open to me. Everything and everybody . . . That's what I want these kids to have. That'll give them a chance at life . . . You don't have to hide and crawl under a rock just 'cause you black" (13). Thus, we get a glimpse of what this sport means to Roosevelt. Even though he is middle class and educated, Roosevelt has not been spared the constraints and humiliation of being black. Golf is his way of mastering the game—of life and of commerce, as well as golf itself (see Elam, 2010, and Stewart, 2010).

In the meantime, Roosevelt Hicks enters into an agreement with a white investor named Bernie Smith, who wants to buy a local radio station, WBTZ, but needs a minority owner to take advantage of the Federal Communications Commission (FCC) Minority Tax Certificate. Harmond tells Roosevelt that he is merely being used, but Roosevelt sees it as a way to "get in the door." In addition to getting a percentage of the station, Roosevelt will also get a salary as the station manager, and he will end up with his own radio show, "Radio Golf." Roosevelt also suggests that Bernie Smith may be willing to become a partner in Bedford Redevelopment if the city council does not declare the Hill blighted, a proposal that Harmond roundly rejects. This is one point at which we realize that the goals of the two men are different: Roosevelt, whose focus is primarily business, is willing to do what others have done before him to "get in the door," including partner with a well-known, white businessman whose motives are purely monetary, while Harmond, whose personally owned real estate company was inherited, believes that advancement can be accomplished without making deals with men like Bernie Smith, but also believes that one way of achieving his goals is through politics.

The optimism of Harmond Wilks—his confidence in his ability to change the course of events with his mayoral candidacy and to restore the Hill

District—borders on arrogance, even as his sincerity shows through. When he informs Sterling Johnson of his intentions to "bring back" the Hill, Sterling simply replies: "How you gonna bring it back? It's dead" (15). Still, Harmond has complete confidence in his own ability to bring about the resurrection of the Hill and to do so on his own terms.

The tide begins to turn when Mame reports that someone is painting a house on the development site. The man painting the house is Old Joe Barlow, who is the owner and who wants to fix it up for his daughter. However, when he first walks into the office, Harmond doesn't know who he is. Old Joe Barlow has come to the office to enlist the help of Harmond Wilks, whom he wants to act as his lawyer. Old Joe shows Harmond the summons he has received for painting the house at 1839 Wylie, and Harmond makes a phone call and gets the summons dismissed. But when Roosevelt Hicks comes in and recognizes Old Joe as the old man disrupting their plans by painting the condemned house, a heated exchange ensues. Old Barlow insists that he is the owner of the house—that his mother had a duly registered deed, and that he intends on using the house for this daughter and her family.

When Old Joe hires Sterling Johnson to paint his house, Sterling shows up at the office to get reimbursed for the paint. He is informed that the house is going to be torn down "rightly or wrongly." His response to that is, "You can't just tear down the man's house. That's the kind of shit they did to the Indians. They sign a treaty and as soon the Indians walk out the door they start plotting how to break it" (51).

After an investigation, Harmond discovers that Old Joe's claims about his ownership of the house and that his family never paid taxes on the house are true. It is due to lack of paying taxes that the house was considered abandoned and sold to Harmond's real estate company. However, Harmond eventually also discovers that it was his own father who had paid the taxes on the house for years until his death, because of the importance of family. After checking, Harmond realizes that the notice of the auction, required to be posted in the paper at least thirty days before the auction, was never done. And then he discovers that his real estate company bought the house before it went to auction, which was illegal. It then sold the house to Bedford Redevelopment, which planned to tear it down to make way for their commercial development.

When he informs Roosevelt of all of this, Roosevelt clearly sees the problem as Harmond's. He doesn't care how Harmond resolves the problem, as long as he does so without interfering with the redevelopment company's plans. Harmond attempts to give ten thousand dollars to Old Joe for the house, but Old Joe rejects the offer. After Sterling Johnson tells Harmond to go look at the house, he does so and discovers that it is beautifully built and full of architectural details that he admires. He has also discovered that his grandfather, Caesar Wilks, was the brother to Black Mary, Old Joe's mother.[4]

Thus, Harmond and Old Joe are related. These discoveries and realizations change Harmond's attitude about the house.

Harmond then decides that the house needs to be preserved, and he takes it upon himself to re-do the architectural drawings of the redevelopment site, which is now built around the house. When he shows the new plans to Roosevelt, his partner goes through the roof and points out that there are contracts with a variety of businesses. Nevertheless, Harmond cancels the demolition of the house.

The knowledge of the historic importance of this house, the familial connection between Harmond and Old Joe Barlow, and the illegal way by which the house was obtained threatens the very project that Harmond and Roosevelt have staked their futures on. Harmond's unilateral actions with regard to the redevelopment project—cancelling the demolition, changing the plans—without considering Roosevelt and Mame leads to the very chaos that he has professed to dislike. The question then becomes, who will prevail and why?

THE RULE OF LAW, POLITICS, AND BUSINESS AS USUAL

A free society rests on the rule of law, as opposed to the rule of men. In theory, the rule of law is the rule of just laws equally applicable to all. However, in practice this was not the case for slaves from colonial times to the end of the civil war, and then it was not the case under the Jim Crow laws of the South that imposed a strict racial segregation or the racially discriminatory practices in the North. Although the effects on African Americans were differential, the group as a whole suffered from the unequal access to free trade, public education, political power, and employment. Besides the inequitable treatment under the law, African Americans also had to deal with a culture deeply infused with a racial ideology that pegged them as inferior intellectually, morally, economically, and politically. In their book, *Race in North America: Origin and Evolution of a World View* by Audrey Smedley and Brian D. Smedley (2011), the authors explained exactly how this racialism was infused into American culture by white slaveowners, often overriding the rule of law so central to a supposedly free society.

The United States also developed with a relatively free economic system, although it was never entirely free from political influence, and that influence not only expanded as the years advanced, but business and government took advantage of each other such that a crony capitalism arose that undercut the free market mechanism that people still assumed existed. Thus, people in power were able to benefit disproportionately. In the midst of all this, African Americans were systematically cut out of participation. Even such fortunate African Americans as Harmond Wilks and Roosevelt Hicks felt the constraints that race imposed upon them—Harmond in the loss of the African America past that he hoped to restore and Roosevelt in the lack of respect from his white boss and the difficulty of getting a seat at the table where deals are made. So, using the same resources that white businessmen had used for centuries, Harmond and Roosevelt took advantage of the situation to launch their Bedford Redevelopment company.

Harmond Wilks believes in the law. When Old Joe asks him what he can do about his house, Harmond replies: "There's nothing you can do. It's the law. The law protects you when you pay your taxes. But the law protects the city when a property's abandoned" (34). Yet, after investigating the situation, Harmond discovers that he is the one who broke the law and acquired Old Joe's house illegally. When Old Joe won't be bought off with the ten thousand dollars that Harmond offers, Harmond's other option is to stop the demolition and arrange for the redevelopment project to be built around the house. This would seem to be the just thing to do to abide by the rule of law and observe Old Joe's property rights. However, because of his political ambitions, and his refusal to listen to the advice of Mame or to consult with Roosevelt, he finds himself backed into a corner economically, politically, and legally.

The dependence of the project on the actions of governments (the city council, the federal government) means that Harmond has breached the line between politics and economics and is using the power granted to the government to benefit economically. When the city council finally approves the blight designation for the Hill, Harmond threatens to undo the deal, not only because he wants justice for Old Joe, but because he does not play the political game well. His certainty of his own righteousness makes him ignore Mame's more astute political advice.

Mame has arranged for the Sunday paper to run Harmond's speech, but when she recommends that he drop the inflammatory statements about the police commissioner because they want him to come to the groundbreaking ceremony and give the project the police endorsement, he refuses. However, when Sterling Johnson reads Harmond's words in the paper, one of the phrases that pops out is: "No one is above the law" (42).

When Mame and Roosevelt try to talk to Harmond, he informs them that he has talked Starbucks into going along with the plan. "Everything's coming together. I'm staying on top of everything. Plans change and you got to roll with them" (67). However, Roosevelt tells Harmond that he has been creating problems that Roosevelt has had to solve—that the Bedford Hills project has fallen through because Harmond's new plans violate the contracts they signed with the proprietors and the understandings they had with the federal government. Furthermore, he has rescheduled the demolition of the house. Harmond threatens to go down to the courthouse and file an injunction against the demolition. Mame tells him that this will result in his "throwing everything away" (70). But Harmond tells them: "You got to have rule of law. Otherwise it would be chaos. Nobody wants to live in chaos" (70).

THE PAST THAT HAUNTS THE PRESENT

What brings Harmond and Roosevelt into conflict is the discovery by Harmond that his own father had been paying the taxes on Aunt Ester's house and that he and Old Joe Barlow are cousins related through a woman known as Black Mary. But while Roosevelt is focused on the future, Harmond is drawn ever more deeply into the past. Once Harmond actually goes to see the house, he immediately appreciates both its history and its importance in his own life. Besides the exquisite craftsmanship present in the building, Aunt Ester's house at 1839 Wylie Avenue represents all of African American history and the myths of its people in Wilson's plays. Thus, its destruction represents the final destruction of history of both African Americans and the Hill. Black Mary was Aunt Ester's successor in the house, and it is through her that Harmond Wilks is related to Old Joe. Thus, Aunt Ester's house represents everything Harmond values. Harmond realizes that his father valued family and, therefore, took care of the house while he was alive. But in another sense, it is Harmond who has dropped the ball. He now wants to rectify his error and see justice done for Old Joe, but he has lost sight of what his new convictions will cost Mame and Roosevelt, not to mention himself because he has combined his economic goals with his political ones, and now they are entangled.

Still moved by the unrelenting grief over the death of his twin brother Raymond in Vietnam, Harmond Wilks decides that it is time for him to put aside his past complacency. He tells Mame he wants to move back to the Hill and into the house he grew up in as a boy—a move that Mame considers moving backwards. Harmond is finally moved to take action to fulfill his own desires. But in doing so, he discovers that the rule of law—the very thing that he believed in—will lead to his own downfall.

On one occasion, after returning the golf clubs stolen from Harmond's car, Sterling Johnson tells him: "You can't tear down that man's house. That's the kind of shit they did to the Indians. They sign a treaty and soon as the Indians walk out the door they start plotting how to break it" (51). Then later, Sterling reminds him again: "That's Mr. Barlow's house . . . .He ain't broke no laws. You stole Mr. Barlow's house. As it is Bedford Hills is in possession of stolen property and you and him are the only ones who know you stole it. Everyone else thinks you bought it. That's why he can't call the police. Won't nobody listen to him . . . If you even *whisper* everybody sit up and stop to listen" (60). It is as though Sterling Johnson is Harmond's conscience.

The new rendering of the development plan that Harmon brings to the office suggests that a way might be found to accommodate the past and the present. However, because of the way it is introduced and because of the way in which Harmon rides rough sod over the opinions of both Mame and Roosevelt and because of his own complicity in not taking care of his legal business at the time of the sale of the house, the rule of law that he so vociferously defended at the beginning of the play comes back to indict him and affect his reputation, and therefore his race for mayor. Harmond's attempt to combine politics and economics has become the trap that springs when he attempts to rectify his mistake.

The repercussions of his actions redound against Mame, who loses her chance to do public relations for the Governor. "You jumped but I'm falling too," she tells him. In the end, she is seen as a mere appendage to Harmond instead of being assessed on her own abilities. She tells Harmond that he has always had things go his way—that "you've always been the kid who had the ball" (72). Harmond has picked this moment to follow his own plan instead of following the plan that others laid down for him, including the plan that would have gotten him elected mayor, or governor, or senator, as Mame reminds him.

Harmond has also threatened Roosevelt's investment in the redevelopment project. He has redrawn the plans without consulting his partner and without consulting the other businesses that are a part of the project. Roosevelt tells Harmond that he is forcing a buyout. He is throwing Harmond out of Bedford Development, buying him out with money supplied by Bernie Smith. Thus, Harmond loses both his economic and political way. He is left right where he started with his real estate company and nothing else.

THE CALCULUS OF DISCONTENT

The past has played itself out, and the naiveté of Harmond Wilks has helped it happen. His courting of the past and his inattention to the present have now resulted in the loss of the future. The true dilemma of *Radio Golf* is the price that must be paid in terms of past history in order to embrace the future. Mame Wilks and Roosevelt Hicks are willing to pay this price. Harmond Wilks is not. For him the past looms so large that it gets in the way of the path he is on.

Harmond's ideals, symbolized by the poster of Martin Luther King, Jr., are good ones, but he seems incapable of joining the past he so reveres with the present. In many ways, Harmond's desire to reconstitute the Hill District is a dream, and one that cannot be realized, because it involves changing a past that cannot be undone—a past in which the Hill was shortchanged in ways that other parts of the city were not. But moving forward involves finding a way to accommodate the past without sacrificing the future, and this Harmond seems unable to do.

In the past, Harmond Wilks did everything his father wanted him to do, and he reaped the benefits: he got a good education at Cornell, he inherited his father's real estate business and his father's wealth. Yet, just as he is about to benefit from all of this, his ties to the past undermine his present interests. His reverence for the past, although it takes the form of wanting to "bring back" the Hill, seems to be tied to his memories of his twin brother, Raymond Wilks, who was a high school football hero known by everyone on the Hill, including Sterling Johnson and Old Joe Barlow. Unlike Harmond, Raymond defied his father. Raymond stands as a symbol of the self-directed man that Harmond always wanted to be but wasn't. Harmond took Raymond's high school football trophy to college with him, and he also has it in the redevelopment office. Harmond's last opportunity, once his plans fall through, is to rebel by joining in the painting party at Elder Barlow's house even as it is scheduled for demolition. So he puts war paint on his face, reminiscent of the cowboys and Indians that his brother used to play as a child with Sterling Johnson, and marches off to join the protest. Yet, one is left to wonder if Harmond's fate will be the same as that of the Native Americans he so stereotypically imitates. As the play ends, it seems highly likely that the Hill he envisioned will never come into being—that it will be replaced by the very redevelopment he himself has set in motion.

What at first seems noble, now seems almost suicidal. His plan for working around the old house would have been viable had he not already brought together all of the elements of the project by using government as a means to create economic opportunity. The powers that be will prevail, but everyone has experienced loss. Old Joe will lose his house. Harmond will lose the Hill, the chance to become the first black mayor in Pittsburgh, and probably Mame. Mame has already lost the chance to succeed in her own right by handling all of the public relations for the Governor's office. Sterling Johnson is still protesting, but his status will also likely remain the same. Sterling's final bit of wisdom for self-preservation is to give in. "Giving in is good for your blood pressure too. Your heart and everything else" (75).

Out of the particularities of the African American experience, August Wilson has crafted a play that speaks to the universalities that lie at the intersection of the public and the private—of the law, politics, and economics, and the way in which individual human experiences result in multiple interpretations of the same facts—interpretations which themselves emanate from the intersection of race, class, and gender. As we read through *Radio Golf* or watch actors bring this story to life on stage, we begin to realize just how fluid these interpretations can be.

We also come to realize that the actions of some affect the lives of others more deeply than we sometimes realize. When we seek to follow the principles that define the spirit of our nation—the rule of law, individual rights, limited government, and free enterprise—we find that they are tangled up with the actual history we and others have lived—that the flawed actions of the past have kept these principles from being fully realized for African Americans.

"Over the course of ten plays, Wilson explores the quotidian existence of ordinary black people and rights—or rewrites—African American history. As a result, his dramaturgy impacts how we think about the very construction of history. Even as Wilson considers the specifics of the African American past, his playwriting reaches beyond the particular to touch the cross-cultural" (Elam, 2005).[5]

I cannot help but think that had Harmond Wilks handled the whole situation more deftly, he could have achieved his goal of maintaining history and restoring the Hill. But the Bedford Redevelopment project was never going to recapture the Hill. As Sterling noted early on, it was already gone. All Joe Barlow's recounting of dates shows us the past as it passed. The creative destruction of the market was clearly at work here and elsewhere. But Elam was correct in noting the application of the particular message of *Radio Golf* to other cultures.

Finally, the specter of race remains hovering over the scene—the pretense that past wrongs have been accommodated by superficial gestures that mean nothing. And yet, some things have changed, but the past, once gone, cannot be retrieved. Harmond Wilks cannot go back and change course, his brother cannot avoid death in Vietnam, and Aunt Ester's house cannot now be saved. As Sterling noted early in the play, the Hill is already dead and gone. The physical space can be claimed and redeveloped, but the Hill is lost in time. As Harmond Wilks puts on his symbolic war paint to join the rally at Aunt Ester's house, we are being told that he has as much chance of rallying as the Native Americans he is emulating. And this is the nature of tragedy—that the past can never be retrieved, except in memory

In his last play, *Radio Golf*, Wilson gives voice to all of the contradictions that have arisen in America's past and the way they are instantiated in the African American present. The trade-off that Harmond cannot face—the one between history and economic advancement—remains a puzzle still to be solved.

NOTES

1. Sterling Johnson appeared as a character in Wilson's *Two Trains Running*, which opened in 1990 and represented the year of 1969 in the Twentieth Century Cycle.

2. Old Joe Barlow appeared as a character in Wilson's *Gem of the Ocean*, which opened in 2003 and represented the year of 1904 in the Twentieth Century Cycle. Old Joe alludes to events that happened in this play in *Radio Golf.*

3. The Hill District is an actual place. It is the neighborhood in Pittsburgh in which the playwright himself grew up. See Glasco and Rawson 2011 for details about the actual Pittsburgh locations in the life of August Wilson. Also see Ervin Dyer and Monica Haynes, "Real-Life Drama Surrounds Wilson's Childhood Home," Post-Gazette.com/Arts & Entertainment, January 26, 2003 (http://old.post-gazette.com/ae/20030126wilson0126fnp5.asp) Accessed July 15, 2015.

4. Aunt Ester Tyler, Black Mary, and Caesar Wilks are all characters in Wilson's *Gem of the Ocean*, which opened in 2003 and represented the year of 1904 in the *Twentieth Century Cycle.*

5. Harry J. Elam, Jr., "A Black Thing," *Theatre Journal.* Volume 57, No 4. Black Performance (December 2005. Downloaded from 131.91.169.193 on Tuesday, April 21, 2015. Accessed 21–04–2015 as: 42 UTC.

REFERENCES

Dyer, Ervin and Monica Haynes. 2003. Real-Life Drama Surrounds Wilson's Childhood Home. Post-Gazette.com (Sunday, January 26, 2003). (http://old.post-gazette.com/ae/20030126wilson0126fnp5.asp) Accessed July 15, 2015.

Elam, Harry, J., Jr. 2005. "A Black Thing," *Theatre Journal.* Volume 57, No 4. Black Performance (December 2005. Downloaded from 131.91.169.193 on Tuesday, 21 April 2015. Accessed 21–04–2015 as:42 UTC.

Elam, Harry J., Jr. 2010. Radio Golf in the Age of Obama. In *Nadel*, 186–206.

Glasco, Laurence A. and Christopher Rawson. 2011. *August Wilson: Pittsburgh Places in His Life and Plays.* Pittsburgh, PA: Pittsburgh History & Landmarks Foundation.

Nadel, Alan, ed. 2010. *August Wilson: Completing the Twentieth-Century Cycle.* Iowa City: University of Iowa Press.

Smedley, Audrey and Brian D. Smedley. 2011. *Race in North America: Origin and Evolution of a World View, Fourth Edition.* New York: Westview/Perseus.

Stewart, Anthony. 2010. *An Exercise in Peripheral Vision: Loyalties, Ironies, and Sports in Radio Golf.* In *Nadel*, 173–85.

Wilson, August. 2001. *The Ground on Which I Stand.* New York: Theatre Communications Group.

———. 2007. *Radio Golf.* New York: Theatre Communications Group.

Index

About the Contributors

Andrew Bernstein is a philosopher, novelist, and frequent lecturer on college campuses. He has taught philosophy at several colleges in New York.

Walter E. Block is Harold E. Wirth Eminent Scholar Endowed Chair in Economics at Loyola University, New Orleans, Louisiana.

Susan Love Brown is a political and psychologist anthropologist and Professor of Anthropology at Florida Atlantic University.

Troy Earl Camplin is a consultant, writer, poet, playwright, editor, and interdisciplinary scholar.

Paul A. Cantor is a literary and media critic and is the Clifton Waller Barrett professor in the Department of English at the University of Virginia.

Stephen Cox is Professor of Literature and Director of the Humanities Program at the University of California, San Diego. He is a founding co-editor of *The Journal of Ayn Rand Studies* and editor of *Liberty* magazine.

Carmen Elena Dorobăţ is Lecturer in International Business at Coventry University.

Mimi Reisel Gladstein is Professor of English and Theatre Arts at the University of Texas at El Paso.

Carl S. Horner is Professor Emeritus of American Literature at Flagler College.

Cynthia Hunter is an accomplished marketing and sales professional with experience in the hospitality, manufacturing, and higher education areas.

Heather King is a Professor of English at the University of Redlands. Her research interest centers on eighteenth-century British literature.

William Kline is an Assistant Professor in the Department of Liberal and Integrative Studies at the University of Illinois, Springfield. He is also the Executive Director of Liberty Studies.

Zennure Köseman is an Assistant Professor in the Department of Western Languages and Literatures at Inönü University in Turkey.

Felix R. Livingston is Professor of Economics and Director of the Honorable Entrepreneurship Program at Flagler College.

Matthew McCaffrey is Assistant Professor of Enterprise at the University of Manchester. He is also the editor of *Libertarian Papers*.

Allen Mendenhall is a writer, attorney, and adjunct professor at Faulkner University. He is the managing editor of *Southern Literary Review*.

Virginia Murr is the owner of an editing business and has worked with the Center for Ethics and Entrepreneurship.

Theodore N. Pauls is Associate Professor of Marketing and Chair of the Department of Business at Wheeling Jesuit University.

Jeff Riggenbach is a journalist, author, and podcaster whose books include *In Praise of Decadence, Why American History Is Not What They Say: An Introduction to Revisionism*, and *Persuaded by Reason: Joan Kennedy Taylor and the Rebirth of American Individualism.*

Sarah Skwire is a Fellow at Liberty Fund and the author of a college writing textbook, *Writing with a Thesis.*

Michael Spindler has retired from academia and now writes poetry, short fiction, novels, and nonfiction on a full-time basis.

Gennady Stolyarov II is an actuary, science fiction novelist, philosophical essayist, poet, and composer. He is Editor-in-Chief of *The Rational Argumentator.*

Frederick Turner is Founders Professor of Arts and Humanities at the University of Texas at Dallas.

Michelle Albert Vachris is Professor of Economics at Christopher Newport University and co-editor of the *Virginia Economic Journal.*

Amy Willis is a Liberty Fund Fellow who also works in the Liberty Fund Conference Program.

Gary Wolfram is William E. Simon Professor in Economics and Public Policy at Hillsdale College and President of a consulting firm specializing in taxation and policy analysis.

Derek K. Yonai is the Director of the Center for Free Enterprise and Associate Professor of Economics at Florida Southern College.

Edward W. Younkins is Professor of Accountancy and Director of Graduate Business Programs at Wheeling Jesuit University. He is also Executive Director of the Institute for the Study of Capitalism and Morality.

www.ingramcontent.com/pod-product-compliance
Ingram Content Group UK Ltd.
Pitfield, Milton Keynes, MK11 3LW, UK
UKHW020256051026
15470UKWH00020B/332

9 781498 519298